BUB

D1417025

Czech (& Central European)
Yearbook of Arbitration

Czech (& Central European) Yearbook of Arbitration

Volume II

2012

Party Autonomy versus Autonomy of Arbitrators

Editors

Alexander J. Bělohlávek

Professor
at the VŠB TU
in Ostrava
Czech Republic

Naděžda Rozehnalová

Professor
at the Masaryk University
in Brno
Czech Republic

JURIS

Questions About This Publication

For assistance with shipments, billing or other customer service matters,
please call our Customer Services Department at:
1-631-350-2100

To obtain a copy of this book, call our Sales Department:
1-631-351-5430
Fax: 1-631-351-5712

Toll Free Order Line:
1-800-887-4064 (United States & Canada)
See our web page about this book:
www.arbitrationlaw.com

Printed in the United States of America.
ISBN: 978-1-933833-83-5
ISSN: 2157-9490

JurisNet, LLC
71 New Street
Huntington, New York 11743 U.S.A.
www.arbitrationlaw.com

The title *Czech (&Central European) Yearbook of Arbitration* as well as the
logo appearing on the cover are protected by EU trademark law.

Typeset in the U.S.A. by Juris Publishing, Inc.

"We regret to announce the death of our most reputable colleague Prof. Dr. Iván Szász. We are thankful for his efforts invested in our common project. His personality and wisdom will be deeply missed by the whole editorial team."

Address for correspondence & manuscripts

Czech (& Central European) Yearbook of International Law
Jana Zajíce 32, Praha 7, 170 00, Czech Republic

www.czechyearbook.org

Impressum

Institutions Participating in the CYArb Project

Academic Institutions

University of West Bohemia in Pilsen, Czech Republic
Faculty of Law, Department of International Law &
Department of Constitutional Law
[*Západočeská univerzita v Plzni, Právnická fakulta.*
Katedra mezinárodního práva & Katedra ústavního práva]

Masaryk University (Brno, Czech Republic)
Faculty of Law, Department of International and European Law
[*Masarykova univerzita v Brně, Právnická fakulta,*
Katedra mezinárodního a evropského práva]

Pavol Jozef Šafárik University in Košice, Slovak Republic
Faculty of Law, Department of Commercial Law and Business Law
[*Právnická fakulta UPJŠ, Košice, Slovensko. Katedra obchodného a*
hospodárskeho práva]

VŠB – TU Ostrava, Czech Republic
Faculty of Economics, Department of Law
[*VŠB – TU Ostrava, Ekonomická fakulta. Katedra práva*]

**Institute of State and Law of the Academy of Sciences of the Czech
Republic, v.v.i.**
[*Ústav státu a práva Akademie věd ČR, v.v.i.*]

Non-academic Institutions Participating in the CYArb Project

International Arbitral Centre
of the Austrian Federal Economic Chamber
  [*Wiener Internationales Schiedsgericht (VIAC), Vienna*]

Court of International Commercial Arbitration attached
to the Chamber of Commerce and Industry of Romania
  [*Curtea de Arbitraj Comercial Internaţional de pe lângă Camera*
  de Comerţ şi Industrie a României, Bucharest]

Arbitration Court attached to the Hungarian Chamber
of Commerce and Industry
  [*A Magyar Kereskedelmi és Iparkamara mellett szervezett*
  Választottbíróság, Budapest]

Arbitration Court attached to the Economic Chamber
of the Czech Republic and Agricultural Chamber of the Czech Republic
  [*Rozhodčí soud při Hospodářské komoře České republiky*
  a Agrární komoře České republiky, Prague]

Arbitration Court attached to the Czech-Moravian Commodity
Exchange Kladno
  [*Rozhodčí soud při Českomoravské komoditní burze Kladno*
  (Czech Republic)]

ICC National Committee Czech Republic
  [*ICC Národní výbor Česká republika*]

The Court of Arbitration at the Polish Chamber of Commerce in Warsaw
  [*Sąd Arbitrażowy przy Krajowej Izbie Gospodarczej w Warszawie*]

Slovak Academy of Sciences, Institute of State and Law, Slovak Republic
  [*Slovenská akadémia vied, Ústav štátu a práva. Bratislava, Slovensko*]

| | |

Proofreading and translation support provided by: Agentura SPA, s. r. o., Prague,
Czech Republic, and Juris Publishing, Inc., USA.

Contents

CASE LAW

Section A

Current Case Law of the National Courts regarding Arbitration

Contents

Czech (& Central European) Yearbook of Arbitration

All contributions in this book are subject to academic review.

List of Abbreviations

AAA	American Arbitration Association
ADR	alternative dispute resolution
ALB	Albania
ArbAct	Czech Arbitration Act (Act No. 216/1994 Coll.)
ArbAct [CZE]	Czech Act No. 216/1994 Coll., on arbitration and the enforcement of arbitral awards, as amended
ArbAct [SVK]	Act No 244/2002 Coll. [SVK], on Arbitration, as subsequently amended
ASA	Swiss Arbitration Association
BGB	German Civil Code
BGH	Bundesgerichtshof (Federal Supreme Court), Germany
BGH [DEU]	Bundesgerichtshof, Federal Court of Justice, Germany
BIT	Bilateral Investment Treaty
CA (CD)	Court of Appeal (Civil Division)[UK]
CA/BCCI	Court of Arbitration of the Bulgarian Chamber of Commerce and Industry
Cass	Cour de cassation (Supreme Court of Cassation), France
CC [CZE]	Act No. 40/1964 Coll., Civil Code, as subsequently amended
CC [SVK]	Civil Code of the Slovak Republic – Act No 40/1964 Coll., as subsequently amended
CC CR [CZE]	Czech Constitutional Court
CCP [CZE]	Czech Act No. 99/1963 Coll., Code of Civil Procedure, as amended
CIArb	Chartered Institute of Arbitrators

ComCode [CZE]	Czech Act No. 513/1991 Coll., Commercial Code, as amended
Constitution CR [CZE]	Constitutional Act No. 1/1993 Coll. of the Czech National Council of 16th December 1992 as amended
Convention	European Convention on Human Rights
CZE	Czech Republic
Directive	Council Directive 93/13/EEC of 5 April 1993 on unfair terms in consumer contracts
DIS	German Arbitration Institution
DRC	Democratic Republic Congo
EAP	Emergency Arbitrator Provisions
ECJ	European Court of Justice
ECODIR	Electronic Consumer Dispute Resolution Rules
ECRI - E	Commerce Claims Redress Interchange
ECtHR	European Court of Human Rights
EFNI	European Forum for New Ideas
ECHR	European Convention on Human Rights
EU	European Union
EWCA Civ	England and Wales Court of Appeal (Civil Division) Decisions
EWHC (Comm)	England and Wales High Court (Commercial Court) Decisions
FAA	Federal Arbitration Act
FIDIC	International Federation of Consulting Engineers
HGB	German Commercial Code
HKSAR	Hong Kong Special Administrative Region
IBA	International Bar Association
ICA	International Commercial Arbitration
ICANN	Internet Corporation for Assignment Names and Numbers
ICC	International Chamber of Commerce
ICCA/BG	International Commercial Arbitration Act of the Republic of Bulgaria
ICSID	The International Centre for the Settlement of Investment Disputes
Int. A.L.R.	International Arbitration Law Review
IPRG	Swiss Private International Law Act
LCIA	London Court of International Arbitration
Lloyd´s Rep.	Lloyd´s Law Review
LPS [CZE]	Charter of Rights and Freedoms of the Czech Republic

MAL	Model Law of International Commercial Arbitration
MKIK	Arbitration Court attached to the Hungarian Chamber of Commerce and Industry
Model Law	UNCITRAL Model law on International Commercial Arbitration
NAFTA	North American Free Trade Agreement
NCC [CZE]	*New* Civil Code of the Czech Republic
NS ČR	Czech Supreme Court
NS ČR [CZE]	Supreme Court of the Czech Republic
OCA	Obligations and Contracts Act
ODR	Online Dispute Resolution
OLG	High Regional Court
POL	Poland
PRC	People´s Republic of China
QBD(CC)	Queen´s Bench Division (Commercial Court) [UK]
RC [CZE]	Czech Regional Court
RCA	Romanian Chamber of Commerce and Industry
RSFSR	The Russian Soviet Federative Socialist Republic
SALC	Stockholm Arbitration & Litigation Center
SC CR [CZE]	Supreme Court of the Czech Republic
SCC	Stockholm Chamber of Commerce
SVK	Slovakia
TFEU	Treaty on the Functioning of the European Union (Lisbon Treaty)
UDRP	Uniform domain Name Dispute Resolution Policy
UN	United Nations
UNCC	United Nations Compensation Commission
UNCITRAL	United Nations Commission on International Trade Law
ÚS ČR [CZE]	Constitutional Court of the Czech Republic
USSR	Union of Soviet Socialist Republics
VIAC	Vienna International Arbitral Centre
WJA	World Jurist Association
YAF	Young Arbitrators Forum
ZPO [DEU]	German Civil Procedure Code (Zivilprozeßordnung)
ZRK [SVK]	Act No. 244/2002 Coll. [of the Slovak Republic], on Arbitration, as subsequently amended.

Articles

Czech (& Central European) Yearbook of Arbitration

Vasily N. Anurov

Autonomy of the Arbitration Agreement: Danger of Broad Interpretation

Key words:
Autonomy of the arbitration agreement | arbitration clause | non-existence | invalidity of the underlying contract | arbitrability | illegality of the underlying contract | fraud | bribery | corruption

Abstract | The autonomy of the arbitration agreement is recognized as a fundamental principle of international commercial arbitration. Initially, the concept of autonomy was elaborated to reinforce an arbitration clause, duly executed by the parties, despite the possible invalidity of the underlying contract. Although this clause was considered to be a contractual provision, it retained its independence from the contract due to the specific goals sought by the parties. In time this principle became so embedded in the minds of academics and practicing lawyers that the link between the arbitration clause and the underlying contract ceased to attract their attention. Anxiety over arbitration provisions was transformed into the overzealous belief in their domination over other contractual terms. As a consequence, the various obstacles put up by national legal instruments to prevent unfair tricks in international business transactions were overcome by inclusion of the arbitration clause, which entails the settlement of disputes not in a public, but in a private manner. The aim of the following paper is to demonstrate the unjustifiably broad application of the arbitration agreement's autonomy by examining relevant cases in arbitration and judicial practice.

Vasily N. Anurov is a candidate of jurisprudence, lecturer at the Faculty of Private International Law, Moscow State Law Academy, Arbitrator of the Vilnius Court of Commercial Arbitration. Also, he holds LL.M in Mineral Law and Policy with distinction (Dundee, Scotland). e-mail: vasily.anurov@ googlemail.com

| | |

I. Introduction

1.01. To refer all disputes that can arise between parties to commercial arbitration is a well-established tradition in international transactions. In most cases this method of dispute resolution is chosen when the underlying contract (UC) is drafted. Thus, relevant provisions of the arbitration agreement are embodied in a text of the contract under the title of "arbitration clause" (AC).

1.02. It is in the nature of this clause to play a significant role in contractual relationships and to potentially be more important than the underlying contract. The importance of the clause comes into play when one of the parties attempts to challenge the existence or validity of the contract. Being part of the contract, the AC could hold nonetheless if the mutual consent of the parties to submit their disputes to the arbitration's jurisdiction   is considered to be separate from the other contract provisions. The independent character of the arbitration agreement (AA) also allows it to confer on the party acting in good faith the ability to seek the main goal of arbitration – namely settlement of the dispute on the merits.

1.03. That the doctrine of autonomy of the arbitration agreement (AAA) is upheld in the international practice of commercial arbitration is more than indisputable. The doctrine is entrenched in various international standards that make recommendations to states to adopt their national legislation acts in a certain manner and is also entrenched in the Arbitration Rules of well-known arbitration institutes to all potential parties of the arbitration agreement. A perfect example of such a standard is Article 16 (1) of the UNCITRAL Model Law on International Commercial Arbitration (Model law)[1] which expresses the idea that the non-existence or invalidity of the underlying contract does not automatically affect the arbitration agreement. Article 6 (4) of the ICC Rules of Arbitration (ICC Rules)[2] envisages the implied presumption of the validity of this agreement in order to confirm the arbitral tribunal's jurisdiction to adjudicate a dispute in question.

1.04. Both the Model law and the ICC Rules do not deny that hypothetically the same defects can affect both the contract and the agreement. To

---

[1]   UNCITRAL Model Law on International Commercial Arbitration 1985, approved by UNCITRAL on June 21, 1985 and recommended by the General Assembly of UN on December 11, 1985 (resolution 40/72) (with amendments as adopted in 2006), Vienna, 2008.

[2]   ICC Rules of Arbitration in force as from January 1998, cost scales effective as of January 1, 2008, ICC publication no. 808, available at: http://www.iccwbo.org/court/arbitration/id4199/index.html (accessed on July 10, 2011).

insist on the opposite view would be to defy common sense. A steadfast link between arbitration and other contractual provisions is revealed in the fact of their belonging to one document – a contract signed by the parties as a result of their negotiations. Of course, the arbitration agreement can be concluded in a separate document but in order to address the most controversial issues this paper will not cover such cases.

1.05.   It is generally agreed that the arbitration agreement should share the fate of the underlying contract if the party opposing the arbitration procedures manages to prove that "a contract was never concluded or that the parties were still in the process of negotiation."[3] The consequences are the same for cases of forgery or where there is coercion or compulsion in the signing of the contract.[4] Also, the lack of the legal capacity of one of the parties usually encompasses both the contract (UC) and the arbitration clause (AC).[5] Notably, all these cases are distinguishable by their obvious character. As a result of such a "formulaic" approach arbitral tribunals or state courts do not find it necessary in such cases to delve into the factual circumstances of the case, and will not consider even the exemplary guidelines set down by prominent scholars.

1.06.   The aim of this paper is to analyze the implementation of this doctrine and demonstrate its ambivalent character. While the autonomy of the arbitration agreement should be proclaimed an essential principle of commercial arbitration, it should not be invoked dogmatically or applied too broadly. This more restrained approach is reflected not in legal rules but in various cases where the concurrence of circumstances required arbitrators or judges to deviate from the widespread tendency to separate the arbitration agreement from the underlying contract. While the making of such awards and judicial decisions deserves encouragement, the unsuccessful attempts of such parties and their objections to the unjustifiably broad application of the doctrine of autonomy also deserve consideration, at least for their potential to provide illumination.

---

[3]   JULIAN D.M. LEW, LOUKAS A. MISTELIS, STEFAN M. KROLL, COMPARATIVE INTERNATIONAL COMMERCIAL ARBITRATION, The Hague: Kluwer Law International 104 (2003).

[4]   ALAN REDFERN, MARTIN HUNTER, LAW AND PRACTICE OF INTERNATIONAL COMMERCIAL ARBITRATION, London: Sweet & Maxwell 303 (4th ed. 2004).

[5]   GUIDITTA C. MOSS, INTERNATIONAL COMMERCIAL ARBITRATION. PARTY AUTONOMY AND MANDATORY RULES, Oslo: Tano Aschehoug 283 (1999).

II. The General Approach to the Principle

1.07.   Ironically, the principle of the autonomy of the arbitration agreement (AAA) is being elucidated in the English academic literature devoted to international arbitration by reference to *V/O 'Souznefteexport'* v. *Joc Oil, Ltd*, which illustrates the Soviet approach to the abovementioned principle.[6] The main source the English scholars used in their arguments is a Bermuda court decision made in the enforcement stage of the arbitral award in 1990. This research is based on the arbitral award, which was issued by the Foreign Trade Arbitration Commission (VTAC) of the Chamber of Commerce of the USSR in 1984 as a source for elaborating the fundamental principles and ways of tackling the problem.[7]

1.08.   The thrust of the dispute was in part the non-payment of the contract on delivery of oil and oil products. Joc Oil, Ltd, acting as purchaser, chose an extremely marginal method in the pleadings. Under the assumption of the absolute non-existence of the UC, it challenged the validity of the AC and the competence of the arbitral tribunal. The attorney for the defendant referred to the well-known principle of classical Roman law – *ex nihilo nihil fit*.[8]– or, out of nothing comes nothing. In response to this [alleged] authority, the attorney for the plaintiff also chose to respond philosophically – employing the ancient Greek puzzle of Achilles and the turtle. Its sense is that Achilles would never overtake the turtle if the period of time is divided into eternally short moments. The Russian attorney asked arbitrators to imagine themselves on the side of Achilles and the turtle on the side of the UC in order to comprehend the lack of common sense in the defendant's position.[9]

1.09.   To return to legal ground, it is now necessary to draw attention to some unique Soviet legal rules which are not in force at the present time. According to these rules any foreign economic transaction had to be signed by two representatives, acting on the basis of the power of attorney, and issued by the chairman of V/O. These representatives were to be included in the official journal of foreign trade and were considered to be duly authorized from the date of the relevant publication. The awkwardness of this regulation was perceived by all

---

[6]   Julian D.M. Lew, Loukas A. Mistelis, Stefan M. Kroll, *supra* note 3, at 104-105, Alan Redfern, Martin Hunter, *supra* note 4, at 283-284.

[7]   *V/O 'Souznefteexport'* v. *Joc Oil, Ltd*, VTAC Case No. 109/1980, Award of July 9, 1984, 2 ICA 135-167 (2007).

[8]   Alexey A. Kostin, *Brief Recollections of a Long Arbitration*, 2 ICA 131 (2007).

[9]   *Ibid.*, at 131-132.

participants in foreign economic activity, as the chairman of V/O was obliged to instruct his subordinates to sign the foreign economic contracts rather than sign them himself. So had the chairman done in the *Joc Oil. Ltd.* case.

1.10. The defendant hitched to the fact that the plaintiff had not fulfilled the mandatory requirements for the conclusion of the foreign economic contract and considered it, including the AC void *ab initio*. The arbitral tribunal upheld this position in part. It examined the issues of the non-existence of the arbitration clause and the UC separately. Referring to the procedural nature of the arbitration clause, the arbitral tribunal underscored that an AA could not be assessed as a foreign economic contract. Therefore, the special requirements to the conclusion of the arbitration agreement should not apply to the AC which customarily could be signed by one person. Thus, the arbitral tribunal recognized the validity of the AA despite the invalidity of the underlying contract.

1.11. Undoubtedly, this approach can be hardly criticized, as it encourages the development of arbitration as an effective system of international dispute resolution. But one might ask, practically speaking, what could happen? Couldn't the parties acting in bad faith use ever more simplified regulation and apply it to arbitration agreements to circumvent the mandatory rules of national legislation? Unfortunately, the answer is yes, they can. It would not be difficult to conceive of hypothetical situations where arbitration could be used as a remedy to get around some inconvenient limitations in corporate law, for example, special requirements for the conclusion of major transactions or transactions with interest. The compulsory approval of the board of directors or general meeting of shareholders would not be needed if the executive director concludes the transaction with arbitration and applicable law clauses. The methodology for convincing such persons is very simple, particularly if they are promised certain fidelity payments, notoriously referred to as "kickbacks."

III. Procedural Limitation of the Principle

1.12. As mentioned above, some defects of the underlying contract also affect the arbitration clause. In *V/O 'Souznefteexport'* v. *Joc Oil, Ltd* the arbitral tribunal classified these defects as defects of the will of the contracting parties.[10] In *AOOT Kalmneft* v. *Glencore International A.G.*[11] the plaintiff confirmed that it had been a victim of fraud.

---

[10] *V/O 'Souznefteexport'* v. *Joc Oil, Ltd, supra* note 7, at 157.

[11] *AOOT Kalmneft* v. *Glencore International A.G. and Another*, QBD (CC) Case, Judgment of July 27, 2001, 1 Lloyd's Rep. 128 [2002].

According to the plaintiff's presumption the deceptive scheme lay in the involvement of an intermediary – Briarwise International Ltd (Briarwise) which was considered by the plaintiff to be an associated company of the defendant. On the basis of two bilateral agreements, AOOT Kalmneft (Kalmneft) was supposed to supply crude oil to Briarwise and Glencore International A.G. (Glencore) agreed to purchase the oil cargoes from Briarwise. Indeed, there was one more trilateral prepayment agreement between these parties where Kalmneft and Briarwise bore joint and several liability in cases of non-delivery of crude oil to Glencore. According to the prepayment agreement Briarwise accumulated substantial debts of money to be paid to Kalmneft for shipped oil cargo. When the payments were stopped Kalmneft accordingly suspended delivery of crude oil. Since the prepayment was transferred to Briarwise as a lump sum at the beginning of the transaction, so Glencore claimed compensation and only at this stage did Kalmneft learn of the prepayment agreement which contained an arbitration clause

1.13.   The key issue of the dispute was whether the First Deputy General Director of Kalmneft was duly authorized to sign the prepayment agreement. Glencore referred to the power of attorney duly issued by the General Director of Kalmneft. Also, part performance of the agreement should have verified the fact of consequent ratification of the validity of the power of attorney.

1.14.   Since Kalmenft strongly opposed arbitration proceedings, so the sole arbitrator faced this choice: to make a preliminary decision regarding his jurisdiction or to suspend this issue until settlement of the dispute on the merits. The sole arbitrator chose the first variant as "a more cost-efficient and speedier way of resolving the dispute."[12]

1.15.   For our purposes, a salient feature of this case was that the conclusion of the existence of the arbitration clause automatically predetermined assessment of the existence of the UC. Having recognized jurisdiction, the sole arbitrator actually made up his mind regarding the key issue of the merits of the dispute. Therefore, the thorough investigation undertaken by the plaintiff in order to adduce sufficient evidence of fraud would have been useless.

1.16.   Unfortunately, Judge Colman didn't uphold the plaintiff's position. The scope of his analysis was limited to a literal interpretation of the relevant rules of English law, which envisage the discretionary power of the arbitral tribunal to rule on its own jurisdiction in a preliminary

---

[12]   *Ibid.*, at 139.

award or award on the merits.[13] Successful challenging of the decision on jurisdiction could have been achieved only if the party seeking this remedy had provided clear evidence refuting the arbitral tribunal's position. The argument that the preliminary award is premature is considered to be insufficient ground for setting aside the decision: "Once an arbitrator has decided under his powers under s. 31(4) to rule on his own jurisdiction, the only function of s. 67 is to challenge the arbitrator's conclusion either that he had jurisdiction or that he did not. Above all the Court has no power to set aside a ruling that the arbitrator has jurisdiction on the grounds that it would be better if he reconsidered the matter in the light of more evidence that might be available at a hearing on the merits."[14]

1.17. Such an approach demonstrates the adherence to the conservative point of view which is inflexible when solving controversial issues. It is actually avoidance of non-standard situations that fall outside the usual models.

1.18. Undoubtedly, this case compels one to review the broad interpretation of the principle of the autonomy of the arbitration agreement. When the arbitrators can't separate the actions of signing or ratifying the AC and the UC, their power to make a preliminary decision on jurisdiction should be confined. Otherwise, the party acting in bad faith may guess at the final award and begin to take measures to stave off the negative consequences, for example by transferring assets to favourable jurisdictions.

IV. Ignoring the Principle

1.19. As demonstrated above, the existence of the arbitration clause is strongly supported by arbitral tribunals and state courts even if one of the parties refers to the non-existence of the UC. In most of these cases the principle of the arbitration agreement's autonomy plays a key role in the formulation of the reasoning of awards or court decisions.

1.20. Thus we see in the following case, there is no doubt at all that the insurer acquiring the rights of subrogation are considered to be bound by the AC set out in the UC initially concluded between the charterer (assignor) and the owner of the vessel. In *West Tankers Inc. v. Ras Riunione Adriatica Sicurta SpA, Generali Assicurazioni Generali SpA*[15]

---

[13] Sections 30 (1), 31 (4), 67 of the Arbitration Act 1996, June 17, 1996, UK Parliaments Acts, Chapter 23, see also at: http://www.statutelaw.gov.uk/ (accessed on July 10, 2011).

[14] *AOOT Kalmneft v. Glencore International A.G. and Another, supra* note 11, at 139.

[15] *West Tankers Inc.* v. *Ras Riunione Adriatica Sicurta SpA, Generali Assicurazioni Generali SpA*, QBD (CC) Case No. 2007-575, Judgment of October 2, 2007, EWHC 2184 (Comm.) [2007].

the owners of the vessel "Front Comor" brought an application against the charterer and its insurer, seeking an anti-suit injunction that the defendants were bound by the arbitration agreement and couldn't refer any disputes to a state court. So the proceedings, initiated by the insurer in the courts of Syracuse, would have been stopped in terms of complying with the requirements of English law.

1.21. Obviously, the insurer didn't consider itself bound by the AC in disposing its right to claim for compensation, paid to the charterer according to the insurance policy. This position could be substantiated by implementation of the principle of AAA. If the arbitration provisions are of an autonomous nature and should be assessed as an agreement, separate from the underlying contract, why can't the assignor transfer to the assignee *only the rights of substantial character, excluding the right to refer to the arbitration?* Incidentally, the arbitral tribunal in *V/O 'Souznefteexport'* v. *Joc Oil, Ltd* came to the conclusion that "the arbitration agreement can't be the subject matter of cession at all. Being considered as autonomous procedural contract, it requires separate consent by the assignee to be subject under the jurisdiction, chosen by the parties in the contract."[16]

1.22. Surprisingly, in *West Tankers Inc.* v. *Ras Riunione Adriatica Sicurta SpA, Generali Assicurazioni Generali SpA* Judge Smith didn't express any doubt concerning an inextricable connection between the AC and the UC in terms of the assignee's obligation to refer its claim to the arbitration. The principle of AAA was not mentioned at all. On the contrary, the AC was called an "incidental burden," implicitly and automatically accepted by the assignee regarding the transferred rights.[17] Thus, the principle of AAA is being applied or ignored depending on whether or not its implementation is favourable to the arbitration proceedings.

V. The Principle as a Substitute for Arbitrability

1.23. Invalidity of the UC doesn't mean the clause never existed. From a legal point of view what the claimant tries to deny is not the fact of the agreement, but its legal consequences. Purportedly, the final aim of the contract could not be achieved because of the defects of the parties' mutual will, the non-compliance with mandatory legal rules or the illegal activity of one of the parties or both of them. The last mentioned situation is the most curious, as it usually only concerns the underlying

---

[16] *V/O 'Souznefteexport'* v. *Joc Oil, Ltd, supra* note 7, at 159.

[17] *West Tankers Inc.* v. *Ras Riunione Adriatica Sicurta SpA, Generali Assicurazioni Generali SpA, supra* note 15, at para. 23.

contract. The party, acting in bad faith can resort to various illegal instruments: collusion, bribe, fraud, in order to achieve the conclusion of a lucrative transaction. The AA is deprived of any commercial sense as it only serves for dispute resolution. Therefore, one can hardly imagine a situation, when the object of illegal actions is directly connected to the arbitration agreement. The only problem the arbitral tribunal or state courts face is the question of the extent to which the illegality of the underlying contract affects the arbitration agreement.

1.24. It has become traditional to consider that illegal or immoral contracts make the arbitration clause invalid.[18] But this general rule has some exceptions. Kreindler's opinion is that "corruption is a less egregious form of illicitness and/or ... it does not taint effective assent to the arbitration agreement."[19] In *Fiona Trust & Holding Corporation & Others* v. *Yuri Privalov & Ors*[20] Judge Longmore actually erased the difference between bribery and misrepresentation or non-disclosure. His arguments can be considered a contemporary interpretation of the principle of AAA based on the following factual circumstances.

1.25. The claimants, being associated with the Russian Sovcomflot group as owners of the vessels, initiated court proceedings against the natural persons and companies involved in the conclusion of charterparties, which were disadvantageous for the claimants. Some of the defendants were the directors or employees of Sovcomflot, who received bribes for entering into the transactions. The owners considered the transactions as rescinded deals and claimed for damages arising from tort of conspiracy and bribery. Meanwhile, the charterers began to enforce the arbitration clause by appointing a sole arbitrator. Therefore, the claimants had to seek an interlocutory injunction to restrain the arbitration proceedings. At the first instance Judge Morison satisfied the claim and granted the requested injunction. But in the Court of Appeal Judge Longmore reversed the decision and allowed the stay of the owners' rescission proceedings. His arguments can be narrowed down to the following proposition.

1.26. First of all, it is necessary to bear in mind that all allegations regarding illegality should concern not only the underlying contract but also the arbitration agreement. The mere speculation that one of the party

---

[18] Hew R. Dundas, *A Siberian Contribution to English Law: Public Policy, Illegality and the Enforcement of International Arbitration Awards. The Case Soinco S.A.C.I.* v. *Novokuznetsky Aluminium Plant and Subsequent Cases*, 3 ICA 63 (2004).

[19] Richard H. Kreindler, *Aspects of illegality in the formation and performance of contracts*, 6-1 Int. A.L.R. 16 (2003).

[20] *Fiona Trust & Holding Corporation & Others* v. *Yuri Privalov & Ors*, CA (CC) Case No. 2006 2353 A3, Judgement of January 24, 2007, EWCA Civ 20 [2007].

would not have entered into the contract at all, had the party been informed of the illegal activity of its representatives, would not be considered sufficient reason to challenge the arbitration agreement.[21] The arbitral tribunal's jurisdiction covers all claims based on the invalidity of the underlying contract regardless of its illegality. Thus, such grounds as fraud and bribery can be assessed in the same way as issues of *non est factum* or misrepresentation.

1.27.   This approach barely hides the desire to create more advantages for international commercial arbitration rather than a system of national courts. It should be noted, that two cases cited in this article in connection with the illegality of the underlying contract primarily concern crimes perpetrated against Russian residents. Also it is no secret that the English judges repeatedly expressed their negative view of the current Russian political and judicial system. At the present time there is no effective cooperation on enforcement of judgements between these countries. In this situation the English arbitrators, acting as private persons, have more authority than the Russian judges or officials do. It's a shame that the popularization of international commercial arbitration should be used as an instrument in the implicit confrontation between two judicial systems.

1.28.   The principle of AAA as it is being developed at the present time is tainted by a double standard. Why should exemptions from implementation of this principle be limited only to the following so-called "overtly illegal contracts": "(a) facilitation or promotion of drug-trafficking, (b) terrorism, (c) subversion, (d) prostitution, (e) child abuse, (f) slavery, and (g) other forms of human rights violations"?[22] It is obvious that these types of crimes could hardly be involved in international trade. Corruption, influence peddling, bribery are frequently met in commercial activity and greatly harm national economics. If these facts can be assessed by arbitrators, the AC will be used as an obstacle to the crime victims' achievement of justice, as this function traditionally belongs to the state courts.

1.29.   To avoid the negative effects of too broad an application of the principle of AAA, it is necessary to recall the other principle of international commercial arbitration – arbitrability. As stated before, there is no need to bother with the defects of the arbitration agreement in cases where the underlying contract is illegal. The legal consequences of the arbitration clause matter more. The arbitration proceedings should be stayed, if the state court or other judicial

---

[21]   *Ibid.*, at para. 25.
[22]   Richard H. Kreindler, *supra* note 19, at 2.

authority declares it has jurisdiction over the dispute. Fraud and bribery are always considered to be dangers to the legal order and social safety. Therefore the dispute ceases to be a private case between opposing parties but requires the intervention of the public authority. Protection of the public interest should outweigh the right of the parties to invoke alternative forms of dispute resolution.

VI. Conclusions

1.30. The principle of AAA as it is being developed in the contemporary academic literature needs review. This article has demonstrated how in many cases it may lead not to an adequate alternative to the judicial system but to the emergence of a new phenomenon, which could be called "jurisdiction heaven," where the interests of small groups of businessmen may take priority over the national legal systems of developing countries.

1.31. To prevent such negative effects it would be better to narrow the implementation of the principle of AAA by establishing certain procedural limitations and to revive the principle of arbitrability. Arbitrability should prohibit the arbitral tribunal's ability to assess the illegality (such as fraud, bribery and corruption) of the underlying contract.

| | |

Summaries

DEU [*Zur Autonomie des Schiedsvertrags: die Gefahr der weitgefassten Auslegung*]

Die Autonomie des Schiedsvertrags gilt der internationalen Schiedsgerichtsbarkeit in Handelssachen als grundlegendes Prinzip. Das Autonomiekonzept war ursprünglich zur Stärkung von ordentlich durch die Parteien abgeschlossenen Schiedsklauseln trotz potenzieller Nichtigkeit des bezogenen Vertrags entwickelt worden. Derartige Klauseln galten zwar als Vertragsbestimmung, wahrten aber ihre Unabhängigkeit vom Restvertrag aufgrund der besonderen von den Parteien verfolgten Ziele. Im Laufe der Zeit wurde dieses Prinzip dem juristischen Denken in Lehre und Praxis so sehr zur zweiten Natur, dass die Verbindung zwischen der Schiedsklausel und dem Vertrag, auf den sie sich bezieht, nicht länger von juristischem Interesse schien. Befürchtungen hinsichtlich der Durchsetzbarkeit von Schiedsbestimmungen schlugen in einen übereifrigen Glauben an deren Vorrang vor allen anderen Vertragsbestimmungen über. Als Konsequenz wurde die Einbindung von Schiedsklauseln in Verträge, was ja die Beilegung etwaiger Streitigkeiten in privater Form (im Gegensatz zu einer öffentlichen Verhandlung) nach sich zieht, zu einem Werkzeug, mit dem Parteien die verschiedensten Hindernisse umschiffen, welche ihnen von nationalen Rechtsinstrumenten in den Weg gelegt wurden, um unlauteren Handlungen im internationalen Geschäftsverkehr vorzubeugen. Die vorliegende Arbeit setzt sich zum Ziel, die unstatthaft breite Anwendung der Autonomie von Schiedsverträgen anhand relevanter schiedsgerichtlicher und gerichtlicher Beispielfälle darzulegen.

CZE [***Autonomie rozhodčí smlouvy: nebezpečí široké interpretace***]

Autonomie rozhodčí smlouvy je uznávána jako základní princip mezinárodního rozhodčího řízení v obchodních věcech. Původně se koncept autonomie vyvinul jako instrument posílení rozhodčí doložky, mezi stranami řádně uzavřené, navzdory možné neplatnosti smlouvy hlavní. Přestože byla tato doložka považována za jedno ze smluvních ustanovení, zachovávala si svou nezávislost na smlouvě díky specifickým cílům, které strany touto doložkou sledovaly. Časem se tato zásada v myšlení akademiků a právníků z praxe zabydlela natolik, že spojení mezi rozhodčí doložkou a hlavní smlouvou přestalo přitahovat jejich pozornost. Obavy o rozhodčí doložky se přetavily do přehnané víry v jejich převahu nad jinými ustanoveními smlouvy. V důsledku tohoto vývoje byly nejrůznější překážky vytvořené národními právními nástroji za účelem předcházení nekalému jednání v mezinárodních obchodních transakcích překonány vložením rozhodčí doložky, která s sebou přináší urovnávání sporů soukromou, nikoli veřejnou cestou. Cílem následujícího příspěvku je poukázat na nedůvodně extenzivní aplikaci principu autonomie rozhodčí smlouvy rozborem relevantních případů z rozhodčí a soudní praxe.

| | |

POL [***Autonomia umowy arbitrażowej: ryzyko szerokiej wykładni***]

Autonomia umowy arbitrażowej w znacznym stopniu przyczynia się do bardziej efektywnego rozwoju międzynarodowego arbitrażu handlowego. Jednak szeroka wykładnia tej reguły może równie dobrze naruszyć interesy pozwanego w postępowaniu arbitrażowym, lub przynajmniej uniemożliwić pozwanemu dochodzenie swoich praw w skuteczny sposób. Niniejszy artykuł zajmuje się analizą krytyczną niekonsekwentnego wdrażania wspomnianej reguły i rozważa konieczność jej rewizji w niektórych przypadkach niezgodności z prawem umowy właściwej.

Czech (& Central European) Yearbook of Arbitration

FRA [*L'autonomie de la convention d'arbitrage : le danger de l'interprétation large*]

L'autonomie de la convention d'arbitrage participe largement au développement effectif de l'arbitrage commercial international. Toutefois, l'interprétation large de ce principe pourrait véritablement empiéter sur les intérêts du défendeur dans les procédures d'arbitrage, ou tout au moins, empêcher le défendeur de faire usage de ses droits d'une manière efficace. Cet article est l'analyse critique de l'application incohérente du principe susmentionné, et pose la question de son bien-fondé dans certains cas d'illégalité du contrat sous-jacent.

RUS [*Независимость арбитражного соглашения: опасность широкого толкования*]

Независимость арбитражного соглашения в значительной степени способствует эффективному развитию международного коммерческого арбитража. Однако широкое толкование этого принципа может также нарушать интересы ответчика в арбитражном процессе или, по крайней мере, не позволять ответчику успешно отстаивать свои права. Эта статья посвящена критическому рассмотрению непоследовательности реализации вышеупомянутого принципа. В ней также поднимается вопрос его пересмотра в некоторых случаях незаконности рассматриваемого договора.

ESP [*Autonomía del acuerdo de arbitraje: El peligro de una amplia interpretación*]

La autonomía del acuerdo de arbitraje contribuye significativamente al desarrollo eficaz del arbitraje comercial internacional. En cualquier caso, una amplia interpretación de este principio podría interferir en los intereses del demandado en los procedimientos de arbitraje o, al menos, impedir que el demandado reivindique sus derechos de forma efectiva. Este artículo realiza un análisis crítico de la implementación inconsistente del principio arriba mencionado y plantea la cuestión de su revisión en algunos casos de ilegalidad del contrato subyacente.

Alexander J. Bělohlávek

Autonomy in B2C Arbitration: Is the European Model of Consumer Protection Really Adequate?

Key words:
contract of adhesion | ADR arbitrability | autonomy | Czech law | evidence | French law | harmonization | international dimension | venue of proceedings | costs of proceedings | German law | liability | EU law | principles of arbitration | procedural autonomy | proportionality | average consumer | Austrian law | arbitral award | law of contract | consumer | Spanish law | abuse of law

Abstract | Consumer protection has become a legal phenomenon to reckon with on a global scale, with repercussions for, among others, contracts concluded between consumers and business entities – i.e., B2C contracts. While the path chosen by EU law is one of special legal protection (on the basis of special legislation) and the introduction of restrictions, the model applied in the United States is based on protection afforded according to the general law of contract principles. The author maintains that the model applied in the United States is more efficient as it does not prevent markets which are based on a high degree of autonomy (but also responsibility) on the part of all contractual partners, including the consumer, from prospering. He argues that "liability" is the other side of the coin labeled "autonomy" and must be applied with a broad brush, both in terms of substantive-law aspects and procedural aspects. This also extends to arbitration agreements concluded between consumers and business entities. He maintains there is no need for special restrictions when it comes to incorporating arbitration clauses in consumer contracts, and that instead, the lawmaker should focus on seeing to it that the basic principles of arbitration are observed. In concluding he finds that the European model often leads to the abuse of the system of consumer protection by the consumers themselves and that the German model represents an interesting and efficient model, striking a compromise between the restrictive system established under EU law and the U.S. model.

Prof. Dr. Alexander J. Bělohlávek holds the chair of legal studies at the faculty of economics of the Technical University of Ostrava [Czech Republic] and a visiting professorship at the Department of International and European Law of the faculty of law at Masaryk University in Brno [Czech Republic]. He is an attorney-at-law in Prague [Czech Republic] (with a branch office in N.J. [USA]), president of the World Jurist Association (Washington D.C., USA), and arbitrator in Prague [CZE], Vienna [Austria], Kyiv [Ukraine], Moscow [Russia], Almaty [Kazakhstan], Vilnius [Lithuania], Chisinau [Moldava], at the ICC, and under UNCITRAL rules, among others.
e-mail: office@ablegal.cz

| | |

I. Arbitration versus the Protection of Consumers in Terms of Procedure

2.01. Arbitration is usually considered to be only one of several forms of alternative dispute resolution, i.e., a form of dispute resolution which takes a route different from that of proceedings before [state/general] courts. Aside from arbitration, there is mediation, mediation in combination with arbitration, expert procedure,[1] assisted conciliation procedure, and various procedures which may be labeled arbitration, but lack one or more of the defining features of arbitration – such as the voluntary character of arbitration or the right to appoint one's arbitrator. Examples would include on-line dispute resolution, mediation-like methods, or certain procedures for resolving consumer disputes which are recognized and supported by the state, such as in Spain or Portugal. A special regime for resolving consumer credit disputes exists in the United Kingdom where all such cases must be resolved by a financial ombudsman in accordance with the 1974 Consumer Credit Act.[2] In terms of their formal aspects, these procedures are notably different from arbitration and the "results" of such procedures (in the sense of any authoritative decisions) are not enforceable internationally under the New York Convention.

2.02. Arbitration is not a panacea, and certainly not suitable for resolving *all* types of disputes. It has its proponents and detractors. In fact, one can hardly speak of any type (group) of dispute as being particularly suited, *a priori*, for resolution via arbitration rather than before a [general] court (nor is the opposite conclusion universally true). This also applies to consumer disputes (i.e., disputes related to consumer contracts – contracts concluded with consumers) which are usually referred to as B2C disputes. Consumers deserve a certain degree of special protection in cases where they are forced to accept the terms, i.e., *contracts of adhesion* presented to them by the business entity with whom they may

---

[1]   *Cf.*, for instance, ALEXANDER J. BĚLOHLÁVEK & RENÁTA HÓTOVÁ, ZNALCI V MEZINÁRODNÍM PROSTŘEDÍ (V SOUDNÍM ŘÍZENÍ CIVILNÍM A TRESTNÍM, V ROZHODČÍM ŘÍZENÍ A V INVESTIČNÍCH SPORECH) (*Experts in International Proceedings (Civil and Criminal Litigation, Arbitration, and Investment Disputes)*), Praha: C. H. Beck (2011) [also available in Polish – Warsaw: C. H. Beck (2011), Russian – Kyiv: Taxon (2011), and Romanian–Bucharest: C. H. Beck (2012)].

[2]   Consumer Credit Act (1974), in the amended wording of 2006 – Consumer Credit Act (2006). The current wording of the Consumer Credit Act (1974) is available at: http://www.legislation.gov.uk/ukpga/1974/39/contents#485933 (accessed on January 14, 2012). The changes introduced in 2006 have been analyzed e.g. on the pages of the Office of Fair Trading at: http://www.oft.gov.uk/about-the-oft/legal-powers/legal/cca/CCA2006/ (accessed on January 14, 2012).

wish to engage in a transaction. It would be wrong, however, to categorically declare that this particular kind of dispute is best resolved by way of litigation, as opposed to resolution by means of a procedure before arbitrators or another dispute resolution (ADR) method.

2.03.　It is also important to point out that arbitration and ADR today are completely different from what they were at the end of the 1980s. In the era of a bi-polar global system that was strictly divided along political, military, and economic lines and the host of political problems caused by that separation, the main issue to be overcome by arbitration and ADR was that of the recognition and enforcement of foreign decisions. Today, this phenomenon is being steadily mitigated and arbitration (and ADR in general) have taken on a much different role; that of replacing state power and public authority in those cases where the latter are, for a variety of reasons, dysfunctional or inefficient.

II. Pushing the Boundaries of Consumer Protection

2.04.　One need not deny the unquestionable significance and necessity of consumer protection in order to see that the intensity of this kind of protection is somewhat fraught with problems –whether this protection is made available through special laws as is typically the case in Europe, or based on general legal principles and the application of the general law of contract as is the case in the United States. If one postulates that the parties to a contract enjoy equal standing, the weaker party deserves special protection. However, intensifying this protection often opens up possibilities for the *weaker party* (e.g., the *consumer*) to abuse the standard – and naturally, such abuse of the law should not be protected in any way. A typical example would be the increasing number of cases in which consumers exercise their right to walk away from a contract within the statutory withdrawal period after actively using the purchased goods and thus achieving the purpose for which they were bought (especially in the case of seasonal products). In addition, even consumers may be held liable to an adequate and customary extent for their actions, i.e., for entering into a contract and assuming obligations under the same. The experience in the Czech Republic shows that the overwhelming majority of consumer disputes take the form of claims by businesses against consumers who are unwilling or unable to honor their financial obligations, compared to a small number of consumer action cases against businesses on the grounds of their defective performance. We have seen that the rather cumbersome mechanism of litigation no longer affords sufficient protection to businesses, which are now being held hostage by consumers due to the special protection enjoyed by them. Situations in which consumers default on their payment obligations because of their inability to properly assess their own financial possibilities are typically cases of the abuse of special consumer-protection laws. It is precisely in this kind of case that the absence of a swift and efficient dispute resolution method, coupled with the denial of access to otherwise available methods of finding justice (that include due process guarantees) is in conflict with the rule of law. On the other hand, it is difficult to see how litigation could ever abandon its traditional and essential elements of civil procedure, including those which may be at fault for making litigation tangibly more protracted than ADR procedures. Hence, arbitration is and should be a suitable option in many countries for resolving the above-described situation, provided that the parties' agreement to be bound by arbitration is an indisputable expression of their true will.

2.05.   In addition, the fact that the special protection of consumers (and in particular, the level of intensity to which it has been taken in the EU) focuses only on the remedy of the consequences rather than on the prevention of the causes[3] is deserving of criticism. After all, consumer protection legislation deals with the nullity, *qua* unconscionability, of certain provisions in consumer contracts – but no legislation (much less mandatory provisions of law) prevents banks from launching massive, cleverly designed advertising campaigns just before the summer holidays or Christmas season including such slogans as *"with us, you can afford it."* No one requires consumer credit agencies[4] to give qualified advice to consumers regarding their potential inability to live up to their financial obligations or to perform a thorough credit check in the real interest of the consumer who is about to take out a loan. These are the circumstances that the lawmaker ought to take into account before they pass what is often very intensive consumer protection legislation; these circumstances should also be taken into account when assessing the proportional of special consumer protection at the expense of contractual autonomy. It is, after all,

---

[3]   It is true that in EU law, Consumer Credit Directive 2008/48/EC (which replaces and supersedes the earlier provisions of Directive 87/102/EEC) sets forth in its Article 20 that "Member States shall ensure that creditors are supervised or regulated by a body or authority independent from financial institutions." However, the definition of the scope of this supervision is only cursory. In terms of the unfair advertising practices of consumer credit agencies, individual countries have taken a very lackadaisical approach to supervision.

[4]   On the issue of consumer credits and arbitration, see e.g. Zdeněk Nový, *Spotřebitelské úvěry a rozhodčí řízení* (*Consumer Credits and Arbitration*), (8) JURISPRUDENCE 22 (2010), among others.

beyond contention that consumers will usually enter into any kind of contract at the prospect of attaining what are often to them *luxurious* goods, without paying heed to any of the information provided to them by the business on the other end of the contract, and irrespective of the form in which this information is presented (i.e., in a separate document or a separately signed document highlighting certain content, etc.). What is more, the sheer amount of information which must be presented to the consumer due to obligatory rules often goes beyond what an *average [typical] consumer* is able to digest; in particular, consumers are unable to fathom the very real underpinnings of such information. Resolving the need for consumer protection by inflating the volume of obligatory information which businesses must make available to the consumer or by engaging in a crusade against any and all alternative forms of the enforcement of businesspersons' rights, is political window dressing which – as I have noted above – does not address the root cause of the problem, but merely represents a rather mock cure of the consequences. Sadly, it is not by accident that this approach resembles the kind of policy so often endorsed by authorities in the past – outwardly attractive measures which do not resolve anything, such as the blanket moratorium of debt in times of crisis (applied, for example, to promissory notes by the Paris Commune) or, to go further into the past, pogroms against groups of people who offered credit, but at higher interest rates. Efforts to maximize remedies at a stage at which the rights under a B2C contract must be enforced authoritatively are in my view as ill-advised as the effort to make an unruly child *touch a hot stove once*, so that he/she gets a taste of the painful consequences of such imprudence. Even if arbitration is not a *cure-all*, you can't very well extol the virtues of the free market on the one hand, only to maximize protective policies on the other.[5]

---

[5]   In this respect, Judgment 2004-10-01 by the Latvian Constitutional Court of 17 January 2005, among others, hits the mark (an electronic version may be available at: www.satv.tiesa.gov.lv/upload/2004-10-01E.rtf (accessed on July 11, 2008). Upon reviewing the conscionability of arbitration clauses in consumer contracts, the Constitutional Court concluded that under standard market conditions, anyone may choose to either accept or refuse a proposal to contract (and thus the specific terms of contract that come with it) – nobody can be forced to enter into a contract. The "invisible hand of the market"(a descriptive term deliberately used by the Constitutional Court in the reasons for its decision) exercises its influence on the content of those contracts which are concluded. It is thus the market environment itself which allows the contracting parties (here: consumers) to arrive at the decision to enter into a given contract or not (and they must bear the consequences, both positive and negative, which arise from such a decision). To the extent that individual market participants abuse their position by dictating their own terms to others, who normally, barring such abuse, would not consent to them, protection

Alternative dispute resolution (and, in particular arbitration) is generally the right method of dispute resolution, but only with respect to a rather small group of civil-law disputes, and is a method within which one should always insist on the utmost professionalism; after all, it is precisely the quality of the decision on the merits and the opportunity of the parties to exert influence on the composition of the *arbitration forum* which serve as the antidote to the procedural shortcuts taken in arbitration, as compared to litigation. Arbitration *can* also serve as a method for attaining the proportionate satisfaction of the parties' various protected interests in consumer disputes,[6] but only if a high standard of arbitration is guaranteed and only if those principles which are specific to arbitration and which are non-negotiable in any form of adversarial procedure are afforded protection.

III. Risk of Consumer Abuse of Special Protection (Abuse of the Law)

2.06. Experience has shown that, even though a certain system for protecting the *weaker party* is necessary, the *weaker party* will often abuse these standards. National jurisdictions should be tasked with identifying defense mechanisms against such unfair practice by consumers[7] and

---

can and must always be sought exclusively in the mechanisms provided by legislation on the protection of competition. The Latvian Constitutional Court also ruled on the issue of the removal of an arbitrator due to lack of impartiality, and did so fully in line with the decision-making practice of the ECtHR (i.e., in particular, but not limited to the decision in *Suovaniemi* v. *Finland*).

[6] In this respect, see for instance the ruling of the Czech Constitutional Court in II. ÚS 2164/10 of 5 November 2011, which states with a specific view to the protection of consumers within the context of arbitration (cit.): "The protection of party autonomy cannot be absolute if there exist other fundamental rights of individuals or constitutional principles or other public interests recognized by the constitution with the capacity to proportionally curb the autonomy of will." However, one cannot set forth a one-size-fits-all criteria in this respect; also in the case of consumer protection, one must differentiate from among a broad spectrum of possibilities, depending on the specific facts of the case and the legal state of affairs.

[7] *Cf.* for instance Decision 28079370102010100498 of the Court of Appeals in Madrid of 12 November 2010 (*Juan Pedro* v. *Metrovacesa S.A.*), annotated by Fernando Mantilla-Serrano in 11 (4) ITA (2011) (the legal proposition and basic outline of the decision have been lifted from the cited annotation). According to this decision, (i) the principle of good faith prevents consumers who themselves initiated an arbitration procedure with reference to the arbitration clause in "their" consumer contract from invoking the unconscionability of that clause in later proceedings on the annulment of the arbitral award; (ii) a consumer's defense of the unconscionability of an arbitration agreement must be dismissed if it is raised only in proceedings on the annulment of the arbitral award in spite of the fact that the consumer could have done so during the actual arbitration procedure; (iii) a Party who

the individual EU Member States should make full use of their procedural autonomy.

2.07. One could name numerous examples of loopholes in consumer protection laws that have been found and exploited by consumers. Under the special regime in place in the EU today, one commonly sees consumers consent to arbitration at first, keeping the option to challenge the arbitration clause as unconscionable up their sleeve, only to be exercised in the case of a later court procedure on the nullification of the arbitral award (in the event that the consumer does not prevail on the merits). Hardly ever does one hear stated clearly, and much less from competent authorities, that the purpose of EU law (just as much as that of national jurisdictions outside the EU) is not this kind of abuse of consumer protection. National jurisdictions (possibly making use of their procedural autonomy) must find ways to prevent these cases of abuse.[8] For that matter, the ECJ itself ruled in *Asturcom* that certain restrictions in this regard are compatible with the acquis (i.e., EU law). The courts thus may rule as unconscionable the consumer's omission to challenge the arbitration clause in arbitration proceedings, but only to a certain degree. They cannot do so in the case of the complete passivity of the consumer, i.e., in cases in which the consumer does not in any way participate in the arbitration procedure or file a court action for the annulment of the arbitral award.[9] Such a list of examples must be considered, of course, non-exhaustive, especially considering that the specific application of EU law (and, in particular, the entire realm of procedural law) is part of the Member States' legislative autonomy. Based on this conclusion alone, however, one cannot build a concept of balanced (equitable) positions of the parties to a dispute (if one takes into account the specific character of consumer contracts). After all, not only the case of a completely passive consumer in arbitration should be covered, but also the case of a consumer who willfully and with ulterior motives chooses not to use the defense of unconscionability (in time). What is more, from the

---

is aware of a violation of discretionary provisions of lex arbitri but does not invoke this fact within a set time period (or, as the case may be, "as soon as feasible," if no time period was given), has thus waived his right to invoke this particular defense. This also extends to the option of invoking the unconscionability (nullity) of the arbitration agreement. In this matter, the court very elegantly applied the principle of good faith to both consumer protection *and* the protection of the commercial business entity that is the consumer's contractual partner.

[8]   Compare ECJ Judgment of 26 October 2006, C-168/05, *Elisa María Mostaza Claro* v. *Centro Móvil Milenium SL*.

[9]   ECJ Judgment of 6 October 2009, C-40/08, *Asturcom Telecomunicaciones SL* v. *Cristina Rodríguez Nogueira (Asturcom)* [2009] ECR I-09579, CELEX 62008CA0040.

vantage point of procedural law, the omission of the defense of the unconscionability of the arbitration clause in the arbitration procedure on the one hand and the omission to file a court action for the annulment of an arbitral award fall within two different categories.

2.08. The vulnerability of consumers stems from the fact that they engage in relations with a business entity which, as such, enjoys a strong bargaining position and privileged access to information. For the business, concluding consumer contracts is a standard transaction within the scope of their operations which they engage in many times over. One may expect them to find their bearings more easily compared to a consumer who is less experienced and often less able to draw upon active and efficient legal assistance. The stress here is to be placed on something which is particularly relevant within the context of arbitration, namely, it is the consumer who is often only to a limited degree in a position to successfully demand a change of the terms of contract. Likewise, the circumstances under which consumer contracts are concluded are often characterized by the somewhat laconic (but nonetheless fitting) phrase "take it or leave it."[10] On the other hand, and this is absolutely essential, especially in proceedings concerning consumer contracts, one must always recognize the limit of such protection, which (to simplify somewhat) must be of the standard which would be extended to the average consumer.[11] Consumer protection may be a fundamental pillar of EU legislation, but the fact that businesses must bear the entire risk inherent in contractual relations, whereas consumers de facto cannot be held liable is unacceptable. This approach would constitute an abuse of law and would be at odds with the fundamental principles of a society governed by the rule of law, which demands, among other things, that everyone be held liable to a proportionate degree for their own legally binding actions. Essentially then, one is tasked with estimating the degree to which the average, or typical consumer is knowledgeable, and to which degree the average consumer has the opportunity and ability to protect

---

[10] See also the note below on what is known as contracts of adhesion.

[11] See also recital (18) of the Preamble to Directive 2005/29/EC, according to which the degree of observance of today's average consumer must be reviewed more stringently than before (i.e., no longer is it sufficient for the consumer to pay merely cursory or customary attention; he needs to be reasonably observant and circumspect). An analogy can be found in NS ČR Judgment 32 Cdo 4661/2007 of 23 October 2008, available in electronic form at: http://www.nsoud.cz/rozhod.php?action=read&id=45311&searchstr=32+Cdo+4661%2F2 007 (accessed on May 24, 2009). On the term "average consumer," see also NS ČR Judgment 23 Cdo 1201/2009 of 29 June 2010.

himself[12] before applying this finding to the actual case at hand (in factual and legal terms) and its solution. Not even the EU standards afford absolute protection to consumers who fail to protect their own interests responsibly or who even abuse consumer protection law.[13]

2.09. The textbook case of a legitimate and desirable degree of special protection for consumers can be found in contracts of adhesion. These are contracts which the consumer may accept or refuse in their entirety; their content cannot be influenced by the consumer's actions or modified by attempting to negotiate a contractual consensus between the parties. Often, the modification of contracts or general terms of a contract, in deviation from the one-size-fits-all standard used by the commercial contract partner, is impossible for the individual consumer who enters into a legal relation with a larger business. This places businesses in a position of considerable power, as they may incorporate provisions in their contracts which put them at a significant advantage. This, coupled with the dearth of information on the part of the consumer, makes the contract highly imbalanced. The

---

[12] On this issue see also, for instance, NS ČR Judgment 32 Odo 229/2006 of 30 May 2007, according to which (cit.): (1) The vantage point of the "average consumer" is that of a consumer who is reasonably well-informed and reasonably observant and circumspect, taking into account social, cultural, and linguistic factors. (2) In advertising for goods and services of daily consumption, almost all consumers today expect a certain amount of exaggeration in advertising and hyperbole that is not to be believed. Adopted from the annotation in Dana Ondrejová, *Generální klauzule nekalé soutěže v aktuální rozhodovací praxi Nejvyššího soudu ČR* (*The Blanket Clause of Unfair Competition in the Current Decision Practice of the Czech Supreme Court*), 15 (4) SOUDNÍ ROZHLEDY 121, 126 (2009). The judgment is also available in electronic form at: http://www.nsoud.cz/rozhod. php?action=read&id=36076&searchstr=32+Odo+229%2F2006 (accessed on May 23, 2009).
See also BGH Judgment I ZR 167/97 of 20 October 1999 ("Orient-Teppich Muster") – one of the most frequently cited decisions in German law in connection with unfair competition. Although the decision was rendered at a time at which the legislation applied is no longer operative, the fundamental principles of the decision still hold true. In the decision, the court addressed the degree of observance one may expect from the average consumer, which depends on the importance of a given text for the specific individual. Then there is e.g. NS ČR Judgment 32 Odo 229/2006 of 30 May 2007, in which the court held that an average consumer was a consumer who is reasonably well-informed and reasonably observant and circumspect.

[13] These conclusions may be drawn e.g. from the following decisions: (•) ECJ Judgment of 4 June 2009, C-243/08, *Pannon GSM Zrt* v. *Sustikné Győrfi Erzsébet* [Pannon GSM] [2009] ECR I-04713;, CELEX: 62008CA0243, (•) Judgment of the Court of Appeals in Madrid [Spain] 28079370102010100498, 12 November 2010 (in *Juan Pedro* v. *Metrovacesa S.A.*), among others. These decisions, and other facts, also indicate that a violation of consumer protection law in connection with the conclusion of arbitration agreements does *not* automatically result in what is known in various jurisdictions as "absolute" (i.e., irremediable) "nullity" (such as the Czech Republic), "Unwirksamkeit" (inoperativeness, Germany), etc.

problem is exacerbated in the international context of cross-border transactions (i.e., in relations with an international dimension). It is therefore altogether unsurprising that the EU has devoted special attention to this issue by passing rather extensive harmonization laws.

2.10. In addition, active electronic communication has greatly facilitated the conclusion of consumer contracts between parties from different countries and thus has increased the overall volume of such contracts several times over. However, one must assume that consumers encountering business partners outside their home country are even less knowledgeable of the legal provisions (of such other country) that may apply to their relation. On the other hand, the same holds true for certain groups of businesses – small enterprises which may have the wherewithal to do business outside their country thanks to electronic media, but are less informed about the consumer legislation in the countries in which they were able to gain a foothold.

IV. The Model of Consumer Protection Applied in the EU: A Restrictive Approach

2.11. The protection of consumers in the European Union rests on the following five groups of fundamental rights: (i) the right to the protection of health and safety, (ii) the right to the protection of economic interests, (iii) the right to information and education, (iv) the right to compensation of damages, and (v) the right to a fair trial.[14] The normative basis in the EU is given in Article 169 TFEU (ex Article 153 TEC). The European Communities began creating consumer protection laws as early as 1984 – primarily, Council Directive 84/450/EEC concerning misleading advertising,[15] followed by Council Directive 85/577/EEC to protect consumers in contracts negotiated away from business premises.[16] However, the first EU laws with a fundamental impact on consumer protection legislation were Council

---

[14] *Cf.* for instance LUBOŠ TICHÝ & RAINER ARNOLD & PAVEL SVOBODA & JIŘÍ ZEMÁNEK & RICHARD KRÁL, EVROPSKÉ PRÁVO (*EU Law*), Praha: C. H. Beck 742 (3rd ed. 2006), and others.

[15] Directive of the Council 84/450/EEC of 10 September 1984 relating to the approximation of the laws, regulations and administrative provisions of the Member States concerning misleading advertising (CELEX: 31984L0450; published in OJ L 250, 19 September 1984, pp. 17–20), in the wording of 97/55/EEC (implemented in the Czech Republic by way of Act No. 40/1995 Coll., on the regulation of advertising and on changes and additions to Act No. 468/1991 Coll., on radio and television broadcasting, as amended).

[16] Directive of 25 July 1985 (CELEX: 31985L0577; published in: OJ L 372, 31 December 1985, pp. 31—33).

Directive 93/13/EEC (hereinafter the "Directive") and Commission Recommendation 98/257/EC (the "Recommendation"). Further, above all, the reference here is to the case law of the ECJ which only in recent years (especially in decisions dating from the period from 2006 to 2010) has begun to specify the issue of consumer protection within the context of arbitration and to delineate its limits with respect to consumer disputes (i.e., from the vantage point of consumer protection rather than from the vantage point of arbitration). The central role in assessing the "unfairness" of arbitration clauses in consumer contracts is undoubtedly played by Council Directive 93/13/EEC (the "Directive") which stipulates that consumers may challenge standard provisions in consumer contracts (other than those concerning the price or the subject matter of contract[17]) as unfair. In the view expressed in the Directive, disproportionate (unfair) provisions create a marked imbalance at the expense of the consumer and are thus at odds with the proportionality requirement. It is left to the courts to decide whether the pertinent criteria have been met. The Directive also contains an Annex – an overview of such terms of contract that may prima facie be considered unfair (subject to contrary evidence). The terms in this list (contained in the Annex to the Directive) are not always unfair and other circumstances and terms are not necessarily fair just because they are not included in this list. For those terms included in the list, an increased likelihood of unfairness is anticipated based on long-term observations. The various language versions use different terms to describe the character of the list, but all of them indicate that we are looking at examples – at a guideline rather than a binding standard. This can be seen most clearly from the German version which

---

[17] In ECJ Judgment of 3 June 2010, C-484/08, *Caja de Ahorros y Monte de Piedad de Madrid* v. *Asociación de Usuarios de Servicios Bancarios* [*Ausbanc*], the Court ruled that neither the Directive nor the EC Treaty are precluding national legislation which authorizes a judicial review as to the (un)fairness of contractual terms, also where these relate to the definition of the main subject matter of the contract or the adequacy of the price and remuneration, and even in cases in which those terms are drafted in plain, intelligible language. In the case at hand, a contractual provision on rounding had come under scrutiny. According to the Spanish Supreme Court (*Tribunal Supremo*), a rounding provision may well constitute a material part of a credit agreement (i.e., here, a mortgage credit agreement for buying an apartment). Article 4 (2) of the Directive precludes any review of the potentially abusive character of contractual terms related to the definition of the main subject matter – essentially, courts are not in a position to rule on the abusive character of such contractual terms under the Directive. The Spanish Supreme Court held, however, that Spain had not implemented Article 4 (2) of the Directive into its national law, and that under Spanish law the entire contract was open to such judicial review. Judgment published in OJ C 209/6, 31 July 2010. CELEX: 62008CJ0484. Original language of the decision: Spanish.

characterizes the annex as "als Hinweis dienende [...] Liste", *i.e., loosely translated, a* "list which serves as an 'indication' or 'guidance.'" It is therefore wrong and somewhat self-serving to consider the relevant contractual understandings to be unfair prima facie. There is an important qualitative difference between the indicative character of guidance or instruction, on the one hand, and a prima facie assumption (even a refutable one) on the other. Two of the terms that are considered potentially unfair concern arbitration, i.e., first, item (i) [of the Annex to the Directive] concerning provisions which irrevocably bind the consumer to terms with which they had no real opportunity of becoming acquainted before the conclusion of the contract. This is applicable if the consumer enters into an arbitration agreement in the form of a contract of adhesion. Second, there is item (q) [of the Annex to the Directive], which concerns provisions "excluding or hindering the consumer's right to take legal action or exercise any other legal remedy, particularly by requiring the consumer to take exclusively to arbitration disputes not covered by legal provisions, unduly restricting the evidence available to him/her or imposing on him/her a burden of proof which, according to the applicable [procedural] law, should lie with the other party to the contract."

2.12. One might want to ask whether *items (i) and (q) of the Annex to the Directive should be interpreted each by itself, or cumulatively.*[18] In the second case (cumulative interpretation), the character of any cancellation of (or withdrawal from) a contract, or the defense of the nullity of any provisions in the consumer contract with respect to the arbitration agreement (or, in a broader scope, any provision of procedural impact) would have to be reviewed, irrespective of the type of procedure, the competencies vested in the arbitrators (or generally in the forum which is to decide the dispute), the law that applies (and the manner in which it should be applied), the respective standing of the parties to the proceedings, or the prescribed course of action in such a situation. Taking this cumulative approach, any contractual understanding of a procedural character would have to be reviewed under the aspect of item (i) of the Annex to the Directive, even if the understanding did not otherwise raise any concern in terms of whether it might be unfair from the point of view of item (g) of the Annex to the Directive. By contrast, in the case of a separate and independent review, one would not have to put contractual understanding to the test of item (i) as long as they do not run counter to the principles embodied in

---

[18] *Cf.* Susan Schiavetta, *Does the Internet Occasion New Directions in Consumer Arbitration in the EU?* (3) JILT 3 (2004).

item (g). In the case of such interpretation, item (i) of the Annex to the Directive would be void of any logic and call into question the overall concept (purpose and objective) of the Directive.

V. Comparison of Selected National Approaches within the EU

2.13. All EU Member States generally recognize the need for protection of the weaker party, but their understanding of the interplay between arbitration and consumer protection is highly diverse. To give just a couple of examples, the policies of a few states will now be examined.

2.14. In spite of the long-standing Austrian tradition of creating a very friendly environment for arbitration, and in spite of the broad range of disputes which are fit for arbitration, Austrian law (when compared to German law and even Czech law) is significantly more restrictive when it comes to the arbitrability of consumer disputes. Section 617 of the Austrian Code of Civil Procedure (ZPO) allows the conclusion of arbitration agreements only for disputes which are already pending, and even then only subject to the fulfillment of special criteria, especially as regards the form of the arbitration agreement (which must be signed in person by the consumer, who must have received instructions regarding the differences between arbitration and litigation; there are also restrictions regarding the seat of arbitration, etc.).

2.15. Following lengthy discussions, a substantive amendment to the Arbitration Act was finally passed *in the Czech Republic* towards the end of 2011; it is set to come into force on 1 April 2012.[19] The amendment preserves the arbitrability of consumer disputes, but sets forth special requirements in terms of the form and content of the arbitration agreement and for acting as an arbitrator in consumer disputes.

2.16. The *German model* is considered particularly tolerant and well-balanced. German law principally does not forbid arbitration clauses in consumer contracts and thus accommodates arbitration even more than Austrian law, with its tradition of promoting this form of dispute

---

[19] Act No. 19/2012, amending (*inter alia*) Act No. 216/1994 Coll., on arbitration and on the enforcement of arbitral awards, as amended. Detailed information on this amendment to the Czech Arbitration Act can be found in a separate news item in this volume of the CYArb. We should mention at this point that arbitration is an extremely popular form of dispute resolution in the Czech Republic. According to estimates by the Czech Ministry of Justice, up to 150,000 arbitral awards have been handed down annually in recent years, most of them on the basis of B2C contracts.

resolution intensively. Special rules for consumer contracts can only be found in Sec. 1032 (5) of the German Code of Civil Procedure (ZPO) according to which arbitration agreements to which a consumer is a party must be contained in a document signed in the parties' own hand. At the same time, the written form may be replaced by the electronic form. The document which contains the arbitration clause must not contain any provisions other than those which concern arbitration. The exceptions are cases in which a contract to which a consumer is a party is concluded in the form of a notarial deed.[20] Some commentators argue that the above-described requirements apply not only to B2C contracts (disputes) but also to contracts (disputes) between two consumers.[21] The German courts have interpreted the Directive with respect to arbitration less restrictively than those in other EU Member States. In a dispute decided in 2005,[22] the German courts ruled that an arbitration clause between a consumer and a business entity was valid in accordance with the national arbitration law (i.e., the Code of Civil Procedure – ZPO) and the former German Act Governing Standard Business Terms which served to implement the Directive.[23] The court found that the arbitration clause met none of the criteria of a prohibited term of contract. According to the German courts, *arbitration agreements are not "surprising" for consumers,*[24] or in conflict with the parties' good faith, and in and of themselves, a priori, do not put the party that accepted the [general] terms of contract at a disadvantage. The court also ruled that the *Directive principally does not rule out arbitration clauses in consumer contracts and that arbitration procedures (and arbitration agreements) conform to the requirements of the Directive.*[25] The German model, in particular, may

---

[20]   *Cf.* for instance Jörg Tröder, *Die Einbeziehung von Schiedsabreden in notarielle Urkunden,* MITTEILUNGEN DER RHEINISCHEN NOTARKAMMER 379-383 (2000).

[21]   *Cf.* Peter Schmitz, *Schiedsvereinbarungen in der notariellen Praxis,* (12) RHEINISCHE NOTAR-ZEITSCHRIFT 591, 601 (2003) (in Footnote No. 106, the author refers to the Commentary on the Zivilprozessordnung (Code of Civil Procedure)). In the cited article, the author states that the relevant criterion for whether a party in a specific legal relationship qualifies as a consumer is the character (qualitative assessment) of the potential future dispute which the parties submit to arbitration.

[22]   BGH Decision of 13 January 2005, annotated *in* (i) NJW 1125 (2005) and (ii) SCHIEDS VZ 95 (2005).

[23]   The latter-cited law has since been abolished and replaced by provisions that were incorporated into the German Civil Code.

[24]   See for instance the following decisions: (•)BGH Decision III ZR 265/03 of 13 January 2005, published *in* 162 BGHZ 9 et seq.; (•)BGH Decision III ZR 164/06 of 1 March 2007, annotated *in* NJW-RER 1456 (2007); (•) Decision Sch 3/06 by the OLG Frankfurt a. M. of 20 July 2007, annotated *in* OLG REPORT FRANKFURT A. M. 647 (2008), among others.

[25]   See for instance BGH Decision III ZR 256/03 of 13 January 2005.

be thought to represent an intriguing compromise between the American model of protection of consumer rights (which is based on general legal principles) and the protection granted on the basis of special laws (lex specialis). Since the amendment of the ZPO in 1997, Germany has undergone a very interesting transition; while arbitration was rather neglected in the past, it enjoys significant support today as a full-value alternative to litigation. Germany is also known for the high degree of protection given to the weaker party, even though party autonomy is also strongly promoted in those relations, including the option to enter into arbitration agreements between consumers and businesses. Germany has fully implemented the consumer protection standards set forth in EU law, but its legal concept relies on the application of general law and the mechanisms afforded by lex generalis. All told, the German approach is rather balanced, while many other European countries alternate between various rather extreme solutions without being able to offer what appears to be ultimately called for, an adequate degree of proportionality. *Spanish law* contains a positive definition of objective arbitrability which covers all relations (disputes) that are subject to the freedom of contract. This category is somewhat broader than that which allows for the conclusion of a settlement on the subject matter of the dispute. In particular, labor-law disputes are also fit for arbitration. Generally, Spanish law does not rule out arbitration procedures even for resolving consumer disputes. Consumer disputes in arbitration are thus subject to general legislation in the area of consumer protection, especially as regards unfair arbitration clauses. There exists a special rule, however, which restricts arbitration in consumer disputes if the arbitration award is to be (solely) based on the principle of equitable discretion.[26]

2.17.   The new *French law* of 1995 essentially incorporates the Directive verbatim. Arbitration in consumer disputes is principally permitted, unless the consumer can show that the arbitration agreement was unfair. This is an exception to the general prohibition of arbitration procedures for disputes to which non-commercial entities (private individuals) are a party, and allows for the resolution of consumer disputes also on the domestic level by arbitration – something which

---

[26]   Act No. 26/1984 of 19 July 1984, on the protection of consumers and users, published *in* BOE No. 175 and No. 176, issue dated 24 July 1984. The original version is available electronically at: *http://civil.udg.edu/normacivil/estatal/contract/lgdcu.html* (accessed on November 2, 2009); see in particular the provisions of the cited law on implementation.
See also Judgment No. 15/1989 of the Spanish Constitutional Court of 26 January 1989, published *in* Annex to the BOE, No. 43, issue dated 20 February 1989.

was impossible in the past.[27] Consumer disputes, albeit with certain restrictions, are also fit for arbitration in cases with an international dimension.[28] During the second stage of the implementation of the Directive, Article 2061 of the Code Civile (i.e., the French Civil Code) was amended;[29] it no longer refers to the commercial nature of arbitration and stipulates that arbitration agreements are validly concluded if they are done so for the benefit of a commercial relationship (i.e., in connection with business operations). This rules out arbitration for any legal relations in which only one party is a business and the other is a consumer. Some have argued that this provision applies exclusively to arbitration agreements concluded before the new law came into force, i.e., prior to 15 May 2001.[30] According to the case law of the French Court of Cassation ("Cass.")[31] of 2005, the provision also applies to arbitration agreements concluded before the [new] law took effect. It does not apply to contracts with an international dimension.[32] Although this approach also met with

---

[27] Philippe Fouchard, *Clause abusives en matière d'arbitrage*, (1) REV. ARB. 149 (2005).

[28] See the following decisions by French courts: (•) Cour de appel de Paris of 24 March 1995 (in *Bin Saud Abdel Aziz* v. *CIC Paris*), published *in* REV. ARB. 259, 263 (1996) and (•) Cour d´appel de Paris of 7 December 1994 (in *Jaguar /V2000/*), published *in* REV. ARB. 245 (1996) and the subsequent Cass. Decision of 21 May 1997 (in the same matter, i.e., *Jaguar /V2000/*), published *in* REV. ARB. 537 (1997).

[29] Code Civile, Article 2061, in the wording of French Law No. 2001-420 of 15 May 2001. Other legislation also makes reference to this provision of the French Civil Code.

[30] Decision of the Cour de commerce de Paris of 2004 in *AGRR* v. *ACE Insurance*, published *in* REV. ARB. 641 et seq (2004). Adopted from: JEAN-FRANÇOIS POUDRET ET SÉBASTIEN, BESSON & STEPHEN BIRTI, COMPARATIVE LAW OF INTERNATIONAL ARBITRATION, London: Sweet & Maxwell 43 (2nd ed. 2007). The decision in question (*AGRR* v. *ACE Insurance*) has met with criticism; see e.g. Orléans. (1) LES CAHIERS DE L'ARBITRAGE 2 (2004), GAZ. PAL. 24, 21/22 May 2004, or Ignotus Auctor, *Paris Commercial Court*, REV. ARB. 451 (2004). These critics have pointed out that Article 2061 of the Code Civile, in spite of being incorporated in a book of substantive law, is of rather procedural character and ought therefore to apply to all arbitration agreements as of the moment in which it came into force. This development in matters of the interpretation of Article 2061 of the Code Civile is referenced *in* JEAN-FRANÇOIS POUDRET, SÉBASTIEN BESSON & STEPHEN BIRTI, COMPARATIVE LAW OF INTERNATIONAL ARBITRATION, London: Sweet & Maxwell 43 (2nd ed. 2007).

[31] Cass. Decision in *SCP Ménard-Quimbert* v. *Beauchard*, *in* REV. ARB. 1011 et seq (2005). Adopted from: JEAN-FRANÇOIS POUDRET, SÉBASTIEN BESSON & STEPHEN BIRTI, *supra* note 30.

[32] *Cf.* for instance Gabrielle Kaufmann-Kohler, *Online Dispute Resolution and Its Significance for International Commercial Arbitration*, *in* LIBER AMICORUM IN HONOUR OF ROBERT BRINNER, Paris: ICC Publishing, Publication 693, 445 (G. Aksen, K.-H. Böckstiegel, M. J. Mustill, P. M. Patocchi, A. M. Whitesell eds., 2005); Louis Degos, *Les nouvelles dispositions de la loi française relative à la clause compromissoire*, 12 (5) IBLJ/RDAI 653 et seq (2001).

criticism in the published literature,[33] it appears that it is here to stay. It remains doubtful how this provision will be interpreted in conjunction with the Commercial Code, i.e., whether B2C contracts are invalid as a result of the amended Article 2061 of the Code Civile [FRA] or whether they are subject to the special L.132-1 regime of the amended Commercial Code. For the time being, French case law provides no clear-cut answer. In matters of international arbitration, the decision-making practice of recent times indicates that the French courts are increasingly open to the recognition and enforcement of arbitration clauses in consumer disputes.[34] A typical example is represented by arbitration clauses concluded between freelance businesspersons (in particular "advocates" – attorneys-at-law) and their clients concerning disputes over attorneys' fees, among others.[35]

2.18. Some countries have gone further in their attempt to protect the consumer than is required by the standard set out in the Directive. This is the case of the *United Kingdom* which implemented part of the Directive for England and Wales by way of the 1996 Arbitration Act,

---

See the following decisions: (•) Cass (civ., 1re) of 21 May 1997 (in *Meglio* v. *V2000*), annotated (by V. Hauzé) *in* RCDIP 87 (1998), and (•) Cass. (civ., 1re) of 21 May 1997 (in *Renault* v. *V2000*), annotated (by C. Jarrosson) *in* REV. ARB. 537 (1997).

The two latter-cited decisions are referenced (with the same source) by Gabrielle Kaufmann-Kohler, *Online Dispute Resolution and Its Significance for International Commercial Arbitration*, *in* LIBER AMICORUM IN HONOUR OF ROBERT BRINNER, Paris: ICC Publishing, Publication 693, 445, Note No. 22 (G. Aksen, K.-H. Böckstiegel, M. J. Mustill, P. M. Patocchi, A. M. Whitesell eds., 2005)

[33] See for instance Philippe Delebecque, *Arbitrage et droit de la consommation*, (104) DROIT & PATRIMOINE 50 (May 2002). Refraining from making her own assessment, Gabrielle Kaufmann-Kohler has drawn attention to this point of critique (among other things by referencing the same source), in *Online Dispute Resolution and Its Significance for International Commercial Arbitration*, *in* LIBER AMICORUM IN HONOUR OF ROBERT BRINNER, Paris: ICC Publishing, Publication 693, 445 (G. Aksen, K.-H. Böckstiegel, M. J. Mustill, P. M. Patocchi, A. M. Whitesell eds., 2005).

[34] See Decision Cass. (civ. 1er) of 30 March 2004 (in *Rado* v. *Painewebber*). Annotated *in* REV. ARB. 115 (2005).

For the rest, this kind of openness can be found in the courts of England and Germany, which appear to have advanced much further than the decision-making practice of French courts.

[35] See for instance the following decisions of the highest French court: the Court of Cassation: (•) Cass., Civ. 1er, 97-41.860, of 4 May 1999, published e.g. *in* BULLETIN CASS. under C112945; (•) Cass., Civ. 1er, 04-11.384, of 22 November 2005, published e.g. *in* BULLETIN CASS. under C51400, available in electronic version e.g. at: http://www.easydroit.fr/ jurisprudence/Cour-de-Cassation-Chambre-civile-1-du-22-novembre-2005-04-11-384-Publie-au-bulletin/C51400/ (accessed on February 17, 2012); Cass., Civ. 1er, 04-12.655, of 22 November 2005, published e.g. *in* BULLETIN CASS. under C51402; (•) Cass., Civ. 1er, 04-20.350, of 4 June 2006, published e.g. *in* BULLETIN CASS. under C51437; (•) Cass., Civ. 1er, 03-16.640, of 20 June 2006, published e.g. *in* BULLETIN CASS. under C51135.

which combines the principles of the Directive with the philosophy that "regular" arbitration is not an adequate means of resolving disputes in the case of what is known as small claims. However, the 1996 Arbitration Act in and of itself does not incontrovertibly suggest that arbitration agreements are unfair for disputes below a certain threshold value. The British Office of Fair Trading, however, published its Unfair Contract Terms Guidelines pursuant to which arbitration clauses are automatically unfair if they are to be applied to disputes with a value of no more than GBP 5 000. Regarding the pertinent consequences, the OFT requires the business to either exclude the applicability of the arbitration clause or at the very least to instruct the consumer that he or she has the right to choose between litigation and arbitration.[36]

VI. The U.S. Model Based on the Application of General Legal Principles

2.19.   In the United States, arbitration on the federal level is governed by the Federal Arbitration Act (FAA).[37] Since the FAA came into existence long before anyone considered the need for special consumer protection,[38] it contains no special provisions in this respect. Be that as it may, the U.S. Supreme Court has consistently interpreted this absence of specific provisions for the resolution of consumer disputes to mean that the FAA does in fact apply to consumer disputes. In *Allied-Bruce Terminix Cos* v. *Dobson*,[39] the Supreme Court ruled[40] that when it passed the FAA Congress had the needs of consumers in mind (just as much as the needs of any other party)."[41] It confirmed this doctrinal trend in its ruling of *Buckeye Check Cashing, Inc.* v. *Cardegna*.[42] Even so, arbitration clauses in consumer contracts are

---

[36]   Christopher R. Drahozal & Raymond J. Friel, *Comparative View of Consumer Arbitration*, 71 ARB. 131, 134 (2005).

[37]   FAA – 9 U.S.C. Sections 1 through 16 (2006); Congress passed this act in 1925.

[38]   *Cf.* Christopher R. Drahozal & Raymond J. Friel, *supra* note 36, at 137.

[39]   Supreme Court Decision 93-1001 of 18 January 1995 (in *Allied Bruce Terminix Companies, Inc. et Terminix International Company, Petitioners* v. *G. Michael Dobson et al.*), *in* 513 U.S. 265 (1995). An electronic version is available e.g. at: http://www.law.cornell.edu/supct/html/93-1001.ZO.html (accessed on August 7, 2011).

[40]   This would have been an opportunity to turn away from the paradigm established by the U.S. Supreme Court decision in *Southland Corporation* v. *Keating* (465 U.S. 1 (1984)). The Supreme Court, however, confirmed the latter-cited decision, and on the contrary declared that the FAA should take preference over the special law of individual states.

[41]   *Cf.* Christopher R. Drahozal & Raymond J. Friel, *supra* note 36, at 134.

[42]   126S.Ct. 1204, 163 L.Ed. 2d 1038 (2006), 546 U.S. 440 (2006). Arbitrators must review the validity of consumer contracts and the consequences of their potential nullity in accordance with the arbitration clause contained in the same. This is in confirmation of

extremely widespread in the United States. You will find them in the kind of contracts that citizens (consumers) make on a daily basis, in the course of providing for their basic needs,[43] in medical and healthcare services,[44] etc.[45] In response to the popularity of arbitration in consumer contracts, the AAA has drawn up recommended procedures for consumer disputes, known as the *Consumer Due Process Protocol.*[46]

2.20. However, based on the application of the general law of contract, arbitration clauses *may indeed be invalid in an individual case*, if the procedure of choice (i.e., arbitration) is found to be associated with *disproportionate costs of proceedings*, thus discouraging consumers from enforcing their rights.[47] A *cost test* is used to determine this.

---

the generally acknowledged principle of severability of the arbitration agreement from the main contract (also in consumer relations).

Cf. for instance Jeffrey P. MacHarg & Albert Bates Jr., *Non-Signatories and International Arbitration: Understanding the Paradox*, in COMPARATIVE LAW YEARBOOK OF INTERNATIONAL BUSINESS, Alphen aan den Rijn: Kluwer Law International 3, 6 (A. Alibekova & D. Campbell eds., 2007). Audley Sheppard, *The Moth, the Light, and the United States Severability Doctrine*, 23 JOURNAL OF INTERNATIONAL ARBITRATION 479, 482 (2006), and here p. 482 in particular; Alito Samuel, *Separability and the United States Supreme Court Decision in Buckeye* v. *Cardegna*, 22 JOURNAL OF INTERNATIONAL ARBITRATION 477 (2006); Richard L. Barnes, *"Prima Paint" Pushed Compulsory Arbitration under the "Erie" Train*, BEPRESS LEGAL REPOSITORY, THE BERKELEY ELECTRONIC PRESS 3 (2006), available in an electronic version at: http://law.bepress.com/cgi/viewcontent.cgi?article=9522&context=expresso&sei-redir= 1#search=%22Buckeye%20Check%20Cashing%2C%20Inc.%20vs%20Cardegna%22 (accessed on August 11, 2011), among others.

[43] See for instance the decisions: (•) *Allied-Bruce Terminex Co., Inc.* v. *Kaplan*, 465 U.S. 1 (1984); (•) *Terminex Int'l Co.* v. *Stabbs*, 930 S.W.2d 345 (Ark. 1996).

[44] See for instance the decisions: (•) *Sosa* v. *Paulos* (Utah, a decision from 1996), 924 P.2d 357; (•) *Engalla* v. *Permanente Medical Group* (California, a decision from 1997), 938 P.2d 903; (•) *Buraczynski* v. *Eyring* (Tennessee, a decision from 1996), 919 S.W.2d 314.

[45] *Cf.* for instance Stephen K. Huber & E. Wendy Trachte-Huber, *Top Ten Developments in Arbitration in the 1990s.* JDI; an electronic version is available at: http://findarticles.com/p/articles/mi_qa3923/is_200011/ai_n8955348/pg_2/?tag=mantle_s kin;content (accessed on August 14, 2011). The above-mentioned authors cite the same examples.

[46] Statement of Principles of the National Consumer Disputes Advisory Committee. *Cf.* for instance STEPHEN K. HUBER & BEN H. SHEPPARD JR. (eds.), 23 AAA YEARBOOK ON ARBITRATION & THE LAW, Huntington (NY): AAA /University of Houston – Law Center/ JurisNet (2011) (special appendix), among others.

[47] See for instance these decisions: (•) Supreme Court [USA] in *Tree Financial Corp.* v. *Randolph*, 531 U.S. 79 (2000); (•) Court of Appeals of the District of Columbia in *Cole* v. *Burns International Security Services*, 105 F.3d 1465 (D.C. Cir. 1997); (•) US Court of Appeal, Ninth Circuit, in *Ting* v. *AT&T*, 3190 F.3d 1126, p. 1150 (9th Cir. Cal. 2003); (•) *Ingle* v. *Circuit City Stores*, 328 F.3d 1165 (in particular 1175–1176; 9th Cir. 2003); (•) *Szetela* v. *Discover Bank*, 118 cal. Rptr. 2d 862 (in particular 867-68x Ct. App. 2002). Cited also *in* Gabrielle Kaufmann-Kohler, *supra* note 32, at 446.

However, this defense against arbitration clauses is only available if the clause in question was agreed in a contract of adhesion with no option to amend it (*take-it-or-leave-it*). For the most part, the applicable case law highlights the need for an individual assessment of the costs of the proceedings[48] (e.g., in terms of how far the venue of proceedings is from the consumer's place of residence)[49] and whether the consumer had the opportunity to study the wording of the proposed contract,[50] etc. The most common litmus test in U.S. case law, however, is the degree to which consumers may be denied the right to *class action*.[51] In this respect, unconscionability is (with few exceptions) assessed in accordance with the general principles of law of contract, as opposed to special legislation for the protection of consumers. The respective bargaining position of the contracting parties is taken into account.[52] In

---

[48]   Decision of the New York State Supreme Court in *Brower* v. *Gateway 2000, Inc.*, 676 N.Y.S. 2d 569, 1998, N.Y. App. Div. *Cf.*, for instance, Joseph T. Mc Laughlin, *Arbitrability: Current Trends in the United States*, 12 ARB. INT. 123 (1996), or Linda Alle-Murphy, *Are Compulsory Arbitration Clauses in Consumer Contracts Enforceable? A Contractual Analysis*, 75 TEMPLE LAW REVIEW 125 (2002); ZHENG SOPHIA TANG, ELECTRONIC CONSUMER CONTRACTS IN THE CONFLICT OF LAWS, Oxford / Portland (Oregon): Hart Publishing 155 (2009), among others.

[49]   Within the context of European jurisprudence, the distance from the venue of arbitration was assessed in matters which were subsequently referred to the ECJ for a preliminary ruling, e.g.: (•) ECJ Judgment of 6 October 2009 C-40/08 in *Asturcom* (with reference to a court procedure pending in Spain) and (•) ECJ Judgment of 4 June 2009 C-243/08 in *Pannon GSM* (with reference to a court procedure pending in Hungary). The distance between the consumer's place of residence and the venue in arbitration on a transcontinental scope was also reflected by the Polish Supreme Court, in its Decision No IV CSK 200/06 of 22 February 2007, in which the enforcement of an arbitral award rendered in the United States against a Polish consumer was denied on the grounds of the Polish consumer's de facto inability to effectively participate in the proceedings.

[50]   Judgment by the U. S. District Court for the Northern District of Illinois Eastern Division 07 C 4946 of 18 April 2008 (in *Jose Trujillo et al.* v. *Apple Computer, Inc.* et *AT&T Mobility, LLC*), 578 Supp 2d 979; the judgment is also available in electronic form at: http://law.justia.com/cases/federal/district-courts/illinois/ilndce/1%3A2007cv04946/ 212324/93 (accessed on August 27, 2011). See also for instance ZHENG SOPHIA TANG, *supra* note 48, at 156.

[51]   *Cf.* for instance Julia Hörnle, *Legal Controls on the Use of Arbitration Clause in B2C E-Commerce Contracts*, 2 (1) MASARYK UNIVERSITY JOURNAL OF LAW AND TECHNOLOGY 34 (2008).

[52]   See for instance the following decisions: (•) Judgment by the U.S. Court of Appeals, Second Circuit, 01-7870, 01-7872 and 01-7860, of 1 October 2002 (in *Christopher Specht, John Gibson, Michael Fagan, Sean Kelly, Mark Gruber, Sherry Weindorf et al.* v. *Netscape Communications Corporation and America Online, Inc.*), 306 F 3d 17 (2d Cir 2002) (*cf.* for instance JAY DRATLER JR., LICENSING OF INTELLECTUAL PROPERTY, New York: ALM Properties, Inc., LAW JOURNAL PRESS (1994) Sec. 1.06[1], p. I–50); (•) Judgment by the U. S. District Court for the Northern District of Illinois Eastern Division, 07 C 4946, of 18 April 2008 (in *Jose*

the past, the courts of several states, notably California[53] and Alabama, but also elsewhere, have repeatedly attempted to take the restrictive road and declare arbitration clauses to be unconscionable. In a number of cases, these attempts to use a special approach outside the general principles of contract interpretation have been quashed by the U.S. Supreme Court, whose long-term view has been that the Federal Arbitration Act applies preferentially, and has repeatedly stressed the need to use general assessment criteria. In this respect, we need to point out that only a *grave breach* of fundamental contract-law principles and abuse of the position of the more powerful party can result in a finding of unconscionability.[54] The courts usually submit the *actual contracting process* to particular scrutiny and thus regularly dismiss the defense of the inoperativeness of arbitration clauses in those cases in which the consumer had the opportunity to read the terms of the contract prior to entering into it,[55] but chose not to do so.[56] One also occasionally encounters the argument that unfair arbitration clauses may generally be unenforceable and represent an obstacle to actually following through with the arbitration procedure.[57]

2.21.   Some claim that the divergent approach to arbitration in consumer disputes in the United States on one hand and in Europe on the other hand rests on two differences;[58] the first is related to the differences in the very legislative concept of consumer protection and the second is related to the nature of the American system of dispute resolution. Supposedly, consumers in the United States enjoy a lower degree of

---

Trujillo et al. v. *Apple Computer, Inc.* et *AT&T Mobility, LLC*), 578 Supp 2d 979; (•) *McKee* v. *At & T*, 164 Wash 2d 372. *Cf.* for instance ZHENG SOPHIA TANG, *supra* note 48, at 156.

[53]   *Cf.* for instance the decision by the Supreme Court of California in *Ting* v. *AT&T*, 319 F3d 1126 (9th CirCal. 2003).

[54]   See for instance the U.S. Supreme Court decision in *Iberia Credit Bureau* v. *Cingular Wireless LLC, Sprint Spectrum Company, Centennial Wireless*; 379 F3d 159, paras. (167) and (168).

[55]   Incidentally, the practice of U.S. courts in this respect does not deviate from the requirements of EU law.

[56]   See for instance the decisions in (•) *Grimm* v. *First National Bank of Pennsylvania*, 578 2d 785; (•) *MA Mortenson* v. *Timberline Software*, 140 Wash 2d 568; (•) *Mortenson* v. *Timberline Software*, 83 Wash App 819; (•) *Olle* v. *5401 Western Ave Residential*, 569 F Supp 2d 41; (•) *US ex rel Wilson* v. *Kellogg Brown*, 525 F3d 370; (•) *Falbe* v. *Dell*, WL 1588243.
See for instance JONATHAN HILL, CROSS BORDER CONSUMER CONTRACTS, Oxford: Oxford University Press (2008), but also ZHENG SOPHIA TANG, *supra* note 48, at 156.

[57]   See the decision *Pine Ridge Homes, Inc.* v. *Stone*, 2004 WL 1730170 (Tex. App. – Dallas 2004).

[58]   *Cf.* Christopher R. Drahozal & Raymond J. Friel, *supra* note 36, at 131.

protection than in Europe (under EU law).[59] The importance of arbitration clauses in consumer contracts has also been confirmed by the Canadian Supreme Court in the *Dell* case in which the Court decided that arbitration clauses in consumer contracts were valid irrespective of the fact that they deprived consumers of their right to file class action.[60]

VII. Conclusion

2.22.   In the final analysis, two concepts which at first glance are quite divergent – the European concept and that applied in the United States – do not differ as much as has occasionally been claimed. One true difference between them is the formal framework within which they are enforced; the American approach does not set forth any special restrictions on the autonomy of contractual parties. The European model (i.e., the model based on EU law) is populist and bureaucratic more than anything else and prevents market mechanisms from deploying their true power by imposing restrictions on party autonomy and relieving consumers to some degree of their responsibility (liability). Ultimately, the EU model amplifies the effects of the economic recession rather than promote a dynamic development of contractual relationships. What is more, this model often tempts consumers to abuse the special protection extended to them. At the same time, many European countries today find that the kind of solution provided by standard litigation does not live up to the requirements of the market (which calls for a solution that is efficient in all respects). One possible avenue towards motivating both businesses and consumers is arbitration. The German model is an adequate compromise; while it does implement a special framework in line with EU law, it is essentially based on general legislation and the general principles of law of contract. Restricting the autonomy of contracting parties, should be seen as counter-productive even regarding dispute resolution. There is no sound reason for prohibiting arbitration in consumer disputes. All that is required is the establishment of sufficiently effective mechanisms of supervision and control to ensure that all of the principles on which arbitration as a dispute resolution procedure is based are consistently enforced.

| | |

---

[59]   *Ibid.*

[60]   That being said, the Canadian approach differs in certain aspects (also from province to province).

Summaries

FRA   [*L'autonomie des parties dans les procédures d'arbitrage portant sur des litiges de consommation: Le modèle européen de protection des consommateurs est-il réellement adéquat?*]

La protection des consommateurs s'impose comme un phénomène juridique supranational, ce qui se manifeste également dans l'autonomie des parties aux contrats conclus entre le consommateur et l'entrepreneur. Si le droit de l'UE a choisi la voie d'une protection juridique spéciale (basée sur des textes particuliers) et des restrictions, le modèle appliqué aux États-Unis se fonde sur une protection qui émane des principes généraux du droit des contrats. Nous croyons que le modèle américain, plus efficace, n'entrave pas le développement du marché, lequel repose sur un degré élevé d'autonomie, mais aussi sur la responsabilité de toutes les parties contractantes, et notamment des consommateurs. La responsabilité va ainsi de pair avec l'autonomie, qu'il convient d'appliquer dans une large mesure tant dans le domaine du droit matériel qu'au niveau procédural. Les conventions d'arbitrage conclues entre le consommateur et l'entrepreneur sont également concernées. Nous sommes persuadés qu'il est inutile de prévoir des restrictions spéciales pour intégrer des clauses d'arbitrage dans les contrats de consommation. La législation devrait plutôt s'orienter vers le contrôle du respect des principes fondamentaux de la procédure d'arbitrage. En outre, le modèle européen conduit souvent vers l'abus du système de protection de la part des consommateurs. Le modèle allemand, qui représente un compromis entre le système restrictif du droit européen et le modèle en vigueur aux États-Unis, nous semble intéressant et efficace.

CZE   [*Autonomie ve spotřebitelských sporech v rozhodčím řízení: je evropský model ochrany spotřebitele skutečně přiměřený?*]

Ochrana spotřebitele se stává fenoménem práva v nadnárodním měřítku. To se projevuje i v autonomii stran smluv uzavíraných spotřebitelem a podnikatelem. Zatímco právo EU jde cestou speciální právní ochrany (na základě zvláštních předpisů) a zaváděním restrikcí, model aplikovaný v USA je založen na ochraně poskytované na základě obecných principů smluvního práva. Podle názoru autora je model aplikovaný v USA více efektivní a nebrání rozvoji trhu založeného na vysokém stupni autonomie, avšak také na odpovědnosti všech smluvních stran, tj. i spotřebitelů. Odpovědnost je rubem autonomie, kterou je zapotřebí aplikovat v široké míře jak z hmotněprávního tak z procesního hlediska. Platí to i pro rozhodčí smlouvy uzavírané mezi spotřebitelem a podnikatelem. Podle autora není zapotřebí zavádět zvláštní restrikce pro sjednávání rozhodčích doložek ve spotřebitelských smlouvách. Právní úprava by se měla zaměřit spíše na kontrolu dodržování základních principů rozhodčího řízení. Evropský model také často vede k tomu, že systém ochrany je spotřebitelem zneužíván. Autor považuje za zajímavý a efektivní německý model, který představuje kompromis mezi systémem restrikcí podle práva EU a modelem USA.

| | |

POL [***Autonomia w sporach konsumenckich w ramach postępowania arbitrażowego: czy europejski model ochrony konsumenta jest rzeczywiście adekwatny?***]
Ochrona materialno-prawna i procesowa w myśl prawa UE ma charakter restrykcyjny, natomiast model amerykański opiera się na konsekwentnej realizacji zasad prawa umownego. Znajduje to swoje odzwierciedlenie również w postępowaniu arbitrażowym. Model amerykański jest bardziej efektywny, natomiast model unijny hamuje rozwój rynku, nie prowadzi do zwiększania zakresu odpowiedzialności konsumenta i często bywa nadużywany. Ciekawy kompromis stanowi prawo niemieckie.

DEU [***Autonomie in Verbraucherstreitigkeiten im Schiedsverfahren: ist das europäische Verbraucherschutzmodell wirklich angemessen?***]
Der materiell-rechtliche und verfahrensrechtliche Schutz nach dem EU-Recht ist auf Einschränkunfen aufgebaut, während das Modell der USA auf der konsequenten Durchsetzung der Prinzipien des Vertragsrechts basiert. Das äußert sich auch im Schiedsverfahren. Das Modell der USA ist effektiv, wogegen das EU-Modell eine Bremse für die Marktentwicklung darstellt, nicht zu größerer Verantwortung des Verbrauchers führt und des Öfteren auch missbraucht wird. Einen interessanten Kompromiss bietet das deutsche Recht.

RUS [***Автономия в потребительских спорах при третейском производстве: действительно ли сообразна европейская модель защиты потребителя?***]
Материально-правовая и процессуальная защита потребителей в понимании права ЕС базируется на ограничениях, в то время как модель США – на последовательном продвижении принципов договорного права. Это проявляется и при третейском производстве. Модель США более эффективна, чем модель ЕС, тормозящая развитие рынка, не приводящая к повышению

степени ответственности потребителя и иногда становящаяся объектом злоупотребления. Любопытный компромисс представляет собой немецкое право.

ESP   [***Autonomía en pleitos de consumo en procedimientos arbitrales: ¿Es el modelo europeo de la protección al consumidor el más adecuado?***]

Conforme al derecho de la UE, la protección jurídico-material y procesal están basadas en restricciones, mientras que el modelo estadounidense se basa en una escrupulosa imposición de los principios del derecho contractual. Se refleja también en el procedimiento arbitral. El modelo estadounidense es más efectivo, en cambio, el modelo de la UE supone un freno al desarrollo del mercado, no lleva al consumidor para que aumente su nivel de responsabilidad y, a veces, se abusa del mismo. El compromiso óptimo constituye el derecho alemán.

Bernd Ehle

Effective Use of Demonstrative Exhibits in International Arbitration

Key words:
International Arbitration
| Demonstrative Exhibits |
Presentation of Evidence |
Visual Aids | Charts |
Graphics | Advocacy |
Persuasion | Hearings |
Complex Technical Cases

Abstract | *This article discusses the use of visual aids, known as "demonstrative exhibits," in international arbitration proceedings. This term refers to graphical representations and other illustrative material that enable parties' counsel to introduce and communicate the evidence itself in a more effective manner to the arbitrators. The author references the origins of such tools of communication in U.S. criminal law and civil law proceedings, in which the overarching goal is to win over the jury, and then explains that such means of persuasion as are common practice in U.S. court rooms cannot be transposed to pleadings before arbitration panels and tribunals without further modifications (in that arbiters will, as a rule, come from a different background than jury members). The author discusses the degree to which the use of "demonstrative exhibits" may make sense (or even be advisable) in international arbitration proceedings, especially in cases with a high degree of technical complexity. He also stresses that the country of origin and the specific legal culture of arbitrators must always be taken into account, closing his paper with a number of practical considerations for parties' counsel and arbitrators.*

Dr. Bernd Ehle, LL.M.
(Northwestern),
MCIArb, Avocat
(Geneva), Rechtsanwalt
(Germany), is a Partner
at LALIVE
(Geneva/Zurich). The
author specializes in
international disputes
and has acted as
counsel and arbitrator
in numerous
international arbitral
proceedings governed
by various procedural
and substantive laws.
He acts as co-chair of
the Geneva Group of
ASA, the Swiss
Arbitration
Association, and is a
committee member of
the European Branch
of the Chartered
Institute of Arbitrators
(CIArb).
e-mail: behle@lalive.ch

| | |

I. Introduction

3.01. Demonstrative exhibits are often an important tool for effective advocacy in international arbitration. In particular in fact-intensive cases involving complex factual matrices, large volumes of documentary evidence, or technical issues, demonstrative exhibits such as tables, charts, and graphics can be an effective way to summarize and highlight the key facts which a party wishes to convey to a tribunal. Although not evidence in themselves, such exhibits allow parties to clarify and present evidence already on record in a compelling way.

3.02. However, international arbitration practitioners must be cognizant of the limitations of demonstrative exhibits, and use them cautiously. In particular, they should tailor any such exhibits to their audience, for example by taking into consideration the arbitrators' cultural and legal background. Indeed, some arbitrators will be more receptive than others to certain forms for demonstrative exhibits. In addition, practitioners must be careful to ensure that demonstrative exhibits fairly, accurately, and completely reflect the evidence which is already on record. Usually, counsel are also required to provide copies of any demonstrative exhibits they intend to use to opposing counsel and the arbitrators sufficiently in advance in order to give them the opportunity to verify their accuracy and the underlying evidence.

3.03. This article provides a brief overview of the use of demonstrative exhibits in international arbitration. It first defines what demonstrative exhibits can consist of and their historical use in litigation in the United States, as well as the psychological aspects behind their effectiveness. It then turns to address the use of demonstrative exhibits in modern international arbitration practice, and in particular their admissibility in arbitration proceedings.

II. What Are "Demonstrative Exhibits"?

3.04. Demonstrative exhibits present evidence through visual aids expressly created for the proceedings to assist the advocate in the art of persuasion.[1] Examples of demonstrative exhibits are charts, graphs, drawings, maps, scale models, photographs, computer animations, and documents enlarged so that everyone in the hearing room can focus on them.[2]

---

[1] Andrew Burr & Keith Pickavance, *The Use of Visualisations in Case Presentation and Evidence*, 26 (1) CONSTRUCTION LAW JOURNAL 3 (2010).

[2] Nicholas Fletcher, *The Use of Technology in the Production of Documents*, in DOCUMENT PRODUCTION IN INTERNATIONAL ARBITRATION – 2006 SPECIAL SUPPLEMENT,

3.05. Black's Law Dictionary defines "demonstrative evidence" in the following terms:

> Physical evidence that one can see and inspect (*i.e.*, an explanatory aid, such as a chart, map, and some computer simulations) and that, while of probative value and usually offered to clarify testimony, does not play a direct part in the incident in question.[3]

3.06. More often than not, demonstrative exhibits do not constitute real or primary evidence, but so-called secondary or indirect evidence, *i.e.*, illustrations of existing primary evidence already part of the record such as documents or witness and expert testimony.[4] Accordingly, demonstrative exhibits rarely have probative value. They can, however, form part of an effective persuasion strategy, visually stimulating the audience (*i.e.*, the members of the arbitral tribunal) and communicating the advocate's evidence and arguments.

III. The Origin of Demonstrative Evidence or Exhibits

3.07. Demonstrative exhibits appear to have their origins in United States criminal and civil litigation. Their use is inherent in the U.S. court system which involves juries consisting of non-lawyers and which requires a particular style of advocacy: important facts need to be "told" to the jury and "talked into the record." U.S. trial lawyers must therefore make sure to grab the jurors' attention, direct it to the key issues of their client's story and thereby increase the jury's level of understanding and retention of the arguments made.[5] Demonstrative exhibits form part of every U.S. trial lawyer's "arsenal" to effectively

---

ICC International Court of Arbitration Bulletin 107, 109 (2006); Andrew Burr & Keith Pickavance, *supra* note 1, at 3, 14-16; R. Doak Bishop & James H. Carter, *The United States Perspective and Practice of Advocacy, Chapter 22, in* The Art of Advocacy in International Arbitration, New York: Juris Publishing, Inc. 519, 561 (R. D. Bishop ed., 2010).

[3] Black's Law Dictionary, Saint Paul, Minnesota: Thomson-West (B.A. Garner ed., 8th ed. 2004).

[4] See Christoph Liebscher, *Beweisaufnahme im Schiedsverfahren, in* Praxishandbuch Schiedsgerichtsbarkeit, Wien: Verlag Österreich 165, 185 (H. Torggler ed., 2007); Rodger D. Young & Steven Susser, *Effective Use of Demonstrative Exhibits and Demonstrative Aids*, 79 (11) Michigan Bar Journal (2000), available at: http://www.michbar.org/journal/article.cfm?articleID=151&volumeID=13&viewType=arc hive (accessed on November 9, 2011).

[5] R. Doak Bishop, *Advocacy in International Commercial Arbitration: United States, Chapter 10, in* The Art of Advocacy in International Arbitration, New York: Juris Publishing, Inc. 309, 351 (R. D. Bishop ed., 2004); R. Doak Bishop & James H. Carter, *supra* note 2, at *Chapter 22*, 519, 561 (2010).

communicate with the jury; for example, by turning complex information into interesting, persuasive graphics. Such evidence is admissible, provided the process adopted in deriving the evidence from the data used for the demonstrative exhibit may be officially traced and examined.[6]

3.08. In the United States, modern courtrooms are often equipped with technology that facilitates the use of visual aids for jurors. These include video cameras that can provide close-up views of exhibits, witnesses' sketches, in addition to individual monitors provided for each juror to view documents. The latter can be particularly useful to counsel in assisting the jury in understanding witness testimony or when attempting to impeach a witness' credibility, considering that the documents can be called up instantly on the monitors, and each juror can have individual control over the information displayed on the screen.[7]

3.09. Demonstrative evidence is even a subject taught at American law schools, and there is an entire market for the forensic animation business: companies such as *Courtroom Visuals*,[8] *Trialtech*,[9] *Executive Exhibits*,[10] *Animators-at-Law*,[11] and *Litigation Graphics*[12] offer complete creative graphics and multi-media support for trial attorneys. Professionals in this field belong to the Demonstrative Evidence Specialists Association, which publishes an informational newsletter entitled "*Visual Persuasion.*"[13]

---

[6] Keith Pickavance, *The Use of Visualisations in Case Presentation and Evidence*, Lecture given at the Chartered Institute of Arbitrators European Branch Spring Meeting in Istanbul on May 2, 2008: See the test applied in *State of Connecticut* v. *Alfred Swinton*, SC 16548, May 11, 2004.

[7] Debra Baker, *Electronic Future Is Now*, 84 ABA JOURNAL 93 (May 1998); RODERICK D. BLANCHARD & WILLIAM M. HART, LITIGATION AND TRIAL PRACTICE, Clifton Park, NY: Thomson Delmar Learning 552-553 (6th ed. 2006).

[8] Courtroom Visuals Inc., available at: www.courtroomvisuals.com (accessed on November 9, 2011).

[9] Trialtech Inc., available at: www.trialtech.com (accessed on November 9, 2011).

[10] Executive Exhibits LLC, available at: www.executiveexhibits.com (accessed on November 9, 2011).

[11] Animators at Law Inc., available at: www.animators.com (accessed on November 9, 2011).

[12] Litigation Graphics, available at: www.litigraph.com (accessed on November 9, 2011).

[13] Demonstrative Evidence Specialists Association, available at: http://desa.org (accessed on November 9, 2011).

IV. The Psychology behind the Use of Demonstrative Evidence

3.10. The idea behind the technique of using demonstrative evidence goes beyond the adage "a picture is worth a thousand words." Scientific research in the United States has shown that people generally learn through hearing *and* seeing: 81% of the general public are so-called "visual learners" rather than "auditory learners," *i.e.*, they better understand and retain information when it is not only conveyed through verbal explanation, but also through images. In particular, research done on jurors has shown that while they retain only 10% to 20% of new information presented to them orally, they retain 65% to 85% of the information presented visually or in a combination of oral testimony and visual aids.[14]

3.11. Interestingly, these statistics do not apply to practicing attorneys: psychologists have also determined that approximately 55% of all practicing lawyers are auditory learners as opposed to visual learners, *i.e.*, they tend to remember information more accurately when they hear it.[15]

3.12. There are further reasons for the use of visual aids to persuade juries: today's society is a "show me" society, which means that it is particularly "visual," having grown up with television replacing written and spoken words as vehicles of mass communication. More than previous generations, people today see events at the same time that they hear about them, with the result that they are more inclined to attach credibility to visual stimuli.[16]

3.13. Finally, charts, graphs, and computer animations facilitate the understanding of complex and potentially tedious information, by

---

[14] Michael S. Kun, *Use Of Demonstrative Evidence In Employment Litigation: A Defense Counsel's Perspective*, paper presented at the 2007 retreat of the LOS ANGELES COUNTY BAR ASSOCIATION on 13 April 2007, available at: www.ebglaw.com/showarticle. aspx?Show=6673 (accessed on November 9, 2011); KENNETH LOPEZ & THE ANIMATORS AT LAW, ATTORNEY COMMUNICATION STYLE STUDY, Washington: Animators at Law 2-7 (2007); Mary Quinn Cooper, *The Use of Demonstrative Exhibits at Trial*, 34 UNIVERSITY OF TULSA LAW JOURNAL 567, 568 (1999); John Selbak, *Digital Litigation: The Prejudicial Effects of Computer-Generated Animation in the Courtroom*, 9 (2) BERKELEY TECHNOLOGY LAW JOURNAL 338, 352 (1994) available at: http://btlj.org/data/ articles/vol9/Selbak.pdf (accessed on November 9, 2011).

[15] See, *e.g.*, Rodger D. Young & Steven Susser, *supra* note 4, at 1538; KENNETH LOPEZ, *supra* note 14, at 2-7.

[16] Rodney Jew & Martin Q. Peterson, *Envisioning Persuasion: Painting the Picture for the Jury*, 31 (10) TRIAL 74(1995).

using interesting and comprehensible formats.[17] If jurors are not listening to a lawyer's oral argument and lose interest, the lawyer will not be able to convey his client's version of the facts to them, let alone ensure that they retain it in deliberation.[18]

V. Are Demonstrative Exhibits Effective before Arbitral Tribunals?

3.14. While U.S. trial lawyers must persuade a jury – people from the general public – counsel in arbitration proceedings must effectively communicate with the arbitrators, mostly lawyers, who tend to be auditory learners.[19] Therefore, the psychology behind demonstrative evidence described above cannot be applied directly to international arbitrators – it can even be counterproductive if overused.[20]

3.15. Besides the fact that jurors and arbitrators may in many cases be different "learners," there are other fundamental differences between the two that indicate that the U.S.-style litigation arsenal should not be fully employed in an international arbitration setting:

- Arbitrators are trained and practicing lawyers, and as such, have learned how to analyze a case, identify crucial issues and focus on them – in other words, they do not require the same level of guidance as jurors do to understand a case;

- Due to their "legal sophistication," arbitrators may not be as impressed as jurors are by dramatic three-dimensional computer-animated presentations which mainly aim at "hammering home" certain key issues;

- Arbitrators will have worked through the parties' written submissions before the hearing and prefer to be presented only with the important and relevant evidence and material in a succinct and well-reasoned manner rather than with each party's entire case;

- Arbitrators often ask counsel questions during pleadings; they can be inhibited from doing so if pleadings are dominated by

---

[17]   Edward M. Josiah, *The Use of Digital Demonstrative Exhibits and Presentations for International Arbitration*, GREYHAWK NEWSLETTER KEEPING TIME (June 2008): "*The difference between winning and losing in international arbitration is oftentimes the ability to transpose complexity into simplicity [...]. In short, demonstrative exhibits are an extraordinary means of simplifying complex issues and, therefore, should be considered an integral part of any proceeding.*"

[18]   Michael S. Kun, *supra* note 14.

[19]   See *supra* paragraph 3.11.

[20]   See Nicolas Fletcher, *supra* note 2, at 108; Michael S. Kun, *supra* note 14.

visual aids, which tend to be very linear,[21] and can become impatient if they have to follow a pre-established path paved with demonstrative exhibits;[22]

- Arbitrators are regularly selected by parties due to specific qualifications, including familiarity and experience with the subject matter in dispute (e.g., construction or telecommunication); as a result, certain basic explanations are often unnecessary;

- Arbitrators are paid service providers for a professional resolution of a dispute, *i.e.*, they have both an incentive and a professional obligation to study the case and listen attentively to counsel's oral arguments and the witnesses' or experts' testimony; and

- Arbitrators are generally experienced "court-sitters" and, unlike most jury members who are called for jury duty and hope to never be called again, are not sitting in proceedings for their first time and indeed hope to be called upon again.[23]

3.16. The differences between the audiences of U.S. court trials and arbitral proceedings do not however imply that counsel in arbitration should refrain from using demonstrative exhibits as part of their persuasion strategy.[24] The arbitral process has the potential of being used more creatively than court proceedings, and the procedural flexibility inherent to arbitral proceedings and their greater informality caters well to demonstrative evidence of a nature that may not be acceptable before state courts.[25]

3.17. When it comes to presenting a client's case at a hearing, arbitration practitioners can indeed learn from their U.S. litigation counterparts: certain well-chosen visual aids may very well be effective in capturing the arbitrators' interest, in helping them focus on and clarify certain issues and thus in saving time in their assessment of the case that they

---

[21] Jean-Georges Betto, Jason Fry, Marc Henry, Elie Kleiman & Philippe Pinsolle, *International Arbitration: New Trends*, (3) INTERNATIONAL BUSINESS LAW JOURNAL 371, 373 (2006).

[22] JANE JENKINS & JAMES STEBBINGS, INTERNATIONAL CONSTRUCTION ARBITRATION LAW, Alphen aan den Rijn: Kluwer Law International 264 (2006).

[23] Michael S. Kun, *supra* note 14.

[24] Jeff Dasteel & Richard Jacobs, *American Werewolves in London*, 18 (2) ARB. INT'L 165, 182 (2002): "*There is no reason to believe that multimedia presentations so typical in the US would not be effective in London as well*"; Arthur H. Aufses III, *Thinking About ADR, in* THE LITIGATION MANUAL, Chicago, Illinois: American Bar Association 67, 74 (J. G. Koeltl & J. Kiernan eds., 1999): "*Even if the setting is informal and the parties are at whispering distance, a lawyer should not abandon his attempt to communicate a sense of conviction and urgency. Graphics and demonstrative evidence are as effective with arbitrators as with a jury.*"

[25] JANE JENKINS & JAMES STEBBINGS, *supra* note 22; ROBERT F. CUSHMAN, JAMES J. MYERS, CONSTRUCTION LAW HANDBOOK, New York: Aspen Law & Business Publishers (1999).

would otherwise have to spend working through voluminous documents. Explaining issues while portraying them in a visual medium can also help reduce the overall time spent on oral arguments – a valuable achievement when hearings take place under time constraints, as they usually do.

3.18. A survey of AAA construction arbitrators has indeed shown that the use of photos, pictures or videos, and the use of graphics or other visual aids were, respectively, the third and fourth types of presentation techniques that they found helpful or persuasive. Moreover, 89% of the arbitrators overwhelmingly replied "yes" to the question: "Do graphics and other forms of demonstrative evidence assist you in arriving at an appropriate award?"[26]

3.19. Similarly, as part of a comparative study on typical practices in conducting arbitration proceedings followed in various parts of the world, arbitration practitioners from diverse legal backgrounds, through a hypothetical case submitted to them, answered in the affirmative when asked whether demonstrative exhibits should be used in order to save hearing time and costs in the presence of voluminous and complicated data.[27]

VI. Demonstrative Exhibits in Modern International Arbitration Practice

3.20. There are few doctrinal references to the use of demonstrative exhibits in international arbitration. While some authors find that such use is not common outside the United States,[28] others take the view that employing a variety of different visual aids in presenting one's case at the hearing has become commonplace in international arbitration and that most arbitral tribunals "are prepared to grant the parties considerable leeway in employing such aids, provided that the aids accurately reflect the evidence on record."[29] Some authors relate the

---

[26] Dean B. Thomson, *Arbitration Theory and Practice: A Survey of AAA Construction Arbitrators*, 23 HOFSTRA LAW REVIEW 137, 164 (1994-1995).

[27] Judge Howard M. Holtzmann & Prof. Giorgio Bernini, *Hypothetical Case for Use in a Comparative Study of Arbitration Practice in Various Legal Systems*, 3 ICCA CONGRESS SERIES 19, 77 (1986).

[28] See, *e.g.*, R. Doak Bishop, *Toward a Harmonized Approach to Advocacy in International Arbitration*, Chapter 15, in THE ART OF ADVOCACY IN INTERNATIONAL ARBITRATION, New York: Juris Publishing, Inc. 451, 451, 486 (R. D. Bishop ed., 2004); R. Doak Bishop & James H. Carter, *supra* note 2, at *Chapter 22*, 519, 561 (2010).

[29] David Roney & Anna Müller, *The Arbitral Procedure*, in ARBITRATION IN SWITZERLAND – A HANDBOOK FOR PRACTITIONERS, The Hague: Kluwer Law International 68 (G. Kaufmann-Kohler, B. Stucki eds., 2004); see also Pierre-Yves Tschanz, *Advocacy in*

increasingly frequent use of demonstrative exhibits in hearings to the "Americanization" of the arbitral process.[30]

3.21. Especially in complex technical cases, such as disputes dealing with construction projects,[31] those involving a factual background spanning a lengthy period, technology transfers,[32] business valuation disputes,[33] and intellectual property disputes,[34] demonstrative techniques are frequently utilized to present a case in a user-friendly form to the arbitrators.[35] The most useful and common forms of demonstrative

International Commercial Arbitration: Switzerland, Chapter 7, in THE ART OF ADVOCACY IN INTERNATIONAL ARBITRATION, New York: Juris Publishing Inc. 195, 218 (R. D. Bishop ed., 2004): *"Charts, tabulations, pictures and enlarged copies of key exhibits are often used at the witness hearing and during oral argument. The procedural rules usually allow demonstrative exhibits at the hearings, provided that no new evidence is contained therein and that copies are provided to opposing counsel and the arbitrators."*

[30] Michael Young & Larry Shore, *Procedural Issues in International Arbitration – a Cultural Battleground?*, IN-HOUSE PERSPECTIVE 5, 9 (2005): the *"Americanisation"* of the arbitral process *"is attributed to the growing influence of US lawyers, often representing US companies that, in the past five to ten years, have come to be parties in a significant percentage."*

[31] *Demonstrative Evidence in Construction Disputes, in* 10 VISUAL PERSUASION, available at: www.campbellleboeuf.com/vispers[1].10.pdf (accessed on November 9, 2011). See also Dean B. Thomson, *supra* note 26, who states that AAA construction arbitrators listed photos, followed by summary or comparison charts, drawings, plans or details, various types of graphs, and time-related schedules as types of helpful visual evidence.

[32] Pravin Anand, *Arbitration in the Context of Technology Transfer Agreements: The Case of India*, 7 J. INT´L ARB. 87, 89 (1990).

[33] Robert Wisner, J. William Rowley & Neil Campbell, *Chapter 8: Effective Use of Economic Experts in International Arbitration: Counsel's Role and Perspective, in* EU AND US ANTITRUST ARBITRATION, Alphen aan den Rijn: Kluwer Law International paras. 8-056 to 8-057, 237, 248-249 (Gordon Blanke & Phillip Landolt eds., 2011).

[34] *Chapter 8: Organization and Conduct of Arbitral Proceedings and the Taking of Evidence, in* TREVOR COOK & ALEJANDRO I. GARCIA, INTERNATIONAL INTELLECTUAL PROPERTY ARBITRATION, Alphen aan den Rijn: Kluwer Law International 175, 211 (2010); *see also* Art. 51 of the WIPO Arbitration Rules ('Agreed Primers and Models'), whereby *"the Tribunal may, where the parties so agree, determine that they shall jointly provide: (i) a technical primer setting out the background of the scientific, technical or other specialized information necessary to fully understand the matters in issue; and (ii) models, drawings or other materials that the Tribunal or the parties require for reference purposes at any hearing."*

[35] GARY BORN, INTERNATIONAL COMMERCIAL ARBITRATION, Alphen aan den Rijn: Wolters Kluwer 1782-1873 (2009): *"Demonstrative evidence can be very useful in technically complex disputes, where the tribunal must understand and assess unfamiliar disciplines or a large body of evidence."* See also Werner Stieger, *Zum Umgang mit technischem Sachverhalt: Beweisführung und Beweiswürdigung in Schiedsverfahren*, (7/8) ZEITSCHRIFT FÜR IMMATERIALGÜTER, INFORMATIONS - UND WETTBEWERBSRECHT 493, 505 (2010); Michael E. Schneider, *Commentary to Article 184 of the Swiss Private International Law Statute*, INTERNATIONAL ARBITRATION IN SWITZERLAND, The Hague: Kluwer Law International (S. V. Berti, H. Honsell, N. P. Vogt, Anton K. Schnyder eds., 2000) note 33;

exhibits are likely the following: (a) charts, for example illustrating the steps in a damage calculation, (b) timelines arranging a complex set of events in a chronological fashion, and (c) highlighting of extracts from a document on screen where the case turns on a close reading of that particular document.[36]

3.22. Graphic evidence has also been used successfully at the United Nations Compensation Commission (UNCC) and the Iran-U.S. Claims Tribunal.[37] Maps play an important role not only in boundary and territorial disputes, where they can even amount to primary and not merely indirect evidence,[38] but also in energy cases (e.g., to depict pipelines trails).

3.23. In international arbitral proceedings where arbitral tribunals tend to be constituted of arbitrators from various countries and regions of the world, counsel should always bear in mind the arbitrators' cultural and legal background when deciding on the nature and scope of the demonstrative evidence to be applied.[39] The late Professor Thomas Wälde expressed the view on the OGEMID discussion forum he had created that "European notions seem to be more traditional and allow only a more narrow focus on what is a legitimate subject of professional discussion while in the US – most certainly due to the greater role of the jury and perhaps also greater curiosity about novel technologies – we have a wider scope for what is considered part of the professional skill arsenal."[40] This view is shared by Doak Bishop who stated that "[s]ome Continental and British arbitrators have indicated a disdain for such evidence. In this atmosphere, counsel should be careful and conservative about the introduction of such evidence."[41] He concludes with an important piece of practical advice: "If in doubt, ask the

---

idem, *Kommentar zu Artikel 184 Bundesgesetz über das Internationale Privatrecht, in* DAS INTERNATIONALE PRIVATRECHT (BASLER KOMMENTAR) note 33 (H. Honsell, N.P. Vogt, A.Schnyder, eds., 2006).

[36] Nicolas Fletcher, *supra* note 2, at 107 et seq.; JANE JENKINS & JAMES STEBBINGS, *supra* note 22; R. Doak Bishop, *supra* note 28, at *Chapter 15*, 451, 486-487.

[37] Stanton Belland, *The Iran-United States Claims Tribunal: Some Reflections on Trying a Claim*, 1 J. INT'L ARB. 237, 249 (1984).

[38] Robert Pietrowski, *Evidence in International Arbitration*, 22 (3) ARB. INT'L 397-398 (2006).

[39] Pierre-Yves Tschanz, *supra* note 29, at 208. See also Charles R. Ragan, *Arbitration in Japan: Caveat Foreign Drafter and Other Lessons*, 7 (2) ARB. INT'L 93, 112 Fn 72 (1991) where the author suggests prudence even in the choice of colors in demonstrative aids, which may be considered offensive in some cultures.

[40] OGEMID, message by Professor Thomas Wälde, sent on 13 October 2005 at 10:47 a.m.

[41] R. Doak Bishop, *supra* note 5, at *Chapter 10*, 309, 352 (2004); R. Doak Bishop & James H. Carter, *supra* note 2, at *Chapter 22*, 519, 562 (2010).

arbitrators at the preliminary hearing about their attitudes towards its use."[42]

VII. The Admissibility of Demonstrative Exhibits

3.24. To be admissible in U.S. civil procedure, a demonstrative exhibit must comply with standards of "authentication" (*i.e.*, it should convey what it is meant to convey), "representational accuracy" (*i.e.*, it should fairly depict the underlying evidence), and "identification" (*i.e.*, it must be an exact match of the underlying evidence or the testimony illustrated). Furthermore, demonstrative evidence before U.S. courts must pass the "three hurdles" of admissibility: relevancy, materiality, and competency.[43]

3.25. In international arbitration, there are no such fixed rules. The introduction of demonstrative exhibits lies within the discretion of the arbitrators who are free to determine the admissibility, relevance, materiality and weight of evidence, as expressly recognized by several arbitration laws and rules.[44]

3.26. In practice, international arbitral tribunals generally admit almost any kind of evidence submitted to them, but retain their discretion to assess its cogency and probative value.[45] In light of the fact that demonstrative

---

[42] *Ibid.*

[43] See Rules 401 et seq. Federal Rules of Evidence; *Schuler v Mid-Central Cardiology*, 729 NE2d 536, 246 Ill Dec 163 (CA Ill, 4th Dist 2000); Rodger D. Young & Steven Susser, *supra* note 4, at 1538.

[44] See Article 9(1) of the 2010 IBA Rules on the Taking of Evidence in International Arbitration ("IBA Rules"). The IBA Rules quite permissively define "Document" as *"writing, communication, picture, drawing, program or data of any kind, whether recorded or maintained on paper or by electronic, audio, visual or any other means."* See also, *e.g.*, Rule 34(1) of the ICSID Arbitration Rules; Section 34(2)(f) of the Arbitration Act 1996; Article 20(6) of the AAA ICDR Arbitration Rules; Articles 182 and 184 of the Swiss Private International Law Statute; JEAN-FRANÇOIS POUDRET & SÉBASTIEN BESSON, COMPARATIVE LAW OF INTERNATIONAL ARBITRATION, London: Sweet & Maxwell 642 (2nd ed. 2007); Robert Pietrowski, *supra* note 38, at 375, 378, 408.

[45] JULIAN LEW, LOUKAS A. MISTELIS & STEFAN KRÖLL, COMPARATIVE INTERNATIONAL COMMERCIAL ARBITRATION, The Hague: Kluwer Law International §§ 22-29, 22-45 (2003); Martin Hunter, *Modern Trends in the Presentation of Evidence in International Commercial Arbitration*, 3 AM. REV. INT'L ARB. 204, 211 (1992). See also PHILIPPE FOUCHARD, EMMANUEL GAILLARD & BERTHOLD GOLDMAN, INTERNATIONAL COMMERCIAL ARBITRATION, The Hague: Kluwer Law International §§ 1257, 1258 (2nd ed. 1999); ALAN REDFERN & MARTIN HUNTER, LAW AND PRACTICE OF INTERNATIONAL COMMERCIAL ARBITRATION, London: Sweet & Maxwell § 6-65 (4th ed. 2004); Martin Hunter *in* Judge Howard M. Holtzmann & Prof. Giorgio Bernini, *supra* note 27: *"If a party wishes to present material in this form it would be unusual, and possibly improper (because a party must be given a proper opportunity to present his case) for the tribunal to refuse to accept it."*

evidence usually provides no real evidence, but merely substitutes for or complements counsel's spoken word and illustrates primary evidence,[46] it appears to be a common procedural standard in international arbitration that

(1) demonstrative exhibits may not be used to introduce new primary evidence;[47] and

(2) demonstrative exhibits must fairly, accurately and completely reflect the real evidence and be otherwise unobjectionable.[48]

3.27. Out of caution not to violate rules of due process, arbitral tribunals will be careful to issue directions ensuring that parties have appropriate notice of the use of demonstrative evidence, in order to prevent unfair surprise and to guarantee an adequate opportunity for response to such evidence.[49] This avoids the possibility of one party benefitting from the opportunity to use demonstrative exhibits and later deciding against it with the expectation that the other party would be precluded from such use. Some arbitration practitioners also state that a party should not be prevented from using demonstrative exhibits on the grounds that another party to the proceedings lacks access to the same technology.[50]

3.28. Moreover, out of regard for due process, copies of demonstrative exhibits to be used (such as print-outs of charts) should be provided to opposing counsel and the arbitrators sufficiently in advance, following the general rule that parties to an international arbitration are required to produce the documents upon which they rely to prove their case.[51] This was expressly required by the arbitral tribunal in an arbitration involving the Bank for International Settlements, when it issued a procedural order whereby "demonstrative exhibits and other visual aids, including those using computer technology, could be used by the parties as long as the material was only based on evidence already in the

---

[46] GARY BORN, *supra* note 35, at 1860: *"Demonstrative evidence is not, strictly speaking, factual evidence or probative of facts; rather, it is a way of explaining, depicting, or arranging evidence that has otherwise been properly submitted."*

[47] Pierre-Yves Tschanz, *supra* note 47, at 218.

[48] Edward M. Josiah, *supra* note 17: for example, photographs must be authenticated as to the date taken, and it must be verified that no alterations have been made.

[49] Bernard Hanotiau, *Massive Productions of Documents and Demonstrative Exhibits in Written Evidence and Discovery, in* INTERNATIONAL ARBITRATION: NEW ISSUES AND TENDENCIES, Paris: ICC Publications 357, 361 (T. Giovannini & A. Mourre eds., 2009).

[50] GARY BORN, *supra* note 35, at 1860; Jean-Georges Betto, Jason Fry, Marc Henry, Elie Kleiman & Philippe Pinsolle, *supra* note 21.

[51] See, e.g., Rule 24 of the ICSID Arbitration Rules and Article 20(4) of the 2010 UNCITRAL Arbitration Rules; see also Pierre-Yves Tschanz, *supra* note 29, at 218.

record and had been shown to the opposing party prior to the hearings for verification purposes."[52]

3.29. Arbitration practitioners further recommend that arbitrators grant opposing counsel the opportunity to review and verify the underlying data on which demonstrative evidence is based.[53] It is rightly suggested that if such an opportunity is not given and a doubt arises with respect to data presented by demonstrative evidence, the tribunal should order the production of the original data at the request of opposing counsel or at its own initiative.[54]

VIII. Conclusion: Some Considerations for an Effective Use of Demonstrative Exhibits in Arbitration Proceedings

3.30. Demonstrative exhibits can be an effective tool of persuasion for counsel and there is no doubt that they will increasingly find their way into international arbitration hearings, given the sophistication and accessibility of computer animations and other technologies that facilitate the creation of graphics.

3.31. Besides complying with the abovementioned procedural rules, counsel in arbitral proceedings should however keep in mind a number of practical considerations when using visual aids:

    (1) Demonstrative exhibits are merely props that help illustrate the underlying evidence and cannot substitute for the principal means of evidence such as documents and witness testimony.

    (2) Demonstrative exhibits should be used with caution; they cannot replace substance, precision, logic, and a well-argued case.[55] In addition, if demonstrative exhibits are overused, counsel risks sending the arbitrators an unwanted message, namely that he or she is trying to distract them from the weakness of his or her client's case with the use of an

---

[52] Scott Armstrong Spence, *Organizing an Arbitration Involving an International Organization and Multiple Private Parties – The Example of the Bank for International Settlements Arbitration*, 21 (4) J. INT'L ARB. 309, 322 (2004).

[53] Judge Howard M. Holtzmann & Prof. Giorgio Bernini, *supra* note 27.

[54] *Ibid.*

[55] Pierre-Yves Tschanz, *supra* note 29, at 205: "*The arbitrators must think that the case is good, not that counsel is brilliant. The merits of the case must appear to owe as little as possible to counsel's skills*"; Nicolas Fletcher, *supra* note 2, at 108: "*...care needs to be taken to ensure that presentational gimmicks do not prevail over substance and that time is not wasted on unnecessary attempts to deploy or demonstrate counsel's full range of technological skills which do not advance the tribunal's understanding of the case*"; see also Michael S. Kun, *supra* note 14.

overwhelming high-tech presentation.[56] Doak Bishop described this in the following terms: "The style of presentation should be dignified and sincere. Bombastic oratory and wild gesticulations, as if playing to the audience in the last row of the theatre, are hardly ever effective in arbitration."[57]

(3) The volume and complexity of information communicated through demonstrative exhibits should be balanced against the arbitrators' capacity to absorb such information, otherwise counsel risks allowing visual aids to detract from the effectiveness of his or her oral pleadings.[58]

(4) The use of demonstrative exhibits should always be audience-driven with respect to the composition of the arbitral tribunal as well as the arbitrators' personality and their cultural and legal background, in particular in an international setting.

(5) When demonstrative exhibits are used to support witness or expert testimony, counsel should make sure to prepare the witnesses and experts on how and when to use them effectively and determine whether they are a true benefit or a dramatization of the issues.[59]

(6) Finally, on a more practical note, counsel should always keep track of demonstrative exhibits and give them exhibit numbers when produced at the hearing to facilitate referencing during the remainder of the proceedings. Furthermore, for maximum impact, counsel should select the type of exhibit and the presentation medium with care so that they work best within the particular presentation arena.[60]

3.32. Arbitral tribunals, on their end, are well advised to give clear directions on the use of demonstrative exhibits so as to avoid any procedural

---

[56] R. Doak Bishop, *supra* note 28, at *Chapter 15*, 451, 486-487 (2004): "*If it is just as easy to put a normal-sized photocopy of a document in front of the arbitrators as showing them an enlarged copy, then there is usually no significant benefit in "blowing up" the document to an enlarged size. A copy of the highlighted document that the arbitrators can keep is generally more useful anyway.*" See also Rodger D. Young & Steven Susser, *supra* note 4, at 1538.

[57] R. Doak Bishop, *supra* note 28, at *Chapter 15*, 451, 479 (2004).

[58] Jean-Georges Betto, Jason Fry, Marc Henry, Elie Kleiman & Philippe Pinsolle, *supra* note 21.

[59] Richard H. Kreindler, *Benefiting from Oral Testimony of Expert Witnesses: Traditional and Emerging Techniques, in* 4 (3) Transnational Dispute Management 6, 13, 15, 17 (June 2007).

[60] Edward M. Josiah, *supra* note 17, who gives the example of a case where the best and most effective option would be to prepare an interactive time-phased two-dimensional site plan which would show the actual progression of work.

uncertainty in this respect.[61] This is best done at the outset of the arbitration, for instance by establishing a specific procedural rule along the following lines:

"No new documents may be presented at the Hearing. However, demonstrative exhibits may be shown using documents or data on record previously submitted in accordance with the procedural timetable. A hard copy of any such demonstrative exhibit shall be provided [...] days in advance by the Party producing the exhibit to the other Party and to each member of the Arbitral Tribunal. The Arbitral Tribunal, at its own initiative or upon request by a Party, may order the production of the underlying data on which such demonstrative exhibits are based."

| | |

Summaries

DEU [*Der wirkungsvolle Einsatz visueller Mittel in internationalen Schiedsverfahren*]

Der Artikel bespricht den Einsatz visueller Mittel, sogenannter „demonstrative exhibits", in internationalen Schiedsverfahren. Es geht dabei um graphische Darstellungen und andere Anschauungsmittel, anhand derer die Parteivertreter den Schiedsrichtern das eigentliche Beweismaterial eingängiger vermitteln können. Der Autor verweist auf die Ursprünge derartiger Kommunikationsmittel im US-amerikanischen Straf- und Zivilprozess, in dem es in erster Linie eine Jury zu überzeugen gilt. Er erklärt, dass die in amerikanischen Gerichtssäälen praktizierten Überzeugungsmechanismen nicht ohne weiteres vor Schiedsgerichten zum Einsatz kommen sollten, weil Schiedsrichter in der Regel andere Voraussetzungen mit sich bringen als die Mitglieder einer Jury. Der Autor bespricht, inwiefern die Verwendung von „demonstrative exhibits" im Rahmen internationaler Schiedsverfahren sinnvoll oder sogar geboten ist, insbesondere bei technisch komplexen Fällen. Er betont, dass dabei jeweils auf die Herkunft und Rechtskultur der Schiedsrichter Rücksicht zu nehmen ist, und schliesst seinen Beitrag mit einer Reihe praktischer Erwägungen für Parteivertreter und Schiedsrichter.

---

[61] See, *e.g.*, NAFTA Chapter 11/UNCITRAL Award of 28 January 2008, *Canadian Cattlemen for Fair Trade* v. *United States*, Digest by Charles H. Brower, ITA, citing Procedural Order n°1 regarding the Hearing on the Preliminary issue dated 20 October 2006.

CZE **[Účinné používání vizuálních prostředků v mezinárodním rozhodčím řízení]**
Článek pojednává o používání vizuálních prostředků, tzv. „demonstrative exhibits", v mezinárodním rozhodčím řízení. Jedná se přitom o grafické znázornění a jiné názorné pomůcky, s jejichž pomocí mohou zástupci stran zprostředkovat rozhodcům vlastní důkazní materiál jednodušeji. Autor odkazuje na původy takových komunikačních prostředků v americkém trestním a občanskoprávním řízení, v němž jde v prvé řadě o to, přesvědčit porotu. Prohlašuje, že přesvědčovací mechanismy praktikované v amerických soudních síních by před rozhodčími soudy neměly být používány bez úpravy, protože rozhodci pocházejí z jiného prostředí (mají jiné předpoklady) než členové poroty. Autor pojednává o tom, do jaké míry má používání „demonstrative exhibits" v rámci mezinárodního rozhodčího řízení smysl nebo je dokonce žádoucí, zejména u technicky komplexních případů. Zdůrazňuje, že je přitom vždy důležité mít na zřeteli původ a právní kulturu rozhodců, a končí svůj příspěvek řadou praktických úvah pro zástupce stran a rozhodce.

| | |

POL **[Skuteczne stosowanie dowodów rzeczowych w arbitrażu międzynarodowym]**
Niniejszy artykuł przedstawia zarys zastosowania pomocy wizualnych czy też dowodów rzeczowych w postępowaniu w ramach arbitrażu międzynarodowego. Autor określa, co może składać się na dowody rzeczowe oraz bada ich zastosowanie w perspektywie historycznej w sporach sądowych w Stanach Zjednoczonych, a także rozważa psychologiczne aspekty ich skuteczności. Ponadto, artykuł podejmuje kwestię dopuszczalności i ograniczeń w stosunku do dowodów rzeczowych we współczesnej praktyce arbitrażu międzynarodowego, prezentując na zakończenie praktyczne wskazówki wykorzystywania tychże dowodów.

FRA **[L'emploi efficace des aides visuelles, ou demonstrative exhibits, dans l'arbitrage international]**
Le présent article livre un panorama de l'emploi des aides visuelles, ou «demonstrative exhibits» dans les procédures arbitrales internationales. L'auteur définit ce qui doit être entendu par «demonstrative exhibits,» examine l'usage qui en a été fait historiquement aux Etats-Unis en matière contentieuse et se penche sur les aspects psychologiques expliquant leur efficacité. L'article examine également la question de

Czech (& Central European) Yearbook of Arbitration

l'admissibilité et des limites des demonstrative exhibits dans la pratique moderne de l'arbitrage international avant de conclure par quelques lignes directrices relatives à leur usage.

RUS [*Эффективное применение наглядных материалов в международных арбитражных процессах*]

В статье дается обзор применения визуальных средств, или наглядных материалов, в международных арбитражных процессах. Автор показывает, что могут собой представлять наглядные материалы, и изучает историю их применения в судебных процессах в США, а также рассматривает психологические аспекты эффективности таких материалов. Далее в статье рассматриваются вопросы допустимости применения наглядных материалов и ограничений на их использование в современной практике международного арбитража, а в завершение дается ряд практических рекомендаций по работе с такими материалами.

ESP [*Uso efectivo de pruebas demostrativas en el arbitraje internacional*]

Este artículo proporciona una visión general sobre el uso de ayudas visuales o pruebas demostrativas en los procedimientos de arbitraje internacional. El autor define en qué pueden consistir las pruebas demostrativas y examina su historial de uso en litigios de Estados Unidos, así como los aspectos psicológicos que concurren en el trasfondo de su efectividad. El artículo versa posteriormente sobre la admisibilidad y las limitaciones de las pruebas demostrativas en la práctica del arbitraje moderno internacional, para concluir con algunas indicaciones prácticas sobre su uso.

Czech (& Central European) Yearbook of Arbitration

Dan Engström | Cornel Marian*

Restrictive Absolutes: Using Party Autonomy to Reconcile Absolute Immunity with the Liberal Standard for Restrictive Immunity Adopted by the Swedish Supreme Court in the *Sedelmayer* Decision

Key words:
Sovereign Immunity |
Commercial exception |
Enforcement Proceedings |
Party Autonomy |
Sedelmayer decision

Abstract | *In the Sedelmayer case, the Swedish Supreme Court affirmed its unequivocal endorsement of restrictive immunity in enforcement proceedings against sovereign states. Although the Swedish Supreme Court's rationale went so far as to suggest that restrictive sovereign immunity is universally accepted as customary international law, that view was soon dismissed when the highest court in Hong Kong ruled in favor of absolute immunity in FG Hemisphere Associates. In stark contrast to the Hong Kong decision, the Swedish Sedelmayer decision incorporates a very liberal commercial exception that places the burden on the state to prove that the property against which enforcement is sought is used for "official purposes" only. The Swedish Sedelmayer decision is noteworthy in that: (1) it continues to give credence to the UN Convention on Sovereign Immunity despite the Convention not being ratified, and (2) it establishes the temporal link that "use and intended use" are to be determined exclusively with reference to the time of the enforcement proceedings. In light of these divergent rulings, this article deduces that the tensions between the absolute and restrictive doctrines*

Dan Engström is the managing partner of Stockholm Arbitration & Litigation Center (SALC) Advokatbyrå, which is the first law firm in Sweden with a practice exclusively limited to litigation and dispute resolution. SALC's members serve as counsels and arbitrators in Sweden and abroad.
e-mail: dan.engstrom@salc.se

Cornel Marian is an associate with the Stockholm Arbitration & Litigation Center (SALC) Advokatbyrå. He is a US-trained attorney, admitted before the courts of the State of New York. He

---

* The views expressed in the article belong solely to the authors and are not representative of the views of the firm or its clients. The errors are those of the authors alone.

Czech (& Central European) Yearbook of Arbitration

to sovereign immunity are real. Until the UN Convention is in a position to reconcile any such conflicts, this article proposes the use of party autonomy as an alternative to resolving any future conflicts. By exploring the gaps in codified international law on sovereign immunity, the article concludes that bilateral investment treaties (BIT) are an ideal mechanism to clarify and set out the party intent on the scope of commercial activity, which can be immune from enforcement.

received his LLM in international commercial arbitration from Stockholm University.
e-mail:
cornel.marian@salc.se

| | |

I. Introduction

4.01.   A thorny issue divides the arbitration community that does not cut across the lines between civil and common law legal regimes. Neither does this division follow the demarcation of developed and developing countries. On the issue of sovereign immunity, legal cultures are divided by diametric views on the role of the state and its liability when it acts in a private capacity.[1]

4.02.   Sovereign immunity in enforcement proceedings dictates that states' assets cannot ordinarily be attached, garnished or be subject to distraint. Neither can a state court exert jurisdiction over a sovereign state unless the state consents. The commercial exception holds that where the state acts in a private capacity, state assets are subject to the jurisdiction of domestic courts and may be enforced against in civil proceedings. There is hence a division in terms of the state being viewed as an *absolute* or indivisible entity, so that all of the state's assets are deemed immune from any attachment, and the state being viewed as a *restrictive* entity, where the state is not immune when it behaves as a private actor. In terms of restrictive immunity, only those state assets that are non-commercial in nature are immune. Despite clear progress toward consolidating these two positions,[2] recent case law reveals that the gap between absolute and restrictive immunity remains wide.

---

[1]   KAJ HOBÉR, INTERNATIONAL COMMERCIAL ARBITRATION IN SWEDEN, Oxford: Oxford University Press 1.53-54 (2011). These divergent views may be traced to Cold War ideology on the role of the state. "As far as Soviet law was concerned, this theory was based on the assumption that the State, the sovereign, is always one: it is always one single subject, although the manifestations of its legal personality may be manifold." *Ibid.*, at 1-56.

[2]   UN General Assembly, Convention on Jurisdictional Immunities of States and their Property, A/59/49, December 2, 2004 (not in force) [hereinafter "UN Convention on Sovereign Immunity"].

4.03. This article begins by comparing the two holdings of a recent court decision in Hong Kong and in Sweden that address the commercial exception to sovereign immunity in jurisdictional and enforcement proceedings respectively [II]. The article proceeds to focus on the holding in the Swedish case and the factual background that reveals a liberal standard for restrictive immunity in execution [III]. The article then discusses the scope of the commercial exception defined by the Swedish Supreme Court [IV], only to conclude with a review of the impact of the UN Convention of Sovereign Immunity [V] and Party Autonomy for resolving potential conflicts [VI].

II. A Tale of Two (or Four) Immunities

4.04. Two recent court decisions, one in Hong Kong and another in Sweden, have unveiled the innate debate on absolute and restrictive sovereign immunity.[3] At the very least, these two court decisions awakened the debate that was left dormant with the fall of the USSR on the breadth of immunity protection enjoyed by a state. Absolute immunity and restrictive immunity differ at the jurisdictional and enforcement phases. The grounds for granting an exception are narrower for enforcement than for jurisdictional proceedings against a state, whereby a state enjoys greater immunity in enforcement proceedings. The two decisions reviewed in this article address the two polar opposite approaches adopted by courts in terms of absolute and restrictive immunity,[4] further confirming that the path towards harmonizing standards of immunity (not only between *absolute* and *restrictive* but also as divided for *jurisdictional* and *enforcement* proceedings) may be longer than expected.

4.05. On the one hand, the Hong Kong decision reinforces the conclusion that, despite being in the minority, absolute immunity is still a prevalent and powerful legal doctrine.[5] In *FG Hemisphere Associates*, the Hong Kong Court of Final Appeal held that foreign states enjoy absolute immunity from jurisdiction. The issue came up on appeal following the FG Hemisphere Associates' attempt to garnish payments

---

[3] *DR Congo* v. *FG Hemisphere* Associates, [2011] HKEC 747, Hong Kong Court of Final Appeal. See also *Sedelmayer* v. *Russian Federation*, Ö 170-10, July 1 2010, Swedish Supreme Court [hereinafter "Sedelmayer, Swedish Supreme Court"].

[4] JULIAN D. M. LEW, LOUKAS A. MISTELLIS & STEFAN KROLL, COMPARATIVE INTERNATIONAL COMMERCIAL ARBITRATION, The Hague: Kluwer Law International para. 27-53 (2003). ("In most laws the exceptions to immunity from execution are narrower than the exceptions to immunity from jurisdiction.")

[5] For a thorough background on the FG Associates case, see Oliver Jones, *Let the Mainland Speak*, 41 HONG KONG LAW JOURNAL (2011).

from China Railway Group that were directed to the government of the Democratic Republic Congo (DRC). FG Hemisphere Associates sought the enforcement of two favorable ICC arbitration awards against DRC. The district court did not take up the issue of immunity and while the Court of Appeal held that Hong Kong adheres to restrictive immunity, the Hong Kong Court of Final Appeal reversed this decision.

4.06. Whereas the previous silence on sovereign immunity led notable legal scholars to conclude that absolute immunity may be enjoying less support in jurisdictions such as People's Republic of China (PRC),[6] the Hong Kong Court of Final Appeal recently held in *FG Hemisphere Associates* that: (1) absolute immunity is unequivocally part of the PRC's legal culture and (2) there is no room for deviation from the "one nation, one system" principle in this context.[7] The majority decision's reasoning was succinct: "[T]he HKSAR cannot, as a matter of legal and constitutional principle, adhere to a doctrine of state immunity which differs from that adopted by the PRC. The doctrine of state immunity practiced in the HKSAR, as in the rest of China, is accordingly a doctrine of absolute immunity."[8] The issue was reached following the submission by the Hong Kong Secretary of Justice received from the Office of the Commissioner of the Ministry of Foreign Affairs, that characterized the position adopted by the Central People's Government to say that: "[t]he consistent and principled position of China is that a state and its property shall, in foreign courts, enjoy absolute immunity, including absolute immunity from jurisdiction and from execution, and has never applied the so-called principle or theory of 'restrictive immunity.'"[9]

4.07. As a result of *FG Hemisphere Associates*, Hong Kong clearly departed from its previous position – grounded in English case law – that provided for a commercial exception to sovereign immunity both in jurisdiction and execution proceedings. In light of the Court's analysis, this position may signal a temporary lapse in Hong Kong jurisprudence until the PRC judicial discourse takes a different course. At this point,

---

[6] KAJ HOBÉR, *supra* note 1, at paras. 1.65-74. Such position is understandable considering that China in fact has signed (but not ratified like Sweden) the UN Convention on Sovereign Immunity. *Ibid.*, at para. 1.74.

[7] The principle is particularly important in Hong Kong where the legal doctrine is deemed to be integrated with that of Mainland China but a level of separation of the local judiciary is still maintained. *DR Congo* v. *FG Hemisphere Associates*, [2011] HKEC 747 at paras. 39-57 (Bokhary Permanent Judge, dissenting).

[8] *DR Congo* v. *FG Hemisphere* Associates, [2011] HKEC 747, at para. 183. The dissent reviewed 1997 Hong Kong judiciary's reliance on US precedent when determining the scope of sovereign immunity to be restrictive. *DR Congo* v. *FG Hemisphere Associates*, [2011] HKEC 747 (dis. J. Bokhary) at paras. 88-92.

[9] *DR Congo* v. *FG Hemisphere Associates*, [2011] HKEC 747, at para. 197.

however, the holding of the Hong Kong Court of Final Appeal appears permanent and speaks loudly of the presence of absolute immunity in current legal discourse.

4.08. On the other hand, the Swedish decision, which is central to this article, reinforces the point that restrictive immunity is upheld by the majority and, in the Swedish context, it is broadly interpreted in enforcement proceedings. In the *Sedelmayer* decision, the Swedish Supreme Court accomplished three notable ends. First, it confirmed that Swedish law endorses restrictive immunity for cases involving commercial exceptions, whereby property not used for official purposes is determined not to be immune from enforcement.[10] Second, the Swedish Supreme Court reasserted its reliance on the UN Convention on Sovereign Immunity as a persuasive instrument despite the fact that the UN Convention has not come into force. Its reliance may be seen in that the Swedish Supreme Court still applied the UN Convention even though, in accordance with its own articles, thirty states have yet to ratify the Convention to put it into force, a fact which further prevents Sweden from formally incorporating the UN Convention into its own domestic law.[11] Third, the Court's decision underlines how politically charged court decisions involving sovereign immunity are and how critical it is to observe the separation between the executive and the judiciary. The *Sedelmayer* decision naturally drew staunch criticism from the Russian government. The Russian Foreign Ministry voiced its objections to the Swedish Foreign Ministry and Prime Minister over the decision of the Swedish Supreme Court, thereby conjuring the belief that the government is viewed as one with courts lacking independence from other branches of the government. Such criticism from the Russian government is not indicative of the idea, and the authors are not alleging, that Russian courts are necessarily likely to endorse absolute immunity.[12] In fact, the outcry against the *Sedelmayer* decision from the Russian executive branch should not be imputed to its judiciary. Just as independent critics have reproved the Russian government's response to the Swedish Supreme Court decision by underlining that the response ignored the separation and independence of the judiciary from the rest of the Swedish government,[13] the authors

---

[10] See *infra* III.

[11] See *infra* IV.

[12] KAJ HOBÉR, *supra* note 1, at paras. 1.61-64.

[13] Commentary by Grigori Amnuel, see Sergei Basimov & Vadim Trukhachev, *Sedelmayer: 'Russia will pay me'*, PRAVDA (July 8, 2011), English version available at: http://english.pravda.ru/business/finance/08-07-2011/118432-Franz_Sedelmayer-0/ (accessed on August 31, 2011).

are careful to acknowledge the independence of the Russian courts. Concluding that Russian courts endorse absolute immunity based on the government criticism alone would be a mistaken supposition. It would unnecessarily distort the issue that Russian courts are not independent, which is a separate issue for review. Yet, the *Sedelmayer* decision and the Russian response underscore that restrictive immunity is a prevailing position adopted by Western courts, which is not endorsed or accepted universally. In this context, the Swedish Supreme Court decision stands in sharp contrast to similar enforcement proceedings in Germany (and elsewhere) where the courts have interpreted the commercial exception to sovereign immunity restrictively.[14]

III. The *Sedelmayer* Saga: A Broad Commercial Exception

4.09. To those familiar with arbitration in Russia, Franz J. Sedelmayer's name has become recognizable as a result of a decade-long arbitration and litigation proceedings against the Russian Federation. In July 1998, Mr. Sedelmayer, a successful German businessperson who formally served in the German Armed Forces, obtained a favorable arbitration award against Russia for USD 2 350 000 plus arbitration costs.[15] In July 2011, nearly thirteen years after the rendering of the final award, Mr. Sedelmayer succeeded in securing enforcement of the award against property partly owned by the Russian government as a result of a final court decision of the Swedish Supreme Court.

III.1. SCC Arbitration Proceedings

4.10. The dispute arose from a failed joint venture between a US company, of which Mr. Sedelmayer was the primary shareholder, and the St. Petersburg's police force. In the final days of the USSR (or the last years of perestroika), Mr. Sedelmayer entered into a joint agreement with the city of St. Petersburg's police force with the purpose of delivering

---

[14] Emmanuel Gaillard, *Effectiveness of Arbitral Awards, State Immunity from Execution and Autonomy of State Entities*, in 4 STATE ENTITIES IN INTERNATIONAL ARBITRATION IAI SERIES ON INTERNATIONAL ARBITRATION, Paris: Juris Publishing Int. 179-193, 183 (Emmanuel Gaillard & Jennifer Younan eds., 2008). See also Alexis Blane, *Sovereign Immunity as a Bar to the Execution of International Arbitral Awards*, 41 (2) NEW YORK UNIVERSITY JOURNAL OF INTERNATIONAL LAW AND POLITICS 453 (2009) (*"The promise of such transportable execution ... may be fatally flawed. When losing state parties do resist award enforcement, the domestic law of sovereign immunity provides a near-absolute bar to attempts to enforce and execute those awards against a state."*)

[15] *Franz Sedelmayer v. Russian Federation*, Arbitration Award, the Arbitration Institute of the Stockholm Chamber of Commerce (July 7, 1998).

equipment and training personnel to the police force in exchange for a 25-year lease on critical real estate. Both parties signed the Protocol of Intent in July 1990 and Mr. Sedelmayer proceeded to invest in the real estate and to provide equipment to the police force.[16]

4.11. In the course of the early reorganization of the Russian Federation in the early 1990s, a federal fund was organized to administer the internal resources for all federal assets, including the property owned by the joint venture which would thus be transferred into governmental hands. The move was not even subtle. A presidential directive was signed expressly requiring the transfer of the property owned by the joint venture to the federal authorities. Mr. Sedelmayer sought redress against the Russian government in the domestic courts, failing which, he sought an investment arbitration with the Arbitration Institute of the Stockholm Chamber of Commerce (SCC), pursuant to the 1989 bilateral investment treaty (BIT) entered between the Soviet Union and the Federal Republic of Germany.[17]

4.12. Despite staunch dissent, the tribunal found that Russia had violated the expropriation provisions of the bilateral agreement entered into by the Soviet Union and the Federal Republic of Germany.[18] The tribunal found that, in reliance upon its agreement with the St. Petersburg police force, Mr. Sedelmayer had invested and made requisite repairs to the disputed real estate, and therefore, awarded compensation to Mr. Sedelmayer for his investment in the real estate and the loss of his right to use the premises.[19] The tribunal also awarded him additional compensation for expropriated property. Russia proceeded to challenge the arbitration award on grounds that Swedish courts lack jurisdiction to review the matter maintaining that the award should thus be deemed invalid.[20] The Russian Federation was unsuccessful in its challenge proceedings before the district court[21] and at the appellate level.[22]

---

[16] *Ibid.*, at 1-7.

[17] *Ibid.*

[18] The dissent held that: (1) Mr. Sedelmayer was not a qualified investor as the contracting party was a US corporation based in Missouri and (2) Mr. Sedelmayer did not initiate proceedings against the proper respondent when it filed the proceedings against the Procurement Department. *Franz Sedelmayer* v. *Russian Federation*, Arbitration Award, the Arbitration Institute of the Stockholm Chamber of Commerce (July 7, 1998) (Pr. I. Zykin dissenting).

[19] *Ibid.*, at 111.

[20] See *Ibid.*, at 106-110 & 118. See generally SCC commentary *Mr. Franz* v. *the Russian Federation*, (2) STOCKHOLM INTERNATIONAL ARBITRATION REVIEW 37-146 (2005).

[21] *Russian Federation* v. *Sedelmayer*, T 6-583-98, Stockholm District Court, December 18, 2002. See also SCC commentary *Mr. Franz* v. *the Russian Federation*, *supra* note 20, at 115-131.

Czech (& Central European) Yearbook of Arbitration

III.2. Enforcement Proceedings outside Sweden

4.13. Despite the SCC award and the finality of the judicial review in Sweden, the Russian Federation refused to abide by the arbitration award. Mr. Sedelmayer then turned to the German courts to enforce the arbitration award against assets owned by the Russian Federation in Germany. Some of these efforts were very original, even perhaps controversial or unorthodox. In Cologne, Mr. Sedelmayer sought to attach the payments made by Lufthansa, the German airline company, for *over-flight* rights in Russia. The issue reached the German Supreme Court, where the Court held that fees for over-flight rights may not be garnished and would infringe on the sovereign's immunity of the state. The Court reasoned that garnishment can be levied only over the property deemed to be within the national borders and that a contrary decision would inadvertently impose hardship on the airline carrier, not on the debtor.[23] In multiple other attempts, Mr. Sedelmayer was unsuccessful in enforcement of the award against real estate owned by the Russian Federation in Germany.[24] These proceedings are still pending in Germany.

III.3. Enforcement Proceedings in Sweden

4.14. Mr. Sedelmayer ultimately prevailed in enforcing the SCC arbitral award in Sweden.[25] Following a successful investigation into Russian assets, Mr. Sedelmayer moved against real estate assets owned by the Russian Federation in Lidingö, a Northern suburb of Stockholm. At an early stage, the Swedish Enforcement Authority (the national authority responsible for the collection of defaulted debt) found that the assets owned by the Russian Federation could be attached in payment for the arbitration award.[26] However, the Enforcement Authority later ruled that rental fees could not be garnished, and this decision was affirmed by the Nacka district court. It was only on appeal to the Svea Court of Appeal that Mr. Sedelmayer prevailed and was allowed to attach against the real estate property and to garnish the rental payments. The

---

[22] *Russian Federation* v. *Sedelmayer*, T 525-03, Svea Court of Appeal, June 15, 2005. See also SCC commentary *Mr. Franz* v. *the Russian Federation, supra* note 20, at 132-135.

[23] *Sedelmayer* v. *Lufthansa*, German Supreme Court, BGH Order VII ZB 9/05, October 4, 2005, paras. 14-15.

[24] Oberlandesgericht Köln, 22 U 98/07 (Judgment, March 18, 2007). See also Landgericht Köln, 3 O 7/07 (Judgment, January 18, 2007).

[25] It would be interesting to see to what extent the Swedish Supreme Court decision will be persuasive in similar proceedings in Germany.

[26] *Sedelmayer* Swedish Supreme Court decision, paras. 1-2.

Supreme Court issued an opinion affirming in detail the Court of Appeal's decision.

4.15. The details on the property itself are *critical* for determining the scope of the commercial exception to sovereign immunity. The property was previously owned by the Russian trade delegation in Stockholm until, in 1976, the trade delegation moved to a nearby location in the same suburb. Despite the Russian Federation's claim that the property was used for "official purposes," the Swedish Supreme Court determined the contrary. The court found persuasive that, although the Russian Federation was the registered owner, sixty residents were also registered at the property, including two corporations, ten Swedish citizens and no Russian diplomats.[27] The Court did not find convincing Russia's evidence that the basement of the building was used as an archive, the premises used as a garage for the trade mission, and that four apartments were used for Russian dignitaries.[28] Moreover, the Court determined that the timing for the petition was highly relevant. To determine use, the date *when* the petition for enforcement was filed became determinative for the court of how the property would be used.[29] These two critical factors: (1) establishment of "use or intended use" for non-commercial purposes and (2) referral to a temporal element to determine use, both of which emerged from previous Swedish law, generally silent on the matter, are discussed below.

IV. *Sedelmayer* as Restrictive Sovereign Immunity in Swedish Enforcement Proceedings

4.16. In refusing to grant and reverse the appellate decision in *Sedelmayer*, the Swedish Supreme Court broadly interpreted the commercial exception to sovereign immunity during the course of the enforcement of an arbitration award. The *Sedelmayer* decision was the first decision to recognize restrictive immunity in enforcement proceedings in Sweden, although it was not the first court ruling on restrictive immunity in general.[30] The Court has unequivocally clarified that it

---

[27] *Ibid.*, para. 18.

[28] *Ibid.*, para. 19.

[29] *Ibid.*, para. 20.

[30] *Sedelmayer* Swedish Supreme Court decision, para. 11 ("There are no rulings of later date in which the Supreme Court has had to decide on the issue of immunity from enforcement measures."). See also KAJ HOBÉR, *supra* note 1, at 1.131-39. In *LIAMCO*, the Svea Court of Appeal came close to pronouncing on the issue but the issue was settled between the parties before a binding rule would come to light. Before the *Sedelmayer* decision, Professor Hobér noted that "[i]n a technical sense, the question of immunity in recognition proceedings is thus still unresolved by Swedish courts." *Ibid.*, at 1.136. See also

endorses the majority consensus on restrictive sovereign immunity. In reaching its decision, the Court followed a clear "textual" approach to restrictive sovereign immunity by: (1) setting the parameters for sovereign immunity, (2) distinguishing the commercial exception in enforcement proceedings to be narrower than for the jurisdictional inquiry, and (3) clarifying the scope of the commercial exception by reviewing the facts. As the decision adds considerably to Swedish case law, the last of these points, which requires close scrutiny, is addressed separately in the next section.

4.17. As to the first point, sovereign immunity is a truism necessary for the existence of international law. The doctrine is "based on comity and equality of states" and is necessary for the "functioning of all governments."[31] The Court reaffirmed this position by observing that "[i]mmunity from enforcement in state property is a consequence of the view that states are equal" and by defining the scope of sovereign immunity, in relation to the commercial transactions that are deemed to be excluded. Restrictive immunity has been part of the fabric of Swedish case law since 1999, albeit in the context of jurisdictional inquiry, when the Court resolved a case involving payments allegedly owed by Iceland to a Swedish municipality.[32] The Court reasoned that a foreign state *could be* ordered to pay when it acted in a private capacity but the facts revealed that the agreement reached between Iceland and a local Swedish school for training students in aircraft maintenance and engineering was not deemed to have been entered into by the sovereign state in a private capacity.[33] Because the dispute arose from a bilateral agreement that fostered educational training, the Court deemed that it lacked jurisdiction to hear the dispute. So in *Västerås Municipality*, the Court held that, despite the recognized commercial exception to sovereign immunity, the claimant could not invoke jurisdiction against the state assets – even for the purpose of exerting jurisdiction over the dispute. In all, *Sedelmayer* extended the analysis used in *Västerås Municipality* cases and applied it to arbitral proceedings.

LIAMCO v. *State of Libya*, 20 ILM (1981) 895-896 (cited almost completely in *Ibid.*, at 1.136-37).

[31] JULIAN D. M. LEW, LOUKAS A. MISTELLIS & STEFAN KROLL, *supra* note 4, at paras. 27-35. See also *Sedelmayer* Swedish Supreme Court decision, para. 9.

[32] *Västerås Municipality* v. *Iceland*, NJA 1999 p. 821. See also *Sedelmayer* Swedish Supreme Court decision, para. 11 ("*There are no rulings of later date in which the Supreme Court has had to decide on the issue of immunity from enforcement measures*").

[33] *Västerås Municipality* v. *Iceland*, NJA 1999 p. 821.

4.18. As to the second point, the Court echoed the majority consensus that the commercial exception provides a narrower scope for reviewing the State's conduct at the jurisdictional phase than at the enforcement stage.[34] The Court saw a distinction between immunity from jurisdiction and immunity from enforcement and recognized the majority position that the grounds for granting an exception to a state's immunity from enforcement are narrower than the grounds for granting an exception to immunity from jurisdiction.[35] The Court reasoned that "it has been viewed as a bigger intrusion [upon] a state's sovereignty to subject its property to distraint than [it is to subject] the state to the jurisdiction of foreign courts."[36] But in contrast to the Iceland case where the Court established restrictive immunity while still denying jurisdictional immunity, the Swedish Supreme Court held that the facts of *Sedelmayer* fell within the narrow limits of the commercial exception in enforcement proceedings against the Russian Federation, which leads to the third point of inquiry, that of the scope of the commercial exception in enforcement proceedings, which draws heavily on the standards for use from the UN Convention on Sovereign Immunity.

V. The Application and Implication of the UN Convention on Sovereign Immunity

4.19. When the Swedish Supreme Court defined the scope of the commercial exception, it notably relied on the definition from the UN Convention on Sovereign Immunity. The *Sedelmayer* decision demonstrates the Swedish Supreme Court's continuous adherence to the UN Convention on Sovereign Immunity despite the Convention not coming into force.[37] In relation to the *Sedelmayer* Supreme Court decision, two points of tensions are derived from the Swedish Supreme Court's use of the UN Convention definition of sovereign immunity concerning the Court's interpretations of the UN Convention: (1) determining the relevant standard for "use and intended for use by the State for non-commercial purposes," and (2) the temporal determination of establishing use.

---

[34] *Sedelmayer* Swedish Supreme Court decision, para. 9.
[35] *Sedelmayer* Swedish Supreme Court decision, paras. 6, 9. JULIAN D. M. LEW, LOUKAS A. MISTELLIS & STEFAN KROLL, *supra* note 4, at paras. 27-53.
[36] *Sedelmayer* Swedish Supreme Court decision, para. 9.
[37] *Bostadsrättsföreningen Villagatan 13* v. *Belgian Republic*, NJA 2009 s 905 (NJA 2009:91).

4.20. First, the Court's legal standard relies on the provisions of UN Convention Article 19(c),[38] which hold that a state is not immune in enforcement proceedings in so far as:

> it has been established that the property is specifically in use or intended for use by the State for other than government non-commercial purposes and is in the territory of the State of the forum, provided that post-judgment measures of constraint may only be taken against property that has a connection with the entity against which the proceeding was directed[39]

4.21. In determining the commercial exception, the Court interpreted the provision "for other than government non-commercial purpose" to mean "that immunity from enforcement measures c[ould] be claimed at least with respect to property that is used for a state's official functions."[40] This interpretation inadvertently places the burden on the state to prove that the property is used for "official" purposes. Having such an onerous burden of proof on the sovereign state is indeed troublesome. As Russia submitted, "the property comprises of premises used for official purposes of such nature that they cannot be further divulged without breaching Russian Federation's right to integrity."[41] It is difficult to comprehend how a government shall handle sensitive or classified matters when it bears the burden to prove in a foreign jurisdiction facts that may be of a sensitive nature. For example, in the German enforcement proceedings, the property against which Mr. Sedelmayer sought enforcement in Germany was alleged to include former real estate used by Soviet security services. It is therefore inconceivable how a state would be within its powers to use real estate for classified purposes and yet not need to disclose the actual purposes of such property to prove its "official use." With such a heightened standard, it would be the duty of the sovereign state to come up with a protective mechanism perhaps by submitting the hearing to closed chambers in the course of litigation or by modifying bilateral agreements so that they wisely exclude such property from enforcement proceedings (see next section).

---

[38] *Sedelmayer* Swedish Supreme Court decision, para. 13 (Court relies on the English translation because a Swedish copy, the Court states, is not available).

[39] UN Convention on Sovereign Immunity, Art 19(c). Note that the German Supreme Court disposed of the issue of garnishing Lufthansa payments to the Supreme Court on the grounds that the assets were not within the territorial jurisdiction of the German courts.

[40] *Sedelmayer* Swedish Supreme Court decision, para. 11.

[41] *Sedelmayer* Swedish Supreme Court decision, para. 19. "Right of integrity" as it appears in the unofficial translation may be best translated as "security", as in "without breaching the security of the Russian Federation."

4.22. Second, the temporal element of when intent is determined is of critical concern. The Court reasoned that: "The relevant time of use for this assessment is, in conformity with what must be considered to have been established internationally, when the application was received by the Enforcement Authority. Thus, changes in the use of apartments and premises that have taken place thereafter shall not be taken into consideration."[42] On this point, the Court responded to Russia's pleading that "as from 1 July 2010 all apartments will be used by people who have diplomatic immunity." This assurance made by Russia, of course, was deemed insufficient. It is realistic, however, to see the potential tensions caused upon referral to the temporal element when establishing "intended use" because while the temporal element is certainly useful in determining current "use" it may be misleading in terms of defining "intended use." Moreover, the UN Convention itself does not call for establishing current use. Article 19(c) provides for such "intended use" that would subject the property to immunity. Housing property can always be intended for "official" use and it is only necessary to show that at some point a diplomat is likely to move in, for tensions with the Court holding and the provisions of Article 19(c) to become evident.

4.23. As a final point related to the weight of the UN Convention, it is notable that the Court found that "the [C]onvention is largely – but not entirely – a codification of customary law."[43] The statement is consistent with the missions of the International Law Commission and other entities under the supervision of the General Assembly such as UNCITRAL to harmonize and codify customary law. The Court, however, did not take up the specific issue of whether the provisions of UN Convention Article 19(c), or the provisions regarding the commercial exception to sovereign immunity in enforcement proceedings to be more precise, amounted to customary law. The authors' position is that Article 19(c) does not encapsulate customary international law in so far as absolute immunity—as reflected in the recent decision by the Hong Kong Court of Final Appeals—is a viable impediment to determining a customary consensus of restrictive immunity.[44]

---

[42] *Sedelmayer* Swedish Supreme Court decision, para. 20.

[43] *Sedelmayer* Swedish Supreme Court decision, para. 11.

[44] *DR Congo* v. *FG Hemisphere Associates*, [2011] HKEC 747, at para. 121 (The court ruled that it did not review whether restrictive immunity is a matter of customary law, while noting that "[i]f it were necessary to do so, I would accept that China has been a persistent objector to restrictive immunity.")

VI. Party Autonomy and Negotiation of BITs as Points for Consolidating National Differences on Sovereign Immunity

4.24. In instances where conflicts between absolute and restrictive immunity jurisdictions are prevalent and—so long as the UN Convention has not been implemented—bilateral treaties may reconcile potential discrepancies in defining the scope of sovereign immunity in enforcement proceedings. As investors derive consent to arbitration from the state by means of investment agreements or most often BITs, sovereign states may conspicuously rely on party autonomy to define the scope of a sovereign's consent to the execution of an award against commercial property.

4.25. For starters, there is no conflicting issue in international law that would prevent clearly demarcating a party's limitation of consent to commercial property. In an observation to the Swedish court proceedings challenging the *Sedelmayer* arbitration award, Domenico Di Pietro presented an alternative position where BITs as international mechanisms turn the issue of enforcement into a matter of international law, which falls outside the domestic courts.[45] To this extent, an arbitral award arising from a BIT may be viewed as not being "justifiable."[46] While this position may be persuasive, some investor-state arbitration awards remain to be rendered pursuant to the rules of arbitration institutes other than those of the International Centre for the Settlement of Investment Disputes (ICSID), thereby being subject to the enforcement mechanisms delineated in the New York Convention and not the Washington Convention. That being said, the scope of sovereign immunity is an issue of enforcement separate from the grounds for refusing enforcement under the New York Convention. While the New York Convention sets the grounds for refusing enforcement of an award, the New York Convention does not deal with *how* enforcement shall take place. Conceptually, bilateral investment treaties may clearly define the scope of sovereign immunity enjoyed by one state for purposes of the enforcement of awards. Other treaties may also shed light on this issue.

4.26. Clarifications on the mechanisms for enforcement of investor-state arbitration awards are appearing to be common in recent bilateral investment treaties. Since early BITs did not envision many (if not

---

[45]   Dominico Di Pietro, *The Issue of Justiciability of Foreign Investment Arbitral Awards in Sedelmayer v. Russia and OEPC v. Ecuador*, (2) STOCKHOLM INTERNATIONAL ARBITRATION REVIEW 137 (2005).
[46]   *Ibid.*

most) arbitration issues currently arising in international investment disputes, the more recent BITs provide detailed mechanisms on the conduct of arbitration proceedings and, even on issues such as *enforcement* and *appeal of final awards*. The US Model Arbitration Agreement, which is adopted in full between US and Uruguay, specifies in Article 34 the mechanisms for enforcement of final awards. One of these is an automatic enforcement clause, mandating that the signatory states "shall provide for the enforcement of an award in its territory."[47] Moreover, in the event that a state fails to abide by a final award, the US Model BIT provides that a "commission" be established to review the failure of a state to abide by a final award.[48]

4.27. Because the mechanisms for enforcement of investor-state arbitration awards may be negotiated by the parties, there is no impediment to the signatory countries negotiating the scope of immunity protection in enforcement proceedings to the extent that these do not conflict with the New York Convention and the ICSID Convention. The clear division between absolute and restrictive immunity indicates the absence of a customary standard for sovereign immunity. The failure of the implementation of the UN Convention on Sovereign Immunity underscores that parties may (and possibly even shall) freely negotiate the scope of immunity protections when signing bilateral treaties.

4.28. But even if the UN Convention becomes operational by virtue of at least thirty signatories, in respect to jurisdiction, the Convention supports the position that states enjoy considerable flexibility when defining the scope of the commercial exception. While UN Convention Article 10(1) states that a state may not invoke immunity from *jurisdiction* when the issue arises out of a commercial transaction, Article 10(2) indicates that parties to a commercial transaction may agree otherwise. Moreover, the autonomy of the parties to agree on the scope of judicial proceedings may be extended to enforcement as well. Article 19(c) indicates that property would not be subject to sovereign immunity when "*it has been established* that the property is in use or intended for use" for non-commercial purposes.[49] Although courts may determine use and intended use, the literal reading of Article 19(c)

---

[47] US Model BIT, Article 34(7).

[48] *Ibid.* Article 34(8). Under the US-Uruguay BIT, such issues are reverted to state-to-state disputes pursuant to art. 37; See Treaty between the United States of America and the Oriental Republic of Uruguay concerning the Encouragement and Reciprocal Protection of Investment, US-Uruguay, November 4, 2005.

[49] See UN Convention on Sovereign Immunity, Art. 19(c)(emphasis added).

indicates that *contracting states* may equally "establish" the limits of the commercial exception through treaty negotiations. [50]

4.29. A foreseeable problem may arise between contradictory provisions in bilateral investment treaties and domestic laws, and the consequential resolution of such conflicts by domestic courts. The US embraces the doctrine of restrictive sovereign immunity with the commercial exception being clearly defined under federal statute.[51] In the event that sovereign immunity mechanisms could indeed be negotiated by virtue of a bilateral treaty,[52] any conflicts between the Foreign Sovereign Immunity Act (FSIA) and a later bilateral treaty would be resolved, under the Supremacy Clause, in favor of the later-signed bilateral treaty.[53] Although such conflicts may arise, ordinarily the international treaty as adopted and ratified domestically shall supersede domestic legislation to the contrary.

VII. Conclusion

4.30. Twenty years after the Cold War ended, the legal principles dictated by the two camps are still present in the approaches to sovereign immunity ranging from absolute immunity to restrictive immunity, which center on the exclusion of commercial conduct from both jurisdictional and enforcement proceedings. With a sweeping decision that enraged Russian officials, the Swedish judiciary excluded assets that were not used for "official purposes" from being immune even when these were owned by the state. The *Sedelmayer* decision has clarified the Swedish legal position that: (1) judicial review of the

---

[50] In prior drafts, the UN Convention expressly stated that "consent to jurisdiction" did not imply "consent to enforcement." UN General Assembly, International Law Commission Report on the work of the Forty-third session 1991 Draft of UN Convention, A/46/10, Art. 18 at 56 (1991)[hereinafter "1991 Draft"]. In subsequent drafts, these provisions were deleted in favor of phrases relying on positive consent of the states, enabling states to waive by consent sovereign immunity.

[51] 28 U.S.C. § 1605(a)(2)[USA]. See also *Republic of Argentina* v. *Weltover*, 504 U.S. 607 (1992)(broadly interpreting the commercial exception to exclude immunity claims from *jurisdiction* when the state issued bonds and thus acted as a private actor).

[52] BITs are not executive agreements but treaties for ratification by the Senate, see US Constitution Article II(2). See *e.g.*, Treaty between US and Russia Federation Concerning the Encouragement and Reciprocal Protection of Investment 1992 (not ratified by Russia). *Cf.* The Treaty between the Government of the United States and the Government of the Republic of Georgia Concerning the Encouragement and Reciprocal Protection of Investment, signed March 7, 1994, Senate Treaty Doc. 104-13.

[53] U.S. Constitution Art. VI. See also *Edye* v. *Robertson*, 112 U.S. 580 (1884). *Cf. Reid* v. *Covert*, 354 U.S. 1 (1957)(ruling that the federal Constitution supersedes any bilateral treaties entered by the US Government).

commercial exception is of a narrower scope in enforcement than in jurisdictional proceedings, and (2) that the Swedish judiciary opts for a broad definition of commercial transaction such that in enforcement proceedings, the state appears to carry the burden of proving that the property is used for "official"/non-commercial purposes.

4.31.   In all, two tools may harmonize the debate and minimize the sources of tension between divergent holdings. The first tool is the UN Convention on Sovereign Immunity, which the Swedish Supreme Court has innovatively and consistently applied as persuasive authority on two separate occasions despite the fact that the UN Convention has not come into force. The UN Convention has an effective working definition for a commercial exception that would benefit from local interpretation. The second tool is the principle of party autonomy, which by virtue of the UN Convention on Sovereign Immunity, supports the idea that states may clearly demarcate and define the desired scope of sovereign immunity in its bilateral treaties. These two tools may curb the divergent views on the scope of the commercial exception to sovereign immunity and may further mitigate the risk of further conflicts in relation to these sensitive issues.

|||

Summaries

FRA   [*Les absolus restrictifs: se servir de l'autonomie des parties pour concilier l'immunité absolue et la norme libérale d'immunité restrictive adoptée par la cour suprême suédoise dans l'affaire Sedelmayer*]

Dans l'affaire Sedelmayer, la Cour Suprême suédoise a affirmé sa reconnaissance sans équivoque de l'immunité restrictive dans les procédures d'exécution conduites à l'encontre d'états souverains. Même si la Cour Suprême suédoise est allée jusqu'à suggérer que l'immunité souveraine restrictive est universellement reconnue comme le droit international coutumier, ce point de vue a ensuite été rejeté lorsque la plus haute instance de Hong Kong a tranché en faveur de l'immunité absolue dans l'affaire FG Hemisphere Associates. En totale opposition avec la décision de Hong Kong, la sentence suédoise dans l'affaire Sedelmayer reconnaît une exception commerciale ultralibérale qui exige de l'état qu'il prouve que le bien qui fait l'objet de la procédure d'exécution est utilisé « à des fins officielles » uniquement. La décision suédoise dans l'affaire Sedelmayer est remarquable en ce: (1) qu'elle continue à accréditer la Convention Européenne sur l'Immunité Souveraine alors que cette Convention n'est toujours pas ratifiée, et (2) qu'elle établit le lien temporel selon lequel « usage et usage prévu » doivent être déterminés exclusivement en fonction du moment où se déroule la procédure d'exécution. À la lumière de ces points de vue divergents, cet article déduit que les tensions entre les doctrines absolues et restrictives de l'immunité souveraine existent réellement. Tant que la Convention Européenne n'est pas en mesure de concilier ces positions, cet article propose d'utiliser l'autonomie des parties comme un moyen alternatif de résolution des futurs litiges. En explorant les zones troubles du droit international codifié en matière d'immunité souveraine, l'article en arrive à la conclusion que les traités d'investissement bilatéraux (TIB) sont l'outil idéal pour clarifier et présenter l'intention des parties en termes d'activité commerciale, lequel peut cependant être exempté d'exécution.

CZE   *[Omezená absoluta: využití principu smluvní autonomie k odstranění rozporů mezi absolutní imunitou a liberálním standardem omezené (restriktivní) imunity přijatým švédským Nejvyšším soudem v rozhodnutí Sedelmayer]*

V případu Sedelmayer Nejvyšší soud Švédska potvrdil své jednoznačné stanovisko podporující omezenou imunitu v řízeních o výkon rozhodnutí vedených proti suverénním státům. Odůvodnění rozhodnutí švédského Nejvyššího soudu zašlo dokonce až tak daleko, že považovalo omezenou imunitu státu za univerzálně přijímanou zásadu zvykového mezinárodního práva; tento názor byl však brzy odmítnut rozhodnutím nejvyššího soudu v Hongkongu, který rozhodl ve věci FG Hemisphere Associates ve prospěch absolutní imunity. V ostrém kontrastu k hongkongskému rozhodnutí zakotvuje švédské rozhodnutí ve věci Sedelmayer velmi liberální obchodní výjimku, která přenáší důkazní břemeno na stát v tom smyslu, že stát je povinen prokázat, že majetek, jenž má být ve vykonávacím řízení postižen, je využíván pouze pro „úřední účely". Švédské rozhodnutí ve věci Sedelmayer je pozoruhodné ze dvou důvodů: 1) spoléhá na Úmluvu OSN o imunitě států navzdory skutečnosti, že tato Úmluva dosud nebyla ratifikována, a 2) zakotvuje časové propojení v tom směru, že „užívání a zamýšlené užívání" mají být zjišťovány výlučně vzhledem k době vedení vykonávacího řízení. Ve světle těchto rozdílných rozhodnutí vyvozuje tento článek závěr, že napětí mezi absolutní a restriktivní doktrínou imunity států je reálné. Do doby, než bude Úmluva OSN schopna takovéto konflikty řešit, navrhuje tento článek využívání principu smluvní autonomie jako alternativy řešení budoucích sporů. Na základě zkoumání mezer v kodifikovaném mezinárodním právu o imunitě států dospívá článek k závěru, že dvoustranné dohody o ochraně investic (BIT) jsou ideálním mechanismem pro vyjasnění a ozřejmení úmyslů stran co do rozsahu obchodní činnosti, která může být nadána imunitou ve vykonávacím řízení.

| | |

POL [*Względne absoluty: Wykorzystywanie autonomii stron w celu pogodzenia immunitetu bezwzględnego z liberalną normą immunitetu względnego, przyjętą przez Szwedzki Sąd Najwyższy w postanowieniu Sedelmayer*]
Artkół omawia decyzję Sedelmayer dotyczącą szwedzkiego Sądu Najwyższego oraz jego wpływ na zdefiniowanie zakresu dotyczącego wyjatku handlowego w stosunku do suwerennego podmiotu. W artykule stwierdza się, że autonomia stron, która została wykazana w odpowiednich konwencjach, często określa odpowiednie zabezpieczenia dla państw i może być wykorzystana do wyjaśnień udziału szwedzkiego Sądu Najwyższego.

DEU [*Das 'Eingeschränkte Absolute': Parteienautonomie als Werkzeug, um absolute Immunität mit dem liberalen Standard für eingeschränkte Immunität in Einklang zu bringen, den der Oberste Gerichtshof Schwedens in seiner Entscheidung in Sachen Sedelmayer gesetzt hat*]
Der Artikel diskutiert die Sedelmayer Entscheidung des schwedischen obersten Gerichtshofes und ihre Implikationen für die Definition des Umfanges der kommerziellen Ausnahmen fuer staatliche Immunität. Der Artikel stellt fest dass Parteiautonomie, wie in einschlägigen Übereinkommen gefunden, oftmals die relevanten Schutzmaßnahmen fuer Staaten definiert und somit zur Erklärung der Entscheidung des schwedischen obersten Gerichtshofes herangezogen werden kann.

RUS [*Абсолютные принципы ограничения: использование независимости стороны для приведения полного иммунитета в соответствие с либеральным стандартом ограниченной неприкосновенности, принятым шведским Верховным судом при принятии решения по делу о Sedelmayer*]
В статье обсуждается решение Верховного суда Швеции по делу Зедельмайер, и его последствия для определения диапазона действия коммерческого исключения из иммунитета государства. В статье делается вывод, что автономия сторон, установленная соответствующими Конвенциями, часто определяет соответствующие средства защиты для государств и, таким

Czech (& Central European) Yearbook of Arbitration

образом, может быть использована для объяснения и согласования решения Верховного суда Швеции.

ESP [*Absolutos restrictivos: El uso de la autonomía de las partes para reconcililar la inmunidad absoluta con la norma liberal relativa a la inmunidad restrictiva adoptada por el tribunal supremo sueco en la decisión Sedelmayer*]

El artículo analiza la decisión de la Corte Suprema de Suecia en el caso Sedelmayer y sus implicaciones para la definición del alcance de la excepción comercial a la inmunidad soberana. El artículo concluye que a través de la autonomía de la voluntad, que se encuentran en los convenios pertinentes, las partes a menudo definen las protecciones correspondientes para los Estados y, por lo tanto, ello puede ser utilizado para explicar el fallo de la Corte Suprema de Suecia.

Leonila Guglya

Waiver of Annulment Action in Arbitration: Progressive Development Globally, Realities in and Perspectives for the Russian Federation (*Different Beds – Similar Dreams?*)

Key words:
Arbitration | Domestic
Arbitration | Award |
Arbitration Clause |
Annulment | Waiver of
Annulment |
Renunciation of
Annulment | Swiss
Private International Law
Act | Russian Federation |
New York Convention

Risk comes from not knowing what you're doing.
–Warren Buffett

Abstract | *The article is devoted to a discussion of waivers of annulment – an "extreme" form of party autonomy in international arbitration, allowing parties to oust the review of the award made in arbitration between them by the national court of the seat of arbitration. This type of waiver, eventually gaining popularity lately, is assessed in two different contexts. First – as a phenomenon belonging to the international arbitration setting, largely following the model reflected in Art. 192 (1) of the Swiss Private International Law Act of 1989, and, second – as a domestic arbitration notion, specific to the Russian Federation. The two approaches, having developed independently, share enough common features, such as, for instance, their place in the relevant procedural framework – as an issue of admissibility, the formal prerequisites with which the parties have to comply to make the renunciation of the annulment valid, the main substantive requirement for their validity – intent. The interpretational paradigms applicable in Switzerland and in the Russian Federation, the only two states, the courts of which have a publicly known record in handling renunciations, however, vary. While*

Leonila Guglya is a researcher at the University of Geneva in Switzerland and an International Business Law lecturer at the Swiss Education Group. She holds an S.J.D. (Doctor of Juridical Science) degree from Central European University (Budapest, Hungary); an LL.M degree in International Dispute Settlement from the MIDS (Master in International Dispute Settlement) Program (Geneva, Switzerland); an LL.M. degree in International Business Law from Central European University; as well as degrees of Specialist in Law and Bachelor in Law from

the Swiss courts normally resort to a restrictive interpretation in search of the will of the parties to waive, the Russian courts are substantially more flexible, allowing in even a general reference to the arbitration rules containing "finality" wording.

the University of "*Kyiv-Mohyla Academy*" (Kyiv, Ukraine). e-mail: leonilla.guglya@gmail.com

| | |

I. Introductory Note

5.01. Waiver (or renunciation) of annulment allows the parties to consensually dispose of the annulment action pertaining to their award by virtue of the addition of a separate provision to their arbitration clause or by an agreement made at the later phase, presumably – even during the pendency of the annulment proceedings. The concept, bringing party autonomy in arbitration on a new level, is more widely known with regard to the international arbitration setting, but could also relate to domestic arbitration proceedings. Facing the geographical spread of the legislative reflection of the concept, as well as a growing trend towards reliance on waivers by the parties opposing annulment requests in Switzerland and the Russian Federation, this article will grapple with several of the concept's aspects. In particular, to begin, some general remarks will be made on annulment and waiver, *inter alia*, dwelling on geography, the aims and the consequences of the latter for the award. Second, approaches to the interpretation of the waivers made by the parties arbitrating in Switzerland and the Russian Federation by the respective national courts will be addressed in greater detail and, where appropriate, will be compared. The discussion will conclude by suggesting that waivers, if handled with due care and understanding, and when duly matched to the circumstances, might serve to increase the efficiency of arbitration proceedings.

II. Annulment Action in Arbitration: The Basics

5.02. Annulment action in arbitration, in both – international and domestic settings– in several respects is a limited form of control of the national judiciary over the justice rendered by arbitrators. The annulment system is designed to reconcile, to the extent possible, the inspirations of the parties who have resorted to arbitration instead of litigation before the state court and the control over the fairness of the dispute resolution process, entrusted to the national judiciaries. As well-stated by William W. Park,

Although no system will perfectly reconcile these rival goals of finality and fairness, a middle ground provides judicial review for the grosser forms of procedural injustice. To this end, legislators and courts must engage in a process of legal fine tuning that seeks a reasonable counterpoise between arbitral autonomy and judicial control mechanisms.[1]

5.03.　In the case of annulment, the *legal fine tuning* referred to above mainly touches upon three important dimensions:

    a)　The right to initiate annulment, which belongs solely to the party to the arbitration proceedings (and, in certain exceptional cases, also to the third party affected by the award[2]);

    b)　The time limit, during which the annulment action may be brought;[3]

    c)　The scope of the grounds which could be considered during the annulment.

5.04.　Structurally, the annulment proceedings could basically be seen as a two-stage process. The first stage of the process relates to the admissibility of the annulment action, *inter alia*, pertaining to the timing of submission of a respective request, its scope, the procedural identity of the submitting party as well as the circumstances which could preclude such submission. It is only should the first stage be passed, that the court will examine the annulment grounds. The waiver normally impacts the first stage of the annulment proceedings by making such proceedings inadmissible as far as all or some of the annulment grounds (depending on the scope of the waiver) are concerned.

---

[1]　William W. Park, *Why Courts Review Arbitral Awards*, *in* Recht der Internationalen Wirtschaft und Streiterledigung im 21. Jahrhundert: Liber Amicorum Karl-Heinz Böckstiegel, Köln: Carl Heymanns 595 (R. Briner, L. Y. Fortier, K.-P. Berger & J. Bredow eds. , 2001); reprinted 16 Int'l Arb. Rep. 27 (Nov. 2001), 596-597.

[2]　See, for instance, Art. 18(2) of the Economic Procedural Code of Ukraine, 1992, as amended on 2 February 2011, according to which:

    The parties to the disputes pertaining to the challenge of the domestic arbitration awards as well as those dealing with the enforcement of the domestic arbitration awards, are the parties to domestic arbitration [as well as] the parties who have not participated in the consideration of the domestic arbitration case, in case the arbitral tribunal has ruled on the issues of their rights and obligations [...]

[3]　Most arbitration laws dealing with the annulment also put an emphasis on the allocation of the burden of proof concerning the annulment grounds to the party seeking the latter.

III. The Waiver of Annulment: A Bit of Geography

5.05.   Being viewed so far as a phenomenon *"of a minor importance"* by the
commentators,[4] the waiver of annulment seems to be subject to
constant spread, and thus might, potentially, gain more significance in
the future, especially in jurisdictions where the approach of the courts
to arbitration is seen as problematic. A growing number of states
provide for the possibility of waiver of the grounds of annulment of
international arbitration award, both in full and in part (Mauritania,[5]
Peru,[6] Sweden,[7] Switzerland,[8] Tunisia,[9] Turkey[10]) or in full only

---

[4]   Laurent Lévy, *Observations following the judgments by the Swiss Supreme Court
rendered on 10 November 2005 in (1) case 4P.98/2005/svc and (2) CASE 4P.154/2005/svc
(The "Republic of Lebanon* v. *FTMI & FTML" Cases),* 1 STOCKHOLM INT'L ARB. REV.
181-191, 190-191 (2006); Laurent Lévy, Tetiana Bersheda, *Recent Swiss Developments on
Exclusion Agreements, Observations on the Decisions of the Swiss Federal Court of 6 March
2008 (DFC 134 III 260) and 21 August 2008 (4A_194/2008),* 3 STOCKHOLM INT'L ARB. REV.
67-82, 82 (2008).

[5]   Art. 59(4)(b), *Loi mauritanienne portant code de l'arbitrage (No 2000-06),* 4 REVUE DE
L'ARBITRAGE (Comité Français de l'Arbitrage) 935 – 960 (2001):
  *The parties who have neither domicile, nor principal residence, nor are established in
  Mauritania, may expressly agree to exclude all recourse against an arbitral award, in
  full or in part. In case they will be seeking recognition and enforcement on the territory
  of Mauritania of the arbitral award so rendered, the Articles 61, 62, 63 [applicable to
  the recognition and enforcement of foreign arbitral awards] are subject to the
  mandatory application.*

[6]   Art. 63(8), Legislative Decree No. 1071 Legislative Decree Regulating Arbitration
Unofficial translation by Fernando Cantuarias S. and Roger Rubio. Published as Legislative
Decree No. 1071 on 28 June 2008, in effect from 1 September 2008:
  *When none of the parties to the arbitration is Peruvian or has his domicile, habitual
  residence or place of main activities in Peruvian territory, an express agreement can be
  concluded to waive any application to set aside or to limit such application to one or
  more grounds set out in this Article. If the parties have waived any application to set
  aside and enforcement of the award is sought in the Peruvian territory, the provisions in
  Title VIII [Recognition and Enforcement of Foreign Awards] shall apply").*

[7]   Sec. 51 *The Arbitration Act of 1999 (SFS 1999:116),* in INTERNATIONAL HANDBOOK ON
COMMERCIAL ARBITRATION, Deventer: Kluwer Law International 1 – 16 (J. Paulsson ed.,
1984, Last updated: December 2000 Supplement No. 32):
  *Where none of the parties is domiciled or has its place of business in Sweden, such
  parties may in a commercial relationship through an express written agreement
  exclude or limit the application of the grounds for setting aside an award as are set
  forth in section 34. An award which is subject to such an agreement shall be recognized
  and enforced in Sweden in accordance with the rules applicable to a foreign award.*

[8]   Art. 192 Swiss Private International Law Act, Chapter 12: *International Arbitration,* 18
December 1987, *in* INTERNATIONAL HANDBOOK ON COMMERCIAL ARBITRATION, Deventer:
Kluwer Law International 1 - 6 (J. Paulsson ed., 1984, Last updated: September 1988
Supplement No. 9):
  *If none of the parties have their domicile, their habitual residence, or a business
  establishment in Switzerland, they may, by an express statement in the arbitration*

(Belgium,[11]France,[12] and Panama[13]). The model of the waiver of annulment currently used in international arbitration setting is, allegedly, "*Swiss-made.*"[14]

> *agreement or by a subsequent written agreement, waive fully the action for annulment or they may limit it to one or several of the grounds listed in Art. 190(2). If the parties have waived fully the action for annulment against the awards and if the awards are to be enforced in Switzerland, the New York Convention of June 10, 1958 on the Recognition and Enforcement of Foreign Arbitral Awards applies by analogy.*

9   Art. 78(6) of the Tunisian Arbitration Code, Promulgated by Law No. 93-42 of 26 April 1993, in force 27 October 1993:

> *The parties who have neither domicile, principal residence, nor business establishment in Tunisia, may expressly agree to exclude totally or partially all recourse against an arbitral award. If they request the recognition and enforcement in Tunisia of an arbitral award made subject to this exclusion in Tunisia, Articles 80, 81 and 82 of this Code [provisions applicable to the recognition and enforcement of foreign arbitral awards] apply mandatorily.*

10   Arts. 15(A)(3), 15(B)(2) *International Arbitration Law (Law No. 4686 of 21 June 2001),* in INTERNATIONAL HANDBOOK ON COMMERCIAL ARBITRATION, Deventer: Kluwer Law International 1 - 14 (J. Paulsson ed., 1984, Last updated: March 2005 Supplement No. 43):

> *The parties may, in part or in full, renounce the right to initiate an action for setting aside the award. A party whose domicile or habitual residence is not in Turkey may renounce that right completely in an express clause in the arbitration agreement or in writing, following the signature of the arbitration agreement. Alternatively, in the same manner, the parties may renounce the above right for one or more of the reasons as set forth above for setting aside the award [see Article 15A(2)(1), above]. If renounced the award is only subject to arbitrability and public policy tests.*

11   1717(4) *Judicial Code, Sixth Part: Arbitration (adopted 4 July 1972 and last amended on 19 May 1998),* in INTERNATIONAL HANDBOOK ON COMMERCIAL ARBITRATION, Deventer: Kluwer Law International 1 - 12 (J. Paulsson ed., 1984, Last updated: April 2007 Supplement No. 49):

> *The parties may, by an express statement in the arbitration agreement or by a later agreement, exclude any application for the setting aside of an arbitral award, in case none of them is a physical person of Belgian nationality or a physical person having his normal residence in Belgium or a legal person having its principal office or a branch office in Belgium.*

It should be noted that the present version of the text was preceded by a different one, according to which

> *The Belgian Court can take cognizance of an application to set aside only if at least one of the parties to the dispute decided in the arbitral award is either a physical person having Belgian nationality or residing in Belgium, or a legal person formed in Belgium or having a branch (une succursale) or some seat of operation (un siège quelconque d'opération) there*

(Judicial Code - Sixth Part: Arbitration (adopted 4 July 1972 and amended 27 March 1985), in INTERNATIONAL HANDBOOK ON COMMERCIAL ARBITRATION, Deventer: Kluwer Law International 1 – 10 (J. Paulsson ed., 1984, Last updated: May 1986 Supplement No. 5). Nevertheless, according to the commentators, "*an outright removal of annulment in arbitrations involving parties not anyhow connected to Belgium" has diverted from the state more arbitrations than it attracted [...]. This is the reason why the legislator has chosen to align itself for the future with the Swiss system's opting-out model,*" Bernard Hanotiau and

5.06. In its turn, Russian law allows parties to waive annulment in domestic arbitration proceedings.[15] The laws of the Dominican Republic[16] and the United Arab Emirates[17] also seem to allow the parties to waive

---

Guy Block, *La loi du 19 mai 1998 modifiant la législation belge relative à l'arbitrage*, in 16 (3) ASA BULLETIN (ASSOCIATION SUISSE DE L'ARBITRAGE) 528 – 538, 531-534 (1998).

[12] Art. 1522(1) and 1522(2), French Arbitration Law as Amended by the Decree No. 2011-48 of 13 January 2011:

> *By way of a special agreement the parties may, at any time, expressly waive their right to bring an action to set aside. Where such right has been waived, the parties nonetheless retain their right to appeal an enforcement order on one of the grounds set forth in Article 1520 [the set aside grounds which are also applicable in course of the recognition and enforcement of foreign arbitral awards.*

Pursuant to article 3 of the Decree, waiver of annulment proceedings is possible only where the arbitral tribunal was constituted after 1 May 2011.

[13] Art. 36 and 38(5) of *Décret-loi n° 5 du 8 juillet 1999*, 3 REVUE DE L'ARBITRAGE (Comité Français de l'Arbitrage) (2005):

> *Si l'arbitrage est un arbitrage commercial international au sens du présent décret-loi, les parties pourront prévoir, ou le règlement d'arbitrage pourra établir, la renonciation des parties au recours en annulation prévu à l'article précédent. S'il s'agit d'une sentence prononcée sur le territoire panaméen en matière internationale, au sens du présent décret-loi, et que les parties ont renoncé, directement ou par le biais du règlement applicable, à exercer un recours en annulation, l'exécution de la sentence impose d'obtenir l'exequatur de la Chambre des affaires générales de la Cour suprême de justice (« Sala de Negocios Generales de la Corte Suprema de Justicia ») comme prévu pour les sentences étrangères.*

[14] See, for instance, Bernard Hanotiau and Guy Block, *supra* note 11, at 531. It should be noted, however, that the relevant legal frameworks of Turkey and Panama, the first – still maintaining the empowerment of the court at the seat to review the award on the arbitrability and public policy grounds, while the second – allowing the implicit waiver (via the reference to the arbitration rules) seem to deviate from the Swiss approach. See *supra* notes 11 and 14 respectively.

[15] Art. 40 of the Federal Law of the Russian Federation "*On domestic Arbitration in the Russian Federation*," dated July 24, 2002, No. 102-ФЗ, reads:

> *If the [domestic] arbitration agreement does not provide that the arbitration award is final, the award might be challenged by one of the parties to the competent court no latter than in the 3-months term from the time such a party received the award.*

[16] The Commercial Arbitration Law of Dominical Republic suggests the possibility of the waiver by providing in its Art. 40(1) that: "*If the parties have not given up the right to exercise any remedy against the award in advance, the Court of Appeals for the Department for the place where the award is rendered has jurisdiction pertaining to the annulment of an award in the Dominican Republic. [...]*". In the meantime, the commentators suggest that the waiver referred to above is subject to limitations. Relying on the Art. 39(3) of the same law, which allows the court to assess the procedural due process, arbitrability and public policy issues *ex officio*, they advise that the waiver of these three grounds is precluded. See The International Comparative Legal Guide to International Arbitration 2011, A Practical Cross-Border Insight into International Arbitration Work, prepared by the Global Research Group in association with CDR and available at: http://www.iclg.co.uk/khadmin/Publications/pdf (accessed on December 29, 2011), p. 336.

[17] For the text of the provision see *infra* note 40.

annulment of domestic arbitration awards, but nevertheless, are not very specific in this regard.

5.07. Meanwhile, certain states are reluctant to allow ousting of their set aside competences. For instance, according to the Croatian Arbitration law,[18] the Egyptian Arbitration law,[19] the Romanian and the Greek Codes of Civil Procedure,[20] the parties cannot derogate in advance from their right to contest the award by an application for setting aside. In Italy and Portugal waivers of the annulment are forbidden outright.[21] Ukrainian courts, which, presumably, could have sided with their Russian neighbours in allowing the parties to dispose of annulment domestically, often express concerns over the legality of some of the domestic arbitration proceedings, in particular by alleging that certain of those are carried out without a valid legal cause, for money laundering purposes or the like.[22]

5.08. The reluctance to allow waivers of this type often dwells on their incompatibility with public policy. In the most basic terms, they are

---

[18] Art. 36(6) Croatian Law of Arbitration, 2001. This provision, namely, reads: "*The parties cannot derogate in advance their right to contest the award by an application for setting aside.*"

[19] Art. 54(1) of the Egyptian Arbitration Law. This provision reads: "*The admissibility of the action for annulment of the arbitral award shall not be prevented by the applicant's renunciation of its right to request the annulment of the award prior to the making of the award.*"

[20] Art. 364-1 of the Romanian Code of Civil Procedure, Book IV, Code of Civil Procedure, Arts. 340-370. On Arbitration (as amended by Law No. 59 of 23 July 1993), which provides: "*The parties cannot, in their arbitration agreement, waive the right to institute proceedings to set aside the award. This right may be waived, however, after the award is made*"; Art. 900 of the Greek Code of Civil Procedure, Book VII (as amended by Law 2331/1995), which reads: "*A renunciation of the right to file an action for setting aside of an arbitral award before such award was rendered shall be null.*"

[21] Art. 829(1) of the Italian Code of Civil Procedure, providing that the recourse is available "*notwithstanding any waiver*"; Art. 28(1) of the Portuguese Law on Arbitration, according to which "*The right to apply for setting aside of the arbitral award may not be excluded.*"

The International Comparative Legal Guide to International Arbitration 2011, supra note 15, discusses several other states where the waiver of annulment proceedings is not allowed. Among those states: Brunei (p. 48); Indonesia (p. 89); Malaysia (p. 110); Pakistan (p. 118); Albania (p. 141); Estonia (p. 150); Hungary (p. 158); Lithuania (p. 166); Macedonia (p. 173); Austria (p. 214); UK (p. 235); Liechtenstein (p. 270); Luxembourg (p. 279); Netherlands (p. 287); Portugal (p. 297); Spain (p. 306); Paraguay (p. 354); Israel (p. 385); South African (p. 409); Canada (p. 427).

[22] For instance, according to the Generalization of the Practice of the Ukrainian courts in application of the Law of Ukraine "*On domestic Arbitration*", issued by the Supreme Court of Ukraine on 11 February 2009, "*The analysis of the domestic arbitral awards confirms that the domestic arbitral tribunals often decide the cases overlooking the procedures provided for in the law, this way infringing the rights of the third parties and the state [...].*"

Czech (& Central European) Yearbook of Arbitration

seen as being *second-level* waivers – after the waiver of the jurisdiction of the national courts in favour of the arbitration *proper*, the waivers of annulment are seen as a radical step,[23] one that overreaches in ousting the national courts from the dispute settlement picture, an action with which many are not yet ready to agree.[24] Seemingly meeting this concern, a *"median"* approach has been introduced in the waiver-related provision in Turkish law, according to which, even when annulment is renounced, the court is still entitled to conduct arbitrability and public policy checks,[25] and, so too does this appear to be the case, in the Commercial Arbitration Law of the Dominican Republic.[26]

IV. The Aims of the Waiver

5.09. The main aim of the waiver approach is two-fold. On the one hand, it provides a workable solution by relaxing the arbitration-related workload of the national court or courts. On the other hand, it is often seen as adding attractiveness to arbitration by making it less subject to the influence of the local judiciaries.[27] On the flip side, however, the waiver of this type is criticized for, allegedly, allowing, or at least tolerating abuses in arbitration settings, which would not be traced unless the award would ultimately end up before the state judiciary following the enforcement request, which, at times, would never happen.[28] Some authors also reasonably warn that the elimination of annulment might result in multiple attachments of assets in the enforcing jurisdictions which allow for such provisional measures.[29]

---

[23] Juan Carlos Landrove, *Les limites de l'ordre public posées à la liberté contractuelle : un exemple tiré du droit international privé suisse*, in « LE DROIT DÉCLOISONNÉ, » INTERFÉRENCES ET INTERDÉPENDANCES ENTRE DROIT PRIVÉ ET DROIT PUBLIC, Genève [etc.]: Schulthess éd. romandes 343-355, 351 (2009).

[24] *Ibid.*, at 349; GERHARD WALTER; WOLFGANG BOSCH; JÜRGEN BRÖNNIMANN, INTERNATIONALE SCHIEDSGERICHTSBARKEIT IN DER SCHWEIZ –KOMMENTAR ZU KAPITEL 12 DES IPR-GESETZES, Berne: Stämpfli Verlag 259 (1991).

[25] For the text of the provision see *supra* note 10.

[26] See *supra* note 16.

[27] This provision was enacted in order to enhance the efficiency of the arbitral process, as well as to unburden Swiss courts by avoiding dilatory appeals related to disputes insufficiently connected with Switzerland. Message of the Federal Council (Government) to the Federal Assembly (Parliament) of November 10, 1982, FF 1983 I 255, no. 2107.27. Laurent Hirsch, *Contractual Exclusion of Annulment Actions against International Arbitral Awards Made in Switzerland*, 2 STOCKHOLM INTERNATIONAL ARBITRATION REVIEW 43-96, 43, 45 (2006).

[28] The situation quite widely speculated on in this respect deals with the award denying all claims which, being subject to the annulment proceedings, could never be subject to the recognition and enforcement scrutiny.

[29] William W. Park, *supra* note 1, at 601.

5.10. Once the international arbitration setting is concerned, the major *"value"* of annulment lies in its *erga omnes* effect, according to which the award, annulled at the seat, by virtue of Art. V(1)(e) of the New York Convention, would not – subject to limited exceptions[30] – be granted enforcement in any other state. Recognition and enforcement, in its turn, has a limited effect, only for the state where enforcement is granted, and thus, clearly, furnishes the party who wishes that the award would not be enforced with a substantially lower degree of predictability. To add, in the opinion of Albert Jan van den Berg, the disposal of the annulment opens up enhanced enforcement forum-shopping possibilities, which might, in the long run, prejudice the gains of such a step. Namely,

> *A losing party must be afforded the right to have the validity of the award finally adjudicated in one jurisdiction. If that were not the case, in the event of a questionable award a losing party could be pursued by a claimant with enforcement actions from country to country until a court is found, if any, which grants the enforcement. A claimant would obviously refrain from doing this if the award has been set aside in the country of origin and this is a ground for refusal*

---

[30] *Pabalk Ticaret Sirketi* v. *Norsolor*, CA Paris, 19 November 1982; 4 REV. ARB. 465, 472 (1983); Cass 1e civ., October 9, 1984, 3 REV. ARB. 431(reviving the award set aside by the Vienna Court of Appeal, 1985); *Polish Ocean Line* v. *Jolasry*, Cass. 1e civ., 10 March 1993, 2 REV. ARB. 255 (enforcing the award suspended in Poland, 1993); *Hilmarton Ltd.* v. *Omnium de Traitement et de Valorisation*, Cass 1e civ., March 23, 1994, 2 REV. ARB. 327 (enforcing the first award, set aside in Switzerland, enforcing the second award made following and in result of annulment of the first award, recognizing the decision annulling the judgment granting recognition to the first award, and, finally, reverting back to the recognition of the first award and quashing other decisions and orders on the basis of *res judicata*, 1994); *Republique Arabe d'Egypte* v. *Chromalloy Aero Services*, CA Paris, January 14, 1997, 3 REV. ARB. 395 (granting enforcement to the award annulled by the Egyptian courts, 1997); *ASECNA* v. *N'Doye*, Cass. 1e civ., October 17, 2000, 4 REV. ARB. 648 (enforcing the award set aside in Senegal, 2000); *Clerico* v. *Cavaterra*, CA Paris, October 10, 2002 (enforcing the award challenged at that time before the Court of Appeal of Rome); *Direction Generale de l'Aviation Civile de l'Emirat de Dubai* v. *International Bechtel*, CA Paris, September 29, 2005, 3 REV. ARB. 695 (enforcing the award set aside in Dubai, 2006); *Bargues Agro Industries* v. *Young Pecan Company*, 1 REV. ARB. 154 (enforcing the award rendered in Belgium while the annulment proceedings were in progress before Belgian courts, 2006); *PT Putrabali Adyamulia* v. *Rena Holding*, 3 REV. ARB. 507 (enforcing the award annulled in England, 2007); *In re Arbitration of Certain Controversies between Chromalloy Aeroservices and the Arab Republic of Egypt*, 939 F. Supp. 907 (D.D.C. 1996) (enforcing the award set aside in Egypt); *Yukos Capital S.A.R.L. (Luxembourg)* v. *OJSC "Oil Company 'Rosneft'"* (*OJSC "Jugasknefgaz")(Russian Federation)*, Decision of the Court of Appeals of Amsterdam, dated April 28, 2009, in case No. LJN BI2451, left unchanged by the Supreme Court of Netherlands (enforcing the award annulled in the Russian Federation), etc.

of enforcement in other Contracting States [of the New York Convention].[31]

5.11. Assessing the same situation with emphasis placed on its varied aspects, William W. Park has noted:

[...] the absence of any court scrutiny at the arbitral situs would adversely affect the victims of defective arbitrations, and in some cases the interests of the reviewing state itself.[32]

5.12. On the brighter side, the waiver of annulment could potentially be helpful in eliminating *"out of place"* annulments, say those made on *"local"* rather than generally accepted grounds.[33] From a somewhat different angle the possibility to waive annulment seems, at times, to be seen as a feature emphasizing the independence of international arbitration from its seat, denying outright the existence in the national courts called to deal with the annulment of the *"safeguard"* duty of not allowing awards failing to meet certain standards out. This idea, in relation to the Swiss courts, was expressed in the following manner:

[...] Swiss courts should not be concerned whether the award is flawed if the award is enforced only outside Switzerland, whereas Swiss courts should perform some check of the award if the award is to be enforced in Switzerland.[34]

V. The Nature of the Award Not Subject to the Annulment

5.13. All of the states that allow the parties to waive annulment in the international arbitration setting, with the exception of Turkey, expressly provide in their relevant laws that, in case of the full waiver, the award will be treated as a foreign award subject to the respective rules and procedures of recognition and enforcement. Partial renunciation of annulment (with respect to certain grounds only), not being expressly dealt with in the text of the relevant statutes, should be expected to produce the same effect as far as the renounced grounds are concerned. This development, clearly not anticipated or provided for by the drafters of the New York Convention, currently seems to

---

[31] ALBERT J. VAN DEN BERG, THE NEW YORK ARBITRATION CONVENTION OF 1958 - TOWARDS A UNIFORM JUDICIAL INTERPRETATION, Boston: Kluwer Law International 355 (1981).

[32] William W. Park, *supra* note 1, at 599.

[33] Jan Paulsson, *Enforcing Arbitral Awards Notwithstanding a Local Standard Annulment*, 9 (1) ICC BULLETIN (1998).

[34] Laurent Hirsch, *Contractual Exclusion of Annulment Actions against International Arbitral Awards Made in Switzerland*, 8 STOCKHOLM INTERNATIONAL ARBITRATION REVIEW 43, 96 (2006:2).

amount to a new "*source*" of non-domestic awards, for the purposes of Article I(1) of the treaty.[35] To this extent, the choice of the term "*foreign*" normally used in the law is somewhat misleading.

5.14.   Being deemed non-domestic, the award, should thus be subject to the application of the New York Convention given that the states are Contracting States thereto, at least insofar as the reciprocity reservation is not made. The three states allowing the waiver, which have made a reciprocity reservation – Belgium, France and Turkey – might potentially face problems with the application of the Convention, depending on the interpretative approach adopted (e.g. deeming the award rendered in the same Contracting State as falling within the scope of the reservation or not). Leaving the issues of connecting factors and interpretations aside, Swiss law expressly deals with the issue, by suggesting that the Convention will apply to the awards subject to the full waiver of annulment.

5.15.   Pertinently, it should be presumed that the failure to seek annulment of the award within the time limit prescribed by the law would not have the same effect as the written waiver in the sense described above, entailing nothing more than the forfeiture of the relevant right.[36]

5.16.   In the domestic arena the significance of the waiver of annulment is somewhat minimized by the fact that, most often, the same grounds would be applicable if the recognition and enforcement of awards is concerned, with the annulment as waived having no influence on the future recognition and enforcement prospects. In this light, a domestic waiver might have a cost-saving effect by *de facto* consolidating the inspirations of the parties (both – enforcement and contra-enforcement ones) in a sole proceeding, rather than splitting them between the two fora (the two different state courts), with unclear interrelation.

5.17.   Dwelling on the balance of the parties' rights in the situation when the annulment is waived, the Presidium of the Higher Arbitrazh Court stated:

---

[35]   Art. I(1) of the New York Convention provides:

   This Convention shall apply to the recognition and enforcement of arbitral awards made in the territory of a State other than the State where the recognition and enforcement of such awards are sought, and arising out of differences between persons, whether physical or legal. It shall also apply to arbitral awards not considered as domestic awards in the State where their recognition and enforcement are sought (emphasis added).

[36]   See, for instance, 55(3) Hungarian Arbitration Act, Act LXXI of 8 November 1994 on Arbitration, *Hungarian Rules of Law in Force* (1995) No. VI.1, pp. 12-32, providing that: "*Failing to keep the time limit defined in subsection (1) entails the forfeiture of right. In case of an additional award the time limit shall be calculated from the delivery thereof.*"

> *According to Art. 238(4) of the Arbitrazh Procedural Code of Russian Federation,[37] the arbitrazh court, upon consideration of the request for the enforcement of the domestic arbitration award has to check for the presence or the absence of the grounds, provided for in Art. 239 of the same code. These grounds are identical to the grounds for the annulment of the domestic arbitration award by the arbitrazh court. For this reason, the violations that could have taken place during the consideration of the case by the domestic arbitration court and could stand as grounds for the annulment of the award, might be located during the enforcement stage. Under such circumstances, the termination of the annulment proceedings [in case of the waiver of the annulment] does not deprive the petitioner from the further possibility to protect his rights and interests in court.[38]*

VI. Substantive and Formal Requirements to the Waiver

5.18.　The renunciation of annulment in international arbitration proceedings is normally allowed only between the parties not linked to the seat of arbitration (not being its nationals, not having their domicile, place of habitual residence or place of business in such a state). The relevant status of the parties is accessed by the court as of the moment of contracting the annulment out[39] (as well as, arguably, at the time of submission of the annulment request). In domestic arbitration, at least as far as the example of the Russian Federation is concerned, to the contrary, the waiver is only allowed in the proceedings not having a foreign element.

5.19.　The renunciation, both in the international arbitration setting and domestically, is also subject to formal requirements – it should be made in writing.

---

[37]　Art. 238. The order of consideration of the requests for the enforcement of the domestic arbitration awards

　　4. In the course of consideration of the case, the arbitrazh court shall establish the presence or the absence of the grounds for the denial of enforcement, provided for in the Art. 239 of this code, by virtue of the scrutiny of the evidence presented to the court in justifying request and objections.

[38]　*"Overview of the Practice of Consideration by the Arbitrazh Courts of the Cases Related to the Recognition and Enforcement of Foreign Court Decisions, Challenge of the Arbitral Awards and Recognition and Issuance of the Bills of Enforcement for Enforcement of Arbitral Awards,"* attached to the information letter of the Presidium of the Higher Arbitration Court of Russian Federation dated December 22, 2005, No. 96, Sec. 9.

[39]　A.X._ v. B.X._ and Y_, 4A_514/2010. Para. 4.1.2.

5.20. In both contexts, should the waiver be proven, the annulment request would be considered inadmissible and the commenced annulment proceedings would have to be terminated without reaching the merits phase.[40] The court concerned is expected to approach the issue of the waiver *ex officio*[41] or upon request of the party alleging its existence as an issue of admissibility.[42]

VII. Interpretations

5.21. The legal requirements being the same, it is, however, of interest to have a look at the tests applicable in assessing the waiver, carried out by the courts which are *"bringing"* the renunciations to life (or dismissing them). While numerous jurisdictions have *de facto* adopted the renunciation regime, only two of them are known to have a case law record of its application – Switzerland (as far as the international arbitration is concerned) and the Russian Federation (pertaining to the domestic arbitration setting).

VII.1. The Swiss Approach

5.22. A number of works have reflected on the renunciation cases considered by the Swiss Federal Tribunal,[43] counting ultimately over a dozen of the

---

[40] Exceptionally, the Civil Procedural Law of the UAE, which also seems to allow the waiver of annulment, however, not necessarily a reciprocal one, positions the renunciation outside the admissibility limits in providing in its Art. 216(2): *"Renunciation by one of the parties of its right to seek annulment, made before the award was made, does not preclude the admissibility of the annulment request"* (Loi sur la procédure civile des Émirats arabes unis - Titre III: L'arbitrage, Revue de l'Arbitrage, Comité Français de l'Arbitrage 1993 Volume 1993 Issue 2) pp. 343 – 350).

[41] A.X._ v. B.X._ and Y_, *supra* note 39, para. 3(1).

[42] *Ibid.*, para. 4.

[43] Laurent Lévy, *supra* note 4. Laurent Lévy, Tetiana Bersheda, *supra* note 4; Nora Krausz, *Waiver of Appeal to the Swiss Federal Tribunal: Recent Evolution of the Case Law and Compatibility with ECHR, Article 6, in* 28 (2) JOURNAL OF INTERNATIONAL ARBITRATION 137 – 162 (2011); JEAN-FRANÇOIS POUDRET & SÉBASTIEN BESSON, COMPARATIVE LAW OF INTERNATIONAL ARBITRATION, London: Sweet & Maxwell Ltd. 781 (Stephen Berti & Annette Ponti trans., 2nd ed. 2007); Sébastien Besson, *Etendue du contrôle par le juge d'une exception d'arbitrage; renonciation aux recours contre la sentence arbitrale: deux questions choisies de droit Suisse de l'arbitrage international,* 4 REV. ARB. 1071, 1080–82 (2005); François Knoepfler, *Note à l'arrêt du Tribunal Fédéral du 24 juin 2002 dans la cause A. AG v. B. SA, 4P.54 2002,* 21 ASA BULL. 137 (2003); Carl Ulrich Mayer, *Exclusion Agreements According to Article 192 of the Swiss Private International Law Act,* 17 ASA BULL. 191, 198 (1999); Andrea Marco Steingruber, *Sports Arbitration: How the Structure and Other Features of Competitive Sports Affect Consent as It Relates to Waiving Judicial Control,* 20 AM. REV. INT'L ARB. 59, 82 (2009); Domitille Baizeau, *Waiving the Right to Challenge an Arbitral Award Rendered in Switzerland: Caveats and Drafting*

published decisions devoted to the topic.[44] The Federal Tribunal has adopted a restrictive case-by-case-based[45] interpretation of the annulment waivers,[46] searching for a specific,[47] [unmistakably] clear,[48] outright,[49] doubtless/ undoubtful,[50] indisputable,[51] expressly stated[52] common intent of the parties to exclude annulment, regardless of the nature and cause of the award.[53] The Federal Tribunal has proven to be not convinced by indirect renunciations posited through general references to the finality of the award,[54] *inter alia*, those embodied in the institutional arbitration rules,[55] finding, however, that a specific reference to the particular legal provisions (i.e. PILA Art.192(1)) is not a requirement to make the waiver valid.[56] Following the waiver, the party, allegedly, is no more able to address the court relying on the *de facto* annulment grounds positioned within the framework of a somewhat different procedural step, for instance, during the revision.[57]

Considerations for Foreign Parties, 7 (3) INT'L ARB. L. REV. 69, 71, 74 (June 2005); François Perret, *Note to the Decision of the Federal Tribunal of February 4, 2005*, 23 ASA BULL. 521 (2005); Cesare Jermini & Manuel Arroyo, *Pitfalls of Waiver Agreements under Article 192 PILS in Multi-Contract Settings: Some Remarks on Swiss Federal Court Decision 134 III 260*, 27 ASA BULL. 103 (2009), etc.

[44] The relevant decisions in English could be found at: http://www.praetor.ch/search-results/?akID[11][atSelectOptionID][]=39 (accessed on December 29, 2011). The translations are prepared by ZPG law firm, in particular – by Dr. Charles Poncet and his team, and relate to the judgments of the Swiss Federal Tribunal rendered after 1 January 2008.

[45] X._ v. Y._ SA, 4A_486/2010. Para. 2.1(2); X._ v. Y._, 4A_464/2009. Para. 3.1.1; X._ v. AY._ Holding B.V., 4A_256/2009. Para. 2.2(1); X._ v. AY._ Holding B.V., 4A_258/2009. Para. 2.2(1); X._ A.S. v. Y._ GmbH, 4A_224/2008. Para. 2.6.2;

[46] "*During the last twenty years, the Federal Tribunal has developed a restrictive approach, setting strict conditions for the validity of waivers*," Nora Krausz, *supra* note 43, at 162.

[47] X._ A.S. v. Y._ GmbH, 4A_224/2008. Para. 2.6.2.

[48] X._ v. AY._ Holding B.V., 4A_256/2009. Para. 2.2(1); X._ v. AY._ Holding B.V., 4A_258/2009. Para. 2.2(1); X._ A.S. v. Y._ GmbH, 4A_224/2008. Para. 2.6.3.

[49] X._ v. Y._ SA, 4A_486/2010. Para. 2.1(2).

[50] X._ A.S. v. Y._ GmbH, 4A_224/2008. Para. 2.6.3.

[51] A.X._ v. B.X._ and Y_, 4A_514/2010. Para. 4.1.2 (3).

[52] X._ v. Y._, 4A_464/2009. Para. 3.1.1.

[53] A.X._ v. B.X._ and Y_, 4A_514/2010. Para. 4.1.2 (3).

[54] X._ v. Y._ SA, 4A_486/2010. Para. 2.1(2); A.X._ v. B.X._ and Y_, 4A_514/2010. Para. 4.1.1; X_SPA v. Y_ 4A 500/2007. Para. 3.1(1).

[55] X._ v. Y._, 4A_464/2009. Para. 3.1.2.

[56] *Ibid.*, para. 3.1.1; X_SPA v. Y_4A 500/2007. Para. 3.1(1).

[57] X._ v. Y._, 4A.234/2008. Para. 2.1(3). Without ruling on the issue explicitly, the Federal Tribunal explained:

> *It appears difficult to admit that a Party which expressly renounced an appeal, including therefore the right to avail itself of the ground for appeal at Art. 190 (2) (a) LDIP, could still seize the Federal Tribunal sideways by relying on the same ground,*

5.23. Bringing the criteria reflected on above to life, the following stipulations made by the parties were, *inter alia*, found to be valid as annulment waivers:

> *Neither party shall be entitled to commence or maintain any action in a court of law upon any matter in dispute arising from or concerning this Agreement or a breach thereof except for the enforcement of any award rendered pursuant to arbitration under this Agreement.* **The decision of the arbitration shall be final and binding and neither party shall have any right to appeal such decision to any court of law."** *(emphasis supplied by the Federal Tribunal).*[58]

> *The parties expressly agree to waive their rights to*
> *a) challenge any determination(s) or award(s) by the Arbitrator through set aside proceedings or any other proceedings;*
> *b) oppose enforcement of the Arbitrator's determination(s) or award(s) in any jurisdiction.*[59]

> *[...] the parties renounce from now any ordinary or extraordinary appeal against the decision which will be issued.*[60]

5.24. In the meantime, the clauses quoted below were deemed insufficient for waiver purposes:

> *(P) The arbitration award, even if passed by the majority of the arbitrators, shall be final and binding for both Parties hereto. Both Parties to this Contract shall accept the award and proceed accordingly.*

> *(Q) All further rules and procedures of the arbitration shall be in accordance with the applicable Rules of Conciliation and Arbitration of the International Chamber of Commerce.*[61]

> *discovered before the time to appeal had expired, within the framework of a petition for revision, failing which Art. 192 PILA would become meaningless.*

[58] X._ v. Y._ SA, 4A_486/2010. Para. 2.2(2). Interpreting the above language, the Federal Tribunal, *inter alia*, stated:
> *This intent to rule out any appeal against such a decision, clearly expressed in the emphasized sentence of the arbitral clause is reinforced and indirectly confirmed by the preceding sentence; it appears indeed that the state courts could not be seized by any party except to obtain the enforcement of an award issued by the Arbitral tribunal* (*Ibid.*, para. 2(4)).

[59] A.X._ v. B.X._ and Y_, 4A_514/2010. Para. 4.1.2 (2) The Federal Tribunal, *inter alia*, noted that: "*this clause is clearly a valid appeal waiver. It undisputedly conveys the parties' joint intent to waive any appeal against any award of the sole arbitrator regardless of the nature and cause of the award*" (*Ibid.*, para. 4.1.2 (3)).

[60] X_SPA v. Y_ 4A 500/2007. Para. 3.2(2).

[61] X._ v. Y._, 4A_464/2009. Para. 3.1.2. The Federal Tribunal, *inter alia*, noted that:
> *[...] reading paragraph (P), it seems [...] that the author of the text has tried to emphasize above all the fact that the award would have a final and binding character*

> [...] disputes arising from the agreement are decided *"finally, excluding the jurisdiction of the general courts, in accordance with the rules of the arbitral tribunal of the International Chamber of Commerce."*[62]

> *All controversies arising from this contract must be resolved in friendly consultations between the parties. Should this fail to lead to an agreement within 60 days after one party gives notice of the dispute to the other, such disputes shall be finally decided according to Rules of conciliation and arbitration of the International Chamber of Commerce in Paris by three arbitrators appointed according to such rules.*

> *X._____ A.S. and Y._____ GmbH undertake to recognize and to submit themselves to the award. The seat of the arbitral tribunal is Bern/Switzerland where the hearing shall take place as well.*[63]

5.25. Since the legislative provisions of most of the other states allowing the renunciation of annulment were modeled after the Swiss law, the probability is rather high that similar approaches will be adopted in these other states should the relevant situations arise (with the exception of Panama, where the renunciation of annulment by virtue of the arbitration rules is explicitly permitted by the law[64]).

---

for both parties even if it was the result of a mere majority decision. In any case, the clause does not in any way manifest, with the precision required, the intent of the Parties to renounce in advance any right to appeal. As to the reference to the ICC Arbitration Rules, of which Art. 28 (6) states that parties "shall be deemed to have waived their right to any form of recourse insofar as such waiver can validly be made", case law has for a long time emphasized that it is not sufficient to justify the application of Art. 192 (1) PILA (Id).

[62] X._ v. AY._Holding B.V., 4A_256/2009. Para. 2.2; X._ v. AY._Holding B.V., 4A_258/2009. Para. 2.2. The Federal Tribunal explained that:

First, the reference to the exclusion of the jurisdiction of the "general courts" merely expresses that an arbitral tribunal, instead of the state courts, should decide on any disputes. An intent of the parties to waive an appeal against the arbitral award to the Federal Tribunal cannot be derived herefrom. Second, designating an award "final", according to customary language usage in civil procedural law, does not exclude an appeal by way of extraordinary legal remedies but merely the (free) review of the award by way of ordinary legal remedies, such as, for example, an ordinary appeal (Id.).

[63] X._ A.S. v. Y._GmbH, 4A_224/2008. Part. A. Not being convinced in seeing the above clause as the renunciation of annulment, the Federal Tribunal added:

In order to interpret the disputed clause as a renunciation to any appeal against the award, including the appeal based on Art. 190 ff. PILA in connection with Art. 77 BGG, an additional sentence should have been included, in which it would have been made clear, for instance, that the parties renounced any legal recourse against the arbitral award (Ibid., para. 2.1(3)).

[64] *Supra* note 14.

VII.2. The Russian Approach

5.26. Unlike their Swiss colleagues, Russian judges are more relaxed in their search for the reflection of the parties' intent pertaining to the waiver, being persuaded even by a general reference to the finality of the award in the arbitration rules or in the charter of/ provision on the arbitration center, of which the parties were reasonably aware.

5.27. The renunciation regime in Russian domestic arbitration is a *sui-generis* creation which has developed independently from its Western counterpart, eventually, having been established already during the early Soviet period. A number of legislative acts, starting as early as 1918, allowed the resort to domestic arbitration in certain types of disputes involving individuals. Among these are: the Decree of the Higher Central Executive Committee of February 16, 1918,[65] which allowed domestic arbitration in civil cases except for those cases falling within the exclusive competence of the special courts or other similar establishments; disputes arising out of the employment and social security agreements; or criminal cases brought by a private person (such as libel);[66] the Civil Procedural Code of RSFSR of 1922, which provided somewhat more detailed regulation of the domestic arbitration in Arts. 199 – 203, as well as in the specific Annex;[67] the Civil Procedural Code of RSFSR 1964,[68] which contained as a separate attachment a Provision on so-called *"Domestic Arbitration."* Nevertheless, neither of the above Acts mentioned any possibility of judicial recourse against domestic arbitration awards, providing, solely, for the possibility of the courts' involvement if the parties would not comply with the awards voluntarily.

5.28. Eventually, in the Soviet system, individuals were allowed a risk of choice in opting for an alternative dispute resolution mechanism. The legal entities, in the mean time, were deprived of such a freedom,

---

[65] Декреты Советской Власти. Том I. 25 Октября 1917 Г. – 16 Марта 1918 Г. М.: Гос. Издат-Во Политической Литературы (*1 Decrees of the Soviet Power, 25 October 1917 – 16 March 1918, Moscow: State Publishing House for the Political Literature*) 1957, the text in Russian is available at: http://www.hist.msu.ru/ER/ Etext/DEKRET/18-02-16.htm (accessed on December 29, 2011).

[66] *Ibid.*, para. 1.

[67] Гражданский Процессуальный Кодекс РСФСР 1922 г.-Приложение.-Положение о третейском суде// СУ РСФСР, 1924, № 78, ст.783 [*Civil Procedural Code of RSFSR 1922, Annex. – Provision on the Domestic Arbitration ("the Third-Party Court"), 78 Collection of the Decrees of RSFSR 783 (1924)*].

[68] Civil Procedural Code of the RSFSR, as adopted by the Supreme Council of RSFSR on 11 June 1964, Annex 3, text in Russian available at: http://base.consultant.ru/cons/cgi/online.cgi?req=doc;base=LAW;n=2237;from=28169-0;div=LAW;rnd=0.36848524170232133 (accessed on December 29, 2011).

presumably, since their *"fortune"* was more important for the state.[69] This situation was only changed in 1992, already in the Russian Federation, by the *Temporary Provision on the Domestic Arbitration in Economic Disputes,"* the promulgation of which was necessitated by a development in the situation. The Temporary Provision afforded no possibility for challenging domestic arbitration awards either.

5.29. Currently, domestic arbitration in the Russian Federation is governed by both – Civil Procedural and Arbitrazh Procedural Codes of the Russian Federation[70] (depending on the parties being individuals or legal entities), as well as by Federal Law *"On domestic arbitration in Russian Federation,"*[71] which, eventually, is a *lex specialis.* All three instruments dwell on the possibility of the challenge of domestic arbitration awards on limited grounds. The challenge grounds mentioned in all three laws are the same, being consistent with those applicable in international arbitration, basically, following the pattern of Art. 34 of the UNCITRAL Model Law. Unlike the Codes, Art. 40 of the Law, however, allows the parties to waive the annulment proceedings should their agreement specify that the award [to be] rendered in arbitration is *"final."*[72]

5.30. The provision has been subject to some interpretation in the *"Overview of the Practice of Consideration by the Arbitrazh Courts of the Cases Related to the Recognition and Enforcement of Foreign Court Decisions, Challenge of the Arbitral Awards and Recognition and Issuance of the Bills of Enforcement for Enforcement of Arbitral Awards,"* attached to the information letter of the Presidium of the Higher Arbitration Court of Russian Federation dated December 22, 2005, No. 96.[73] Namely, section 9 of the said Overview discussed the case considered by the Arbitrazh Courts in Russia, in which one of the parties challenged a domestic arbitration award based on the arbitration clause reflecting on

---

[69] Постановление Совета труда и обороны от 14 марта 1923 г.; Постановление ЦИК СССР № 5 и СНК СССР № 298 от 3 мая 1931 г. об утверждении Положения об арбитраже [*Decree of the Labour and Defense Council of 14 March 1923; Decree of the Central Executive Committee (CEC) of USSR No, 5 and of the People's Commissioners' Council of USSR No. 298, of 3 May 1931, adopting the Provision on Arbitrazh*].

[70] Civil Procedural Code of Russian Federation, dated November 14, 2002, 138-FZ, (Text No. 4532) and Arbitrazh Procedural Code of Russian Federation, dated July 24, 2002, No. 95-ФЗ, respectively.

[71] Federal Law of Russian Federation *"On Domestic Arbitration in Russian Federation,"* dated July 24, 2002, No. 102-ФЗ, available online at: http://www.akdi.ru/gd/proekt/ 089498GD.SHTM (accessed on December 29, 2011).

[72] For the text of the provision see *supra* note 15.

[73] The text of the document in Russian is available at: http://law7.ru/legal2/se14/pravo1 4257/page2.htm (accessed on December 29, 2011).

the finality of the latter. According to the Overview, the Court dismissed the annulment request, having established that the arbitration agreement, providing for finality of the award, was valid, being concluded by the duly authorized representatives of the parties.

5.31. Several reported cases applied Art. 40 of the Law on domestic arbitration to situations where the alleged waiver was reflected in the text of the applicable arbitration rules referenced in the arbitration agreement – all of these cases – finding a waiver to be valid.

5.32. For example, in its decision rendered in January 2010, the Federal Arbitrazh Court of the Western Siberian Circuit quashed the decision of the lower court, the Arbitrazh Court of Novosibirsk region,[74] setting aside the domestic arbitration award rendered by the Siberian Court of Arbitration in the dispute between an LLC and a private entrepreneur.[75] The award was annulled by the lower court on the basis of the established violations of the fundamental principles of Russian law.

5.33. Applying Art. 40 of the Law on domestic arbitration to the facts of the case, the appellate court made reference to the language of Art. 59 of the Arbitration Rules of the Siberian Court of Arbitration, dealing with the entry of the award into legal force.[76] According to this provision,

1. The award gains force and becomes binding upon the parties right after being rendered; [...]

2. If the parties have not agreed otherwise, the award shall be final.

5.34. Reading the above in conjunction with Art. 7(3) of the Law on domestic arbitration, according to which, "*unless the parties agreed otherwise, in case the dispute is submitted for consideration to the permanent [domestic] arbitration institution, the arbitration rules of such permanent institution shall be considered a part of the arbitration agreement,*" the court found that the award was not subject to challenge, since the parties failed to explicitly "*agree that the award could be set aside,*" as the clause seemed to suggest. It thus found itself incompetent to consider the request.[77]

---

[74]   Decision of the Arbitrazh Court of Novosibirsk Region, dated 23 October 2009.

[75]   Decree of the Federal Arbitrazh Court of the Western Siberian Circuit dated 11 January 2010, in case No. A45-12292/2009, text in Russian available online at: http://arbitrage.ru/sudebnaya-praktika/436-Okonchatelnost-resheniya-mojet-ustanavl ivatsya-reglamentom-suda.html (accessed on December 29, 2011).

[76]   The Arbitration Rules of the Siberian court of arbitration are available in Russian at: http://sts.arbitrage.ru/index.php?option=com_content&task=view&id=87&Itemid=24 (accessed on December 29, 2011).

[77]   The court relied on Art. 150(1)(1) of the Arbitrazh Procedural Code of Ukraine, according to which the Arbitrazh court shall terminate the proceedings in case it finds the dispute lies outside of its jurisdiction.

5.35. Similarly, the Federal Arbitrazh Court of the Moscow circuit interpreted the language of Art. 63(1) (now Art. 88(1)) of the Rules of the Permanent Interregional Domestic Arbitration Court,[78] according to which

> *If the parties failed to specifically agree to the contrary, the award of the IAC is final and is not subject to challenge [...]*

as an effective waiver of annulment.[79]

5.36. The same court dealt with a somewhat trickier situation when considering the challenge to the decision of the arbitrazh court of the city of Moscow[80] dismissing the case dealing with the challenge of the arbitration award rendered by the domestic arbitration court of the OJSC «*Gazprom*».[81] Still finding that the award at stake is final and, thus, no challenge is possible, it relied on two documents: on the arbitration rules of the domestic arbitration court, as well as on the Provision, governing the structure as well as the activities of the latter.

5.37. The relevant Provision,[82] in its Art. 12, dealing with the award of the arbitration court and its enforcement, read:

> *12.1. The award of the arbitration court is final and binding on the parties.*
>
> *12.2. If the arbitration agreement does not provide that the award is final, the award might be challenged by one of the parties to the competent court. [...]*

Art. 51(1) of the Rules of the court,[83] in its turn, provided: "*the award of the domestic arbitration court is final and binding upon the parties.*"

---

[78] The Rules in Russian are available at: http://www.masarbitrag.ru/reglament.php (accessed on December 29, 2011).

[79] Decree of the Federal Arbitrazh Court of the Moscow circuit, dated 6 June 2006, in case No. КГ-А40/6020-06-П. The text in Russian is available at: http://arbitrage.ru/sudebnaya-praktika/305-Reshenie-treteiskogo-suda-ne-podlejit-osparivaniu-esli-pravilami-suda-ustanovlena-ego-okonchatelnost.html (accessed on December 29, 2011).

[80] Decision of the Arbitrazh Court of the city of Moscow, dated 4 June 2008, in case No. A40-20842/08-69-222

[81] Decree of the Federal Arbitrazh Court of the Moscow Circuit, dated 11 August 2008, in case No. КГ-А40/7211-08. Text in Russian is available at: http://arbitrage.ru/sudebnaya-praktika/137-Okonchatelnost-resheniya-suda-mojet-bit-ustanovlena-reglamentom-suda.html (accessed on December 29, 2011).

[82] Adopted by the decision of the Council of Directors of the OJSC "*Gazprom*", dated 23 April 2003, No. 454. Text available in Russian at: http://gazprom.ru/f/posts/95/658856/polozhenie_o_ts.pdf (accessed on December 29, 2011).

[83] Adopted by the Oder of the OJSC "*Gazprom*" dated 23 July 2003, No. 73. Text available in Russian at: http://www.gazprom.ru/f/posts/95/658856/reglament_01.01.2011.pdf (accessed on December 29, 2011).

5.38. After finding that according to Art. 2 of the Law on Domestic Arbitration, the rules of the domestic arbitration institution could be contained in the different instruments, *inter alia*, in the relevant provisions and rules [of procedure], the court acknowledged the lack of clarity created by the language of the Provision. It, nevertheless, further applied the *lex posterior derogat legi priori* principle, deeming a clearer language of the Rules prevailing, this way making the award final and not being subject to challenge.

5.39. Finally, the Federal Arbitrazh Court of the Western-Siberia circuit, after finding finality language in Section 11 of the Provision on the Domestic Arbitration Court at the Siberian Bank of the Russian Sberbank, dismissed the allegations of the party to the effect that neither the above provision nor the Arbitration rules of the said institution were attached to the parties' contracts, which contained an arbitration clause, since Sec. 8.7 of the contract explicitly mentioned, that the parties *"have taken cognaissance of the Arbitration Rules."*[84]

VIII. Concluding Remarks

5.40. The brief discussion above has outlined the major points of the *status quo* pertaining to the reflection of the concept of the waiver of annulment in the national legislations as well as in the judicial practice. It allows one to conclude that such a waiver is technically possible, being, however, subject to the specific rules adopted in the particular jurisdiction that permits it. For instance, as shown in the case law overview, the standards applied in the interpretation of the waiver by the Swiss courts are somewhat more restrictive than those at stake in the courts of the Russian Federation. Nevertheless, neither of the models establishes a threshold which would be hard to meet, should the respective agreement containing the waiver be drafted carefully, taking into consideration, among other things, the existing jurisprudence as well as the peculiarities of the enforcement regime in the potential enforcing jurisdictions.

5.41. The benefits of the waiver of annulment should be assessed on a case-by-case basis. While the decision to waive should not be taken easily, at times resorting to this solution could have positive effects, *inter alia*, in terms of procedural and cost efficiency. In addition, the possibility of

---

[84] Decree of the Federal Arbitrazh Court of Western Siberia Circuit, dated 16 February 2004, in case No Ф04/665-100/А45-2004. Text in Russian available at: http://arbitrage.ru/sudebnaya-praktika/310-Esli-v-reglamente-ustanovlena-okonchatel nost-resheniya-to-ono-ne-podlejit-osparivaniu.html (accessed on December 29, 2011).

waiving the potential intrusion of the courts of the seat within the post-arbitration phase might be viewed as a solution worth considering as far as the jurisdictions known for their not-that-friendly arbitration-related stance are concerned. While, in such a case, the waiver would not solve all problems connected to the seat, which could arise in arbitration, e.g. court assistance at the phase of the arbitration proper would have to be handled as is – to the extent available, it would at least safeguard the ready award from redundant attacks or an irregular annulment.

| | |

Summaries

FRA [*Abandon de recours en annulation dans le cadre de l'arbitrage : développement global progressif, réalités et perspectives de la Fédération de Russie (des lits différents, des rêves similaires?)*]

Cet article consiste en une discussion à propos des recours en annulation, une forme « extrême » d'autonomie des parties disponible dans l'arbitrage international, qui permet aux parties de refuser la révision de la sentence rendue à leur égard lors de l'arbitrage par le tribunal national du siège de l'arbitrage. Ce type d'abandon, qui gagne depuis peu en popularité, est étudié dans deux contextes différents. Premièrement, en tant que phénomène relevant du cadre de l'arbitrage international, qui suit en grande partie le modèle évoqué à l'Art. 192 (1) de la Loi sur le Droit Privé International suisse de 1989, et, deuxièmement, en tant que notion d'arbitrage nationale, spécifique à la Fédération de Russie. Ces deux approches, qui se sont développées de manière indépendante, partagent cependant un certain nombre de caractéristiques telles que notamment, leur place dans le système procédural concerné – en termes de recevabilité, les conditions formelles requises que les parties doivent remplir pour rendre l'abandon du recours en annulation valide. Les paradigmes applicables en matière d'interprétation en Suisse et dans la Fédération de Russie, les deux seuls états où les tribunaux sont connus pour avoir traité des abandons, varient cependant. Tandis que les tribunaux suisses privilégient en général une interprétation restrictive de la démarche de renonciation des parties, les tribunaux russes sont sensiblement plus souples, allant même jusqu'à permettre de se référer aux règles d'arbitrage contenant le terme « finalité ».

CZE [*Vzdání se práva na zrušení rozhodčího nálezu v rozhodčím řízení: progresivní vývoj v celosvětovém měřítku, realita současné Ruské federace a perspektivy do budoucna (Jiné postele – podobné sny?)*]
Článek je věnován diskusi o vzdání se možnosti zrušení rozhodčího nálezu – „extrémní" formě smluvní autonomie v mezinárodní arbitráži, která stranám umožňuje vyloučit přezkum rozhodčího nálezu, vydaného v rozhodčím řízení vedeném mezi nimi, národním soudem v sídle rozhodčího řízení. Tento druh vzdání se práva, který v poslední době konečně získává své příznivce, je hodnocen ve dvou různých kontextech. Za prvé jako jev patřící do sféry mezinárodního rozhodčího řízení, který do značné míry sleduje model zakotvený v článku 192 odst. 1 švýcarského zákona o mezinárodním právu soukromém z roku 1989. A za druhé jako pojem národního rozhodčího řízení specifický pro Ruskou federaci. Tyto dva přístupy, které se vyvinuly nezávisle na sobě, sdílejí dosti shodných prvků, například postavení v rámci příslušného procesního rámce – jako otázka přípustnosti, formální náležitosti, které musí strany splnit, aby bylo vzdání se možnosti zrušení rozhodčího nálezu platné, a hlavní hmotněprávní podmínkou jejich platnosti je úmysl. Výkladová paradigmata použitelná ve Švýcarsku a v Ruské federaci, jediných dvou státech, jejichž soudy jsou veřejně známy svým rozhodováním o vzdáních se tohoto práva, se však liší. Zatímco švýcarské soudy se při hledání vůle stran k vzdání se tohoto práva běžně uchylují k restriktivnímu výkladu, ruské soudy jsou podstatně flexibilnější, a dovolují dokonce i obecný odkaz na rozhodčí pravidla obsahující ustanovení o „konečnosti".

| | |

POL [*Zrzeczenie się skargi o stwierdzenie nieważności w arbitrażu: Rozwój progresywny w perspektywie globalnej, stan rzeczywisty i perspektywy Federacji Rosyjskiej (śpimy w różnych łóżkach, ale mamy podobne sny?)*]
Niniejszy artykuł omawia przypadki zrzeczenia się unieważnienia – "ekstremalnego" przejawu autonomii stron w postępowaniu arbitrażowym, umożliwiającego stronom wykluczyć ponowne rozpatrzenie orzeczenia arbitrażowego przed sądem krajowym w miejscu odbywania się arbitrażu. Ten typ zrzeczenia się, zyskujący w ostatnim czasie na popularności, analizowany jest w dwóch różnych kontekstach. Po pierwsze – jako zjawisko w ramach arbitrażu międzynarodowego, w znacznym stopniu nawiązujące do szwajcarskiego modelu zawartego w art. 192 szwajcarskiej ustawy PILA

(międzynarodowe prawo prywatne), i po drugie – jako pojęcie krajowego arbitrażu, charakterystyczne dla Federacji Rosyjskiej.

DEU [*Der Verzicht auf Aufhebungsklage in Schiedssachen: die progressive Entwicklung im weltweiten Maßstab, die Realitäten in der Russischen Föderation und die Perspektiven für selbige (Andere Betten – Ähnliche Träume?)*]

Dieser Artikel bespricht den Rechtsmittelverzicht als "Extremform" der Parteiautonomie in internationalen Schiedssachen; er erlaubt es den Parteien, die Prüfung von Schiedssprüchen durch das für den Schiedsort zuständige nationale Gericht außer Kraft zu setzen. Diese in jüngerer Zeit immer populärer werdende Form des Rechtsverzichts wird in zwei verschiedenen Zusammenhängen bewertet. Zum einen – als ein dem Umfeld der internationalen Schiedsgerichtsbarkeit zugehöriges Phänomen, das größtenteils dem in Artikel 192 des schweizerischen IPRG (Bundesgesetz über das Internationale Privatrecht) zum Ausdruck gebrachten Schweizer Modell nachempfunden ist, und zum anderen – als Begriff der nationalen Schiedsgerichtsbarkeit und Besonderheit der Russischen Föderation.

RUS [*Отказ от аннулирования исков в арбитражном суде: прогрессивное развитие в мировом масштабе, реалии и перспективы для Российской Федерации (Разные постели - Похожие сны?)*]

В статье рассматривается вопрос добровольного отказа сторон от права обжалования арбитражного решения в суде страны в которой проходило арбитражное разбирательство, являющийся, фактически, одной из крайних форм автономии сторон, обратившихся с целью решения спора в арбитраж. Вопрос рассмотрен с двух точек зрения - как институт международного арбитражного процесса, базирующийся, в основном, на так называемой "Швейцарской" модели, основы которой отображены в статье 192(1) Швейцарского закона о международном частном праве, и как институт третейского правосудия в праве Российской Федерации.

ESP [*Renuncia a la acción de anulación del laudo arbitral: desarrollo progresivo global, realidades y perspectivas en la Federación Rusa (Camas diferentes –¿ sueños similares?)*]

El artículo discute las renuncias a la anulación – una forma "extrema" de la autonomía de la voluntad en el arbitraje internacional que permite a las partes librarse de la revisión del laudo arbitral por el tribunal nacional de la sede del arbitraje. Este tipo de anulación, que últimamente ha ganado mucha popularidad, se ha evaluado en dos contextos diferentes. En primer lugar. como un fenómeno perteneciente al establecimiento del arbitraje internacional, en gran parte siguiendo el modelo suizo reflejado en el art. 192 de la Ley Suiza de Derecho Internacional Privado (PILA) y, en segundo lugar, como una noción de arbitraje nacional, una especialidad de la Federación Rusa.

Dániel Bán | László Kecskés

Changing Aspects of Unsigned Arbitration Agreements

Key words:
relative structure of
arbitration agreement
| non-signatories |
implied consent | public
policy

Abstract | *Although the prevailing approach has been to prohibit extensive interpretation of arbitration agreements, increasingly, proceedings before arbitration courts involve persons who did not conclude an arbitration agreement ("joining non-signatories" or "extending the arbitration clause"). However, the extension of jurisdiction through involvement of third parties is not without its risks. This can be observed both at the start and conclusion of the arbitral application of law. The arbitration court that decides on its own competence on the basis of the Kompetenz – Kompetenz doctrine may face significant contract law dilemmas just upon answering the preliminary questions as to jurisdiction: whether or not the arbitration agreement – on which the court's competence is based – exists, and if such an agreement exists, whether the agreement is valid. If, the arbitration court is too liberal in handling the extension of the arbitration clause to third parties, it may lead to unfavorable consequences in the course of the acknowledgement and enforcement of the court's decision. Thus, with regard to the initial arbitral application of law, the problem is to be considered one of jurisdiction, while with regard to the conclusion of the arbitral law's application, the problem must be seen as involving the enforceability of the arbitral award.*

Dániel Bán, Attorney-at-law; Perényi & Bán Law Firm (Budapest) External lecturer; Civil Law Department, Faculty of Law, Pécs University of Sciences Founding member of "Magánjogot Oktatók Egyesülete (Society of Civil Law Teachers) Scope of his research: contract law, private international law, arbitration. e-mail: bandaniel@ ajk.pte.hu

László Kecskés, Professor and Head of the Civil Law Department, Faculty of Law, Pécs University of Sciences; Doctor of the Hungarian Academy of Sciences; President of the Arbitration Court attached to the Hungarian Chamber of Commerce and Industry (Budapest) Scope of his research: civil law, private international law, arbitration, EU law and approximation of laws e-mail: kecskeslaszlo@ ajk.pte.hu

| | |

I. Procedural Consequences of Changes in Civil Law Dogma

6.01. The legitimacy of arbitration proceedings is based on an agreement between parties to submit their disputes to arbitration.[1] Hence, reference to arbitration as a *consensual method* for the settlement of disputes is not rare.[2] Only those persons who conclude an arbitration agreement may be involved in arbitration proceedings, and the proceeding itself may be conducted only on the matter submitted by the parties to arbitration. Therefore, no arbitration proceeding may be conducted without consensus between the parties to submit their dispute to arbitration.[3] In short: there is no arbitral jurisdiction where there is no arbitration agreement.[4]

6.02. The view on arbitration clauses was recently specified by a change in thought requiring the placement of arbitration agreements in written form and [the parties'] compliance with this condition. This process of change can be explained in part by the influence of technical novelties in contract law. Even with the appearance of the telegram, telex and fax it is more than obvious that questions on new type-forms of contracts cannot always be answered through the classical dogma of contract law. In addition, the pressure of practical problems is increased by the fact that technical evolution [typically] outstrips legislative modes of legal development. As we see, in contrast to earlier historical periods, today, the exchange of letters or telegrams is no longer the most advanced method for concluding contracts. Countless contracts now may be concluded by the completion of an uploaded electronic application form ("by a click"), by exchange of electronic messages (without an electronic signature), or by *Skype* conversation. In addition, the "team-work" in technical development and the emergence of unexpected situations, or emergencies, may create further specialized methods for contract conclusion: for example, the exchange of radio messages

---

[1]   CAROLE MURRAY, DAVID HOLLOWAY & DAREN TIMSON-HUNT, SCHMITTHOFF'S EXPORT TRADE. THE LAW AND PRACTICE OF INTERNATIONAL TRADE, London: Sweet & Maxwell 539 (2007).

[2]   *Ibid.*, at 538.

[3]   *Ibid.*, at 539.

[4]   The author of the first Hungarian monograph concerning the questions of arbitration, Tihamér Fabinyi (1890, Hisnyóvíz, Hungary – 1953, Boston, USA) in his comprehensive work provides brief and precise wording in this respect: "The arbitration agreement constitutes the justification for the arbitration court." See: TIHAMÉR FABINYI, A VÁLASZTOTT BÍRÁSKODÁS (*Arbitration*), Vác: A szerzö 114 (1926).

between a captain and air-traffic controller during a distress landing could be considered a peculiar form of contract.

6.03. Thus, as a matter of course, legislators must attempt – as far as possible – to keep pace with technical evolution. According to Section 2 Article 38 of Act 11 of 1960, which put the Hungarian Civil Code into effect, the requirement that an agreement be put in writing would be met by an electronic document, if the document were signed with an electronic signature. Section 3 Article 5 of the Hungarian Arbitration Act (Act LXXI of 1994) considers the arbitration agreement as prepared in writing if it is contained in an exchange of messages, which provide a permanent record of the agreement. According to Article 7 Option I of the UNCITRAL Model Law on International Commercial Arbitration "the requirement that an arbitration agreement be in writing is met by an electronic communication if the information contained therein is accessible so as to be useable for subsequent reference; [where] "'electronic communication' means any communication that the parties make by means of data messages; [and where] 'data messages' means information generated, sent, received or stored by electronic, magnetic, optical or similar means, including, but not limited to, electronic data interchange (EDI), electronic mail, telegram, telex or telecopy."

6.04. These examples demonstrate that technical developments make necessary a change in and enlargement of the legal requirement of writing concerning contracts. Nevertheless, many lawyers believe the process of the elaboration is but a legal symptom of technical evolution. However, it is obviously more: the dissolution of formal requirements has both a technical (or so-called "external") ground, and a very important legal ("internal") ground, one rooted in legal developments of the 19th century. This study will examine these legal grounds – as these relate to unsigned arbitration agreements.

6.05. Our starting-point is that – although extensive interpretation[5] of arbitration agreements is commonly prohibited in both theory and practice – persons who never concluded an arbitration agreement are increasingly involved in arbitration proceedings before arbitration courts and it is also common for arbitrators to proceed in cases that were not expressly submitted by the parties to their jurisdiction. Such a situation may occur, for e.g., in arbitration proceedings initiated pursuant to an arbitration agreement that was concluded with a subsidiary having financial difficulties, when the plaintiff wishes to

---

[5]   In Hungarian legal practice, in order No. Gf. II. 20.033/2005/2 published under No. BDT2005.1225, the Győr Court of Appeal stipulated as a principle the prohibition of extensive interpretation.

involve the defendant's mother company having solid capital. It is also often the case that while the plaintiff establishes business relations with several companies within a group of companies that only one of the agreements concluded with such partners includes an arbitration clause. In such cases, on the basis of the arbitration clause, the plaintiff frequently strives to sue the company that did not sign the arbitration agreement. Moreover, primarily U.S. authors report cases where the defendant sued before an ordinary court (in order to evade the severity of the court) and submitted a jurisdictional objection on the basis of an arbitration agreement concluded by its subsidiary or mother company – not the company involved in the proceeding.[6]

6.06. The specialist literature refers to such occurrences as *"joining non-signatories,"* or *"extending the arbitration clause."*[7] The term *"joining non-signatories"* is widely used primarily by common lawyers, and refers to the joining of third parties to the proceeding, while the latter term is more typically used by continental lawyers when they refer to the extension of arbitration agreements. However, with regard to the requirement of there being a close connection between the consensus of the parties manifested in the arbitration agreement and the jurisdiction of the arbitration court, the extension of jurisdiction by way of the involvement of third parties is not without risks.

6.07. The extension of arbitration agreements to a third party is in fact a peculiar reflection of the disintegration of the relative structure of agreements involving procedural law consequences: *the contract law doctrine of relative structure transforms into a jurisdictional doctrine within the domain of arbitration agreements*, therefore, the structural relaxing of the arbitration agreement requires significantly more consideration than that of standard civil law agreements.

6.08. The risks related to the extension of jurisdiction as a result of the extension of the agreement can be observed both at the initiation and conclusion of the arbitral application of law. The arbitration court that decides on its own competence on the basis of the *Kompetenz – Kompetenz* doctrine[8] may face significant contractual law dilemmas

---

[6] William W. Park, *Non-signatories and International Contracts. An Arbitrator's Dilemma*, MULTIPLE ACTIONS IN INTERNATIONAL ARBITRATION: CONSENT, PROCEDURE AND ENFORCEMENT, Oxford: Oxford University Press 3 (B. MacMahon ed., 2009).

[7] *Ibid.*, at 2.

[8] In respect of the latest EU law developments concerning the doctrine of "Kompetenz – Kompetenz" see: László Kecskés & Zoltán Nemessányi, *Veszélybe került a választottbíráskodás számára fontos "Kompetenz – Kompetenz" dogma? Kvázi hatásköri bíróságként járt el az Európai Bíróság a West Tankers ügyben (Is the doctrine of "Kompetenz – Kompetenz" essential for arbitration at threat? The European Court of*

already upon answering the *preliminary questions on jurisdiction*: whether or not the arbitration agreement on which it bases its competence exists, and if such agreement exists, whether or not the agreement is valid. If, the arbitration court handles the extension of the arbitration clause to third parties over-generously, this may have unfavorable consequences in the course of the *acknowledgement* and *enforcement* of its decision. Thus, with regard to the *initiation* of the application of arbitral law the problem is to be considered as one of jurisdiction, while with regard to its *conclusion*, as an issue involving the enforceability of the arbitral award.

II. Dilution of the Relative Structure of Arbitration Agreements

II.1. Contract Law Techniques for the Extension (Dilution) of Arbitration Agreements: Implied Consent

6.09.   It has become one of the generally accepted cornerstones of contract law that in addition to the contractual terms expressly stipulated by the parties, contracts may also include certain implied conditions and terms.[9] These implied terms are inferred and *implied into* the contract by the arbitrator (judge) primarily on the basis of the intention of the parties, the nature and purpose of the contract, and the requirement of good faith, fair dealing and reasonableness. Therefore, the purpose of this interpretive activity is to reveal the *true* intention of the parties at the time of the conclusion of the contract.

6.10.   Implied consent is in fact the application of this *implication* for the purpose of including a third party into an arbitration agreement. The basis of this solution is that the party's inclusion is implied in the statements, or in a wider sense, by the party's conduct that such party also accepted the arbitration agreement as binding to himself. In certain cases the conduct of a person who did not formally conclude an arbitration agreement may rightly give a reasonably-thinking outsider the impression that such person committed himself to participation in the arbitration proceeding. However, deducing the true *intention* of a third person from the *impressions made* by the conduct of such third person upon another person is undoubtedly problematic. Getting at the parties' true intention in such behavior involves considerable risks. For

---

Justice proceeded as a quasi-jurisdictional court in the West Tankers case.), 3 Európai Jog 14-23 (2009).

[9]   See: PECL Art. 6:102, UNIDROIT-Principles Art. 5.1.1., 5.1.2. and DCFR II. – 9:101.

example, as early as the 15th century, the English King's Bench warned against engaging in the examination of the intention of the parties in respect of legal issues, since, as they claimed, in most cases only the devil (or not even the devil) could tell what the parties' true intention was.[10] Upon examining the doctrine of implied conditions Sturge also emphasizes that there is no consensus even among Anglo-Saxon lawyers in respect of the actual use of this institution. As a result of the over-exaggerated belief in the "true" intention of the parties this method may become the means for achieving contradictory results: by applying this doctrine, obligations that were actually never undertaken could be deemed to be part of the contractual obligations, while the effect of obligations that were actually taken could be diminished under the mask of the fictitious figure of the "reasonably-thinking person."[11] It may be due in part to the foregoing that in his extensive comparative study Gyula Eörsi[12] referred to the theory of implied conditions as a means of legal policy, rather than as a means of dogma.[13] On this point, Tibor Várady concurs. Moreover, according to Várady, as a result of the strengthening and institutionalization of arbitration, a previously unknown issue also must be faced, namely, that there might be a conflict between the loyalty of the arbitration court towards the parties and its loyalty towards the institution of international commercial arbitration.[14] In recognition of the above issue, Várady emphasizes that the strengthening of the position of arbitration and the extension of its scope must not be transformed into a forcing of arbitration on the parties. Therefore, it is essential that the examination of the *true intention of the parties* solely serve the purpose of preventing the party who implicitly submitted himself to the jurisdiction of the arbitration court from evading the proceedings, and that such examination not result in implications read by the *arbitration court of its true intention* into the statements of the parties.[15]

---

[10] Roscoe Pound, *The Role of the Will in Law*, 68 (1) HARVARD LAW REVIEW 1 (1954).

[11] L. J. Sturge, *The Doctrine of Implied Condition*, 41 LAW QUARTERLY REVIEW 171(1925).

[12] Gyula Eörsi (1922 – 1992) was professor of civil law at the Eötvös Lóránd University (Budapest) and the former President of the Arbitration Court attached to the Hungarian Chamber of Commerce and Industry (MKIK).

[13] As expressed by Eörsi: *"the technique of implication serves the transfer of the case from the scope of delictual liability into the scope of contractual liability by fictional means: the implication into the contract of consequences complying with certain objectives of legal policy."* See: GYULA EÖRSI, ÖSSZEHASONLÍTÓ POLGÁRI JOG (*Comparative Civil Law*), Budapest: Akadémiai Kiadó 422 (1975).

[14] Tibor Várady, *Választottbíráskodás a felek ellenére?* (*Arbitration in Contravention of the Intention of the Parties*), (1) MAGYAR JOG 52 (1995).

[15] *Ibid.*

6.11. Despite the risks involved therein, implied consent often assists the arbitration court to establish its jurisdiction in disputes between parties where one did not conclude (more precisely, did not sign) an arbitration agreement. For example, it frequently occurs that the person participating in the negotiations preceding the conclusion of the contract containing the arbitration agreement, and in the development of the content of such contract, ultimately does not formally become the subject of the contract.[16] This was the case in a dispute that came before the arbitration court attached to the International Chamber of Commerce (ICC): instead of the person actually proceeding upon the conclusion of the contract, it was instead a third person who finally signed such contract in order to remove the transaction from the scope of the VAT obligation. The arbitration court established that the person who had not signed the contract, did however play a major role in the development of the content thereof and was thus the actual subject of the contract and of the arbitration agreement contained therein.[17]

6.12. In the so-called *Trelleborg* case a similar train of thought was followed by the Sao Paulo State Court. The court established that Trelleborg Industri AB, the mother company of the defendant was subject to the scope of the arbitration agreement, despite the fact that the arbitration agreement was signed only by the subsidiary. In its reasoning the court emphasized that the active participation of the mother company in the transaction at issue could be established on the basis of the documents in the case.[18] In this case the court obviously relied on the theory referenced in the relevant literature as the "group of companies doctrine." The essence of this theory is the following: if within a group of companies a company signed an arbitration agreement, but another company did not sign such agreement, but the latter also participated in the drawing up of the contract that included the arbitration agreement, the scope of the arbitration clause may also extend to the non-signatory company.[19] Therefore, it is essential to underscore that membership within a group of companies is not sufficient in itself to justify extension of the scope of the arbitration agreement to the non-signatory member. Such extension also requires that the relevant

---

[16] William W. Park, *supra* note 6, at 8.

[17] See the decision delivered in ICC Case No. 11160. Quoted by William W. Park, *supra* note 6, at 27.

[18] Flavio Pereira Lima & Daniel Calhman de Miranda, *Extension of the Arbitration Agreement to Non-Signatories Pursuant to Brazilian Law, in* 1 ARBITRATION IN BRAZIL, Brasil: Impressão régra 19 (F.P. Lima ed., 2010).

[19] *Ibid.*, at 20.

member of the group actively participate in the transaction including the arbitration agreement, namely active participation admits the conclusion that the company truly intended to submit itself to the jurisdiction of the arbitration court.[20]

6.13. Nevertheless, the issue may arise as to what is to be considered "active participation" in respect of the contract containing the arbitration agreement, or the arbitration agreement itself. This issue is to be resolved by the proceedings' arbitrator (judge) upon consideration of all circumstances of the case, the conduct displayed by the parties already at the phase of the conclusion of the contract, or in the course of the enforcement of claims. Naturally, the conduct displayed in the course of the enforcement of claims best clarifies the situation: if in the arbitration proceeding the person not a signatory to the arbitration agreement brings an action, or submits a jurisdiction objection to the court, stating that claims against it are to be enforced by way of arbitration, such conduct will be deemed by law as acceptance of the arbitration agreement.[21] Although in a less obvious manner than in the above-described case, if a person participates in the formulation of the content of the future contract already in the course of the negotiations preceding the conclusion of such contract, such behavior may also constitute the person's acceptance of the binding force of the arbitration agreement. In this respect, Park emphasizes that from the perspective of the determination of the content of the contractual obligation the relevance of the contractual negotiations significantly exceeds that of the performance phase, and therefore, active participation in the course of the former may serve to more fully justify extension of the scope of the arbitration agreement.[22]

6.14. Active participation in the relevant transaction (which includes an arbitration agreement) may be realized, even if apparently several different transactions have been entered into by and between various persons, and even when not all of these transactions include an arbitration agreement.[23] In such cases, if it can be established that the documents seeming to be different agreements in fact establish *a*

---

[20] *Ibid.*, at 21.

[21] William W. Park, *supra* note 6, at 9. It should also be considered within the scope of the conduct displayed in the course of the enforcement of claims, if as a result of breaching formal requirements, the parties concluded an invalid arbitration agreement, however, "they expressly submitted to the judgment and implemented their transactions accordingly." See: GÉZA UJLAKI, A VÁLASZTOTTBÍRÁSKODÁS KÉZIKÖNYVE (*Compendium of Arbitration*), Budapest: Dick Manó kiadása 55 (1927).

[22] William W. Park, *supra* note 6, at 21.

[23] Stavros Brekoulakis, *The Notion of the Superiority of Arbitration Agreements over Jurisdiction Agreements: Time to Abandon It?* 24 (4) J. INT´L ARB. 350 (2007).

uniform contractual obligation in respect of several subjects, the scope of the arbitration agreement can be extended to all subjects of the contractual obligation.[24] By way of the above technique, complex transnational commercial transactions otherwise serving a single economic purpose may be prevented from being separated from procedural law aspects.[25]

6.15. We may consider the extension of legal succession in substantive law to the arbitration agreement as another form of implied consent to the arbitration agreement. This approach may be observed also in the practice of the Arbitration Court attached to the Hungarian Chamber of Commerce and Industry (MKIK): on several occasions the proceeding arbitration panel – faced with a lack of any agreement between the parties to the contrary – considered legal succession based on substantive law in respect of the commercial relationship, as indication of the simultaneous entry of the legal successor into the arbitration agreement.[26] Éva Horváth[27] deduces this solution from the expectability requirement towards the legal successor. According to her position, it may be rightfully expected from the legal successor in substantive law who examines the legal relationship "inherited" thereby, that if such relationship also includes an arbitration agreement, the legal successor should expressly state its intention to ignore this arbitration agreement. In the absence of such statement, it is obvious that the legal successor entered into the legal relationship taking into consideration (also) the possible future arbitration proceeding.[28]

The relation between arbitral clauses and legal succession in substantive law raises special issues with regard to assignment. The problem lies in the fact that assignment does not result in general legal succession, but only in a change in the subject of the *position of the*

---

[24] William W. Park, *supra* note 6, at 8.

[25] The same concept is hidden also behind the following reasoning of the Paris Cour d'appel: "arbitral clauses contained in international transactions have sui generis validity and effect, which requires the extension of the arbitral clause to also those persons who participated in the performance of the contract and the dispute arising from such contract, provided that it can be established that the conduct displayed by such persons supports the presumption that they were aware of the existence and extent of the arbitral clause..." See the judgments delivered by the Cour d'appel in the *Korsnas Marma* v. *Durand-Auzias* case on November 30, 1988 and in the *Ofer Bros.* v. *Tokyo Marine and Fire Insurance* case on February 14, 1989. Quoted by: Stavros Brekoulakis, *supra* note 23, at 351.

[26] Éva Horváth, *A választottbíráskodás néhány gyakorlati kérdése (Some Practical Issues of Arbitration)*, 3 GAZDASÁG ÉS JOG 5 (2001).

[27] Professor of law and former President of the Arbitration Court attached to the Hungarian Chamber of Commerce and Industry.

[28] Éva Horváth, *supra* note 26, at 5.

obligee, therefore, assumption of the *obligations* under the arbitration agreement (waiver of the right to submit a dispute to an ordinary court, and the obligation to enforce claims before an arbitration court) does not automatically follow from the assignment. Although the Hungarian Supreme Court has not been receptive to the above argument so far,[29] such an argument nevertheless was made in the non-litigious proceeding heard by the Metropolitan Court (Budapest) under number 9.Gpk.40.168/2007. In the decision, delivered in the above referenced case, the Metropolitan Court pointed out that a change in the subject of the arbitration agreement would require the same civil law agreement as if the change occurred in the subject of any other contractual relationship. Since the arbitration agreement indicates (also) the unity of rights and obligations, the change in the subject thereof may not take place by a mere assignment: instead, it requires the conclusion of an agreement combining assignment and the assumption of obligations.[30]

6.16. It seems that in Hungarian legal thinking the connection of assignment and the extension of the scope of the arbitration agreement is making little progress for the time being, primarily because of dogma. The example set by foreign legal practice may aid progress out of the standstill: for instance, according to Park's definite position, in order to improve the efficiency of arbitration, French legal practice frequently deems it expedient that the *rights and obligations* (jointly) following from the arbitration agreement "be contracted for following" substantive law rights and obligations – although the above practice (which may sometimes be excessive in its attempts to sidestep dogma) is intended to prevent the differentiation of the person of the obligor under substantive law and the defendant actionable before the arbitration court solely as a result of legal succession in substantive law.[31]

---

[29]   According to the approach prevalent in the practice of the Hungarian Supreme Court, the assignee shall be bound by the arbitral clause contained in the contract concluded between the assignor and the assigned party, since the validity and effect of the arbitral clause is not affected by legal succession on the side of either of the parties. A summary of relevant judicial practice can be found in: KATALIN MURÁNYI, ÖSSZEFOGLALÓ AZ ÁLLAMI BÍRÓSÁGOKNAK A VÁLASZTOTTBÍRÓSÁGI ELJÁRÁSHOZ KAPCSOLÓDÓ GYAKORLATÁRÓL ÉS JAVASLATOK A VÁLASZTOTTBÍRÁSKODÁSRÓL SZÓLÓ TÖRVÉNY ÉS A MAGYAR KERESKEDELMI ÉS IPARKAMARA MELLETT SZERVEZETT VÁLASZTOTTBÍRÓSÁG ELJÁRÁSI SZABÁLYZATA MÓDOSÍTÁSA ÉS KIEGÉSZÍTÉSE TÁRGYÁBAN. (*Summary of the Practice of State Courts Related to Arbitration Proceedings and Proposals for the Amendment and Supplementation of the Arbitration Act and the Rules of Procedure of the Arbitration Court Attached to the Hungarian Chamber of Commerce and Industry*), Budapest: Manuscript 14 (2010).

[30]   The position of the Metropolitan Court is quoted and analyzed in: *Ibid.*, at 15.

[31]   William W. Park, *supra* note 6, at 15.

II.2. Procedural Law Technique of Extension: Estoppel

6.17. The institution of estoppel is in fact the Anglo-Saxon procedural law sanction corresponding to the principle of *venire contra factum proprium* ("non-conformity with prior conduct.") The essence of this institution is that if a person, by way of his positive conduct, inspires well-founded confidence in another person regarding the truthfulness of a fact, such person subsequently may not refer *vis-à-vis* the other person to the untruthfulness of such fact.[32] Thus, estoppel practically prevents the parties from proving to the contrary of their own facts. From the perspective of arbitration agreements, the above institution means that if the dispute is related to a contract in, or in relation to which the parties stipulated the enforcement of claims by way of arbitration, the party signing the arbitration agreement may not claim the inapplicability of the arbitral clause.[33] The court assumed this position in a case in which two groups of companies cooperated for the purpose of the construction of a power plant in Saudi Arabia. Within the framework of the cooperation various contracts were concluded between the members of the two groups of companies. Among these contracts there were some that also included arbitral clauses, and some that included no arbitral clause. The dispute was raised in relation to the statement by one of the companies that also signed the arbitral clause that it was persuaded to sign the contract (that also included an arbitral clause) by way of misrepresentation. With a view to such misrepresentation, the company brought an action for damages before an ordinary court against a company which was a member of the other group of companies; although the defendant company had not signed the arbitration agreement itself, its mother company had signed the agreement. The court considered the defendant's jurisdictional objection well-founded despite the fact that the defendant had not concluded the arbitration agreement. This finding was based on the reasoning that if the plaintiff had acknowledged the arbitration agreement as binding to itself, in a dispute that arose in relation to this legal relationship, it subsequently could make no reference to the inapplicability of the arbitral clause – not even against a party that had not signed the arbitration agreement.[34] A similar decision was delivered in a dispute between Illinois beverage traders: only the wholesale trade agreement included an arbitral clause; however, in the lawsuit initiated

Czech (& Central European) Yearbook of Arbitration

---

[32] Friedrich Kessler & Edith Fine, *Culpa in contrahendo, bargaining in good faith, and freedom of contract: A comparative study*, 77 HARVARD LAW REVIEW 447 (1963-1964).

[33] William W. Park, *supra* note 6, at 13.

[34] *Ibid.*, at 14.

by the subcontractor of the wholesale trader directly against the manufacturer signing the wholesale trade agreement the ordinary court remitted the case to the arbitration court with reference to the fact that the manufacturer undertook to submit itself to arbitration in respect of all disputes related to this transaction (and simultaneously waived its right to enforce claims before an ordinary court).[35]

6.18. On the basis of the above-mentioned decisions it may be established that persons signing an arbitration agreement may not refer to the inapplicability of such arbitration agreement within the scope of the cases affected thereby, even against persons that did not sign the arbitration agreement. This consideration is based on the fact that by signing the arbitration agreement the parties assume an obligation to submit their specific dispute to arbitration. Therefore, in the cases falling within the objective scope of the arbitration agreement the parties to the agreement may not claim on sound foundation that the arbitration court should not proceed in a particular case.

6.19. The application of estoppel in the above-described manner seems justified in cases where the other (litigious) party, which did not conclude an arbitration agreement, *wishes to settle the dispute by arbitration* (if, as plaintiff, it sues the signatory before an arbitration court, or if, as defendant, it submits a jurisdictional objection to an ordinary court, claiming that the plaintiff stipulated the jurisdiction of the arbitration court in respect of the relevant dispute). However, the situation is more complex if the party, not a signatory to the arbitration agreement, *does not wish* to participate in the proceeding before the arbitration court and brings an action before an ordinary court, or submits a jurisdictional objection to the arbitration court.

6.20. The above issue, in combination with the institution of the consignation of lawsuits, has special significance in respect of the enforcement of claims related to transportation and freight forwarding contracts. The transportation contract between the forwarding agent and the carrier frequently includes an arbitration clause. However, whether such clause may also affect the principal of the forwarding agent, if the principal wishes to directly enforce its claims following from the transportation contract, is questionable:[36] Is it possible for the principal to bring an action against the carrier before an arbitration court? Or, is it possible for the carrier to submit a jurisdictional objection in the proceeding before an ordinary court? Answering the

---

[35] *Ibid.*

[36] Under Hungarian law Section 2 Article 517 of the Civil Code provides such right to the principal.

first question is probably easier; in such cases, by having recourse to the institution of estoppel, in the arbitration proceeding the carrier can be prohibited from claiming *vis-à-vis* the principal (as third party) the inapplicability of the arbitral clause, since it is obvious that:

- by signing the arbitration agreement included in the transportation contract concluded with the forwarding agent the carrier agreed that possible claims arising from the transportation relationship would not be enforced before an ordinary court;

And,

- the principal, although it did not conclude an arbitration agreement, wishes to settle the dispute by arbitration.

6.21. However, let us examine what the situation would be, if the principal initiates a lawsuit against the carrier before an ordinary court. Could the carrier's jurisdictional objection be considered well-founded in a lawsuit initiated by a person with whom the carrier concluded no arbitration agreement? In such cases the institution of estoppel cannot be applied. In this case, the most probable basis for the solution giving preference to arbitration could be the approach prevailing in the case of the previously referenced legal succession in substantive law: in fact, the principal wishes to enforce its rights following from the contract which stipulated the arbitration proceeding for the very purpose of enforcing such rights. The above reasoning is even more convincing in the case of the so-called atypical forwarding, when the forwarding agent concludes the contract with the carrier including the arbitral clause not on its own, but on behalf of its principal. Therefore, in the case of atypical forwarding, it would not be appropriate, if in the course of the proceedings initiated by the forwarding agent before the arbitration court the carrier could submit a well-founded jurisdictional objection. Nor would it be appropriate if the forwarding agent could bring an action against the carrier before an ordinary court. In these cases the freight forwarder acts as the litigation agent who is in fact enforcing the claim of one of the parties to the arbitration agreement against the other party who is also a signatory to such agreement. In our view, for this very reason, the contract on the consignation of the lawsuit is to be interpreted as including that the litigation consignatory acknowledges the arbitration agreement between its principal and the third party as binding to itself. On the other hand, the litigious party in opposition to the litigation consignatory is prevented from contesting the arbitral clause by the institution of *estoppel*.

III. Risks to International Arbitration as a Result of the Dilution of the Relative Structure of Arbitration Agreements: Questions on the Recognition and Enforcement of Foreign Arbitral Awards

6.22.   It is a frequent occurrence that a judgment delivered in a particular state is to be enforced in another state, and that the losing party domiciled in the latter state uses its best endeavors in order to prevent the recognition and the enforcement of the judgment. In this case the issue of the extension of the scope of the arbitration agreement may repeatedly arise, however, no longer as a preliminary jurisdictional issue, but as the possible reason for the *rejection of recognition and enforcement*.[37]

6.23.   With respect to the extension of the scope of arbitration agreements to third parties, the following provisions of the New York Convention on the Recognition and Enforcement of Foreign Arbitral Awards have primary significance:

a)   pursuant to Section 1(b) of Article IV, the party applying for recognition and enforcement shall, at the time of the application, *supply* the original agreement referred to in Article II or a duly certified copy thereof. According to Section 1 of Article II, an arbitration agreement is *an agreement in writing* under which the parties undertake to submit to arbitration all or any differences which have arisen or which may arise between them in respect of a defined legal relationship, whether contractual or not, concerning a subject matter capable of settlement by arbitration. Pursuant to Section 2 of Article II, the term "agreement in writing" shall include an arbitral clause in a contract or an arbitration agreement, signed by the parties or contained in an exchange of letters or telegrams.

b)   Section 1(a) of Article V stipulates that recognition and enforcement of the award may be refused, at the request of the party against whom it is invoked, only if that party furnishes proof that the said agreement is *not valid* under the law to which the parties have subjected it or, failing any indication thereon, under the law of the country where the award was made (lex loci arbitri).

c)   according to Section 2(b) of Article V, recognition and enforcement of an arbitral award may also be refused, if the

---

37   CAROLE MURRAY & DAVID HOLLOWAY & DAREN TIMSON-HUNT, *supra* note 1, at 590-591.

competent authority in the country where recognition and enforcement is sought finds that the recognition or enforcement of the award *would be contrary to the public policy* of that country.

According to the abovementioned, the lack, or the invalidity of an arbitration agreement, or where the recognition or enforcement of the award would be contrary to the public policy of the country where recognition and enforcement is sought, may result in the refusal of the recognition and enforcement of the award.

6.24.   In light of the foregoing, the possible risks involved in the extension of the scope of the arbitration agreement to third parties may be easily understood. If the arbitration forum established its jurisdiction in a dispute despite the fact that one of the parties to such dispute concluded no arbitration agreement within the meaning of Article II of the Convention, this may readily result in the refusal of the recognition or enforcement of its award. It may also prevent the enforceability of the award, if the agreement concluded between the parties is to be deemed invalid under the law to which the parties have subjected it or, failing any indication thereon, under the law of the country where the award was made (*lex loci arbitri*). However, upon assessing invalidity, we may not disregard the consideration that in a particular case the law governing in respect of the formal and material validity of the agreement – especially in lack of the stipulation of governing law – may be diverse. Special rules applicable to arbitral clauses typically specify only formal requirements, thus the material validity of agreements (for example the issue of error of intention), or their existence are to be assessed on the basis of the general contractual provisions of the otherwise applicable law.[38] Therefore, it is of great importance whether the agreement is deemed non-existent, or invalid due to material or formal reasons, although all of the above mentioned elements prevent recognition and enforcement.

6.25.   However, as drawing a distinction is sometimes extremely difficult, it is not surprising that countries where the award is to be recognized and enforced frequently strive to avoid, rather than solve this issue. We may consider the fact that the concept of the protection of public policy gained remarkable strength in relation to the refusal of the recognition and enforcement of arbitral awards, as a symptom of the above-described practice.[39] The conclusion that reference to the fact that an

---

[38]   Stavros Brekoulakis, *supra* note 23, at 359.

[39]   The uncertainty characteristic of public policy can be observed both in the protection of domestic and international public policy. In more detail see: László Kecskés & Zoltán Nemessányi, *Magyar közrend – nemzetközi közrend – közösségi közrend (Hungarian public policy - International public policy – Community public policy)*, 3 EURÓPAI JOG 21-34 (2007).

award is contrary to public policy may easily become the means of overshadowing contract law issues is well exemplified by the *Oleaginosa Moreno* case, in which the Brazilian court refused to recognize the award by a foreign arbitration court with reference to Brazilian public policy, upon the following reasoning: the recognition of the award of the arbitral tribunal presupposes the existence of the jurisdiction of such arbitral tribunal, while the establishment of the jurisdiction is subject to the existence of the arbitration agreement. However, the court judged that in the initial case there was no satisfactory evidence to prove the establishment of such arbitration agreement, since the parties concluded only an oral agreement.[40] It is obvious that the above reasoning generously mingles the issue of the existence and the issue of the validity of arbitration agreements, with the tacit argument that the conflict with public policy is suitable for covering both of these issues, since both the lack of an arbitration agreement and its invalidity will result in the lack of the jurisdiction of the arbitration court. As Park notes, it is not surprising at all for any "civilized" legal system, if it does not enforce an arbitral award without examining whether the losing party indeed submitted itself to the jurisdiction of the arbitration court. It is even less surprising that each person concerned wishes to answer the above question on the basis of its own law.[41] Thus, conflict with public policy may seem to be the lowest common denominator among the reasons for the refusal of the recognition and enforcement of arbitral awards, and is considered by some as a certain kind of general clause for the refusal of the recognition and enforcement of arbitral awards.[42] Nevertheless, this approach may pose significant risks. The overstressing of the concept of public policy may easily result in the degradation of the private autonomy of the parties and consequently in a decrease in the efficiency of international arbitration.

6.26. A dispute arising from a commercial agency contract and submitted to the Munich Court of Appeal (OLG München) demonstrated a spectacular conflict between the excessive protection of public policy and international arbitration based on freedom of contract.[43] The defendant was a company incorporated in San Jose (California), which as principal concluded a commercial agency contract with the plaintiff incorporated in Manching, Germany. According to the contract,

---

[40] Flavio Pereira Lima & Daniel Calhman de Miranda, *supra* note 18, at 14.

[41] William W. Park, *supra* note 6, at 24.

[42] In respect of Hungarian legal practice Katalin Murányi reports a similar approach. See: KATALIN MURÁNYI, *supra* note 29, at 60, 71.

[43] See order No. U. 1781/06 of the OLG München delivered on May 17, 2006.

disputes arising therefrom were to be settled in Santa Clara, California, on the basis of the rules of the American Arbitration Association and the provisions of California law.[44] Upon the termination of the contract by the defendant, the agent filed a claim in Germany for the payment of the so-called compensation due thereto under Section 89b of the German Commercial Code (HGB). The court of first instance established its lack of jurisdiction and rejected the claim. However, OLG München proceeding pursuant to the appeal lodged by the plaintiff set forth the following argument: Section 89b of the Commercial Code (HGB), constituting the legal ground for the claim, is intended to transpose into German law Articles 17 and 18 of Council Directive 86/653/EEC on the coordination of the laws of the member states relating to self-employed commercial agents, and the direct effect and cogent nature of these Articles had already been declared by the European Court of Justice.[45] According to the position of the court, the provisions of Community law requiring absolute enforcement may not be evaded either by a jurisdictional or an arbitration agreement. Nevertheless, if there is a potential risk that the arbitration forum stipulated by the parties and located in a state other than a member state fails to apply the cogent provision of EU law, this may result in the undermining of the effect of EU law. On the basis of the foregoing, the appellate court concluded that an arbitration agreement which stipulates an arbitration forum located in a state other than a member state, which *in all probability* will fail to apply the cogent provisions of EU law – or any other law of corresponding content – may not be taken into consideration.[46]

6.27.   The judgment delivered by OLG München was strongly criticized, primarily because the decision clearly moved away from the previous, less severe public policy practice of the German Supreme Court,[47] and also because it pointed towards the restriction of private autonomy and

---

[44]   The facts of the case are described in detail in: Giesela Rühl, *Extending Ingmar to Jurisdiction and Arbitration Clauses: The End of Party Autonomy in Contracts with Commercial Agents?* 15 (6) EUROPEAN REVIEW OF PRIVATE LAW 893 (2007).

[45]   See ECJ Judgment of 9 November 2000, No. C-381/98, *Ingmar GB Ltd.* v. *Eaton Leonard Technologies Inc.* [2000] ECR – I 9305.

[46]   Giesela Rühl, *supra* note 44, at 894.

[47]   The practice of the BGH up till now considered jurisdictional and arbitration agreements invalid only if such agreements prevented the application of a provision required to have absolute prevalence, and if as a result of such prevention the order of the prescribed forum was contrary to German public policy. Thus, the BGH does not consider it as sufficient reason, if a provision which is to prevail absolutely is disregarded, but it also requires that the order delivered in the above manner be contrary to public policy. See: *Ibid.*, at 896.

excessive paternalism.[48] Such excessive protection of public policy can lead to the consequence that the extension of the scope of arbitration agreements to third parties may be prevented, even if, on the basis of the general rules of contract law and the transactional conduct and practice of the parties, such extension would otherwise be considered justified.

6.28. In light of the foregoing it is obvious that the extension of arbitration agreements to third parties may pose serious risks as regards the recognition and enforcement of foreign arbitral awards. If the proceeding arbitration panel of the country where recognition and enforcement is sought too liberally interprets the issue of whether to extend the arbitration agreement to a third party, the recognition and enforcement of the arbitral award could be refused on the basis of all circumstances of the case, either with reference to the lack of an arbitration agreement, or its invalidity, or even for public policy reasons. As regards this latter reason, with a view also to the possible consequences of an exaggerated concern for public policy, it must be emphatically noted that conflict with public policy should be consistently considered a specific reason for refusal and not as an "ultimate reason for all other reasons." As we have seen, the overstressing of the concept of public policy may lead to a result that is contrary to the objective of the extension of arbitration agreements: while the extension of arbitration agreements to third parties, as a means of settling jurisdictional (preliminary) questions, directly enhances the efficiency of arbitration, it may easily backfire, due to public policy concerns, as regards recognition and enforcement.[49]

IV. UNCITRAL – Responses to Practical Challenges

6.29. The issues arising in relation to the determination of governing law, recognition and enforcement of awards primarily originate from the diverse evaluation of the formal validity requirements set for arbitration agreements. Diverse evaluation may stem from the regulatory grounds,[50] while in other cases it follows from the intuition of the person applying the law. Naturally, the first consideration

---

[48]   *Ibid.*, at 902-903.

[49]   CAROLE MURRAY, DAVID HOLLOWAY & DAREN TIMSON-HUNT, *supra* note 1, at 592.

[50]   Due to the diversity of national laws, the formal requirements set for arbitration agreements are not uniform: the concept of "written form" may be determined differently by the various legal systems (compare with footnote 15), moreover, there are legal systems that do not at all require a written form (for example, New-Zealand law). See: Éva Horváth, *Mi lesz veled New York-i Konvenció? (What Will Become of the New York Convention?)*, 7 MAGYAR JOG 400 (2010).

influences the latter, and ultimately, the (arbitrator's) judge's attitude towards the extension of the arbitration agreement to a third party will be jointly determined by these two considerations. It is obvious that the sharp edge of [the need for] practicality is best blunted, if the difference between the various laws, at least with respect to formal requirements, can be successfully minimized. By doing so, one may avoid potential disregard of either the more relaxed formal requirements of the chosen law, or of the determination of jurisdiction predicated upon an arbitration agreement extended to a third party with a view to the *lex loci arbitri*. Either could be disregarded because of the more severe rules of the state where enforcement is sought, which could in turn undermine the enforceability of the award. In recognition of the above-described need, in 2006 UNCITRAL decided to amend the Model Law on International Commercial Arbitration,[51] and to make recommendations in respect of Articles II and VII of the New York Convention.[52]

6.30. The 2006 amendment of the Model Law specifies two options for the determination of arbitration agreements. According to the first option, the arbitration agreement shall be in writing. However, the requirement of written form is to be interpreted more broadly than it had been before.[53] The second option moves even further, in that it stipulates that the arbitration agreement is an agreement by the parties to submit to arbitration all or certain disputes which have arisen or which may arise between them in respect of a defined legal relationship, whether contractual or not. It can be seen that the above provision does not set any formal requirements for arbitration agreements.

6.31. Although more moderately than Option II of Article 7 of the Model Law, the Recommendation regarding the interpretation of Articles II (2) and VII (1) of the New York Convention is also aimed at the

---

[51] UNCITRAL Model Law on International Commercial Arbitration 1985, with amendments as adopted in 2006.

[52] Recommendation regarding the interpretation of article II (2), and article VII (1), of the Convention on the Recognition and Enforcement of Foreign Arbitral Awards (New York, 1958) - adopted by UNCITRAL on 7 July 2006.

[53] Option I. Art. 7 (3): "An arbitration agreement is in writing if its content is recorded in any form, whether or not the arbitration agreement or contract has been concluded orally, by conduct, or by other means." Option I. Art. 7 (4): "The requirement that an arbitration agreement be in writing is met by an electronic communication if the information contained therein is accessible so as to be useable for subsequent reference; "electronic communication" means any communication that the parties make by means of data messages; "data messages" means information generated, sent, received or stored by electronic, magnetic, optical or similar means, including, but not limited to, electronic data interchange (EDI), electronic mail, telegram, telex or telecopy."

relaxing of formal requirements. According to Article II (2) of the Convention, the term "agreement in writing" shall include an arbitral clause in a contract, or an arbitration agreement signed by the parties, or contained in an exchange of letters or telegrams. According to the Recommendation, "the circumstances described in Article II (2) shall be applied recognizing that they are not exhaustive."[54] Namely: Article II (2) may not be considered exhaustive, which means that awards based on agreements that do not comply with any of the above terms may also be recognized and enforced.

6.32. According to Article VII (1), the provisions of the present Convention shall not affect the validity of multilateral or bilateral agreements concerning the recognition and enforcement of arbitral awards entered into by the Contracting States, nor deprive any interested party of any right he may have to avail himself of an arbitral award in the manner and to the extent allowed by the law or the treaties of the country *where such award is sought to be relied upon.* However, the Recommendation is intended to extend the provisions under Article VII (1) – which, according to its wording, applies only to arbitral *awards* – also to arbitration *agreements.*[55] According to the Recommendation, the above provision of the Convention should be interpreted and applied to allow any interested party to avail itself of rights it may have, under the law or treaties of the country where an arbitration agreement is sought to be relied upon, to seek recognition of the validity of such an arbitration agreement.[56]

6.33. It can be observed that both the amendment of the Model Law and the Recommendation issued for the purpose of the interpretation of the Convention are aimed at the relaxing of formal requirements set for arbitration agreements. The more flexible approach to the requirement of the written form or the omission of such formal requirement clearly encourages the practice of the expansive interpretation of the personal scope of arbitration agreements. If a written form is no longer considered a requirement for the validity of arbitration agreements, the techniques applied so far only as a means of extension may gain more

---

[54] "Recommends that Article II, Paragraph 2, of the Convention on the Recognition and Enforcement of Foreign Arbitral Awards, done in New York, 10 June, 1958, be applied recognizing that the circumstances described therein are not exhaustive."

[55] Éva Horváth, *supra* note 50, at 400.

[56] "Recommends also that Article VII, Paragraph 1, of the Convention on the Recognition and Enforcement of Foreign Arbitral Awards, done in New York, 10 June, 1958, should be applied to allow any interested party to avail itself of rights it may have, under the law or treaties of the country where an arbitration agreement is sought to be relied upon, to seek recognition of the validity of such an arbitration agreement."

relevance in respect of the interpretation of arbitration agreements. However, in this case the relaxing of the above-described, somewhat rigid public policy approach would be even more important, as the relaxing of formal requirements would not be of much use, if the validity of the verbal agreement is recognized. However, such enforcement in foreign countries of the award of the arbitration court whose jurisdiction follows from such agreement continues to be impeded due to public policy reasons.

V. Conclusion

6.34. First and foremost, it needs to be emphasized that the relaxing of the formal requirements regarding arbitration agreements *is not a simple technical issue,* but is one of the concomitant manifestations of the *dilution of the relative structure of agreements.* In respect of arbitration agreements, the process of structural dilution results in the extension of the scope of the agreement and thereby the expansion of the jurisdiction of the arbitration court. The foregoing circumstances indicate a shift toward the involvement of third parties into the arbitral procedure.

6.35. By application of the techniques developed in international arbitration (contractual, corporate law and procedural law), there are two approaches available for the implementation of such extensions which we may refer to as being "subjective" and "objective" in scope. With the first *subjective* approach there is the plain case of the involvement of a third party in the agreement, while in the other *objective* approach the third party's involvement is not indispensable, in that although only the parties to the agreement are involved in the procedure, the procedure itself extends in part to issues that were not submitted to arbitration. Such extensive interpretation of the arbitration clause is typically justified by the argument that the consensus manifesting itself in the arbitration clause is also a certain kind of *abstract consent* to the conducting of the arbitration procedure.[57] This otherwise frequently criticized[58] practice is sometimes also referred to as *separation within the arbitration agreement,* since, instead of the separation of the arbitration clause from the (main) contract, this practice concerns the separation within the arbitration agreement of the abstract "intention aimed at arbitration" from other elements of the arbitral clause.[59]

---

[57] Stavros Brekoulakis, *supra* note 23, at 362.
[58] On criticism see in more detail: *Ibid.,* at 360.
[59] Tibor Várady, *supra* note 14, at 61.

6.36. However, as shown by these examples, in the course of the extension of the scope of arbitration agreements by way of the dilution of their relative structure serious *difficulties* may arise due to aspects of both *contract* and *procedural law.*

Contract law uncertainty is primarily indicated by the fact that the issues concerning the existence, material and formal validity of the arbitration agreement are frequently intermingled. Unfortunately, often the problems related to the formal validity and unity of intention (the consensus) are jointly examined, and the issue of consensus is reduced to the simple issue of formal validity. A frequent consequence of this approach is that standard practice stubbornly adheres to the existence and material validity of agreements in compliance with formal requirements.[60] As we have already noted in relation to public policy jurisdiction, this approach needs to be changed: a more sophisticated approach to issues of formal validity and the problem of the unity of intention would be highly desirable. In this respect, however, the latest UNCITRAL developments which point in the direction of a removal of constraints of form give reason for optimism.

6.37. As regards procedural issues: in the opinion of many, over-extension of the scope of arbitration agreements has resulted in the frequent and unjustified preference of such clauses over jurisdiction agreements.[61] The judgment delivered in the *Paul Smith v. H & S International Holding* case[62] is an example of such obvious partiality. In this case the contract concluded between the parties included both arbitration and jurisdiction agreements: on the one hand, the contract stipulated that disputes were to be settled by the ICC Arbitration Court, while on the other hand it specified the exclusive jurisdiction of English courts. On this basis the English court considered that the parties agreed on arbitration, and the reference to exclusive English jurisdiction was in fact a reference to the *lex arbitri,* namely, the specification of the governing law of the arbitration proceeding. Thus, from the contesting clauses the court gave preference to the arbitral clause, and considered the jurisdiction agreement as a mere choice of law.[63]

6.38. However, the *"pro-arbitration" trend* that has prevailed in the last two decades may bring unpleasant surprises, primarily for the relevant parties, not only in respect of the general tendencies, but also at the

---

[60] Stavros Brekoulakis, *supra* note 23, at 357-358.

[61] *Ibid.,* at 341.

[62] For the judgment see: *Paul Smith Ltd.* v. *H & S International Holding Inc.,* 2 LLOYD'S REPORT 27 (1991).

[63] Stavros Brekoulakis, *supra* note 23, at 349.

level of specific disputes.[64] On the one hand, the *increase in the protection of public policy,*[65] and on the other – through the mediation of EU law – the *excessive severity of consumer protection*[66] may be observed as possible reactions to the excessive extension of the scope of arbitration agreements.

6.39. Moreover, one must also keep in mind that the unfounded extension of the scope of arbitration agreements is ultimately unfavorable to arbitration itself. In addition to the fact that such unfounded extensions may easily undermine confidence in private autonomy, it may also cut arbitration proceedings free from the parties' intention, which sooner or later would result in the loss of the consensual nature of arbitration, as an alternative method for the settlement of disputes. Nevertheless, it is to be emphasized that it does not follow from the foregoing that the extension of the scope of the arbitration agreement to a third party is in itself contrary to the principles of contract law based on private autonomy. In fact, and as we have described, the involvement of third parties in proceedings frequently corresponds to the intention of the parties, to their business relationship, and contractual practice.

6.40. Essentially, the emergence of the principle of *in dubio pro arbitratio* ("when in doubt, for arbitration") is to be ensured by relying on and not in defiance of private autonomy. If arbitration were separated from the consensus based on private autonomy, we would strike at the very root of the institution, without which arbitration would be easily blown away.

| | |

---

[64]   *Ibid.*, at 363.

[65]   This is the reason why René David calls attention to the fact that the relaxing of the validity requirements for arbitration agreements can be justified only to a certain extent, as excessive relaxing may ultimately endanger the legitimacy of arbitration, and result in the more severe state (court) revision of arbitral awards. See: RENÉ DAVID, ARBITRATION IN INTERNATIONAL TRADE, Deventer / Netherlands: Kluwer Law and Taxation Publishers 197 (1985).

[66]   According to several experts, this manifestation is connected with the fact that *commercial* arbitration has recently become a means of alternative dispute resolution also in consumer disputes (namely, in *non-commercial* cases). Accordingly, excessive consumer protection is in fact a possible means of defense against arbitration originally stipulated for commercial disputes. See: Dagmar Coester – Waltjen, *Einige Überlegungen zu Schiedsgerichtsvereinbarungen und ihrer Wirksamkeit, in* CONVERGENCE AND DIVERGENCE IN PRIVATE INTERNATIONAL LAW. LIBER AMICORUM KURT SIEHR, Schultess: Eleven International Publishing 615 (2010).

Summaries

FRA   [*Modifier certains aspects des conventions d'arbitrage non signées*]

Même si l'approche établie prône l'interprétation stricte des conventions d'arbitrage, les procédures menées devant les tribunaux arbitraux impliquent de plus en plus des personnes qui n'ont pas conclu une convention d'arbitrage (« non signataires joints » ou « extension de la clause d'arbitrage »). Cependant, l'extension de compétence induite par la participation de tierces parties n'est pas sans risques. Ceci s'observe tant au début qu'à la conclusion de la procédure arbitrale. Le tribunal arbitral, qui décide de sa propre compétence sur la base de la doctrine Kompetenz – Kompetenz, peut se trouver face à d'importants dilemmes de droit contractuel simplement en répondant aux questions préliminaires de compétence, et notamment en déterminant si la convention d'arbitrage, sur laquelle se fonde la compétence du tribunal, existe ou non, et le cas échéant, si celle-ci est bien valide. Si le tribunal arbitral est trop libéral lorsqu'il traite l'extension de la clause d'arbitrage vis-à-vis de tierces parties, cela peut avoir des conséquences néfastes en matière de reconnaissance et d'exécution de la décision du tribunal. Ainsi, eu égard à l'application arbitrale initiale de la loi, cette question doit être considérée comme un problème de compétence, tandis que du point de vue de la conclusion de l'application de la sentence arbitrale, il faut l'envisager comme un aspect relevant de l'applicabilité de la sentence arbitrale.

CZE   [*Měnící se problematika nepodepsaných rozhodčích smluv*]
Přestože převažujícím trendem je zákaz extenzivního výkladu rozhodčích smluv, je faktem, že účastníky stále většího počtu řízení před rozhodčími soudy jsou osoby, které rozhodčí smlouvu neuzavřely ("přibírání osob, které nejsou signatáři" nebo "rozšiřování rozhodčí doložky"). Rozšiřování pravomoci (příslušnosti) cestou přibírání třetích osob do řízení s sebou ovšem nese určitá rizika. To lze pozorovat jak na začátku, tak na konci procesu aplikace práva v rozhodčím řízení. Rozhodčí soud, který rozhoduje o své vlastní pravomoci (příslušnosti) na základě doktríny Kompetenz-Kompetenz, může čelit zásadním smluvněprávním dilematům již při řešení předběžných otázek týkajících se pravomoci (příslušnosti): tedy zda rozhodčí smlouva – na níž je pravomoc soudu založena – existuje, a pokud taková smlouva skutečně existuje, zda je platná. Pokud bude rozhodčí soud zacházet s rozšiřováním rozsahu rozhodčí doložky na třetí osoby příliš liberálně, mohlo by to mít nepříznivé následky v procesu uznávání a výkonu nálezu. Proto pokud jde o aplikaci práva na počátku rozhodčího řízení, je nutné na tento problém pohlížet jako na otázku pravomoci

(příslušnosti), zatímco pokud jde o závěrečnou fázi aplikace rozhodčího práva, je nutné považovat tento problém za otázku vykonatelnosti rozhodčího nálezu.

|||

POL [*Zmiany aspektów niepodpisanych umów arbitrażowych*]
Niniejsza praca poświęcona jest zmieniającej się ocenie formalnych wymogów w zakresie zapisów na sąd polubowny. Po pierwsze należy zauważyć, że rozluźnienie wymogów formalnych jest jedną z konsekwencji rozmywania się względnej struktury zapisów. Stosowane techniki uogólniania wymogów często umożliwiają rozszerzanie właściwości trybunału arbitrażowego. Zaś autonomia stron i rozszerzona właściwość trybunału często prowadzą do poważnych sporów.

DEU [*Nicht unterzeichnete Schiedsvereinbarungen unter sich wandelnden Vorzeichen*]
Die vorliegende Studie setzt sich mit der im Wandel begriffenen Beurteilung der formalen Voraussetzungen für den gültigen Abschluss von Schiedsvereinbarungen auseinander. Zunächst einmal ist festzustellen, dass die Aufweichung der formalen Anforderungen eine direkte Folge der Verwässerung relativer Vertragsstrukturen ist. Verwässerungsstrategien machen es oft möglich, die Entscheidungskompetenzen des Schiedstribunals auszuweiten. Allerdings begegnen wir oft ernsthaften Konflikten im Spannungsfeld zwischen Parteiautonomie und Ausweitung der schiedsgerichtlichen Zuständigkeit.

RUS [*Изменчивые аспекты неподписанных арбитражных соглашений*]
В этой статье затрагиваются различные подходы к оценке формальных требований к арбитражным соглашениям. В первую очередь, нужно отметить, что смягчение формальных требований является одним из последствий ослабления соответствующей структуры соглашений. Способы ослабления часто дают возможность расширить юрисдикцию арбитражного суда. Как бы то ни было, автономность сторон и расширение юрисдикции часто приводят к серьезным конфликтам.

ESP [*Aspectos cambiantes de los acuerdos de arbitraje no firmados*]

Este estudio trata sobre la evaluación cambiante de los requisitos formales relativos a los acuerdos de arbitraje. En primer lugar, es preciso constatar que la relajación de los requisitos formales es una de las consecuencias de la dilución de la estructura relativa de acuerdos. Las técnicas de dilución a menudo posibilitan la extensión de la jurisdicción del tribunal de arbitraje. En cualquier caso, la autonomía de las partes y el ámbito jurisdiccional nos demuestran con frecuencia graves conflictos.

Crenguta Leaua

The Applicability of Party Autonomy in the Appointment of Arbitrators

Key words:
party autonomy
| appointment of
arbitrators |appointing
authority | arbitration
institution | state courts |
human rights | fair trial

Abstract | *The concept of party autonomy in arbitration is frequently referred to in the context of the choice of the substantive law or of the applicable rules. While the relationship between parties and arbitrators has been extensively explored, the question of the implications of party autonomy for the process of arbitrator appointments has received less attention. This article submits that the relationship between party autonomy and tribunal appointment also deserves exploration, whether the appointment is undertaken by the parties, by the co-arbitrators, or by various other persons or institutions that act as appointing authorities, since the constitution of the arbitral tribunal reveals the potential vulnerabilities of arbitral awards in the annulment or enforcement process before various state courts. The article also addresses the limits of party autonomy in the appointment of arbitrators and the role of these limits in ensuring that the requisite conditions for fair trial and due process in arbitral proceedings have been met.*

Crenguta Leaua Dr.
iur.; university lecturer
in Business Law at the
University of
Economics in
Bucharest and visiting
lecturer in
International
Commercial
Arbitration at "Petru
Maior" University in
Tg, Mures, Romania;
vice-president of the
Court of International
Commercial
Arbitration attached to
the Chamber of
Commerce and
Industry of Romania;
member of the ICC
Commission on
Arbitration as a
representative of the
Romanian national ICC
Committee; managing
partner of "Leaua &
Asociatii" law firm in
Bucharest, Romania.
e-mail:
crenguta.leaua@
leaua.ro

| | |

I. General Consideration of the Principle of Party Autonomy in Arbitration

7.01. The principle of party autonomy refers to the role of the autonomous will of the parties in replacing the exercise of the state authority. Party autonomy, as developed by academic writers, is expressed both in the parties' choice of substantive law applicable to the dispute and of the procedures shaping the rules to be applied in the arbitration.

7.02. With regard to the choice of substantive law the principle refers to the rule, grounded in a number of international conventions, that the arbitral tribunal shall apply the law designated by the parties as applicable to the substance of the dispute. See for e.g., the Geneva Convention (1961),[1] the Rome Convention (1980)[2] and the UNCITRAL Model Law. Many of the arbitration rules of the arbitral institutions also reflect these provisions. Limitations to the parties' freedom of choice usually stem from lack of bona fide authenticity, illegality, or offence against public policy.[3]

7.03. As to the procedural rules, party autonomy doctrine maintains the parties' right to choose the rules of procedure that are to be applied in the arbitral proceedings. This right is also supported by international conventions, such as the New York Convention (1958)[4] which provides, in art. V (1) d, that an award may be refused recognition *"if the procedure was not in accordance with the agreement of the parties, or, failing such agreement, was not in accordance with the law of the country where the arbitration took place,"* or the UNCITRAL Model Law which states in art. 19, that *"Subject to the provisions of this Law, the parties are free to agree on the procedure to be followed by the arbitral tribunal in the conduct of the proceedings,"* and is further supported by a number of the rules of various arbitral institutions.[5]

7.04. The appointment of arbitrators is a matter of procedure, but is not expressly referred to in either of the abovementioned international conventions, which instead refer to the procedure to be applied by the

---

[1] European Convention on International Commercial Arbitration, Geneva, 1961.

[2] The Rome Convention on the Law Applicable to Contractual Obligations, 1980. For a comprehensive analysis of the principle of the party autonomy in arbitration, see NATALYA SHELKOPLYAS, THE APPLICATION OF EC LAW IN ARBITRATION PROCEEDINGS, The Hague: Europa Law Publishing 264 et seq. (2003).

[3] ALAN REDFERN & MARTIN HUNTER, LAW AND PRACTICE OF INTERNATIONAL COMMERCIAL ARBITRATION, London: Sweet & Maxwell 97-98 (2nd ed. 1999).

[4] Convention on the Recognition and Enforcement of Foreign Arbitral Awards, New York, 1058.

[5] See the comments of ERIK SCHAFER, HERMAN VERBIST CHRISTOPH IMHOOS, ICC ARBITRATION IN PRACTICE, The Hague: Kluwer Law International 75 (2005).

arbitral tribunal once constituted. However, party autonomy is reflected (and thus acknowledged) in this phase of the arbitration proceedings as well. In fact, scholars refer to party autonomy as *"the principal controller of the appointment process."*[6]

7.05. In arbitral proceedings arbitrators are appointed by the person or institutions so designated in the rules and in the legal provisions applicable to the arbitral proceedings. Apart from appointment by the parties, the arbitrators may be appointed by the other arbitrators, by the arbitral institutions, by other persons who the parties haven chosen to perform the role of appointing authority or by the local courts of law.

7.06. The parties' will plays a definite role in each of these methods and must be observed both in the drafting of the arbitral agreement and in the various procedural options existing at the time of the initiation of the arbitration. The parties may indicate the number of arbitrators or their appointment.

II. Party Autonomy concerning the Number of Arbitrators

7.07. Article 10 (1) f the UNCITRAL Model Law provides that *"The parties are free to determine the number of arbitrators."* This is a direct expression of party autonomy.

7.08. The number of arbitrators, in most of the cases, is defined by the parties in the arbitral agreement. The determination may be made in the arbitration agreement or by reference to a certain arbitration rule. The will of the parties on the number of arbitrators may be expressed in writing or, under certain legislation, may be inferred from the tacit acceptance and lack of any objection to the number of arbitrators. In one case, Romanian courts of law, when confronted with an annulment procedure following an arbitration case where only two arbitrators issued the arbitral award, and not three as provided both by the arbitration rules and the arbitration law, rejected the request for annulment, based on the fact that the challenging party had not objected to the number of arbitrators during the arbitration proceedings, but only upon filing the challenge.[7]

7.09. In the absence of such provisions in the arbitral agreement, in the case of institutionalised arbitration, reference to the arbitration rules of the institution may lead to the institution's participation in the decision on

---

[6] JULIAN D. M. LEW, LOUKAS A. MISTELIS AND STEFAN M. KROLL, COMPARATIVE INTERNATIONAL COMMERCIAL ARBITRATION, The Hague: Kluwer Law International 236 (2003).

[7] Decision of the Bucharest Court of Appeal no. 200 of 9 February 2007.

Czech (& Central European) Yearbook of Arbitration

the number of arbitrators. The parties' role in this decision is indirect, performed through the parties' deference to the arbitration institution and its rules. Similarly, in ad hoc arbitrations when parties agree on the application of certain rules, such rules may indicate the number of arbitrators, as well.

7.10.   Should neither the parties nor the arbitration rules specify the number of arbitrators, the applicable law at the place of arbitration has, in most of the cases, a provision that may be applied. In the absence of such a provision, the local courts may also decide on this issue, in order to unblock the arbitration.

7.11.   There are certain limitations upon the parties' freedom to choose the number of arbitrators, for e.g., under some forms of legislation, where the arbitral tribunal may be required to have an even number of arbitrators.[8] Such is the requirement in the English Arbitration Act.

III. Party Autonomy concerning the Appointment of Arbitrators

7.12.   The appointment of arbitrators may be made by the parties, or, in the absence of their agreement on this appointment, by the various appointing authorities.

III.1. Appointment Made by the Parties

7.13.   Under most laws and arbitral rules, the parties are provided with the first option of appointing the arbitrators, and only in the absence of that appointment, do the appointing authorities come into play. The most preferable situation, although very rare in practice, is for the parties to agree on all the members of the arbitral tribunal. If they should fail to agree, the alternative is for each party to appoint one of the three members of an arbitral tribunal, with the third arbitrator being appointed by another method.

7.14.   This appointment may be made by the parties either in the arbitration agreement, or at the time the arbitral proceedings are initiated, within the time frame provided by the applicable rules. Certain national arbitration laws make the validity of the arbitration agreement in ad hoc arbitration (as does the Romanian Civil Procedural Code) conditional upon the designation of the name of the arbitrators. The will of the parties is therefore reflected (i) in the appointment of the arbitrators in the arbitral agreement, when possible; (ii) in the choice of the applicable arbitration rules which allow the parties to appoint the

---

[8]   JULIAN D. M. LEW, LOUKAS A. MISTELIS AND STEFAN M. KROLL, *supra* note 6, at 231.

arbitrators and describe the conditions of such appointment; and (iii) in the very choice of the arbitrator or arbitrators to be appointed.

III.2. Appointment Made by the Other Arbitrators

7.15. In cases where the appointment is made by the other arbitrators, scholars have noted that "of the various methods of appointing a third arbitrator, this is perhaps the most satisfactory."[9] This opinion may explain the fact that the most common solution for the appointment of the presiding arbitrator in the case of arbitral tribunals constituted of three arbitrators is for the presiding arbitrator to be appointed by agreement of the two party-appointed arbitrators. This method is adopted in the Vienna International Arbitration Centre (VIAC), the Court of International Commercial Arbitration attached to the Romanian Chamber of Commerce and Industry (RCA). Under other rules this may be an option should the parties agree in this respect, as is also evident in the rules of the International Court of Arbitration–ICC Paris (ICC Rules).

7.16. The will of the parties is indirectly manifested in this method of arbitrator appointment: (i) by stipulation in the arbitral agreement of the method for the appointment of the third arbitrator by agreement of the party-appointed arbitrators or inclusion in the agreement of the applicable arbitration rules to be used for the appointment of the third arbitrator; and (ii) in certain cases, by the consultations the parties have with the party–appointed arbitrator concerning the profile or even the identity of the third arbitrator. (This consultation is considered acceptable under the international standards concerning the independence and impartiality of arbitrators.[10])

III.3. Appointment Made by the Arbitral Institutions

7.17. The arbitral institutions may perform the role of appointing authority either in institutionalised arbitration or in ad hoc arbitration.

7.18. In institutionalized arbitration, the rules of the arbitral institutions generally provide for the role of certain persons or bodies within such institutions as appointing authority. For example, such provisions may be found in the ICC Rules, where the Court acts as appointing authority, or the rules of the London Court of International Arbitration

---

[9]   ALAN REDFERN & MARTIN HUNTER, *supra* note 3, at 200.
[10] Recent doctrine also mentions this approach as one of the possibilities – Thomas H. Webster, *Party Control in International Arbitration, in* 19 (2) ARBITRATION INTERNATIONAL 130 (2003).

(LCIA), where this role is assigned to certain divisions, or of VIAC, where the Board is given this role. The American Arbitration Association (AAA) and the Arbitration and Mediation Centre of the World Intellectual Property Organization (WIPO) have similar arrangements.

7.19. In ad hoc arbitration, one option is for the parties to agree in the arbitration clause that a particular arbitral institution should act as appointing authority; the institution will provide this service. If the UNCITRAL rules are applicable and the parties failed to agree on an appointing authority, any of them may apply to the Secretary-General of the Permanent Court of Arbitration at The Hague to designate an appointing authority, which also may be an arbitral institution.

7.20. The will of the parties is indirectly manifested in this method of arbitrator appointment: (i) by their choice of the applicable arbitration rules in the arbitral agreement; and (ii) in certain cases, by the expression of their views on the proposals made by the arbitral institution for the potential arbitrators (see for example the WIPO Arbitration Rules).

III.4. Appointment Made by Other Persons or Institutions

7.21. In institutionalised or ad hoc arbitration, the parties may agree on any person they trust to act as the appointing authority, and that person may not be an arbitration institution. One such example in institutionalised arbitration is that of the president of the Chamber of Commerce and Industry of Romania, who acts as appointing authority under the rules of the RCA. In ad hoc arbitrations, the option is often similar where the president of a certain chamber of commerce and industry, or another professional association (such as the associations of traders in various geographical areas or the president of the Bar Associations) acts as appointing authority.

7.22. The will of the parties is also manifested in this method of arbitrator appointment, but is manifested indirectly through the arbitral agreement in its specification of the person or institution to perform the role of appointing authority or of the applicable arbitration rules that are to provide for this role.

III.5. Appointment Made by the Local Courts

7.23. Under a number of national arbitration laws, in the absence of any expression in the arbitral clause or in the arbitral rules of the parties' choice regarding the appointing authority, the local courts shall act as appointing authorities.

7.24.   This occurs when the only role the parties play in the process of appointing the arbitrators is by omission, namely by failing to agree on any other method of appointment. However, in certain situations, the local courts do involve the parties in the appointment process, albeit to a certain – very limited – extent, for instance, by requiring that the parties inform the court of their views on the profile of a suitable candidate.

IV. Limitations to Party Autonomy concerning the Appointment of Arbitrators

7.25.   In its general application,[11] the principle of party autonomy is subject to a number of limitations which may affect the parties' freedom to choose an arbitrator, and these may arise from the parties' own previous agreements, or from the law. These limitations apply to the parties, but also to the appointing authorities.

IV.1. Limitations Provided by the Arbitration Agreement

7.26.   When choosing the arbitrators, both parties or the institutions or persons acting as appointing authorities must observe the provisions covering the previous will of the parties that might have been expressed in the arbitration agreement. Amendment of the arbitration agreement by the parties is possible, but may be done only by the parties' mutual consent and not unilaterally, meaning those instances where the appointment of the party-appointed arbitrators (if party appointment of the arbitrator is the procedure previously agreed on) is made by will of only one of the parties.

7.27.   The arbitration agreement may stipulate that certain requirements be fulfilled by the parties' candidates for appointment (such as their possession of a certain level of experience, language skills, or professional qualifications). This was traditionally the recognized practice of the Court of International Commercial Arbitration attached to the Chamber of Commerce and Industry of Romania in an arbitration file where the parties requested that the sole arbitrator meet the criteria of being a professor of conflicts of law.[12]

---

[11]   Michael Pryles, *Limits to Party Autonomy in Arbitral Procedure, in* 24 (3) JOURNAL OF INTERNATIONAL ARBITRATION 327, 331 (2007); Irene Welser, Susanne Wurzer, *Formality in International Commercial Arbitration, in* AUSTRIAN ARBITRATION YEARBOOK, Vienna: C.H. Beck/Stampfli/Manz, 228-230 (C. Klausegger, P. Klein, F. Kremslehner, A. Petsche, N. Pikowitz, J. Power, I. Welser, G. Zeiler eds., 2008).

[12]   Arbitration Award no. 13 of 14 March 1973.

IV.2. Limitations Provided by Applicable Arbitration Rules

7.28. The choice of the applicable arbitration rules may affect the freedom of the parties or the freedom of the appointing authority to select an arbitrator.

7.29. The rules may provide a list of arbitrators which may limit their choices on the parties or the appointing authority, even if the list is rather ample and includes a wide range of professional arbitrator profiles. This is the approach of the Court of International Commercial Arbitration attached to the Chamber of Commerce and Industry of Romania, which provides a list of over 150 arbitrators, for institutionalised arbitration (for ad hoc arbitrations administrated by the Court the limitation does not exist). According to Romanian jurisprudence, where prevalence was not given to the parties' agreement on the presiding arbitrator's appointment is not to be considered ground for challenging the arbitral award, if the applicable arbitration rules provide for other methods of appointing the presiding arbitrator.[13]

7.30. The rules may provide that a certain body within the arbitral institution confirm the parties' appointment of the arbitrators. This is precisely the provision in the ICC Rules, where party-appointed arbitrators must be confirmed by the Court.

7.31. Other rules may indirectly restrict the parties' choice to appointment of only those arbitrators willing to perform this role for a rather low fee (many arbitral institutions provide for fixed or capped arbitrator fees, which, in time consuming cases, may lead to arbitrators being paid at very low hourly rates). An example is the Court of Arbitration attached to the Chambers of Commerce and Industry of Hungary or of Bulgaria.

7.32. In other cases, specification of the use of a certain language as the language of arbitration may limit the choice of arbitrators to solely those having good command of a given language, as is the example in Dubai or Poland.[14]

7.33. Last, arbitration rules may require that the chairman of the arbitral tribunal possess certain professional qualifications as seen in the DIS Rules which require that the chairman be a lawyer.

---

[13] Decision of the Bucharest Court of Appeal no. 1870 of 2 December 2003.

[14] See Thomas H. Webster, *supra* note 10, at 124.

IV.3. Limitations Provided by the Applicable Law

7.34. The applicable law may contain various relevant provisions concerning the appointment of arbitrators. Such norms, to the extent they concern public order, may place new strictures on the will of the parties expressed in the arbitration agreement, may void certain provisions of the arbitration agreement, or may otherwise affect the effectiveness of the parties' will in the process of appointing the arbitrators.

7.35. One issue of public order concerns the legal requirements for the valid appointment of a person to act as arbitrator. Generally, such requirements are limited to questions of the candidate's capacity, but in certain cases issues of citizenship may also be applicable, particularly for domestic arbitrations (this requirement is expressed in the Romanian Civil Procedural Code, and is applicable for ad hoc arbitration, where, in domestic arbitrations, arbitrators must be Romanian citizens; this requirement does not exist in international commercial arbitration).

7.36. The issue of capacity also concerns the effects of the nomination of an appointing authority. If the appointing authority is an institution, it must have the legal capacity provided by the laws of the country of incorporation, possibly also by the law applicable to the arbitration. Its capacity may be limited by the scope of its activity as defined in its bylaws. Similarily, a natural person designated by the parties as appointing authority must be endowed with the capacity required by the law to regularly act in this role in order to claim full legal capacity.

7.37. Beyond these restrictions, some laws impose still others, such as imperative provisions on the number of arbitrators,[15] as we see in the Netherlands or Egypt. Other countries' legislation requires that the chairman of the arbitral tribunal be a lawyer – as stipulated by the Chinese Arbitration Act 1994.

7.38. Another issue rising out of the general legal principle of *"res inter alios acta aliis neque nocere neque prodesse potest"* is the effectiveness of the designation of a certain appointing authority. Parties cannot impose their will upon other persons or institutions by empowering them to act as appointing authority in the absence of that person or institution's will. The nominees' consent is expressed in the form of a contract and in their acceptance of a certain fee. The procedure they are to follow must be agreed on prior to such persons entering into the roles the parties have assigned to them. This is an inherent limitation of party will. Therefore, in cases where the parties have chosen other persons or

---

[15]   See JULIAN D.M. LEW, LOUKAS A. MISTELIS AND STEFAN M. KROLL, *supra* note 6, at 225.

institutions to act as appointing authority, the effectiveness of this designation is subject to the will of those persons to act in this role. The situation is similar for arbitral institutions who have the activity of appointing authority included in the list of services they provide, when there is a slight difference in the sense that a refusal of the arbitral institution is still possible, but rather on issues of payment of the fees than out of any unwillingness to offer this service. The only genuine exception is that of the state courts, that act as appointing authority not as a direct effect of the will of the parties, but of the provisions of the law vesting them with this role, in the absence of any other agreement of the parties. The jurisprudence of the Romanian courts of law has underlined that such appointments made by the courts of law may not take place in every circumstance when a party has failed to appoint an arbitrator by a certain applicable deadline, because in cases where the parties have expressed their consent to an institutionalised arbitration, the arbitration rules of that institution provide for another appointing authority.[16] The role of the courts of law as appointing authority is subsidiary to the will of the parties.

V. Limitations of Party Autonomy and the Right to Fair Trial

7.39. Finally, among the limitations that party autonomy may be subject to as far as choosing the number of arbitrators or appointing arbitrators is concerned, by virtue of law, are the requirements of a fair trial as part of public policy. These deserve special attention.

7.40. Within the doctrine of arbitration the applicability of the European Convention on Human Rights (ECHR) to arbitral proceedings has been a constant feature of discussion in the recent years, with some authors considering that the arbitration agreement constitutes a waiver of the application of art. 6 of the ECHR,[17] based on certain jurisprudence of the European Court of Human Rights. Other scholars maintain that art. 6 of the ECHR does apply in arbitration as well,[18] while yet others have argued that only part of the principles of art. 6 of the ECHR would apply in arbitration;[19] Another group maintains that such application is

---

[16] Decision of the Bucharest Court of Appeal no. 110/R of 25 January 2010.

[17] See ALAN REDFERN & MARTIN HUNTER, *supra* note 3.

[18] See for instance Matscher, *L'arbitrage et la Convention, art. 6 (suite), in* LA CONVENTION EUROPÉENE DES DROITS DE L'HOMME. COMMENTAIRE ARTICLE PAR ARTICLE, Paris: Economica 281 et seq (L.-E. Pettiti, E. Decaux, P.-H. Imbert eds., 1995).

[19] CHRISTOPH LIEBSCHER, THE HEALTY AWARD – CHALLANGE IN INTERNATIONAL COMMERCIAL ARBITRATION, The Hague: Kluwer Law International 112 et seq. (2003).

to be included in the constitutional law and made part of public policy.[20] However, the concept of a fair trial does not rely solely on the ECHR provisions or the jurisprudence of the European Court of Human Rights. "Fair trial" is a concept to be found in most domestic laws, in various forms, and even if one considers that the ECHR does not directly apply to arbitration, the fundamental principles of fair trial and due process must still be seen to apply. Such principles would apply on the basis of the national laws or of art. VI(1)b of the New York Convention (1958).[21] A number of state courts' decisions which refer to the principle of fair trial as part of public policy applicable in arbitration proceedings as well have been analyzed in the recent doctrine.[22]

7.41. The rules of a fair trial and due process also extend to the process of the appointment of arbitrators. The appointment procedure is mentioned as being among the issues to be considered when assessing the equal treatment of the parties, for the purpose of either deciding on the annulment of an arbitral award or on the recognition and enforcement of an award under the New York Convention (1958). [23]

7.42. Scholars have stressed that: *"submitting the appointment process to party autonomy carries the danger that the stronger party can impose appointment procedures which are disadvantageous to the weaker party,"*[24] as would be the case in an arbitration agreement providing that in the absence of both parties' agreement, one party would be entitled to appoint the chairman of the arbitral tribunal. Such a clause, under certain forms of legislation, would be considered invalid.[25] In some countries a remedy for these arbitration clauses is provided, for example under section 1034 (2) of the German arbitration law or article

---

[20] See for example Sebastien Besson, *Arbitration and Human Rights, in* 24 (3) ASA BULLETIN 395 (2006), JULIAN D. M. LEW, LOUKAS A. MISTELIS AND STEFAN M. KROLL, *supra* note 6, at 95.

[21] JULIAN D. M. LEW, LOUKAS A. MISTELIS AND STEFAN M. KROLL, *supra* note 6, at 95, GEORGIOS PETROCHILOS, PROCEDURAL LAW IN INTERNATIONAL ARBITRATION, Oxford: Oxford University Press sec. 4.51 (2004).

[22] See Alexander J. Bělohlávek, *Arbitration from Perspective of Right to Legal Protection and Right to Court Proceedings (The Right to Have One's Case Dealt with by a Court): Significance of Autonomy and Scope of the Right of a Fair Trial, in* 1 CZECH (& CENTRAL) EUROPEAN YEARBOOK OF ARBITRATION: THE RELATIONSHIP BETWEEN CONSTITUTIONAL VALUES, HUMAN RIGHTS AND ARBITRATION, New York: Juris Publishing, Inc. 47 (A. J. Bělohlávek, N. Rozehnalová eds., 2011). See also Sebastien Besson, *supra* note 20, at 47 et seq.

[23] For an extended comparative law perspective, see CHRISTOPH LIEBSCHER, *supra* note 19.

[24] JULIAN D. M. LEW, LOUKAS A. MISTELIS AND STEFAN M. KROLL, *supra* note 6, at 252.

[25] German decision, Bundersgerichtshof, 19 December 1968, quoted by JULIAN D. M. LEW, LOUKAS A. MISTELIS AND STEFAN M. KROLL, *supra* note 6, at 253, where an arbitration clause provided for such an appointment was considered to be invalid.

1028 of the Netherlands Civil Code of Procedure, where the courts of law are granted with an appointing authority "if the arbitration agreement grants preponderant rights to one party with regard to the composition of the arbitration tribunal which place the other party at a disadvantage."[26] Arbitration awards rendered by a sole arbitrator appointed by a party, only, are also at risk of being successfully challenged.[27]

7.43. Other examples given as situations where the appointment process might be considered to violate the requirements of a fair trial are those when only the members of a particular organization can be appointed as arbitrators even in cases with non-members. These situations may lead to the successful challenge of the arbitral award.[28]

7.44. As far as the activity of the appointing authority is concerned, in 2007 the Romanian High Court of Cassation and Justice delivered a decision[29] refusing the enforcement in Romania of an ICC arbitral award due to the violation of the Romanian public order, which, in the findings of the High Court of Cassation and Justice, includes the ECHR provisions, due to a provision of the Romanian Constitutions providing for direct application in Romania of the international treaties Romania has ratified in the area of human rights. The violation of the due process requirement consisted in a number of procedural incidents in which parties were not treated equally, among which was the decision of the ICC to appoint a sole arbitrator, as requested by the Claimant, instead of a three-member arbitral tribunal, as had been requested by the Respondent, in spite of the value of the dispute exceeding 5 mil. USD. This composition of the arbitral tribunal was considered by the High Court of Cassation and Justice as giving undue prevalence to the Claimant's request, as long as appointing sole arbitrators in a rather small claim, which is contrary to the ICC's usual practice considering the appointing sole arbitrators in small claims, (i.e. claims below the threshold for small claims of 1,5 mil Eur[30]). While deciding in this respect, the High Court of Cassation and Justice of Romania upheld that appointing authorities should not deviate from their own practice

---

[26] JULIAN D. M. LEW, LOUKAS A. MISTELIS AND STEFAN M. KROLL, *supra* note 6, at 253.

[27] Supreme Court of Queensland, *Resort Condominium International Inc.* v. *Ray Balwell Resort Condominium Pty Ltd*, (1995) and Supreme Court of India, *Sumitomo Heavy Industries Ltd* v. *ONGN Ltd India* (1999), quoted by JULIAN D. M. LEW, LOUKAS A. MISTELIS AND STEFAN M. KROLL, *supra* note 6, at 250.

[28] See JENS PETER LACHMANN, HANDBUCH FUR DIE SCHIEDSGERICHTSPRAXIS, Köln: Otto Schmidt Verlag para. 577 (2nd ed. 2002).

[29] Decision no. 1834 of 16 May 2007.

[30] ERIK SCHAFER, HERMAN VERBIST CHRISTOPH IMHOOS, *supra* note 5, at 38.

and guidelines when deciding the composition of arbitral tribunals in the absence of good cause, as such deviation may be construed to be a violation of the due process requirements, and as showing undue favour to one of the parties in the arbitration.

VI. Conclusions

7.45. The principle of party autonomy in arbitration is frequently referred to in the context of substantive law choice or the choice of the applicable rules. However, party autonomy is also widely reflected in the appointment process of arbitral tribunals. This principle is not absolute – there are a number of limitations imposed by the applicable laws, in order to insure that the requirements of a fair trial and due process have been met. These provisions are considered part of procedural public order and may impact the validity of the arbitral award or its enforceability under the New York Convention (1958).

| | |

Summaries

FRA [*L'applicabilité de l'autonomie des parties dans la désignation des arbitres*]
Le concept d'autonomie des parties dans le cadre de l'arbitrage est fréquemment évoqué en termes de choix du droit substantiel ou des règles de fond. Alors que le rapport entre les parties et les arbitres a été exploré en profondeur, la question des implications de l'autonomie des parties dans le processus de désignation des arbitres est moins étudiée. Cet article suggère que le rapport entre autonomie des parties et désignation du tribunal mérite également d'être étudié, que ce choix soit réalisé par les parties, les co-arbitres ou d'autres personnes ou institutions agissant en qualité d'organes de désignation, étant donné que la constitution du tribunal arbitral révèle les vulnérabilités potentielles des sentences arbitrales dans les procédures d'annulation ou d'exécution devant différentes juridiction nationales. Cet article aborde également la question des limites de l'autonomie des parties dans la désignation des arbitres, et le rôle de ces limites à garantir que les conditions requises pour assurer un procès et un traitement équitables dans le cadre de l'arbitrage soient remplies.

CZE [*Aplikovatelnost zásady autonomie vůle stran při jmenování rozhodců*]

Zásada autonomie vůle stran v rozhodčím řízení je často zmiňována v souvislosti s volbou hmotného práva nebo použitelných pravidel. Zatímco vztah mezi stranami a rozhodci byl již předmětem podrobných studií, otázce dopadů aplikace zásady autonomie vůle stran na jmenování rozhodců byla věnována mnohem menší pozornost. V tomto článku je obhajována teze, že vztah mezi autonomií vůle stran a jmenováním rozhodců si rovněž zasluhuje důkladné prostudování, ať již jmenování provádí strany, ostatní rozhodci v senátu nebo různé jiné osoby či instituce, které působí jako orgány pro jmenování (appointing authorities), neboť ustavení rozhodčího senátu odhaluje potenciální slabé stránky rozhodčích nálezů při řízení o jejich zrušení nebo výkonu vedeném u různých obecných soudů. Článek se rovněž věnuje hranicím autonomie vůle stran při jmenování rozhodců a funkci těchto hranic při zajišťování toho, aby byly v rámci rozhodčího řízení splněny stanovené podmínky spravedlivého a řádného procesu.

| | |

POL [*Stosowalność autonomii stron do wyznaczania arbitrów*]

Niniejszy artykuł analizuje zastosowanie zasady autonomii stron w kontekście wyznaczania arbitrów, czy to przez strony, czy też przez innych rozjemców w składzie, lub inne osoby i instytucje posiadające uprawnienia do ich wyznaczania. Ponadto, omawia granice autonomii stron przy wyznaczaniu arbitrów oraz wpływ, jaki mają w tym zakresie wymogi dotyczące sprawiedliwego procesu i należytego postępowania w ramach arbitrażu w kontekście powoływania trybunału arbitrażowego jako jednego z elementów stanowiących potencjalnie słaby punkt orzeczenia arbitrażowego podczas późniejszego postępowania w sprawie uchylenia lub wykonania tegoż orzeczenia.

DEU [*Anwendbarkeit der Parteiautonomie auf die Bestellung von Schiedsrichtern*]

Der vorliegende Artikel analysiert die Anwendung des Prinzips der Parteiautonomie im Kontext der Ernennung von Schiedsrichtern (sei es durch die Parteien selbst, durch bereits ins Schiedspanel bzw. -tribunal gewählte Kollegen oder durch andere Personen oder Institutionen, die das Recht zur Bestellung des Schiedsrichters wahrnehmen). Der Artikel spricht außerdem die Grenzen an, die der Parteiautonomie bei der Bestellung von Schiedsrichtern gesetzt sind, sowie die Auswirkung der Forderung nach einem gerechten Prozess und des Rechtsstaatsprinzips in diesem Bereich der Schiedsverfahrensführung – dies im Kontext der Tatsache, dass die Zusammensetzung des Schiedstribunals im Rahmen der späteren Aufhebung bzw. Vollstreckung des Schiedsspruchs einen der potenziellen Angriffspunkte bzw. Schwachstellen des Schiedsspruchs darstellt.

RUS [*Применимость принципа самостоятельности сторон при назначении арбитров*]

В статье анализируется применимость принципа самостоятельности сторон в контексте назначения арбитров, выполняемого либо сторонами процесса, либо другими арбитрами, либо различными иными уполномоченными лицами или организациями. Кроме того, рассматриваются пределы самостоятельности сторон при назначении арбитров и влияние требования обеспечения справедливого суда и соблюдения норм отправления правосудия в контексте положения об арбитражном суде, которые также могут быть уязвимы в решении арбитражного суда в ходе дальнейших процедур его исполнения либо отмены.

ESP [*Aplicabilidad de la autonomía de las partes en la designación de árbitros*]

El artículo analiza la aplicación del principio de autonomía de las partes en el contexto de designación de árbitros, tanto por las partes, como por los coárbitros, o por otras personas o instituciones que actúen como autoridades designadoras. Asimismo, se hace referencia a los límites de la autonomía de las partes en la designación de árbitros y al impacto que en el contexto de la constitución del tribunal de arbitraje pueden tener los requisitos necesarios para un proceso justo y un proceso ordinario en el ámbito de los procedimientos de arbitraje, como parte de las vulnerabilidades potenciales del fallo de un arbitraje en el procedimiento posterior de anulación o de ejecución.

Martin Maisner

Liability and Independence of the Arbitrator

Key words:
International Arbitration
| arbitrator| arbitral
tribunal | general liability
| indemnity | arbitrators
liability | personal
immunity | arbitrator's
misconduct | arbitrator's
disqualification | arbitral
immunity | statutory
immunity | absolute
judicial immunity |
quasi-judicial immunity
| jurisdictional theory
| contractual theory |
contractual liability |
arbitrator's duties | tort
liability

Abstract | This article describes the potential sources of the arbitrator's liability as seen from different perspectives – civil and criminal liability, liability derived from jurisdictional theory, contractual theory, hybrid theory and autonomous theory. The undisputed duties of an arbitrator based on both indemnity endorsing and liability oriented jurisdictions are described, as well as the possible types of arbitrator's liability viewed from the technical point of view and from the different views of common law and continental law countries, where the common law countries incline toward absolute quasi-judicial indemnity while the continental law countries apply different levels of liability. The presented court decisions from different jurisdictions specify the different views of potential liability or indemnity of an arbitrator compared to the general approach of the jurisdiction. The conclusion however confirms that the issue is highly controversial especially in international arbitration where there is no general lead or approach applied worldwide which raises the question of whether an international understanding on a basic principle or at least a wider discussion should be initiated, but preferably ending in some form of an international convention agreeing on some basic generally accepted rules.

JUDr. Martin Maisner, PhD. is a partner at ROWAN LEGAL. He is a renowned expert in the area of ICT Law, Outsourcing, ICT dispute resolution and CyberSecurity. He has written many publications and articles, has given lectures and presentations at international conferences; regularly lectures at several universities including Prague University of Economics, Masaryk University in Brno and Pan-European University in Bratislava. He is also an active arbitrator in both domestic and international arbitration disputes including specialised ICT and intellectual property cases and has represented clients in

8.01. The liability or indemnity of the arbitrator in international arbitration is an issue referred to in almost any publication on the practice of international arbitration. The reasons are obvious. Different doctrines have been applied in different jurisdictions and there is an evident difference in the basic approach of common law and civil law countries to this issue. There are strong arguments for keeping the indemnity of the arbitrator and on the other hand very sound arguments that advocate retaining instruments for enforcement of at least the basic arbitrator's duties.

arbitrations in Prague, Geneva, Zurich, Hague and London.
e-mail: maisner@rowanlegal.com

8.02. David Bristow and Jesmond Parke, both practising arbitrators and mediators, have referred[1] to the situation as a "drift towards claims against mediators and arbitrators in the US" and as a "warning to ADR Practitioners in Canada." Susan D. Franck in her excellent study[2] stressed that because of perceived misconduct by arbitrators and the risk of party manipulation, the arbitration process has come under increasing attack through civil actions against arbitrators and the issue of arbitrator´s immunity has received increased attention.[3]

8.03. Although different jurisdictions have dealt with this issue very differently, they offer an astonishing number of solutions to this problem. Meanwhile, there is no international widely accepted standard that addresses the issue of liability or its scope for international arbitrators.

I. General Liability in Relation to Different Arbitration Theories

8.04. There are two basic sources of arbitrator's potential liability – it always concerns a breach of duty – the difference is whether the breach was based upon contract or tort. Even if the common law approach seems to be very different from the civil law approach, both systems admit that the arbitrator has certain duties.

---

[1]   See David I. Bristow, Jesmond Parke, *Gathering Storm of Mediator & Arbitrator Liability*, DISPUTE RESOLUTION JOURNAL (Aug-Oct 2000).

[2]   See Susan D. Franck, *The Liability of International Arbitrators: A Comparative Analysis and Proposal for Qualified Immunity*, 20 (1) NEW YORK LAW SCH. J. INT'L & COMP. L. (2000).

[3]   See Gerold Hermann, *Does the World Need Additional Uniform Legislation on Arbitration?* 15 ARB. INT'L (1998), (noting that there are emerging tactics of recalcitrant parties attacking the independence of arbitrators).

8.05. Any discussion in this regard must begin by addressing the phenomenon of judicial or quasi-judicial immunity which is widely favoured in common law countries to sometimes an overly broad arbitral immunity backed both by court judgments.[4] The English courts have constantly recognized that arbitrators are in a quasi-judicial position and therefore should enjoy immunity from charges of negligence and mistakes of law in fact. In practice the courts here refer to the civil or private law immunity of the arbitrator in the exercise of his judicial functions although in fact such immunity is an exception to the general principle that a person with professional expertise may be liable in damages should he prove negligent of exercising due care and skill.[5]

8.06. The rationale for arbitrator immunity rests on a principle that was clearly set by the 7th UN Congress:

(16) Without prejudice to any disciplinary procedure or any right of appeal or to compensation from the State, in accordance to national law, judges should enjoy personal immunity from civil suits for monetary damages for improper acts or omissions in the exercise of their judicial functions.[6]

8.07. The immunity of the arbitrator is derived from the concept of judicial immunity which itself maintains that judges should remain immune from the pressures exerted by the parties during and after trial "in order that [they] can make [their] decision[s] with calmness of mind and see the justice be done."[7] The justification for granting arbitrators full judicial immunity is based on the ground that arbitrators and judges should be treated alike because "courts and arbitrators are in the same business, namely the administration of justice."[8]

8.08. Critics of this concept object that there are serious differences between judges and arbitrators: First – the judge's power derives directly from the state and the law of the nation under specific rules and judges receive a certain level of training and education. Second – judges are

---

[4] See e.g. *Lendon v. Keen (*1916) 1 K.B.994, 999 per Michael Hwang, *Claims against Arbitrators for Breach of Ethical Duties*, CONTEMPORARY ISSUES IN INTERNATIONAL ARBITRATION AND MEDIATION, THE FORDHAM PAPERS, Leiden: Martinus Nijhoff Publishers (A. W. Rovine ed., 2007).

[5] *Ibid.*, at 226.

[6] *The UN Basic Principles on the Independence of the Judiciary*, as adopted by the 7th UN Congress and endorsed by the General Assembly in 29 November 1985.

[7] Ramon Mullerat, Juliet Blanch, *The Liability of Arbitrators: A Survey of Current Practice*, International Bar Association, Commission on Arbitration, Chicago (21 September 2006).

[8] J. Donaldson in *Bremen Schiffbahn v. South India Shipping Corp.Ltd*, 1981, AC 909-921.

not chosen or nominated and definitely are not remunerated by the parties compared to the arbitrator who is usually nominated by one of the parties and paid either directly or through an arbitration institution. Third – judges are only accountable to the state while arbitrators are accountable to the parties and sometimes to the arbitral – usually private – body or institution. Fourth and finally – judges decisions are rarely final – they can be institutionally fully revised or corrected in an appeal process – while the arbitrator's award is mostly final and cannot be revised but only vacated for a limited range of reasons. The position of an arbitrator is therefore similar to the judge's position but only in certain aspects. The dissimilarities are substantial and may have a severe effect on the parties and on the decision-making procedure. Critics in this camp also raise serious objections that immunity may lead to lack of diligence and proper care on the part of an individual arbitrator and the available sanctions like vacation of the award or withholding of the arbitrator's fee are not sufficient or adequate to enforce the duties of an arbitrator or to ensure due arbitration procedure.[9]

8.09. The various jurisprudential theories – applicable in both civil law and common law systems -respond differently to this problem. Generally the *jurisdictional theory* emphasizes the quasi-judicial immunity concept that the arbitrator's position should be treated like the position enjoyed by judges (judgment theory) or maintains that arbitrators are performing a public function as temporary judges (delegation theory).[10] If we disregard the substantial differences just described, there is another more important reason to challenge that approach: when a mistake is made by the state court (in fact by a judge) which is not corrected for various reasons during the appellate process and this mistake is later discovered and proven, the damages caused by this defect in judgment in the majority of jurisdictions is compensated by the state, even if the judge enjoys immunity. However, there is no such procedure or possibility for compensation in arbitration. An obvious comparison is posed – if the state concedes under certain circumstances its judiciary powers, it should also take care of the compensation of damaged parties in cases of a defective procedure or an obvious mistake made by the arbitrator. Such provision would not by any means jeopardize the freedom of an arbitrator to seek the truth and render a fair award. Such ideas unfortunately are not welcomed by any state officials, not mentioning the fact that the arbitrator is not

---

[9] See Ramon Mullerat, Juliet Blanch, *supra* note 7, at 8.
[10] See Anastasia Tsakatoura, *The Immunity of Arbitrators*, LEX E-SCRIPTA (2002).

always tied to the forum and the reasons for adopting such schemes are substantially weaker than in case of a judge.

8.10. The *contractual theory* gained very substantial support as early as the 19th century. The theory can be summarized in these few words:

it is the agreement to arbitrate that alone gives the arbitrators the authority to make the award. They in turn, in resolving the dispute, are acting as agents or "mandataries" of the parties.[11]

8.11. The existence of the contractual relationship seems to be obvious and widely accepted, but there are still serious questions to be raised. In implying that the contractual relationship between the parties and the arbitrators appointed by them is clear, does the contract extend to the third arbitrator appointed by the party-appointed arbitrators without direct implication of the parties?[12]

8.12. In a contractual relationship it seems to be logical, that the arbitrator should be liable for performing his contractual duties as would any other professional. Under the contractual approach, the liability of an arbitrator is yet another term of the *receptum arbitri* negotiated between the parties and the arbitrator. Accordingly, the extent of arbitrator liability is subject to modifications, but within the set limits of the mandatory provisions of national legislation.[13]

8.13. In this regard we must face another problem related to the international conflict of jurisdiction. Jurisdiction for civil claims against arbitrators lies at the arbitrator's main seat of business or at the arbitrator's habitual residence or at the seat of the arbitration which is the place of performance of the contractual relationship with the arbitrator. A further question is posed when there is a three-person arbitral tribunal. Are there three individual *recepta arbitri*, each possibly governed by the different jurisdictions? Confusing. Should we declare that three arbitrators form a certain type of partnership to achieve the same result? The logical solution would be that *receptum arbitri* forms a contract between the parties, perhaps themselves also forming a partnership and the three members of the arbitral tribunal form a partnership for that purpose.[14]

---

[11] See Adam Samuel, Jurisdictional Problems in International Commercial Arbitration – A Study of Belgian, Dutch, English, French, Swedish, Swiss, US and West German Law, Zurich: Schulthess Polygraphischer Verlag (1989).

[12] See Ramon Mullerat, Juliet Blanch, *supra* note 7, at 2.

[13] See Christian Hausmaninger, *Civil Liability of Arbitrators – Comparative Analysis and Proposals for Reform*, J. Int´l Arb. 7 (1990).

[14] See Pierre A. Kareer, *Responsibility of Arbitrators and Arbitral Institutions, in* The Leading Arbitrators' Guide to International Arbitration, New York: Juris Publishing, Inc. 614 (L. W. Newman, R. D. Hill eds., 2nd ed. 2008).

8.14. The *Hybrid theory* (or mixed theory) states that it is the relationship and not the arbitrator that performs a legal function (which then leads one to the conclusion that there isn't a strong basis for granting full quasi-judicial immunity); nor is the award a contract. Specifically, *"The parties, by their arrangement, created and fixed the limits of their private jurisdiction."* The arbitrator's duty is to judge, but the power to do so is conferred to him by the agreement of the parties.[15] Many experts believe that this is where the actual responsibility lies. Unfortunately, such a conclusion would entail the systematic harmonization of widely accepted international standards.

8.15. The most recent – and probably most promising – position is the *autonomous theory*, which maintains that arbitration should be separate from all three above-described theories and should acquire an autonomous character. This may solve the differences between jurisdictions, between common law and civil law concepts, and work to establish the most suitable rules for international arbitration. Unfortunately, that would require the creation of specific, suitable, and widely acceptable rules and the extremely difficult process of bringing about their international implementation. Such efforts would undoubtedly encounter serious opposition from all directions since it implies the partial surrender of legal sovereignty.

II. Duties of the Arbitrator

8.16. It should be stressed at the very beginning that [generally speaking] international arbitrators do have a sense of duty regarding the proper performance of their arbitral function.[16] Nonetheless, the specific duties of an arbitrator (regardless of whether they are pronounced as contractual liabilities or duties that emanate from the national jurisdiction on arbitration, or from adopted arbitration rules or other source) are usually similar, although they may be differently specified.

8.17. Some experts describe the duties of the arbitrator simply as "the duty to act judicially and the duty of due diligence."[17] Other authors are more specific – they determine a duty to

    a) act fairly and impartially,

    b) act with due care,

    c) act independently,

---

[15] See Anastasia Tsakatoura, *supra* note 10.

[16] See Jan Paulsson, *Ethics, Elitism, Eligibility*, 14 (4) J. INT'L ARB. 13,17 (1997).

[17] See NIGEL BLACKABY, CONSTANTINE PARTASIDES, ALAN REDFERN AND MARTIN HUNTER, REDFERN & HUNTER ON INTERNATIONAL ARBITRATION, Oxford: Oxford University Press (5th ed. 2009).

      d)   act with due diligence, complete the reference and issue an award

      e)   and sometimes even further specify duties (such as to draft the terms of reference as suggested by ICC rules).[18]

8.18.   Another definition of the main duties may be as follows:

      a)   To act in an independent and impartial way, treating the parties equally during the entire proceedings, giving each party a reasonable opportunity to put his case;

      b)   To settle the dispute between the parties and give a valid award not open or susceptible of challenge;

      c)   To carry out his mission within the fixed time limit created by law or by contract;

      d)   To carry out his function in good faith with diligence, and avoid undue delays (since justice delayed is justice denied), abstentions, and withdrawals;

      e)   To carry out his function to the point of delivering the award and not resign without good cause before the award is rendered; therefore, his functions cannot cease unless there are very solid reasons for this;

      f)   To respect and maintain the confidentiality of the arbitration (this principle being recognized across the board by the regulations on arbitration).[19]

8.19.   Since the potential liability of an arbitrator may originate basically in the breach of the arbitrator's duty it is important to specify which duties apply in a particular arbitration proceeding and how they are to be interpreted. There is no uniform code applied universally in international arbitration even if national legislation or different arbitration rules describe in different words a very similar scope of duties.

III. Different Types of Potential Liability for Arbitrator's Misconduct

8.20.   With regard to the arbitrator's misconduct or breach of his ethical duties, there are basically two possibilities particular to the situation – by the arbitrator's active breaching of his stated duty or by nonfeasance (inactivity).

8.21.   Basically, the claims may be brought for the following reasons:

      a)   Claims for delay by arbitrators

---

[18]   See PETER ASHFORD, HANDBOOK ON INTERNATIONAL COMMERCIAL ARBITRATION, New York: Juris Net, LLC 45 (2009).

[19]   See Ramon Mullerat, Juliet Blanch, *supra* note 7, at 3-4.

b) Claims for failure to disclose conflicts of interest
c) Claims for being corrupt
d) Claims for negligence[20]

IV. Interesting Court Decisions on Arbitrator Liability

1999 Canada, Ontario

Cohen case

8.22. In May 1999, Ontario courts in the *Cohen* case pondered the problem of an arbitrator accused by the arbitrating parties of negligence in the conduct of an arbitration and in his decision. The parties did not want to pay the arbitrator anything as they claimed the arbitration was of no benefit to them. The arbitrator had ruled in favour of the landlord after the arbitration which involved a landlord and tenant over rent to be paid by the tenant. On appeal from this award the court allowed the appeal and set aside the decision of the arbitrator, finding that he had made two errors which resulted in the arbitrator exceeding his jurisdiction.

8.23. Both parties to the arbitration refused to pay the arbitrator his fees and the arbitrator applied to an assessment officer to have his account assessed pursuant to section 56(1) of the Ontario Arbitration Act under which an arbitrator's account for fees and expenses may be assessed by an assessment officer in the same manner as would a solicitor's bill under the Solicitors Act. The assessment officer found the arbitration of no benefit to the parties and assessed the account at nil. The arbitrator appealed to the Ontario Superior Court of Justice. The arbitrator argued that his errors were errors in judgment, not amounting to negligence and he should be paid; the parties argued that the services provided by the arbitrator were negligently provided and were worth nothing and the arbitrator should not be paid. The issue remained: Was the arbitrator negligent?

8.24. The court found that: "although the arbitrator made serious errors in his report which ultimately rendered the report worth little or no value to the clients, he was not negligent." Consequently he should be paid for his services. The court further found that the arbitrator prepared "lengthy, well organized reasons" and that but for two important matters he had "acted fairly and capably."[21]

---

[20] See Michael Hwang, *supra* note 4, at 231-245.
[21] See David I. Bristow, Jesmond Parke, *supra* note 1.

2005, Finland

Urho, Sirkka and Juuka Ruola v. *X* (KKO 2005:14)

8.25. On January 31 2005 the Finnish Supreme Court handed down a ruling on the principles applicable to the liability of arbitrators. The Supreme Court had not previously ruled on the issue. The Finnish Arbitration Act (967/1992) does not contain specific provisions regarding the liability of arbitrators, unlike the arbitration rules of the Board of Arbitration of the Central Chamber of Commerce of Finland, which include an exclusion of liability clause (Section 43a of the rules). Based on these rules, an arbitrator shall not be liable for any loss incurred by the parties in arbitral proceedings save for loss resulting from wilful misconduct or gross negligence. The following Supreme Court decision, however, concerns ad hoc arbitration where such limitation cannot be applied.

8.26. The initial arbitral award was handed down in 1995. The case originally concerned a dispute arising from a share and purchase agreement between three private sellers and a company whose shares were owned by a Finnish bank. Later, other banks acted as intervening parties in the proceedings. Both the sellers and the company acted as claimants and defendants in the course of the proceedings. The arbitral tribunal consisted of three arbitrators (one appointed by each party) plus the chairman of the arbitral tribunal, appointed by the other two arbitrators. The tribunal dismissed all claims presented by the sellers and ordered them to pay compensation to the company and legal costs to the relevant banks.

8.27. The sellers filed an application to declare the arbitral award null and void in the district court. This was confirmed by a final judgment of the Court of Appeals in 1997. The nullity was based on the ruling that the chairman of the arbitral tribunal was considered disqualified as both before and during the proceedings he had acted for the company, the banks and companies belonging to same group of companies by providing expert legal opinions. The chairman had not informed the sellers of these opinions. The fact that the opinions concerned completely different issues from the pending arbitral proceedings was considered irrelevant. Due to the nullity of the award the sellers had to recommence the arbitral proceedings. The sellers also filed a claim against the chairman demanding that he should pay them €166,729.70 plus interest as compensation for damages.

8.28. Both the district court and the Court of Appeal considered that, on the basis of Section 9 of the Arbitration Act, the chairman should have informed the sellers of the tasks that he was performing for the company and the banks in question. The chairman was not considered to be dependent on the company or the banks. However, the courts considered that as a result of the following factors, the chairman had neglected his duties under the Arbitration Act:

a) the large number of statements given;
b) their timing prior to the proceedings;
c) the considerable compensation received as a result of the statements; and
d) the importance of the arbitral proceedings.

The courts considered that the compensation payable should be determined in accordance with the Tort Liability Act (412/1974), Chapter 5, Section 1. This regulation states that only where especially weighty reasons exist may compensation be payable for economic loss that is not connected to personal injury or damage to property.

8.29. In light of previous jurisprudence and the fact that the chairman's conduct was only to be categorized as slight negligence, the court ruled that no weighty reasons existed to support recovery of the economic loss. The Court of Appeal further considered that the connection between the sellers and the arbitrators was similar to a contractual relationship, but still maintained that the damages should be evaluated based on the Tort Liability Act. Consequently, the lower courts dismissed the claim.

8.30. The Supreme Court took a different approach to the question of an arbitrator's liability. The court maintained that the sellers incurred additional legal costs because of the chairman's disqualification. However, it stressed that arbitrator's liability is triggered only in exceptional circumstances. This is necessary in order to guarantee the independence and impartiality of arbitrators.

8.31. The court also ruled that the chairman should have informed the sellers of his connection to the other party and the intervening banks. The court emphasized the importance of Section 9 of the Arbitration Act, which sets out the duty to disclose any circumstances that are likely to give rise to justifiable doubts as to the arbitrator's impartiality and independence. The court stressed that this duty is not limited only to facts that could disqualify the arbitrator and considered that the threshold for the duty to disclose is low.

8.32. The court further considered that a causal connection existed between the chairman's failure to provide information to the sellers and the damage caused. The court emphasized that the chairman may also have foreseen this causal relation. The court considered that had the chairman informed the sellers of the expert legal opinions he delivered to the other party and the intervening banks in accordance with

Section 9 of the Arbitration Act, liability for damages would not have actualized. The sellers could have either consented to continue the proceedings or demanded that the chairman be considered disqualified. Even had the Arbitral Tribunal dismissed the claim regarding disqualification, the matter could have been assessed by a district court. The court also stated that where the claim for disqualification would have succeeded before the district court, liability for damages could not have actualized as the decision regarding the arbitrator's disqualification would have been made within the powers granted to the arbitral tribunal.

8.33. The court evaluated whether there was a contractual relationship between the parties and the arbitrators as the arbitral tribunal consisted of three arbitrators. The court stated that although the parties had not appointed the chairman, they had (by agreeing to the arbitration proceedings) accepted him as being elected in accordance with the law. On this basis, the court considered that the chairman's liability was no different from the liability of the other members of the arbitral tribunal.

8.34. Furthermore, the court considered that the liability of an arbitrator is not tort liability; in arbitration proceedings the parties "purchase" the dispute resolution from the arbitrators. Thus, the relationship is comparable to a contractual relationship. The court considered that the chairman had failed to prove that the nullity of the original arbitral award and the ensuing damages were not his fault. The court added that given his education and background, the chairman should have understood that the drafting of legal opinions for the intervening banks during the arbitral proceedings against considerably high remuneration was likely to give justifiable doubts as to his impartiality and independence.

8.35. The Supreme Court revoked the decisions of the lower courts. The Supreme Court ruled that the compensation payable should be based not on the Tort Liability Act but on contractual liability. The ruling remained final but the amount of compensation was returned to the district court to be decided. One of the five members of the Supreme Court gave a dissenting opinion but his conclusion was unanimous with the majority.[22]

---

[22] Described and shortened by Castrén & Snellman available at: http://www.castren.fi/ (accessed on September 13, 2011).

Czech (& Central European) Yearbook of Arbitration

2005, Austria

X v. *Arbitrators (Austrian Supreme Court)*

8.36.   Another relevant case in this context was decided by the Supreme Court on June 6, 2005. It dealt with the alleged liability of arbitrators for various claimed deficiencies of the arbitration. The arbitrators had rendered an award that was not set aside and was not subject to setting-aside proceedings. The unsuccessful party argued that any application to set aside the award would be futile due to the limited grounds on which such applications may generally be based. It claimed that the arbitrators were liable for their alleged violations of their contractual relationship with the parties. In return, the arbitrators argued that if they were contractually liable at all under Austrian law, it was a precondition for such liability that their award had been set aside (i.e. limited contractual liability). Further, they argued that an arbitrator's liability cannot be broader than the liability of state court judges, which requires gross negligence, and this was not present in the case at hand. This argument assumed the public law status of the arbitrator. Basing its findings solely on the contractual concept, the court determined that the (limited) contractual liability of arbitrators required the award to have been set aside. In justifying this approach, the court observed that the Austrian concept of the (limited) contractual liability of arbitrators, although rather restrictive, is still broader than the concept of arbitrators' liability in other jurisdictions (e.g. Germany), which further limits an arbitrator's liability for breach of his or her duties to failures that are penalized by public law.

8.37.   Austrian law considers the appointment of arbitrators to be an act of public law. By contrast, the mutual rights and obligations of the arbitrator and the parties regulating certain aspects of an arbitrator's entitlement to remuneration and his or her liability are governed by the contractual relationship between them.[23]

2006, Austria

*X.*v. *Austrian Federal Economic Chamber* (6 Ob 207/06v)

8.38.   In its judgment of November 30 2006 (6 Ob 207/06v) the Supreme Court ruled on whether an arbitrator whose appointment had successfully been challenged during the arbitral proceedings could claim fees. The issue had arisen in arbitration before the Vienna International Arbitral Centre (VIAC) of the Austrian Federal Economic

---

[23]   Described and shortened by Shönherr Restanwalte available at http://www.sc hoenherr.eu/locations/austria (accessed on September 13, 2011).

Chamber as the institution administering the arbitration proceedings. Since under both the applicable Rules of Arbitration and Conciliation of 2001 and Austrian arbitration law the arbitrator was obliged to disclose any facts which could give rise to doubts as to his independence early in the proceedings, the VIAC, acting as the trustee to which the parties had paid the deposit, refused to pay the arbitrator for his services rendered in the arbitration as he had neglected this duty. The arbitrator subsequently filed a claim against the Austrian Federal Economic Chamber (i.e. the institution to which the VIAC is attached) for payment of his fees. Within this litigation, the Supreme Court analyzed the relationship between the parties and the arbitrator. In this respect it held that the relationship was a contractual relationship which was governed by the Civil Code and its provisions on contracts for services to the extent that neither Sections 577 and following of the Code of Civil Procedure (i.e. the Austrian law on arbitration) nor the characteristics of the contractual relationship provided otherwise. The court applied the regulations on contracts for services in order to determine the mutual rights and duties arising out of the contractual relationship. Therefore, the court assumed that a contractual relationship existed between the parties and the arbitrator. Considering that the arbitrator had neglected his contractual duty of disclosure at an early stage of the arbitration, the court held that the arbitrator was not entitled to his fees.[24]

2006, USA, Texas

Pullara v. American Arbitration Association, Inc.

8.39. The arbitration of Michael Pullara's dispute with Becker Fine Builders, Inc. (Becker), a Houston builder, arising out of an agreement to remodel Pullara's apartment, did not turn out as Pullara had hoped. Pullara had hired Becker to renovate his apartment. The construction contract required any dispute to be submitted for arbitration to the American Arbitration Association (AAA). A dispute arose concerning a delay in completion of the project, and Becker filed a demand for arbitration with the AAA.

8.40. The American Arbitration Association (AAA) arbitrator, Stephen B. Paxson, awarded Becker a total of $97,442.29 against Pullara. Approximately one year later, however, Pullara discovered something Paxson had allegedly not disclosed before being selected as arbitrator – namely, that for many years Paxson had acted as general counsel for the Greater Houston Builders Association (GHBA). Before being selected

---

[24] *Ibid.*

as arbitrator, Paxson had disclosed his membership in GHBA, but apparently not his representation of that organization. To begin the arbitration process, the AAA sent a list of ten arbitrators to Becker and Pullara. A brief biography and set of disclosures were provided for each arbitrator on the list. Paxson, one of the listed arbitrators, disclosed he was a member of the GHBA, a trade association for residential builders in the Houston area. But, Pullara contends Paxson failed to disclose he had served as counsel for the organization for over a decade. Using the information disclosed, Pullara and Becker each struck three arbitrators from the list. Paxson was one of the arbitrators not struck by either party, and the AAA appointed him to arbitrate the dispute.

8.41.   Finding himself beyond the standard ninety-day deadline to seek to vacate the award under Section 171.088 of the Texas Civil Practice and Remedies Code, Pullara did not move to set aside the award. Instead, he *sued* Paxson and the AAA *for damages* he alleges were caused by Paxson's failure to disclose his work as general counsel for the GHBA. Pullara contends Paxson's alleged failure to disclose the attorney-client relationship with GHBA revealed a bias in Becker's favour, which Pullara believes was a material fact he was entitled to know when he chose the arbitrators to strike from the AAA's list.

8.42.   Pullara appealed the trial court's having granted summary judgment against him in favour of the defendants. The Apellate court affirmed the judgment of the trial court because Pullara's claims are barred by the doctrine of arbitral immunity.

8.43.   The Appellate judges ruled that an arbitrator's role is functionally equivalent to that of a judge. As with the judiciary, it is necessary to protect arbitrators from undue influence and safeguard their independence. To those ends, judicial immunity has been extended to arbitrators as well as their sponsoring organizations. The appellees asserted that Pullara's claims were barred by the doctrine of arbitral immunity. The judgment was affirmed.[25]

2008, USA, New Jersey

Malik v. *Ruttenberg* (Docket No. A-6615-06T3)

8.44.   The Appellate Division of the State of New Jersey was presented with a situation where an attorney involved in the arbitration allegedly had assaulted one of the parties. The party involved had previously asked the arbitrator to remove this attorney from the proceedings. This request was denied by the arbitrator and the assault allegedly took place during a recess outside of the arbitration room.

---

[25]   Opinion by Chief Justice Morriss.

8.45. The party that was allegedly assaulted brought an action against the American Arbitration Association and the arbitrator, claiming that both knew of this attorney's dangerous tendencies, but failed to exercise reasonable care to control them. The American Arbitration Association and the arbitrator sought dismissal of the complaint based upon a claim of immunity.

8.46. The Appellate Division noted that whether or not a common law or statutory immunity applies to a party is a question of law. If immunity applies and bars civil liability, it trumps any theory of negligence. In its analysis, the Court noted that there are few doctrines that were more solidly established at common law than the immunity of judges from liability for damage for acts committed within their judicial jurisdiction. This immunity is necessary for the independent and impartial exercise of judicial judgment that is vital to the judiciary. The opinion of the Court noted that the common law extended absolute judicial immunity to the work of quasi-judicial figures such as arbitrators. An alleged wrongful act does not expose a judge to liability so long as the act was undertaken in an official capacity and an arbitrator is similarly protected. The Appellate Court found that an arbitrator's duty to control the proceedings was clearly within the scope of a judicial function. The acts of the arbitrator were found to be protected by judicial immunity, as was the arbitral organization in its job of administering arbitration. In finding that "immunity trumps liability" the Appellate Division dismissed the complaint filed against the arbitrator and the American Arbitration Association.[26]

2009, Netherlands

ASB Greenworld v. NAI and arbitrators (BJ7834)

8.47. Sagro Aannemingsmaatschappij Zeeland initiated institutional arbitration proceedings under the rules of the Netherlands Arbitration Institute against a German company and against ASB Greenworld. Greenworld appeared in the arbitral proceedings and raised the plea that the arbitral tribunal lacked jurisdiction on the ground that there was no valid arbitration agreement. Arbitrators dismissed the plea and awarded the claim as filed by Sagro. Subsequently Greenworld filed an application to the Court in order to set the arbitral award aside for absence of a valid arbitration agreement. The Court denied the application but the Court of Appeal later indeed did quash the arbitral award for absence of a valid arbitration agreement. Later appeals to the

---

[26] Lewis J. Pepperman, *Arbitrator's Immunity from Civil Liability*, available at: http://www.njlawblog.com/ (accessed on September 13, 2011).

Netherlands Supreme Court were dismissed. This did not end the proceedings. Greenworld subsequently held the arbitrators and the Netherlands Arbitration Institute personally liable, for committing an unlawful act (or tort) under Dutch law. The claim was dismissed in two instances and Greenworld appealed to the Netherlands Supreme Court, which led to a landmark decision on arbitrator liability in The Netherlands.

8.48. Held: The mere fact that a decision is set aside does not make the decision wrong. Arbitrators render judicial or quasi-judicial functions that render them comparable to judges. Like judges, arbitrators should be at liberty to judge cases. When arbitral awards are set aside, this does not necessarily mean the decisions were wrong and decisions can only be held to be unlawful in exceptional cases.

8.49. As a general rule formulated by the Netherlands Supreme Court, arbitrators can only incur personal liability in the event of intent, wilful misconduct or if arbitrators manifestly fail to exercise due care and skill. The appeal failed.[27]

V. Conclusion

8.50. The scope of the presented, and relatively recent, decisions from different jurisdictions demonstrates the status and development of the situation. The problems and their solutions in national jurisdictions are not as simple as they may at first seem and the approaches in the national jurisdictions differ. On the other hand, they do have something in common with one another; the certainty of the arbitrator's liability has been finally accepted or granted even from very opposite standpoints. The liability is always substantially limited to the most important duties of the arbitrator – the duty to report a relationship to the parties because of potential breach of impartiality, the duty not to prevent or delay proceedings by the arbitrator's unjustified resignation, or the duty to deliver (i.e. the proceedings and the award) in due time. The question of *male fidei* acts is covered by their criminal liability and lies outside the scope of this thesis.

8.51. Common law countries traditionally prefer absolute or almost absolute (quasi-judicial) immunity for the arbitrator while *vacatur* or *rehearsal* should be the only remedies possible. This is the main idea being developed in the environment where the judicial or arbitral community is expected and believed to prevent excesses and to rectify the undesired behaviour of the members of the arbitral community. It is

---

[27] Published by Hein Kernkamp, *ASB Greenworld* v. *NAI and arbitrators, in* KERNKAMP'S NETHERLANDS CIVIL COURT CASE SUMMARIES (December 7, 2009).

the correct approach for said legal environment – and yet common law courts have denied quasi-judicial immunity to the arbitrator who was several months behind schedule in issuing an award – i.e., just for delay (which every person practicing as an attorney or an arbitrator in dispute resolution has experienced in a at least some of the proceedings – usually suffering without any penalty or other legal consequences). What is important to highlight is that a legal environment where an extreme emphasis is placed on treating arbitrators like judges may work to deny the arbitrator *any immunity* for such breach of his duties as a delay in his performance as an arbitrator.

8.52.   Civil law countries are more inclined to adopt the legal standpoint that arbitrators are liable for certain very specific deeds or omissions, while – at the end of the day – the conditions under which the liability is in reality incurred limit the real and enforceable scope of arbitrators' liability to an extent very similar to that seen in common law countries.

8.53.   A completely different situation is found in the area of international arbitration. The international character of the proceedings, the fact that the arbitrators frequently act and serve in a legal environment which is not their domestic environment, with a potential for incurring liability and encountering interpretation which is not always predictable – makes the ice a little thinner than desirable and therefore usually the result is contractual – and almost unlimited – indemnity of the arbitrator, of the arbitral institution or both. This status (heavily influenced by the common law tradition) is now being questioned by new arbitration markets emerging from the remains of the former Soviet Union sphere of influence. These potential for influence of these markets is great since the local courts are not efficient and experienced enough to face the challenges of effectively resolving international disputes and the number of international business relationships (*ergo* contracts and subsequently disputes) has risen exponentially. A typical cultural feature in said region is however, the deep suspicion against any authority or subject, who may act (in exchange for a fair compensation) without any liability for his acts or omissions; in a multicultural, globalised world, such suspicion cannot be just plainly rejected. The doubts about the future of international arbitration as we know it have a very serious base. The future of arbitration – especially international commercial arbitration shall not be what the arbitrators want, but what the parties of the dispute accept, and there are no arbitration cases without the parties willing to take part in them.

8.54.   The author is well aware of the controversial nature of this issue. However, controversial issues are not solved by leaving them unmentioned, untouched and undiscussed. A possible solution might be holding an international convention, or at least drawing up guidelines (comparable to those issued by the IBA *in re* Conflict of Interest) that would not be generally binding, but at least be in existence and be there to be referred to. How narrow the scope of liability or how wide the scope of indemnity will be is not so important – just drawing the line will offer some orientation and add the solemnity of international wide acceptance to the attempt to work toward a solution. In the multicultural and sometimes troubled environment of current international arbitration, such steps might shine a beam of bright light on the often dark and winding path of human disputes.

||| |

Summaries

DEU [*Haftung und Unabhängigkeit des Schiedsrichters*]

Dieser Artikel beschreibt die möglichen Quellen einer Haftung auf Seiten des Schiedsrichters aus verschiedenen Blickwinkeln – die zivilrechtliche und strafrechtliche Verantwortung sowie eine aus der Rechtsprechungstheorie, Vertragstheorie, einer gemischten Theorie sowie einer autonomen Theorie hergeleitete Belangbarkeit. Vorliegende Arbeit beschreibt die unstrittigen Pflichten von Schiedsrichtern sowohl in Rechtssystemen, die von einer Haftungsfreistellung ausgehen, als auch in haftungsorientierten Rechtssystemen, ebenso wie die möglichen Formen einer schiedsrichterlichen Haftung aus technischer Hinsicht und aus der (uneinheitlichen) Sicht von Common Law-Ländern (also Ländern mit richterlichem Gewohnheitsrecht nach angloamerikanischem Muster) einerseits und Ländern mit kontinentalem Rechtssystem andererseits, wobei gilt, dass Common Law-Länder zu einer absoluten quasi-richterlichen Haftungsfreistellung tendieren, während das kontinentale Recht mehr oder minder von verschiedenen Graden der Haftung ausgeht. Die hier beschriebenen gerichtlichen Entscheidungen aus verschiedenen Jurisdiktionen zeigen die unterschiedlichen Auffassungen einer potenziellen Haftung bzw. Nichthaftung von Schiedsrichtern auf, im Vergleich zum allgemeinen Ansatz der Jurisdiktion. Abschließend finden wir aber bestätigt, dass das Thema höchst kontrovers v. a. in der internationalen Schiedsgerichtsbarkeit behandelt wird, wo keine generelle Richtschnur und kein allgemeiner, weltweit zur Anwendung kommender Ansatz existieren. Dies wirft die Frage auf, ob hier nicht Anstoß zur Findung eines internationalen Konsensus bezüglich eines grundlegenden Haftungsprinzips (oder doch wenigstens zu einer breiteren Diskussion) gegeben werden sollte; eher noch bedürfte es eines internationalen Übereinkommens in der einen oder anderen Form, in dessen Rahmen einige grundlegende, allgemein anerkannte Regeln festgehalten würden.

CZE **[*Odpovědnost a nezávislost rozhodce*]**
Tento článek popisuje možné zdroje odpovědnosti rozhodce z nejrůznějších hledisek – občanskoprávní a trestní odpovědnost, odpovědnost vyvozená z jurisdikční teorie, smluvní teorie, teorie smíšené a teorie autonomní. Předmětem rozboru jsou nezpochybnitelné povinnosti rozhodce vycházející jak z právních řádů, které schvalují princip beztrestnosti, tak z právních řádů, které se přiklánějí k určité odpovědnosti rozhodce, jakož i potenciální druhy odpovědnosti rozhodce z technického hlediska a z rozdílných pozic v zemích common law a v zemích kontinentálního práva, kdy země common law inklinují k absolutní kvazijudiciální beztrestnosti, zatímco země kontinentálního práva aplikují různé úrovně odpovědnosti. Předkládaná soudní rozhodnutí z různých jurisdikcí popisují různé náhledy na možnou odpovědnost nebo beztrestnost rozhodce ve srovnání s obecným přístupem dané jurisdikce. Závěr nicméně potvrzuje, že tato otázka je vysoce kontroverzní zejména v mezinárodním rozhodčím řízení, kde neexistuje žádné obecné vodítko nebo přístup, které by bylo aplikováno na celém světě. To vyvolává otázku, zda by neměla být iniciována mezinárodní dohoda o základním principu nebo přinejmenším širší diskuse, pokud možno však ve formě mezinárodní úmluvy zachycující dohodu o určitých základních obecně akceptovaných pravidlech.

|||

POL **[*Odpowiedzialność i Niezawisłość Arbitra*]**
Niniejszy artykuł opisuje potencjalne źródła odpowiedzialności arbitra z różnych perspektyw – odpowiedzialności cywilnej i karnej, odpowiedzialności wynikającej z teorii jurysdykcyjnej, teorii umownej, teorii hybrydowej i teorii autonomicznej. Przedstawione orzeczenia sądowe z różnych jurysdykcji wskazują na różnice w poglądach na temat potencjalnej odpowiedzialności lub zwolnienia od odpowiedzialności arbitra na tle ogólnego podejścia w orzecznictwie. Jednakże wniosek potwierdza, iż jest to niezwykle kontrowersyjny temat, zwłaszcza jeżeli chodzi o arbitraż międzynarodowy, gdzie brak ogólnego wzorca lub podejścia globalnego, co prowadzi do pytania, czy nie warto by stworzyć międzynarodowej koncepcji podstawowych zasad, lub choćby rozpocząć szerszej dyskusji na ten temat.

FRA *[Responsabilité et Indépendance de l'Arbitre]*

Cet article décrit les sources potentielles de responsabilité de l'arbitre, étudiées sous différents points de vue, et notamment la responsabilité civile et pénale, la responsabilité associée à la théorie des compétences, à la théorie contractuelle et à la théorie de l'autonomie. Les décisions de tribunaux relevant de différentes juridictions présentées identifient les différentes perspectives de responsabilité potentielle ou d'indemnisation d'un arbitre par rapport à l'approche générale de la juridiction. La conclusion confirme néanmoins qu'il s'agit bien d'un aspect très controversé au niveau de l'arbitrage international qui ne prévoit pas l'application d'une tendance ou d'une démarche de principe à l'échelle mondiale, ce qui nous interroge quant à la nécessité de définir un accord international sur un principe fondamental, ou tout au moins d'initier une discussion à plus vaste échelle.

RUS *[Ответственность и Независимость Арбитра]*

В данной статье под разными углами зрения рассматривается вопрос о том, откуда берется ответственность арбитра. Это гражданская и уголовная ответственность, ответственность, берущая начало в теории юрисдикции, теории договоров, гибридной теории и независимой теории. Представленные решения судебные решения в различных юрисдикциях позволяют по-разному взглянуть на возможную ответственность или гарантию возмещения ущерба арбитра в сравнении с общепринятым подходом в юрисдикции. Однако заключение наводит на мысль о том, что в этом вопросе очень много противоречий, особенно в международном арбитраже, в котором отсутствует генеральная линия или повсеместно применяемый подход, в результате чего поднимается вопрос о необходимости прийти к международному соглашению по некоему базовому принципу либо, по крайней мере, о необходимости более широкого обсуждения.

ESP *[Responsabilidad e Independencia del Árbitro]*

El artículo describe las potenciales fuentes de responsabilidad del árbitro desde diferentes perspectivas – responsabilidad civil y criminal, responsabilidad derivada de la teoría jurisdiccional, de la teoría contractual, de la teoría híbrida y de la teoría autónoma. Las resoluciones judiciales presentadas correspondientes a diferentes jurisdicciones especifican los diferentes puntos de vista de la responsabilidad o indemnización de un árbitro en comparación con el enfoque general de la jurisdicción. La conclusión, en cualquier caso, confirma que esta cuestión es altamente controvertida, especialmente en el arbitraje internacional, donde no existe una línea o enfoque general aplicado en todo el mundo, lo que plantea la cuestión de si debería iniciarse o no un acuerdo internacional sobre un principio básico, o al menos un debate más amplio.

Czech (& Central European) Yearbook of Arbitration

Nikolay Natov

The Autonomy of Arbitrators in Determining the Law Applicable to the Merits of a Case

Key words:
arbitrators' autonomy | limits of the arbitrator's autonomy | choice by the parties | choice by the arbitrators | conflict-of-law rules | mandatory rules

Abstract | *This article deals with the legal and practical aspects of arbitrator autonomy in determining the law applicable to the merits of a case. It is based on Bulgarian legislation and practice as compared to some other states' legislation, to main international instruments, to the UNCITRAL Rules and Model Law and to the ICC Rules. Its thesis is that arbitrators enjoy broad freedom in determining the substantive law. This freedom is mainly limited by the public policy rules of the seat of arbitration, of the state under whose law the award has been rendered, and of the place of the award's eventual recognition and enforcement. Arbitrators are not bound to apply the conflict-of-law rules of the seat of arbitration. They must apply the law chosen by the parties. In the absence of the parties' choice arbitrators apply the law of their choosing. In this they may resort to conflict-of-law rules or may directly choose the substantive rules. Without being obliged to give any guaranties arbitrators must render an award that is enforceable at law. When dealing with an international case, arbitrators should respect the mandatory rules of the seat while their regard for the foreign mandatory rules may be subject to certain conditions.*

Nikolay Natov, Professor of PIL at the Faculty of Law, The St. Kliment Ohridski University of Sofia, Bulgaria; Arbitrator and conciliator for Bulgaria at the ICSID; from 1993 to 2007 – arbitrator at CA/BCCI; since 2008 – Head International Arbitration Court of Legal Interaction Alliance (Sofia, Bulgaria); ICC *ad hoc* arbitrator – 3 cases; author of 4 books, over 100 articles on various aspects of private international law (in Bulgarian and English). e-mail: natov.nikolay@ gmail.com

| | |

9.01. For those familiar with private international law the correct determination of the law applicable to the merits of an international arbitration case is undoubtedly of crucial importance to the outcome of the dispute. The relationship between the substantive law to be applied and the result of the arbitration is more than evident. Nor should one forget the significance of the financial aspects of international arbitral awards, upon which the applicable substantive law has a direct influence. The consequences of wrongly determined law could be hard on the loser or on both parties to the dispute.

9.02. Consequently, the subject matter of this article will concern the autonomy of arbitrators in determining the law applicable to the merits of a case. Its contribution, drawn from the author's practical experience, will lie in its attempt to address the following: what autonomy is and its limits are; when arbitrators should apply public policy; whether the choice of law made by the parties to the dispute is mandatory for the arbitrators and if so, to what extent; how the arbitrators determine the substantive law in the absence of the choice of the parties; what methods for determining the substantive law arbitrators apply; what the duty of arbitrators may be to render an award enforceable at law; and what the role of the mandatory (overriding) rules may be for international arbitration.

9.03. The analysis will be based on the International Commercial Arbitration Act of the Republic of Bulgaria. The Act will be compared to similar statutes in other states, to the basic international instruments in this matter – the New York Convention and the European Convention. Some examples from the practice of the Court of Arbitration of the Bulgarian Chamber of Commerce and Industry will be extracted to illustrate the approach of the arbitrators in the country. The UNCITRAL Model Law of International Commercial Arbitration (the MAL), the UNCITRAL Model Arbitration Rules as well as the ICC Rules of Arbitration will also be used as bases for generally considering arbitrator autonomy.

9.04. The article's thesis maintains that arbitrators enjoy broad freedom in determining the law applicable to the substance of an international arbitration, but that this freedom is limited. Arbitrators are not bound by state judges to determine the substantive law and are not obliged to apply all the rules that a state judge must apply in settling an international case.

9.05. If the parties to an international arbitration case have chosen the substantive law the arbitrators must respect that choice and apply it. Usually the law is taken from a country different from the law of the seat of arbitration or is drawn from the national law of one of the parties or from the national law familiar to some of the arbitrators (generally speaking, a foreign law). Taking first into account the mandatory (overriding) rules of the seat of arbitration, the tribunal must apply this law to the extent it doesn't contravene public policy. This last condition places one of the few limitations upon the freedom of arbitrators. If there happen to be gaps in the law chosen by the parties the arbitrators must bridge these gaps by applying the rules of the law specifically devoted to that purpose. By applying the law the parties have chosen arbitrators are not obligated to follow the conflict-of-law rules of the seat of arbitration unless the arbitrators decide, based on the circumstances present in every particular case, that they must.[1]

9.06.   When the parties agree that the chosen law shall encompass the conflict-of-law rules, arbitrators should apply these rules. Usually such a broad scope granted by the parties is accompanied by the request of the law that the choice be made explicit; otherwise the arbitrators will be obliged to apply only the substantive rules of the chosen law. In such cases the substantive rules of the chosen law limit the freedom of arbitrators.

9.07.   When the parties fail to choose the substantive law, use of the conflict-of-law rules of the law of the seat is not also obligatory for the arbitrators. The question of whether to apply them is left to their discretion. If they decide to apply the conflict-of-law rules these could coincide not only with the seat of arbitration's rules, but also with the private international law rules belonging to another country.

9.08.   The arbitrators may directly choose the substantive rules applicable to the merits of the case and the choice may be made without recourse to any conflict-of-law rule. These substantive rules could be the rules of any national law.

9.09.   In both situations above – when the parties have chosen or when they have failed to choose – the arbitrators must take into consideration the parties' intentions, the terms of the contract and its commercial use. These last two considerations place certain limitations upon arbitrator freedom.

9.10.   According to Article 38, paragraph 1 of the International Commercial Arbitration Act of the Republic of Bulgaria[2] (ICAA/BG): "The

---

[1]   Usually the seat is selected for practical reasons as for instance for its geographical proximity or neutrality, therefore the role of the seat should not be overestimated – for more details see GARY B. BORN, INTERNATIONAL COMMERCIAL ARBITRATION, The Hague: Wolters Kluwer Law & Business 1679 et seq. (2009).

[2]   The International Commercial Arbitration Act (ICAA) was promulgated in the State Gazette (SG.) No 60/5 Aug 1988; amend. SG. 93/2 Nov 1993, amend. SG. 59/26 May 1998, amend. SG. 38/17 Apr 2001, amend. SG. 46/7 May 2002, amend. SG. 102/1 Nov 2002, amend. SG. 59/20 Jul 2007.

arbitration tribunal shall decide on the dispute in accordance with the law chosen by the parties. Unless otherwise agreed, the choice of law shall concern the substantive law and not the conflict-of-law rules." Paragraph 2 of the same Article adds that "[i]f the parties have failed to designate the applicable law the arbitration tribunal shall apply the law pointed out by the conflict-of-law rules which it considers applicable." In paragraph 3, the Act continues, "[i]n all cases the arbitration tribunal shall apply the terms of the contract and shall take into account the trade usages." No doubt this rule is a replica of Article VII, paragraph 1 of the European Convention on International Commercial Arbitration.[3] Article 17 of the ICC Rules of Arbitration is similar.

9.11. A detailed review of this passage from the ICAA/BG demonstrates as follows: First, the rule allows the parties to an international arbitration dispute to choose the law applicable to the substance of the dispute. Party autonomy (or will autonomy) is not compulsory for the parties, but an option. Second, according to the above-quoted ICAA/BG rule the law chosen by the parties is compulsory for the arbitral tribunal and it is the arbitrators' duty to comply. Third, the parties may decide only to choose the substantive rules of the applicable law. If so, the arbitrators will apply those rules in the same manner that the rules are applied in their country of origin. A second option is for the parties to choose the conflict-of-law rules of the applicable law. In such situations the arbitrators should follow the connecting factors of the chosen PIL and apply the substantive rules indicated by these factors. This option could nonetheless lead to *renvoi* in two forms: remission and transmission with all the vagueness that accompanies the application of the conflict-of-law rules of the PIL. The arbitrators must apply the rules whether the rules chosen are the substantive or the conflict-of-law rules.

9.12. Here the ICAA/BG passage cited above adds that element which is important for establishing the limits of arbitrator freedom in the determination of the substantive law. As we noted earlier, if the parties agree that the conflict-of-law rules shall be encompassed by the law applicable to the dispute, their agreement must be explicit. Should an explicit agreement be lacking, the arbitrators are bound to apply the chosen substantive rules. Bulgarian drafters strictly follow the rule expressed in Article 28 (1) MAL entitled *"Rules applicable to [the] substance of [the] dispute,"* the second paragraph of which reads: "...Any designation of the law or legal system of a given State shall be construed, unless otherwise expressed, as directly referring to the substantive law of that State and not to its conflict of laws rules."

---

[3]   Promulgated in Bulgaria in the SG 57/21 July 1964.

9.13. If there are gaps in the chosen law and the issues of the substance of the case cannot be regulated completely by the selected substantive law, the autonomy of the arbitrators in finding rules to fill in these gaps is restricted by the obligation to exclusively use the substantive rules of the law chosen by the parties. They can only use the rules of this law that are especially devoted to filling gaps. That requirement puts specific limits on the arbitrator's autonomy in such situations.

9.14. Fourth, the arbitrators shall decide which law to apply in cases where the parties aren't given a choice. The arbitrators may then enjoy broad freedom in determining this law. The rules to be chosen are left to the arbitrators' discretion.[4] What they may do first is consider which conflict-of-law rules to apply in order to find a substantive law. Two options emerge here: the rules could be the conflict-of-law rules of the seat of arbitration or the conflict-of-law rules drawn from another country's private international law, which the arbitrators deem to be appropriate.

9.15. Article 38 (2) ICAA/BG does not explicitly extend the freedom of arbitrators to directly make a choice on the substantive rules. But the rule should be interpreted as favoring that possibility. This interpretation follows from the phrase "considers applicable" attributed to the "conflict-of-law rules" that point out a law. An implicit meaning located within this paragraph of the rule may be found, which opens up another possibility for the arbitrators. According to this passage should the arbitrators consider in a particular case that no conflict-of-law rule exists at all or can't be applied, then they may directly choose the substantive rules of law that are to regulate the merits of the case. In such situations, if substantive rules have been chosen directly by the arbitrators, these could be the rules of any national law that the arbitrators consider applicable.[5]

9.16. On the other hand, in contrast to the Bulgarian state courts' duty to apply the conflict-of-law rules of the Bulgarian PIL, should arbitrators happen to decide to apply the conflict-of-law rules, they are not bound to apply the Bulgarian conflict-of-law rules.[6] Although this obligation is

---

[4]   Иван Владимиров (Ivan Vladimirov), Арбитражът в Международното Частно Право (*Arbitration in Private International Law*), София: Издателска къща СОФИ – Р (Sofia: Publishing House SOFI-R) 168 (2000).

[5]   This interpretation is accepted in the doctrine – see for instance the explanation of the *voie directe* and *voie indirecte* by Margaret L. Moses, The Principles And Practice Of International Commercial Arbitration, Cambridge: Cambridge University Press 77-78 (2008).

[6]   Живко Сталев (Zhivko Stalev), Арбитраж по Частноправни Спорове (Arbitration on Private Legal Disputes), София: Издателска къща СИЕЛА (Sofia: Publishing House CIELA) 126 (1997).

not imposed on the arbitrators, Bulgarian arbitration practice shows that arbitrators are at times reluctant to decline use of the Bulgarian Code of Private International Law (i.e., their domestic conflict-of-law rules) and implicitly follow its principles. However, this same practice points to the fact that arbitral tribunals in Bulgaria do not forget "the more subtle and informal character of arbitration as compared to the work of judicial authorities."[7]

9.17. Fifth, the terms of the contract are to be applied by the arbitrators as well. The third paragraph of Article 38 ICAA/BG makes adhering to the terms of the contract compulsory for the arbitrators. This corresponds to the mandatory character of the contract for its parties. Bulgarian Law treats the contract as law for the parties. Under Article 20 (a) of the Obligations and Contracts Act, "Contracts shall have the force of law for the parties that have concluded them."[8] Since the parties agreed on the terms of their contract and the terms have the force of law, the effect of these facts for the determination of the law applicable to the merits of an international arbitration case is the same as if the parties had chosen that law. And since the arbitrators are bound to apply the law chosen by the parties, they are similarly obligated to apply the terms of the contract between these same parties.

9.18. Sixth, the trade usages are to be taken into account by the arbitrators when they consider the applicable law. No doubt the international trade usages are meant here by the second indent of Article 38, paragraph 3 ICAA/BG. Due to the fact that trade usages are not themselves law, arbitrators may not apply them. However in all cases the arbitration tribunal shall take the trade usages into account.

9.19. In sum, it should be pointed out that despite these restrictions in accordance with Bulgarian law as we see it applied in the field, arbitrators have a great deal of freedom in determining the law applicable to the merits of a case.

---

[7]   Nikolay Natov (coord.), Boriana Musseva, Vassil Pandov, Dafina Sarbinova, Nikolay Bandakov, Stanislav Yordanski, Teodora Tsenova, Tsvetan Krumov, Zahari Yanakiev, *Bulgaria, in* APPLICATION OF FOREIGN LAW, Munich: Sellier – European Law Publishers GmbH 145, 158 (C. E. Mota, J. L. I. Buhigues, G. Palao eds., 2011).

[8]   Obligations and Contracts Act (OCA), Incl. the denomination of 5 July 1999; Corr. SG. 2/3 Jan 1950, Promulgated in SG. 275/22 Nov 1950, amend. SG. 69/28 Aug 1951, amend. SG. 92/7 Nov 1952, amend. SG. 85/1 Nov 1963, amend. SG. 27/3 Apr 1973, amend. SG. 16/25 Feb 1977, amend. SG. 28/9 Apr 1982, amend. SG. 30/13 Apr 1990, amend. SG. 12/12 Feb 1993, amend. SG. 56/29 Jun 1993, amend. SG. 83/1 Oct 1996, amend. SG. 104/6 Dec 1996, amend. SG. 83/21 Sep 1999, amend. SG. 103/30 Nov 1999, amend. SG. 34/25 Apr 2000, suppl. SG. 19/28 Feb 2003, amend. SG. 42/17 May 2005, amend. SG. 43/20 May 2005, amend. SG. 36/2 May 2006, amend. SG. 59/20 Jul 2007, amend. SG. 92/13 Nov 2007, amend. SG. 50/30 May 2008; Art. 1. (Repealed, SG No. 12/1993)

9.20. As discussed, the autonomy of arbitrators is to a certain extent limited. We have examined two limitations that are legally recognized, but there are others. Public policy is thought to set the first limit upon arbitrator autonomy. Arbitrators' choices must meet the test for public policy when foreign law has been chosen as applicable to the substance of the dispute. The question is: what criteria to apply? National criteria or international ones? Or should both be taken into consideration?

9.21. In the first place arbitrators must take into account the public policy of the seat of arbitration. If they don't, they risk having the award based on the application of a substantive law that contravenes the public policy rules of the seat. This may lead to setting aside under that public policy law due to the contradiction between the award and the public policy rules of the country where the award was rendered.[9]

9.22. If the seat of the arbitration is in one country but the law applicable to the arbitration *(the Lex arbitri)* is that of another country, then the award must conform to the public policy rules of that other country. If in such delocalization of the arbitration, the award is based on the application of a substantive law that contravenes the public policy rules of the country under whose law the award has been rendered such an award will be at risk of annulment, too.

9.23. Second, arbitrators should also bear in mind the public policy rules of the country where the award is to be recognized and enforced. If they render an award by applying a substantive law that contravenes the public policy rules of the country of recognition and enforcement there is always the risk that the award may be denied recognition and enforcement due to its contradiction of the public policy of that country. Such a situation is envisaged by Article V, paragraph 2 (b) of the New York Convention. The text provides for the review of the conformity of an award, rendered by an international arbitration, with the public policy rules of the country where recognition or enforcement are sought. The same rule was adopted by the national arbitration legislation of other countries.[10] Its background is MAL – Art. 34, (2) (b) (ii).

9.24. The principles of public policy that national courts apply, which could revoke or deny recognition and enforcement of an international arbitration award, are mostly recognized as "international public

---

[9] See Art. IX, European Convention; Art. 47 (3) of the ICAA/BG which states that if the arbitral award contradicts the public policy of the Republic of Bulgaria, the Supreme Court of Cassation may revoke it.

[10] See for instance the Swiss Private International Law Statute, Art. 190 (2)(e); the French Code of Civil Procedure, Art. 1502 (5) and Art. 1594; the English Arbitration Act, Sec. 68 (2) (g).

policy."[11] The arbitrators are bound to respect and obey the rules of international public policy – "these rules being derived from the comparison of the fundamental requirements of various domestic legal systems and from public international law."[12]

9.25.   The application of public policy rules reveals another difference between international arbitrations and state courts. State courts, before which international arbitral awards could be revoked or denied recognition and enforcement, apply their own national requirements and public policy criteria. Most of these criteria and requirements are adjusted to international public policy standards. The courts strive to ensure that the international arbitration award is in accordance with these national requirements and criteria.

9.26.   In fact, the consequences of applying public policy may be grave for the selected substantive law. These consequences may be far reaching and have as their final result disregard for the choice made by the parties or by the conflict-of-law rule. By declining application of some rules of the chosen law by reasoning of consideration of national or transnational public policy, the arbitrators exercise one of their main duties in the international arbitration – to render an enforceable award that meets the requirements of international public policy.[13]

9.27.   The award must successfully pass the test of public policy in two countries alternatively – that of the seat of the arbitration or the other country under whose law the award was rendered. This must be done to avoid having the award set aside at the seat of the arbitration.

9.28.   Arbitrators should also ponder how their award will be recognized during the eventual future procedure for the award's recognition and enforcement in the various jurisdictions. Obviously, to ensure their award will be recognized and enforced in these jurisdictions, the international arbitrators should also do their best to ascertain that the award successfully passes the test of public policy in the country of its eventual future recognition and enforcement. This is extremely important and especially when it concerns a country where the enforcing courts are required to apply the public policy test *ex officio*.[14] Of course arbitrators are not expected to give guarantees but, as Art. 35

---

[11]   Emmanuel Gaillard, *The Role of the Arbitration in Determining the Applicable Law, in* THE LEADING ARBITRATORS' GUIDE TO INTERNATIONAL ARBITRATION, New York: Juris Publishing, Inc. 171, 197-198 (L. W. Newman, R. D. Hill eds., 2nd ed. 2008)

[12]   *Ibid.*, at 198.

[13]   *Ibid.*, at 201; MARGARET L. MOSES, *supra* note 5, at 81-83.

[14]   NIGEL BLACKABY, CONSTANTINE PARTASIDES & ALAN REDFERN, MARTIN HUNTER, REDFERN AND HUNTER ON INTERNATIONAL ARBITRATION, Oxford: Oxford University Press 656 (2009).

of the ICC Rules requests "... the Arbitral Tribunal shall act in the spirit of these Rules and shall make every effort to make sure the Award is enforceable at law." The eventual result of the work of the international arbitration is a final enforceable award.[15]

9.29. Thus, together with consideration of international public policy, other factors must be made part of their deliberations. Arbitrators should bear in mind i) the public policy of the seat of arbitration or ii) the same rules of the country under whose law the award is to be rendered as well as iii) the public policy of the jurisdiction where the award is to be eventually recognized and enforced.

9.30. These three groups of rules constitute the first and the most important limitation upon arbitrator autonomy in determining the applicable law.

9.31. When the parties agree that only the substantive rules of the chosen law will apply, the arbitrators are limited by this decision. They cannot apply some other rules but only those agreed to by the parties. In such situations the parties prevent the possibility of burdening the process of decision-making by anticipation of the *renvoi*. They do not accept remission or transmission (the two forms of *renvoi*) because the nature of both is to introduce uncertainty in the considerations of the merits due to the difficulty of determining the applicable substantive law.[16]

9.32. If the substantive law chosen by the parties doesn't contain complete regulation for the particular case or is impaired by gaps the arbitrators are free to fill in these gaps by choosing rules for that purpose. In this, however, the autonomy of the arbitrators is again limited to the substantive law chosen by the parties. This means that the arbitrators must stay within the selected substantive law and try to find in that law the rules to address those gaps. They are not permitted to go beyond these boundaries and directly choose another country's substantive law in the search for answers. They may apply foreign law as an exception only and when it is clear that the chosen law doesn't have the appropriate rules.

9.33. The international arbitrators must respect the intentions of the parties. This is undoubtedly the arbitrators' duty when the parties have expressly chosen the law. It remains their duty to respect the parties' intentions even when the parties have failed to expressly choose the law or have done so but in an implicit way. This is because the arbitrators are bound to make every effort to understand (or even decode) the parties' intentions. They are required to delve into the details of the contract and extract from those details the intentions of the parties that

---

[15]   *Ibid.*, at 517.
[16]   See MARGARET L. MOSES, *supra* note 5, at 73-74.

were implemented in the contract's clauses. This very method is applied by the Court of Arbitration of the Bulgarian Chamber of Commerce and Industry.[17]

9.34. The parties' intentions should be derived from their previous relations, from their correspondence, from the results of their meetings and talks, from the practice they have established among themselves. In so doing, the arbitrators first of all seek the intentions of the parties with regard to the methodology they envisaged would be applicable in ascertaining the substantive law. Thus, the arbitrators are totally bound by the parties' intentions. This duty to ascertain the parties' intentions further limits arbitrator autonomy in determining the substantive law applicable to the merits of the case.

9.35. With regard to the arbitrators' duty to take the terms of the contract into account: Bulgarian arbitrators constantly verify that this has been done and in cases where the parties have not chosen the law and the contract contains a foreign element that links the contract to foreign law, the arbitrators apply that law.[18] Clearly such foreign elements may be obtained from the terms of the contract.

9.36. Furthermore, it should be noted that the freedom of arbitrators to determine the law may be further limited by the terms of the contract. If, for instance, the parties have introduced a clause into the contract under which the conflict-of-law rules of a given country are to be applied by the arbitrators in order to determine the substantive law applicable to the case, the freedom of the arbitrators to determine this law is limited by the said term of the contract. Such a clause could also request that the arbitrators apply the private international law of the seat of the arbitration.[19]

9.37. Commercial usage marks yet another limit to the autonomy of international arbitrators. Bulgarian arbitrators make use of the "commercial usage" test when deciding international cases.[20] By determining the substantive law the arbitrators should take into account international commercial usage. It could be argued that the consideration of commercial usage places the final border around arbitrator autonomy. The applicability of commercial usage may be

---

[17] See: Practice of the Court of Arbitration of the Bulgarian Chamber of Commerce and Industry (CA/BCCI) – in short CA/BCCI Practice, Case No. 223/91; Case No. 2/94, available at: http://www.bcci.bg (1989 – 1995) (accessed on June 15, 2011) .

[18] CA/BCCI Practice, Award No. 84/95 available at: http://www.bcci.bg (accessed on June 15, 2011) (1996).

[19] See Emmanuel Gaillard, *supra* note 11, at 186.

[20] CA/BCCI Practice, Award No. 24/91 available at: http://www.bcci.bg (accessed on June 15, 2011) (1989 – 1995).

drawn from various sources. First, commercial usage could be a term agreed upon by the parties – and if the parties have so agreed, the arbitral tribunal must apply that usage. Second, such usage may be a rule of the applicable substantive law. If there is no such agreement by the parties but the applicable substantive law requires their application then the arbitrators must apply that usage. Third, the arbitrators could deem international commercial usage to be directly applicable. In other words, regardless of the selected substantive law, the international commercial usage is to be applied along with that law.

9.38. In sum, even when broad, the autonomy of arbitrators is limited in various respects. The public policy to be applied only as an exception may place the most restrictive limit upon their freedom.

9.39. Another question concerns the character of the choice of law made by the parties. Is this choice mandatory for international arbitrators and if so – to what extent?

9.40. When parties, acting within the framework of their freedom to select the substantive law make their choice, the consequence is that a substantive law applicable to the merits of the case is found. As previously stressed, party autonomy is a well recognized principle in private international law and the arbitrators are bound to respect this principle and apply the law chosen by the parties.[21] The arbitrators cannot deviate from the choice and apply another law except when for public policy reasons the applicability of some rule (or rules) is declined and the arbitrators are left to find other rule(s) meeting the public policy test.

9.41. After the parties have reached an agreement on the applicable law, they commonly turn that agreement into a clause of the contract, but the clause itself at times may also contain stabilization conditions. In the second half of the 20th century academics debated over the validity of such stabilization clauses in international commercial contracts.[22] Such clauses no doubt serve to express the parties' autonomy to determine the substantive law to be applied to their contract. The consequence of the stabilization clause is that it allows the applicable law to be "frozen" (stabilized) – usually as it stood at the time of the conclusion of the contract or at any other time deemed important by the parties. Normally stabilization clauses may be found in contracts between a private party and a public party, for e.g., a State whose law is selected by the parties as applicable to the

---

[21] Cindy G. Buys, *The Arbitrators Duty to Respect the Parties' Choice of Law in Commercial Arbitration*, 79 (1) St. John's L. R. 59 (2005).
[22] See Emmanuel Gaillard, *supra* note 11, at 172.

contract. The purpose of having a stabilization clause is to protect private parties from the legislative power of the State which is a party to the contract too. Without going deeper into the theoretical debate or discussing whether the use of stabilization clauses could result in application to the merits of the case of a substantive law that no longer exists or whether the use of such clauses would effectively lead to putting the parties above the law and whether this is acceptable or not, I would like to mention the following: instead of drafting such clauses and incorporating them into international contracts, States should enact statutes or sign international treaties with stabilization norms within them. Such norms give much more surety to private parties and their business, especially in the field of international investment and contracts between private investors and States.

9.42. Even if the parties have selected the substantive law for their contract and have agreed on a stabilization clause about this law or on a clause under which it may appear that part or the entire contract might be declared void, the arbitrators must respect the parties' will. This is because the duty of the arbitrators encompasses not only the choice of the applicable law but the terms of the contract as well. So they first are bound to apply the substantive law based on the fact that it was chosen by the parties. They also should apply this law as it stands, as it is stabilized by the "freezing" clause because the clause is itself a term of the contract and as such is further stabilized by arbitrator duty too. This also applies when under the selected law a given contract should be declared partially or wholly null and void. These issues are tied more to the process of ascertaining the content of foreign law, than they are to the problem of determining the applicable substantive law.[23]

9.43. Concerning whether the parties have chosen the substantive law in an explicit or implicit way: In both situations the arbitrators are obligated to respect their choice.[24] If the choice is not clear or is implicit the arbitrators should make every effort to discover the actual will of the parties as to the applicable law.

9.44. If, after taking into account all the circumstances of the case, the arbitrators come to the conclusion that the will of the parties in choosing a substantive law was discredited, because, for instance, either the parties or one of them did not have the capacity to enter

---

[23] *Ibid.*, for more details at 172 – 177.

[24] CA/BCCI Practice, Case No. 2/94 available at: http://www.bcci.bg (1996) (accessed on June 15, 2011) – by testing the will of parties the arbitrators in this case discovered their implicit choice of law and applied it.

such an agreement, or because of fraud, these facts would provide the ground for declaring the choice of law clause of the contract null and void. The consequence of this nullification of the clause would be the possibility that the arbitrators would themselves choose the law applicable to the merits of the case. But even then, before doing so the arbitrators should consider the intentions of the parties during the process of negotiations for the contract as to the applicable law. Only if it is certain that no indications of the intentions of parties exist should the arbitrators feel free to choose the applicable law.

9.45.   Another example of an instance when arbitrators may disregard the will of the parties on the applicable law is found when the will of the parties fails to meet the formal requirements of that law because it is not in the requested written form, not notarized, etc. Even here the arbitrators should attempt to rectify the formal invalidity to the extent possible and only if doing so proves impossible should they themselves choose the applicable law.

9.46.   In sum – the arbitrators are bound by the parties' choice of the applicable law. They must respect the explicit as well as the parties' implicit choice. The arbitrators should always seek out the intentions of the parties. The chosen law's applicability should be declined only after it has failed to meet the public policy test. The arbitrators may disregard the parties' choice when the parties will proves to be invalid due to fraud, incapacity of party/parties, or due to lack of the formal validity of the choice of law clause of the contract. If some or both reasons are present the arbitrators should be the ones to choose.

9.47.   If the parties have failed to determine the applicable law, the arbitrators must determine it. Questions remain: how may the arbitrators determine the substantive law in the absence of the parties' choice and what methods should they apply?

9.48.   Generally, three methods are distinguished for determining the applicable law in the absence of the choice of the parties. All three methods grant broad autonomy to arbitrators.[25]

9.49.   The methods are as follows: Use of the UNCITRAL method of application of conflict-of-law rules that the arbitrators deem proper; Use of the Swiss method of application of conflict-of-law rules of the PIL of the seat of arbitration; or use of the method of direct choice by the arbitrators.

---

[25]   Emmanuel Gaillard, *supra* note 11, at 188.

9.50. The UNCITRAL method is one of the most popular. It is adopted by many countries worldwide including Bulgaria. As mentioned above (Paragraph 1, supra) Art.38 (1) ICAA/BG implements this method in Bulgarian arbitration legislation. Under the UNCITRAL Rules and under MAL, in the absence of a choice by the parties the arbitrators are to identify the proper conflict-of-law rule and apply it to the dispute. Then, by following the choice made by that rule the arbitrators should determine the substantive law applicable to the merits of the case. In other words the choice of the arbitrators is that of the conflict-of-law rule which they deem to be appropriate. The method at hand gives arbitrators very broad autonomy as to the choice of the specific conflict-of-law rule they will apply.

9.51. Within this method there is private international law and the arbitrators apply that rule. Various approaches exist as to determining which state's private international law shall be applied.

9.52. Article VII, paragraph 1 of the European Convention provides the first legal expression of this method. It states: "Failing any indication by the parties as to the applicable law, the arbitrators shall apply the proper law under the rule of conflict that the arbitrators deem applicable."

9.53. The UNCITRAL Arbitration Rules of 1976 was the original source for this method. According to Article 33 of the Rules, in the absence of a choice of law by the parties, "the arbitral tribunal shall apply the law determined by the choice of law rules which it considers applicable." Article 28 (2) MAL (as amended in 2006) has the identical regulation. The same rule was adopted in the English Arbitration Act of 1996 in Sec. 46 (3) and in the Zivilprozessordnung (the German arbitration statute of 1997) in Art. 1051, paragraph 2.

9.54. To answer the question concerning which conflict-of-law rule of exactly what PIL shall be applied in order to determine the applicable substantive law, the arbitrators may first seek to ascertain the national legal systems to which the case at hand is connected. They then select the conflict-of-law rules of those systems and if they all point to the same substantive law, the arbitrators are to apply this law to the merits of the dispute. The benefits of this method are the possibility of foreseeing the result and the respect shown to the parties' legitimate expectations. But if the various conflict-of-law rules of the national legal systems that are linked to the dispute should lead to different results, i.e. different substantive laws, this approach will obviously prove ineffective. However, even if that method should fail, the arbitrators still have a second option – they may rely on the generally accepted principles of private international law as these later have been adopted by the legislation of many states.[26] This approach may be seen in the practice of Bulgarian arbitrators.[27] As parties to Case 20/04 of the CA/BCCI failed to choose the substantive law, the arbitrators applied the generally accepted principle of the "characteristic performance of the contract" and decided that the applicable law would be the law of the domicile of the defendant who was, under the contract, to execute the characteristic performance.

9.55.   Arbitrators may also take into consideration the same generally accepted principles as those adopted by the main international instruments in the field:[28] doctrine or international arbitral practice.[29]

9.56.   As far as the Swiss method is concerned its subject is the application of the conflict-of-law rules of the seat of arbitration's private international law that are specifically drafted for application in international arbitration cases. The Swiss Statute on Private International Law of 1987 so provides in Art. 187, that in the absence of a choice of substantive law by the parties, the arbitrators shall apply the rules of law "with which the case has [the] closest connection." This is a conflict-of-law rule specifically drafted to be applied by international arbitrations. No doubt it is flexible enough to give the arbitrators the freedom to choose the substantive law which – under the circumstances of every particular case – they deem to be most closely connected to the case at hand.[30]

9.57.   The direct choice method is estimated as being most open to the arbitrators' freedom to select the substantive law applicable to the merits of the case. How it differs from the previous two methods lies in the possibility that it gives to arbitrators to directly choose the substantive rule they deem appropriate for settling the dispute without need of recourse to any conflict-of-law rule. They may, but are not obligated to apply some conflict-of-law rules and may resort directly to a substantive rule.[31]

---

[26]   Especially by the states with old and/or developed traditions in the international commercial arbitration like the UK, France, Germany, the US, Australia, Canada, the Netherlands, Sweden, Italy.

[27]   It has been constantly applied by Bulgarian arbitrators since 1994: see CA/BCCI Practice, Case No. 20/94; Case No. 18/2000; Case No. 20/2004, available at: http://www.bcci.bg (1989 – 1996; 2000 – 2001 and 2004 – 2005) (accessed on June 15, 2011).

[28]   For instance: the 1980 Rome Convention on the Law Applicable to Contractual Obligations and the 1980 Vienna Convention on the International Sale of Goods.

[29]   The practice of the ICC, ICSID, The Hague Permanent Court of Arbitration, the LCIA, the Court of Arbitration at the Stockholm Chamber of Commerce etc.

[30]   Galliard gives as a second example here Art. 39 of the Egyptian Law No. 27 of 1994, see Emmanuel Gaillard, *supra* note 11, at 190.

[31]   Emmanuel Gaillard, *supra* note 11, at 190-191 notes that the direct choice method

9.58. When dealing with a given case arbitrators face another question of highly practical importance. The question concerns the role of the mandatory (overriding)[32] rules for international arbitration and may usually appear before the process for determining the applicable law has begun, during that process, or after.

9.59. The mandatory (overriding) rules are rules of law that purport to apply regardless of whether the law was chosen by the parties or selected on the basis of the conflict-of-law rule.[33] The attitude of the arbitrators towards such rules is debated in the theoretical literature. No doubt these rules should be respected in any legal proceeding. But, as practice shows, there are various approaches to international arbitration which may range from neglect to complete obedience.[34]

9.60. Bulgarian law uses the term "special mandatory rules" and regulates the rules in the Code of Private International law in the following manner:

"Special Mandatory Rules

Art. 46. (1) The provisions of the Code shall not impact [the] application of the mandatory rules of Bulgarian law, which, in view of their subject and purpose, shall be applied, not depending on the reference to the foreign law.

(2) The court may take in[to] consideration the mandatory rules of the other state, to which the relationship is in a close connection, if these rules as per the law of the other state shall be applied, not depending on which law has been defined as applicable accordingly to the conflict-of-law rules of the code. In order to decide if to apply such special mandatory rules, the court shall take in[to] consideration their nature and their subject, as well as the consequences of their application or of the avoidance of their application."[35]

'has been adopted by a number of modern national arbitration statutes, the foremost examples being Article 1496 (1) of the French New Code of Civil Procedure and Article 1054 (2) of the Netherlands Code of Civil Procedure (introduced by the 1986 Netherlands Arbitration Act). This method has gained enormous ground through its recent adoption by the majority of the most widely used arbitrations institutions including the AAA, the LCIA, the ICC and the Stockholm Chamber of Commerce." More details about the three methods see there at 188-191; also see MARGARET L. MOSES, *supra* note 5, at 78-79.

[32] DICEY AND MORRIS ON THE CONFLICT OF LAWS, London: Sweet & Maxwell 32 (L. A. Collins ed., 13th ed. 2000).

[33] Andrew Barraclough; Jeff Waincymer, *Mandatory Rules of Law in International Commercial Arbitration*, 9 MELBJLINTLAW 1, 1-5 (2005).

[34] *Ibid.*, at 7-10.

[35] The Code of Private International Law (CPIL) was promulgated in the 42 (17) SG. May 2005, amend. 59 (20) SG. July 2007, 47 (23) SG. June 2009.

9.61. According to Bulgarian theory, PIL paragraph 1 of this Article is interpreted as imposing a duty upon the Bulgarian court to apply the special mandatory rules of its national law before seeking recourse in the conflict-of-law rules. In contrast, when the court is faced with the special mandatory rules of a foreign law there is no duty to apply them. If such rules are selected as applicable by a conflict-of-law rule or by the parties, the Bulgarian court should then ponder the broader questions on the nature of these rules, their subject, as well as the consequences of their application or non-application. Only after so doing may it decide whether or not the special mandatory rules apply.[36]

9.62. Both national judges and international arbitrators should apply the mandatory rules. In the theory of international arbitration the application of these rules is held to be accepted as "uncontroversial"[37] and such an approach should be supported. The importance of the special mandatory rules, in principle, limits the freedom of the arbitrators to choose the applicable law and could sometimes preclude their freedom. As to the mandatory rules of the seat of arbitration, the arbitrators should respect them. In contrast to the conflict-of-law rules of the seat which arbitrators are not obliged to apply, the seat's mandatory rules are based on the fundamental values of the given country such as for instance its national sovereignty and as such it is the duty of the arbitrators to apply them.[38]

9.63. As far as the mandatory rules of another country are concerned arbitrators should apply or disregard them depending on whether these are the rules of a country whose law is applicable to the arbitration *(Lex arbitri)*, or are the rules selected by the parties. The *Lex arbitri's* mandatory rules should be applied by the arbitrators; otherwise their award would be at risk of being set aside or being denied recognition and enforcement for public policy reasons. The parties' chosen foreign law mandatory rules could be disregarded by the arbitrators or applied by them depending on their consideration of various facts as for instance the nature of these rules, their subject, as well as the consequences of their application or non-application.

| | |

---

[36] НИКОЛАЙ С. НАТОВ (NIKOLAY S. NATOV), КОМЕНТАР НА КОДЕКСА НА МЕЖДУНАРОДНОТО ЧАСТНО ПРАВО. КНИГА ПЪРВА, ЧЛЕН 1 – 47 (*1 Commentary of the Code of Private International Law, Article 1 – 47*), София: Издателска къща СИЕЛА (Sofia: Publishing House CIELA) 393-395 (2006).

[37] See Andrew Barraclough, Jeff Waincymer, *supra* note 33, at 10 et seq.

[38] MARGARET L. MOSES, *supra* note 5, at 80-81.

Summaries

FRA [*Autonomie des Arbitres en Matière de Détermination du Droit Applicable au Fond d'une Affaire*]

Cet article traite des aspects juridiques et pratiques de l'autonomie des arbitres en matière de détermination du droit applicable au fond d'une affaire. Il se fonde sur la législation et la pratique bulgares, et dresse une comparaison avec la législation d'autres états, les principaux instruments internationaux, les Règles et la Loi-Type de la CNUDCI, ainsi que les Règles de la CCI. La thèse part du principe que les arbitres bénéficient d'une grande latitude pour déterminer le droit substantiel. Cette liberté se trouve cependant limitée par les règles d'ordre public en vigueur dans le lieu d'arbitrage de l'état dont le droit régit la sentence, et du lieu où cette sentence est éventuellement reconnue et appliquée. Les arbitres ne sont pas tenus d'appliquer les règles de conflit de lois du siège de l'arbitrage. Ils doivent en revanche appliquer le droit choisi par les parties. Si les parties n'ont pas exprimé leur choix, ce sont les arbitres qui choisissent le droit qu'ils souhaitent appliquer. Ils peuvent alors recourir aux règles de conflit de lois ou choisir directement les règles substantielles. Même s'ils n'ont pas à fournir de garanties d'aucune sorte, les arbitres ont le devoir de rendre une sentence légalement exécutable. Lorsqu'il s'agit d'une affaire internationale, les arbitres doivent respecter les règles obligatoires du lieu d'arbitrage, tandis qu'ils peuvent se conformer aux règles statutaires étrangères dans certaines conditions.

CZE [*Autonomie rozhodců při určování práva rozhodného pro meritum věci*]

Tento článek se zabývá právními a praktickými aspekty autonomie rozhodců při určování práva rozhodného pro meritum věci. Vychází z bulharské legislativy a praxe v porovnání s právními předpisy některých jiných zemí, základní mezinárodní právní úpravou, Pravidly a Vzorovým zákonem UNCITRAL a Pravidly ICC. Výchozím předpokladem je, že rozhodci jsou při určování použitelného hmotného práva nadáni poměrně širokou volností. Tato volnost je omezena především normami veřejného pořádku zakotvenými v právu místa konání rozhodčího řízení, státu, podle jehož práva byl rozhodčí nález vydán, a místa případného uznání a výkonu nálezu. Rozhodci nejsou povinni aplikovat kolizní normy místa konání rozhodčího řízení. Musí aplikovat právo zvolené stranami. V případě absence volby práva stranami aplikují rozhodci právo, které určí sami. V tomto ohledu mohou buď vycházet z kolizních norem, nebo použitelné hmotněprávní normy určit přímo. Rozhodci sice nemusí dávat žádné záruky, jsou ale povinni vydat nález, který bude dle práva vykonatelný. V případě řešení mezinárodních sporů by rozhodci měli respektovat kogentní normy místa řízení; respektování cizích kogentních norem je naproti tomu pouze dobrovolné a závisí na splnění určitých podmínek.

| | |

POL [*Autonomia Arbitrów w Zakresie Ustalania Prawa Regulującego Meritum Sprawy*]

Praca dotyczy prawnych i praktycznych aspektów autonomii arbitrów w zakresie ustalania prawa regulującego meritum sprawy. Opracowanie to zostało oparte na ustawodawstwie i praktyce bułgarskiej w zestawieniu z ustawodawstwem kilku innych państw, głównych instrumentów międzynarodowych, Regulaminem i Prawem Modelowym UNCITRAL oraz Regulaminem ICC. Do kluczowych kwestii należą granice swobody arbitrów i ich obowiązki w tym zakresie.

DEU [*Autonomie von Schiedsrichtern bei der Bestimmung des in der Sache Anzuwendenden Rechts*]

Diese Arbeit befasst sich mit den rechtlichen und praktischen Aspekten der Ermessensfreiheit von Schiedsrichtern bei der Bestimmung des auf die inhaltlichen (materiellrechtlichen) Aspekte eines Rechtsstreits anzuwendenden Rechts. Sie basiert auf der bulgarischen Rechtsprechung und Praxis im Vergleich zur Gesetzgebung anderer Staaten, wichtigen internationalen Instrumenten, der UNCITRAL-Schiedsgerichtsordnung sowie dem UNCITRAL-Modellgesetz und den ICC-Regeln. Schlüsselaspekte sind die Autonomie der Schiedsrichter und deren Grenzen sowie die diesbezüglichen Pflichten der Schiedsrichter.

RUS [*Независимость Судей Арбитражного Суда в Определении Права, Применимого При Рассмотрении Дел По Существу*]

В данной работе рассматриваются юридические и практические аспекты независимости судей арбитражного суда в определении права, применимого при рассмотрении дел по существу. В основу положены законодательство и практика, принятая в Болгарии, которые сопоставляются с нормами других государств и базовым международным инструментарием, правилами ЮНСИТРАЛ и типовым законом, а также Правилами МТП. В центре внимания работы — свобода судей, ее рамки и связанные с ней обязательства.

ESP   [*Autonomía de los Árbitros a la Hora de Determinar el Derecho Aplicable Sobre los Fundamentos de un Caso*]

El trabajo aborda los aspectos jurídicos y prácticos relativos a la autonomía de los árbitros a la hora de determinar el derecho aplicable sobre los fundamentos de un caso. Está basado en la legislación y práctica búlgaras en comparación con la legislación de otros estados, con los instrumentos jurídicos internacionales principales, con las normas y el modelo de ley de UNCITRAL y con las normas de la CCI. Los puntos fundamentales son la libertad de los árbitros, sus límites y sus obligaciones dentro de estos.

Mateusz Pilich

Law Applicable to the Merits of the Dispute Submitted to Arbitration in the Absence of the Choice of Law by the Parties (Remarks on Polish Law)

Key words:
International
Commercial Arbitration |
Law Applicable | Merits
of the Dispute | Choice of
Law | Arbitrators'
Discretion | Polish
Arbitration Law | Direct
Approach | Indirect
Approach

Abstract | *The object of this study is an analysis of the present tendencies of the requirements imposed on arbitration tribunals in Poland with respect to the law applicable to the substance of the dispute in the absence of a choice made by the parties. In 2005, Polish arbitration law (fifth part of the Civil Procedure Code) was significantly modified. One of the provisions added by the legislator – Article 1194, Paragraph 1 CPC – imposes a general obligation to settle the dispute in accordance with the "applicable law," which might possibly be interpreted as imposing the obligation to apply international private law. The author finds, however, that such an interpretation is not supported by the Code itself nor by the present tendencies in the law of arbitration. At the level of arbitration doctrine and jurisprudence, there are two major approaches practicable with respect to the problem: the "indirect method" (application of conflict rules by the arbitrators) or the "direct method" (designation of applicable law without the use of such mechanism). Neither Article 1194, Paragraph 1 of the Polish CPC nor the other provisions of the Code are an obstacle to the application of these two methods.*

Mateusz Pilich, Dr. iur., Assistant Professor – Chair in International Private and Trade Law at the Faculty of Law, University of Warsaw, Poland; Member of the Office for Studies and Analyses at the Supreme Court of Republic of Poland.
e-mail: m.pilich@ wpia.uw.edu.pl

|||

I. Introduction

10.01. The subject matter of this paper concerns a problem basic to the law of international commercial arbitration which, despite being rather well understood by foreign scholars, has only occasionally been touched upon in the Polish legal literature[1] – namely, the difficulty of determining the law applicable to the substance of the dispute. This lacuna in the literature may be surprising, given the importance of private international law matters to the disputing parties who neither elect the applicable law nor authorize the arbitrators to settle the case *ex aequo et bono*. Discussion of the problem has gained importance especially since the thorough change in Polish arbitration law took place in 2005.[2]

10.02. The reason why determination becomes a serious problem stems from the very essence of the legal institution of arbitration. The arbitral tribunal fulfills its obligation as moderator not by following its own will, but by following the will of the interested individuals. From the standpoint of particular States, one would be led to believe their laws should never be overlooked by the subjects of legal relationships which give rise to disputes settled in the course of arbitration proceedings. After all, the underlying function of the substantive law rules is to determine the scope of the autonomy of will of the parties to the given relationship, which simply cannot be isolated from any applicable State law.[3]

10.03. However, although one may concede that arbitration does not provide a "way out" from State legislation, it must be stressed that the arbitrators' attitude to such legal rules may deviate, all the same, from that represented by State court judges. The arbitral tribunal may settle the dispute between individuals and in this sense assist the judicial system in fulfilling its obligation, yet it remains a private institution –

---

[1]   See Maria Anna Zachariasiewicz, *Z problematyki prawa własciwego dla stosunkow rozstrzyganych przez arbitraz miedzynarodowy (From the Problematics of the Law Applicable to the Relationships Submitted to the International Arbitration), in* 1 PROBLEMY PRAWNE HANDLU ZAGRANICZNEGO (*Legal Problems of the International Trade*), Katowice: Uniwersytet Śląski 137 (1977); Dominik Mazur, *Prawo właściwe w międzynarodowym arbitrażu handlowym (Law Applicable in the International Commercial Arbitration)*, 12 (1) KWARTALNIK PRAWA PRYWATNEGO (*Private Law Quarterly*) 115 (2003).

[2]   See the Law amending the Code of Civil Procedure of 28 July 2005 (Journal of Laws 2005, No. 178, pos. 1478).

[3]   It is esp. the case with the doctrine of "self-regulatory contracts"; *cf.* Jadwiga Pazdan, *Czy mozna wylaczyc umowe spod prawa (May the Contract Be Excluded from the Scope of the State Law)*, 10 PANSTWO I PRAWO (*Law and State*) 13-14 (2005) with further references.

one not legally connected with any State territory or law in a strict sense and it does not administer justice.[4] Furthermore, while, the arbitrators must apply a set of substantive rules, in the absence of the parties' authorization to decide the case *ex aequo et bono,* they can never be absolutely sure how to determine it[5] —except of course, upon the parties' election of the applicable substantive law, which is not the subject-matter of our interest.

10.04. At the first glance, it seems unjustified to claim that the designation of the arbitration venue implies referral to the substantial law as in force within the territory of the State of arbitration.[6] Quite unfortunately, the issue of determining which law to apply to the merits is much more complex. Generally speaking, this problem is resolved by recourse to either the so-called *indirect* (in French *la voie indirecte*) or *direct methods* (*la voie directe*)[7] of applicable law designation. The distinction between the methods is predicated upon the various ways arbitrators' justify their decisions when applying a given substantive legal regulation. We will now examine these methods in brief.

---

[4] Various concepts of arbitration have been thoroughly explained in the literature; *cf.* i.a. PETER SCHLOSSER, DAS RECHT DER INTERNATIONALEN PRIVATEN SCHIEDSGERICHTSBARKEIT, Tübingen: J. C. B. Mohr (Paul Siebeck) 28 et seq. (1989). It is enough to remark that according to the "jurisdictional" theory, arbitration is an equivalent of the system of the State judiciary. Although it is logically true, from the constitutional standpoint it seems impossible for an organ created voluntarily by the parties to exercise authority in the strict sense. The State does not cease to control this legal sphere, as on the one hand it limits the arbitrability of disputes, and on the other hand it issues the exequatur and foresees certain legal remedies against the arbitral award; *cf.* Horacio A. Grigera Naón, *Choice-of-law Problems in International Commercial Arbitration in* 29 STUDIEN ZUM AUSLÄNDISCHEN AND INTERNATIONALEN PRIVATRECHT, Tübingen: J.C.B. Mohr (Paul Siebeck) 16-17 (1992), with further references.

[5] MAURO RUBINO-SAMMARTANO, INTERNATIONAL ARBITRATION: LAW AND PRACTICE, The Hague: Kluwer Law International 426 (2nd ed. 2001); PETER SCHLOSSER, *supra* note 4, at 163.

[6] Andrzej W. Wiśniewski, Maria Hauser-Morel, *Wyrok, zasady wyrokowania, inne sposoby zakończenia postepowania arbitrażowego* (*Arbitral Award, Ruling Principles in Arbitration, Other Ways of Finishing the Arbitral Proceedings*), *in* 8 SYSTEM PRAWA HANDLOWEGO. ARBITRAŻ HANDLOWY (*Commercial Law System. Commercial Arbitration*), Warszawa: C. H. Beck 503 (Andrzej Szumański ed., 2010).

[7] JULIAN D. M. LEW, LOUKAS A. MISTELIS, STEFAN M. KRÖLL, COMPARATIVE INTERNATIONAL COMMERCIAL ARBITRATION, The Hague: Kluwer Law International 427 (2003).

II. Methods of Designating the Law Applicable as to the Merits of the Arbitration Dispute

II.1. Indirect Method

10.05. The "indirect method" of solving the question of which law to apply to the merits of the arbitration dispute represents no single legal notion, but rather encompasses various ways the arbitral tribunal may ground the applicability of the substantive law. Their common denominator is the assumption of the need to search the applicable law using the rule of conflict. J. D. M. Lew believes that resolution may consist in applying either a rule or a set of rules laid down by the given State (application of a system of private international law) or the rules having non-State provenance (*application of a non-national system of private international law*). The main criterion for the distinction of these sets of rules would be the existence of the duty to apply a specific private international law system,[8] although it is unlikely that it would have any real practical or doctrinal significance. One can only recognize the contrast between the method of applying the conflict rules as in force in the arbitration venue on the one hand, and the other indirect methods which do not presuppose an a priori prominence of the one given legal system over the other; as a matter of fact, one is hard put to find a common denominator for such various ways of settling the conflict of laws, since the particular solution is not bound to rely (though it obviously can rely) on the arbitrators operating according to typical "textbook" rules of private international law.

10.06. Therefore, if we set aside the abovementioned (yet currently outmoded) obligation to apply the seat of arbitration's private international law, there are two main subcategories of the indirect method that are still adopted in the case law: namely, the *cumulative* application of conflict rules belonging to the legal systems connected to the subject-matter of the case, and referral to what are deemed to be *general* principles of private international law[9]. One might also indicate other possibilities: that of applying a system of rules of conflict freely chosen by the arbitrators themselves (still without any strict obligation),[10] and even — in spite of certain controversies that have

---

[8]   JULIAN D. M. LEW, APPLICABLE LAW IN INTERNATIONAL COMMERCIAL ARBITRATION, The Hague: Kluwer Law International 289 (1978).

[9]   Pierre Lalive, *Les règles de conflits de lois appliquées au fond du litige par l'arbitre international siégeant en Suisse,* 7 REVUE DE L'ARBITRAGE 155 (1976).

[10]   PHILIPPE FOUCHARD, EMMANUEL GAILLARD, BERTHOLD GOLDMAN, ON INTERNATIONAL COMMERCIAL ARBITRATION, The Hague: Kluwer Law International 871 (E. Gaillard, J. Savage eds., 1999).

arisen by granting such a wide margin of discretion to the arbitral tribunal —an option for self-creation of an *ad hoc* rule.

10.07. All these methods deserve at least a short comment, one informed by the evaluation of their advantages and disadvantages. The obligatory application of conflict rules in force in a given State is usually associated with theories about the so-called jurisdictional or "hybrid" nature of the arbitration.[11] Sauser-Hall's well-known report on private international law in arbitration[12] describes the nature of the arbitration as a "hybrid" or *"sui generis* legal institution," intertwining two constitutive factors: contractual and jurisdictional. The arbitration fulfills a function comparable to the State courts' jurisdiction. There is a strong interrelation between the arbitral proceedings and the law of the State within which the arbitral tribunal has its "seat" (*siège d'arbitrage*). In the absence of the parties' election of the law, the arbitrators would be bound to apply the substantive law of this State.[13] It was thus inspired by Sauser-Hall that the International Law Institute adopted the famous Amsterdam Resolution of 1957.[14] According to Article 11 of the Resolution: "The rules of choice of law in force in the state of the seat of the arbitral tribunal must be followed to settle the law applicable to the substance of the dispute." (*Les règles de rattachement en vigueur dans l'Etat du siège du tribunal arbitral doivent être suivies pour déterminer la loi applicable au fond du litige*).

10.08. This jurisdictional concept was heavily criticized. Many authors underscore that irrespective of the appearance of legal stability and foreseeability for the parties, the concept diminishes the voluntary and transnational significance of international commercial arbitration, and it disregards the very reason for the parties,' the arbitrators' or the arbitral institution's choice of the place of arbitration.[15] This latter

---

[11] OKEZIE CHUKWUMERIJE, CHOICE OF LAW IN INTERNATIONAL COMMERCIAL ARBITRATION, Westport, Connecticut: Quorum Books 126 (1994).

[12] Georges Sauser-Hall, *L'arbitrage en droit international privé,* 44 ANNUAIRE DE L'INSTITUT DE DROIT INTERNATIONAL 469 (1952), supplemented in 47 ANNUAIRE DE L'IDI 394 (1957).

[13] JULIAN D. M. LEW, LOUKAS A. MISTELIS, STEFAN KRÖLL, *supra* note 7, at 79-80.

[14] ARBITRATION IN PRIVATE INTERNATIONAL LAW (*"L'arbitrage en droit international privé"*), Resolution taken at the 14th Session of Amsterdam (French text – authoritative) is available at: http://www.idi-iil.org/idiF/resolutionsF/1957_amst_03_fr.pdf (accessed on April 27, 2011); English text – translation is available at: http://www.idi-iil.org/idiE/resolutionsE/1957_amst_03_en.pdf (accessed on April 27, 2011).

[15] Filip De Ly, *Conflicts of Law in International Arbitration – An Overview, in* CONFLICT OF LAWS IN INTERNATIONAL ARBITRATION, Munich: Sellier. European Law Publishers 6 (F. Ferrari, S. Kröll eds., 2010); PHILIPPE FOUCHARD, EMMANUEL GAILLARD, BERTHOLD GOLDMAN, *supra* note 10, at 867.

venue may have no actual link to the circumstances of the case.[16] The ambiguity of the "seat of arbitration" is also noted. In a permanent institutional arbitration, the term: "seat" may be understood to be the territory of the State in which the institution organizing or administering the arbitration is seated, inasmuch as the ad hoc arbitration casts many doubts in this regard, which cannot be overcome even with a highly casuist approach.[17] The case law that emphasizes the binding character of the given system of private international law usually highlights the obligation to apply the rules in force in the place of the arbitral proceedings.[18] Such an approach is occasionally accepted in certain contemporary codifications of arbitration law.[19]

10.09. In sum, we must conclude that the very idea of applying private international law as in force in the territory of a certain State (and in particular in the arbitral tribunal's seat or in the arbitration venue) cannot be cast aside. The arbitrators are allowed to make use of this law, as well as of any other. The matter should not be, however, to assume an *a priori* obligation which would bind arbitrators in every case.[20] To name a certain legal system (be it that of the arbitral tribunal's seat or of the arbitration venue) as the *"lex fori"* of the arbitration is also unacceptable, the latter having virtually no "forum" at all.[21]

10.10. The other approach (which, however, lies outside the scope of the present paper) would be to designate the law as that applicable in the international investment arbitration under the Washington

---

[16] OKEZIE CHUKWUMERIJE, *supra* note 11, at 126-127.

[17] JULIAN D. M. LEW, *supra* note 8, at 248-249; in Polish literature, *cf.* Maria A. Zachariasiewicz, *supra* note 1, at 141-142.

[18] See esp. ICC arbitral awards No.: 4187/1982, 2735/1976 and 6719/1994, cited after: MAURO RUBINO-SAMMARTANO, supra note 5, at 429; see also OKEZIE CHUKWUMERIJE, *supra* note 11, at 126; JULIAN D. M. LEW, *supra* note 8, at 255 et seq.

[19] JEAN-FRANÇOIS POUDRET, SÉBASTIEN BESSON, COMPARATIVE LAW OF INTERNATIONAL ARBITRATION, London: Sweet & Maxwell Ltd. 583-584 (2nd ed. 2007); Alexander J. Bělohlávek, *Law Applicable to the Merits of International Arbitration and Current Developments in Private International Law: Conflict-of-Law Rules and the Applicability of the Rome Convention, Rome I Regulation and Other EU Law Standards in International Arbitration,* 1 CZECH YEARBOOK OF INTERNATIONAL LAW, New York: Juris Publishing, Inc. 36 (A. Bělohlávek & N. Rozehnalová eds., 2010). It is believed, however, that even arbitrators sitting in such jurisdictions are exempted from the above-mentioned obligation, if the parties have so decided; speaking otherwise, the parties' will takes a priority; *cf.* PHILIPPE FOUCHARD, EMMANUEL GAILLARD, BERTHOLD GOLDMAN, *supra* note 10, at 866.

[20] OKEZIE CHUKWUMERIJE, *supra* note 11, at 127.

[21] TADEUSZ ERECINSKI, KAROL WEITZ; SAD ARBITRAZOWY (*Arbitration Tribunal*), Kraków: LexisNexis Polska 322 (2008).

Convention.[22] According to Article 42 (1), second sentence of the Convention, where the parties have not agreed upon an applicable law, the tribunal shall apply the law of the Contracting State party to the dispute, including its conflict of laws rules, and such rules of international law as may be applicable. If we take into account the specificity of this form of arbitration (between the private party and the State within whose territory the investment is placed), such a solution seems fully justified. It is enough to remark that such provisions do not usually form part of the bilateral investment treaties (BITs) entered into between Poland and some other States, although the arbitration clause forms a standard part thereof. It is claimed, however, that in practice, tribunals in BIT arbitrations apply the substantive provisions of the relevant treaty itself and other sources of international law, with host State law rules also having a role in certain questions by virtue of BIT provisions (for e.g. the legality of a covered investment, the calculation of compensation for expropriation, etc.).[23]

10.11. Some States tend to set down special rules of conflict addressed to the arbitration tribunal. A well-known example is Article 187 (1) of the Swiss Private International Law Act (IPRG)[24] according to which, in the absence of the choice of law applicable to the merits of the dispute by the parties, the arbitral tribunal shall settle the case in accordance with the law which is most strictly connected to the subject-matter of the dispute. A similar provision is to be found in Section 1051 (2) of the German Code of Civil Procedure (ZPO). Their mandatory character and the following obligatory applicability are questioned by some scholars. The dominant viewpoint, however, seems to be that the obligation should be placed on the arbitrators and not on the parties themselves. The parties are eventually left to abstain from its application to the dispute, for instance by the choice of the rules of arbitration which may work to settle in a certain way the issue of the

---

[22] Convention on the Settlement of Investment Disputes between States and Nationals of Other States of 18 March, 1965 so far not signed by the Republic of Poland; available at: http://icsid.worldbank.org/ICSID/ICSID/RulesMain.jsp (accessed on April 27, 2011).

[23] LUCY REED, JAN PAULSSON, NIGEL BLACKABY, GUIDE TO ICSID ARBITRATION, The Hague: Kluwer Law International 71-72 (2nd ed. 2011). The confirmation of this conclusion in the recent practice concerning Poland seems the partial *ad hoc* award in *Eureko B.V.* v. *Republic of Poland,* available at: http://ita.law.uvic.ca/documents/Eureko-PartialAwardandDissentingOpinion.pdf (accessed on April 27, 2011).

[24] Swiss Private International Law of 18 December 1987 available at: http://www.admin.ch/ch/d/sr/c291.html (accessed on April 27, 2011); Polish translation: JERZY POCZOBUT, KODYFIKACJE PRAWA PRYWATNEGO MIĘDZYNARODOWEGO (*Codifications of the Private International Law*), Warszawa: Wydawnictwa Uniwersytetu Warszawskiego 89 et seq. (1991).

law applicable to the substance of the arbitration award.[25] On the other hand, it is doubtful whether such a general provision would restrict arbitrators' discretion at all. The "closest connection" criterion does not provide any point of connection in a proper sense. Hence it is the arbitrators themselves who finally determine which law to apply to the merits of the dispute.[26]

10.12. To some extent, the rules of international arbitration law may support such views as to the indirect method which do not assume there to be any binding character to statutory private international law and leave a wide margin of discretion to the arbitral tribunal. In the light of Article VII (1), second sentence of the European Convention on International Commercial Arbitration,[27] failing any indication by the parties as to the applicable law, the arbitrators shall apply the proper law under the rule of conflict that the arbitrators deem applicable. A somewhat similar rule is contained in the instruments of the UN Commission for International Trade Law (UNCITRAL).[28] All these rules of law obligate the arbitral tribunal to use the indirect method but they offer virtually no precise solution, which grants the maximum liberty to the arbitral tribunal.[29] In any case, no State system of law may claim primacy.[30]

10.13. Under such circumstances, the arbitrators are certainly allowed to choose the applicable rule of conflict from among the systems of law connected to the subject-matter of the dispute. Even though no option may be ruled out here, it is very rare to find the specific provision taken from one particular legal system. By way of illustration, we mention

---

[25] JEAN-FRANÇOIS POUDRET, SÉBASTIEN BESSON; *supra* note 19, at 585-586.

[26] *Ibid.*; PHILIPPE FOUCHARD, EMMANUEL GAILLARD, BERTHOLD GOLDMAN; *supra* note 10, at 869-870.

[27] European Convention on International Commercial Arbitration, Done at Geneva on 21 April, 1961 (40 Journal of Laws 1964, pos. 270).

[28] *Cf.* Article 33(1) of the 1976 Arbitration Rules available at: http://www.uncitral.org/uncitral/en/uncitral_texts/arbitration/1976Arbitration_rules.html (accessed on April 27, 2011); Polish translation: (3) PROBLEMY PRAWNE HANDLU ZAGRANICZNEGO (*Legal Problems of the International Trade*) 161 et seq. (1979); (4) BIULETYN ARBITRAZOWY (*Arbitration Bulletin*) 53 et seq. (2007); Article 28(2) of the 1985 Model Law on International Commercial Arbitration; available at: http://www.uncitral.org/pdf/english/texts/arbitration/ml-arb/07-86998_Ebook.pdf (accessed on April 27, 2011). The UNCITRAL 1976 Rules have been revised recently and now contain a more flexible provision of Article 35(1); see the 2010 Revised Version, http://www.uncitral.org/pdf/english/texts/arbitration/arb-rules-revised/arb-rules-revised-2010-e.pdf (accessed on April 27, 2011).

[29] Ole Lando, *The Law Applicable to the Merits of the Dispute, in* ESSAYS ON INTERNATIONAL COMMERCIAL ARBITRATION 134 (P. Šarčević ed., 1989).

[30] DAVID D. CARON, LEE M. CAPLAN, MATTI PELLONPÄÄ; THE UNCITRAL ARBITRATION RULES, Oxford: Oxford University Press 131-132 (2006).

ICC arbitral award No. 1422/1966:[31] the litigious contract between the Italian producer and the Swiss distributor for the sale of goods to the USA and Mexico contained no law choice. The arbitral tribunal, whose seat was in Paris, found itself competent to assume a certain margin of discretion in specifying the substantive law. After a thorough examination of various parts of the contract it was concluded that objectively, the law was most closely linked to Italy, that the law of that State would apply, and that moreover such a solution agreed with the general principles of law of the civilized nations. The same result was approved by invoking both rules of French and Swiss private international law: the former as the *lex arbitri,* and the latter as the law of the seat of one of the parties. The award shows then some adherence to the traditional English concept of the *proper law of contract* or to the French theory of the *localisation objective;*[32] at the same time, we do encounter cumulative application of two sets of the State conflict rules being adopted.

10.14. This "cumulative" approach seems especially attractive to the arbitrators applying the indirect method. Simultaneous designation of the same substantial law by the conflict rules laid down by various lawmakers allows arbitrators to obtain a sufficiently stable and foreseeable result. At the same time it makes it easier to present the result as natural, just and consistent with the parties' expectations, and enables arbitrators to avoid the reproaches usually made against recourse to the concept of the arbitration's seat, since the rules of conflict applied cumulatively are not imposed but objectively create the "best solution."[33]

10.15. An argument against any application – not only cumulative but whichever – of the State conflict law has been put forward by the adherents of the "anational" concept of arbitration. They claim that in applying those private international law systems most strictly connected to the subject matter of the dispute, arbitrators in fact shift their duty to determine the applicable law on to the lawmaker, which contradicts the supposed autonomy of the arbitration: in this way, the arbitral tribunal executes practically a certain State policy, the expression of which is the rule of conflict.[34]

---

[31] (101) JOURNAL DU DROIT INTERNATIONAL 884 et seq. (1974).

[32] Horacio A. Grigera Naón, *supra* note 4, at 41; for the French doctrine of *"localisation objective,"* see HENRI BATIFFOL, PAUL LAGARDE, 2 DROIT INTERNATIONAL PRIVE, Paris: Libraire générale de Droit et de Jurisprudence 265-266 (7th ed. 1983).

[33] PHILIPPE FOUCHARD, EMMANUEL GAILLARD, BERTHOLD GOLDMAN, *supra* note 10, at 872; DAVID D. CARON, LEE M. CAPLAN, MATTI PELLONPÄÄ; *supra* note 30, at 132.

[34] JULIAN D. M. LEW, LOUKAS A. MISTELIS, STEFAN KRÖLL; *supra* note 7, at 430-431.

10.16. The disadvantage of – or better, the natural restraint to application of – the cumulative approach is the deadlock which can occur when the rules of conflict having a relevant connection to the subject-matter of the case nonetheless differ.[35] A reasonable compromise for their application would probably consist then in searching for a solution that would prove representative of the majority of the rules; arbitrators could also compare substantive provisions specified by various rules of conflict in order to determine whether their content justifies the same solution as to the merits.[36]

10.17. Another concept within the framework of the indirect method concerns application of the *general* principles of private international law, which seems to imitate an established doctrine used to support the substantive solution. By "general" is meant the principles universally accepted in various legal systems (at least those taken into account as being closely connected to the dispute). To be sure, the question arises whether, in the face of deep differences between various private international law systems, such basic and fundamental principles (other than the general idea of conflicts of law) do exist.[37] As arbitral praxis bears out this is just the way of justifying a solution which is held to be the most reasonable and fair in the arbitrators' eyes; viewed in its particulars, what is ever at issue is choice of the proper "connecting factor." Hence, invoking general principles of private international law becomes instead but a turn of speech serving in fact to hide the discretionary choice of law still made by the arbitrators themselves.[38]

10.18. Of course, such remarks should not imply rejection of the "general principles" method, provided that those arbitrators' decisions are serious in their motivation, grounded in comparative jurisprudence, and in the international law instruments containing provisions of private international law (including draft conventions or the treaties which still might not be in force).[39]

---

[35] PHILIPPE FOUCHARD, EMMANUEL GAILLARD, BERTHOLD GOLDMAN; *supra* note 10, at 872.

[36] DAVID D. CARON, LEE M. CAPLAN, MATTI PELLONPÄÄ; *supra* note 30, at 132.

[37] PHILIPPE FOUCHARD, EMMANUEL GAILLARD, BERTHOLD GOLDMAN, *supra* note 10, at 873; JULIAN D. M. LEW, LOUKAS A. MISTELIS, STEFAN KRÖLL, *supra* note 7, at 433.

[38] PHILIPPE FOUCHARD, EMMANUEL GAILLARD, BERTHOLD GOLDMAN, *supra* note 10, at 873-874; similarly OKEZIE CHUKWUMERIJE, *supra* note 11, at 129.

[39] PHILIPPE FOUCHARD, EMMANUEL GAILLARD, BERTHOLD GOLDMAN, *supra* note 10, at 874.

II.2. Direct Method

10.19. The law on the conflict of laws was created as a tool for the State courts. This is why its application may seem to be at odds with the nature of arbitration. Even if the parties cannot agree as to which law to apply, arbitrators usually become involved in the settlement of such controversies only to the minimal extent necessary.[40] It is this concern which has lead to the increasing popularity of the so-called "direct method," which is basically the immediate application of the substantive rules of law, by the arbitral tribunal, i.e. without invocation of any conflicts provision.[41] The first to adopt such an approach was the French arbitration law, according to which in the absence of the choice of law by the parties, the arbitral tribunal applies the legal rules (*règles de droit*) which it considers appropriate.[42] Some other legal systems followed suit (i.e. the law of the Netherlands, Lebanon and Algeria). *Voie directe* has become also a governing standard in the arbitration rules, squeezing out the abovementioned indirect approach.[43]

10.20. As to the standpoint of the arbitration rules of Polish leading arbitration institutions in this respect, the situation seems rather unclear. According to Section 8, first sentence of the Arbitration Rules of the Court of Arbitration at the Polish Chamber of Commerce in Warsaw,[44] the arbitral tribunal shall resolve a dispute pursuant to the law applicable to the relationship concerned and – provided that it was authorized to do so by the parties – pursuant to the general rules of law or equity (*ex aequo et bono*). Next, Sec. 14 (1) of the Rules of the Court of Arbitration at the Polish Confederation of Private Employers "Lewiatan"[45] states that the arbitral tribunal shall apply the substantive law of the country unanimously selected by the parties and in cases where the parties have not chosen any, the law of the country which is most closely connected to the examined legal relationship shall apply.

---

[40] JULIAN D. M. LEW, *supra* note 8, at 371.

[41] JEAN-FRANÇOIS POUDRET, SÉBASTIEN BESSON, *supra* note 19, at 586; MAURO RUBINO-SAMMARTANO, *supra* note 5, at 434.

[42] *Cf.* Article 1496 of the French Code of Civil Procedure, now replaced with the identical Article 1511 (Decree No. 2011-48 of 13 January 2011 Concerning the Reform of the Arbitration, OJFR No. 11 14/01/2011 p. 777); JEAN-LOUIS DEVOLVÉ, JEAN ROUCHE, GERALD POINTON, FRENCH ARBITRATION LAW AND PRACTICE, Alphen aan den Rijn: Kluwer Law International 146 (2003).

[43] JULIAN D. M. LEW, LOUKAS A. MISTELIS, STEFAN KRÖLL, *supra* note 7, at 434-435; PHILIPPE FOUCHARD, EMMANUEL GAILLARD, BERTHOLD GOLDMAN, *supra* note 10, at 876.

[44] See: http://www.sakig.pl/pdf/terms.en.pdf (accessed on April 27, 2011).

[45] http://www.sadarbitrazowy.org.pl/upload/RulesoftheCourtofArbitrationatPCPELewiatan 17May2010.pdf (accessed on April 27, 2011).

At first glance, the latter rules seem to be more in agreement with the direct method than with the former, which limits itself to repetition of the Polish Code of Civil Procedure.

10.21. At least where the French law is concerned, the direct approach seems to be practically on par with granting the unrestricted discretion of arbitrators in determining the applicable substantive law. There is virtually no indication and no legal standard as to their choice. It is remarkable that the notion of "rules of law" as provided in Article 1496 (now Article 1512) of the French Code cannot be identified with the "law" as such; while the latter points quite precisely at the system of rules laid down by the State, the former may stem from various sources and not necessarily have such a formal character – the supra- or non-national origin of such rules being conceivable as well.[46] It is believed that only two specific limitations may be derived from the content of the above-cited provision: first, that the arbitral tribunal in France cannot issue an award based exclusively on the general principles of law (*par amiable composition*), unless authorized to do so by the parties, and second, that it cannot violate "international public policy."[47]

10.22. The theory itself of direct application of the substantive rules by the arbitral tribunal does not differ much from the abovementioned doctrine of the *proper law*. In both cases, arbitrators look for that system of law (a set of legal rules) which is most closely connected to the subject matter of the dispute and which best serves its settlement. Practically speaking, the main difference between the indirect and direct approach is that in the latter, the arbitral tribunal is exempt from the obligation of searching for a specific conflicts rule to justify their decision as the substantive legal basis of the award. Of course, this also does not mean that no grounds for the choice of law applicable are expected.[48] On the other hand, the strength of the connection between the examined case and the law chosen by the arbitrators may not necessarily prove to be the determining factor; the arbitral tribunal may still take into account whether, for instance, the substantive law fits the subject matter of the dispute or makes the contract valid (*favor contractus*).[49]

---

[46] Gonzalo Parra-Aranguren, *Choice of Law Applicable to the Dispute in Recent Legislation on International Commercial Arbitration*, in PRIVATE LAW IN THE INTERNATIONAL ARENA – PRIVATRECHT IN DER INTERNATIONALEN ARENA: LIBER AMICORUM KURT SIEHR, The Hague: T.M.C. Asser Press 560 (J. Basedow ed. 2000).

[47] JEAN-LOUIS DEVOLVÉ, JEAN ROUCHE, GERALD POINTON, *supra* note 42, at 144-145.

[48] JULIAN D. M. LEW, LOUKAS A. MISTELIS, STEFAN KRÖLL, *supra* note 7, at 434-436.

[49] PHILIPPE FOUCHARD, EMMANUEL GAILLARD, BERTHOLD GOLDMAN, *supra* note 10, at 875-876.

10.23. Some decades ago, one of the most fashionable questions in the legal discourse was the applicability of the so-called *lex mercatoria*. It is enough to recall here that this term stands for a conglomerate of various legal rules and standards, based mainly on international trade customs and contractual practice, approved not only by the traders themselves but also in the case law, the purpose of which was to regulate international exchange in civil and commercial matters.[50] The concept of the *lex mercatoria* may be understood as an expression of the objection against assignation of a purely "national" nature to the legal regulation of international contracts.[51] Its *spiritus movens* is fear of the advantage one of the parties to the transnational arbitration could potentially have[52] due to the application of the substantive law well known to the other party. Some authors believe that the existence of a neutral set of rules makes the solution more just and objective.

10.24. Arbitration case law provides numerous examples of the application of the *lex mercatoria*, sometimes expressly approved by the State courts.[53] Nevertheless such cases do not constitute an unquestionable standard. First, the *lex mercatoria* is by no means a closed and complete system of legal rules, its content being based in recent decades, on the hypotheses of its authors, and supported by the editing of certain "private law restatements" such as, for example, the UNIDROIT Principles.[54] Second, from the standpoint of the parties themselves,

---

[50] BERNADETTA FUCHS, LEX MERCATORIA W MIĘDZYNARODOWYM OBROCIE HANDLOWYM (*Lex Mercatoria in the International Commerce*), Kraków: Kantor Wydawniczy „Zakamycze" 17 (2000); MATEUSZ PILICH, DOBRA WIARA W KONWENCJI O UMOWACH MIĘDZYNARODOWEJ SPRZEDAZY TOWAROW (*Good Faith in the Convention on Contracts for the International Sale of Goods*), Warszawa: C. H. Beck 107 et seq. (2006); Jerzy Poczobut, *Ewolucja pojęcia międzynarodowego prawa handlowego* (*Evolution of the Notion of the International Trade Law*), 1 PROBLEMY PRAWA PRYWATNEGO MIĘDZYNARODOWEGO (*Problems of the Private International Law*), Katowice: Wydawnictwo Universytetu Śląskiego 21 et seq. (Maksymilian Pazdan ed., 2007).

[51] Berndt von Hoffmann, *O stosowaniu "legis mercatoriae" w międzynarodowym arbitrażu handlowym* (*On the Application of the 'Lex Mercatoria' in the International Commercial Arbitration*), 12 PROBLEMY PRAWNE HANDLU ZAGRANICZNEGO (*Legal Problems of International Trade*), Katowice: Wydawnictwo Universytetu Śląskiego 11-12 (Maksymilian Pazdan ed., 1988).

[52] *Cf.* Article I (1)(a) of the European Convention on International Commercial Arbitration (see *supra* note 27), where the substantive scope of the regulation has been defined by the subjective criteria: the habitual residence (*résidence habituelle*) or the seat (fr. *siège*) of the parties in diet seqerent Contracting States.

[53] See esp. judgments: of the French *Cour d'appel de Paris*, the case *Valenciana* and the Austrian *Oberster Gerichtshof,* the case *Norsolor*, cited after: EMMANUEL GAILLARD, JOHN SAVAGE, *supra* note 10, at 879-880.

[54] UNIDROIT Principles are sometimes called one of the sources of the *lex mercatoria*, which seems misleading, because they were created not by traders themselves but by

choice of non-State legal standards, which were not duly promulgated and which also give the international traders no guarantee of legal certainty,[55] may seem too casual and arbitrary, amounting to the exceeding of the scope of the arbitrator's mandates.[56] Third, while the arbitral tribunal is certainly not bound by the private international law of the place of arbitration, it is obliged to apply the procedural law of the *locus arbitri*, which may limit the extent of its discretion in this respect. Again, where the law of the arbitration venue provides that in the absence of the parties' choice, the arbitral tribunal shall settle the dispute according to the "law" most closely connected to the case, it must be read as an obligation to apply the rules of law laid down by a State. Under such circumstances the application of the *lex mercatoria* would create a significant threat to the stability of the arbitral award, even though this consequence itself does not justify setting aside the award or the denial of its recognition and execution by the court.

III. Approach to the Law Applicable to the Substance of the Dispute under the Polish Code of Civil Procedure

10.25. Polish law does not in principle regulate the issue of which law to apply to the merits of the dispute submitted to arbitration. The only provision touching upon it indirectly is Article 1194 of the Code of Civil Procedure (CCP). As stated in par. 1, the arbitral tribunal shall settle the dispute according to the law applicable to the given relationship, and if the parties have expressly authorized it to do so – according to the general principles of law or equity. In every case (par. 2), however, due respect shall be given to the contract provisions and to the trade customs which are appropriate to the particular relationship. Since Part Five of the Code adopts all the basic assumptions of the UNCITRAL Model Law – including the principle of equal treatment of

---

scholars; KLAUS PETER BERGER, THE CREEPING CODIFICATION OF THE NEW LEX MERCATORIA, Alphen aan den Rijn: Kluwer Law International 191 (2010).

[55] The conviction of the existence of the international "merchants' society" (*societas mercatorum*), which is governed by its own law, is denied by certain authors who point to the fact that the level of its self-organization, as well as the way in which the autonomous customary law is developed, depend on various factors, first and foremost on the specificity of a given branch of trade; *cf.* Luís de Lima Pinheiro, *The "Denationalisation" of Transnational Relationships – Regulation of Transnational Relationships by Public International Law, European Community Law and Transnational Law, in* AUFBRUCH NACH EUROPA: 75 JAHRE MAX-PLANCK INSTITUT FÜR PRIVATRECHT, Tübingen: J.C.B. Mohr (Paul Siebeck) 440 et seq. (J. Basedow ed., 2001).

[56] Ole Lando, *supra* note 29, at 154-155.

foreign and international arbitration – it is true that Article 1194 CCP should be applied to any arbitration taking place in Poland,[57] irrespective of the legal characterization of the arbitration dispute.[58]

10.26. The above-cited provision contains no rule of conflict and does not even designate the method which should be used by the arbitrators settling the dispute. It is not, however, devoid of any meaning. Its sense lies in the words: *"law applicable to the given relationship."* Such an expression unambiguously indicates that the arbitral tribunal must apply the system of rules laid down and sanctioned by the State. Had the drafters of the law intended otherwise, they would have chosen a more general term: "rules of law." Such a consequent differentiation between the "law" and "rules of law" may be found under Article 28 of the Model Law, which in principle has not been transferred to Article 1194 of the Polish Code. Notwithstanding this fact, both are interpreted in a similar way, as in the absence of the choice of law by the parties, arbitrators shall settle the dispute in accordance with the rules of the given system of law and hence, without an authorization by the parties themselves, any rules or standards other than the substantive law of the given State shall be excluded from applying.[59]

10.27. The first question to be posed with regard to the purpose of Article 1194 (1) CCP is whether the drafters of the law have limited the catalogue of methods which can be referred to by the arbitrators in searching for the law applicable as to the merits. At first glance the language of the provision provides some support for the arguments of the adherents of the view that Polish law exclusively admits the indirect approach.[60] Admittedly, it is remarkable, that the expression: "applicable law" (*loi applicable, anwendbares Recht*) usually evokes an association with the branch of private international law, since it connotes the result of specifying the given system of substantive rules according to the connecting factor of the rule of conflict[61]. Moreover, as underlined in the literature, applying the rules of conflict undoubtedly fosters a sense of confidence in the arbitral award.[62]

---

[57] See Article 1154 CCP.

[58] TADEUSZ ERECINSKI, KAROL WEITZ, *supra* note 21, at 323; Tadeusz Erecinski, *in* 5 KODEKS POSTEPOWANIA CYWILNEGO: KOMENTARZ (*Code of Civil Procedure. Commentary*), Warszawa: LexisNexis Polska 703 (T. Erecinski, J. Ciszewski eds., 2nd ed. 2007).

[59] *Ibid.*

[60] See TADEUSZ ERECINSKI, KAROL WEITZ, *supra* note 21, at 324.

[61] See i.a. WITALIS LUDWICZAK, MIEDZYNARODOWE PRAWO PRYWATNE (*International Private Law*), Warszawa: PWN 15 (4th ed. 1990).

[62] Alexander J. Bělohlávek, *supra* note 19, at 39 et seq.

10.28. It seems more justified, however, to interpret this provision in a different way, stressing the weight of the arbitral tribunal's decision. Polish law, unlike Article 28 (1) and (2) of the UNCITRAL Model Law contains no conflict rule.[63] One of the reasons for this could be respect for the autonomous character – one of the main principles – of the arbitration law. Arbitrators fulfill their duties towards the will and in the interest of the parties and cannot be bound directly by the law of any State. The arbitrators' discretion, which has long been recognized among Polish scholars,[64] has been declared in numerous provisions of the Code, in particular in Articles 1155 (1), 1181 (1), 1184 (2), 1185, 1187 (1) and 1189 (1) CCP. Hence it should be basically the parties' will with regard to the applicable law which takes precedence, and unless the parties themselves have made no use of that competence, the decision must shift instead to the arbitral tribunal than to the provisions of the law of the locus arbitri.

10.29. Moreover, the arbitrators are free to make use of any of the methods (approaches) described in this paper. Even the "direct approach" does not contradict Polish public policy. Violation of the *ordre public,* which would obviously justify setting aside the award (Article 1206 (2), point 2 CCP) or denial of its recognition and execution in Poland (Article 1214 (3)(2) CCP, Article V (2)(b) of the New York Convention[65]) occurs only where the qualified infringement of certain fundamental mandatory provisions of the Republic of Poland takes place.[66] In this context, finding rules of substantive law as immediately binding.[67] has been repeatedly rejected in both the legal literature and jurisprudence of the Supreme Court. If we take this into account, the problem concerning the methods of specifying which law to apply to the merits of the

---

[63] Motives on the 2005 Draft Law Amending the Code of Civil Procedure, which introduced new Polish arbitration law in the form of the Part Five of the CCP, make practically no comment on this Article; cf. Parliamentary Printout of the 6th Term of Office (*druk sejmowy IV kadencji*) No. 3434.

[64] Maria Anna Zachariasiewicz, *supra* note 1, at 143 et seq.

[65] The Convention on the Recognition and Enforcement of Foreign Arbitral Awards, done at New York, 10 June 1958 (9 Journal of Laws 1962, pos. 41).

[66] Mateusz Pilich, *Klauzula porządku publicznego w postępowaniu o uznanie i wykonanie zagranicznego orzeczenia arbitrażowego (Public Policy Exception in the Proceedings on the Recognition and Enforcement of the Foreign Arbitral Award)*, 12 KWARTALNIK PRAWA PRYWATNEGO *(Private Law Quarterly)* 157 et seq. (2003).

[67] See i.a. the judgments of Polish Supr. Court: 8.2.1937, C III 1254/35, ZU OSN 1938, poz. 44; 3.9.2009, I CSK 53/09, Biul. SN 2009/12, 9; Rafal Morek, *Mediacja i arbitraż (art. 183¹-183¹⁵, 1154-1217 KPC). Komentarz,* 230-231 (2006); critically, *cf.* Przemyslaw Ballada, *Zagadnienie obowiązku stosowania prawa materialnego w postępowaniu przed sądem polubownym (Question of the Obligation to Apply the Substantive Law in the Proceedings before the Arbitration Tribunal),* (1) RUCH PRAWNICZY, EKONOMICZNY I SOCJOLOGICZNY *(Legal Economic & Sociological Movement)* 87 (2002).

dispute seems to be of minor importance, as the award is subject to a more comprehensive evaluation, obviously not in light of the (mis)application of the rules of conflict, but in light of the award's content and legal effects as a whole. After all, if no rule of law obliges the arbitrators to apply particular provisions of private international law, it would be hard to perceive the arbitral award as violating Polish public policy only because the applicable law has been referred to without any rule of conflict whatsoever. To fulfill the obligation to provide grounds for the arbitral award (Article 1197 (2) CCP), it is enough that the arbitrators explain their motives for applying a given system of substantial law. By no means is there any duty to invoke a particular rule of private international law.

IV. Summary and Conclusion

10.30. Use of the so-called "indirect method" in settling the conflict of laws applicable to the merits in the absence of the parties' law choice seems to have become a dominant trend in the development of arbitration law. This tendency is quite clear, given both the rising number of arbitration rules which leave the decision to the arbitrators in such cases, and the fact that few State jurisdictions oblige arbitrators to apply any rules of conflict.[68]

10.31. In this context, Polish law has taken a rather liberal approach, remarkably deviating from the pattern of Article 28 of the UNCITRAL Model Law. Despite the seeming tenor of Article 1194 (1) CCP, Polish law does not take any specific position on the way the law applicable to the substance of the arbitral dispute must be specified. One should note that a more strict interpretation could work, disadvantageously, to promote Poland as an arbitration-friendly jurisdiction. The time has come to step up: why not admit the applicability of the international "restatements of contract law," just as in for e.g. the UNIDROIT Principles, if both parties to the arbitration are traders? Common knowledge of such sources of "soft law" and greater experience with their doctrinal and practical application remove the threat of undermining the basic values of legal certainty or the parties' confidence in the arbitration. The future evolution of Article 1194 (1) CCP should lead to the loosening of the "legal straitjacket" and open a wider scope of discretion to arbitrators.

| | |

---

[68]   See Article 834 (1) of the Italian Code of Civil Procedure – abrogated in 2006 – which had constituted a particular rule of conflict for the arbitration; JEAN-FRANÇOIS POUDRET, SÉBASTIEN BESSON, *supra* note 19, at 585.

Summaries

FRA [*Droit applicable au fond d'un litige réglé par arbitrage lorsque les parties ne disposent pas du choix du droit*]

L'objectif de cette étude est une analyse des tendances actuelles dans les exigences posées sur les tribunaux d'arbitrage en Pologne, en ce qui concerne la loi applicable au fond du différend en absence du choix par les parties. En 2005, la loi d'arbitrage polonaise (la cinquième partie du Code de procédure civile) a été sérieusement altérée. Un des dispositions ajoutées par le législateur – l'article 1194, paragraphe 1 CPC prévoit une obligation générale pour régler le litige conformément à la « loi applicable », ce qui pourrait éventuellement être interprété comme imposant une obligation à appliquer le droit international privé. Cependant l'auteur estime que cette interprétation ne trouve aucun appui dans le Code même et dans les tendances actuelles en droit d'arbitrage. Sur le plan de la doctrine et de la jurisprudence d'arbitrage, il y a deux principales approches possibles du problème: la « voie indirecte » (l'application des règles de conflit par les arbitres) ou la « voie directe » (la désignation de la loi applicable sans l'utilisation d'un tel mécanisme). Ni l'article 1194, paragraphe 1 CPC polonais, ni d'autres articles du Code ne sont l'obstacle à l'application de deux méthodes.

CZE [*Právo rozhodné pro meritum sporu předloženého k projednání a rozhodnutí v rozhodčím řízení v případě absence určení rozhodného práva stranami*]

Tato studie se zabývá analýzou současných trendů v požadavcích kladených na rozhodčí soudy v Polsku, pokud jde o právo rozhodné pro meritum sporu v případě, že si jej účastníci nezvolili. V roce 2005 byl zásadním způsobem pozměněn polský zákon o rozhodčím řízení (5. část občanského soudního řádu). Jedním z ustanovení, která zákonodárce doplnil (čl. 1194 odst. 1 OSŘ), je všeobecná povinnost řešit spory v souladu s "rozhodným právem", což by mohlo být vykládáno i tak, že vzniká povinnost použít mezinárodní právo soukromé. Autor však má za to, že takovýto výklad nelze opírat ani o samotný OSŘ, ani o současné trendy v rozhodčím právu. Z hlediska právní nauky a arbitrážní judikatury existují dva hlavní přístupy k problému: "nepřímé určení" (rozhodci použijí kolizní normy) a "přímé určení" (rozhodné právo je určeno bez aplikace norem mezinárodního práva soukromého). Jak čl. 1194 odst. 1 polského OSŘ, tak ani jeho další články nebrání v použití kterékoliv z obou možností.

POL   [*Prawo regulujące meritum sporu przekazanego do rozstrzygnięcia przez sąd polubowny w razie braku wyboru prawa przez strony*]
Głównym celem tej pracy jest analiza przeważających tendencji w zakresie przepisów kolizyjnych zgodnie z art. 1194(1) Kodeksu postępowania cywilnego, dotyczącego prawa regulującego meritum międzynarodowego arbitrażu handlowego. Prawo arbitrażowe jest generalnie otwarte na różne podejścia w tym względzie, w związku z czym polskie prawo powinno być interpretowane jako uznające zarówno "pośrednią", jak i "bezpośrednią" metodę wyznaczania obowiązującego prawa przez arbitrów.

DEU   [*In der Sache anzuwendendes Recht bei Schiedsstreitigkeiten, in denen die Parteien keine Rechtswahl getroffen haben*]
Hauptzweck der vorliegenden Arbeit ist die Analyse der vorherrschenden Trends in punkto Kollisionsrecht gemäß § 1194 Abs. 1 der polnischen Zivilprozessordnung, betreffend das Recht, das im internationalen Handelsschiedsrecht auf die Hauptsache anzuwenden ist. In dieser Hinsicht steht das Schiedsrecht im allgemeinen verschiedenen Ansätzen offen, und polnisches Recht sollte von daher so ausgelegt werden, dass es sowohl eine "indirekte" als auch eine "direkte" Methode zur Bestimmung des von Schiedsrichtern anzuwendenden Rechts anerkennt.

RUS   [*Право, применимое арбитражным судом при рассмотрении спора по существу, при отсутствии указания права, выбранного сторонами*]
Основная цель данной работы состоит в анализе доминирующих тенденций в случае конфликта права согласно Статье 1194(1) Гражданского процессуального кодекса Польши, касающейся права, применимого при рассмотрении арбитражных споров в международной торговле. В этом смысле, арбитражное право оставляет многочисленные варианты трактовки, поэтому польское право следует толковать двояко, а именно, признающее как «прямые», так и «косвенные» способы указания применимого права судьями арбитражного суда.

ESP   [*Derecho aplicable sobre los fundamentos del pleito, sometido a arbitraje ante la ausencia de elección de fuero por las partes*]
El objetivo principal de este documento es analizar las tendencias dominantes en el conflicto de leyes en virtud del artículo 1194(1) del Código de Procedimiento Civil de Polonia, lo que afecta al derecho aplicable sobre los fundamentos del arbitraje comercial internacional. La ley de arbitraje suele estar abierta a diversos enfoques en este sentido;

por ello, la ley polaca deberá interpretarse como si reconociera el método tanto "indirecto" como "directo" de designación del derecho aplicable por parte de los árbitros.

Karl Pörnbacher |Inken Knief

Liability of Arbitrators – Judicial Immunity versus Contractual Liability

Key words:
Contractual Liability |
Decision-making Process |
England | France |
Germany | Independence
of Arbitrators |
Institutional Rules |
Judicial Immunity |
Liability of Arbitrators |
Intentional Wrongdoing |
Negligence | Res Judicata

Abstract | *The issue of the liability of arbitrators plays out between the conflicting priorities of contractual liability and judicial privilege. Arbitrators take on the double role of service providers hired and paid for by the parties to the dispute and of the authority dispensing justice. Accordingly, some argue in favor of the immunity of arbitrators in the sense of being relieved of liability, due to the arbitrator's "status" as a "quasi-court"; others reject such immunity, based on the concept of contractual liability. This article first provides an overview of the status quo of arbitrator liability under the rules of various arbitral institutions and under the laws of various countries, hailing both from the sphere of common law and from the sphere of civil law.*

The present paper then develops its own position regarding the liability of arbitrators, which takes into account both the contractual approach and the approach that takes its bearings from the "judicial function" of arbitrators. In the view of the authors, ruling out the liability of arbitrators for ordinary negligence in reaching their verdict is called for because of the need to protect the arbitrator's independence. However, outside of the decision-making process, as such (and in cases of willful intent), the service character of an arbitrator's work requires principally unlimited liability on the arbitrator's part for any kind of culpable conduct.

Karl Pörnbacher is a partner at Hogan Lovells' Munich office and head of the firm's German arbitration practice. The focus of his work is on national and international arbitration and litigation and alternative dispute resolution. His practice comprises disputes resulting from projects, energy, M&A, insurance and reinsurance and general commercial relationships. Mr. Pörnbacher is president of the arbitration court of the German-Polish Chamber of Commerce. Due to his specific experience he is frequently involved in cross-border disputes involving Poland and other Central and Eastern European Countries, both as arbitrator and counsel.
e-mail:
karlpoernbacher@hoga nlovells.com

| | |

I. Introduction

11.01. The question of the arbitrator's liability reveals a basic clash inherent to the law of arbitration.[1] On the one hand, the arbitrator is a service provider to the parties. By the arbitrator's contract, he is contractually engaged to resolve the parties' dispute, with the expected expertise, in the most efficient manner, and on the sound basis of the applicable rules of law – in return for considerable fees. By contractual standards, the arbitrator owes the parties to arbitration to exercise his function with utmost diligence and care. If he fails to do so, contractual standards would naturally provide that he must fully and personally compensate the parties for any damage resulting from his breach of obligation. This is the most basic rule of any developed law of contracts.

Dr. Inken Knief is a senior associate within the arbitration group of Hogan Lovells in Munich. Her practise comprises the area of international arbitration, under various institutional rules and national arbitration regimes. e-mail: inken.knief@hoganlovlls.com

11.02. On the other hand, by the parties' agreement, the arbitrator exercises the judicial function of resolving disputes between the parties with a final binding effect that is recognized by the law. His arbitral awards enjoy full *res judicata*, just as state court decisions. They even enjoy more protection than state court decisions: Generally, there is no appeal but only a very limited possibility for a challenge. Within that challenge, any *révision au fond* is inadmissible. Further, by his adjudicative function, the arbitrator is awarded with (and obliged to) independence in his decision-making. The independence of the arbitrator and the *res judicata* effect of his awards, however, seem to forbid threatening the arbitrator with contractual liability, and submitting his decision to judicial review, above an action to set the award aside.

11.03. This article outlines the antipodes contractual liability versus judicial immunity, and attempts to develop a feasible conceptual approach to the subject of arbitrator immunity. Part One will provide an overview of the law of arbitrator liability as it stands in institutional rules, national laws, and the law of contracts. Part Two deals with the concepts of contractual liability versus judicial immunity. Part Three attempts to align the controversial concepts and develop a sensible approach to the concept of arbitrator liability.

---

[1]   This article benefits from the valuable research as well as the thoughtful comments of Dominik Steghöfer, who deserves special mention and thanks.

II. The Arbitrator's Liability under Institutional Rules, National Arbitration Regimes and Arbitrator's Contracts

11.04. The scope and extent of the arbitrator's liability is governed, in institutional arbitrations, by the rules of the arbitral institution under which the parties have agreed to arbitrate, in *ad hoc* arbitrations, by the applicable national law. The applicable national law also provides the framework for contractual agreements of the parties, intending to exclude or extend the arbitrator's liability.

II.1. The Arbitrator's Liability under Institutional Rules

11.05. The vast majority of Institutional Rules provides for a partial exclusion of the arbitrator's liability, either in form of a guarantee of the arbitrator's immunity, or in form of a waiver of the arbitrator's liability. Institutional Rules differ as regards the extent to which liability is waived, or immunity is granted. The common denominator seems to be that arbitrators will not be held liable for simple negligence with regard to their taking of legal decisions.

11.06. Providing for the most extensive exclusion of liability, the ICSID Convention and the Rules of the American Arbitration Association (AAA) provide for complete immunity of the arbitrator, even in case of intentional misconduct. Article 21 of the ICSID Convention provides that *"[t]he Chairman [and] persons acting as conciliators or arbitrators shall enjoy immunity from legal process with respect to acts performed by them in the exercise of their functions, except when the Centre waives this immunity."* To the same effect, Article R-48 (c) of the AAA Rules provides: *"Parties to an arbitration under these rules shall be deemed to have consented that neither the AAA nor any arbitrator shall be held liable to any party in any action for damages or injunctive relief for any act or omission in connection with any arbitration under these rules."*

11.07. The ICC Rules 2012, in Article 40, contain a waiver of liability which in principle even encompasses intentional acts; however, insofar different from the ICC Rules 1998, only if this is permitted under the applicable national law. Art. 40 of the ICC Rules 2012 states: *"The arbitrators, any persons appointed by the arbitral tribunal [and] the emergency arbitrator [...] shall not be liable to any person for any act or omission in connection with the arbitration, except to the extent such limitation of liability if prohibited by applicable law."* To the same effect, Article 8 of the VIAC Rules provides that *"[l]iability of the arbitrators [...] for any* *act or omission in relation to arbitration proceedings, insofar as such exclusion is admissible by law, is excluded."*

11.08. Article 16 of the UNCITRAL Rules 2010 *per se* excludes intentional wrongdoings from the waiver, providing that *"[s]ave for intentional wrongdoing, the parties waive, to the fullest extent permitted under the applicable law, any claim against the arbitrators, the appointing authority and any person appointed by the arbitral tribunal based on any act or omission in connection with the arbitration."* Similarly, Article 31.1 of the LCIA Rules provides for an exclusion of liability, *"save where the act or omission is shown by that party to constitute conscious and deliberate wrongdoing committed by the body or person alleged to be liable to that party."*

11.09. The Swiss Rules and the SCC Rules extend the arbitrator's liability also to cases of qualified negligence. Article 44 of the Swiss Rules states: *"None of the Chambers or their staff, arbitrators, tribunal-appointed experts or the secretary of the arbitral tribunal shall be liable for any act or omission in connection with an arbitration conducted under these Rules, save where the act or omission is shown to constitute deliberate wrongdoing or extremely serious negligence."* Similarly, Article 48 of the SCC Rules provides that *"[n]either the SCC Institute nor the arbitrator(s) are liable to any party for any act or omission in connection with the arbitration unless such act or omission constitutes wilful misconduct or gross negligence."*

11.10. Finally, the DIS Rules distinguish between arbitrator liability for acts in regard to deciding legal matters in cases of intentional misconduct and other acts of gross, but not simple negligence. Section 44 of the DIS Rules provides: *"44.1: All liability of an arbitrator for any act in connection with deciding a legal matter is excluded, provided such act does not constitute an intentional breach of duty. 44.2: All liability of the arbitrators, the DIS, its officers and its employees for an act or omission in connection with arbitral proceedings is excluded, provided such acts do not constitute an intentional or grossly negligent breach of duty."*

II.2. The Arbitrator's Liability under National Arbitration Regimes

11.11. National arbitration regimes are equally diverse in their approach to the subject of arbitrator immunity.[2] This corresponds to the lack of

---

[2] For an overview see the country reports in PRACTITIONER'S HANDBOOK ON INTERNATIONAL COMMERCIAL ARBITRATION, Oxford: Oxford University Press (F.-B. Weigand, 2nd ed. 2010) and the JAN PAULSSON, INTERNATIONAL HANDBOOK ON COMMERCIAL ARBITRATION, The Hague: Kluwer Law International (2010).

uniformity in different national law systems also with regard to state court judge immunity.[3] In light of the diversity of national law approaches to the arbitrator's immunity, the drafters of the UNCITRAL Model Law concluded that a satisfying provision harmonizing the national arbitration statutes on the subject was not attainable.[4] The UNCITRAL Model Law has therefore remained silent on the subject.

11.12. The vast majority of national arbitration regimes seek to protect arbitrators from civil liability, again with differences as regards the extent of such protection. Only some Middle Eastern countries seem to hold arbitrators personally liable for all wrongful conduct, including negligence.[5] As regards the dogmatic concept behind the arbitrator's immunity, common law jurisdictions seem to follow mostly a concept of judicial immunity, viewing arbitrators as functionally comparable to judges.[6] By contrast, most civil law traditions rather focus on the contractual character and the origin of the arbitrator's appointment.

II.2.1. USA

11.13. US courts have frequently dealt with the liability of arbitrators, with case law dating back to the 19th century. As a general rule, arbitrators in the United States enjoy absolute immunity from civil liability for all actions related to their decision-making, including cases of gross negligence and even intentional misconduct.[7] This extremely broad concept of immunity corresponds to US doctrine regarding state court judges who are immune from suit even when they have acted maliciously or corruptly.[8]

---

[3] For an overview of national law see approaches to the state judge's liability, ECJ C-224/01, Judgment of 30 September 2003, 2003-I, 10239 (Köbler).

[4] UNCITRAL, Fourteenth Session, Vienna 19-26 June 1981, International Commercial Arbitration–Possible Features of a Model Law on International Commercial Arbitration, UN Doc. A/CN.9/207, para. 70.

[5] See GARY B. BORN, INTERNATIONAL COMMERCIAL ARBITRATION, Alphen aan den Rijn: Kluwer Law International 1659 (2nd ed. 2009).

[6] For the differentiation between the concept of judicial immunity and the concept of contractual liability see, FRANZ T. SCHWARZ, CHRISTIAN W. KONRAD, A COMMENTARY ON INTERNATIONAL ARBITRATION IN AUSTRIA, Alphen aan den Rijn: Wolters Kluwer 178 et seq. (2009).

[7] Peter B. Rutledge, *Toward a Contractual Approach for Arbitral Immunity*, 39 GA. L. REV. 151, 151 et. seq (2004); Susan D. Franck, *The Liability of International Arbitrators: A Comparative Analysis and Proposal for Qualified Immunity*, 20 N.Y.L. SCH. J. INT'L & COMP. L. 1, 31 (2000); for a relatively recent discussion in case law see e.g. *Stasz v. Schwab*, 121 Cal. App. 4th 420 (Cal. Ct. App. 2004).

[8] Sara Roitman, *Beyond Reproach: Has the Doctrine of Arbitral Immunity Been Extended Too Far for Arbitration Sponsoring Firms?* 51 (2) BOSTON COLLEGE LAW REVIEW 557, 562

11.14. Recent US case law seems to have limited somewhat the traditionally extensive concept of immunity. In a few cases, arbitrators have been denied immunity, e.g. in case of the arbitrator's failure to render the award in the time limit prescribed by the arbitration agreement,[9] or in cases of wilful and malicious wrongdoing.[10] In addition, according to the prevailing doctrine, arbitrators who have acted negligently or in bad faith are prevented from collecting their fees.[11] These developments have prompted state legislators to introduce statutory provisions explicitly granting arbitrators absolute immunity.[12]

II.2.2. England

11.15. Following the common law concept of quasi-judicial immunity, the English Arbitration Act 1996 grants arbitrators explicit statutory immunity from civil liability *"for anything done or omitted in the discharge or purported discharge of their function unless the act or omission has shown to be in bad faith"* (§ 29(1)), or unless the arbitrator resigns from his office on grounds that a court finds unreasonable (§ 29(3)).[13]

11.16. Article 29 of the English Arbitration Act codifies English case law prior to the enactment of the English Arbitration Act 1996. According to the responsible Departmental Advisory Committee, it notably serves to protect the impartiality of the arbitrators and the finality of the award by preventing a losing party from re-litigating issues resolved by arbitration in a subsequent action against the arbitrators.[14]

(2010), referring to *Jones* v. *Brown*, 6 N.W. 140, 142 (Iowa 1880): *"[A] judge of any court, whether of limited or general jurisdiction, is not liable in a civil action for acts done in his judicial capacity, and within his jurisdiction, even though it be alleged that the acts complained of were done maliciously and corruptly."*

[9]   *Baar* v. *Tigerman*, 140 Cal. App. 3d 979 (Cal. Ct. App. 1983).

[10]   *Lundgren* v. *Freeman*, 307 F.2d 104 (9th. Cir. 1962).

[11]   Susan D. Franck, *supra* note 7, at 10. Essentially, this constitutes civil liability, but capped at the amount of fees owed; see for a similar rule Art. 13 (6) of the Indian Arbitration and Conciliation Act which allows the courts to determine whether the arbitrator is entitled to any fees in case the award is set aside.

[12]   See Californian Code of Civil Procedure, Sect. 1297.119: *"An arbitrator has the immunity of a judicial officer from civil liability when acting in the capacity of arbitrator under any statute or contract"*; an identical rule for non-international arbitration was enacted, but expired in 1997. This allowed the Court of Appeals for the Second District to affirm the nonfeasance-exception in *Morgan Phillips Inc* v. *JAMS/Endispute, LLC*, 140 Cal. App. 4th, 795, 44 Cal. Rptr. 3rd 782 (Cal. Ct. App. 2006). See also Sect. 14 of the Revised Unified Arbitration Act 2000.

[13]   *Cf.* Art. 29 and 25 of the English Arbitration Act 1996.

[14]   Departmental Advisory Committee on Arbitration Law, 1996 *Report on the Arbitration Bill*, ARB. INT. 1997, 275 § 132.

II.2.3. France

11.17. French law follows a contractual concept as regards the arbitrator's liability holding that as arbitrators assume no public office, any action for damages in respect of the performance of their functions is governed only by ordinary tort or contract law.[15] As regards the extent of arbitrator liability, French law provides for a comparatively wide regime of liability, holding arbitrators liable in the event of gross fault, fraud, or connivance with one of the parties.[16] As reason for the exemption of cases of simple negligence from liability, the Reims Tribunal of First Instance has held that *"[o]therwise the protection, independence and authority of the arbitrators would be restricted to an extent that would be incompatible with the task of judging which is conferred to them."*[17]

11.18. Further, under French law, the liability of arbitrators only holds where errors in the actual decision-making process are concerned. Beyond the decision-making, the arbitrator's liability seems to be subject to no limitations.[18] In this vein, as a matter of example, French courts have held arbitrators liable for non-disclosure of facts and circumstances raising doubts as to their independence and impartiality.[19]

II.2.4. Germany

11.19. German law equally follows the civil law concept of contractual liability, primarily subjecting the standard for arbitrator's liability to a contractual regime.

11.20. On that basis, the German Supreme Court (BGH) has found in constant holdings that arbitrators, in exercising their office, are in principle liable for a breach of contract under the arbitrator's contract, and not entitled to immunity under § 839 of the German Civil Code (BGB).[20] Approximating the arbitrator's liability to the state court

---

[15] Cass. 2e civ., Jan. 29, 1960, *Veuve J. Houdet et Fils* v. *Chambre arbitrale de l'union syndicale de grains et farines de Bordaux*, Dalloz, jur. 262 (1960); 1960 REV. ARB. 121.

[16] JEAN-FRANÇOIS POUDRET & SÉBASTIAN BESSON, COMPARATIVE LAW OF INTERNATIONAL ARBITRATION, London: Sweet & Maxwell para. 446 (2nd ed. 2007) citing TGI Paris Bompard, REV. ARB. 1996, 476; EMMANUEL GAILLARD, JOHN SAVAGE, FOUCHARD GAILLARD GOLDMAN ON INTERNATIONAL COMMERCIAL ARBITRATION, The Hague: Kluwer Law International para. 1082 (1999); F.-B. Weigand, *supra* note 2, at para. 6.203.

[17] TGI Reims, Sept. 27, 1978, *Florange* v. *Brissart et Corgié*, No. 482/77, unpublished.

[18] EMMANUEL GAILLARD, JOHN SAVAGE, *supra* note 16, at paras. 1090 et seq.

[19] CA Paris, July 2, 1992, *Raoul Duval* v. *Merkuria Sucden*, 1996 REV.ARB. 411.

[20] § 839 provides in relevant parts: "(2) *If an official breaches his official duties in a judgment in a legal matter, then he is only responsible for any damage arising from this if the breach of duty consists in a criminal offence. This provision is not applicable to refusal*

judge's liability, the German Supreme Court has, however, further ruled that the arbitrator's contract impliedly grants arbitrators the same degree of immunity as afforded to state court judges under § 839 BGB, as far as the exclusion of liability is admissible under German law of contracts.[21]

11.21. Applying the German Supreme Court's holdings, the arbitrator is released from liability to the extent that state court judges are afforded immunity, i.e. to the extent that the judge or arbitrator's wrongdoing does not amount to a criminal offense. Arbitrators are however only excluded from liability, as far as such exclusion is limited to the extent permissible under German contract law which means that liability for intentional wrongdoings may not be excluded (§ 276(3) BGB). In other words, for arbitrators, different than for state court judges, intentional wrongdoings, falling short of a criminal offense, may result in personal liability.[22] Although the German Supreme Court's theory of an "implied waiver" has been criticised in German legal writing as unrealistic,[23] German doctrine widely accepts the contractual regime for the arbitrator's liability as outlined by the BGH.[24]

11.22. Along the lines of § 839 BGB, the exclusion of the arbitrator's liability only extends to acts related to the arbitrators' actual decision-making process. According to German legal writing this includes the arbitrator's taking of evidence, their establishment of the relevant facts, the application of the law, or any other action in the conduct of the arbitral proceedings, closely related to the actual decision-making.[25] Further, as far as the decision-making is concerned, arbitrators are

---

or delay that is in breach of duty in exercising a public function. (3) Liability for damage does not arise if the injured person has intentionally or negligently failed to avert the damage by having recourse to appeal."

[21] BGHZ 15, 12, 14 et seq.

[22] BGHZ 15, 12, 14, referring to § 276 para. 3 BGB; Münch in MüKoZPO 3rd ed. 2008, Vorbem. zu den §§ 1034ff., para. 29. In fact, a significant number of authors wish to grant arbitrators the same immunity afforded to judges who are not liable even for certain intentional acts below the threshold of criminal liability which attaches only to especially egregious violations of due process, see e.g. JENS GAL, DIE HAFTUNG DES SCHIEDSRICHTERS IN DER INTERNATIONALEN HANDELSSCHIEDSGERICHTSBARKEIT, Tübingen: Mohr Siebeck Verlag 199 (2009). This view is, however, incompatible with the contractual approach by the BGH.

[23] Jens-Peter Lachmann, Die Haftung des Schiedsrichters nach deutschem Recht, AG 1997, 170, 178.

[24] Ibid., at 179.

[25] Musielak ZPO § 1035 para. 25 (8th ed. 2011); Münch in MüKoZPO 3rd ed. 2008, Vorbem. zu den §§ 1034ff., para. 30.; see also with regard to the state court judge's liability, Decision of the German Supreme Court dated 4 November 2011, III, ZR 32/10, Beck RS 2010, 29173.

arguably only liable under the condition that the concerned party has attempted to challenge the award within the prescribed time limits (*arg.* § 839(3) BGB).

11.23. For those duties which are only ancillary to the decision-making, arbitrators are personally and fully liable under the arbitrator's contract. As a matter of example, they may be held liable for breaches of the duty of confidentiality, or the duty to disclose conflicts of interest, as well as for breaches of the obligation to deliver a formally correct award according to § 1054 German Code of Civil Procedure (ZPO), or the duty to issue an award in time.[26]

II.2.5. The Arbitrator's Liability under the Arbitrator's Contract

11.24. The national law regimes also provide the framework for contractual provisions on the arbitrator's liability which will be commonly found in arbitrator's contracts. As regards the question of whether the parties can limit the arbitrator's liability, it seems widely uncontested that the parties, by their contractual autonomy, may in principle do so. However, most national laws provide for a mandatory minimum standard of liability, generally comprising intentional wrongdoing, which consequently cannot be excluded by the parties' agreement.[27]

11.25. A more complex question is whether the parties can also extend the arbitrator's liability in the arbitrator's contract, exceeding the national law standard. On the one hand, arbitration is fundamentally of a contractual nature, so that one might conclude that the parties should generally be free to extend the arbitrator's liability to the degree they wish, for example also including simple negligence. This solution would certainly be a consequence of the purely contractual approach to the arbitrator's liability, as suggested by the German Supreme Court. If the partial release from liability is derived from the parties' implied

---

[26] Münch in MüKoZPO 3rd ed. 2008, Vorbem. zu den §§ 1034ff., para. 30. In a recent decision regarding the state court judge's liability for wrongful delays in issuing their decisions (§ 839(2) 2 BGB), the German Supreme Court, emphasizing the constitutional guarantee of the judicative independence, has further limited the judge's liability for actions falling outside of the scope of § 839(2)1 BGB to cases where the judge's conduct must be considered as outright inconceivable (*unvertretbar*), see Decision of the German Supreme Court dated 4 November 2011, III, ZR 32/10, Beck RS 2010, 29173. It remains to see whether the German Supreme Court will extend these findings also to arbitrators.

[27] For French law, see F.-B. Weigand, *supra* note 2, at para. 6.207 (The contractual liability can be excluded by agreement with the parties, except for cases of "serious" fault and intentional misconduct); for German law, see § 276(3) BGB: "The obligor may not be released in advance from liability for intention."

intention to approximate the arbitrator's liability to the state court judge's liability, the parties should arguably be able to expressly contest such presumption, and agree on a stricter regime of liability.[28]

11.26. On the other hand, one might take the view that standards for the finality and legal certainty of the arbitral proceedings, and the arbitrator's independence are not subject to private agreement, but are basic principles of public policy which must be observed by the parties. In this vein, it is accepted under English law, that Article 29 of the English Arbitration Act 1996, providing for the arbitrator's immunity, forms part of English mandatory law, and that the parties therefore cannot bargain for extended liability.[29] By contrast, US authors, although on the basis of the similar US approach to the arbitrator's judicial immunity, suggests that the parties should be allowed to bargain for the extent of liability in exchange for a reduction of the arbitrator's fees.[30]

III. The Case For and Against Arbitrator Liability

11.27. As noted above, the subject of arbitrator liability lies in an area of conflict between the principle of contractual liability on the one hand and the principle of judicial immunity on the other. In order to align these principles and come to a sensible solution, it is important to understand the nature and extent of these principles.

III.1. Contractual Liability

11.28. The principle of contractual liability, essential in any developed law of contracts, has full force also with regard to arbitrators. Arbitrators, different from state courts judges, are primarily service providers to the parties. By the arbitrator's contract, they are entrusted with resolving the parties' dispute, thereby observing their contractual obligations of diligence and care as regards a proper establishment of the relevant facts, a fair and comprehensive taking of evidence, a sound and weighed application of the applicable law to the facts, and an expeditious and balanced conduct of the proceedings. In light of the arbitrator's expert status, one might well argue that the arbitrator is even exposed to a

---

[28] Jens-Peter Lachmann, *supra* note 23, at 179-180.

[29] See *supra* note 14, at § 133.

[30] Peter B. Rutledge, *supra* note 7, at 201; see also Emmanuela Truli, *Liability* v. *Quasi-Judicial Immunity of the Arbitrator: The Case against Absolute Arbitral Immunity*, 17 AM. REV. INT'L ARB. 383, 402 et seq., arguing for qualified immunity as the default rule and the ability for the parties to contractually waive all liability.

higher standard of diligence than others.[31] In return for his services, the arbitrator receives significant recompense.

11.29. From a contractual angle, there seems to be no reason why the arbitrator should be privileged as compared to other service providers, such as lawyers. The restitutive and the preventive function of contractual liability require that a party to a contract must compensate its contractual counterpart for all damages arising from a breach of its contractual obligations. This obligation to compensate for damages incurred from a breach of obligations is a precondition for the contractual entrustment with obligations in the first place. The parties to a contract reasonably expect that the mutual contractual obligations will be performed with dutifully and care, failing which any damages incurred by the breach of obligations must be compensated. Further, the threat of contractual liability is seen as the most important instrument to hold parties to their contractual obligations. It is common sense that if a breach is not redressed with negative consequences for the wrongdoer, the obligation as such loses force.

11.30. These restitutive and preventive functions of contractual liability also apply to arbitrators. Immunity from liability might remove the arbitrator's incentive to act dutifully and diligently in arbitration by shielding him from the consequences of his wrongdoing.[32] As a consequence, arbitrators could freely proceed with the arbitration as they see fit, thereby violating the parties' procedural rights and applicable legal standards – without the consequence of even losing their fees. This danger is not merely theoretical. Carelessness, cursoriness or personal unconcern can be observed in state court proceedings, notably in cases where there is no further judicial appeal. Unfortunately, it has also been observed in arbitral proceedings where arbitral awards are from the start only subject to minimal review.

11.31. Such careless handling of the arbitral process, against the contractual duties imposed on the arbitrator, would not only leave the parties disappointed in their reasonable expectations to obtain decent service for their money. It would also damage the reputation of arbitration as an alternative means of dispute resolution. In order to be accepted as a dispute resolution method equal or even preferable to state court litigation, the arbitral process needs to meet the expectation of the highest quality and diligence. Negligent conduct in the proceedings or

---

[31]   See for Austrian law, FRANZ T. SCHWARZ, CHRISTIAN W. KONRAD, *supra* note 6, at para. 8-013.

[32]   Peter B. Rutledge, *supra* note 7, at 175; Emmanuela Truli, *supra* note 30, at 399.

decision-making mars the reputation of arbitration as a high-quality method of dispute resolution, and thereby removes the most important reasons for choosing arbitration.

11.32. Some authors propose that the absence of an adequate sanction for contractual breaches is compensated by the existence of "soft sanctions" applied within the arbitration circuit. Indeed, international arbitration is by no means an anonymous market on the supply side. In fact, it is notoriously hard to get into, and to remain a popular choice as an arbitrator, reputation is everything. Arbitrators rumoured not to apply the highest standards in their work might thus quickly be removed from the marketplace. This mechanism is especially effective if institutions such as the ICC are involved which take an active role in case management and purge arbitrators from their rosters if performance is subpar.[33] However, as effective as these mechanisms may be, they are not apt to replace the sanction of contractual liability, as, most importantly, they do not compensate an injured arbitral party for its damage.

11.33. In sum, from a contractual angle, there is no reason to privilege arbitrators over other service providers, and release them from contractual liability. Fundamental arguments pro contractual liability apply with equal force also to arbitrators. Notably, in the absence of liability as a sanction for contractual breaches, arbitrators may not apply the required diligence in the arbitral process, and thereby thwart the parties' expectations, as well as harm the reputation of the arbitral process. Further considerations on the subject, must bear in mind the importance of these considerations, inherent to the concept of contractual liability as such. It seems that any shielding from contractual liability of the arbitrator can only take place as an exception, and for prevailing reasons of public policy.

11.34. On a final note, the suggestion that skilled professionals would be less inclined to act as arbitrators if they were facing liability for their actions[34] seems far-fetched. Many professions face full liability for any service below the standard of care, yet are not lacking applicants. Arbitration is a considerable market and liability insurance is available also to arbitrators. Additional costs for such insurance could be priced into arbitrator's fees, allowing parties and arbitrators to bargain for a

---

[33] *Cf.* Art. 12 (2) ICC Rules 1998; Christian Hausmaninger, *Civil Liability of Arbitrators – Comparative Analysis and Proposals for Reform*, J. INT'L ARB. 7, note 9 (1990).

[34] See *Tamari* v. *Conrad*, 552 F.2d 778, 780-81 (7th Cir. 1977), which did, however, concern arbitrators acting for the Chicago Board of Trade "at nominal pay," in contrast to international commercial arbitrators who receive substantial fees.

contractual exclusion of liability in exchange for lower fees depending on the parties' preferences.[35]

III.2. Judicial Immunity

11.35. International scholars mostly advance the "quasi-judicial"[36] function of the arbitrator in favour of his immunity. Due to his judicial function, the arbitrator should be afforded the same privileges as state court judges who, under most legal system, enjoy immunity from most personal suits.[37]

11.36. There is considerable force in that argument, although, of course, arbitrators are not, in fact judges.[38] Judges are appointed and paid for by the state (and often sworn in to their duty to adhere to the law), while an arbitrator receives his appointment and his fees by the parties. Arbitrators might refuse to be appointed, or bargain for certain terms, while judges do not have this option. Judges may be, depending on the legal system, under scrutiny either by the electorate or subject to disciplinary action. Certain procedural safeguards, such as the duty to observe precedent and the independence of the judiciary from political influence, are lacking in arbitration.[39]

11.37. However, the comparison between state courts judges is still compelling in two regards. First, arbitrators, like state court judges, are entitled to resolve a dispute by making final and binding decisions with full *res judicata* effect. Second, arbitrators, like state court judges, are afforded (and obliged to) independence in the making of their decisions. Both points, with varying emphasis, normally serve to justify the immunity of state courts judges in state court proceedings.[40] One would suspect that they might therefore also serve to release the arbitrator from contractual liability.

---

[35] JULIAN M. LEW, LOUKAS A. MISTELIS, STEFAN MICHAEL KRÖLL, COMPARATIVE INTERNATIONAL COMMERCIAL ARBITRATION, The Hague: Kluwer Law International paras. 12-41 (2003); Peter B. Rutledge, *supra* note 7, at 175.

[36] *Hoosac Tunnel Dock & Elevator Co.* v. *O'Brien*, 137 Mass. 424, 426 (Mass. 1884).

[37] FGG para. 1074.

[38] Susan D. Franck, *supra* note 7, at 23; Christian Hausmaninger, *supra* note 33, at 17.

[39] There are of course other safeguards that prevent abuses of the arbitrators' discretion: The adversarial process, the right of judicial review and procedures for removal of arbitrators all provide a certain level of protection.

[40] See *supra* note 3.

III.3. Contractual Liability and the Binding Effect of Arbitral Awards

11.38. As regards the final and binding effect of arbitral awards, scholars and courts across different jurisdictions frequently argue that if the parties could re-litigate their case by holding the arbitrator liable for wrongful decisions, this would undermine the finality of the award.[41] In this context, it has also been argued that post-arbitral litigation about the conduct of the arbitrators could entail a loss of confidentiality.

11.39. While it is clear that, indeed, attempts to hold the arbitrator liable, over and above an action to set the award aside have a "destabilizing effect"[42] and "undermine the arbitral process's central objectives of finality and speed;"[43] it seems, however, doubtful whether such actions could actually touch upon the *res judicata* effect of arbitral awards. At least from a civil law perspective, an action for damages brought against the arbitrator could have no bearing on the final and binding effect of the initial arbitral award. The new law suit concerns neither the same request nor the same parties as the initial award, and can therefore have no effect on the latter's *res judicata* effect. This argument, by the way, equally applies with regard to state court proceedings.

11.40. Further, even acknowledging a certain "destabilization of the award" in case a party is attempting to litigate one and the same question over again, now under the guise of the arbitrator's liability – this argument is not held sufficient to release other legal professions from liability. By way of example, a negligent conduct of the proceedings on the lawyer's side is generally awarded with strict contractual liability. There is no doubt, that also in damages claims related to the lawyer's professional liability, this may essentially result in the re-litigation of the case, including the question of what the judge would have decided on the merits if the lawyer had complied with its professional duties. This aspect, however, is generally not held sufficient to release the lawyer from liability. It is thus inconceivable why it should release the arbitrator from his or her contractual liability.

11.41. In sum, the binding effect of the arbitral award as such does not justify an exemption of the arbitrator from liability. The *res judicata* effect of the award does not forbid new legal actions regarding the arbitrator's contractual liability. The destabilizing effects of such actions are certainly undesirable, but are generally taken into account also in regard to similar cases of the lawyer's contractual liability. A similar

---

[41] *Supra* note 14, at 132.
[42] EMMANUEL GAILLARD, JOHN SAVAGE, *supra* note 16, at para. 1084.
[43] GARY B. BORN, *supra* note 5, 1662.

line of argument is essentially valid for the further argument that post-arbitral litigation about the conduct of the arbitrators could entail the loss of confidentiality. No arbitration proceeding can be kept completely confidential in case of recognition and enforcement proceedings before a state court.

III.4. Contractual Liability and the Independence of Arbitrators

11.42. As a further argument justifying the arbitrator's immunity from civil liability, international scholars and courts have emphasized the arbitrator's independence in his decision-making process. It is part of the system of arbitration that parties, by submitting their dispute to arbitration, agree that an arbitrator shall decide on the merits of the case on the basis of his own judgement and discretion. Civil liability could impede the arbitrator's task to make an independent decision – which is central to the arbitral process.[44]

11.43. Notably, an arbitrator concerned with personal liability to one of the parties could be influenced in the making of his decision.[45] A troublesome consequence would be for an arbitrator to make undue efforts to please the parties, for example by giving in to dubious requests for additional hearings or expert witnesses.[46] Further, an arbitrator averse to being sued might have every incentive to remain as conservative as possible on legal issues. It would be undesirable, if an arbitrator, in order to avoid the risk of being held liable, only provided non-transparent and vague reasons for his decisions, so that no toehold for a liability suit could be found; or if he were to avoid any evolution of the law, feeling bound to potentially outdated or inapplicable precedents.

---

[44] GARY B. BORN, *supra* note 5; see also TGI Reims, Sept. 27, 1978, *Florange* v. *Brissart et Corgié*, No. 482/77, unpublished (As the most important reason for the exemption of cases of simple negligence from liability, the Reims Tribunal of First instance has held that *"[o]therwise the protection, independence and authority of the arbitrators would be restricted to an extent that would be incompatible with the task of judging which is conferred to them."*).

[45] GARY B. BORN, *supra* note 5.

[46] A useful illustration of how great the danger of liability to a profession's efficiency may be is the reported amount of doctors in the United States ordering tests they consider unnecessary (or avoiding dangerous fields of medicine altogether) in order to avoid malpractice suits, See e.g. *Defensive Medicine Among High-Risk Specialist Physicians in a Volatile Malpractice Environment*, JAMA 293:2609-2617 (2005); available at: http://jama.ama-assn.org/content/293/21/2609.full (accessed on January 27, 2012). In arbitration, such "defensive medicine" could only exacerbate the cost and time problem the process is already facing.

11.44. In light of the central importance of the arbitrator's independence in exercising the powers conferred to him, it seems justified and advisable to grant arbitrators a certain degree of immunity in their decision-making, in order to protect arbitrators from undue influence in the form of subtle threats or even simple concerns. The minimum standard for such immunity would arguably be an exemption from contractual liability for only negligent wrongdoings. One might argue that such a minimal standard is inherent and central to the adjudicative function of the arbitrator, and should thus be considered as mandatory law. The parties may thus not extend the arbitrator's liability for mere negligence of arbitrator conduct.

IV. Conclusion

11.45. The reasons underlying the concept of contractual liability apply with equal force also to arbitrators. As provider of services, arbitrators owe their diligent performance of the task conferred to them, in return for their considerable remuneration. In the interest of the parties, and in the interest of the institution of international arbitration, arbitrators should therefore generally be held responsible for their breaches of contract, and only be exempted from contractual liability exceptionally and for prevailing reasons of public policy.

11.46. The independence of the arbitrator constitutes such a prevailing concern that it justifies a limitation of the arbitrator's liability. Any influence on the arbitrator's decision-making, resulting from the threat of personal liability, may hinder the arbitrator in fulfilling his adjudicative function which is at the heart of the arbitral process. The arbitrator should therefore be released from personal liability as regards negligent wrongdoings. Such exemption from personal liability should be seen to form part of a mandatory minimum standard of immunity, which is not subject to the parties' autonomy.

11.47. The question remains as to what further extent immunity from personal suits should be granted, namely whether immunity should also encompass grossly negligent or even intentional wrongdoings. International scholars argue that an arbitrator's independence would be threatened with almost equal force by the allowance of actions based upon gross negligence, as by the allowance of claims based upon simple negligence.[47] Admittedly, the qualification as gross or simple negligence is ultimately a matter of judgement, leaving ample room for legal

---

[47] GARY B. BORN, *supra* note 5.

uncertainty.[48] However, mere difficulties in a legal assessment do not justify generally disposing of a (sensible) differentiation. And further, the differentiation between gross negligence and intent may also be difficult.

11.48. In light of the importance of the instrument of contractual liability as a sanction, arbitrators should not be shielded from liability where they have, by intention or by gross negligence, done away with the parties' rights. Insofar, arbitrators should be subjected to the same rules as other service providers. Most legal systems, in any case provide that an exclusion of the arbitrator's liability for intentional wrongdoings by contract is inadmissible. For cases of gross negligence, there is no necessity to presume that the parties may have wanted to imply that the arbitrator not be held liable, or to extend the protection of the arbitrator's independence beyond bearable standards. All contractual liability claims based on the arbitrator's wrongful decision-making should further require that the injured party has attempted to vacate the award within the time limit prescribed by the applicable national law.

11.49. Finally, the protection of the arbitrator's independence, resulting in his immunity *vis-à-vis* contractual claims resting on simple negligence, only encompasses the actual decision-making process. All other wrongful actions of the arbitrator, unconnected to his decision-making are subject to ordinary contractual liability. Although the distinction between those obligations which are connected with the arbitrator's decision making, and those which are not may at times be difficult to find, it is however not impossible. In case of doubt, national courts are called to draw the lines and create sensible criteria. In international writing, authors have suggested as ancillary obligations outside of the actual decision-making process, namely the obligation to ensure adequate service of documents in *ad hoc* proceedings, the obligation of confidentiality, the obligation to disclose potential conflicts, the obligation to render an award in time, or the obligation to complete his mandate.[49]

| | |

---

[48] For the critical view of the concept of gross negligence taken in England see *Armitage* v. *Nurse* [1997] EWCA Civ 1279.

[49] See e.g. Musielak ZPO § 1035 para. 25 (8th ed. 2011) with further references.

Summaries

DEU [*Belangbarkeit von Schiedsrichtern – Richterimmunität versus vertragliche Haftung*]

Das Problem der Haftung des Schiedsrichters bewegt sich im Spannungsfeld zwischen vertraglicher Haftung und Richterprivileg. Schiedsdrichter sind von den Parteien bezahlte Dienstleister und haben Rechtsprechungsfunktion zugleich. Dementsprechend wird das schiedsrichterliche Haftungsprivileg teils aus dem Konzept vertraglicher Haftung begründet, teils aufgrund des "Status" des Schiedsrichters als "Quasi-Gericht" abgelehnt. Dieser Artikel gibt zunächst einen Überblick über den Status Quo der Schiedsrichterhaftung unter den Regeln der verschiedenen Schiedsinstitutionen sowie einiger ausgewählter Länder sowohl aus dem Rechtskreis des Common Law als auch des Civil Law.

Der Artikel entwickelt eine eigene Position zur Schiedsrichterhaftung, die sowohl den vertraglichen als auch den an der Justizfunktion des Schiedsrichters orientierten Ansatz berücksichtigt. Nach Auffassung der Autoren gebietet der Schutz der Unabhängigkeit im Ergebnis den Ausschluss der Haftung für einfache Fahrlässigkeit bei der Entscheidungsfindung. Außerhalb der eigentlichen Entscheidungsfindung (sowie bei vorsätzlichem Handeln) erfordert jedoch der Dienstleistungscharakter der schiedsrichterlichen Tätigkeit eine grundsätzlich unbeschränkte Haftung für jede Form schuldhaften Handelns.

CZE [*Odpovědnost rozhodců – soudcovská imunita versus smluvní odpovědnost*]

Řešení otázky odpovědnosti rozhodců se pohybuje mezi kolidujícími prioritami smluvní odpovědnosti a soudcovské imunity. Rozhodci mají dvojí úlohu – jednak jako poskytovatelé služeb najatí a placení stranami sporu, jednak jako orgán vykonávající spravedlnost. Někteří proto argumentují ve prospěch imunity rozhodců ve smyslu zbavení odpovědnosti, a to z důvodu „postavení" rozhodce jako „kvazi-soudního" orgánu; jiní takovou imunitu odmítají s odvoláním na koncept smluvní odpovědnosti. Článek nejprve nabízí nástin současného pojetí odpovědnosti rozhodce dle pravidel různých rozhodčích institucí a dle právních předpisů řady zemí patřících buď do oblasti common law, nebo naopak do sféry kontinentálního práva (civil law).

Příspěvek následně rozvíjí vlastní stanovisko autorů ohledně odpovědnosti rozhodců, které přihlíží jak ke smluvní teorii, tak k teorii, která vychází ze „soudcovské funkce" rozhodců. Dle názoru autorů je potřeba vyloučit odpovědnost rozhodců za běžnou nedbalost při vydávání rozhodnutí, a to z důvodu nutnosti ochrany rozhodcovské nezávislosti. Nicméně nad rámec procesu rozhodování jako takového (a v případech úmyslného zavinění) platí, že povaha práce rozhodce, tedy poskytování služby, zásadně vyžaduje neomezenou odpovědnost na straně rozhodce za jakékoli zaviněné jednání.

||

POL   [*Odpowiedzialność arbitrów – immunitet jurysdykcyjny a odpowiedzialność umowna*]

Niniejszy artykuł prezentuje zarys przeciwstawnych koncepcji odpowiedzialności umownej i immunitetu jurysdykcyjnego w kontekście odpowiedzialności arbitrów. Autorzy są zdania, iż arbitrzy jako usługodawcy powinni zasadniczo być pociągani do odpowiedzialności za naruszenie swych zobowiązań umownych, z wyjątkiem sytuacji, kiedy czyn zabroniony jest bezpośrednio związany z procesem decyzyjnym i zostaje popełniony przez zwykłe niedbalstwo. Z wyłączeniem faktycznego procesu decyzyjnego, który podlega ochronie z tytułu funkcji sądowniczej arbitra, każde inne naruszenie zobowiązań umownych przez arbitra pociąga za sobą pełną odpowiedzialność cywilną.

FRA   [*Responsabilité des arbitres – L'immunité judiciaire par rapport à la responsabilité contractuelle*]

Cet article résume les concepts opposés de la responsabilité contractuelle et de l'immunité judiciaire dans le contexte de la responsabilité de l'arbitre. Les auteurs défendent l'opinion que les arbitres, étant prestataire de service, devraient être tenus responsable pour une violation de leurs obligations contractuelles, à l'exception des cas où la malfaisance est en relation directe avec la prise de décision et commis par simple négligence. En dehors de la prise de décision soi-même, protégée par la fonction judiciaire de l'arbitre, tous cas de violation des obligations contractuelles par l'arbitre sont sanctionnés avec sa responsabilité civile.

RUS   [*Ответственность арбитров–судебный иммунитет против договорных обязательств*]

В этой статье предлагается обзор противоположных концепций договорных обязательств в сравнении с судебным иммунитетом в контексте ответственности арбитра. Авторы придерживаются мнения, что арбитры, как поставщики услуг, должны в принципе нести ответственность за нарушение своих договорных обязательств, за исключением случаев, если неправомерное действие, непосредственно имеющее отношение к принятию решения, совершено по простой небрежности. Помимо того, что фактический процесс принятия решений закреплен законодательной функцией арбитра, любое несоблюдение арбитром его договорных обязательств является предметом полной гражданской ответственности.

ESP [*Responsabilidad de los árbitros – Inmunidad judicial versus responsabilidad contractual*]

Este artículo se propone esbozar conceptos opuestos de la responsabilidad contractual versus la inmunidad judicial en relación con la responsabilidad de los árbitros. El autor considera que los árbitros en calidad de proveedores de servicio deberían, en principio, asumir su responsabilidad en caso de transgredir sus obligaciones contractuales, salvo cuando el acto ilícito esté relacionado directamente con la toma de decisión o se haya cometido por simple negligencia. Más allá del proceso real de la toma de decisión que está protegido por la función judicial del árbitro, cualquier incumplimiento por parte del árbitro de sus obligaciones contractuales está garantizado por plena responsabilidad civil.

Czech (& Central European) Yearbook of Arbitration

Barbara Helene Steindl

Party Autonomy under the 2012 ICC Arbitration Rules

Key words:
*ICC arbitration | 2012
ICC Rules | multi-party |
multi-contract | joinder of
party | applicability
ratione temporis | party
autonomy | emergency
arbitrator | case
management techniques*

Abstract | *Since the revision of the 1998 ICC Arbitration Rules and the entering into force of the 2012 ICC Arbitration Rules on January 1, 2012, ICC arbitration has changed. The contribution highlights several important innovations, and explains their meaning as well as the intention behind the change. Furthermore, an analysis is given of the extent to which the 2012 ICC Arbitration Rules limit, allow for, and even promote party autonomy. Light is shed on the development of the 2012 ICC Arbitration Rules, their applicability ratione temporis, on which mandatory and dispositive requirements have been established for the Request and the Answer's content and how compliance with those requirements may assist to save time and cost. In addition, the new provisions on multi-party and multi-contract arbitration, the case techniques for more efficient case management introduced by the 2012 ICC Arbitration Rules and the new Emergency Arbitrator will be discussed.*

RA Mag. Barbara Helene Steindl, LL.M. (Columbia) MCIArb acts as counsel and arbitrator in international arbitrations under all major arbitration rules. Most of her work involves construction, investment protection, cross-border trade, distribution and sports arbitration. Mrs. Steindl is admitted to the Vienna bar and has passed the New York Bar exam. She is a former deputy counsel of the ICC International Court of Arbitration and acts as the LCIA's YIAG representative for Central Europe. She works in English, French and German. e-mail: b.steindl@bkp.at

| | |

I. Party Autonomy and the Revision of the 1998 Rules

I.1. Party Autonomy in International Arbitration

12.01. Party autonomy as it appears in international arbitration is a multifunctional concept. It is exercised with respect to the selection of the applicable law both as regards procedure and substance. Within those two categories, in arbitration, the parties are free, to the extent permitted by mandatory law and public policy:

> ➤ to determine the content of their arbitration agreement;
> ➤ to appoint individuals of their choice as arbitrators, and detail the procedure of the arbitrators' appointment, primarily, as well as in case of default;
> ➤ to determine the length and conduct of the arbitration proceedings;[1]
> ➤ to limit or extend the powers of the arbitrators and the basis upon which the case will be decided (law, international principles, ex aequo et bono);
> ➤ to frame the extent of the judicial review of awards and
> ➤ to even influence award enforcement (e.g. to waive certain objections in enforcement action).

As far as dispute resolution is concerned, international arbitration is the procedure that seems most responsive to the parties' wishes. Thus, party autonomy is called a major advantage of international arbitration and – for the experienced and skilled – rightfully so.

---

[1] *Cf.* Article V.1(d) 1958 Convention on Recognition and Enforcement of Foreign Arbitral Awards, (hereinafter "New York Convention"): "*Article V 1. Recognition and enforcement of the award may be refused, at the request of the party against whom it is invoked, only if that party furnishes to the competent authority where the recognition and enforcement is sought, proof that:* [...] *(d) The composition of the arbitral authority or the arbitral procedure was not in accordance with the agreement of the parties, or, failing such agreement, was not in accordance with the law of the country where the arbitration took place; or* [...].; *Cf.* Article 19.1 and 19.2 1985 (with 2006 amendments) UNCITRAL Model Law on International Commercial Arbitration: "*Determination of rules of procedure (1) Subject to the provisions of this Law, the parties are free to agree on the procedure to be followed by the arbitral tribunal in conducting the proceedings. (2) Failing such agreement, the arbitral tribunal may, subject to the provisions of this Law, conduct the arbitration in such manner as it considers appropriate. The power conferred upon the arbitral tribunal includes the power to determine the admissibility, relevance, materiality and weight of any evidence.*"

I.2. The Revision of the 1998 Rules and the Launch of the 2012 Rules

12.02. This contribution explores party autonomy and its limits under the 2012 ICC Arbitration Rules (hereinafter the "2012 Rules"). The ICC Arbitration Rules underwent their first major revision in 1975 and their second revision in 1998. Having seen the 1998 ICC Arbitration Rules (hereinafter the "1998 Rules") apply in practise for a period of ten years during which arbitration practise swiftly developed and demands for effective dispute resolution requested a framework able to deal with increasingly complex procedural situations, a review of the rules seemed warranted in 2008. The general guiding principles for the rules revision were, in short:

> ➢ bring the 1998 Rules in line with today's practise where deemed necessary, while retaining, to the greatest extent possible, the key and distinguishing features as well as the flexibility of ICC arbitration;
>
> ➢ make ICC's practise in handling arbitrations more transparent;
>
> ➢ make ICC arbitration still more time and cost efficient and
>
> ➢ leave the parts of the rules that do not create problems untouched – thus only make changes where necessary.

12.03. In October 2008, a special Task Force on the Revision of the ICC Rules of Arbitration[2] was established by the ICC's Commission on Arbitration. This task force discussed and refined the drafts produced by the Drafting Subcommittee that started its work in March 2009. The task force further approved the draft 2012 Rules when they were ready to be laid before the ICC Commission on Arbitration. The Commission eventually submitted the draft to the ICC World Council for approval.[3] In total, the actual process of reviewing the 1998 Rules expanded over a time-period of roughly two years. The 2012 Rules were finally approved by the ICC World Council held in Mexico City on 11 June 2011. The 2012 Rules entered into force on 1 January 2012.

I.3. The Structure of This Contribution and the Comparative Version of the 2012 Rules

12.04. In line with the 2012 Rules' scope, this contribution focuses on the procedural aspect of party autonomy. But for the applicability ratione

---

[2] The author was a member of the ICC Task Force on the Revision of the ICC Rules of Arbitration and contributed to the respective Task Force meetings during the drafting process.

[3] See Article 7 of Appendix I to the 1998 Rules.

temporis of the 2012 Rules and their administration solely by the ICC International Court of Arbitration (the "Court"[4]), the author will work through some of the most interesting new provisions in the sequence in which they appear in the 2012 Rules. The changes made to the 2012 Rules are visualized in mark-up mode (deleted portions of the 1998 Rules are in italicized square brackets; portions added to the 1998 Rules are underlined, and mere orthographic changes have been neglected).

II. Party Autonomy Maintained as to the Applicability of the 2012 Rules

II.1. Applicability Ratione Temporis under the 2012 Rules

12.05. Every rules revision inevitably leads to the question of which version applies to the case at hand. Although the 1998 Rules' general transitory provision remained almost unaltered, the issue shall be quickly revisited to mark the difference vis-á-vis the newly introduced special transitory provision of Article 29.6 2012 Rules that restricts the applicability of the Emergency Arbitrator Provisions.[5] In general, the 1998 as well as the 2012 Rules[6] provide that the parties are free to determine a specific version of ICC Rules to apply to their arbitration. In general, there are two major points in time that the parties may take into account to decide which version of the ICC Rules shall apply to the resolution of their dispute.

II.1.1. The Parties Have a Choice between the Flexible and the Fixed Approach

12.06. First, there is the point in time when the actual arbitration commences that parties may chose as determinative for the applicable ICC Rules version. This point in time also serves as the fall back position pursuant to Article 6.1 2012 Rules if the applicable ICC Rules version has been left undetermined. To the extent the parties do not see the necessity to

---

[4] The ICC International Court of Arbitration is defined as the "Court" by Article 1.1 2012 Rules.

[5] See VI. below for specific regulations concerning the applicability of the newly introduced Emergency Arbitrator Provisions.

[6] Article 6.1 2012 Rules: *"Effect of the Arbitration Agreement: Where the parties have agreed to submit to arbitration under the Rules, they shall be deemed to have submitted ipso facto to the Rules in effect on the date of commencement of the arbitration [proceedings], unless they have agreed to submit to the Rules in effect on the date of their arbitration agreement."*

bind themselves to a specific ICC Rules version, but prefer benefitting from a continuously updated set of rules in line with the latest developments of arbitration practise at the cost of some uncertainty regarding the rules' content, they may prefer the flexible approach and rely on the version in force when their arbitration finally commences. In light of this, the burden placed on the ICC Task Force to revise the rules cautiously and maintain the core features of ICC arbitration is only a sign of the respect owed to the parties which – in the overwhelming number of cases – place their trust in ICC by relying on the flexible approach. This very consideration and the fact that the Emergency Arbitrator Provisions (the "EAP") indeed qualify as a major change led ICC to *inter alia* limit their application to proceedings under ICC arbitration agreements concluded on or after 1 January 2012. Thus, parties relying on the flexible approach will not be bound by the EAP if their arbitration agreement dates back to 31 December 2011 or earlier.[7] Second, there is the point in time of the parties' submission to arbitration which is frequently the time at which the contract including the arbitration clause is concluded. This is a fixed date and, if this date is chosen as determinative for the ICC Rules version, the applicable version's regulations are known from the outset. Thus, if parties appreciate certain features of an ICC Rules version that they fear may be varied by future rules revisions, they are able to freeze this version of the rules[8] under which they desire to arbitrate. It shall, however, be noted that like under previous versions, pursuant to the 2012 ICC Rules,[9] the cost scales for the filing, administrative and arbitrator's fees are not subject to the individual choice of the parties.[10] Those scales are more frequently adapted and different cost scales were in force during the 1975 as well as the 1998 Rules' term.

---

[7] See VI. below for the two other limitations to the EAP's application: The explicit and implicit opt-out by the parties.

[8] For instance the 1998 Rules for arbitrations commencing after 1 January 2012.

[9] Article 37[1].1 2012 Rules: "*The costs of the arbitration shall include the fees and expenses of the arbitrators and the ICC administrative expenses fixed by the Court, in accordance with the scale in force at the time of the commencement of the arbitration [proceedings], as well as the fees and expenses of any experts appointed by the Arbitral Tribunal and the reasonable legal and other costs incurred by the parties for the arbitration.*"

[10] *Cf.* Article 4.1 of Appendix III regarding the May 2010 cost scale of the 1998 Rules: "*The Scales of Administrative Expenses and Arbitrator's Fees set forth below shall be effective as of 1 May 2010 in respect of all arbitrations commenced on or after such date, irrespective of the version of the Rules applying to such arbitrations.*"

III. Party Autonomy Cut as to the Institution which Administers Arbitration under the 2012 Rules

12.07. There have been incidents in the past, however rare, where arbitration institutions other than the Court attempted to administer arbitration proceedings under the 1998 Rules. Since the 2012 Rules are the ICC's work product, require proper administration by a plurality of well thought-out, interrelated and tested ICC procedures, and distinguish tasks specifically reserved for the ICC's bodies, rule-conforming administration of proceedings under the 2012 Rules may only be offered by the Court. It is thus for the benefit of both the parties to ICC arbitrations, the enforceability of their award and naturally also the Court that Article 1.2 2012 Rules[11] now expressly spells out that no other body than the Court is authorized to do so. Article 6.2 2012 Rules[12] even supersedes any contradicting party agreement. Unlike with ad hoc arbitration rules or national arbitration frameworks, here, it is not up to the parties' choice to select the 2012 Rules and combine them with a foreign arbitration institution as their administrator or appointing authority. By the terms of Articles 1.2 and 6.2 2012 Rules, the 2012 Rules as a set of institutional arbitration rules are intrinsically tied to the Court and its bodies and their administration by foreign arbitral institutions is prohibited. The parties and other arbitration institutions have no say in this.

IV. Party Autonomy Promoted as to the Request for Arbitration's Place of Filing and the Shortening of the Arbitration's Start-Up Phase

IV.1. The Claimant's Choice as to the Place of Filing and the Parties' Choice as to the Shortening of the Arbitration's Start-Up Phase

12.08. ICC arbitration is practised globally and by allowing for the Request for arbitration (the "Request"[13]) to be filed with designated ICC offices

---

[11] Article 1.2 2012 Rules: "*The Court does not itself [settle] resolve disputes. It administers the resolution of disputes by arbitral tribunals, in accordance with the Rules of Arbitration of the ICC (the "Rules"). The Court is the only body authorized to administer arbitrations under the Rules, including the scrutiny and approval of awards rendered in accordance with the [has the function of ensuring the application of these] Rules. It draws up its own internal rules which are set forth in Appendix II (the "Internal Rules").*"

[12] Article 6.2 2012 Rules: "*By agreeing to arbitration under the Rules, the parties have accepted that the arbitration shall be administered by the Court.*"

[13] *Cf.* Article 4.1 2012 Rules.

outside ICC's French headquarters, ICC made an important step in supporting the enforceability of ICC awards if the latter is tied to the place where the arbitration is filed and administered. Without doubt, the increase of time and cost efficiency of ICC arbitration was the primary goal demanded by users from the latest rules revision. In line with this, according to Articles 4.3,[14] 5.1 and 5.5 2012 Rules, the information in the Request and in the Answer to the Request (the "Answer")[15] about the parties, the case and some crucial procedural points must now be more complete in order to allow the arbitration to proceed more swiftly, especially during its first phase until the transfer of the file to the arbitral tribunal.

12.09. Due to space limitations, the footnotes in subsection IV only restate the marked-up text of Article 4.3 2012 Rules dealing with the Request. However, since the amendments made to the description of the Request in Article 4.3 2012 Rules are exactly mirrored by the amendments introduced to the description of the Answer and counterclaim of Articles 5.1 and 5.5 2012 Rules, this does not hamper the discussion of what is now required from the Answer and counterclaim. For the new duties and choices arising in equal measure for both claimant as well as respondent, in IV.1.1 to IV.1.2.5 below, only the specific sections of Article 4.3 2012 Rules are cited in the text. It shall suffice to merely refer to the pertinent sections of Articles 5.1 and 5.5 2012 Rules (which are in fact providing for the same duties and choices for Respondent and its Answer and counterclaim) in the footnotes.

---

[14] Article 4.3 2012 Rules: "*The Request shall[, inter alia,] contain the following information: a) the name in full, description, [and] address <u>and other contact details</u> of each of the parties; <u>b) the name in full, address and other contact details of any person(s) representing the claimant in the arbitration;</u> c[b]) a description of the nature and circumstances of the dispute giving rise to the claims <u>and of the basis upon which the claims are made;</u> d[c]) a statement of the relief sought, [including], <u>together with the amounts of any quantified claims and,</u> to the extent possible, an <u>estimate of the monetary value of any other claims</u> [indication of any amount(s) claimed]; e[d]) [the] <u>any</u> relevant agreements and, in particular, the arbitration agreement(<u>s</u>); <u>f) where claims are made under more than one arbitration agreement, an indication of the arbitration agreement under which each claim is made;</u> g[e]) all relevant particulars <u>and any observations or proposals</u> concerning the number of arbitrators and their choice in accordance with the provisions of Articles [8,] <u>12</u>[9] and 13[0], and any nomination of an arbitrator required thereby; and h[f]) <u>all relevant particulars and any observations or proposals</u> [any comments] as to the place of arbitration, the applicable rules of law and the language of the arbitration. <u>The claimant may submit such other documents or information with the Request as it considers appropriate or as may contribute to the efficient resolution of the dispute.</u>*"

[15] *Cf.* Article 5.1 2012 Rules.

IV.1.1. The Claimant's Choice as to the Place of Filing

12.10. As a practical matter, under the 1998 Rules, Requests could only be filed with the ICC's Secretariat in Paris. Article 4.1 2012 Rules[16] now provides claimants with a choice where to file their Request[17] and allows for the Secretariat's daily administrative functions to be carried out at any of the ICC Secretariat's offices specified in the Internal Rules. In addition to its traditional Paris office, ICC has currently one other office in Hong Kong which was created in November 2008. A list of designated ICC offices is kept by the Secretary General. The ICC Hong Kong office provides a safe harbour for ICC arbitration when the resulting award may need to be enforced in mainland China. Under Chinese arbitration law, arbitration institutions administering proceedings with their place of arbitration in China need to be registered with the Chinese authorities just as China's most popular arbitration institution, CIETAC, is. For the ICC and other foreign arbitration institutions not being registered with the Chinese authorities, a sensible way to support the enforceability of awards rendered in China-related arbitrations and bearing "a foreign element" (e.g. a non-Chinese party) is to select Hong Kong as the place of arbitration, to have the arbitration administered by the ICC Hong Kong office, and thus benefit from the bilateral enforcement agreement between China and the Hong Kong Special Administrative Region.

IV.1.2. The Parties' Must Comply with the Mandatory Content of the Request for Arbitration and the Answer and Counterclaim

12.11. Pursuant to the wording of Articles 4.3, 5.1 and 5.5 2012 Rules, more detailed information must now be provided in the Request as well as in the Answer and counterclaim. By requesting the additional information from the parties discussed below, the 2012 Rules foster party autonomy: On the one hand, by complying with the prerequisites set

---

[16]   Article 4.1 2012 Rules: *"Request for Arbitration A party wishing to have recourse to arbitration under these Rules shall submit its Request for Arbitration (the "Request") to the Secretariat [which] at any of the offices specified in the Internal Rules. The Secretariat shall notify the claimant and respondent of the receipt of the Request and the date of such receipt."*

[17]   *Cf.* Appendix II's Article 5.3: *"Offices [Branches] of the Secretariat may be established outside the headquarters of the ICC. The Secretariat shall keep a list of offices designated [as branches] by the Secretary General. Requests for Arbitration may be submitted to the Secretariat at [its seat or at] any of its offices [branches], and the Secretariat's functions under the Rules may be carried out from [its seat or] any of its offices [branches], as instructed by the Secretary General, Deputy Secretary General or General Counsel."*

forth by Article 4.3 2012 Rules, the parties may directly influence the time and cost of the arbitration. Otherwise, Article 4.3 g) and h)[18] 2012 Rules mainly request procedural specifications that are decisive for tailoring the arbitration to the parties' needs, and that are open to the parties' agreement. The latter changes can therefore be understood as ICC's attempt to emphatically motivate the parties to exercise their discretion even during the pending arbitration – or to communicate the failure to reach agreement and have the respective decision-makers (cf. IV.1.2.3) care for what is necessary at a much earlier point in time.

IV.1.2.1. Identification of the Parties, Their Counsel and Proof of Authority

12.12. To facilitate swift communication with the Secretariat and potential future service of the Request by electronic communication, not only the parties' address but also their *"other contact details"* (e-mail, telephone, fax) shall now be included in the Request and Answer (Article 4.3 a) 2012 Rules[19]). Further, the name, address and other contact details of *"any persons representing"* the parties in the arbitration must now be stated (Article 4.3 b 2012 Rules[20]), whether in-house or external. Given recent cases in which party's co-counsel provoked arbitrator conflicts,[21] full disclosure of each party's legal team must be welcomed. The duty to fully identify a party's representative is accompanied by Article 17 2012 Rules[22] which now specifically empowers the Secretariat to request proof of authority of a party representative. In particular when Requests are filed by state entities which are frequently represented by multiple changing in-house individuals, the Secretariat must be in a position to verify who represents the party at a certain point in time and where the authorized representative can be reached. The 2012 Rules facilitate this task.

---

[18] Article 5.1 e) and f) 2012 Rules for the Answer.

[19] Article 5.1 a) 2012 Rules for the Answer.

[20] Article 5.1 b) 2012 Rules for the Answer.

[21] *Cf. inter alia Hrvatska Elektroprivreda, d.d.* v. *The Republic of Slovenia* (ICSID Case No. ARB/05/24) and the Tribunal's Ruling of 6 May 2008: Here, the participation of a party's co-counsel pertaining to the same UK chambers than the presiding arbitrator (thus raising a conflict) had not been disclosed. Once discovered, the co-counsel was refused by the ICSID Tribunal.

[22] Article 17 2012 Rules: *"Proof of Authority: At any time after the commencement of the arbitration, the arbitral tribunal or the Secretariat may require proof of the authority of any party representatives."*

IV.1.2.2. The Basis of Claims and Their Quantification

12.13. Not only the factual but also the legal basis upon which the claims and counterclaims are made shall now be set forth in the Request and counterclaim. This at least requires the party's indication of whether it brings contractual or tort claims (Article 4.3 c) 2012 Rules[23]). To the extent a party desires to provide a more extensive legal basis and assessment of their claims in order to shorten the proceedings and to allow for a fuller reply by the respective opponent party in turn, the party is free to do so. Furthermore, in order to assist the Secretariat in calculating the advance on costs, Article 4.3 d) 2012 Rules[24] reformulates the parties' duty to state the total amount of their (counter) claims. The parties shall now give the amount of their quantified claims and to the extent possible, an estimate of the monetary value of any other claims (i.e. claims that are not yet quantifiable). Notwithstanding that it largely depends on the parties and their skills to convincingly reason why (counter)claims are not yet quantifiable, party autonomy for deciding whether to quantify claims, and at which point in time seems to have been retained to a large extent.

IV.1.2.3. Particulars, Observations and Proposals by the Parties to Promote Party Autonomy

12.14. Pursuant to Article 4.3 g) 2012 Rules,[25] the Secretariat is no longer satisfied with the parties' merely giving the relevant particulars of the party's respective agreement, but in the Request and Answer, they shall now also state their *"observations or proposals"* on the number of arbitrators and the appointment mechanism. Article 4.3 h) 2012 Rules[26] additionally requests the parties to submit *"all relevant particulars, and any observations or proposals"* on the place of arbitration, the applicable rules of law, and the language of the arbitration. Those amendments are again deemed to facilitate and shorten the arbitration start-up phase by advancing the constitution of the arbitral tribunal and by striving to clarify much earlier whether the Court's decision on the place of arbitration[27] or the arbitral tribunal's decisions on the

---

[23] Articles 5.1c) and 5.5 a) 2012 Rules for the Answer and counterclaim.
[24] Article 5.5 b) 2012 Rules for the Answer and counterclaim.
[25] Pursuant to Article 5.1 e) 2012 Rules for the Answer.
[26] Article 5.1 f) 2012 Rules for the Answer.
[27] See Article 18.1 2012 Rules, pursuant to which the Court fixes the place of arbitration unless agreed upon by the parties. Early agreement on the place of arbitration will also

applicable rules of law[28] and the language on the arbitration[29] are required. Also, once the aforementioned three parameters have been determined, the Court is in a much better position to select the ideal arbitrator for the file. In practice the start-up phase for ICC arbitration proceedings was unnecessarily prolonged whenever the parties' delayed their agreement on the number of arbitrators, the particulars of their appointment, and the place of arbitration. By asking for *"observations and proposals"* on these issues, it is hoped that claimants will proactively review whether the appointment mechanism has been properly provided for; failing which the claimants shall – when filing the Request – for instance, propose an interpretation of any ambiguous terms of the arbitration agreement, the number of arbitrators, or shall suggest changing from the pre-defined number of arbitrators or appointing mechanism if they do not suit the case at hand. If claimant complies with Article 4.3 g) 2012 Rules in its Answer, respondent is obliged to reply with *"any observations or proposals ... in light of the claimant's proposals ... ."*,[30] the observations and proposals which should then complete the information required for the appointment of the arbitrators within, and at the latest, 30 days of the respondent's receipt of the Request.[31,32]

---

help the Secretariat and the Court to take potential characteristics of the local arbitration act into account when administering the arbitration.

[28] See Article [15]21.1 2012 Rules, pursuant to which the arbitral tribunal determines the appropriate rules of law that apply to the merits, unless agreed upon by the parties. *Cf.* the comparable situation under Article 19.1 2012 Rules concerning the rules governing the proceedings: *"The proceedings before the arbitral tribunal shall be governed by these Rules and, where these Rules are silent, by any rules which the parties or, failing them, the arbitral tribunal may settle on, whether or not reference is thereby made to the rules of procedure of a national law to be applied to the arbitration."*

[29] See Article 20 2012 Rules, pursuant to which the arbitral tribunal determines the language of the arbitration unless agreed upon by the parties. Early agreement on the language of the arbitration will help the Secretariat choose the right language for its communication with the parties.

[30] See Article 5.1 e) 2012 Rules.

[31] See Article 5.1 first clause 2012 Rules.

[32] Even in case respondent requests an extension of the time for submitting the Answer, Article 5.2 2012 Rules provides that in this case, the application for such extension must contain *"all relevant particulars and any observations or proposals concerning the number of arbitrators and their choice,"* failing which no extension will be granted.

IV.1.2.4. Multi-party, Multi-contract and the Relevant
(Arbitration) Agreements

12.15. Pursuant to the terms of Article 4.3 e) 2012 Rules,[33] the parties must provide *"any agreements"* that are relevant for their case, including the arbitration agreement(s) on which (counter)claimant relies in its Request or counterclaim. Depending on the complexity of the underlying contractual framework and whether and in which way third party contracts interrelate with the very contract under which the (counter)claimant's claims are made, this duty may be a heavy burden (e.g. third party concession and construction agreements that are determinative for claims under the consultancy agreement under which claimant's claims are made) or a simple exercise (e.g. separate sales contract). However, (counter)claimants who are unable to strictly comply with the duty to submit *"any relevant agreements"* may trust that the Secretariat and the Court will not construe these terms in an excessive way and notify the Request, subject, however, to the arbitral tribunal's later review if (counter)respondent objects to the Request's or the counterclaim's compliance with Article 4.3 2012 Rules.[34] Pursuant to the entirely new provision of Article 4.3 f) 2012 Rules,[35] the (counter)claimant must further identify the arbitration agreement for each claim brought, in the event the claimant raises claims under multiple arbitration agreements.

12.16. The presentation of the underlying (arbitration) agreements will enable the Court to make its prima facie decision on jurisdiction, however, under the 2012 Rules, only if invited by the Secretary General to do so.[36]

12.17. Another focal point of the rules revision shall briefly be touched upon: Multi-contract, multi-party and joinder of party scenarios. The 2012 Rules for the first time spell out and to some extent liberalize the Court's practise when it comes to the joinder of parties against which claims are introduced,[37] to claims between multiple parties (including "cross claims" between multiple claimants or multiple respondents[38]) and to claims based on multiple contracts which shall be determined in one arbitration.[39] Here again, party autonomy is limited due to

---

[33] Pursuant to Article 5.5 c) 2012 Rules for the counterclaim.

[34] Articles 5.1 and 5.5 2012 Rules for the Answer and counterclaim.

[35] Article 5.5 d) 2012 Rules for the counterclaim.

[36] *Cf.* footnote 50 below for a short introduction of the new mechanism of prima facie decisions on jurisdiction.

[37] For the filing procedure see Article 7 2012 Rules.

[38] For the filing procedure see Article 8 2012 Rules.

[39] For the filing procedure see Article 9 2012 Rules.

mandatory content requirements as far as the Request for Joinder,[40] the Answer to such a request[41] and the document introducing claims in a multi-party setting[42] are concerned.[43] Then again, it is left to party autonomy to join a party at a rather late stage: Pursuant to Article 12.7 2012 Rules, a joined party may nominate an arbitrator jointly with the claimant(s) or respondent(s). Thus, in order not to neglect the joined party's possibilities to influence the constitution of the arbitral tribunal, Article 7.1 2012 Rules foresees that no party may be joined after the confirmation or appointment of any arbitrator. However, if all parties including the joined party agree to the joinder notwithstanding the arbitrator confirmation or appointment already effected, the joinder may proceed.[44]

12.18. Article 6.4 (i) 2012 Rules deals with the substantive requirements for joinder and multi-party claims while Article 6.4 (ii) 2012 Rules deals with the ones for multi-contract claims. In short, parties may be joined and claims can be made against a joined party as well as between other multiple parties if, as to all parties concerned, *"the Court is prima facie satisfied that an arbitration agreement under the Rules that binds them all may exist"* (Article 6.4 (i) 2012 Rules).[45] By this clause, in order for an arbitration with a joined party or with multiple parties to proceed, all parties concerned must be bound by one and the same arbitration agreement. If, however, the claims introduced in one arbitration are based on multiple contracts and therefore rely on more than one arbitration agreement, in short, such claims can only be brought if *"the Court is prima facie satisfied (a) that the arbitration agreements under which those claims are made may be compatible, and (b) that all parties to the arbitration may have agreed that those claims can be determined together in a single arbitration."* (Article 6.4 (ii) 2012 Rules).[46] By this

---

40   The Request for Joinder's content is described by Articles 7.1 to 7.3 2012 Rules.

41   The Answer to the Request for Joinder's content is described by Article 7.4 2012 Rules.

42   This document's content is described by Article 8.2 2012 Rules.

43   The mandatory content corresponds to the content required for the Request by Article 4.3 c) to f) 2012 Rules; *cf.* IV.1.2.2 and IV.1.2.4 above.

44   Article 7.1 penultimate clause 2012 Rules.

45   Article 6.4 (i) 2012 Rules: *"In all cases referred to the Court under Article 6(3), the Court shall decide whether and to what extent the arbitration shall proceed. The arbitration shall proceed if and to the extent that the Court is prima facie satisfied that an arbitration agreement under the Rules may exist. In particular: (i) where there are more than two parties to the arbitration, the arbitration shall proceed between those of the parties, including any additional parties joined pursuant to Article 7, with respect to which the Court is prima facie satisfied that an arbitration agreement under the Rules that binds them all may exist;"*

46   Article 6.4 (ii) 2012 Rules: *"In all cases referred to the Court under Article 6(3), the Court shall decide whether and to what extent the arbitration shall proceed. The*

clause, in order for an arbitration with claims on the basis of multiple contracts to proceed, (a) the underlying arbitration agreements shall not contradict each other (e.g. as regards the place of arbitration, the number of arbitrators selected and their appointment) and (b) the parties to the arbitration must at least have had reason to anticipate that their claims, although arising under several contracts, may be arbitrated in a single proceeding. According to the Court's practise, this may for instance be the case if the underlying (arbitration) agreements have been concluded by the same parties respectively and if the claims are related to the same economic transaction. If claims are brought under multiple contracts and if they simultaneously arise in a multi-party setting or are directed against a party that shall be joined, both tests under Article 6.4 (i) and (ii) 2012 Rules will be looked at.

12.19.   These regulations indeed respect party autonomy, i.e. the parties' right to intentionally preselect with whom they wish to arbitrate claims in a single proceeding. In this regard, the 2012 Rules' limitation to joinder, multi-party and multi-contract arbitration offers important protection to the parties, since multi-party and multi-contract proceedings in general tend to be significantly more complex and thus more time and cost-intensive than bipolar ones.[47]

---

arbitration shall proceed if and to the extent that the Court is prima facie satisfied that an arbitration agreement under the Rules may exist. In particular: (i) [...] and (ii) where claims pursuant to Article 9 are made under more than one arbitration agreement, the arbitration shall proceed as to those claims with respect to which the Court is prima facie satisfied (a) that the arbitration agreements under which those claims are made may be compatible, and (b) that all parties to the arbitration may have agreed that those claims can be determined together in a single arbitration. The Court's decision pursuant to Article 6(4) is without prejudice to the admissibility or merits of any *party's plea or pleas."*

[47]   The same protection of party autonomy is offered by Article 10 2012 Rules which sets forth the preconditions according to which separate arbitration proceedings may be consolidated. Those preconditions are similar than the ones used under Article 6.4 (i) and (ii) 2012 Rules for multi-party and multi-contract settings. Article 10 2012 Rules: *"Consolidation of Arbitrations: The Court may, at the request of a party, consolidate two or more arbitrations pending under the Rules into a single arbitration, where: a) the parties have agreed to consolidation; or b) all of the claims in the arbitrations are made under the same arbitration agreement; or c) where the claims in the arbitrations are made under more than one arbitration agreement, the arbitrations are between the same parties, the disputes in the arbitrations arise in connection with the same legal relationship, and the Court finds the arbitration agreements to be compatible. In deciding whether to consolidate, the Court may take into account any circumstances it considers to be relevant, including whether one or more arbitrators have been confirmed or appointed in more than one of the arbitrations and, if so, whether the same or different persons have been confirmed or appointed. When arbitrations are consolidated, they shall be consolidated into the arbitration that commenced first, unless otherwise agreed by all parties."*

IV.1.2.5. The Parties Are Invited to Add Dispositive Content to the Request for Arbitration

12.20. Moreover, Article 4.3 last clause 2012 Rules[48] expressly invites the parties to submit additional documents and information with their Request and Answer "*as may contribute to the efficient resolution of the dispute.*" Although parties experienced in ICC arbitration may regard this as a matter of course since they submitted substantial Requests and Answers under the 1998 Rules as well, when appropriate, past practise shows that less experienced parties frequently submit skeleton Requests and Answers, leaving it to the Secretariat and the arbitral tribunal to collect the missing data upon the respective opponent party's objection in the course of the proceedings. This obstructs the Secretariat's endeavour to streamline the proceedings. For instance, if pre-arbitral dispute resolution mechanisms have been agreed upon (e.g. negotiation, mediation, conciliation), a claimant able to make a strong case to the effect that the preconditions to resort to arbitration have been fulfilled is well advised to explain this situation in the Request and offer substantive documentary evidence on point. Respondent will then think twice whether to make the otherwise notorious allegation that the pre-arbitral mechanism has not been complied with.[49] If this is the case, this saves time, for the Court is no longer required to take a prima facie decision on jurisdiction.[50] Nonetheless, even in case respondent should make a weak and obstructive allegation that arbitration is premature, if claimant, by way of precaution, has fully worked up the

---

[48] Articles 5.1 last clause and 5.5 last clause 2012 Rules for the Answer and counterclaim.

[49] It may in particular think twice, since the 2012 ICC Rules – alike the 2010 IBA Rules on the Taking of Evidence in International Arbitration – allow arbitrators to take a variety of factors into account (e.g. delaying tactics) when deciding on the costs of the arbitration. *Cf.* Article 37.5 2012 Rules: "*In making decisions as to costs, the arbitral tribunal may take into account such circumstances as it considers relevant, including the extent to which each party has conducted the arbitration in an expeditious and cost-effective manner.*"

[50] Article 6.3 2012 Rules provides for a new and more efficient mechanism of prima facie decisions on jurisdiction by the Court under which the Court will take less prima facie decisions. The new mechanism empowers the Secretary General to decide whether to refer cases to the Court for a prima facie decision on jurisdiction under the criteria mentioned in Article 6.4 2012 Rules. Article 6.3 2012 Rules does not foresee any preconditions for such referral to the Court by the Secretary General, however, it is expected that the Secretary General will only refer cases for a prima facia decision to the Court if the Secretary General has sincere doubts about jurisdiction. Contrary to Article 6.2 1998 Rules, Article 6.3 2012 Rules thus diverts from the approach that the Court must automatically take a prima facie decision on jurisdiction if no Answer is filed or jurisdictional objections are raised. The new principle rather is that jurisdiction is dealt with by the arbitral tribunal, unless the Secretary General refers the case to the Court on an exceptional basis.

issue from its point of view in the Request, the Court will be able to directly issue its prima facie decision on jurisdiction, without (re)approaching claimant on the issue. Thus, depending on the parties' overall strategy for the arbitration, Article 4.3 last clause 2012 Rules[51] fosters party autonomy when it comes to exerting their influence on the time and cost to conclude the arbitration.

V. Party Autonomy Promoted as to the Limits of Effective Case Management

12.21. Enhancing the time and cost-efficiency of arbitration in an appropriate way[52] may be achieved through different tools, one of them being the better organisation of the case by the enhanced use of case management techniques. As much as possible, the course of the proceedings shall not be determined by issues being raised in a coincidental way, but shall rather be determined by the logical flow of efficient legal assessment. Appendix V to the 2012 Rules exemplarily mentions some useful techniques and *inter alia* suggests:

> ➢ Identifying issues that can be resolved by party or expert agreement;
>
> ➢ Seeing which of the remaining issues may be decided on the basis of documents and which require a hearing;
>
> ➢ Limiting the length and scope of written submissions, of requests for the production of documents and of written and oral evidence;
>
> ➢ Apportioning the proceedings on the issues to be resolved through bifurcation and partial awards.

12.22. Prior to their adoption, the arbitral tribunal is obliged to consult with the parties on such procedural measures in a case management conference.[53] Considering that case management techniques that are employed to save time and cost may cut short the parties procedural rights,[54] Article 22.2 2012 Rules[55] only allows the arbitral tribunal to

---

51 Article 5.1 last clause and 5.5 last clause 2012 Rules for the Answer and counterclaim.

52 *Cf.* Article 22.1 2012 ICC Rules: "*Conduct of the Arbitration: The arbitral tribunal and the parties shall make every effort to conduct the arbitration in an expeditious and cost-effective manner, having regard to the complexity and value of the dispute.*"

53 Article 24.1 2012 Rules: "*Case Management Conference and Procedural timetable: When drawing up the Terms of Reference or as soon as possible thereafter, the arbitral tribunal shall convene a case management conference to consult the parties on procedural measures that may be adopted pursuant to Article 22(2). Such measures may include one or more of the case management techniques described in Appendix IV.*"

54 *Cf.* Article V.1(b) New York Convention: "*Article V 1. Recognition and enforcement of the award may be refused, at the request of the party against whom it is invoked, only if that*

adopt such procedural measures to ensure effective case management if those are *"not contrary to any agreement of the parties."* Thus, ICC case management largely defers to party autonomy.[56] Thus, on the basis of Article 22.2 2012 Rules' wording, it is conceivable that an arbitral tribunal must refrain from bifurcating the proceedings or from limiting requests for the production of documents if all parties concerned disagree with those measures. While it may seem sensible to leave procedural measures for *enhanced* efficiency of arbitration to the will of the parties, Article 22.2 2012 Rules touches on the classic area of conflict between the arbitral tribunal's general powers to conduct the proceedings as they deem appropriate[57] and the parties' right to enforce a different way to proceed. Practise will show where the arbitral tribunal's power to determine the proceedings does end and the parties' respective power starts under the 2012 Rules.

VI. Party Autonomy Promoted as to the Forum for Pre-Arbitral Conservatory and Interim Measures

12.23. Prior to the 2012 Rules, a party in need of conservatory or interim measures before the constitution of the arbitral tribunal could in principle only revert to the state courts. As other arbitration institutions do,[58] ICC through Article 29 2012 Rules[59] now also offers

---

party furnishes to the competent authority where the recognition and enforcement is sought, proof that: (a) [...]; or (b) The party against whom the award is invoked was not given proper notice of the appointment of the arbitrator or of the arbitration proceedings or was otherwise unable to present his case; [...]."

[55]   Article 22.2 2012 ICC Rules: "*In order to ensure effective case management, the arbitral tribunal, after consulting the parties, may adopt such procedural measures as it considers appropriate, provided that they are not contrary to any agreement of the parties.*"

[56]   *Cf.* Article V.1(d) New York Convention, footnote 1.

[57]   *Cf.* Article 25.1 2012 Rules: *"The arbitral tribunal shall proceed within as short a time as possible to establish the facts of the case by all appropriate means.";* cf. also sec. 5a of the 2002 (consolidated as of 2007) Rules of the Arbitration Court attached to the Economic Chamber of the Czech Republic and Agricultural Chamber of the Czech Republic: "*Course of Proceedings The arbitrators shall be free to proceed in the trial in a manner they consider appropriate, by ensuring the equal standing of the parties and, providing all parties with an equal opportunity to exercise their rights for the purpose of ascertaining, without unnecessary formalities, all the facts of the case necessary for the resolution of the case (Secs. 18 and 19 paragraph 2 of the Act No.216/1994 Coll.).*"

[58]   *Cf.* Appendix II to the 2010 Arbitration Rules of the Arbitration Institute of the Stockholm Chamber of Commerce.

[59]   Article 29.1 2012 Rules: "*Emergency Arbitrator – A party that needs urgent interim or conservatory measures that cannot await the constitution of an arbitral tribunal ('Emergency Measures') may make an application for such measures pursuant to the Emergency Arbitrator Rules in Appendix V. Any such application shall be accepted only if it*

the parties an alternative approach to pre-arbitral emergency proceedings with the state courts:[60] the Emergency Arbitrator Provisions (the "EAP").[61] However, a transitional period was thought appropriate in order to respect party autonomy and not impose the Emergency Arbitrator on any party.[62] If the parties concluded an ICC arbitration clause prior to 1 January 2012 and did not expressly select an older version of the rules, the 2012 Rules will apply without the EAP. Neither will the EAP apply if parties agree on the 2012 Rules after 1 January 2012 and either expressly or through their agreement on a different pre-arbitral mechanism (as may be foreseen in FIDIC contracts) opt out of the EAP. Respecting party autonomy, by virtue of Article 29.5 2012 Rules, ICC expressly limits the application of the EAP to the signatories of the underlying arbitration agreement and their successors. Given that Applications for Emergency Measures present a powerful tool, non-signatories that may be included in arbitration proceedings by means of constructive consent shall not be subject to the EAP.

12.24. A party filing an Application for Emergency Measures[63] which must be followed by a Request for Arbitration within 10 days[64] may normally expect the appointment of an Emergency Arbitrator within two days.[65] In order to perform these expedited appointments, it has been discussed during the rules revision that ICC will keep an open list of arbitrators that are willing to act as Emergency Arbitrators on a short term notice. The Emergency Arbitrator's order deciding on the Application for Emergency Measures shall be made no later than 15 days upon the transfer of the file.[66] The arbitral tribunal constituted

---

is received by the Secretariat prior to the transmission of the file to the arbitral tribunal pursuant to Article 16 and irrespective of whether the party making the application has already submitted its Request for Arbitration."

[60]   The 2012 Rules do not prevent the parties from reverting to state courts prior to filing an Application for Emergency Measures with the Secretariat and, in appropriate circumstances, even thereafter. *Cf.* Article 29.7 2012 Rules.

[61]   The proceedings before the Emergency Arbitrator (i.e. the EAP) are set forth in detail Appendix V to the 2012 Rules.

[62]   The applicability of the EAP is regulated by Article 29.6 2012 Rules: "*The Emergency Arbitrator Provisions shall not apply if: a) the arbitration agreement under the Rules was concluded before the date on which the Rules came into force; b) the parties have agreed to opt out of the Emergency Arbitrator Provisions; or c) the parties have agreed to another pre-arbitral procedure that provides for the granting of conservatory, interim or similar measures.*"

[63]   See Article 1.1 of Appendix V to the 2012 Rules.

[64]   See Article 1.6 of Appendix V to the 2012 Rules.

[65]   See Cf. Article 2.1 of Appendix V to the 2012 Rules.

[66]   See Article 6.4 of Appendix V to the 2012 Rules.

upon the filing of the Request holds the powers of an appellate body as it is not bound by the Emergency Arbitrator's order and may modify, terminate or annul the same.[67]

12.25. The EAP provide a convenient alternative forum for pre-arbitral emergency proceedings that are not suited for resolution by state courts but also pose certain risks. Those risks have been mitigated by the arbitral tribunal's power to review the Emergency Arbitrator's order and by the 2012 Rules' deference to party autonomy: The EAP apply pro futuro and not retroactively. Finally, for all parties that see reasons to reject the EAP in the future, ICC's new model arbitration clause is offered with alternative wording that opts out of the EAP.[68]

| | |

Summaries

FRA   [*L'autonomie des parties en vertu des Règles d'Arbitrage CIC 2012*]
Depuis la révision des Règles d'Arbitrage CIC 1998 et l'entrée en vigueur, le 1er janvier 2012, des Règles d'Arbitrage CIC 2012, l'arbitrage de la Cour Internationale de Commerce a changé. Cet article met en lumière plusieurs innovations importantes, et explique leur signification ainsi que l'intention sous-jacente à ce changement. Celui-ci analyse en outre dans quelle mesure les Règles d'Arbitrage CIC 2012 limitent, permettent ou favorisent l'autonomie des parties. Il fait la lumière sur le développement des Règles d'Arbitrage CIC 2012, leur applicabilité ratione temporis, le fondement des exigences obligatoires et juridiques conditionnant le contenu de la Demande et de la Réponse, et la manière dont la conformité à ces exigences peut contribuer à économiser du temps et de l'argent. En outre, les nouvelles dispositions en matière d'arbitrage multi-parties et multi-contrats, les techniques légales permettant une gestion plus efficace des affaires introduites par les Règles d'Arbitrage CIC 2012 et le nouvel Arbitre d'Urgence font l'objet d'une discussion.

CZE   [*Autonomie stran dle rozhodčích pravidel ICC 2012*]
Od okamžiku revize rozhodčích pravidel ICC v roce 1998 a vstupu v platnost nových rozhodčích pravidel ICC dne 1. ledna 2012, došlo v rozhodčím řízení ICC k určitým změnám. Příspěvek poukazuje na

---

[67]   See 29.3 2012 Rules.

[68]   See   http://www.iccwbo.org/uploadedFiles/Court/Arbitration/other/Standard_Arbitration_Clauses_ENGLISH.pdf (accessed on February 7, 2012) for the available versions of the ICC 2012 Rules model arbitration clause.

některé významné inovace a vysvětluje jejich význam, jakož i záměr, jímž byla změna motivována. Článek dále rozebírá rozsah, v němž nová rozhodčí pravidla ICC omezují, připouštějí, či dokonce podporují autonomii stran. Osvětluje se vývoj rozhodčích pravidel ICC 2012, jejich použitelnost ratione temporis, na níž jsou založeny kogentní a dispozitivní požadavky týkající se obsahu žaloby a žalobní odpovědi, a dále způsob, jakým může vyhovění těmto požadavkům přispět k úspoře času a nákladů. Předmětem rozboru jsou rovněž nová ustanovení o rozhodčím řízení, jehož se účastní více stran nebo které se týká více smluv, techniky efektivnějšího vedení řízení zavedené rozhodčími pravidly ICC 2012 a nový institut „Emergency Arbitrator".

| | |

POL *[**Autonomia stron w rozumieniu Regulaminu Arbitrażu ICC 2012**]*
Niniejsza praca omawia poprawki do Regulaminu Arbitrażu ICC 1998, wprowadzone wraz z wejściem w życie Regulaminu Arbitrażu ICC 2012. Artykuł zajmuje się w tym kontekście kwestią przyznawania i ograniczania autonomii stron, a także niektórymi istotnymi nowymi rozwiązaniami, takimi jak np. nowe wymogi dotyczące wnoszenia i odpowiadania na pozwy, czy też zasady obowiązujące w trakcie postępowania wielostronnego lub wiążące dla arbitra w sprawach nagłych.

DEU *[**Parteiautonomie gemäß der ICC-Schiedsordnung 2012**]*
Der Beitrag diskutiert die Novellierung der 1998er ICC Schiedsordnung durch das Inkrafttreten der 2012 er ICC Schiedsordnung. Die Frage der Gewährung und Beschränkung der Parteiautonomie durch die 2012 Schiedsordnung wird beleuchtet, sowie einige wichtige Neuerungen, beispielsweise die neuen Erfordernisse an die Schiedsklage und die Antwort, die Vorschriften zu Mehrparteienverfahren und zum Eilschiedsrichter.

RUS *[**Автономия сторон согласно Нормам Арбитража Международной торговой палаты, вступившим в силу в 2012 году**]*
В данной статье обсуждается поправка к Нормам Арбитража МТП от 1998 года, которая была реализована при вступлении в силу Норм Арбитража в 2012 году. В данном контексте в статье рассматриваются вопросы предоставления и ограничения автономии сторон, а также ряд существенных нововведений, таких, как новые требования к исковому заявлению и к ответу,

либо правила для многосторонних процессуальных разбирательств, а также тех, которые контролирует арбитр по чрезвычайным делам.

ESP   [*La autonomía de las partes bajo el Reglamento de arbitraje de la CCI de 2012*]

Este artículo trata de la enmienda al Reglamento de arbitraje de la CCI de 1998, que ha sido implementada una vez entrado en vigor el Reglamento de arbitraje de la CCI de 2012. De ese modo, el artículo examina las cuestiones de concesión y restricción de la autonomía de las partes y ciertas novedades más relevantes, como son los nuevos requisitos para demandar y responder o el reglamento para los arbitrajes con múltiples partes o los del árbitro de emergencia.

Czech (& Central European) Yearbook of Arbitration

Jozef Suchoža |
Regina Hučková Palková
Autonomy of Arbitrators – Decision-making on the Basis of *Ex Aequo et Bono*[*]

Key words:
Arbitrator | ex aequo et bono | amiable compositeur | dispute resolution | principles of equity

Prof. JUDr. Jozef Suchoža, DrSc. is a recognised authority in the field of commercial law. He is the author of several scholarly monographs and of a wealth of specialist articles and studies, and the co-author of the first comprehensive Slovak textbook on commercial law. He is also a member of the Scientific Council at the Institute of State and Law of the Czech Academy of Sciences in Prague, and an international arbitrator on the lists of arbitrators of the Arbitration Court attached to the Slovak Chamber of Commerce and Industry and of the Arbitration Court attached to the Economic Chamber and the Agricultural Chamber of the Czech Republic. He is currently acting as the project manager in charge of a project funded by the Slovak Research and Development Agency (APVV), which focuses on the issue of out-of-court dispute resolution in Slovakia

Abstract | *Arbitration offers possibilities which are impossible in standard litigation. Traditionally, arbitration has been connected to a more flexible decision-making process; the parties have the opportunity to influence more of the aspects involved in the arbitrators' decision-making. Resolution of disputes following the principle of ex aequo et bono and similar principles still remains a mystery. The study focuses on these particular principles which are founded on the concept of equity, insofar as the arbitrator is authorized to resolve the dispute on the basis of unwritten equitable principles. The study analyses the possibility of resolving the dispute following such principles both from the perspective of Slovak and Czech legal systems and from the perspective of selected international instruments. Resolving disputes following equitable principles has no clearly defined criteria because it hinges on another legal concept often subject to conflicting interpretations – equity. The authors have attempted to document some of the interesting opinions published on this topic and, last but not least, to themselves contribute to a partial clarification of this phenomenon.*

| | |

[*] This article is a contribution to the resolution of the **LPP-0076-09** Project "Extrajudicial (alternative) dispute resolution in the Slovak Republic."

I. Introduction – Theoretical Contexts and Insights

13.01. The theoretical analysis presented in this study focuses on the autonomy or, broadly speaking, the legal status of arbitrators in arbitration, specifically in foreign commercial disputes. Proceeding from this premise, we will further concentrate on the issue of resolving such disputes following the principles of equity, i.e., *ex aequo et bono*. The topics subject to our examination have many aspects and give rise to numerous questions. We shall divide them into several categories:

13.02. What is the *legal status of arbitrators,* especially permanent arbitral institutions in the complicated hierarchical network of the institutions which hear and resolve private-law disputes including, but not limited to foreign commercial relationships? What is their legal authority both public and private, their procedural legitimacy and, in the broader sense, their legal status?

13.03. The principally consensual basis of the formation of arbitrators also gives rise to a certain doctrinal and legislative overlap of several levels of relationships: that of the *arbitrator - party* to the arbitration; *party-court* (taking into consideration the process of recognition and review of arbitral awards); court - *bailiff (executor)* (during the involuntary enforcement of arbitral awards). This framework may, in a certain sense, include the much discussed (predominantly academic)

(LPP-0076-09 – Out-of-court/alternative dispute resolution in Slovakia).

JUDr. Regina Hučková Palková, PhD is research associate at the Chair of Commercial Law and Economic Law of the Faculty of Law of Pavol Jozef Šafárik University in Košice. She completed her post-graduate studies in 2009 by successfully defending her dissertation on the topic: "Arbitration procedures in commercial matters – The current state and proposals for future legal development." Her research work continues to address issues in the realm of arbitration as well as out-of-court dispute resolution in a more general context. She manages the grant project "Out-of-court (alternative) dispute resolution in Slovakia." e-mail address for contacting both authors:
regina.palkova@upjs.sk

issue of whether the arbitrator (arbitral tribunal) is a state authority, an indirect derivative of such authority ("cum imperio" jurisdiction) or the result of a specific private-law agreement, the arbitration agreement (clause), which is connected to a commercial contract and the property of the parties ("cum dominio" jurisdiction). The key issue is the proper distinction between private-law and public-law matters in the analysed area. Do the arbitrators exercise public authority?

13.04. One thing is certain; the issue of the legal status of arbitrators must be resolved with respect to all relevant circumstances, including the binding nature of the arbitrators' final award on the merits when it appears to justify an ex post classification of the entire proceeding as a specific one exhibiting certain public-law features.[1] We will return to this issue later.

13.05. The clarification of the legal status of arbitrators is associated with the issue of their liability on several levels; these include private-law liability, criminal liability and others. For practical reasons, deciphering the premises of the arbitrators' liability (liability of permanent arbitral institutions and their founders, as the case may be) requires the clarification and identification of the other party to the liability relationship (the obligee). Nonetheless, there are other aspects of this

---

[1]   *Cf.* JAN VÁŽNÝ, ŘÍMSKÝ PROCES CIVILNÍ (*Roman Civil Procedure*), Praha: Melantrich 5 et seq. (1935).

The author points out that the history of Roman procedure reveals the reaction of the state to the "age-old exercise of rights, self-help." (p. 6). Also: "*The interesting thing is that the state's response to the arbitrary exercise of rights which cannot be suffered in the interest of civil peace is not a replacement for the administration of justice by the state but a referral of the parties to the dispute advising them to submit to the decision of their fellow citizen as an arbitrator. It prohibits the arbitrary enforcement of rights by creditors themselves but grants them the possibility to have their case decided by an arbitrator despite the debtor's disagreement; the creditor is subsequently allowed to enforce such a decision, albeit observing the prescribed forms and modalities*" (p. 6) (underlined by the authors of this study). The author continues: "*These aspects (to wit, 'the participation of a lay civil element in the judiciary') would justify the comparison of the nature of the Roman procedure to arbitration: if arbitration means the parties submitting their case to their selected judge by agreement, the same idea is expressed in the Roman procedure as well... Because the Roman procedure contains a number of other elements, let's call them public, which are foreign to arbitration. It involves the intervention of a state body with jurisdiction whose dare actionem, dare iudicem, iudicari iubere (to name the most significant) is just as decisive for the possibility of a dispute as the initiative of the parties. These two faces of procedure, the mutual influence of private and public elements, is the best explanation of the essence of Roman procedure.*" (p. 12).   See also MILAN BARTOŠEK, DĚJINY ŘÍMSKEHO PRÁVA VE TŘECH FÁZÍCH JEHO VÝVOJE (*History of Roman Law in the Three Stages of Its Development*), Praha: Academia 79 et seq. (1995). *Cf.* also VÁCLAV HORA, III ČESKOSLOVENSKÉ CIVILNÍ PRÁVO PROCESNÍ: OPRAVNÉ PROSTŘEDKY A ZVLÁŠTNÍ ZPŮSOBY ŘÍZENÍ. SE STÁLYM ZŘETELEM KE SLOVENSKU A PODKARPATSKÉ RUSI (*Czechoslovak Civil Procedure Law: Remedial Measures and Special Types of Procedure. with Constant Regard to Slovakia and Carpathian Ruthenia. Vol III.*), Praha: published by the author himself 234 (1929). New ideas regarding arbitration in the Czech Republic (de lege ferenda) in combination with the proposed regulation of private international law were presented by Zdeněk Kučera, K otázkam úpravy medzinárodného práva súkromného (*Regarding the Regulation of Private International Law*), 1 ACTA UNIVERSITATIS CAROLINAE. IURIDICA – AKTUÁLNÍ OTÁZKY MEZINÁRODNÍHO PRÁVA SOUKROMÉHO (*Current Topics in Private International Law*), Praha: Univerzita Karlova – Karolinum 7 et seq. (Z. Kučera, M. Pauknerová, K, Růžička eds., 1998).

liability, first and foremost, the sources of the arbitrators' liability, i.e., its legal basis and principles. The legal status, formation and nature of arbitrators are all institutional issues of arbitration law.

13.06. The procedural aspects of arbitration as a *specific type of legal proceeding* are a relatively separate category.[2] Arbitration, originally serving as a mere addendum to procedural law (general litigation before regular, state courts) gradually developed and became institutionally established as an equal alternative to the resolution of private-law disputes in court proceedings. Such a development, transcending the borders of individual states, was significantly facilitated by the international cooperation of business entities which were looking for effective and rational mechanisms for the resolution of their disputes arising from foreign trade. The basic formal framework was already in place when, for instance, as a result of the application of *ius gentium,* ancient Roman law tolerated proceedings mediated by a party-appointed arbitrator, especially in disputes involving complicated economic and technical matters that require a certain degree of expertise on the part of the arbitrator. It's no wonder that the concept of arbitration has undergone certain transformations in the history of law. Ultimately, it was incorporated in civil procedure rules applicable in the Austro-Hungarian Empire, specifically in the Austrian Civil Procedure Rules (Act nos. 112/1895 and 123/1895 of the Imperial Code) and the Hungarian Civil Procedure Rules (Act nos. I/1911 and LVI/1912). These laws were also applied in Czechoslovakia. They were repealed by Czechoslovak Act No. 142/1950 Coll. promulgating the Civil Procedure Code; however, the concept of arbitration was preserved. Arbitration attained a new dimension in 1963 with the adoption of Act No. 97/1963 Coll., on Private International Law (still applicable, with subsequent amendments), and Act No. 98/1963 Coll., on Arbitration in International Commerce.

13.07. Last but not least, these issues must be analysed with regard to the *determination of the applicable substantive law* which the arbitrator is obliged to apply to the dispute.[3]

---

[2]   *Cf.* Petr Bezouška, Jan Kocina, *Právní povaha rozhodčího řízení – aplikační problémy (The Legal Nature of Arbitration – Application Problems),* 18 (16) PRÁVNÍ ROZHLEDY 585 et seq. (2010).

See also KVĚTOSLAV RŮŽIČKA, ROZHODČÍ ŘÍZENÍ PŘED ROZHODČÍM SOUDEM PŘI HOSPODÁŘSKÉ KOMOŘE ČESKÉ REPUBLIKY A AGRÁRNÍ KOMOŘE ČESKÉ REPUBLIKY (*Arbitration before the Arbitration Court Attached to the Economic Chamber of the Czech Republic and the Agricultural Chamber of the Czech Republic*), Dobrá voda u Pelhřimova: Nakladatelství a vydavatelství Aleš Čeněk 18 et seq. (2003).

[3]   In the broader sense, this involves the delimitation of the applicable law with respect to the conflict-of-law rules (laws) determining which law shall be applied to relations with

13.08. Based on the above, it is also necessary to examine selected arbitration laws which contain certain aspects of the applicable law.[4]

---

an international element. ZDENĚK KUČERA, VYBRANÉ OTÁZKY SROVNÁVACÍHO MEZINÁRODNÍHO PRÁVA SOUKROMÉHO (*Selected Issues of Comparative Private International Law*), Praha: Univerzita Karlova – Karolinum 37 et seq. (1996). See also ZDENĚK KUČERA, MONIKA PAUKNEROVÁ, KVĚTOSLAV RŮŽIČKA, VLASTISLAV ZUNT, ÚVOD DO PRÁVA MEZINÁRODNÍHO OBCHODU (*Introduction to the Law of International Commerce*), Dobrá voda u Pelhřimova: Aleš Čeněk 276 et seq. (2003).

See also NADĚŽDA ROZEHNALOVÁ, PRÁVO ROZHODNÉ V ŘÍZENÍ PŘED MEZINÁRODNÍMI ROZHODCI (TENDENCE V OBLASTI ZÁVAZKOVÉHO PRÁVA S PŘIHLÉDNUTÍM K ÚPRAVÁM V NĚKTERÝCH EVROPSKÝCH ZEMÍCH) (*Applicable Law in Arbitration before International Arbitrators (New Trends in the Law of Obligations in Light of the Laws of Selected European Countries)*), 138 (11) PRÁVNÍK 1066 et seq. (2000). The author explains, *inter alia*, various methods of determining the law applicable to the merits of the case, primarily the *territorial approach* (considered to be the older, traditional method) as well as the *contractual approach*, which the author deems to be more flexible. She highlights several possibilities, specifically (p. 1069):

- abandoning the principle of *lex fori* in order to apply the rules of private international law (usually conflict-of-law rules);
- the *creation of conflict-of-law rules* (in the absence of a choice of law) by the arbitrators themselves;
- the so-called *direct determination of the substantive law* without using conflict-of-law rules;
- the application of legal rules created in a particular community (in the case of international commercial arbitration, law created by international merchants - *lex mercatoria*) or the resolution of disputes outside the sphere of law (deciding cases according to equity, *ex aequo et bono*, etc.)

[4] Act No. 97/1963 Coll., on Private and Procedural International Law as subsequently amended, stipulates as follows (Section 10): "in the absence of a choice of law by the parties, their obligations shall be governed by the law whose application corresponds to a reasonable resolution of the relationship"; conflicts shall be solved according to (certain) generally accepted types of connecting factors such as lex domicilii, lex personalis, lex rei sitae, lex loci actus, lex voluntatis, lex fori, lex causae, lex monetiae (pecuniae) etc.

Cf. also the *European Convention on International Commercial Arbitration* of 21 April 1961 concluded in Geneva, Decree No. 176/1964 Coll. of the Minister of Foreign Affairs which includes the following provision dealing with the applicable (governing) law, Article VII:

"The parties shall be free to determine, by agreement, the law to be applied by the arbitrators to the substance of the dispute. Failing any indication by the parties as to the applicable law, the arbitrators shall apply the proper law under the rule of conflict that the arbitrators deem applicable. In both cases, the arbitrators shall take into account the terms of the contract and trade usages."

Similarly, the UNCITRAL Model Law on International Commercial Arbitration – United Nations document A/40/17, Annex I, adopted by the United Nations Commission on International Trade Law on 21 June 1985, Article 28: "The arbitral tribunal shall decide the dispute in accordance with such rules of law as are chosen by the parties as applicable to the substance of the dispute. Any designation of the law or legal system of a given State shall be construed, unless otherwise expressed, as directly referring to the substantive law of that State and not to its conflict of laws rules.

Failing any designation by the parties, the arbitral tribunal shall apply the law determined by the conflict of laws rules which it considers applicable.

13.09. We shall concentrate specifically on the principle of *"ex aequo et bono,"* which is briefly defined in various arbitration laws as *the resolution of disputes following equitable principles.* The Slovak Arbitration Act, Section 31(4), briefly stipulates the following:

13.10. "The arbitral tribunal only has the right to resolve a commercial dispute according to the principles of equity if the parties to the arbitration explicitly authorize it to do so." Section 31(2) of the Act which, *strictly speaking,* must be considered as mandatory, provides that a dispute arising from domestic commercial and civil relationships shall *always* be resolved by the arbitral tribunal *pursuant to the laws of the Slovak Republic;* consequently, we must *a contrario sensu* assume that the principle of *ex aequo et bono* may not be applied in such disputes. But there are opinions to the contrary.

13.11. *Czech arbitration rules* (Section 25(3) of Act No. 216/1994 Coll.) clearly allow the application of equitable principles both in domestic and international disputes. Concerning disputes with an international element, Czech law requires that the arbitrators adopt the specific approach described in Section 37 of such Act (regarding the choice of the applicable law – or legal system, as well as the application of the law which the *arbitrators shall determine* according to domestic conflict-of-law rules).

13.12. *Hungarian law* features a different method; instead of applying any particular law, the arbitral tribunal resolves a dispute *pursuant to the principles of equity,* although only if explicitly authorized to do so by the parties to the arbitration. (Section 49(3) of Act LXXI of 1994). The same applies under the Rules of Arbitration and Conciliation (the so-called Vienna Rules) of the *Vienna International Arbitral Centre –* VIAC), adopted by the assembly of the Austrian Economic Chamber on 30 November 2000 – effective date 1 January 2001 (see Article 16(2)).

The arbitral tribunal shall only decide *ex aequo et bono* or as *amiable compositeur* if the parties have expressly authorized it to do so.
In all cases, the arbitral tribunal shall decide in accordance with the terms of the contract and take into account the *usages of the trade* applicable to the transaction."
Cf. also Slovak Act No. 244/2002 Coll. on Arbitration, as subsequently amended (Section 31).
Similarly Czech Act No. 216/1994 Coll. on Arbitration and the Enforcement of Arbitral Awards, as subsequently amended (Section 25 (3)).
Cf. also Hungarian Act LXXI of 1994 on Arbitration (Sections 49 and 50).
See also Regulation No. 593/2008 of the European Parliament and the Council of 17 June 2008 on the law applicable to contractual obligations (*Rome I*) – O. J. L 177, 4 July 2008 as well as Regulation No. 864/2007 of the European Parliament and of the Council of 11 July 2007 on the law applicable to non-contractual obligations (*Rome II*) – O. J. L 199, 31 July 2007.

13.13. In this connection, we should pay extra attention to the arbitration rules applicable before the *International Court of Arbitration* of the International Chamber of Commerce in Paris. The Rules of Arbitration adopted by the International Chamber of Commerce (ICC) stipulate that first and foremost, the parties have the right to agree on the rules to be applied by the arbitrators to the merits of the dispute; in the absence of such agreement, the arbitrators shall apply the rules which they determine to be appropriate. The Rules also emphasize that the arbitrators shall always take into account the provisions of the contract and any relevant trade usages. Finally, the Rules stipulate that "the arbitral tribunal shall only assume the powers of an *amiable compositeur* or decide *ex aequo et bono* if the parties have agreed to give it such powers."

13.14. The application of the principle of ex aequo et bono in arbitration gives rise to certain doubts concerning its interpretation, at least as concerns an adequate definition of *"justice (equity)"* in the general sense of the word. In this connection, Victor Knapp states that "… the concept of justice (equity) is intuitively understandable but its definition causes problems comparable to the definition of law or legal awareness. Philosophers and lawyers have been attempting to define justice (equity) for more than two thousand years, but no satisfactory definition or explication of the word 'justice' (equity) has been invented."[5]

13.15. As this information suggests, arbitration laws apply the ex aequo et bono principle, at least as a predictable substitute for the conceivable substantive law which would otherwise apply, based either on a choice of law or on the normative platform of conflict-of-law rules (i.e., private and procedural international law) often including very complicated academic and judicial interpretations of the legal-normative body (entity).

13.16. The choice of the substantive law is no doubt based on an agreement. It is primarily the result of a commercial contract with an international element where the parties to the international commercial transaction may agree on the choice of the applicable substantive law as late as at the opening of the arbitral proceedings. This possibility is naturally anticipated by certain national arbitration laws and international instruments.[6]

---

[5]   VIKTOR KNAPP, TEORIE PRÁVA (*The Theory of Law*), Praha: C. H. BECK 86 (2nd ed. 1995).

Cf. also HERBERT LIONEL ADOLPHUS HART, POJEM PRÁVA (*The Concept of Law*), Praha: Prostor 157 et seq. (2010).

[6]   See for instance the European Convention on Commercial Arbitration of 21 April 1961 (Decree No. 176/1964 Coll.) – Article VII.

13.17. The Slovak Arbitration Act introduced the possibility of resolving a commercial dispute following equitable principles (i.e., ex aequo et bono) in Section 31(4) entitled *"The applicable law and its interpretation."* The structure of Section 31 indicates that the legislator places arbitration which follows the principles of equity on a par with (or above) the resolution of disputes according to the otherwise applicable substantive law. The parties' clause directing the arbitrator to resolve their commercial dispute *according to the principles of equity* de facto temporarily suspends the application of the otherwise applicable substantive law (i.e., "suspends the application of the law").

13.18. However, we must add that subsection 3 of Section 31 of this Act mandates that the arbitral tribunal, when resolving a dispute according to the applicable law, base its decision primarily on the *contents of the commercial contract* entered into between the parties to the arbitration and further consider the *trade usages* applicable to the dispute (to wit, trade usages relevant at the level of the negotiated transaction) as well as the *principles of honest business transactions and good morals*.

13.19. In other words, the Slovak legislator principally envisages two scenarios. The first scenario relates to those cases in which the arbitrator acts (decides) according to settled arbitration rules determined either by an agreement (choice) of the parties (choice of a legal system) or by conflict-of-law mechanisms. The crucial fact is that the interpretation of the applicable law by the arbitrator must be based, first and foremost, on the *commercial contract entered into by the parties*. The commercial contract is one of the decisive components contributing to the content of the applicable (governing) law. The contract makes the *law (the so-called autonomy, lex contractus).*[7]

13.20. Section 31(3) of the Arbitration Act is remarkable in the fact that when interpreting the applicable law, the arbitrator must also take into consideration:
   – *trade usages* (applicable to the dispute), as well as
   – *principles of honest business transactions* (i.e., fair trade) and finally
   – *(principles of) good morals.*

13.21. The second scenario relates to the rare case in which, instead of applying the applicable law, the arbitrator resolves the dispute

---

Also, for instance, the UNCITRAL Model Law on International Arbitration – United Nations document A/40/17, Annex (As adopted by the United Nations Commission on International Trade Law on 21 June 1985) – Article 28. (Rules applicable to the substance of the dispute).

[7]   VIKTOR KNAPP, *supra* note 5, at 52 et seq.

according to the principle ex aequo et bono (pursuant to equitable principles).

13.22. The above analysis gives rise to a number of questions. Suddenly we realize that such concepts like trade usages, principles of honest business and good morals (and their legal specification) are hard to define. But they do represent a precious subject of academic interpretation. These are categories which, from a historical-evolutionary perspective, have their basis in generally recognised values of human existence and mutual communication between people, i.e., in the structure of social relations (interests, needs). This raises another question which demands an answer. What is the relationship between these phenomena (Section 31(3)) and the principles of equity, a.k.a. the principle of ex aequo et bono (Section 31(4))? Do they overlap?

13.23. First of all, it is necessary to emphasize that these terms are employed by many Slovak laws, albeit on a general level. From the perspective of law, they are, in a certain sense, sophisticated concepts.[8] Sporadic attempts of legislators to establish a more detailed definition of these terms albeit limited to the relevant Act, or more specifically for the purposes of the relevant Act, ultimately turn out to be redundant, to say the least, and sometimes almost tautological (for instance acts *contra bonos mores* – deviation from moral rules, etc.).

13.24. The principle of equity is generally connected with the recognized values of a democratic society; under Roman law, with the requirement

---

[8]   See for instance: Civil Code – Section 3 (the *exercise of rights* cannot be *contra bonos mores*), Section 39 (legal acts which are *contra bonos mores* are null and void), Section 424 (*liability for damage* caused by a wilful act *contra bonos mores*), Section 564 (*power of the court to determine*, at the creditor's request, *the time of performance* so that such determination *complies with good morals*) and Section 630 (the *right of the donor* to demand the *return of the gift* if the donee's behaviour toward the donor or members of his or her family *grossly contravenes good morals*). In the Commercial Code, see for instance: Section 44 (*prohibition* of unfair competition, i.e., any act which is *contra bonos mores of competition*) and Section 265 (refusal to enforce any right which contravenes the *principles of honest business transactions*). The Commercial Code (Section 381) defines the category of lost profits (compensation for lost profits) with reference to the criterion of "profits usually achieved by *honest business transactions*, under conditions similar to the terms of the breached contract, in the aggrieved party's industry." *Cf.* also Act No. 250/2007 Coll. on Consumer Protection, as subsequently amended (Section 4(8)). This Act (for the purposes of this Act) defines behaviour contra *bonos mores* as "behaviour violating certain traditions and exhibiting obvious features of discrimination or deviation from moral principles recognised in the business of selling goods and rendering services, or behaviour capable of causing damage to consumers by failing to observe honesty and good faith. In usages and practice, it employs primarily errors, deceit, threats, significant inequality of the contracting parties and breaches of contractual freedom." The concept of "*trade usages*" is incorporated in Sections 1(2), 264 and 730 of the Commercial Code.

of equitable treatment and welfare.[9] "Equity" in the historical-evolutionary sense is based on natural law. The "precise" definition of equity, however, encounters certain problems in interpretation that are caused by the very nature of the analysed phenomenon. These are not only semantic problems, i.e., the need to adequately delimit the characteristic features of the respective phenomenon from its specifically linguistic perspective. It is also necessary to define its legally relevant or rather, legally normative aspect.

13.25. Equity (justice) means the aggregate of several principles of natural law which give rise to and externally attain a certain degree of internal

---

[9] *Cf.* PETER BLAHO, JARMILA VAŇKOVÁ, I CORPUS IURIS CIVILIS. DIGESTA., Bratislava: EUROKODEX 527 (2008). Book I (LIBER PRIMUS), Title I (De iustitia et iure – About Justice and Law) says: "*Law takes its name from justice (iustitia), or, as eloquently defined by CELSUS, the art of good and equity (justice)*" – *ius est ars boni et aequi* (p. 53). Elsewhere PAULUS in Book XIV to Sabinus: "*The word "law" has several meanings: it means natural law when we speak of things that benefit everybody or the majority of people in an individual civitas*" (p. 57). ULPIANUS says: "*Justice is a mute and constant will to give everybody his or her own right. The orders of law are as follows: **live honestly, do not cause harm to others, give everybody what is due to them** – honeste vivere, alterum non laedere, suum cuique tribuere*" (p. 56). *Cf.* also IUSTINIANI INSTITUTIONES. JUSTINIÁNSKE INSTITUCE. (*Justinian Institutions*), Praha: Univerzita Karlova – Karolinum 411. Book III, Title 22, 3, analyses, *inter alia*, consensual obligations (de consensu obligatione) – (p. 269–271). In this connection, the book reads as follows: "These contracts further imply that the parties are mutually obliged to perform what each of them is bound to provide to the other based on good faith and justice" (quod alterum alteri ex bono et aequo praestere oportet). Similarly, Title 24 of the same Book, 5, regarding lease and rent (p. 279). We can say, however, that natural law in Europe originated in antiquity, especially in Greek philosophy. *Cf.* ARISTOTELES, POETIKA, RÉTORIKA, POLITIKA (*Poetics, Rhetoric, Politics*), Bratislava: Tatran 67 et seq. (1980). See also JAN PATOČKA, ARISTOTELÉS. PŘEDNÁŠKY Z ANTICKÉ FILOSOFIE (*Aristotle. Lectures from Classical Philosophy*), Praha: Vyšehrad 14 (1994). Similarly JAN PATOČKA, NEJSTARŠÍ ŘECKÁ FILOSOFIE: FILOSOFIE V PŘEDKLASICKÉM ÚDOBÍ PŘED SOFISTIKOU A SÓKRATEM: PŘEDNÁŠKY Z ANTICKÉ FILOSOFIE (*The Oldest Greek Philosophy: Philosophy in the Pre-classical Era before Sophistry and Sokrates: Lectures from Classical Philosophy*), Praha: Vyšehrad 158 et seq. (1996). See also MILAN MRÁZ, SPRAVEDLNOST A DEMOKRACIE V ARISTOTELOVĚ FILOSOFII (*Justice and Democracy in Aristotle's Philosophy*), Praha: Filosofia 75 et seq. (M. Hrubec ed., 2005). In that connection, Mráz says: "*Aristotle further divides civil law into the categories of natural law (**to dikaion politikon fysikon**) and statutory law (to dikaion politikon nomikon). According to Aristotle, natural law applies everywhere and in the same form, whether people like it or not. Statutory law, on the other hand, differs from city to city and country to country because it is the result of an agreement reflecting specific living conditions and ways of life in the given community. Aristotle believes that only voluntary behaviour can be just or, conversely, unjust (i.e., behaviour observing the law or violating the law)*" (at p. 79 and 80). Elsewhere: "*Aristotle highly esteems equity (**epieikeia**), i.e., an element correcting the statutory law in those cases where the automatic application of general statutory principles would result in an incorrect decision which would actually conflict with the legislator's intent*" (p. 81).

integrity. As we touched upon earlier, ancient literature (for instance the presentation of Roman jurisprudence, especially the Justinian Code dating back to the 6th century) defined justice as including principles such as the principle of equality combined with the principle of good morals (*bonae mores*), good faith (*bona fides*), and estoppel (*abusus iuris*); whereas the requirement of equity (*aequitas*) was a principle of a higher order.[10]

13.26. Considering the question of the relationship between trade usages, principles of fair trade and good morals on the one hand and the resolution of disputes by arbitrators following equitable principles (ex aequo et bono) on the other, we have to admit that there are no clear dividing lines between the compared phenomena. The principle of fair trade falls under the wider context of the bearing principles of commercial law and, in a general sense, ultimately complements the system of private law principles. This principle can also be compared to the application of the general requirement of good morals (especially good morals in competition). There are certain interfaces between them and in a certain sense we could say that their contents more or less overlap. Any attempt to define the compared terms with the aim of their canonisation, whether in an academic or in a legislative (normative) or judicial presentation, are destined to fail. This is not to say, however, that theoretical discussions and differing opinions on the interpretation of the principles of private law and their ramifications for the shaping of commercial obligations (especially foreign commercial obligations) and for the solution of legal disputes arising from them in arbitration would be harmful. Arbitral awards as well as court judgments in specific cases have recently enjoyed exceptional importance and authority in practice. Consequently, a body of judge-made legal precedents has been evolving in the Czech Republic, concentrated primarily in the case law of general courts (or the Constitutional Court) and arbitral tribunals.[11]

---

[10]   *Cf.* JAN HURDÍK, PETR LAVICKÝ, SYSTÉM ZÁSAD SÚKROMNÉHO PRÁVA (*The System of Private Law Principles*), Brno: Masarykova univerzita 197 (2010)
We should take due notice of the authors' following opinion: "*From the conceptual perspective, good morals are characterised by their **lack of definition** and their **lack of ability to be defined**. This undeniable fact has become gradually accepted and respected both by legislators and, to a great extent, by case law which, when faced with the problem of characterising good morals, avoids judicial definitions of this concept because they would unduly restrict the room for application.*" (p. 123).

[11]   *Cf.* KAREL KLIMA, INTERPRETACE PRÁVA ÚSTAVNÍMI SOUDY (TEORETICKÉ REFLEXE) (*Interpretation of Law by Constitutional Courts (Theoretical Essays)*), Plzeň: Vydavatelství a nakladatelství Aleš Čeněk 11 et seq. (2006). A specific practical problem relates to arbitration clauses in unequal relationships and disputes (bordering on injustice), where

13.27. As concerns academic legal science, it is generally accepted that its role is to "systematically process the applicable law and reflect the law in theory and it is clear that legal principles are a suitable instrument and a frequent result of this science."[12]

one party is significantly weaker. The consequences and procedural aspects of that situation are analysed *in* Jana Koláčková, Pavel Simon, *At the Edge of Justice: Arbitration in Unequal Relationships. The Constitutional Limits of Arbitration, in* CZECH (& CENTRAL EUROPEAN) YEARBOOK OF ARBITRATION. THE RELATIONSHIP BETWEEN CONSTITUTIONAL VALUES, HUMAN RIGHTS AND ARBITRATION, New York: Juris Net, LLC 183 et seq. (A.J. Bělohlávek & N. Rozehnalová eds., 2011). *Cf.* also Karel Klíma, *Constitutional Environment and the Phenomenon of Arbitration, in* CZECH (& CENTRAL EUROPEAN) YEARBOOK OF ARBITRATION. THE RELATIONSHIP BETWEEN CONSTITUTIONAL VALUES, HUMAN RIGHTS AND ARBITRATION, New York: Juris Net, LLC 147 et seq. (A. J. Bělohlávek & N. Rozehnalová eds., 2011). Similarly, Regina Palková, *Vybrané problémy rozhodcovskej zmluvy (so zvláštnym zreteľom na oblasť sporov zo spotrebiteľských zmlúv) (Selected Problems of the Arbitration Agreement (With a Special Focus on Disputes Arising from Consumer Contracts))*, 12 (2) JUSTIČNÁ REVUE 225 et seq. (2009).
See also Ludvík David, *O soudcovském právu (About Judge-Made Law)*, 151 (5) PRÁVNÍK 469 et seq. (2011).
Cf. also Libor Hanuš, *Jsou obecné právní principy pramenem práva v právním řádu ČR? (Are General Principles of Law One of the Sources of Law in the Czech Legal System?)*, 147 (1) PRÁVNÍK 1 et seq. (2007).
See also Rudolf Kasinec, *Povaha precedensu ako prameňa práva (The Nature of Precedent as a Source of Law)*, 18 (6) BULLETIN SLOVENSKEJ ADVOKÁCIE 18 et seq. (2011).
[12] JAN WINTR, ŘÍŠE PRINCIPŮ. OBECNÉ A ODVĚTVOVÉ PRINCIPY SOUČASNÉHO ČESKÉHO PRÁVA *(The Realm of Principles. General and Sectoral Principles in Contemporary Czech Law)*, Praha: Univerzita Karlova – Karolinum 263 (2006). *Cf.* also Jozef Prusák, *Princípy v právnej teórii a právnej praxi (Principles in Legal Theory and Legal Practice), in* PRÁVNÍ PRINCIPY. RECHTSPRINZIPIEN. PRINCIPLES OF LAW. COLLOQUIUM, Pelhřimov 999, 43 et seq. (J. Boguszak ed., 1999). *Cf.* also MILOŠ VEČEŘA, FRANTIŠEK WEYR, Brno: Nadace Universitas Masarykiana 304 (2001). In his TEORIE PRÁVA *(Theory of Law)*, Praha, Brno: Orbis 83 et seq. (1936), Weyr also analysed the relationship between law (legal order) and justice. He based his conclusions on a relativisation of the concept of justice. He says: "*To claim that something is >>just<< (= burns with justice) probably means nothing else than that it **complies with a particular rule**. The term "justice"* – as a quality ascribed to something – is therefore a relative term; in other words: something (for instance an act) can be >>just<< only in relation to a particular rule (=compared to that rule). It is therefore logically impossible for something to be **absolutely** just or unjust irrespective of anything else (a rule or a principle). Searching for the principle of absolute justice is therefore logically futile, an intellectually erroneous activity (M. Večeřa at p. 214 et seq.). Some aspects of the Brno "school of the pure science of law" (represented in our country by František Weyr, *inter alia*) were analysed by **Vladimír Kubeš** in his study *"Brněnská škola ryzí nauky právní" (The Brno School of the Pure Science of Law), in* BRNĚNSKÁ ŠKOLA PRÁVNÍ TEORIE (NORMATIVNÍ TEORIE) *(The Brno School of Legal Theory (Normative Theory))*, Praha: Univerzita Karlova– Karolinum 440 (O. Weinberger, V. Kubeš, J. Kosek eds., 2003). Kubeš claims that one of the fundamental features of this science is the positivistic tendency and that the *"pure science of law is a theory of positive law; the idea of natural law is considered to be a concept burdened with an internal conflict."* (p. 12)

II. Autonomy of Arbitrators and Application of the Principle of "Ex Aequo et Bono"

13.28. An arbitrator's autonomy must be examined with respect to the arbitration agreement (arbitration clause). National legislation (the Arbitration Act in Slovakia) defines the prerequisites which every arbitrator must meet. Apart from the common attributes of civil or, broadly speaking, private-law communication (majority and legal capacity) the arbitrator must meet certain professional prerequisites which entitle him or her to discharge the office of arbitrator. Moreover, the selected arbitrator must have a clean criminal record. The requirement of the impartial and objective resolution of disputes is incorporated in the very nature of the procedural law and its supporting principles; arbitration laws allow for the challenging of an arbitrator if there are any doubts regarding his or her impartiality.[13]

13.29. Despite the fact that the appointment of arbitrators in a dispute is principally the result of an agreement between the contracting parties, the arbitrator "may never act as a representative of any party, despite having been appointed by said party."[14]

13.30. The status of arbitrators in a dispute must be analysed with respect to the arbitration agreement and the applicable Arbitration Act. International agreements, primarily those which are binding on the Slovak Republic and incorporated in its legal system, must also be taken into account. These include mainly the Convention on the Recognition and Enforcement of Foreign Arbitral Awards (Decree No. 74/1959

---

[13] *Cf.* KVĚTOSLAV RŮŽIČKA, ROZHODČÍ ŘÍZENÍ PŘED ROZHODČÍM SOUDEM PŘI HOSPODÁŘSKÉ KOMOŘE ČESKÉ REPUBLIKY A AGRÁRNÍ KOMOŘE ČESKÉ REPUBLIKY (*Arbitration before the Arbitration Court Attached to the Economic Chamber of the Czech Republic and the Agricultural Chamber of the Czech Republic*), Dobrá Voda: Aleš Čeněk 43 et seq. (2003).

[14] Květoslav Růžička, *K některým otázkám rozhodčího řízení* (*Regarding Selected Arbitration Issues*), 1 ACTA UNIVERSITATIS CAROLINAE. IURIDICA – AKTUÁLNÍ OTÁZKY MEZINÁRODNÍHO PRÁVA SOUKROMÉHO (*Current Topics in Private International Law*), Praha: Univerzita Karlova – Karolinum 62 (1998); *Cf.* Regina Palková, *Rozhodcovské konanie a mediácia z pohľadu súčasnej legislatívy a praxe (Quo vadis mimosúdne riešenie sporov)* [*Arbitration and Mediation from the Perspective of Contemporary Legislation and Practice (Quo Vadis Extrajudicial Dispute Resolution)*], *in* OBCHODNÉ PRÁVO A JEHO ŠIRŠIE KONTEXTY. ZBORNÍK VEDECKÝCH PRÁC (*Commercial Law and Its Broader Contexts. Collection of Scientific Papers*), Košice: Pavol Jozef Šafárik University 131 et seq. (2010). See also Jozef Suchoža, Regina Palková, *Právna povaha rozhodcovského konania v Slovenskej republike (niektoré úvahy jej zdokonalenia)* [*The Legal Nature of Arbitration in Slovakia (Proposals for Improvement)*], 8 (3) PRÁVNÍ FÓRUM 106 et seq. (2010). *Cf.* also ZDENĚK KUČERA, MONIKA PAUKNEROVÁ, KVĚTOSLAV RŮŽIČKA, VLASTISLAV ZUNT, *supra* note 3, at 293 et seq.

Coll.) and the European Convention on International Commercial Arbitration (No. 176/1964 Coll.). Given the general understanding, especially at the international level, that the status of arbitrators is fundamentally *autonomous,* we need to ask: What is the nature of this autonomy? Autonomy in relation to whom? Autonomy means independence (i.e., freedom from control of other entities) or more precisely, an independent position in arbitration, determined only by the limits posed by the applicable law and the relevant procedural framework. The arbitrator hears and resolves the merits of a dispute endowed with freedom, dignity and seriousness, fully observing the generally recognised arbitration principles and procedures, primarily those which have been gradually established, cultivated, shaped and modernised by the long-term practice of international commercial arbitration, mainly by the International Court of Arbitration of the International Chamber of Commerce in Paris.

13.31. Considering the specific status of arbitrators and the historical-evolutionary circumstances which facilitated, in ancient Rome, for instance, the origin of this institution, the arbitrator was perceived mainly as a conciliation judge. The arbitrators' historical seal and the functional dimension of their conciliatory jurisdiction have lost nothing in value, although the status of arbitrators has also gradually encompassed other powers, such as the power to decide the merits of a dispute. This goes hand in hand with the arbitrator's active intervention in the determination of the applicable substantive law.[15]

13.32. Apart from his or her conciliatory power (*amiable compositeur)* over the parties, during the process of finding the applicable law, the arbitrator is authorized to "make" and interpret the law in a certain sense, especially if he or she is supposed to resolve a dispute according to equitable principles (*ex aequo et bono*). We need to point out that the abovementioned prerogatives of the arbitrator are very difficult to compare to the status of judge (in a court of law) although both share a number of common features.

13.33. Let us concentrate briefly on the status of the arbitrator in a situation in which the parties authorize him or her (probably out of their trust in the arbitrator) to resolve the dispute according to equitable principles.

---

[15] According to the European Convention on International Commercial Arbitration (Article VII): "Failing any indication by the parties as to the applicable law, the arbitrators shall apply the proper law under the rule of conflict that the arbitrators deem applicable." We should also take due note of subsection 2, Section VII, which reads as follows: "The arbitrators shall act as amiables compositeurs if the parties so decide and if they may do so under the law applicable to the arbitration." *Cf.* Article 28 of the UNCITRAL Model Law on International Commercial Arbitration.

In such cases, the arbitrator no doubt enjoys very high respect in the eyes of the parties to the dispute (and their counsel). The parties have given the arbitrator the power (the law says "authorized") to resolve their dispute on the basis of principles which are otherwise determinant in the legislative process (the process of making law). If the laws of a country are to be just (which is not always the case as the parties to the dispute probably realize) both parties know that they will achieve a higher degree of law if the arbitrator hears and decides the merits of the case following the principles of equity (as expressed by the principle of "ex aequo et bono") which is more valuable than the statute itself.

13.34. The parties to the dispute make a pragmatic as well axiological choice. They take into account the rational and value-selective aspects. Presuming that the arbitrator then delivers a decision (an award) in a case applying the principle of ex aequo et bono, we can rightfully ask whether the arbitrator in fact has made a new law, albeit only in the *inter partes* relation (and not *erga omnes*). This issue must be further deciphered with respect to the role of precedent in arbitration, provided that we are comparing such a precedent to the significance and importance of a court precedent per *analogiam iuris*.[16]

13.35. We must also emphasize that the arbitrator's power to make law in situations in which he or she is supposed to decide ex aequo et bono cannot be interpreted as being voluntaristic. Ultimately, such decision-making (especially decisions on the merits) must also be subject to well-known and identifiable legal principles, or known and published analogous decisions (judicial or arbitral precedents), doctrinal interpretations, or must be justified by the arbitrator's brand new ideas aimed at pioneering brave final solutions. Such solutions help to develop the system of arbitral precedents, albeit often locked in the arbitrators' safe deposit boxes (due to the confidentiality of arbitration).

13.36. Recently, some private, permanent arbitral institutions (for instance the Arbitration Court at IAL SE in Bratislava) have attempted to draft

---

[16] HERBERT LIONEL ADOLPHUS HART, *supra* note 5, says as follows: "*This is the importance characteristically attached by courts when deciding unregulated cases to proceeding by analogy so as to ensure that the new law they make, though it is a new law, is in accordance with principles and underpinning reasons recognised as already having a footing in the existing law. It is true that when particular statutes or precedents prove indeterminate, or when the explicit law is silent, judges do not just push away their law books and start to legislate without further guidance from the law. Very often, when deciding such cases, they cite from some general principle or aim or purpose which some considerable relevant area of the existing law can be understood as exemplifying or advancing and which points towards a determinate answer for the instant hard case. This indeed is the very nucleus of the >>constructive interpretation<<.*" (p. 266).

codes of equitable principles.[17] The problem is, however, whether the internal regulations of permanent arbitral institutions can *ex ante* define and specify equitable principles which would have to be observed by the arbitrators in potential disputes. Moreover, the interpretations of such principles are too general, vague and unconvincing compared to their doctrinal definition in the form of principles of private law described in professional legal literature.

III. The Concept of Resolving Disputes as an Amiable Compositeur

13.37. Having analysed the concept of ex aequo et bono in the paragraphs above, we shall hereinafter concentrate on another specific type of arbitration, in comparison with resolving disputes ex aequo et bono. These two concepts are often perceived as synonymous but they exhibit certain differences. *Amiable compositeur* can be characterised as a situation in which the arbitrators are supposed to decide according to the law and legal principles but are allowed to change the effects of the application of the individual rules. On the other hand, the resolution of disputes on the basis of the ex aequo et bono principle represents a decision-making process outside the sphere of law, according to moral principles.[18] As we have already mentioned, these two concepts of resolving disputes in arbitration, their definition and normative delimitation, differ from author to author and from one jurisdiction to another. Some authors insist on distinguishing between ex aequo et bono and amiable compositeur. Others consider these concepts synonymous.[19] Individual opinions are no doubt influenced by the respective author's relation to his or her legal system or legal culture.[20]

---

[17] For instance "The Code of the Principles of Justice" adopted by the Arbitration Court at IAL SE defines these principles (albeit in a very general manner) as a "collection of intellectual ideals incorporated in the internal system of values, morals and philosophy of the arbitrator and connected to the decision-making mechanisms which are a component of the everyday procedure of the arbitrator as a human being." And elsewhere: "the principles of justice are not defined by a casuistic enumeration; they are an abstract from the fundamental principles of the legal order and the internal virtues of the arbitrator."

[18] NADĚŽDA ROZEHNALOVÁ, ROZHODČÍ ŘÍZENÍ V MEZINÁRODNÍM A VNITROSTÁTNÍM OBCHODNÍM STYKU (*Arbitration in International and Domestic Commercial Relations*), Praha: ASPI 238 (2008).

[19] For instance: SIMON GREENBERG, CHRISTOPHER KEE, J. ROMESH WEERAMANTRY, INTERNATIONAL COMMERCIAL ARBITRATION: AN ASIA-PACIFIC PERSPECTIVE, New York: Cambridge University Press 138 et seq. (2011); Similarly EMMANUEL GAILLARD, JOHN SAVAGE, FOUCHARD GAILLARD GOLDMAN ON INTERNATIONAL ARBITRATION, The Hague: Kluwer Law International (1999), who maintain: *"In all statutes and international conventions which allow the parties to empower the arbitrator to rule as an amiable*

13.38. The Czech Republic permits resolving disputes following the ex aequo et bono principle, as analysed above. Czech laws are unfamiliar with the concept of amiable compositeur. Consequently, one cannot expect that this regime of resolving disputes in arbitration can be applied pursuant to the laws of the Slovak Republic. We should point out that Czech laws were partly inspired by Section 28(3) of the UNCITRAL Model

---

compositeur *(which is sometimes referred to as ruling either ex aequo et bono or in equity),* *the amiable compositeur is still considered to be an arbitrator who decides the dispute.* *Thus, the European Convention of April 21, 1961 provides that "arbitrators shall act as* *amiable compositeurs if...".* We believe this clearly indicates that the authors emphasize the status of amiable compositeur in a different way. They continue: *"In acting as amiable compositeur, the arbitrators must give all parties a fair hearing, and their decision will be a genuine arbitral award. Any obligation to state the grounds for the award therefore applies as it does to an award made by an arbitrator not acting as amiable compositeur."* This renowned publication on international arbitration also indicates a preference for the concept of amiable compositeur while the concept of ex aequo et bono is mentioned only marginally or as a supplement: *"Nevertheless, considerable controversy remains as to the exact meaning of amiable composition and, in particular, as to the need to distinguish it from the concept of equity and from the arbitrators' power to rule ex aequo et bono."* Similarly, John B. Tieder, Jr. and Carter B. Reid, *International Contract Law as the Substantive Law Applicable to International Contracts, in* INTERNATIONAL DISPUTE RESOLUTION. CENTER FOR INTERNATIONAL LEGAL STUDIES, Alphen aan den Rijn: Kluwer Law International 122 (D. Campbell ed., 2010): *"General principles of international contract law are not the same as the concepts of amiable compositeur and ex aequo et bono. The latter two concepts, which are really the same thing, allow an arbitral tribunal to apply principles of fairness and equity outside of any legal principles."* For an opposite opinion see A.F.M. Maniruzzaman, *The Arbitrator's Prudence in Lex Mercatoria: Amiable Composition and Ex Aequo Et Bono in Decision Making, in* 18 (12) MEALEY'S INTERNATIONAL ARBITRATION REPORT (2003): *"The legal scholarship on the subject has failed to adequately explain the difference between the two concepts* (ex aequo et bono and amiable compositeur – supplemented by the authors) *though they are perceived to be different in the juristic thinking."* J. F. Poudret and S. Besson completely refuse to consider the two concepts equal – JEAN-FRANÇOIS POUDRET, SÉBASTIEN BESSON, COMPARATIVE LAW OF INTERNATIONAL ARBITRATION, London: Sweet and Maxwell 619 (2007): *"...it can be inferred therefrom that, at least according to these texts* (the authors analyse the text of the UNCITRAL Model Law and Rules of Arbitration) *arbitration ex aequo et bono is not the same thing as amiable composition, but rather, corresponds to arbitration in equity."*

[20] Some legal systems lack provisions regulating the possibility of resolving disputes ex aequo et bono or as amiable compositeur altogether; others only mention amiable compositeur (for instance French law) as opposed to other systems which only accept ex aequo et bono or a derivative thereof in the form of equitable principles (for instance Slovak law, Czech law and others). As Rozehnalová says, there are legal systems which recognise both concepts; these include states which diligently adopted the Model Law in International Commercial Arbitration. Maniruzzaman refers to Swiss law as an example of a law that strictly distinguishes between both concepts: *"... under Swiss law the power to act ex aequo et bono entitles the arbitrator to disregard the relevant legal rules, including mandatory rules, subject only to international public policy, while an amiable compositeur must comply with mandatory rules of law. "*

Law which stipulates that the arbitral tribunal shall decide ex aequo et bono or as amiable compositeur only if the parties have expressly authorized it to do so; in all cases, the arbitral tribunal shall decide in accordance with the terms of the contract and take into account the usages of the trade. The explanatory note to this provision points out that this type of arbitration is not accepted by all legal systems and that the Model Law does not intend to impose this option on any jurisdiction. It only insists that the arbitral tribunal be empowered by the contracting parties in order to exercise such powers;[21] the wording of the Model Law seems to suggest that the Law does not differentiate between the two concepts. The resolution of disputes ex aequo et bono (the same holds true for deciding cases as amiable compositeur) must not be the arbitrator's arbitrary act; in other words, the arbitrator cannot arbitrarily decide that he or she will adopt such course of action. At the same time, arbitrators may not resolve disputes arbitrarily and must base their decisions on objective, rational and clearly articulated considerations.[22]

13.39. The definition of resolving disputes as amiable compositeur and ex aequo et bono varies depending on the individual legal systems. However, the generally accepted position is that arbitrators authorized to decide ex aequo et bono or as amiable compositeurs are not bound by the obligation to apply national law and may rely on other sources of inspiration, including supranational or international rules, when making their decisions.[23] The traditional definition of amiable

---

[21] But legal literature also offers opposite opinions. For instance, MARÍA JOSÉ FALCÓN Y TELLA, EQUITY AND LAW, Leiden: Martinus Nijhoff Publishers 264 (2008): *"....despite the above, ex aequo et bono may even be applied without the consent of the disputants when a special 'ad hoc' Court is set up. Its special character resides in its being set up exclusively for the case in question, and after it has been made manifest that no law is applicable to the issue being dealt with. This implies the establishing of enforced arbitration amongst the parties in disagreement, who must abide by the arbitration."* The authors nonetheless believe that such situations will be very rare in practice. This is confirmed by Friedrich: *"The authorization to arbitrate ex aequo et bono (or amiable compositeur) needs to be explicit. Explicit has the meaning of doubtless and crystal clear. ..... Explicit consent may be given in the course of the arbitral proceedings, but it must be given prior to the decision of the tribunal. Parties may wish to provide a clarification in the arbitration agreement. But it may also be given in the course of the proceedings by conferring a more specific authorization on the arbitral tribunal."* B. Friedrich *in* ARBITRATION IN GERMANY. THE MODEL LAW IN PRACTICE, Alphen aan den Rijn: Kluwer Law International 360 (K.-H. Böckstiegel, S. Kröll, P. Nacimiento eds., 2007).

[22] CHRISTOPH H. SCHREUER, THE ICSID CONVENTION: A COMMENTARY, Cambridge: Cambridge University Press 641 (2001).

[23] MICHAEL JOACHIM BONELL, AN INTERNATIONAL RESTATEMENT OF CONTRACT LAW: THE UNIDROIT PRINCIPLES OF INTERNATIONAL COMMERCIAL CONTRACTS, New York: Transnational Publishers, Inc. 194 (3rd ed. 2004).

compositeur is an arbitrator deciding on the basis of equitable principles, or equity.[24] He or she may deviate from the solutions offered by traditionally applied legal rules and choose less frequent sources of decisions, especially sources which are often classified by expert literature as lex mercatoria. An amiable compositeur is "entitled to resolve the dispute on the basis of generally accepted principles without being bound by the formal aspects of any particular legal system.[25]

13.40. The countries of Latin America have mostly taken over the concept of amiable compositeur, often merged with the concept of ex aequo et bono. Most jurisdictions in that geographical region distinguish between arbitration "de iure" and arbitration conducted by arbitrators acting as amiable compositeurs. In the former case, the arbitrator (*arbitro de derecho*) will not only apply the law applicable to the merits of the dispute; he or she will also apply the applicable procedural laws, unless the parties agreed otherwise.[26] The *arbitro de derecho* must also be a lawyer, or practice law. Such requirements do not apply to an amiable compositeur (*arbitro arbitrador al amigable componedor*).[27]

13.41. The concept of amiable compositeur has its roots in French law, namely the *amicabilis compositor* of Canon Law. The role of the amicabilis compositor was to conciliate rather than render decisions.[28] As we have already mentioned, the resolution of disputes as amiable compositeur is possible if both of the two above-mentioned conditions are met; i.e., the agreement of the contracting parties authorizing the arbitrator to perform this type of arbitration and the possibility to employ this method of arbitration sanctioned by legislation. If the arbitrator fails to adhere to these requirements, his or her decision becomes null and void under the applicable law. In the event of the failure to observe the former requirement, the arbitration contravenes the agreement of the contracting parties whereby they explicitly

---

[24] ICC Case Number 4567, Awards of June 1984 and May 1985, *in* IX Yearbook of Commercial Arbitration, Hague: Kluwer Law International 143-147 (A.v.d. Berg ed., 1986), case quoted according to International Dispute Resolution. Center for International Legal Studies, Hague: Kluwer Law International 122 (D. Campbell ed., 2010).

[25] ICC Case Number 2367, Partial Award of 14 June 1979, *in* VII Yearbook of Commercial Arbitration, Hague: Kluwer Law International 96-105 (P. Sanders ed., 1982), quoted according to D. Campbell, *supra* note 24.

[26] Pieter Sanders, Quo vadis Arbitration? Sixty Years of Arbitration Practice: A Comparative Analysis, London: Kluwer Law International (1999).

[27] *Ibid.*

[28] Jana Herboczková, *Amiable composition in international commercial arbitration*, available at: http://www.law.muni.cz/sborniky/cofola2008/files/pdf/mps/herboczkova_jana.pdf (accessed on August 11, 2011).

submitted their disputes to arbitration which the applicable law permits to be resolved ex aequo et bono (or as amiable compositeur, according to other legal regulations); if the latter requirement is breached, the nullity would be caused by the breach of the applicable law. But as we already mentioned before, such legal systems are not very common. In our current era in which laws on international arbitration are globalized according to the Model Law, the resolution of disputes ex aequo et bono, or as amicable compositeur, is a common component of arbitration laws. But the opposite scenario, i.e., no provision accepting the resolution of disputes ex aequo et bono or as amiable compositeur in a particular legal system can give rise to many difficult situations in practice. According to Rubino-Sammartano, a significant problem can arise in connection with the recognition of foreign arbitral awards which were rendered using the analysed doctrines.[29]

13.42. An interesting solution to the terminological problem of defining ex aequo et bono and amiable compositeur is incorporated in the German legislation which refrained from using these concepts in the normative wording of the law. A similar Solomonic solution was employed by Czech domestic law which, instead of the dual solution incorporated in the Model Law, introduces a certain simplification by using the words "according to equitable principles." We are rather inclined, though, to equate this concept with that of ex aequo et bono. From our perspective, the German wording of the applicable statute somewhat simplifies the problem: *"Das Schiedsgericht hat nur dann nach Billigkeit zu entscheiden, wenn die Parteien es ausdrücklich dazu ermächtigt haben. Die Ermächtigung kann bis zur Entscheidung des Schiedsgerichts erteilt werden.[30]"* But Friedrich maintains the opposite opinion and points out that translations in English automatically domesticate the internationally used concepts of ex aequo et bono and amiable compositeur. In other words, these concepts are not replaced by any general uniform concept of "Billigkeit."[31] Friedrich is convinced that the interconnection between these two concepts is supported by

---

[29] MAURO RUBINO-SAMMARTANO, INTERNATIONAL ARBITRATION. LAW AND PRACTICE, The Hague: Kluwer Law International 459 (2nd ed. 2001).

[30] Trans: *"The arbitral court could decide the dispute ex aequo et bono only if expressly authorized to do so by the parties to the dispute. Such authorisation could be given until the decision of the arbitral court on the merits is issued."*

[31] B. Friedrich, *in* KARL-HEINZ BÖCKSTIEGEL, STEFAN KRÖLL, PATRICIA NACIMIENTO, *supra* note 21, at 359: *"§ 1051 (3) ZPO corresponds to Article 28 (3) ML; yet § 1051 (3) § 1051 (3) ZPO does not mention the terms ex aequo et bono and amiable composition. It refers to decisions in equity. The uncertainty of the meaning of amiable compositeur and ex aequo et bono remains."*

French case law as well. As he says: "...French case law offers an excellent illustration of ex aequo et bono principles applied in practice. A tribunal deciding a case as amiable compositeur must explain why the solution proposed in his eyes is just...".[32]

13.43. The discussion regarding the clarification of the dividing lines between the terms ex aequo et bono and amiable compositeur as well as the limits of their application is closed by Maniruzzaman: *"In the broad senses of the two concepts, however, the tendency of many rather seems to assume that while acting as amiable compositeur (friendly arbitrator) an arbitrator may decide ex aequo et bono (according to equity, justice and fairness),"*[33] following ICC case no. 1780: *"While amiable compositeur has a broader connotation than ex aequo et bono, an arbitrator, acting as amiable compositeur, may not or need not resort to equity or justice and may fall back on other factors to decide a dispute."*[34] The issues analysed in this article remain important and significant, as the activities of the International Chamber of Commerce in Paris prove – the ICC set up a special commission for amiable composition and ex aequo et bono, presided over by Edouard Bertrand and Ronald King. The crucial issues dealt with by the commission were: (1) identification of the fundamental features of amiable compositeur and ex aequo et bono and (2) clarification of the status of arbitrators acting as amiable compositeurs or of making decisions according to ex aequo et bono.[35]

| | |

Summaries

FRA [*Autonomie des arbitres – arbitrage sur la base du principe ex aequo et bono*]
La procédure d'arbitrage offre des possibilités irréalisables dans une procédure classique. On associe traditionnellement l'arbitrage à une grande souplesse, les parties contractantes pouvant intervenir dans bien des aspects des décisions des arbitres.
Les décisions d'arbitrage ex aequo et bono - ou se basant sur des principes équivalents - restent cependant un domaine mal connu. L'étude présente examine ces principes reposant sur la notion de justice

---

32   *Ibid., supra* note 21, at 359.
33   A.F.M. Maniruzzaman, *supra* note 19.
34   *Ibid.*
35   http://www.iccwbo.org/policy/arbitration/id6566/index.html (accessed on July 27, 2011).

et non sur le droit, c'est pourquoi on passe en revue les cas, où l'arbitre est autorisé à prendre une décision fondé sur des principes et non sur des règles écrites de justice. La possibilité de résoudre un conflit de cette manière est analysée du point de vue des législations tchèques et slovaques, d'une part, et du point de vue du droit international, d'autre part. Le problème d'un arbitrage fondé sur un principe de justice est qu'il n'a pas de critères de délimitation bien clairs, car il se heurte à une multiplicité d'interprétation de ce qu'est la justice.

Les auteurs de l'article explorent quelques thèses intéressantes et tentent de contribuer à éclaircir un peu ces questions.

CZE [***Autonomie rozhodců a rozhodování na základě zásady ex aequo et bono***]

Rozhodčí řízení s sebou přináší možnosti, které jsou v klasickém soudním řízení nerealizovatelné. Již tradičně se s rozhodčím řízením pojí širší variabilita rozhodovacího procesu, přičemž smluvní strany mají možnost ovlivnit více aspektů rozhodování rozhodců.

Velkou neznámou i nadále zůstává rozhodování na základě ex aequo et bono a jiných, obdobných zásad. Předmětná studie pojednává právě o těchto zásadách založených na pojetí spravedlnosti, tedy případech, kdy je rozhodce oprávněn rozhodovat na základě nepsaných pravidel spravedlnosti. Možnost rozhodnout spor tímto způsobem je ve studii analyzována jednak z pohledu právních řádů Slovenské a České republiky, jednak z hlediska vybraných mezinárodních úprav. Problém rozhodování na základě zásad spravedlnosti nemá vymezena jasná kritéria, neboť naráží na další různě vykládaný právní jev – spravedlnost.

Autoři se snažili zdokumentovat některé zajímavé názory publikované v této oblasti a v neposlední řadě přispět i vlastními silami k částečnému objasnění tohoto institutu.

| | |

POL [***Autonomia arbitrów – rozstrzyganie na mocy reguły ex aequo et bono***]

Przedmiotowe opracowanie omawia instytucję rozstrzygania na mocy reguły ex aequo et bono, która jest dopuszczalna w wielu regulacjach prawnych, bowiem wiele z nich opiera się na Ustawie modelowej UNCITRAL w sprawie międzynarodowego arbitrażu handlowego, która w bardzo wyczerpujący sposób reguluje wspomnianą możliwość.

DEU [*Schiedsrichterliche Autonomie – Entscheidungsfindung auf der Basis des Prinzips ex aequo et bono*]

Die vorliegende Studie untersucht das Rechtsinstitut von Entscheidungen auf der Grundlage des ex aequo et bono-Prinzips, welches in einer Reihe von Jurisdiktionen zugelassen ist, vor dem Hintergrund, dass viele Rechtsordnungen ihr Schiedsrecht vom UNCITRAL-Modellgesetz über die Internationale Handelsschiedsgerichtsbarkeit (Model Law on International Commercial Arbitration) herleiten, welches diese Möglichkeit in extensiver Weise regelt.

RUS [*Автономия арбитров – принятие решения на основе принципа ex aequo et bono*]

В данной работе анализируется институт принятия решения на основе принципа ex aequo et bono, который допускается во многих законодательствах. Последнее возможно благодаря тому, что эти законодательства исходят из Типового закона UNCITRAL о международном торговом арбитраже, в котором регулируется такая возможность, и даже очень экстенсивно.

ESP [*Autonomía de los árbitros – decisiones basadas en el principio ex aequo et bono*]

El estudio analiza la cuestión de la decisión sobre la base del principio ex aequo et bono, que es aceptado en numerosas legislaciones, una prueba de que muchas legislaciones parten de la Ley Modelo UNCITRAL sobre arbitraje comercial internacional, por la que se regula ampliamente esta posibilidad.

Case Law

Section A

Current Case Law of the National Courts regarding Arbitration

1. Albania

Abbreviations used in annotations:
    ALB   Albania

Alexander J. Bělohlávek

I. Special and General Jurisdiction (Decision of Albanian Supreme Court, Case No. 1637 of 9 March 2004)

Key words:
bank guarantee | counterfeit | general jurisdiction | scope of the arbitration clause | special jurisdiction | special type of dispute | motion for the invalidity of a bank guarantee

Laws Taken into Account in This Ruling:
- European Convention on International Commercial Arbitration (Geneva, 1961);[1]
- Code of Civil Procedure [ALB] – Act No. 8116 of 29 March 1996: Article 32, Article 36, Article 59, Article 270, Article 439, Article 485(a);
- Civil Code [ALB] – Act No. 6340 of 27 June 1981;[2]
- Convention on the Recognition and Enforcement of Foreign Arbitral Awards (New York, 1958).[3]

---

[1]   Ratified in Albania by Act No. 8687 of 9 November 2008.
[2]   The Act was, in the meantime, repealed by a new law.
[3]   Ratified in Albania by Act No. 8116 of 29 March 1996.

Rationes Decidendi:[4]

14.01. The jurisdiction of arbitral tribunals is special jurisdiction, whereas jurisdiction of courts is general jurisdiction.

14.02. Special types of disputes, such as proceedings concerning the invalidity (nullity) of a bank guarantee presented at the conclusion of a contract negotiated within the framework of public procurement, are not covered by an arbitration clause incorporated in the contract. Conversely, such disputes are subject to the [general] jurisdiction of courts.

[Description of Facts and Legal Issues]

14.03. The Ministry of Transport [ALB] and the General Roads Directorate in Tirana [ALB] (joint contracting parties and joint plaintiffs in the proceedings), following a public procurement procedure, entered into an agreement on the supply of works during the reconstruction of the Rrogozhine – Elbasan road. The other contracting party (the supplier/contractor) was BE-HA-SA Ltd. (defendant in the proceedings). The agreement concluded as a result of the public procurement procedure contained an arbitration clause referring to the International Court of Arbitration of the ICC. In the course of the public procurement procedure, the defendant submitted, in compliance with the specifications, a bank guaranteed securing the performance of obligations under the agreement. Only after the conclusion of the agreement, the plaintiffs (both of the above mentioned public entities) lodged a motion with the Tirana District Court [ALB] demanding the declaration of the invalidity of the bank guarantee.[5] The defendant challenged the jurisdiction of the court, invoking the arbitration clause.

[Decision of Court]

14.04. The Tirana District Court [ALB] rejected the jurisdictional challenge and held that the arbitration clause did not cover the bank guarantee, which was an instrument separate from the agreement, let alone interfere with the general jurisdiction of the court in civil matters. This applies all the more because the case concerns a motion for the invalidity of a bank guarantee.[6]

---

[4] The decision was referred to us and the basis of this annotation was drafted by Mr. Shpati Hoxha, attorney-at-law, Tirana, Albania. Decision No. 12 concerning Dossier No. 3052/897 of 13 April 2005.

[5] The available sources explicitly mention *counterfeit*.

[6] The available sources are not sufficiently specific with respect to the merits of the dispute. Considering the information regarding the *counterfeit* bank guarantee, the case probably concerned the nullity of the respective security instrument.

[Decision of Supreme Court]

14.05. The Supreme Court [ALB] concluded that the dispute did not fall within the scope of the arbitration clause. The case concerned proceedings for the declaration of the invalidity (nullity) of a document that was allegedly counterfeit; it was therefore a special type of dispute. Consequently, it was not a dispute covered by the arbitration clause and was subject to the jurisdiction of Albanian courts.[7] The Supreme Court therefore upheld the decision of the lower court.

| | |

II. Decision of Albanian Supreme Court (Case No. 1588/69 of 10 February 2005), and Decision of Same Court (Case No. 11243-00567-00-2006 of 26 September 2007)

Key words:
procedural error | power of attorney | procedural rights | default interest | recognition and enforcement of foreign arbitral awards

Laws Taken into Account in This Ruling:
➤ Code of Civil Procedure [ALB] – Act No. 6340 of 26 June 1981;[8]
➤ Code of Civil Procedure [ALB] – Act No. 8116 of 29 March 1996: Article 312, Article 314, Article 393 et seq., Article 472.

Rationes Decidendi:[9]

14.06. The commencement of the proceedings for the recognition and enforcement of a foreign arbitral award must be notified to the other party (defendant).

14.07. The proceedings for the recognition and enforcement of a foreign arbitral award must guarantee equal procedural rights to all parties.

14.08. The power of attorney for the party's representative (legal counsel) in the proceedings for the recognition and enforcement of a foreign arbitral award must contain an explicit authorization with respect to

---

[7] With reference to Article 36 of the Code of Civil Procedure [ALB].

[8] This Act was, in the meantime, repealed and replaced by Act No. 8116 of 29 March 1996.

[9] The decision was referred to us and the basis of this annotation was drafted by Mr. Shpati Hoxha, attorney-at-law, Tirana, Albania. Decision (•) No. 222 concerning Dossier No. 1588/69 of 10 February 2005 and Decision (•) No. 00-2007-1233 concerning Dossier No. 11243-00567-00-2006 of 10 February 2005.

these proceedings (authorization to file a motion on behalf of and represent the client in these proceedings).

[Description of Facts and Legal Issues]

14.09. In 1998, the plaintiff filed a motion with the Tirana Court of Appeal [ALB] demanding the recognition and enforcement of an arbitral award issued by a foreign permanent arbitral institution against the Council of Ministers of Albania, for the payment of 48 billion Italian Lira. It was a claim for damages payable under a contract negotiated between the parties.

[I. Decision of Court]

14.10. The court granted the claim. Subsequently in 2000, upon a petition of the plaintiff, the court extended the decision by allowing the recognition and enforcement of the order awarding the plaintiff default interest accrued until the actual payment of the claim under the arbitral award. In 2005, the defendant, represented by a State attorney, filed a cassation appeal to the Supreme Court [ALB]. The cassation appeal was based on the defendant's complaint that he had not been duly informed of the proceedings for recognition and enforcement.

[I. Decision of Supreme Court]

14.11. The Supreme Court [ALB] held that the decision of the Tirana Court of Appeal [ALB] was correct on the merits, as concerns the recognition and enforcement of the arbitral award, but failed to honour the defendant's right to be heard and present his defence in the proceedings. The Supreme Court therefore reversed the decision of the lower court and remanded the case for a new trial.

[II. Decision of Court]

14.12. The Tirana Court of Appeal [ALB] retried the case and dismissed the motion for enforcement and recognition. The reasons for the decision were errors discovered in the procedural materials (in the dossier). The decision especially pointed out that the motion (petition) suffered from a defect in that the counsel's power of attorney did not explicitly stipulate his authorization to represent his client in the proceedings for the recognition and enforcement of the arbitral award. The decision was challenged by the plaintiff, arguing that the court had failed to honour his rights and had not given him the opportunity to remedy the procedural defects of his motion.

[II. Decision of Supreme Court]

14.13. The Supreme Court [ALB] held that the latter proceedings before the Tirana Court of Appeal [ALB] had again suffered from a procedural error, because the plaintiff's rights had not been duly honoured. The Supreme Court [ALB] again remanded the case for a new trial.

[Author's Note]

14.14. The author did not manage to obtain any information regarding further developments in the case. It is not out of the question, though, that the proceedings are still pending.

|||

III. Arbitration Clause Excludes Jurisdiction of Court (Decision of Albanian Supreme Court, Case No. 3052/897 of 13 April 2005)

Key words:
dismissal of lawsuit | arbitration clause | exclusion of jurisdiction of court

Laws Taken into Account in This Ruling:
➢ Code of Civil Procedure [ALB] – Act No. 6340 of 26 June 1981;[10]
➢ Code of Civil Procedure [ALB] – Act No. 8116 of 29 March 1996: Article 400 et seq., Article 485(a).

Ratio Decidendi:[11]

14.15. An arbitration clause excludes the jurisdiction of courts.

[Description of Facts and Legal Issues]

14.16. The plaintiff sued the defendant (Ministry of Transport [ALB]) for a certain amount of money. The plaintiff's claim was based on a contract for the implementation of works and supply of services; the plaintiff argued that he had performed his obligations, but the defendant failed to pay. The lawsuit was lodged with the Tirana District Court [ALB].

---

[10]   This Act was, in the meantime, repealed and replaced by Act No. 8116 of 29 March 1996.

[11]   The decision was referred to us and the basis of this annotation was drafted by Mr. Shpati Hoxha, attorney-at-law, Tirana, Albania. Decision No. 12 concerning Dossier No. 3052/897 of 13 April 2005.

[Decision of Court]

14.17. The court dismissed the lawsuit on the grounds of an arbitration clause in the contract. The plaintiff challenged the decision by a cassation appeal to the Supreme Court [ALB].

[Decision of Supreme Court]

14.18. The Supreme Court [ALB] upheld the lower court's dismissal of the lawsuit.

|||

IV. Essential Terms of Arbitration Agreement; Invalidity of Arbitration Clause (Decision of Albanian Supreme Court, Case No. 2303/296 of 31 May 2005)

Key words:

seat of arbitration | invalidity of contract | separability | essential requirements of an arbitration agreement | jurisdiction of court | arbitration clause | scope of an arbitration clause | main contract | service agreement | identification of the arbitral tribunal | motion for the invalidity of contract | lack of court jurisdiction

Laws Taken into Account in This Ruling:

➤ Code of Civil Procedure [ALB] – Act No. 8116 of 29 March 1996: Article 36, Article 404 et seq., Article 472.

Rationes Decidendi:[12]

14.19. A dispute over the invalidity of the [main] contract can be heard and resolved on condition that the issue is explicitly encompassed by the scope of the arbitration clause.

14.20. The arbitration clause must precisely identify the arbitral tribunal and the seat of arbitration, or otherwise the arbitration clause is invalid.

[Description of Facts and Legal Issues]

14.21. The parties had concluded a service agreement, which was subsequently unilaterally terminated by a notice of the defendant. The plaintiff addressed the Tirana District Court with a motion demanding

---

[12] The decision was referred to us and the basis of this annotation was drafted by Mr. Shpati Hoxha, attorney-at-law, Tirana, Albania. Decision No. 932 concerning Dossier No. 2303/296 of 31 May 2005.

that the contract be declared invalid and the plaintiff be awarded damages together with default interest.

[Decisions of Trial Court and Appellate Court]

14.22. The trial court (Tirana District Court) partially granted the motion. The defendant subsequently appealed the decision to the Tirana Court of Appeal. The defendant challenged the jurisdiction of the trial court on the grounds of an arbitration clause in the service agreement. The Court of Appeal granted the appeal and declared a lack of jurisdiction of Albanian courts. The plaintiff lodged a cassation appeal with the Supreme Court [ALB].

[Decision of Court of the Supreme Court]

14.23. The Supreme Court [ALB] reversed the decision of the appellate court. The Supreme Court held that the arbitration clause was invalid, because it did not contain essential requirements set forth in Article 404 of the Code of Civil Procedure [ALB]; in particular, the clause did not identify the arbitral tribunal that was supposed to resolve the case. The arbitration clause must also determine the seat of arbitration. The Supreme Court [ALB] also held that one of the plaintiff's motions had been aimed at the determination of the invalidity of the service agreement. But the arbitration clause itself did not stipulate that it covered disputes regarding the validity of the [main] contract. Consequently, the Supreme Court [ALB] reversed the decision of the lower court and remanded the case for a new trial.

[Author's Note]

14.24. The decision indicates that arbitration clauses relating to Albania [ALB] must be specific and itemized to the utmost extent. At the same time, it might appear that the application of the principle of separability of the arbitration agreement from the main contract is somewhat undermined. This is not the case, however. But in order for the separability principle to apply fully, the scope of the arbitration clause must be specified to the maximum extent, including the connection to the disputes arising in the case of the invalidity of the contract. It is also necessary to precisely identify the arbitral tribunal; according to the decision, this is an essential term of the arbitration agreement.

| | |

V. Laws and Regulations Applicable to Enforcement of Foreign Arbitral Award; Time Limit for Commencement of Enforcement (Decision of Albanian Supreme Court, Case No. 11242-00075-00-2005 of 21 December 2006)

Key words:
foreign arbitral award | limitation of recognition and enforcement | law applicable to recognition | law applicable to enforcement | limitation of actions | recognition of a foreign arbitral award | enforcement of a foreign arbitral award

Laws Taken into Account in This Ruling:

➢ Code of Civil Procedure [ALB] – Act No. 6341 of 26 June 1981;[13]
➢ Code of Civil Procedure [ALB] – Act No. 8116 of 29 March 1996: Article 395;
➢ Civil Code [ALB] – Act No. 6340 of 27 June 1981;[14]
➢ Convention on the Recognition and Enforcement of Foreign Arbitral Awards (New York, 1958).[15]

Rationes Decidendi:[16]

14.25. The recognition of a foreign arbitral award has a functional connection with the enforcement thereof. The decision regarding enforcement therefore inherently implies the recognition of the arbitral award.

14.26. The limitation (refusal) of the recognition and enforcement of a foreign arbitral award is governed by the laws of the state in which recognition/enforcement is sought, as applicable at the time the arbitral award was issued.

14.27. The recognition/enforcement of a foreign arbitral award cannot be granted if the time limit for the commencement of the proceedings for recognition/enforcement has expired under applicable law.

[Description of Facts and Legal Issues]

14.28. The claimant, a foreigner, sold approximately 14 tons of wheat to an Albanian enterprise (respondent). The Arbitral Tribunal of the Association for Trading in Wheat and Fodder issued Arbitral Award

---

13 The Act was, in the meantime, repealed by a new law.
14 The Act was, in the meantime, repealed by a new law.
15 Ratified in Albania by Act No. 8116 of 29 March 1996.
16 The decision was referred to us and the basis of this annotation was drafted by Mr. Shpati Hoxha, attorney-at-law, Tirana, Albania. Decision No. 00-2006-892 concerning Dossier No. 1242-00075-00-2005 of 21 December 2006.

No. 11-336 on 14 October 1993. The Award ordered the respondent to pay USD 1,638,360.33. In 2005, the claimant (plaintiff) filed a motion for the recognition of the Arbitral Award in [ALB] pursuant to Article 395 et seq. of the Code of Civil Procedure [ALB] – Act No. 8116 of 29 March 1996. The Tirana Court of Appeal refused the recognition of the Arbitral Award, because the former Civil Code [ALB] – Act No. 6340 of 26 June 1981 – and the former Code of Civil Procedure [ALB] – Act No. 6341 of 27 June 1981 – demanded that the enforcement proceedings be initiated within one year of the issuance of the decision (or within one year after the decision became enforceable).

[Decision of Court of Appeal]

14.29.   The Supreme Court [ALB] ruled that the decision on enforcement has a functional connection with recognition. The presently applicable Code of Civil Procedure (Act No. 8116 of 29 March 1996) stipulates that enforcement proceedings are initiated by a decision on the opening of the enforcement proceedings issued by the competent court. According to the previous laws, however, which were applicable on the day the arbitral award was rendered, no special court decision on the opening of the enforcement proceedings was required, and the enforcement of the arbitral award could have commenced immediately after the arbitral award was rendered. However, the previous law applicable on the day the award was issued stipulated a one-year time limit (limitation period) for the commencement of enforcement. The claimant (plaintiff) failed to commence the enforcement of the arbitral award within one year of the issuance thereof. The expiration of the limitation period constitutes grounds for the refusal to enforce the foreign arbitral award.

| | |

VI. Scope of Arbitration Clause; Exclusion of Jurisdiction of Court; Related Contracts (Decision of Albanian Supreme Court, Case No. 11217-02125-00-2007 of 13 December 2007)

Key words:
jurisdiction of court | arbitration clause | contract for work | settlement agreement | related contracts | exclusion of jurisdiction of court

Laws Taken into Account in This Ruling:
➢   Code of Civil Procedure [ALB] – Act No. 8116 of 29 March 1996: Article 404;

Rationes Decidendi:[17]

14.30. An arbitration clause also covers any financial performance in connection with the rights and obligations (relationships) falling within the scope of the arbitration clause.

14.31. If a party files a motion with the court that is covered by a valid arbitration clause, Albanian courts must declare a lack of jurisdiction if the matter has not yet been heard before an arbitral tribunal or if the arbitral proceedings are still pending.

14.32. An arbitration clause in a contract, however, does not apply to other contracts that were entered into in connection with or following the contract, unless the related/ensuing contracts (in this case, a settlement agreement) contain an arbitration clause, or unless the original arbitration clause explicitly presumed the application thereof to such other contracts.

[Description of Facts and Legal Issues]

14.33. The dispute concerned claims from a contract for work concerning road construction works. The plaintiff demanded the payment of the price for the work. The parties had negotiated a settlement agreement regarding the price for the work. Whereas the contract for work contained an arbitration clause, the settlement agreement contained no arbitration clause. The plaintiff filed a motion with a court in [ALB] demanding the payment of the price for the work in compliance with the contract for work; the plaintiff simultaneously proposed that the court declare the settlement agreement invalid. The lower courts denied jurisdiction over both claims (payment and declaration of invalidity of the settlement agreement), invoking the valid arbitration clause. The courts also held that in such cases, courts are not entitled to hear the case before the commencement of or in the course of arbitration.

[Decision of Court of Appeal]

14.34. The Supreme Court [ALB] upheld the decision of the lower courts with respect to the claim for the payment of the price for the work under the contract for work, holding that the claim fell within a valid arbitration agreement, and that the arbitral proceedings concerning that matter had not even been initiated yet. At the same time, however, the Supreme Court [ALB] reversed the decisions of the lower courts,

---

[17]   The decision was referred to us and the basis of this annotation was drafted by Mr. Shpati Hoxha, attorney-at-law, Tirana, Albania. Decision No. 00-2006-892 concerning Dossier No. 1242-00075-00-2005 of 21 December 2006.

whereby jurisdiction was denied with respect to the settlement agreement, because this agreement did not contain any arbitration clause. According to the Supreme Court [ALB], it is irrelevant that the settlement agreement concerns claims arising from a contract that does contain an arbitration clause.

| | |

VII. Arbitration Clauses and Agreements on Choice of Foreign Court (Decision of Albanian Supreme Court, Case No. 11118-02384-00-2007 of 17 January 2008: Exclusion of Jurisdiction of Courts)

Key words:
arbitration clause | choice-of-court clause | choice-of-court | exclusion of jurisdiction of court | foreign company

Laws Taken into Account in This Ruling:
➢ Code of Civil Procedure [ALB] – Act No. 8116 of 29 March 1996: Article 485

Rationes Decidendi:[18]
14.35. A valid arbitration agreement excludes the jurisdiction of Albanian courts.
14.36. If at least one of the contracting parties is a company established outside Albania [ALB], the parties have the right to agree on the jurisdiction of an arbitral tribunal abroad or on the jurisdiction of a foreign court.
14.37. Courts are obliged to honour a valid arbitration agreement.

[Description of Facts and Legal Issues]
14.38. The respective case concerned a dispute over contractual liability and compensation for damage under a contract negotiated between two companies. The plaintiff filed a claim for damages with the Shkodër District Court. The plaintiff's claims were based on two separate contracts entered into between the parties.

---

[18] The decision was referred to us and the basis of this annotation was drafted by Mr. Shpati Hoxha, attorney-at-law, Tirana, Albania. Decision No. 00-2008-140 concerning Dossier No. 11118-02384-00-2007 of 17 January 2008.

[Decision of Trial Court]

14.39. The trial court denied jurisdiction, arguing that one of the contracts contained an arbitration clause, and the other contract contained a choice-of-court clause (in favour of a court in Bari/Italy).

[Decision of Court of Appeal]

14.40. The Supreme Court [ALB] upheld the decision of the trial court on the grounds that both contracts excluded the jurisdiction of Albanian courts, the first one by means of an arbitration clause and the second one by means of a choice-of-court clause favouring a foreign court. At the same time, one of the parties was a foreign company (a company established outside [ALB]).

| | |

2. Czech Republic

Abbreviations used in annotations:

ArbAct [CZE]	Act No. 216/1994 Coll., on Arbitration, as subsequently amended (without the changes introduced by the amendment to the ArbAct [CZE] that takes effect on 1 April 2012).
BGH [DEU]	Bundesgerichtshof, Federal Court of Justice, Germany.
CC [CZE]	Act No. 40/1964 Coll., as subsequently amended, Civil Code.[1]
CCP [CZE]	Act No. 99/1963 Coll., the Code of Civil Procedure, as amended.
Charter [CZE]	Charter of Rights and Freedoms of the Czech Republic.[2]
ComC [CZE]	Act [of the Czech Republic] No. 513/1991 Coll., the Commercial Code, as subsequently amended.
Constitution CR [CZE]	Constitutional Act No. 1/1993 Coll. of the Czech National Council of 16th December 1992 as amended.
Convention	European Convention on Human Rights.
ECHR	European Court of Human Rights.
Directive	Council Directive 93/13/EEC of 5 April 1993 on unfair terms in consumer contracts.[3]
NS ČR [CZE]	The Supreme Court of the Czech Republic.
NCC [CZE]	*New* Civil Code of the Czech Republic-Cabinet bill.[4]
RC in[...] [CZE]	Regional Court in [...].
SC CR [CZE]	Supreme Court of the Czech Republic.

---

[1] We expect that a new Code, the New Civil Code (NCC [CZE]), will replace, *inter alia*, the current Civil Code (CC [CZE]); the New Civil Code should take effect on 1 January 2014.

[2] Resolution of the Presidium of the Czech National Council No. 2/1993 Coll. of 16 December 1992 on the promulgation of the Charter of Fundamental Rights and Freedoms as a part of the constitutional order of the Czech Republic, as amended by the Constitutional Act of the Czech Republic No. 162/1998 Coll.

[3] *OJ* L 95 of 21 April 1993, pp. 29–34. CELEX: 31993L0013.

[4] Draft new Civil Code passed by the Chamber of Deputies of the Czech Republic in late 2011. At the time this manuscript was being completed, the Bill was being debated in the second chamber of the Parliament of the Czech Republic (the Senate of the Parliament of the Czech Republic). The Bill anticipates that the new law will take effect on 1 January 2014.

ÚS ČR [CZE]	Constitutional Court of the Czech Republic.
ZPO [DEU]	Zivilprozeßordnung. German Civil Procedure Code.
ZRK [SVK]	Act No. 244/2002 Coll. [of the Slovak Republic], on Arbitration, as subsequently amended.

Alexander J. Bělohlávek

I. Constitutional Court of Czech Republic Abandoned Strict Contractual Interpretation of Contract Theory of Arbitration.
Is This on the Way towards a Modern Symbiosis between a Jurisdictional and Contractual Basis for Arbitration?
(Judgment of Constitutional Court of Czech Republic, Case No. I ÚS 3227/07 of 8 March 2011)

Key words:
autonomy | civil procedure | different authority | jurisdictional theory | supervisory role of the courts | authority | duty to give instructions | rule of law | procedural rules | predictability of decisions | Res Judicata | equality of the parties | contract theory | consumer dispute | will of the parties | annulment of an arbitral award

States involved:
[CZE] - [Czech Republic]. No link to another State identified in the available summary.

Laws and Regulations Taken into Account in This Ruling:
➤ LPS [CZE] Article 36(1), Article 37(3) ;
➤ CCP [CZE] Section 106, Section 118 ;
➤ ArbAct [CZE] Section 18, Section 19(2), Section 25(3), Section 27, Section 28(2), Section 31;
➤ UNCITRAL Model Law Article 34;
➤ ZPO [DEU] Section 1059;
➤ ZRK [SVK] Section 40.

Rationes Decidendi:

15.01. The Constitutional Court of the Czech Republic (ÚS ČR [CZE]) has repeatedly analysed issues connected with arbitration[5] and the basis for arbitration[6]. The landmark decision is the Judgment of the ÚS ČR, Case No. I ÚS 3227/07 of 8 March 2011[7], which has brought about a significant material change in the opinions held by the ÚS ČR [CZE]. The preceding constitutional opinion (which appears long out-dated, even from the perspective of international practice) was based on the presumption that arbitration was mainly the process of determining the

---

[5] For instance:
  ➢ Resolution of the ÚS ČR [CZE], Case No. III. ÚS 460/01 of 1 November 2001, published as Resolution No. 41 *in* 24 SBÍRKA NÁLEZŮ A USNESENÍ ÚSTAVNÍHO SOUDU ČESKÉ REPUBLIKY (*Czech Constitutional Court Reports*) 563 et seq.
  ➢ Resolution of the ÚS ČR [CZE], Case No. IV. ÚS 174/02 of 15 July 2002, published as Resolution No. 20 *in* 27 SBÍRKA NÁLEZŮ A USNESENÍ ÚSTAVNÍHO SOUDU ČESKÉ REPUBLIKY (*Czech Constitutional Court Reports*) 257 et seq.; the majority of the subsequent decisions of the ÚS ČR [CZE] had been referring to this particular resolution, until the ÚS ČR delivered its Judgment No. I ÚS 3227/07 of 8 March 2011, annotated in this article.
  ➢ Resolution of the ÚS ČR [CZE], Case No. III. ÚS 145/03 of 12 September 2003;
  ➢ Resolution of the ÚS ČR [CZE], Case No. IV. ÚS 435/02 of 22 October 2002;
  ➢ Resolution of the ÚS ČR [CZE], Case No. IV. ÚS 511/03 of 4 December 2003;
  ➢ Resolution of the ÚS ČR [CZE], Case No. I. ÚS 339/02 of 26 January 2004;
  ➢ Resolution of the ÚS ČR [CZE], Case No. III. ÚS 166/05 of 29 April 2005;
  ➢ Resolution of the ÚS ČR [CZE], Case No. II. ÚS 2169/07 of 3 September 2007;
  ➢ Resolution of the ÚS ČR [CZE], Case No. II. I. ÚS 3059/08 of 15 January 2009 et al.

[6] For more details, see, for instance: Alexander Bělohlávek, Tereza Profeldová, *Arbitration in Case Law of Constitutional Court of Czech Republic with regard to Nature and Purpose of Arbitration*, *in* 1 CZECH (& CENTRAL EUROPEAN) YEARBOOK OF ARBITRATION: RELATIONSHIP BETWEEN CONSTITUTIONAL VALUES, HUMAN RIGHTS AND ARBITRATION, New York: JurisNet 343 (A. J. Bělohlávek, N. Rozehnalová eds., 2011); Naděžda Rozehnalová, Jan Havlíček, *Rozhodčí smlouva a rozhodci ve světle některých rozhodnutí ... aneb quo vadis ...?* (*Arbitration Agreements and Arbitrators in Light of Certain Decisions ... or Quo Vadis...?*), 7 (3) PRÁVNÍ FÓRUM, 114 et seq. (2010); Pavel Varvařovský, *Rozhodčí řízení v judikatuře Ústavního soudu* (*Arbitration in Constitutional Court Case Law*), 7 (3) PRÁVNÍ FÓRUM 143 et seq. (2010) et al.

[7] The electronic version of the Judgment is available at the ÚS ČR website: http://nalus.usoud.cz/Search/ResultDetail.aspx?id=69584&pos=1&cnt=1&typ=result (accessed on 26 August 2011). The proceedings before the Constitutional Court were initiated following these decisions of the lower courts: (i) Judgment of the Municipal Court in Prague, Case No. 8 Cm 164/2004-28 of 29 October 2004, (ii) Judgment of the High Court in Prague, Case No. 8 Cmo 80/2005-42 of 7 October 2005 and Resolution of the NS ČR [CZE], Case No. 32 Odo 366/2006-64. The arbitral award was rendered in arbitral proceedings before the Arbitration Court Attached to the Economic Chamber of the Czech Republic and the Agricultural Chamber of the Czech Republic under Case No. Rsp 352/03 on 30 April 2004.

contents of the consensus between the parties to the dispute;[8] in other words, it was based on the contract theory. The opinion expressed in the Judgment of the ÚS ČR [CZE] pushes this theory **a great measure towards the jurisdictional theory of arbitration, perceived as a process of finding the law by a private-law entity**, analogous and equivalent to litigation and in compliance with the applicable law. It is therefore safe to say that this 2011 decision of the Constitutional Court of the Czech Republic [CZE] overruled the contract theory[9] and confirmed the jurisdictional basis for arbitration (albeit based on the contractual autonomy of the parties), and thereby confirmed the actual state of affairs that has already been in place for some time in both arbitration proceedings, as such, and in the judicial practice of the courts. The arbitral tribunal was also classified as a **"different authority,"** which is important, especially because arbitrators are directly bound by the applicable law and obliged to apply the applicable law. At the same time, however, the Constitutional Court has honoured the fact that the arbitrators' jurisdiction can only be established by agreement of the parties based on their autonomy and within the limits of the applicable statutory rules. This decision is comparable to the modern approach to arbitration and reflects the actual present situation.

15.02. The Constitutional Court of the Czech Republic [CZE] **expressed its opinion on, *inter alia*, the following issues**, many of which are essential for the definition of the arbitration agreement, arbitration as such, arbitral proceedings and their relationship to litigation:

▶ Arbitration is a **type of civil procedure**. The fundamental difference from civil procedure in court (i.e. litigation) lies in the definition of the managing and decision-making authority. Whereas in court

---

[8]   The ÚS ČR [CZE] used to follow, in this regard, the opinion expressed in the Resolution of the ÚS ČR [CZE], Case No. IV ÚS 174/02 of 15 July 2002, published, for instance as Resolution No. 20 *in* 27 SBÍRKA NÁLEZŮ A USNESENÍ ÚSTAVNÍHO SOUDU ČESKÉ REPUBLIKY (*Czech Constitutional Court Reports*), 257 et seq. It was thoroughly annotated, for instance, in: Alexander J. Bělohlávek, Tereza Profeldová, *supra* note 6, at 343, 350.

[9]   In modern Czech arbitration, even academics have seldom adopted this approach; see, for instance, Alexander Bělohlávek, Tomáš Pezl, *Postavení rozhodčího řízení v systému ochrany práv a ústavního pořádku České republiky a dalších zemí (Status of Arbitration in System of Rights Protection and Constitutional Laws of Czech Republic and Other Countries)*, 12 (7) PRÁVNÍ ROZHLEDY 256–261 (2004); Přemysl Raban, *K odpovědnosti rozhodce a rozhodčího soudu (Regarding Liability of Arbitrators and Arbitration Tribunals)*, 13 (1) BULLETIN ADVOKACIE 25 (2003). Critical or dissenting opinions prevailed; see for instance: Richard Pecha, *K právní povaze rozhodčích nálezů (Regarding Legal Nature of Arbitral Awards)*, 13 (5) BULLETIN ADVOKACIE 41(2003); Květoslav Růžička, *K otázce právní povahy rozhodčího řízení (Regarding Legal Nature of Arbitration)*, 13 (5) BULLETIN ADVOKACIE 32–40 et al. (2003).

proceedings (litigation) it is the court, in arbitration it is the arbitrator or a permanent arbitral institution (hereinafter "arbitrator"[10]).

▶ The fact that arbitration is a type of civil procedure, however, **does not in itself mean that courts are allowed to intervene freely in arbitration.**

▶ **The arbitrator's power to hear and resolve the dispute is based on the joint will of the parties to the dispute** expressed in their arbitration agreement. By means of this procedural agreement, the parties exclude the jurisdiction of the courts (with respect to Section 106(1) CCP [CZE][11]) only conditionally) and establish the jurisdiction of the arbitrator(s).

▶ **Based on the voluntary acts of the parties, the arbitrator therefore performs the duties instead of a court,** which would otherwise have to hear and decide the case. However, the rights of the parties to make dispositions with their disputes are even more far-reaching; the parties to the dispute are, for instance, allowed to determine the identity of the arbitrators, the applicable procedural rules, the venue of arbitration, the type of proceedings (oral or written), or even the criteria that should be applied to the merits[12].

---

[10]   This terminological abbreviation is used directly in the Judgment of the ÚS ČR [CZE] rendered in said case.

[11]   CCP [CZE] (approximate translation, cit.): Examination of procedural requirements – [...] Section 106 – ""(1) *As soon as the court discovers, upon the defendant's objection lodged together with or before the first act of the defendant on the merits, that the agreement of the parties requires the case to be submitted to arbitration, the court must desist from further examination of the case and terminate the proceedings; the court, however, hears the case if the parties declare that they waive the agreement. The court also hears the case if the court determines that the matter is not arbitrable under the laws of the Czech Republic, or that arbitration agreement is null and void or non-existent, or that making the agreement the subject matter of the arbitral proceedings would exceed the scope of jurisdiction vested in the arbitrators by the agreement, or that the arbitral tribunal refused to hear the case. (2) If the court proceedings under Subsection (1) were terminated and a motion for the commencement of arbitral proceedings was lodged in the same case, the original petition for commencement of the proceedings retains its legal effects, provided the motion for the commencement of arbitral proceedings is lodged no later than within 30 days of the delivery of the court's resolution terminating the proceedings. (3) If the arbitral proceedings were opened earlier than the court proceedings, the court stays its proceedings on the absence, nullity or expiration of the agreement until the arbitrator(s) decide(s) on their jurisdiction over the case or on the merits.*""

[12]   The ÚS ČR invokes Section 25(3) ArbAct [CZE].
ArbAct [CZE] (approximate translation, cit.): Section 25 – "(1) *The arbitral award must be passed by a majority of the arbitrators, executed in writing and signed by the majority or all of the arbitrators. The order of the arbitral award must be clear and unambiguous. (2) The arbitral award shall contain the reasons for the award, unless the parties agree to dispense with reasons; this also applies to any arbitral award rendered pursuant to* Section 24(2)

▶No claim can be subject to **arbitration and litigation** at the same time, i.e. the two proceedings **cannot be conducted in parallel**; arbitral awards are also endowed with the same effect as final and binding court decisions,[13] which means that arbitral awards constitute *res judicata*, barring the parties from litigating the same claim again in courts.

▶**In compliance with the principle of autonomy of the parties,** the law **honours the freely expressed will of the parties who wish to have their dispute heard and decided by an arbitrator;** courts are therefore not allowed to intervene in the arbitral proceedings, except in strictly defined situations specified in the ArbAct [CZE]. On the other hand, this does not mean that the purpose of arbitration is to eliminate or reduce the degree of protection that would otherwise be afforded to the parties in civil litigation; arbitration, just like litigation, aims at peaceful resolution of the dispute between the parties. The parties only have a special reason (for instance, expeditiousness or confidentiality of the information discussed in the proceedings)[14] to believe that arbitration is a more suitable solution for them. From this perspective, the submission of a dispute to arbitration means the transfer [of jurisdiction, legal protection] to a **different decision-making and law-**

[ArbAct [CZE]]. (3) *When making the award, the arbitrators apply the substantive law applicable to the dispute; they may, however, resolve the dispute according to the rules of equity, but only if the parties have explicitly authorized them to do so."*

[13]   The ÚS ČR invokes Section 28(2) ArbAct [CZE].

ArbAct [CZE] (approximate translation, cit.): Section 28 – "(1) *The written copy of the arbitral award must be served on the parties and after the service stamped with the legal force clause. (2) If an arbitral award cannot be subject to review under Section 27 [ArbAct [CZE]] or if the time period for filing the petition for review under Section 27 [ArbAct [CZE]] expired without the petition having been filed, the award has the effects of a final and binding court judgment and is enforceable by courts upon delivery."*

ArbAct [CZE] (approximate translation, cit.): Section 27 – "*The parties may agree in their arbitration agreement that the arbitral award can be reviewed by other arbitrators at the request of any or both of the parties. Unless the arbitration agreement stipulates otherwise, the petition for review must be sent to the other party no later than within 30 days of the delivery of the arbitral award to the party requesting the review. Review of the arbitral award constitutes part of the arbitral proceedings and is governed by the provisions of this Act."*

[14]   The ÚS ČR [CZE] says that (cit.): "*Academic writings mention, for instance, the following advantages: more expeditious proceedings due to the usual exclusion of appeal, less formal proceedings and more simple procedural rules, as well as the fact that the arbitrator can be an expert in the respective field that is the subject matter of the dispute."*

See, for instance, Bohuslav Klein, *Pozapomenuté výhody rozhodčího řízení* (*Forgotten Advantages of Arbitration*), 5 (4) PRÁVNÍ FÓRUM, 128 et seq. (2008).

finding authority, rather than a waiver of legal protection[15]; indeed, any other conclusion would render it conceptually unacceptable to consider arbitration a dispute resolution method alternative to litigation.

► The law allows the parties to **exclude the jurisdiction of the court by their arbitration agreement and to vest jurisdiction over their dispute in an arbitrator,** who will **find the law in their respective case and incorporate the result in an authoritative decision – the arbitral award.** The conclusion of the agreement is the result of a decision freely made by the parties, who contemplate the advantages and disadvantages of submitting their case to arbitration.

► The **autonomy of will** is one of the principles observed by a state honouring the rule of law. This autonomy also applies to the process of negotiating arbitration agreements. The law therefore accepts that the parties do not desire to have their dispute resolved by a court and prefer arbitration.

► Hearing the case in arbitral proceedings **does not constitute a denial of legal protection; it only represents the transfer of the latter from the courts to arbitrators.** However, the state cannot entirely waive the possibility of intervening; it must retain certain **supervisory duties** exercised by the courts[16]. The extent of this supervision must be carefully balanced – the rule stipulating that arbitration must also guarantee legal protection must not be eliminated, but on the other hand, the advantages of arbitration and its practical applicability must not be entirely wiped out.

► Indeed, the parties do have a broad opportunity to **agree on procedural rules**[17] governing the arbitral proceedings; on the other hand, though, this opportunity is not without limits. The Arbitration

---

[15]   See a similar case in Germany, Judgment of the Federal Court of Justice (Supreme Court; BGH [DEU]), Case No. III ZR 265/03 of 13 January 2005. Said decision of the German court is available at: http://juris.bundesgerichtshof.de/cgi-bin/rechtsprechung/document.py?Gericht=bgh&Art=en&nr=31677&pos=0&anz=1 (accessed on 9 August 2011). They quote, for instance: Milan Hulmák, Blanka Tomančáková, *Rozhodčí řízení jako vhodný prostředek řešení sporů mezi dodavatelem a spotřebitelem (1. část)* (*Arbitration as Suitable Means for Resolution of Disputes between Supplier and Consumer (Part 1)*), 2 (6) OBCHODNĚPRÁVNÍ REVUE 168 (2010) (see Footnote 33 in said article).

[16]   See, for instance, KAREL KLÍMA, ÚSTAVNÍ PRÁVO (*Constitutional Law*), Dobrá Voda u Pelhřimova: Aleš Čeněk 79 (1st ed. 2002).

[17]   The ÚS ČR invokes Section 19(1) ArbAct [CZE]; this provision is quoted below.

Act (ArbAct) contains in Section 18[18] a **mandatory provision incorporating the principle of equal standing of the parties; the parties must also be provided with a full opportunity to assert their rights. Any agreement of the parties conflicting with this rule would be null and void.** The equality of the parties and the full opportunity to assert their rights are principles that apply even in those cases in which the arbitrator's case management of the proceedings is governed by arbitration rules adopted by a permanent arbitral institution, or in which the arbitrators themselves determine the progress of the proceedings. This is clearly articulated in the second sentence of Section 19(2) ArbAct [CZE][19]. A breach of the mandatory Section 18 ArbAct [CZE][20] constitutes grounds for setting aside the arbitral award listed in Section 31(1)(e) ArbAct [CZE][21]. If the *equality of arms* was not honoured or if any of the parties was denied full opportunity to assert his or her rights, the party was undoubtedly denied the possibility to plead his or her case before the arbitrators within the meaning of the last mentioned provision.

►**Unpredictable acts of the arbitrator** could also constitute such denial of the full opportunity to assert the party's rights, as a result of which the party, for instance, will not be able to plead their case with

---

[18]   ArbAct [CZE] (approximate translation, cit.): Section 18 – *"The parties have equal standing in the arbitral proceedings and must be provided with a full opportunity to assert their rights."*

[19]   ArbAct [CZE] (approximate translation, cit.): Section 19 – *"(1) The parties have a right to agree on how the arbitrators shall administer the proceedings. Matters regarding the case management of the proceedings may be resolved by the chairman of the tribunal, provided he or she was authorized to do so by the parties or by all arbitrators. (2) Unless the parties negotiated an agreement pursuant to Subsection (1), the arbitrators shall case manage the proceedings in any manner they see fit. They case manage the arbitral proceedings in such manner that the facts of the case necessary for the resolution of the dispute are sufficiently ascertained, without any unnecessary formalities, and while giving all parties equal opportunity to plead their case."*

[20]   Cited above.

[21]   ArbAct [CZE] (approximate translation, cit.): Section 31 – *"At the request of any party, the court sets aside an arbitral award if (a) the award was rendered in a case which is not arbitrable (cannot be the subject of a valid arbitration agreement), (b) the arbitration agreement is null and void for other reasons, was cancelled or does not apply to the dispute, (c) one or more arbitrators involved in the resolution of the dispute was/were not authorized to make decisions in the case under the arbitration agreement or otherwise, or lacked the capacity to act as arbitrator, (d) the arbitral award was not passed by the majority of arbitrators, (e) one or more parties did not have the opportunity to plead their case before the arbitrators, (f) the arbitral award orders a party to provide performance that was not requested by the creditor or that is not possible or allowed under domestic law, or (g) it transpires that there are grounds that would otherwise justify a motion for reopening the proceedings (trial de novo) in civil litigation."*

respect to all relevant circumstances, or supplement their statements regarding any facts that the party did not consider relevant from the perspective of their own legal opinion, but which are relevant from the perspective of the arbitrator's legal opinion, and to propose the relevant evidence. **Eliminating any unpredictability** in the arbitrators' decision is all the more exigent because arbitration, as a rule, does not allow appeals,[22] which prevents the parties from responding to any surprising legal opinion at least *ex post facto*. **The arbitrator cannot play the role of a merely passive element; he or she must case manage the proceedings in such manner that his/her decision is not a surprise to the parties.** To that end, civil court proceedings prescribe that courts must give instructions to the parties; there is no reason to absolve the arbitrator of that obligation in arbitral proceedings, considering the fact that in such proceedings the arbitrator acts as the decision-making authority instead of the court. **The duty of the arbitrator to give instructions to the parties** does not conflict with the nature of arbitration; in other words, the specific features of arbitration cannot justify the conclusion that arbitrators do not need to take care that their decisions are predictable.

▶ The Arbitration Act [CZE] (ArbAct [CZE]) does not lay down the arbitrator's obligation to give instructions; it is therefore legitimate **to reasonably apply the Civil Procedure Code** (CCP [CZE]).[23]

---

[22] See Section 27 ArbAct [CZE] (approximate translation, cit.): Section 27 – *"The parties may agree in their arbitration agreement that the arbitral award can be reviewed by other arbitrators at the request of any or both of the parties. Unless the arbitration agreement stipulates otherwise, the petition for review must be sent to the other party no later than within 30 days of the delivery of the arbitral award to the party requesting the review. Review of the arbitral award constitutes part of the arbitral proceedings and is governed by the provisions of this Act."*

[23] The ÚS ČR invokes Section 30 ArbAct [CZE] and subsequently Section 118 CCP [CZE]. The Court simultaneously confirms the opinion expressed in the judgment of the NS ČR [CZE], Case No. 32 Odo 1528/2005 of 25 April 2007 and in the judgment of the NS ČR [CZE], Case No. 23 Cdo 3749/2008 of 26 May 2010.

CCP [CZE] (cit.): Section 118 – "(1) *After opening the hearing, the chairman of the panel requests that the plaintiff (petitioner) present his or her claim (petition for opening the proceedings) or summarize the contents thereof, and requests that the defendant (all other parties to the proceedings) present his or her defence or written pleadings or summarize the contents thereof; submissions lodged by absent parties shall be read or the contents thereof summarized by the chairman of the panel. The defendant (any other party to the proceedings) who has not lodged his or her written submission yet shall be invited by the chairman of the panel to make a statement in the case. If necessary, the chairman of the panel also invites the party to supplement his or her statements and to propose evidence supporting his or her case. (2) Having performed the acts under Subsection (1), the chairman of the panel shall report the results of the preparatory stage of the proceedings and inform the parties accordingly which legally significant statements of fact presented by*

If the courts in proceedings on setting aside an arbitral award failed to address the objection that the arbitrator(s) did not discharge their duty to give instructions to the parties in the course of the arbitral proceedings, the ÚS ČR [CZE] cannot (materially) address this objection either, because the Constitutional Court would thereby violate its duty to act as a protector of constitutionally guaranteed fundamental rights and freedoms, and would interfere with and unduly substitute for the conduct of the lower courts. In such cases, however, the court may grant the constitutional complaint and annul the decisions of the lower courts for violating the party's right to a fair trial.[24]

▶ Although it might be constitutionally relevant in certain cases that the legislator failed to lay down rules regulating a particular issue, this does not apply if the list of grounds for annulment of an arbitral award[25] does not include a conflict with substantive law or public policy. Permitting the review of arbitral awards by the court[26] due to a breach of substantive law is doubtful both from the perspective of

---

the parties can be considered uncontested, which legally relevant statements of fact remained contested and what evidence proposed so far shall be heard or read, and which evidence shall be heard or read despite the fact that the parties did not propose to hear or read the evidence. (3) Unless the law stipulates otherwise, the chairman of the panel shall administer the proceedings, depending on the circumstances of the case."

CCP [CZE] (cit.): Section 118a – "(1) If it transpires during the proceedings that any party has not yet presented all relevant statements of fact or has presented them only insufficiently, the chairman of the panel invites the party to supplement its statements and gives him or her instructions as to which statements are to be supplemented and what the consequences of noncompliance are. (2) If the chairman of the panel opines that the court's legal opinion of the case could differ from the party's legal opinion, the chairman invites the party to supplement the relevant statements of fact to the necessary extent; the chairman shall proceed similarly to Subsection (1). (3) If the chairman of the panel discovers during the proceedings that a party has not proposed evidence yet necessary to prove all of his or her contested statements, the chairman invites the party to identify such evidence without undue delay and gives him or her instructions regarding the consequences of noncompliance. (4) During the hearings, the chairman of the panel also gives the parties instructions regarding other procedural rights and duties of the parties; this does not apply if the party is represented by an attorney or a notary public to the extent of the notary's authorization under special laws."

[24] Consequently, the case was remanded to the trial court, which will have to examine whether the duty to give instructions was breached in the arbitral proceedings and whether or not there are grounds for setting aside the arbitral award. We have had no new information about the new trial in the lower courts and the results thereof up until the day of drafting this annotation.

[25] The grounds are listed in Section 31 ArbAct [CZE]; the provision is quoted above.

[26] See, for instance, Tomáš Pohl, K problematice přezkoumání rozhodčích nálezů soudem (Regarding Review of Arbitral Awards by Courts), (4) PRÁVNÍ FÓRUM 158 et seq. et al. (2008).

interpreting the grounds for annulment of arbitral awards and from the theoretical perspective.

▶ Proceedings on setting aside an arbitral award by the court can never be structured similarly to remedial civil court proceedings, let alone regular appellate proceedings. If the court were allowed to review an arbitral award from the perspective of its compliance with substantive law, it would deny the existence of arbitration. **The supervisory role of the courts** can therefore only concentrate on **examining the crucial procedural issues,** for instance, whether arbitration could actually have been conducted, whether any important procedural rights were denied to the parties, or whether the arbitral award itself is free of any procedural flaws (for instance, it was not passed by the majority of the arbitrators).

[Factual and Legal Circumstances of Case and Court Decisions regarding Setting Aside Arbitral Award]

15.03. Proceedings at the ÚS ČR [CZE] were held following the proceedings on setting aside the arbitral award, which was rendered in the Czech Republic in April 2004. The Arbitration Court attached to the Economic Chamber of the Czech Republic and the Agricultural Chamber of the Czech Republic dismissed the claimant's claim for the payment of [CZK *xxx.xxx.xxx*], and stated that the arbitral award was final and binding, having the effect of a final judgment as soon as it was served on both parties, and was enforceable by the court. The Arbitration Court reasoned that the claimant was not entitled to claim the respective amount of money from the respondent; consequently, the claimant's motion was dismissed.

15.04. The complainant[27] argued that the principle of predictability of decisions was breached in the arbitral proceedings due to the violation of the duty to give instructions, which the arbitrators refused to apply. According to the complainant, the arbitral tribunal breached the duty to give instructions by adopting a different legal opinion on two issues without having informed the claimant thereof, and by failing to invite the claimant to propose evidence proving her allegations regarding the interpretation of a contract according to the intention of the parties, which was – considering the award finally rendered by the arbitrators – fundamental. The complainant argued that the true will of the parties

---

[27] The complainant was a bank, namely Česká spořitelna a.s.
Regarding some aspects of the connection between contracts negotiated in the financial area and arbitration according to Czech laws see also Robert Krč, Karel Marek, *Smlouva o otevření akreditivu* (*Letter of Credit Agreement*), 6 (7) PRÁVNÍ ROZHLEDY 361 et seq. (1998).

should have been ascertained by interrogating witnesses[28]. The complainant herself proposed the examination of witnesses, without being requested to do so by the arbitrators; the arbitrators, however, rejected this evidence without providing any grounds justifying such rejection. The complainant in her constitutional complaint alleged that the courts groundlessly refused (in the proceedings on setting aside the arbitral award) to apply the principle of predictability incorporated in Section 118a CCP [CZE][29], and thereby violated Article 36(1) LPS [CZE][30] and Article 37(3) LPS [CZE][31].

15.05. The complainant also argued that the arbitral award grossly violated substantive law, as a result of which the decision was unpredictable. The complainant's main argument was the acceptance of the so-called contract theory by the Constitutional Court of the Czech Republic [CZE] (according to a number of decisions rendered in the past)[32]. The complainant claimed that if the duty of the arbitrator was [only] to establish (settle) an obligation (relationship) between the parties, rather than to find the law (as opposed to the duties of courts, as the contract

---

[28]   As concerns the significance of such evidence, the complainant invokes the Judgment of the ÚS ČR [CZE], Case No. I. ÚS 220/98 of 6 June 2000, published as Resolution no. 85 *in* 18 Sbírka nálezů a usnesení Ústavního soudu ČR (*Czech Constitutional Court Reports*) 219 et seq.

[29]   The provision is quoted above in this annotation.

[30]   Charter [CZE] (approximate translation, cit.): Chapter Five – The Right to Judicial and Other Legal Protection – Article 36 – "(1) *Everyone may assert, through the legally prescribed procedure, his or her rights before an independent and impartial court, or in specified cases, before a different authority. (2) Unless the law provides otherwise, any person who claims that his or her rights were curtailed by a decision of a public administrative authority may turn to a court for review of the legality of that decision. However, judicial review of decisions affecting the fundamental rights and basic freedoms listed in this Charter may not be removed from the jurisdiction of courts. (3) Everyone is entitled to compensation for damages or losses sustained by him or her as a result of an unlawful decision of a court, another state authority, or a public administrative authority, or as a result of improper official procedure. (4) Conditions and detailed provisions are laid down by statute.*"

[31]   Charter [CZE] (approximate translation, cit.): Chapter Five – The Right to Judicial and Other Legal Protection – [...] Article 37 – [...] (3) "*All parties to the proceedings are equal.* [...]"

[32]   The ÚS ČR [CZE] also invoked the contract theory and the complainant refers especially to:
   ➢ Resolution of the ÚS ČR [CZE], Case No. III. ÚS 460/01 of 1 November 2001, published as Resolution No. 41 *in* 24 Sbírka nálezů a usnesení Ústavního soudu České republiky (*Czech Constitutional Court Reports*) 563 et seq.
   ➢ Resolution of the ÚS ČR [CZE], Case No. IV. ÚS 174/02 of 15 July 2002, published as Resolution No. 20 *in* 27 Sbírka nálezů a usnesení Ústavního soudu České republiky (*Czech Constitutional Court Reports*) 257 et seq. and
   ➢ Resolution of the ÚS ČR [CZE], Case No. IV. ÚS 435/02 of 22 October 2002.

theory of arbitration would demand), the law-finding activity of courts should not be prejudiced by arbitration, and courts should be allowed to review the arbitral award from the perspective of its compliance with substantive law. This conclusion is also supported, in the complainant's view, by the fact that arbitrators are not **"different authorities"** in terms of Article 36(1) LPS [CZE][33]. Both the arbitral proceedings and the arbitral award are of a private-law nature; arbitral awards should therefore be reviewable from the perspective of their compliance with substantive law. They are not, however, and the complainant considers this state of affairs unconstitutional. Section 31 ArbAct [CZE], as opposed to other laws, does not even allow the courts to annul the arbitral award for fundamental procedural irregularities,[34] or for breach of public policy or the fundamental principles of Czech law [CZE]. The complainant argues that this violates her right to a fair trial, and this situation can only be remedied by including in Section 31 ArbAct [CZE] the possibility to set aside an arbitral award for failure to comply with substantive law. The complainant therefore suggested amending the ArbAct [CZE] so that the list of grounds for setting aside an arbitral award is no longer an exhaustive list, but becomes merely illustrative.

15.06. As concerns the facts of the case, the complainant pointed out that the award did not comply with substantive law, because the Restructuring Agreement negotiated between the parties did not stipulate the due date on which the so-called motivation fees were to be paid. From this perspective, the award conflicted with the Restructuring Agreement and breached the principle of *pacta sunt servanda*, as well as the statutory rules regulating the interpretation of the parties' expression of will. The courts failed to protect the complainant against an award rendered in violation of substantive law, by which the courts breached Article 36(1) LPS [CZE].

15.07. However, the complainant argued, in particular, that the arbitral proceedings also suffered from other procedural irregularities. The arbitral tribunal failed to hear the evidence proposed by the complainant and based its decision merely on the allegations of the joint party (i.e. the respondent in the original arbitral proceedings, hereinafter the "respondent"). Even though the complainant proposed interrogating witnesses, whereby the true will of the parties was to be determined, the arbitral tribunal dismissed the proposal and thereby de facto deprived the complainant of the possibility to plead her case; the

---

[33] Cited above in this annotation.

[34] The grounds for setting aside an arbitral award are (*inter alia*) identical to the grounds for a trial *de novo* in court proceedings (see Section 31(g) ArbAct [CZE]), but not to the grounds constituting the so-called *irregularity of proceedings*.

tribunal based its decision merely on the unsubstantiated allegations of the respondent. The lower courts concluded that the failure to hear or read evidence did not constitute grounds sufficient for setting aside an arbitral award pursuant to Section 31(e) ArbAct [CZE]; this conclusion conflicts with Article 36(1) LPS [CZE][35] and Article 37(3) LPS [CZE][36].

15.08. The trial court[37] dismissed the complainant's motion for the annulment of the arbitral award. The court maintained that the arbitral tribunal's refusal to hear the evidence did not constitute grounds for setting aside the arbitral award pursuant to Section 31(e) ArbAct [CZE] (failure to provide an opportunity to plead one's case in the arbitral proceedings). The appellate court upheld the decision of the trial court.[38] The appellate court maintained that the arbitral tribunal had discussed the case with the parties in an oral hearing, and the parties had had full opportunity to present their statements and propose evidence. Setting aside an arbitral award for the tribunal's failure to hear or read evidence proposed by a party would only be possible if the arbitrators, without any justification, refused to hear or read the evidence or examined it only insufficiently. The court, however, cannot evaluate such evidence with regard to its potential impact on the result of the proceedings; such evaluation is reserved for the arbitrators[39]. The cassation appeal to the Supreme Court challenging the decisions mentioned above was dismissed[40]. The Supreme Court upheld the preceding decisions of the lower courts, especially as concerns the opportunity of the party to plead his or her case in the arbitral proceedings. The Supreme Court

---

[35] Cited above in this annotation.

[36] Cited above in this annotation.

[37] Judgment of the Municipal Court in Prague [CZE], Case No. 8 Cm 165/2004 of 11 January 2005 (unpublished).

[38] Judgment of the High Court in Prague [CZE], Case No. 8 Cmo 80/2005-42 of 7 October 2005.

[39] The appellate court also found that the arbitrators had in fact analysed the grounds for rejecting the respective evidence (interrogation) and had issued resolutions regarding that issue.

[40] Resolution of the Supreme Court of the Czech Republic [CZE], Case No. 32 Odo 366/2006-64 of 11 September 2007. Published on the NS ČR [CZE] website at: http://www.nsoud.cz/JudikaturaNS_new/judikatura_prevedena2.nsf/WebSearch/71F1280 0CB05F81AC12575FF007A036C?openDocument (accessed on 26 August 2011). The Supreme Court (NS ČR [CZE]) points out, *inter alia*, that the Civil Procedure Code (CCP [CZE]) does not grant the parties the right to have the evidence that they proposed heard or read; it is the court that decides what evidence (proposed by the parties) shall be admitted in the proceedings. The party is not deprived of the opportunity to plead his or her case before the court by the mere fact that the court refuses to hear or read the evidence proposed by that party, provided the court justifies its refusal to admit the evidence. This interpretation can be extrapolated to Section 31(e) ArbAct [CZE].

mainly emphasized that the parties have no right to have all evidence (which they proposed) heard or read, not even under civil procedure rules regulating litigation.

[Decision of Constitutional Court of Czech Republic on Merits]

15.09. According to the ÚS ČR [CZE], arbitrators or permanent arbitral institutions are *different authorities,* which resolve disputes between the parties, and in doing so apply the applicable law. They do not, however, become public authorities as a result thereof. Arbitrators are still private persons whom the parties to the dispute endow with the power to hear and decide their dispute according to their procedural agreement. If the arbitrator or the permanent arbitral institution is not a public authority, then their decision or any other intervention cannot be directly challenged by a constitutional complaint. The ÚS ČR [CZE] therefore dismissed the part of the complainant's constitutional complaint in which she directly challenged the arbitral award (the Constitutional Court refused to set aside the arbitral award). Indeed, the complainant herself admitted that the part of the constitutional complaint challenging the arbitral award was only included because the complainant wished to proceed cautiously. The Constitutional Court therefore concentrated exclusively on the arguments challenging the court decisions rendered in the proceedings on setting aside the arbitral award.

15.10. The constitutional complaint was joined with the motion to repeal the part of Section 31 ArbAct [CZE] that stipulates that the list of grounds for the annulment of an arbitral award is exhaustive. The complainant pointed out that a conflict with substantive law was missing as a ground for annulment, as well as other situations such as a breach of public policy. The complainant did not suggest, though, that the absence of these grounds curtailed the complainant's constitutional rights. It was the absence of any arguments regarding any potential violation of the complainant's specific constitutional rights that resulted in dismissing the motion as prima facie groundless. The refusal to review the merits of arbitral awards has also been analysed by the ÚS ČR [CZE], thoroughly and from the comparative (international) perspective.[41] The Constitutional Court concluded, however, that the courts had failed to sufficiently address the issue of whether or not the duty to give instructions had been duly discharged, and in the latter case, if the arbitrators had thereby violated the party's right to a fair trial or, as the

---

[41]   The Court made a comparison with Article 34 of the UNCITRAL Model Law, Section 1059 ZPO [DEU] and Section 40 ZRK [SVK].

case may be, deprived the party of the opportunity to plead her case in the arbitral proceedings. Despite the decision on the merits, i.e. the annulment of the decisions of the lower courts and remanding the case for a new trial in order to find out whether the duty to give instructions was duly discharged, the ÚS ČR [CZE] provided an unusually thorough and comprehensive analysis of the majority of the fundamental issues relating to the nature of the arbitration agreement, the substance of arbitration, the fundamental principles of arbitration, and its relation to the process of finding the law and to the acts of courts. Without exaggeration, it is a landmark decision, which offers a new and clear definition of these fundamental issues from the perspective of constitutional law and constitutional principles. However, it is by no means a *surprising decision.* Legal professionals and a large number of academics have clearly confirmed that the definition of the substance of arbitration as previously articulated by the Constitutional Court, especially in the 2002 resolution, and as subsequently adhered to, is no longer sustainable; the Constitutional Court de facto treated arbitration as an equal alternative to litigation from the perspective of many fundamental procedural principles and from the perspective of finding the applicable law in arbitration.[42] It is therefore probably the *proverbial end* of the fifteen-year search for a constitutional opinion on arbitration after the ArbAct [CZE] was adopted in 1994 (effective date 1 January 1995), and arbitration was thereby opened for the majority of civil disputes and disputes without international elements, which were the only arbitrable disputes prior to 1995.[43]

[**Correlation between Decision and Consumer Protection**]

15.11. The respective dispute was not a consumer dispute. However, the Constitutional Court (ÚS ČR [CZE]) modified its case law and explicitly stated that arbitrators were an "authority" that finds and must find the applicable law. It is a significant shift in the case law of the ÚS ČR [CZE] since 2002. Indeed, the ÚS ČR [CZE] thereby also provided a clear answer to the question of what the arbitrators' duty in the arbitral proceedings actually is. Arbitrators are persons (albeit with private-law status) who apply the applicable law, and there is consequently no reason to suspect that the requirements of consumer protection under European (Community) law should not be fulfilled in this regard. Indeed, the same conclusion regarding this issue in connection with

---

[42] See, for instance, Naděžda Rozehnalová, *Rozhodčí řízení – alternativa k řízení soudnímu* (*Arbitration – An Alternative to Litigation*), 5 (4) PRÁVNÍ FÓRUM 121 et seq. (2008).

[43] Pursuant to Act No. 98/1963 Coll., on Arbitration in International Commerce and on Enforcement of Arbitral Awards.

consumer protection was articulated, for instance, by the German Supreme Court (BGH [DEU]). On the other hand, we have to point out that the ÚS ČR [CZE] did not attempt to disguise its rather cautious approach to arbitration clauses in consumer contracts. The Court stated that the law indeed allowed the parties to exclude, in their arbitration agreement, the jurisdiction of the court and to vest jurisdiction over their dispute in an arbitrator who would find the law in their respective case and incorporate the result in an authoritative decision – the arbitral award. The conclusion of the agreement is the result of a decision freely made by the parties, who contemplate the advantages and disadvantages of submitting their case to arbitration. The Constitutional Court, however, explicitly emphasized that the complainant was not a consumer and therefore the Court had not analysed arbitration clauses incorporated in arbitration agreements that (cit.): *"are often abused and frequently have the nature of unreasonable (unfair) terms."* Apparently, the Court reserved the possibility to make specific conclusions, should it be called upon to review a case concerning a consumer dispute in the future. Moreover, the decision was adopted at a time when the Cabinet was finalizing an extensive amendment to the ArbAct [CZE], the purpose of which was, *inter alia*, to lay down rules applicable in consumer dispute arbitration. It is therefore laudable that the ÚS ČR [CZE] at that time refrained from voicing any explicit opinion of arbitration clauses in consumer disputes, and left the entire field of law to the legislator. The Court's reservation (as concerns consumer disputes) is thus constitutionally conformant and strategic. On the other hand, the *critical remark* went rather too far (this is a general negative trait of the Czech decision-making practice). It is clear that in its future decisions, the ÚS ČR [CZE] might apply very strict criteria (to say the least) in connection with arbitration clauses in consumer contracts and with respect to consumer protection. Indeed, the Court's possible future approach to consumer dispute arbitration can be deduced from numerous paragraphs of the present judgment, especially the Court's conclusion regarding full autonomy, which, however, means the expression of a **joint** (i.e. *actual, true* – author's note) **will of the parties**. The arbitration agreement entered into between the parties must therefore clearly indicate that it represents an expression of will of both (all) parties to the agreement. The Constitutional Court of the Czech Republic [CZE] also repeatedly emphasizes the equality of the parties and points out that any agreement of the parties to the contrary would be null and void. This necessarily means that any agreement that would award more procedural rights to one of the parties, to the detriment of others, would be null and void.

15.12. The emphasis placed on the **duty to give instructions** as protection against surprising decisions is probably a feature specific to Czech law (Czech *lex arbitri*). The requirement to furnish both parties with the necessary instructions had been previously and repeatedly voiced, especially (though not exclusively) in the case law of the Supreme Court of the Czech Republic. Although there are certain trends even in the international arena that have the objective of eliminating the so-called *unpredictable decisions*, the prevailing international practice has adopted a rather distrustful approach to any duty to give instructions in arbitration, and has stressed the principle of maximum liability of the parties for the protection of their rights, arguing that a duty to give instructions tends to conflict with the principle of independence and impartiality of arbitrators. Consequently, it is certainly a specific feature of Czech *lex arbitri* and Czech civil procedure, in which this [*duty to give instructions*] imposed on courts [or arbitrators, as the case may be] is considered a *principle*, thanks to the case law of the lower courts, as well as the Constitutional Court. This principle becomes all the more important in connection with consumer disputes, although it applies in arbitration generally.

| | |

II. The Nexus between the Protection of Party Autonomy in Contracting Arbitration Agreements on the One Hand and the Protection of the Weaker Party (Consumer Protection) on the Other (Judgment II. ÚS 2164/10 of the Czech Constitutional Court of 1 November 2011)

Key words:
party autonomy | natural person | jurisdictional objection | protection of the weaker party | consumer protection | legal entity | jurisdiction | proportionality | equality of the parties-arbitrator | arbitration clause | arbitration agreement | weaker party | private law | consumer | permanent arbitral institution | impermissible provision | abusive provision | constitutional principle | public interest | basic rights | stay of proceedings

Laws and Regulations Taken into Account in This Ruling:

➢ Czech Charter of Fundamental Rights and Basic Freedoms. Resolution No. 2/1993 Coll. of 16 December 1992 by the Chair of the Czech National Council, on the declaration of the Charter of Fundamental Rights and Basic Freedoms as part of the constitutional order of the Czech Republic, in the wording of Czech Constitutional Law No. 162/1998 Coll., Charter [CZE]: Article 36(1),[44] Article 38;[45]

➢ Act No. 40/1964 Coll., as subsequently amended, the Civil Code, CC [CZE]: Sec. 51a,[46] Sec. 52 et seq. (provisions concerning consumer contracts / consumer protection), in particular Sec. 55,[47] Sec. 56;[48]

---

[44]   Charter [CZE] (cit.): Chapter Five – The right to judicial and other legal protection – Article 36 – "(1) *Everyone may assert, through the prescribed procedure, their rights before an independent and impartial court or, in specified cases, another body.* (2) *Unless the law provides otherwise, a person who claims that their rights were curtailed by a decision of a public administrative authority may petition the court for a review of the legality of that decision. However, the judicial review of decisions affecting the fundamental rights and freedoms listed in this Charter may not be removed from the jurisdiction of courts.* (3) *Everyone is entitled to compensation for damage caused to them by the unlawful decision of a court, other state bodies, or public administrative authorities, or as a result of an incorrect official procedure.* (4) *Restrictions and further details are stipulated by law.*"

[45]   Charter [CZE] (cit.): Article 38 – "(1) *No one may be removed from the jurisdiction of their lawful judge.* [...]"

[46]   CC [CZE] (cit.): Sec. 51a – "*This chapter implements the pertinent regulations of the European Communities and provides the rules for the protection of consumers in consumer contracts as well as certain obligations in connection with the conclusion of consumer contracts.*"

[47]   CC [CZE] (cit.): - Sec. 55 – "(1) *The terms of consumer contracts may not deviate from the law to the detriment of the consumer. In particular, consumers cannot waive rights granted to them by law, or otherwise weaken their own contractual position.* (2) *The terms of the consumer contracts referenced in Sec. 56 shall be considered null and void.* (3) *In the event of doubt concerning the meaning of a consumer contract, that interpretation which is more advantageous for the consumer shall be favored.*"

[48]   The relevant provisions are cited in a footnote to this annotation further below. CC [CZE] (cit.): - Sec. 56 – "(1) *Consumer contracts may not contain any terms which, in conflict with the requirement of good faith and to the detriment of the consumer, represent a considerable imbalance in the rights and obligations of the parties.* (2) *The provision of paragraph (1) shall not apply to those contractual terms which define the subject of performance under the contract or its price.* (3) *In particular, the following terms are impermissible: a) terms that exclude or restrict the supplier's liability for its actions or failure to act resulting in the consumer's death or injury; b) terms that exclude or restrict the consumer's rights to claim a liability for defects or damages; c) terms that stipulate that the contract shall be binding for the consumer whilst the supplier's performance is linked to the fulfillment of a condition whose realization depends exclusively on the supplier's will; d) terms that allow the supplier to withhold performances already received from the consumer in the event that the consumer does not enter into (or withdraws from) the contract with the*

> Act No. 99/1963 Coll., Code of Civil Procedure, as amended, CCP [CZE] :Sec. 106(1)

> Act No. 216/1994 Coll., on arbitration and the enforcement of arbitral awards, as amended, ArbAct [CZE]: Sec. 1 (1), Sec. 2 (1), Sec. 4, Sec. 7 (1), Sec. 8, Sec. 11, Sec. 12, Sec. 13 (2), Sec. 31 (c);

> Constitutional Act No. 1/1993 Coll. of the Czech National Council of 16th December 1992 as amended, Constitution [CZE]: Article 90.[49]

Rationes Decidendi:

15.13. *Inter alia*, the Czech Constitutional Court drew the following **conclusions:**[50]

▶ The courts must construe procedural rules and principles primarily in terms of the spirit and purpose of the protection afforded by the fundamental rights and basic rights that are guaranteed under the Constitution.

▶ Ad hoc arbitrators must always be natural persons.

---

supplier; e) terms that entitle the supplier to withdraw from the contract without good cause under the contract or the law, but do not entitle the consumer to do the same; f) terms that entitle the supplier to terminate a contract which was concluded for an unlimited period of time for no good cause without observing an adequate notice period; g) terms that oblige the consumer to fulfill conditions with which they could not familiarize themselves prior to entering into the contract; h) terms that allow the supplier to unilaterally change the terms of the contract in the absence of any of the reasons stipulated in the contract for such a change; i) terms stipulating that the price of goods or services shall be specified only at the moment of their performance or that entitle the supplier to increase the price of goods or services without entitling the consumer to withdraw from the contract if the price agreed at the moment of conclusion of the contract is essentially exceeded at the moment of performance; j) terms that bind the consumer to fulfill all of their obligations even if the supplier failed to fulfill their own obligations that arose under the contract; k) terms that allow the supplier to assign the rights and obligations from the contract to a third party even without the consumer's consent if such assignment results in a deterioration of the collectability of the consumer's claim or the security granted for such claim."

[49] Constitution[CZE] (cit.): Article 90 – *"The task of the courts is above all to provide protection of rights, in such manner as determined by law."*

[50] The decision can be accessed on the website of the ConCourt CR [CZE]. In proceedings before the courts, the following decisions were issued:

> Resolution by the Prague 10 Municipal District Court [CZE] C 295/2009-9 of 19 October 2009,

> Resolution by the Prague Municipal Court [CZE] 22 Co 565/2009-20 of 15 June 2010.

The decision was also commented on in the literature, see for instance Jiřina Gojová, *Rozhodčí doložka ve spotřebitelské smlouvě a její ústavněprávní limity (The arbitration clause in consumer contracts and its limits under constitutional law)*, 9 (1) PRÁVNÍ FÓRUM 46-48 (2012).

▶ Transparent and unambiguous rules for determining who will act as arbitrator are a prerequisite for a valid arbitration agreement in consumer disputes.

▶ Respecting and protecting the autonomy of the parties is a deeply fundamental prerequisite for the viability of a state under the rule of law (in the substantive understanding of that term); one might speak of a "*matrix*" of the relation between the individual and the authority of the state, wherein certain "*absolute terms*" are not a part of the "bracketed expression", but extracted as invariable commonalities, "*among them the individual and specific basic rights, which have been given positivist legal definitions in response to their massive violation by authoritarian and totalitarian regimes.*" In the spirit of autonomy, parties to an arbitration agreement may voluntarily and deliberately waive their right to have disputes among them heard before an independent and impartial court.[51]

▶ The primary objective of consumer protection regulations is to protect the weaker party (i.e., the consumer); such protection being a marked trend of modern-day private law.

▶ The protection of **party autonomy** cannot be absolute in those areas in which **other fundamental rights of individuals or constitutional principles (or other constitutionally sanctioned public interests)** may **curtail party autonomy, provided that the considerations of proportionality are observed.**[52]

▶ In individual cases which concern relations between an entrepreneurial subject and a consumer, **arbitration clauses must be examined primarily in terms of the consumer's right to protection**.

▶ Also, the arbitration clause must be analyzed as to whether it might not constitute an abusive and impermissible provision – whereas it is of no concern whether or not the law (i.e., the CC [CZE]) mentions arbitration clauses in its non-exhaustive list of abusive provisions.[53]

▶ Excessive provisions are provisions which give rise to an imbalance of a disproportional degree between the parties (in terms of their respective rights and obligations) and ultimately result in the significant procedural disadvantage of one party compared to the other. This

---

[51] The Constitutional Court referred to its earlier decisions such as:
  ➢ Resolution ConCourt CR[CZE] I. ÚS 2619/08 of 18 November 2008.
  ➢ Resolution ConCourt CR[CZE] II. ÚS 805/06 of 8 January 2007.
[52] The Constitutional Court referred to its earlier decisions, namely Judgment ConCourt CR[CZE] II. ÚS 3/06 of 6 November 2007.
[53] See Sec. 56 (3) CC [CZE], as amended, which does not list the arbitration clause among the items on its indicative list of [*potentially*] abusive and thus impermissible provisions.

imbalance may also exist where disputes are decided *according to the principles of equitable discretion*, which strip the consumer of their protection under the law.

▶ The **right to a lawful judge** (Article 38 (1) of the Charter [CZE]; a right which in the common-law system is subsumed under the right to a fair trial / due process) also finds its (simplified) expression in arbitration, in the form of **transparent and unambiguous rules for determining the arbitrator.**

[Description of Facts and Legal Issues]

15.14. The parties entered into a loan agreement and an agreement on the security assignment of rights which contained an arbitration clause according to which any dispute between the parties could be heard by either one of two arbitrators listed in the agreement (depending on the arbitrator who would be approached with the request for arbitration). Specifically, the arbitration clause stipulated that "[a]*ll disputes shall be finally decided by a single arbitrator chosen by the claimant from the list of members of the Association of Arbitrators or determined by the Chairman of the Association of Arbitrators (if the claimant decides not to exercise its right of choice) in arbitration proceedings conducted pursuant to the Rules of Arbitration of the Association of Arbitrators, whereas the Parties agree that the proceedings shall be conducted solely based on written documentation, without any oral hearings, and that the dispute shall be decided according to the principles of equity*".[54] The request for arbitration was initially brought before the first of the agreed arbitrators; however this arbitrator declined the request. To date, the second of the agreed arbitrators, the Prague-based *Association of Arbitrators*, has not refused to hear the case and decide on the dispute; however, in the meantime, a claim was filed in court.

15.15. The **first-instance court** stayed the judicial proceedings in the matters of the claim for a declaration of the nullity of contract, on the grounds of a punctually filed jurisdictional objection on the grounds of the existence of an arbitration agreement.[55] The **second-instance court**, in hearing the appeal against the lower court's decision, confirmed the first-instance decision, stating that it had found no obstacles to having the case heard and decided in arbitration. According to the court, the parties had not exhausted all options for dispute resolution in

---

[54] This interpretation of the arbitration clause is adopted from the statement of reasons of the relevant ConCourt CR [CZE] judgment.

[55] See Sec. 106 (1) CCP [CZE].

arbitration proceedings (since there was no evidence that the second of the agreed arbitrators had declined to hear the case).

[Constitutional Complaint, Findings, Stated Reasons for the Decision by the Constitutional Court][56]

15.16. The complainant's core argument in its constitutional complaint was that its right to judicial protection and a fair trial pursuant to Article 36 of the Charter [CZE] had been violated, and that the courts should have heard the case pursuant to Sec. 106 (1) Sentence Two of the CCP [CZE]. According to the complainant, the arbitration clause did not stipulate that a request for arbitration would have to be filed with a second arbitrator if the first arbitrator refused to hear the case (contrary to what had been stated in the court decisions). The complainant stressed that it was impermissible that an arbitration clause should determine a *legal entity*, i.e., an *indeterminate arbitrator*, as the arbitrator, and that the arbitration clause was therefore null and void. In the complainant's view, the courts should have reflected this fact.

[Autonomy and Consumer Protection]

15.17. In its reply to the briefs by the counter-party and the accessory to proceedings, the complainant rejected the assertion that the arbitration clause represented the free expression of the will of both parties by pointing out that it had had no realistic opportunity to influence the content of the contractual obligation, and that in the case at hand, contractual autonomy had been reduced to the mere choice of signing the agreement or not, so that the equality of the parties had been merely *formal*. The complainant also invoked the poor quality of the arbitrators, and their financial dependence on the outcome of proceedings which, according to the complainant, would have rendered this particular outcome a foregone conclusion.

15.18. The Constitutional Court primarily found that the matter at hand could well constitute a consumer relationship, i.e., a consumer contract between an entrepreneurial subject and a consumer. At the same time, the Constitutional Court reiterated the view it has consistently favored in its decision-making practice – party autonomy must be enforced to the maximum extent permissible. It was therefore compelled to take the position with respect to the matter of the interdependence between the protection of autonomy on the one hand and the protection of other basic rights on the other, and in this regard concluded that the

---

[56] The other findings made by the ConCourt CR [CZE] are summarized in the introduction to this annotation.

contractual autonomy is not unlimited (absolute) in those cases in which another fundamental right, constitutional principle, or constitutionally sanctioned public interest plays a role. In the present case, the protection of the weaker party (as pursued by consumer protection regulations) represents such a principle. According to the Constitutional Court, the principle of consumer protection takes precedence over the protection of party autonomy.

[EU-compliant Interpretation of Consumer Protection Law]

15.19. Consumer protection has been transposed into Czech law, *inter alia*, based on the Directive. While the Directive has no direct horizontal effect within Czech law (i.e., no binding power between individual parties) it may still be used to accomplish an **EU-compliant interpretation of Czech law** in order to corroborate one's conclusion. Sec. 51a of the CC [CZE] is at the heart of the EU-compliant interpretation of consumer contracts.[57] For the purpose of interpretation, this provision is crucial, whereas the objective of the pertinent European legal norm (i.e., typically, an EU directive) for the purposes of an EU-compliant interpretation (or interpretation pursuant to the "*Von Colson*" principle[58]) should serve as a fundamental yardstick for courts that are concerned with the interpretation of the provisions of national (domestic) law.[59]

15.20. According to the Constitutional Court, the Directive was conceived to improve the consumer's protection against excessive contractual provisions. The point of departure for the assessment of whether an arbitration clause should be considered excessive (in the sense that it deprives the consumer of its right to file a claim in court) is the view, expressed in earlier ÚS ČR [CZE] decisions, that arbitration is not a process of finding justice, but of a supplementary interpretation of the obligation between the parties through arbitrator-made law. According to this view, arbitration serves to clarify and settle mutual rights through the arbitrator's actions on behalf of the parties, whereas the parties delegate their will to the arbitrator by way of the

---

[57] Provision cited in the introduction to this annotation.

[58] ECJ Judgment of 10 April 1984, 14/83, *Sabine von Colson* et *Elisabeth Kamann* v. *Land Nordrhein-Westfalen*, CELEX: 61983CJ0014.

[59] The Constitutional Court invokes the following ECJ judgments:
  ➢ ECJ Judgment of 10 April 1984, 14/83, *Sabine von Colson* et *Elisabeth Kamann* v. *Land Nordrhein-Westfalen*, CELEX: 61983CJ0014 and
  ➢ ECJ Judgment of 10 April 1983, 79/83, *Dorit Harz* v. *Deutsche Tradax GmbH*, CELEX: 61983J0079&lg.

arbitration agreement.[60] According to the ÚS ČR [CZE], this approach necessarily leads to the conclusion that arbitration proceedings are not of the same category or type as judicial proceedings (court proceedings). This is reflected in the generally less forgiving assessment of arbitration clauses (and their mandatory content) seeking to ensure that they do not represent excessive provisions in consumer contracts (e.g., that they do not deprive the consumer of its right to file a claim in court).

[Inconsistencies in the Reasons Given for the Judgment concerning the Nature of Arbitration, and Blatant Conflicts with Other Recent Positions of the Constitutional Court]

15.21. In the view of the author of this annotation, the conclusion drawn in the preceding paragraph is **highly surprising** – especially in relation to **Judgment I ÚS 3227/07 by the ÚS ČR [CZE] of 8 March 2011,**[61] which clearly marked a shift in the Constitutional Court's approach.

---

[60] The Constitutional Court referred to its earlier decisions, namely:
   - ➢ Resolution ConCourt CR [CZE] I. ÚS 339/02 of 26 January 2004,
   - ➢ Resolution ConCourt CR [CZE] IV. ÚS 511/0 of 5 December 2003,
   - ➢ Resolution ConCourt CR [CZE] III. ÚS 166/05 of 29 April 2005,
   - ➢ Resolution ConCourt CR [CZE] Pl. ÚS 37/08 of 28 January 2009,though one could also cite the following decisions:
   - ➢ Resolution ConCourt CR [CZE] III. ÚS 460/01 of 1 November 2001, published *in* 24 SBÍRKA NÁLEZŮ A USNESENÍ ÚSTAVNÍHO SOUDU ČR (2002), Evidentiary resolution No. 41, pp. 563 et seq.
   - ➢ Resolution ConCourt CR [CZE] IV. ÚS 174/02 of 15 July 2002, published *in* 27 SBÍRKA NÁLEZŮ A USNESENÍ ÚSTAVNÍHO SOUDU ČR (2002), Evidentiary resolution No. 20, pp. 257 et seq.; it is this resolution in particular which is invoked in most of the later decisions of the Constitutional Court prior to ConCourt CR Judgment I ÚS 3227/07 of 8 March 2011 annotated herein.
   - ➢ Resolution ConCourt CR [CZE] III. ÚS 145/03 of 12 September 2003; Resolution ConCourt CR [CZE] IV. ÚS 435/02 of 22 October 2002;
   - ➢ Resolution ConCourt CR [CZE] II. ÚS 2169/07 of 3 September 2007;
   - ➢ Resolution ConCourt CR [CZE] II. ÚS 3059/08 of 15 January 2009, among others.
   For the details, see e.g.: Alexander J. Bělohlávek, Tereza Profeldová, *supra* note 6, at 343-361; Naděžda Rozehnalová et Jan Havlíček, *supra* note 6, at 114 et seq.; Pavel Varvařovský, *supra* note 6, at 143 et seq., among others.

[61] This judgment may be accessed at the website of the Constitutional Court, at: http://nalus.usoud.cz/Search/ResultDetail.aspx?id=69584&pos=1&cnt=1&typ=result (accessed on August 26. 2011). Proceedings before the ConCourt CR[CZE] in this matter were preceded by the following decisions of Czech courts: (i) Judgment 8 Cm 164/2004-28 by the Prague Municipal Court of 29 October 2004, (ii) Judgment 8 Cmo 80/2005-42 by the Prague Upper Court of 7 October 2005, and (iii) Resolution 32 Odo 366/2006-64 by the Czech Supreme Court. The arbitral award was rendered in proceedings before the Arbitration Court attached to the Economic Chamber of the Czech Republic and the Agricultural Chamber of the Czech Republic under case ref. Rsp 352/03 on 30 April 2004.

The opinion expressed in the ÚS ČR[CZE] judgment of 8 March 2011 **constitutes a major move towards the jurisdictional theory of arbitration which understands arbitration as the search for justice by a private-law entity** in a manner that is analogous and equivalent to court proceedings and in accordance with the applicable law. In the view of this author, it was this judgment I. ÚS 3227/07 by the ÚS ČR [CZE] of 8 March 2011 which essentially overcame the contract theory of arbitration as obsolete – in line with the approach long taken by the legal community, and more or less by the courts in their standard practice[62] and thus confirmed the jurisdictional basis of arbitration (regardless of the fact that it is based on the parties' autonomy of contract). This very decision of the ÚS ČR [CZE] which states what had already been the de facto standard in arbitration itself and in the decision-making practice of the courts was essentially being confirmed and sanctioned. Specifically, in its decision of 8 March 2011 – which this author considers to be a landmark decision heading in the right direction – the Constitutional Court labeled the arbitrator (the arbitration panel) as **"another (state) body."** This classification has an impact not only on the status of the arbitrator, but on the degree to which statutory law has direct binding power over the arbitrator and on their obligation to apply statutory law.[63] It even appears that the 2nd Senate of the ÚS ČR [CZE] (which passed the decision annotated herein) had been unaware of the judgment of 8 March 2011, which was passed by the 1st Senate of the ÚS ČR [CZE], **since the two decisions are diametrically opposed in terms of capturing the essence of arbitration.** And yet, in my view, it is precisely the judgment of 8 March 2011 which very accurately and with a sure feeling for the facts reflects the actual situation in the Czech Republic, and which found a highly balanced middle ground between the actual needs fulfilled by arbitration,[64] the right to judicial protection, and the specific type of

---

[62] For that matter, even legal theory has only sporadically tended towards this understanding in modern day Czech arbitration; see e.g. Alexander J. Bělohlávek et Tomáš Pezl, *supra* note 9, at 256-261; Přemysl Raban, *supra* note 9, at 25-34. Largely dismissive or critical opinions were more common; see for instance: Richard Pecha, *supra* note 9, at 41-45; Květoslav Růžička, *supra* note 9, at 32-40, among others.

[63] For a detailed annotation of the ConCourt CR [CZE] judgment in question (*inter alia* within the context of consumer protection), see Alexander J. Bělohlávek, *Ústavní soud České republiky opustil striktní smluvní výklad koncepce rozhodčího řízení* (*The Czech Constitutional Court Abandons its Strictly Contractual Interpretation of the Concept of Arbitration*), 12 BULLETIN ADVOKACIE 40-43 (2011), as well as this volume of CYArb for the details.

[64] ConCourt CR[CZE] Judgment I. ÚS 3227/07 of 8 March 2011: *"Arbitration proceedings are a kind of civil-law proceedings. The fundamental difference between civil-*

alternative trial process which is embodied in arbitration proceedings (and which in qualitative terms serves the same role as court proceedings).[65] One must therefore ask oneself whether it is not high time for the plenary assembly of the Constitutional Court to convene in order to issue another fundamental statement regarding the nature of arbitration in the Czech Republic, since some time has passed since the last unified comment in this matter was handed down by the justices. In this context, the ÚS [CZE] judgment of 1 November 2011 (i.e., the decision annotated herein) is all the more surprising since the Constitutional Court itself states, in the statement of reasons of this judgment that arbitration involved a **delegation of the jurisdictional authority of the state** (of the courts) to private-law subjects – the arbitrators;[66] yet in the same paragraph it also claims that the decisions of arbitrators were a form of supplementary interpretation of the contractual parties' relationship through arbitrator-made law. The latter opinion negates the former, according to which "jurisdictional authority" is being "delegated"! After all, the term "supplementary interpretation of the legal relationship through arbitrator-made law" is mutually incompatible with the concept of such "jurisdictional acts" as making decisions on the "equitable application of the law," i.e., decisions on what is lawful and what is not.

15.22. This author finds it particularly excessive that in the judgment annotated herein, the ÚS ČR[CZE] should label the arbitrator a *representative of the party* of sorts. While the Constitutional Court may have merely indulged in *descriptive wording* in order to highlight the *contractual basis* which underlies arbitration proceedings, one must keep in mind the fact that **in principle arbitrators must be impartial and unbiased, which is fundamentally at odds with the position of anyone who should *represent* (= *enforce*) the interests of either party. The impartiality of the arbitrator, which rules out their acting as representatives,** is in many ways made explicit in the ArbAct[CZE] itself[67] and confirmed by extensive international practice, which in fact

---

law proceedings in court (i.e., in civil justice) is in the definition of who plays the role of the governing and decision-making body. In civil justice, this is the court; in arbitration, it is the arbitrator or a permanent arbitral institution."

[65] ConCourt CR[CZE] Judgment I. ÚS 3227/07 of 8 March 2011: *"Based on a voluntary arrangement of the parties, the arbitrator thus acts as a substitute for the (public) court which would otherwise hear and decide the matter."*And elsewhere in the same judgment, e.g.: *"Conducting proceedings before an arbitrator is not a denial of legal protection, but merely its delegation from the courts to the arbitrator."*

[66] Item (26) of the statement of reasons of the ConCourt CR[CZE] judgment.

[67] See in particular Sec. 8 ArbAct [CZE], but also Sec. 1 (1), Sec. 11, Sec. 12, and Sec. 31 (c) of the ArbAct [CZE] (whereas with the exception of Sec. 8 ArbAct [CZE], the above-

understands perfect impartiality on the part of the arbitrator to be a broadly and internationally accepted principle of arbitration.

[Proportionality of Fundamental Rights in Consumer Contracts and the Transparency Requirement]

15.23. The Constitutional Court found that the arbitration clauses in this particular case meet the criteria of excessive provision because they create an imbalance **of a disproportional degree** between the parties **(in terms of their rights and obligations)** which may ultimately lead to the substantial procedural disadvantage of one of the parties. This procedural imbalance may take the form of stripping the consumer of the protection which it is afforded under consumer protection legislation, e.g., because the dispute is decided according to equity principles.

15.24. In this regard, we ought to mention that an amendment to the ArbAct [CZE] which will come into force on 1 April 2012 proscribes decisions according to the principle of equitable discretion in consumer disputes (although the resolution of consumer disputes before an arbitrator is generally permissible, subject to fulfillment of the statutory requirements (Sec. 25 ArbAct[CZE]).[68]

---

cited provisions will not be affected by the amendment to the ArbAct [CZE], set to come into force and effect on 1 April 2012).

ArbAct [CZE] (in the wording in force on the day on which the arbitration clause was drafted, which is identical to the wording in force on the day on which the annotated ConCourt CR[CZE] judgment was passed)(cit.): Sec. 8 – "*A person who is about to be or has been selected or appointed as arbitrator must promptly notify the parties or the court of all circumstances which could give rise to legitimate doubts as to their impartiality and due to which they would be barred from acting as arbitrator.*"

On 1 April 2012, an amendment to the ArbAct [CZE] will come into force which strengthens the independence of arbitrators and amends Sec. 8 ArbAct [CZE] by replacing it with the following completely reworded passage (cit.): Sec. 8 – "*(1) An arbitrator is disqualified from hearing and deciding a matter if, with a view to their involvement in the matter or their relationship to the parties or their representatives, there is reason to doubt their impartiality. (2) A person who is about to be, or has been, selected or appointed as arbitrator must promptly notify the parties or the court of all circumstances which could give rise to legitimate doubts as to their impartiality and due to which they would be barred from acting as arbitrator. (3) Where a dispute arising from a consumer contract is to be decided, the arbitrator must notify the parties prior to the commencement of hearings of whether, over the course of the past three years, they rendered (or participated in rendering) an arbitral award (or whether they are the arbitrator in a pending arbitration proceeding) concerning a dispute involving either of the parties. The time period specified in the preceding sentence commences on the final date of the arbitration proceeding covered by such notification duty, until the commencement date of the arbitration proceeding in which the notification duty arises for the arbitrator.*"

[68] ArbAct [CZE] (in the wording in force on the day on which the arbitration clause was drafted, which is identical to the wording in force on the day on which the annotated

15.25. In the view of the Constitutional Court, the case at hand does not satisfy the criteria of a transparent understanding regarding the identity of the arbitrator (or, as the case may be, the manner in which the arbitrator will be chosen) whereas such transparency is a fundamental prerequisite for entering into an arbitration agreement in consumer disputes in the first place. Above all, the Constitutional Court pointed to the fact that in this case the arbitration clause allowed only one of the parties to choose the arbitrator and that all disputes should be finally decided by a single arbitrator chosen by the claimant from the list of members of the *Association of Arbitrators* or determined by the Chairman of the Association of Arbitrators (if the claimant decides not to exercise their right of choice) in arbitration proceedings conducted pursuant to the Rules of Arbitration of the *Association of Arbitrators,* whereas the Parties agree that proceedings should be conducted solely based on written documentation, without any oral hearings, and that the dispute should be decided according to the principles of equity. Generally speaking, arbitration proceedings regarding consumer disputes must guarantee procedural rights comparable to those which would be guaranteed in proceedings held in the absence of an arbitration agreement made with the consumer (i.e., oral hearings, fair-minded dealings, a body of appeals, absence of other obstacles to the exercise of consumer rights); however, an arbitration procedure held on the terms set out in this case would certainly *not* guarantee such procedural rights.

ConCourt CR [CZE] judgment was passed)(cit.): Sec. 25 – "[...](2) *The arbitral award must contain reasons, unless the parties have agreed that no statement of reasons is required; this also applies to arbitral awards rendered under Sec. 24 (2). (3) In making their decision, the arbitrators shall be guided by the substantive law applicable to the dispute; they may also decide the dispute at their equitable discretion / following the principles of natural equity, but only if they were expressly authorized by the parties to do so."*
On 1 April 2012, an amendment to the ArbAct [CZE] will come into force which amends Sec. 25 ArbAct [CZE] with respect to arbitration proceedings in consumer disputes by rephrasing Sec. 25 (2) and (3) ArbAct [CZE] as follows (cit.): Sec. 25 – "[...](2) *The arbitral award must contain reasons, unless the parties have agreed that no statement of reasons is required; this also applies to arbitral awards rendered under Sec. 24 (2). If the dispute has arisen from a consumer contract, the arbitral award must always contain a statement of the reasons, and instruct the parties of their right to file a request in court for setting aside the award. [...]* (3) *In making their decision, the arbitrators shall be guided by the substantive law applicable to the dispute; they may also decide the dispute at their equitable discretion / following the principles of natural equity, but only if they were expressly authorized by the parties to do so. In disputes which have arisen from a consumer contract, the arbitrators shall always be guided by consumer-protection laws and regulations."* The provision of Sec. 25 (1) ArbAct [CZE] remains unchanged. Those cases in which no "consumer contract" (i.e., a contract made by a consumer, or an agreement of the consumer-contract type) is present remain unaffected by the amendment.

Czech (& Central European) Yearbook of Arbitration

[Requirement of the Possibility of Appeals]

15.26. In the view of this author, the requirement of an *appellate instance* raised by the Constitutional Court (as the requirement of a procedural right which must supposedly be guaranteed where consumer rights are invoked) is questionable. True, Sec. 27 of the ArbAct [CZE][69] allows the parties to agree on the review of arbitral awards within the arbitration system, but this is not common practice. In fact, from a global point of view, this kind of procedure is only incorporated in national arbitration laws in a few isolated cases. The author has no intention of elaborating on whether an appellate procedure makes any sense at all in light of the fact that various commentators have found that it actually waters down the generally acknowledged benefit of arbitration – namely, the swiftness with which a final decision is rendered. Either way, the opinion of the Constitutional Court as *interpreted* in the above paragraph must be considered inherently contradictory: if the Constitutional Court generally accepts that consumer disputes may be submitted to arbitration, it cannot also demand that the arbitral award always be open to scrutiny. This is because arbitral awards should principally not be open to higher-instance reviews, and the parties agree that a review of decisions on the merits ought to remain the exception to this general rule. This, after all, is also recognized by the Czech legal framework for arbitration (*lex arbitri*). The fact is, arbitration in consumer disputes is still permissible, even under the amendment to the ArbAct [CZE] coming into force as of 1 April 2012. For this reason, this author opposes the view that a [multi-]tiered system of procedural review is an indispensable principle which would have to be upheld similarly to, say, procedural *ordre public*. True, to some extent, one may agree that decision-making according to the equity principle indeed limits the option for a review of whether those consumer rights which form the essential core of consumer protection were guaranteed in arbitration. With that in mind, though, it is remarkable that elsewhere in this judgment,[70] the Constitutional Court states that (cit.:) *"arbitration represents a 'departure' of sorts from classical court proceedings, resulting in decisions which are only to a very limited degree open to judicial*

---

[69] ArbAct [CZE] (cit.): Sec. 27 – *"The parties may agree in the arbitration agreement that the arbitral award is open to a review by other arbitrators at the request of either or both of them. Unless where specified otherwise in the arbitration agreement, the request for a review must be sent to the respective other party within 30 days from the day on which the requesting party was served the arbitral award. Reviews of arbitral awards form a part of arbitration and are subject to the provisions of this Act."*
[70] Item (28) of the statement of reasons of the ConCourt CR[CZE] judgment.

review".[71] I find it baffling that the statement of reasons of this ÚS ČR [CZE] judgment is replete with internal contradictions, inconsistencies, and deviations from other recent Constitutional Court decisions (which, by contrast, are largely consistent and show a long-term trend).

15.27. The gist of the Constitutional Court's conclusions, then, is that the arbitration clauses in question did not warrant a transparent procedure and as such were impermissible (in a consumer contract). However, parties to an arbitration clause who waive their right to judicial protection guaranteed by the state must not automatically yield to arbitrariness and caprice. Arbitral awards are enforceable decisions, and state authority thus plays a role with respect to arbitration – and state authority may only be exercised and enforced in such cases as prescribed by law, within the limits drawn by the law, and in such manner as set out in the law, always in observance of fundamental rights and basic freedoms. From the vantage point of constitutional law, an arbitration clause in a consumer contract is only permissible on the assumption that the rules for determining the arbitrator and the agreed procedural rules guarantee equal treatment of all parties. According to the Constitutional Court, this implies increased protection of the weaker party (i.e., the consumer) in cases involving a consumer relationship; it supposedly also implies that the agreed procedural rules guarantee a fair trial (including the potential review of the arbitral award by other arbitrators, as envisioned by the current act on arbitration. I have already commented on how the latter-cited implication could be called into question. This is also borne out by the amendment to the ArbAct [CZE], which represents the outcome of lengthy discussions and extensive legislative work that involved the participation of the professional community, including representatives of the judiciary, consumer protection agencies, etc. For that matter, one of the key declared objectives of the amendment to the ArbAct [CZE] (coming into force on 1 April 2012) was to stipulate mechanisms that would guarantee qualified consumer protection in arbitration.

---

[71]   With reference to Sec. 31 ArbAct [CZE], which gives an exhaustive list of reasons for which a motion for setting aside the arbitral award may be filed or, as the case may be, for which the court may quash the arbitral award.

[Right to a Lawful Judge and Rules for the Appointment of the Arbitrator]

15.28. As an *Obiter dictum*, the Constitutional Court added that arbitration clauses made within the context of consumer contracts must be reviewed with greater stringency than those outside consumer contracts, emphasizing in particular the role of transparency in the selection of the arbitrator who is to decide the dispute. Parties locked in arbitration cannot resign themselves to any old rules: as another remark in passing, the Constitutional Court declared that if one of the fundamental principles for judicial proceedings was **the right to a lawful judge** (Article 38 (1) of the Charter [CZE]), a **similar demand could also be made with respect to arbitration proceedings.** While the latter are conducted in a less formal and more straightforward manner, the objective should be to reach a fair and equitable decision, and this presupposes above all that the choice of arbitrator be governed by transparent and unambiguous rules.

15.29. Item (27) of the statement of reasons of the ÚS ČR[CZE] judgment annotated herein comes across as somewhat inarticulate. The Constitutional Court states that (cit.:) "[i]f the matter is to be decided by a subject (*legal entity*) other than a permanent arbitral institution established under the law (Sec. 13 ArbAct [CZE]), the identity of the arbitrator ought to be determined unambiguously, either by giving a specific name or by clearly determining the manner in which the arbitrator is to be chosen." The wording of this sentence suggests that "*the dispute may be decided by a legal entity.*" While *lex arbitri* does not explicitly require the arbitrator (i.e., the *person who assesses the facts and legal aspects of the case and issues an award on the merits*) to be a "natural person" (or a group of natural persons – i.e., an arbitration panel) this requirement may clearly be inferred from Sec. 4 of the ArbAct [CZE]. For that matter, in other judgments the ÚS ČR [CZE] itself has expressed the requirement that the arbitration forum be determined either by an agreement among the parties in favor of a permanent arbitral institution or a specific natural person, or by a [transparent] arrangement for selecting such a specific natural person as the arbitrator in ad hoc arbitration.[72] The Constitutional Court adds that the wording of the law[73] in this respect clearly *prefers* the requirement of an individualized (specifically defined) arbitrator (see,

---

[72] This – rather ambiguously worded - conclusion of the ConCourt CR[CZE] is even more surprising considering that the Constitutional Court had already taken a position on this issue about three weeks earlier, in resolution (ConCourt CR[CZE]) II. ÚS 3057 of 5 October 2011.

[73] Referencing Sec. 1, Sec. 2 (1), and Sec. 7 (1) ArbAct [CZE].

for instance, "[...]*disputes are decided by independent and impartial arbitrators.*"[74] "[...]*shall be decided by one or several arbitrators*[...]"[75] or "*the arbitration agreement shall as a rule also specify the number and identity of the arbitrators*"[76]). However, in coming to the conclusion of this very item, the Constitutional Court suddenly stipulates that the arbitrator *must* be a natural person. Therefore, it is not entirely clear what purpose is served by this detour taken in Item (27) of the statement of reasons. Given that an arbitral award, unlike a court decision, is open to review in only a small number of cases, based on a final and exhaustive list of grounds for which the arbitral award may be set aside,[77] must disputes in arbitration be decided by an arbitrator who was chosen according to transparent rules. In the matter at hand, however, the choice of arbitrator was based on the will of one of the parties only: the claimant was to select from a list of arbitrators kept by an entity other than a permanent arbitral institution. It is perfectly possible that the list of arbitrators at the time at which the arbitration clause was drafted could have been completely different from such list at the time at which arbitration proceedings were initiated. The choice of the arbitrator thus need not necessarily depend all that much on the will of that party who approaches such entity with their request for arbitration, but may be crucially influenced by the entity that keeps the list of arbitrators (e.g. by adding or removing specific persons to or from the list). According to the Constitutional Court, this makes a transparent choice of arbitrator impossible. The Constitutional Court remarked that the contractual autonomy of the parties who enter into an arbitration agreement is not unlimited. It also stated that the right to choose the arbitrator must not be abused for the benefit of one of the parties. The limit to the parties' autonomy in this particular case is stipulated by Article 2 (3) of the Charter LPS [CZE], according to which everyone may do that which is not prohibited by law, and nobody may be compelled to do that which is not imposed upon them by law. On the one hand, then, a right is being declared to decide freely and at one' own discretion in the way in which a given legal relationship should be open to scrutiny; on the other hand, this right is being restricted by fundamental procedural rules and principles. Thus, according to the Constitutional Court, an arrangement would be permissible under

---

[74]   Sec. 1 ArbAct [CZE].

[75]   Sec. 2 (1) ArbAct [CZE].

[76]   Sec. 7 (1) ArbAct [CZE].

[77]   From this point of view, as discussed earlier in the annotation of this ConCourt CR[CZE] judgment, the Constitutional Court's motivation behind calling for the preservation of an appeal procedure is rather unclear.

which both parties agree on the choice of the arbitrator, i.e., the choice would **not be made dependent on the will of only one of the participants** – otherwise, the contractual clause could give rise to an imbalance of the parties' respective rights and obligations. Even this conclusion, though made in passing, as *obiter dictum*, is not entirely convincing. For this, the Constitutional Court would have had to draw a clear distinction between permanent arbitral institutions and *ad hoc* arbitration (administered by a legal entity which, however, is not a permanent arbitral institution). In particular, the Constitutional Court failed to address the relevance of Sec. 7 of the ArbAct [CZE] in this context, which allows the parties to agree on a *modus operandi* for appointing the arbitrator. After all, in principle it is possible that the parties may agree on an entity (known as the appointing authority) that *chooses* the arbitrator in their stead and on their behalf – an arrangement which enjoys broad international acceptance. It is not so much the case that one could not generally accept the conclusions of the Constitutional Court in this matter, but rather that the issues which are at the heart of the constitutional complaint call for a more comprehensive assessment than that which has been performed by the Constitutional Court. The relevant question is the criteria of independence that ought to be satisfied by the *third party*, i.e., the one that selects the *independent arbitrator* who is then appointed to hear and decide the dispute. The criteria for this independence on the part of the appointing authority and, above all, how these criteria are safeguarded should be the most important points to consider. Sadly however, the Constitutional Court fails to address this. Equally debatable is the Constitutional Court's conclusion that choosing an arbitrator from a list of arbitrators was in conflict with constitutional transparency principles. That the selection of arbitrators should be limited by certain restrictions is nothing extraordinary. Although several permanent foreign arbitral institutions have recently abandoned the practice of keeping *lists of arbitrators*, this practice remains relatively common in the countries of Central and Eastern Europe. The Constitutional Court's opinion that the possibility of changes in such *lists of arbitrators* between the conclusion of the arbitration agreement and the commencement of proceedings (appointment of the arbitrator) was of material importance is hard to accept. For one, such changes are only natural. Besides, they in no way interfere with the requirement under the law that the arbitrator (even if chosen from a list of arbitrators) must meet the criterion of impartiality. After all, what *is* of relevance is that the impartiality of the *appointing authority*, thus warranting the choice of an independent and impartial arbitrator. Of course, one may concur that restricting the right of appointment of the arbitrator (or even the opportunity to have influence on the choice of the arbitrator) by granting this right or opportunity to only one of the parties is in conflict with the basic principles governing arbitration. Whether this is the case in a specific matter or whether the requirement of equal standing of the parties is satisfied must be assessed based on the specific circumstances of the individual case. However, one must also keep in mind those cases in which the defendant is inactive, so that ultimately the appointment of the arbitrator can only be performed by one of the parties. This would concern a situation in which the arbitration clause stipulates a *sufficient and adequate time period* during which the defendant must respond to the claimant's proposal, and in which the failure to do so (i.e., the defendant neither acknowledges nor rejects the proposal) triggers the legal fiction of consent. However, this arrangement would have to be expressly agreed between the parties, and one would have to ensure that the counterparty is given a sufficient and adequate opportunity to consider the proposal. In other words, arbitration recognizes the complete opposite of the civil-law principle according to which *silence does* not *mean consent.* This is because such a procedure is perfectly compatible with the proportionality requirement, since one has to concede that there exists a legitimate interest in preventing the defendant from delaying the hearing and decision of a dispute. Beyond that, one will undoubtedly admit that in the case of consumer relationships, the test of whether proportionality has been preserved will have to be especially stringent. What is surprising, however, is that the Constitutional Court did not even ask or answer these questions, but instead expressed opinions which, with all due respect, may well be called perfunctory, and internally inconsistent as well as inconsistent with the recent position of the ÚS ČR[CZE] itself. The ultimate ruling reached by the Constitutional Court in this specific matter is without doubt worthy of approval, but as we have seen above – and to the bafflement of the author – there are many aspects in which this decision is excessive, and starkly different from the otherwise consistent and balanced decision-making practice of the ÚS ČR[CZE].

| | |

III. *Ad Hoc* Arbitration versus Proceedings before Permanent Arbitral Institutions (Resolution of the High Court in Prague, Case No. 12 Cmo 496/2008 of 28 May 2009)

Key words:
natural person | costs of proceedings | legal person | jurisdiction of a permanent arbitral institution | arbitrator | arbitration clause | ad hoc arbitrator | arbitration agreement | rules of the permanent arbitral institution | permanent arbitral institution | statutes and rules of permanent arbitral institution | hearing | method of appointment of arbitrator

Laws and Regulations Taken into Account in This Ruling:

➢ Act No. 216/1994 Coll., on Arbitration, as subsequently amended, ArbAct [CZE]: Section 2, Section 4, Section 7, Section 13;[78]

➢ Act No. 40/1964 Coll., Civil Code, as subsequently amended, CC [CZE]: Section 39;[79]

➢ Act [of the Czech Republic] No. 513/1991 Coll., the Commercial Code, as subsequently amended, ComC [CZE]: Section 269(3);[80]

➢ Act No. 99/1963 Coll., the Code of Civil Procedure, as subsequently amended. CCP[CZE]: Section 106(1).[81]

Rationes Decidendi:

15.30. In their arbitration agreement, the parties must agree on (an) *ad hoc* arbitrator(s) or on a permanent arbitral institution established under the law (Section 2(1) of the ArbAct). An *ad hoc* arbitrator or arbitrators, should there be more than one, always (a) natural person(s)[82] may be identified directly in the arbitration agreement, or

---

[78] The provisions are quoted in other annotations of Czech [CZE] case law in this CYArb edition.

[79] CC [CZE] (cit.): Section 39 – *"A legal act is invalid if the content or purpose thereof violates or evades the law or is inconsistent with good morals."*

[80] ComC [CZE] (cit.): Section 269 – *"[...] (3) The agreement on certain parts of the contract may be replaced with an agreement of the parties on the manner of the subsequent determination of the subject of the obligation, provided this manner does not depend on the will of one party only. If the missing part of the contract is to be determined by the court or a designated party, the agreement must be executed in writing, and Section 291 shall similarly apply."*

[81] The provision is quoted in other annotations of Czech [CZE] case law in this CYArb edition.

[82] Section 4 of the ArbAct [CZE].

the arbitration agreement may define their number and method of appointment.[83]

15.31. The determination of the method of appointment of arbitrators may only be interpreted as the determination of a method of appointment that does not depend exclusively on the will of one party, as the principle is articulated in Section 269(3) of the ComC.

As opposed to arbitrators appointed *ad hoc*, permanent arbitral institutions may issue their own rules (statutes and rules) that set forth the process of appointment, determine the number of arbitrators (the arbitrators can be selected from a list) and stipulate the manner in which the arbitrators case manage the proceedings and the costs of arbitration payable by the parties. These Rules (statutes and rules) must be published in the Business Journal and the arbitrators' decisions are rendered pursuant to the above mentioned Rules of the permanent arbitral institution applicable on the day the request for arbitration is filed with the arbitral institution.

15.32. Unless the parties agree otherwise, the permanent arbitral institution shall follow these Rules. A permanent arbitral institution follows its own Rules (statutes and rules) published in the Business Journal, unless the parties agree otherwise. If an entity other than a permanent arbitral institution established under a special law, as anticipated under Section 13 of the ArbAct [CZE] carries out activities which, according to the ArbAct [CZE], are reserved for permanent arbitral institutions, it shall be deemed as intending to evade the law and its conduct shall be deemed **contra legem**.

15.33. An entity other than a permanent arbitral institution (Section 13 of the ArbAct [CZE]) is not entitled to issue its own statutes and rules for governing the case management of proceedings and set forth provisions (binding on the parties and applicable unless the parties agree otherwise) which provide for the costs of proceedings and the remuneration of the arbitrators.

15.34. The fact that arbitration principally involves (oral) hearings (Section 19(3) of the ArbAct [CZE]) is, from the procedural perspective, a very important requirement. If the proceedings are to be conducted on the basis of written submissions (despite the fact that the arbitrators may summon the parties to an oral hearing, if necessary) such procedure must be explicitly agreed in the arbitration agreement. Only proceedings before a permanent arbitral institution permit such procedure to be agreed by a mere reference to the statutes (rules) of this permanent arbitral institution.

---

[83] Section 7(1) of the ArbAct [CZE].

[Factual and Legal Circumstances of the Case]

15.35. The plaintiff appealed against the resolution terminating the proceedings; the plaintiff argued that a bill of exchange (promissory note) belonged to the category of abstract securities (negotiable instruments) and, as such, contained no arbitration clause. The plaintiff (appellant) argued that the trial court had erroneously inferred that an arbitration clause incorporated in a contract also covered the relationship established by the bill of exchange.

15.36. The appellate court set aside the resolution terminating the proceedings. However, it focused on the issue of the validity of the arbitration clause (arbitration agreement) as a preliminary question. It determined that the entity (legal person / *XY s.r.o.*) to which the arbitration agreement referred was not a permanent arbitral institution. The appellate court therefore proceeded to the issue of whether the parties had agreed in their arbitration clause that their dispute was to be resolved by (an) arbitrator(s) appointed *ad hoc*. Only a positive answer to this question would preserve the validity of the arbitration agreement; the court maintained that the parties had to either agree on an *ad hoc* arbitrator or on the jurisdiction of a permanent arbitral institution.

15.37. The court stressed that the parties had not agreed on any particular arbitrator but had authorized the party that filed the petition with [*XY s.r.o.*] to choose a single arbitrator from a list of arbitrators administered by such company. However, the right to maintain a list of arbitrators is reserved exclusively for permanent arbitral institutions, not an entity that does not belong to that category. It is also necessary to point out that the determination of the method of appointment of arbitrator must be interpreted only as a determination of a method of appointment that does not depend exclusively on the will of one party, as the principle is articulated in Section 269(3) of the ComC [CZE].[84]

[Arguments of the Court]

15.38. The court therefore concluded that in the present case the parties had not agreed on the jurisdiction of a permanent arbitral institution or on an *ad hoc* arbitrator. Nor had they agreed on a permanent arbitral institution or, as mentioned above. The court also held that considering the conduct and rules adopted by [*XY s.r.o.*], the entity assumed the powers ("copied" the activities) of a permanent arbitral institution thus evading Section 13 of the ArbAct. Consequently, if the arbitration

---

[84] The author believes that a reference to Section 7 of the ArbAct [CZE] would be more suitable.

agreement lacks any direct identification of an *ad hoc* arbitrator or a specific description of the method of his or her appointment, and merely refers, as concerns the selection of the arbitrator and determination of the rules of arbitration, to a legal entity other than a permanent arbitral institution established under the law, and statutes and rules adopted by that corporation which provided for the appointment and selection of arbitrators, as well as the case management of arbitration and the rules governing the costs of proceedings, the arbitration agreement is invalid pursuant to Section 39 of the CC, because it evades the law. The arbitration agreement in the present case is therefore invalid and it is not necessary to examine whether the invalid arbitration agreement also covered disputes related to the contested bill of exchange. Since the arbitration agreement is invalid, the court is obliged to hear the pertinent property dispute pursuant to Section 106(1) of the CCP.

| | |

IV. Arbitration Clause Harming "Weaker" Contracting Party; Permanent Arbitral Institutions versus "Ad hoc" Arbitrators (Resolution of SC CR [CZE], Case No. 31 Cdo 1945/2010 of 11 May 2011)

Key words:
real estate | invalidity | invalid legal act | number of arbitrators | legal act | arbitrator | "ad hoc" arbitrator | arbitration clause | Rules on Arbitration | arbitration agreement | list of arbitrators | weaker contracting party | permanent arbitral institution | appointment of arbitrator | (ownership) title

Laws and Regulations Taken into Account in This Ruling:
➢ Act No. 40/1964 Coll., as subsequently amended, Civil Code, CC [CZE]: Section 39;
➢ Act No. 216/1994 Coll., on Arbitration, as subsequently amended, ArbAct [CZE]: Section 2(1),[85] Section 4,[86] Section 7(1),[87] Section 13,[88] and Section 19.[89]

---

[85] Quoted below.
[86] Quoted below.
[87] ArbAct [CZE] (as applicable on the day this arbitration clause was concluded, cit.): "Section 7 – (1) *An arbitration agreement should, as a rule, determine the number of*

Rationes Decidendi:

The Supreme Court reached the following conclusions in the present case:[90]

15.39. The principle of **party autonomy must not** be (mis-)used to negate [the consequences consisting in the invalidity] of arbitration clauses that violate the law and that **clearly indicate an intention to harm the**

---

arbitrators and their identity, or stipulate the method whereby the number and the identity of the arbitrators shall be determined. The final number of arbitrators must always be odd [...]".

With effect from 1 April 2012, an Amendment to the ArbAct [CZE] also partially modifies (supplements) Section 7 of the ArbAct [CZE]; the respective provision, as amended by the Amendment to the ArbAct [CZE], reads as follows (cit.): Section 7 – "(1) *An arbitration agreement should, as a rule, determine the number of arbitrators and their identity, or stipulate the method whereby the number and the identity of the arbitrators shall be determined. The arbitrator may also be appointed by a person agreed upon by the parties or following a method of appointment specified in the rules on arbitration pursuant to Section 19(4). The final number of arbitrators must always be odd* [...]".

88   Quoted below.

89   ArbAct [CZE] (as applicable on the day this arbitration clause was concluded, cit.): "Section 19 – (1) *The parties have a right to agree on how the arbitrators shall case manage the proceedings. Matters regarding the case management of the proceedings may be resolved by the chairman of the tribunal, provided he or she was authorized to do so by the parties or by all arbitrators. (2) Unless the parties negotiated an agreement pursuant to Subsection (1), the arbitrators shall case manage the proceedings in any manner they see fit. They case manage the arbitral proceedings in such manner that the facts of the case necessary for the resolution of the dispute are sufficiently ascertained, without any unnecessary formalities and while giving all parties equal opportunity to plead their case. (3) Unless the parties agree otherwise, the arbitral proceedings shall be oral. These proceedings are always confidential.*"

With effect from 1 April 2012, an Amendment to the ArbAct [CZE] modifies Section 19 of the ArbAct [CZE] by amending Subsection (2) of Section 19 of the ArbAct [CZE] and inserting a new Subsection (4) in Section 13 of the ArbAct [CZE] as follows (cit.): Section 19 – "[...] (2) *Unless the parties negotiated an agreement pursuant to Subsection (1) or unless the procedure is determined pursuant to Subsection (4), the arbitrators shall case manage the proceedings in any manner they see fit. They case manage the arbitral proceedings in such manner that the facts of the case necessary for the resolution of the dispute are sufficiently ascertained, without any unnecessary formalities and while giving all parties equal opportunity to plead their case. [...] (4) The parties may also determine the procedure to be followed in the rules regulating the arbitral proceedings, provided the rules are included with the arbitration agreement, without prejudice to the application of rules adopted by a permanent arbitral institution.*" Subsections (1) and (3) of Section 19 of the ArbAct [CZE] remain unamended.

90   Available on the website of the SC CR [CZE]: http://www.nsoud.cz/ JudikaturaNS_new/judikatura_prevedena2.nsf/WebSearch/35D7A1839F99F5BAC125789 9002EA885?openDocument (accessed on January 12, 2011). Also published *in* (121) SBÍRKA SOUDNÍCH ROZHODNUTÍ (2011). Cited, for instance, *in* Miloš Tomsa, *K problematice právní úpravy rozhodčího řízení* (*Regarding Laws on Arbitration*), 3 (9) OBCHODNĚPRÁVNÍ REVUE 267-270, 269 (2011). This decision is also referred to in certain later rulings, for instance, in the Resolution of the SC CR [CZE], Case No. 30 Cdo 4415/2010 of 27 July 2011, etc.

"weaker" contracting party (a party to the contractual relationship).[91] A democratic country honouring the principle of the rule of law must not give up on the protection of rights and legitimate interests that could be jeopardized in alternative proceedings conducted instead of litigation. If the arbitration agreement lacks any direct identification of an *ad hoc* arbitrator, or a specific description of the method of his or her appointment, and refers to *"Rules on Arbitration"* issued by a legal entity (corporation) other than a permanent arbitral institution established under the law, the arbitration agreement is invalid pursuant to Section 39 of the CC [CZE].[92]

15.40. Section 2(1) of the ArbAct [CZE][93] provides that an arbitration agreement (or a clause incorporated in the main contract, as the case may be) must include the parties' agreement on either (an) *"ad hoc"* arbitrator(s) or a permanent arbitral institution established under the law.

The *ad hoc* arbitrator must always be a natural person (Section 4 of the ArbAct [CZE][94]).

---

[91] The SC CR [CZE] held that this was the case here.

[92] This *ratio decidendi* was adopted from the database of the SC CR [CZE] (in the section regarding the decision published on the court's website). CC [CZE] (cit.): Section 39 – *A legal act is invalid if the content or the purpose thereof violates or evades the law or is inconsistent with good morals.*

[93] ArbAct [CZE] (as applicable on the day this arbitration clause was concluded, cit.): Section 2 – *"(1) The parties may agree that their disputes over property, except disputes arising from the enforcement of decisions and except incidental disputes, which would otherwise fall within the jurisdiction of the courts, shall be decided by one or more arbitrators or by a permanent arbitral institution (arbitration agreement)."*
With effect from 1 April 2012, an Amendment to the ArbAct [CZE] also partially modifies (supplements) Section 2(1) of the ArbAct [CZE]; the respective provision, as amended by the Amendment to the ArbAct [CZE], reads as follows (cit.): Section 2 – *"[...] (1) The parties may agree that their disputes over property, except disputes arising from the enforcement of decisions and except incidental disputes, which would otherwise fall within the jurisdiction of the courts or which can be submitted to arbitration under special laws, shall be decided by one or more arbitrators or by a permanent arbitral institution (arbitration agreement).[...]"*.

[94] ArbAct [CZE] (as applicable on the day this arbitration clause was concluded, cit.): Part Two – Arbitrators – Section 4 – *"(1) Any citizen of the Czech Republic who is of legal age and has legal capacity can serve as an arbitrator, unless a special law stipulates otherwise. (2) A foreigner can serve as an arbitrator if he or she has legal capacity under the laws of his or her country; it shall suffice, however, if he or she has legal capacity under the laws of the Czech Republic."*
With effect from 1 April 2012, an Amendment to the ArbAct [CZE] modifies Section 4 of the ArbAct [CZE] with respect to arbitration in consumer disputes; the entire Section 4 of the ArbAct [CZE] is amended as follows (cit.): Section 4 – *"(1) Any citizen of the Czech Republic who is of legal age, has no criminal record and has legal capacity can serve as an arbitrator, unless a special law stipulates otherwise. (2) A foreigner may serve as an*

15.41. The *ad hoc* arbitrator(s) must be identified [by his, her or their name(s)], or the arbitration agreement (arbitration clause) may define, in compliance with Section 7(1) of the ArbAct [CZE], the method of appointment and the number of arbitrators. As opposed to ad hoc appointed arbitrators, [only] permanent arbitral institutions may issue their own rules (statutes and rules), which may set forth the process of appointment and determine the number of arbitrators (the arbitrators can be selected from a list), as well as stipulate the manner whereby the arbitrators shall case manage the proceedings and the costs of arbitration payable by the parties. Such rules must be published in the Business Journal.

15.42. If an entity other than a permanent arbitral institution established under a special law (Section 13 of the ArbAct [CZE]) carries out activities that, according to the ArbAct [CZE], are reserved for permanent arbitral institutions, logic dictates that this entity clearly and intentionally violates the law.

15.43. **Proceedings before a permanent arbitral institution also allow** the parties to agree **to deviate from the rules adopted by the permanent arbitral institution.** Unless the parties agree otherwise, the arbitrator(s) shall follow the rules adopted by the permanent arbitral institution, as applicable on the day the request for arbitration is filed with the arbitral institution.

[Description of Facts, Legal Findings and Decisions of Trial Court and Appellate Court]

15.44. The parties entered into a real estate purchase contract (real estate transfer contract); the contract contained an arbitration clause. The arbitration clause stipulated that "[*a*]*ny and all disputes that arise or could arise between the parties or any other claims shall be resolved in arbitration before a single arbitrator, in compliance with Act No. 216/1994 Coll., pursuant to the Rules on Arbitration and the Tariff adopted by* [XY, s.r.o.];[95] *the valid version of these documents is available at the website of the abovementioned association of*

---

arbitrator if he or she meets the condition of majority, no criminal record and legal capacity; the requirement of legal capacity shall be governed by the person's lex personae. It shall suffice, however, if he or she has legal capacity under the laws of the Czech Republic. (3) In order to meet the requirement of no criminal record under Subsections (1) and (2), the person must have no previous final and conclusive conviction for a criminal offence, unless the person's criminal record is expunged and the person is deemed never to have been convicted. (4) An arbitrator designated by an arbitration clause to resolve disputes arising from consumer contracts must be registered on the list of arbitrators administered by the Ministry of Justice (the "Ministry")."

[95] Made anonymous by the author. The decision mentions a specific entity.

arbitrators."[96] The important thing is that [XY, s.r.o.] is not an entity that could be classified as a permanent arbitral institution pursuant to Section 13 of the ArbAct [CZE].[97]

15.45. The subject matter of the dispute was the determination of the (ownership) title to the real estate; the plaintiff argued that the purchase contract was invalid. The District Court in Frýdek Místek, as the trial court, terminated the proceedings initiated by the petition for the determination of the (ownership) title to the particular piece of real estate[98] filed with said court; the reason for termination was a timely jurisdictional challenge. The RC in Ostrava [CZE], as the appellate court, upheld the trial court's decision.[99] An arbitration clause covers not only the rights arising from legal relationships established directly by the contract, but also the issue of the legal validity of these relationships, as well as the rights associated therewith. If the

---

[96] The arbitration agreement is not available. Adopted from the interpretation articulated in the reasons supporting the resolution of the SC CR [CZE], in the part summarizing the contents of the plaintiff's cassation appeal; the text is *reconstructed* from the information regarding various parts of this arbitration clause.

[97] ArbAct [CZE] (as applicable on the day this arbitration clause was concluded, cit.): Section 13 – "(1) *Permanent arbitral institutions can only be established under the law.* (2) *Permanent arbitral institutions can issue their own statutes and rules, which must be published in the Business Journal; these statutes and rules may determine the method of appointment and the number of arbitrators, and may stipulate that the arbitrators shall be selected from a list administered by the permanent arbitral institution. The statutes and rules may also determine how the arbitrators shall case manage the proceedings and render their decisions, and resolve other issues connected with the activities of the permanent arbitral institution and the arbitrators, including rules regulating the costs of proceedings and remuneration of arbitrators.* (3) *If the parties agreed on the jurisdiction of a particular permanent arbitral institution and failed to agree otherwise in the arbitration agreement, they shall be deemed to have submitted to the regulations specified in Subsection (2), as applicable on the day the request for arbitration is filed with the permanent arbitral institution.*"

With effect from 1 April 2012, an Amendment to the ArbAct [CZE] modifies Section 13 of the ArbAct [CZE] by amending Subsection (1) and inserting a new Subsection (4) in Section 13 of the ArbAct [CZE] as follows (cit.): Section 13 – "Permanent Arbitral Institutions – "(1) *Permanent arbitral institutions can only be established by another law or if their formation is explicitly allowed by another law.* [...] (4) *No entity may carry out its activities using a name that evokes a misleading impression that the entity is a permanent arbitral institution under this law, unless a different law or regulation or an international agreement integrated in the legal system authorizes the entity to use the name.*" Subsections (2) and (3) of Section 13 of the ArbAct [CZE] remain (even after the Amendment to the ArbAct [CZE]) unamended.

[98] Resolution of the District Court in Frýdek Místek [CZE], Case No. 15 C 238/2008-18 of 2 February 2009.

[99] Resolution of the Regional Court in Ostrava [CZE], Case No. 57 Co 150/2009-51 of 15 February 2010.

arbitration agreement is included in a real estate purchase contract (real estate transfer contract), the arbitration clause also covers disputes over the determination of the (ownership) title to the real estate.

[Cassation Appeal]

15.46. In her cassation appeal, the plaintiff argued, *inter alia*, that the courts had erroneously interpreted the first sentence of Section 7(1) of the ArbAct [CZE]. The plaintiff emphasized that the parties had only agreed on the number of arbitrators (a single arbitrator), without identifying any particular arbitrator. If we applied the second part of the sentence in Section 7(1) of the ArbAct [CZE] to the present case, then considering the relevant arbitration clause, we could conclude that the parties had neither agreed on the method of determining the number of arbitrators nor the method of identifying the individual arbitrators. The signing of the purchase contract containing the arbitration clause does not imply that the plaintiff became acquainted with the "Rules on Arbitration and the Tariff of [XY, s.r.o.]", to which the arbitration clause refers. The plaintiff therefore claimed that the arbitration clause violated Section 2(1) of the ArbAct [CZE] and Section 7(1) of the ArbAct [CZE] and was an invalid legal act. The plaintiff also argued that if her petition on the merits invoked the invalidity of the purchase contract, it simultaneously implied that the plaintiff had raised the defence of the invalidity of the arbitration clause contained therein.

15.47. The plaintiff also argued that in criminal proceedings conducted before the same court,[100] a connection had transpired between the legal counsel for the defendant and [X.Y., s.r.o.] in other similar cases, which unacceptably violates the principle of impartiality of any eventual arbitral proceedings. The plaintiff claims that her conclusion regarding the invalidity of the purchase contract itself is supported by the acts of a particular natural person [M.T.], for which the person was convicted;[101] the person is still being prosecuted for another part of the committed act relating to the subject matter of the purchase contract. The plaintiff also emphasized that she could not abide by the *Rules on Arbitration and the Tariff* issued by an entity that was not authorized to do so because it was not a permanent arbitral institution. The plaintiff therefore challenged the legal conclusions of the appellate court as concerns the validity of the arbitration agreement.

---

[100] District Court in Frýdek Místek, Case No. 1 T 97/2008; the status of the proceedings has not been specified.

[101] Judgment of the District Court in Frýdek – Místek [CZE], Case No. 80 T 127/2009 of 3 February 2010. It is not clear whether the decision is final.

[Decision of Cassation Court and Cassation Court's Arguments]

15.48. The three-member Panel No. 30 of the SC CR [CZE], which was called upon to hear and decide the cassation appeal according to the court's schedule, arrived at a legal opinion deviating from the preceding decisions.[102] The Supreme Court of the CR [CZE] concluded that the decision of the appellate court was not correct.

15.49. The Supreme Court of the CR [CZE] analysed the issue of whether the arbitration clause in the present case required the resolution of the eventual dispute between the parties to be entrusted to (an) *ad hoc* arbitrator(s); the Supreme Court highlighted that both the trial court and the appellate court in the present case had actually answered the question in the affirmative (despite no detailed analysis of said issue).

15.50. At the same time, the Supreme Court emphasized that we could not dismiss the fact that the selection of the respective arbitrator was subjected to the regime of [X.Y., s.r.o.], which, however, had never been authorized to issue statutes and rules that would, *inter alia*, regulate the way in which the arbitrator(s) case manage(s) the arbitral proceedings or determine the method of appointment of the arbitrator(s), etc. [X.Y., s.r.o.] is a corporation; the line of business of that corporation in the

---

[102] Judgment of the SC CR [CZE], Case No. 32 Cdo 2312/2007 of 21 January 2009. In said decision, the cassation court adopted, *inter alia*, a legal opinion according to which *"[i]f the appellate court in the given case held that the terms of the arbitration agreement had been validly contracted by reference to the rules specified therein (Rules of Arbitration Procedure adopted by Společnost pro rozhodčí řízení a.s.), such a provision appears, to say the least, as a vague and ambiguous provision, in that the rules were made for ad hoc arbitral proceedings and were not incorporated in the arbitration agreement and, as opposed to statutes issued by permanent arbitral institutions (Section 13(2) of the ArbAct), these rules were not published in the Business Journal."* The opinion voiced in said decision corresponds to the Resolution of the High Court in Prague, Case No. 12 Cmo 496/2008 of 28 May 2009, annotated elsewhere in this book.

However, this decision was preceded by another decision, namely Resolution of the SC CR [CZE], 32 Cdo 2282/2008 of 31 July 2008, which reads as follows (cit.): *"The parties to the agreement may validly agree that the disputes arising from their agreement will be decided by an arbitrator selected by the plaintiff/complainant from a list of arbitrators administered by a private entity other than a permanent arbitral institution established within the meaning of Section 13 [ArbAct /CZE/], and that the arbitral proceedings will follow the rules adopted by such a private entity."*

See also, for instance: An overview of decisions rendered by the Supreme Court of the CR in 2010 that were not selected for publication in *Sbírka soudních rozhodnutí a stanovisek (Court Reports)*, 17 (2) SOUDNÍ ROZHLEDY 41-47, 44 (2011); Jan Kocina, *Rozhodčí doložky sjednané ve prospěch "soukromých rozhodčích soudů" (Arbitration Clauses Agreed for the Benefit of "Private Arbitral Tribunals")*, 7-8 BULLETIN ADVOKACIE 48-49 (2011); Tomáš Sokol, *K aktuálním problémům rozhodčího řízení (Regarding Current Problems in Arbitration)*, 19 (9) PRÁVNÍ RÁDCE 4-14, 9 et al. (2011).

decisive period was specified as follows: consultancy services for arbitrators in arbitration, services provided by organizational and economic consultants relating to the services for arbitrators and arbitration, agency services for arbitrators and arbitration.

15.51. The Supreme Court classified such a situation, i.e. when entities other than permanent arbitral institutions issue their own rules that also provide for the method of appointment of arbitrators, as a manifest imposition of conditions that raise reasonable doubts as to the perspective of independent and impartial dispute resolution. The court also held that we could not postulate that the parties had perhaps agreed to have their eventual dispute resolved by an *ad hoc* arbitrator, because no such arbitrator was identified in the arbitration agreement, or rather the arbitration agreement contained no clear terms, in compliance with the law, that would provide for the method of selecting the respective arbitrator; the already mentioned reference (and a very general reference at that) to the rules adopted by [X.Y., s.r.o.] cannot be accepted as an alternative (substitute) method of appointing the *ad hoc* arbitrator due to the reasons specified above. The SC CR [CZE] held that the respective arbitration clause had been a clear attempt to harm the weaker contracting party. This is the first case in which such an opinion was explicitly voiced, at the general level, with respect to arbitration agreements, i.e. not only in connection with contracts concluded by consumers. Although we do not know any details regarding the terms of the main contract concluded in the present case, it might prove difficult to infer that the contract was a typical so-called consumer contract. Consequently, the Supreme Court based its conclusions not on the special protection afforded to consumers, but on general legal principles [civil-law principles], which constitute a principle superior to the special protection of consumers (though not endowed with higher force).

15.52. The trial court's decision and the appellate court's decision were both set aside, and the case was remanded to the trial court for a new hearing.

| | |

V. Consumer Protection and Independent and Impartial Arbitration (Resolution of Constitutional Court of Czech Republic, Case No. II. ÚS 3057/10 of 5 October 2011)

Key words:
absolute invalidity | autonomy | autonomy of will | expression of will | invalidity | unfair terms | unfairness | company name | restriction of the access to court | unfairness of arbitration clause | voidability | equal rights | arbitrator | arbitration clause | arbitral tribunal | freedom of contract | consumer | consumer contract | permanent arbitral institution | free will | appointment of arbitrator

Laws and Regulations Taken into Account in This Ruling:

➤ European Convention on Human Rights (Convention): Article 6(1);

➤ Charter of Rights and Freedoms of the Czech Republic,[103] Charter [CZE]: Article 2(3), Article 36(1);[104]

➤ Act No. 40/1964 Coll., as subsequently amended, the Civil Code, CC [CZE]: Section 52 et seq. (provisions regulating consumer contracts/consumer protection), primarily Sections 52, 55, 56;[105]

➤ Act No. 216/1994 Coll., on Arbitration, as subsequently amended,[106] ArbAct [CZE]: Section 2,[107] Section 13, Section 19, Section 25(3);

---

[103] Resolution of the Presidium of the Czech National Council No. 2/1993 Coll. of 16 December 1992 on the promulgation of the Charter of Fundamental Rights and Freedoms as a part of the constitutional order of the Czech Republic, as amended by the Constitutional Act of the Czech Republic No. 162/1998 Coll.

[104] Charter [CZE] (cit.): Chapter Five – The Right to Judicial and Other Legal Protection – Article 36 – "(1) *Everyone may assert, through the legally prescribed procedure, his or her rights before an independent and impartial court, or in specified cases, before a different authority. (2) Unless the law provides otherwise, any person who claims that his or her rights were curtailed by a decision of a public administrative authority may turn to a court for a review of the legality of that decision. However, the judicial review of decisions affecting the fundamental rights and basic freedoms listed in this Charter may not be removed from the jurisdiction of courts. (3) Everyone is entitled to compensation for damage or losses sustained by him or her as a result of an unlawful decision of a court, another state authority, or a public administrative authority, or as a result of an incorrect official procedure. (4) Conditions and detailed provisions are laid down by statute.*"

[105] The applicable provisions are quoted in a footnote below.

[106] Without the changes introduced by the amendment to the ArbAct [CZE], which takes effect on 1 April 2012.

[107] ArbAct [CZE] (as applicable on the day this arbitration clause was concluded, cit.): Section 2 – "(1) *The parties may agree that their disputes over property, except disputes*

> Council Directive 93/13/EEC of 5 April 1993 on unfair terms in consumer contracts, Directive:Article 3, Article 6(1), par. 1(q) of the Annex to the Directive;

> Constitutional Act No. 1/1993 Coll. of the Czech National Council of 16th December 1992 as amended,Constitution CR [CZE]: Article 2(4).

Rationes Decidendi:

The Constitutional Court of the Czech Republic arrived at the following conclusions, *inter alia:*[108]

15.53. The Constitutional Court [CZE] has repeatedly **stressed the principle of freedom of contract, also in relation to arbitration clauses, which – when incorporated in laws and regulations – are not considered a restriction of the access to court,** i.e. not a violation of Article 36(1) of the Charter.[109] However, it is desirable for **the waiver of the right to have the dispute reviewed by a court to be permissible, unambiguous**

---

arising from the enforcement of decisions and except incidental disputes, which would otherwise fall within the jurisdiction of the courts, shall be decided by one or more arbitrators or by a permanent arbitral institution (arbitration agreement). (2) The arbitration agreement will be valid if the law allows the parties to resolve their dispute (the subject matter of the agreement) by settlement. (3) The arbitration agreement can provide for (a) *an individual and already existing dispute (agreement on arbitrator), or* (b) *all disputes that would arise from a particular legal relationship or a specified category of legal relationships in the future (arbitration clause). (4) Unless the arbitration agreement stipulates otherwise, it governs both the rights directly arising from the legal relationships and the issue of legal validity of these legal relationships, as well as any rights associated with the aforementioned rights. (5) The arbitration agreement is also binding on the legal successors to the parties, unless explicitly excluded by the parties in their agreement."*

[108] The decision is available on the website of the ConCourt CR [CZE]. The litigation involved the following decisions:

> Resolution of the District Court for Prague 2 [CZE], Case No. 18 C 218/2009-59 of 29 October 2010,

> Resolution of the Municipal Court in Prague [CZE], Case No. 58 Co 332/2010 of 16 July 2010.

[109] Charter [CZE] (cit.): Chapter Five – The Right to Judicial and Other Legal Protection – Article 36 – "(1) *Everyone may assert, through the legally prescribed procedure, his or her rights before an independent and impartial court, or in specified cases, before a different authority. (2) Unless the law provides otherwise, a person who claims that his or her rights were curtailed by a decision of a public administrative authority may turn to a court for a review of the legality of that decision. However, the judicial review of decisions affecting the fundamental rights and basic freedoms listed in this Charter may not be removed from the jurisdiction of courts* [Charter /CZE/]. *(3) Everybody is entitled to compensation for damage sustained by him or her as a result of an unlawful decision of a court, another state authority, or a public administrative authority, or as a result of an incorrect official procedure. (4) Conditions and detailed provisions are laid down by law."*

and made out of one's own free will.[110] This requirement entails the obligation of the court to examine the arbitration clause, in each particular case, from the perspective of the reasonability of the clause (see the *Directive*), taking into account the unequal position of the consumer as a party to the arbitration agreement.

15.54. The autonomy of will and freedom of individual conduct are based primarily on Section 2(1) of the ArbAct [CZE].

15.55. The method of concluding and the wording of arbitration agreements (or arbitration clauses, as the case may be) in consumer contracts regulated under Section 52 et seq. of the CC [CZE] must be approached in a specific manner. These provisions are based on the *Directive,* which was adopted with the aim of enhancing the protection of consumers against unfair contractual terms. Article 3(1) and Article 6(1) of the *Directive* indicate that a national court is authorized to examine an arbitration clause incorporated in a contract concluded between a consumer and a professional in light of the *Directive,* even if the consumer him- or herself did not raise the defence of the unfairness of the clause (so-called absolute invalidity).

15.56. Article 3(1) of the *Directive* combined with Paragraph 1(q) of the Annex to the *Directive* stipulate that **arbitration clauses can be considered unfair** terms in consumer contracts.

15.57. Section 56 of the CC [CZE] stipulates that consumer contracts must not contain terms causing a **significant imbalance in the parties' rights and obligations.** Terms that (i) were not individually negotiated and that (ii) cause a significant imbalance in the parties' rights and obligations are invalid.

15.58. The court examines all circumstances of the case. Despite the fact that arbitration clauses are not explicitly listed in the non-exhaustive list of potential unfair terms in consumer contracts as specified in the CC

---

[110] The ConCourt [CZE] invokes the judgment of the ECHR in the case of Complaint No. 1643/06 of 28 October 2010 (*Suda* v. *Czech Republic*), in which the right to a fair trial under Article 6(1) of the Convention was subject to examination. *Suda* v. *Czech Republic* concerned a Czech citizen living in the Czech Republic (the complainant). He was a minority shareholder in a joint stock company. His shares were redeemed by the majority shareholder in compliance with the provisions of the Commercial Code, which anticipated the possibility that the compensation for the shares would in such cases be reviewed by an arbitral tribunal instead of a court. The complainant argued that his fundamental right to a fair trial had been violated in such case, because he was bound by an arbitration clause that he himself had not contracted. See, for instance, Christa Roodt, *Conflicts of Procedure between Courts and Arbitral Tribunals with Particular Reference to the Right of Access to Court,* 19 (2) AFRICAN JOURNAL OF INTERNATIONAL AND COMPARATIVE LAW 236-282 (2011).

[CZE],[111] the court may conclude that a particular arbitration clause must be classified as unfair.

15.59. If the arbitration clause is incorporated in a consumer contract, the wording of the clause must be subject to a more rigorous assessment; the same applies to the criteria regarding the arbitrators who might be called upon to resolve potential future disputes between the contracting parties – the method of their appointment must be subject to a particularly rigorous test. **Considering the nature of consumer contracts, it is necessary to place special emphasis on the rule that both parties must have equal rights in selecting their arbitrators.**

15.60. In the case of an arbitration clause [in a consumer contract] that is, contrary to the law, clearly aimed at causing detriment to the "weaker" contracting party, the principle of party autonomy may not be (mis)used to negate the protection of that party. A democratic country honouring the principle of the rule of law must not give up on the protection of the rights and legitimate interests that could be jeopardized in alternative proceedings conducted instead of litigation.[112]

15.61. The assessment of the validity of an arbitration clause must **take into account the importance of arbitration** as a dispute resolution method, including the appointment of the arbitrator, i.e. the person who **the parties choose** as a result of having confidence in him or her. **The principle of selecting one's arbitrator is not fulfilled by a mere reference to a list of arbitrators.**

15.62. Section 2(1) of the ArbAct [CZE] provides that an arbitration agreement (or an [arbitration] clause incorporated in the main contract, as the case may be) **must include the parties' agreement on either an "ad hoc" arbitrator(s) or a permanent arbitral institution established under the law.**[113] The *ad hoc arbitrator*, always a natural

---

[111] Section 56(2) of the CC [CZE], as amended. We ought to mention that the New Civil Code (NCC [CZE]), the draft version of which was passed by the Chamber of Deputies of the Parliament of the Czech Republic in 2011, and which is now being debated in the Senate of the Parliament of the Czech Republic, expressly broadens this non-exhaustive list to include arbitration clauses.

[112] In this case, the Constitutional Court of the Czech Republic agreed with the opinion expressed in the decision of the Grand Panel of the Civil Law Division and the Commercial Law Division of the Supreme Court of the Czech Republic, Case No. 31 Cdo 1945/2010 of 11 May 2011.

[113] See the ArbAct [CZE] (as applicable on the day this arbitration clause was concluded, cit.): Section 13 – *"Permanent Arbitral Institutions – (1) Permanent arbitral institutions can only be established under the law. (2) Permanent arbitral institutions can issue their own statutes and rules, which must be published in the Business Journal; these statutes and rules may determine the method of appointment and the number of arbitrators, and may*

person (Section 4 of the ArbAct [CZE]),[114] can be identified (*by his, her or their name(s), should there be more than one arbitrator, directly in the arbitration agreement*), or the arbitration agreement (clause) can define the method of appointment and the number of arbitrators – Section 7(1) of the ArbAct [CZE].

15.63. Section 19 of the ArbAct [CZE][115] provides that the parties may agree on how the arbitrators shall case manage the proceedings and, in the absence of such agreement, the arbitrators shall case manage the

---

stipulate that the arbitrators shall be selected from a list administered by the permanent arbitral institution. The statutes and rules may also determine how the arbitrators shall case manage the proceedings and render their decisions and resolve other issues connected with the activities of the permanent arbitral institution and the arbitrators, including rules regulating the costs of proceedings and remuneration of arbitrators. (3) If the parties agreed on the jurisdiction of a particular permanent arbitral institution and failed to agree otherwise in the arbitration agreement, they shall be deemed to have submitted to the regulations specified in Subsection (2), as applicable on the day the request for arbitration is filed with the permanent arbitral institution."

With effect from 1 April 2012, an Amendment to the ArbAct [CZE] modifies Section 13 of the ArbAct [CZE] by amending Subsection (1) and inserting a new Subsection (4) in Section 13 of the ArbAct [CZE] (cit.): Section 13 – "Permanent Arbitral Institutions – (1) *Permanent arbitral institutions can only be established by another law or if their formation is explicitly allowed by another law.* [...] (4) *No entity may carry out its activities using a name that evokes a misleading impression that the entity is a permanent arbitral institution under this law, unless a different law or regulation or an international agreement integrated in the legal system authorizes the entity to use the name."* Subsections (2) and (3) of Section 13 of the ArbAct [CZE] remain unamended.

[114] ArbAct [CZE] (as applicable on the day this arbitration clause was concluded, cit.): Part Two – Arbitrators – Section 4 – "(1) *Any citizen of the Czech Republic who is of legal age and has legal capacity can serve as an arbitrator, unless a special law stipulates otherwise. (2) A foreigner can serve as an arbitrator if he or she has legal capacity under the laws of his or her country; it shall suffice, however, if he or she has legal capacity under the laws of the Czech Republic."*

With effect from 1 April 2012, an Amendment to the ArbAct [CZE] modifies Section 4 of the ArbAct [CZE] with respect to arbitration in consumer disputes; the entire Section 4 of the ArbAct [CZE] is amended as follows (cit.): Section 4 – "(1) *Any citizen of the Czech Republic who is of legal age, has no criminal record and has legal capacity can serve as an arbitrator, unless a special law stipulates otherwise. (2) A foreigner may serve as an arbitrator if he or she meets the condition of majority, no criminal record and legal capacity; the requirement of legal capacity shall be governed by the person's lex personae. It shall suffice, however, if he or she has legal capacity under the laws of the Czech Republic. (3) In order to meet the requirement of no criminal record under Subsections (1) and (2), the person must have no previous final and conclusive conviction for a criminal offence, unless the person's criminal record is expunged and the person is deemed never to have been convicted. (4) An arbitrator designated by an arbitration clause to resolve disputes arising from consumer contracts must be registered on the list of arbitrators administered by the Ministry of Justice (the "Ministry")."*

[115] Quoted below in a footnote to the annotation of this decision.

proceedings in any manner they see fit (the proceedings are oral, unless the parties agree otherwise). **As opposed to arbitrators appointed *ad hoc*, permanent arbitral institutions may issue their own rules (statutes and rules), which may set forth the process of appointment and determine the number of arbitrators (the arbitrators can be selected from a list), as well as stipulate the manner by which the arbitrators shall case manage the proceedings and the costs of arbitration payable by the parties.** Such rules must be published in the *Business Journal [Obchodní věstník].*[116] Decisions[117] are rendered pursuant to the abovementioned Rules issued by the permanent arbitral institution, as applicable on the day the request for arbitration is filed with the arbitral institution.

15.64. If an entity other than a permanent arbitral institution under the ArbAct [CZE] carries out activities that, according to the ArbAct [CZE], are reserved for permanent arbitral institutions, **logic dictates** that this entity **clearly and intentionally violates the law**. It is a manifest attempt to impose conditions that raise **reasonable and justified doubts regarding the perspective of independent and impartial dispute resolution.**

15.65. If the arbitration agreement lacks any direct identification of an *ad hoc* arbitrator, or a **specific description of the method of his or her appointment**, but **only refers to a selection made by a "tribunal/court")**, i.e. a legal entity (corporation) other than a permanent arbitral institution established under the law, **the arbitration agreement is invalid.**

15.66. **The arbitration clause is also likely to be classified as invalid if the clause refers to a legal entity whose company name contains the words *"arbitral court/institution/tribunal"*, despite the fact that it is not a *permanent arbitral institution*** pursuant to Section 13 of the ArbAct [CZE], because such a reference can be considered a fraudulent **term misleading the consumer** as a deceitful company name.

---

[116] See Section 13(2) of the ArbAct [CZE]. Regarding the conditions for the formation of *"permanent arbitral institutions"*, see Section 13(1) of the ArbAct [CZE]. The provision is cited elsewhere in a footnote to the annotation of this decision, together with information regarding the changes to be implemented with effect from 1 April 2012.

[117] Although the Constitutional Court of the Czech Republic in its resolution speaks of the "decision-making subject to the respective *rules*", the author believes that the Constitutional Court means especially the *entire procedure*, which the final decision only brings to an end. It is a somewhat inaccurate statement incorporated in the reasons for the resolution adopted by the ConCourt CR [CZE]; in the author's opinion, though, it will not cause any problems with the interpretation of the ruling.

15.67. The parties may also agree to depart from the rules issued and published by the permanent arbitral institution; in the absence of such agreement, however, the permanent arbitral institution follows the rules.

[Description of Facts and Legal Issues]

15.68. The case concerned an arbitration clause, which read as follows (cit.): "*[a]ny and all disputes arising from or in connection with this contract shall be submitted to and resolved in arbitration before [... company name of the legal entity.... with its registered office in Prague...], by a single arbitrator selected by the Court from the list of arbitrators administered by the Arbitration Court of the Czech Republic. The arbitral proceedings shall follow the Rules of Procedure, the Tariff and other rules adopted by the Arbitration Court of the Czech Republic (rozhodcisoud.net). The parties have explicitly agreed that these rules, as applicable on the day the arbitration was initiated, shall be followed in the arbitral proceedings, within the meaning of Section 19(1)* [ArbAct/CZE/];[118] *the parties authorize the arbitrator selected by the Court to resolve the dispute following the principles of equity.*[119] *The*

---

[118] ArbAct [CZE] (as applicable on the day this arbitration clause was concluded, cit.): Section 19 – "(1) *The parties have a right to agree on how the arbitrators shall case manage the proceedings. Matters regarding the case management of the proceedings may be resolved by the chairman of the tribunal, provided he or she was authorized to do so by the parties or by all arbitrators. (2) Unless the parties negotiated an agreement pursuant to Subsection (1), the arbitrators shall case manage the proceedings in any manner they see fit. They case manage the arbitral proceedings in such manner that the facts of the case necessary for the resolution of the dispute are sufficiently ascertained, without any unnecessary formalities, and while giving all parties equal opportunity to plead their case.*"
With effect from 1 April 2012, an Amendment to the ArbAct [CZE] modifies Section 19 of the ArbAct [CZE] by amending Subsection (2) and inserting a new Subsection (4) in Section 19 of the ArbAct [CZE] (cit.): Section 19 – "[...] (2) *Unless the parties negotiated an agreement pursuant to Subsection (1) or unless the procedure is determined pursuant to Subsection (4), the arbitrators shall case manage the proceedings in any manner they see fit. They case manage the arbitral proceedings in such manner that the facts of the case necessary for the resolution of the dispute are sufficiently ascertained, without any unnecessary formalities, and while giving all parties equal opportunity to plead their case.* [...] (4) *The parties may also determine the procedure to be followed in the rules regulating the arbitral proceedings, provided the rules are included with the arbitration agreement, without prejudice to the application of rules adopted by a permanent arbitral institution.*" Subsections (1) and (3) of Section 19 of the ArbAct [CZE] remain unamended.
[119] ArbAct [CZE] (as applicable on the day this arbitration clause was concluded, cit.): Section 25 – "[...] (3) *When determining the award, the arbitrators apply the substantive law applicable to the dispute; they may, however, resolve the dispute according to the rules of equity, but only if the parties explicitly authorized them to do so.*"
With effect from 1 April 2012, an Amendment to the ArbAct [CZE] modifies Section 25 of the ArbAct [CZE] with respect to arbitration in consumer disputes by amending Subsections (2) and (3) of Section 25 of the ArbAct [CZE] as follows (cit.): Section 25 –

parties have explicitly agreed that no oral hearings before the arbitrator are necessary".[120] This arbitration clause was incorporated in the main contract (the so-called reservation contract). The legal entity referred to in the arbitration clause as the administrator of the dispute was not a permanent arbitral institution within the meaning of the definition of the latter under Section 13 of the ArbAct [CZE].[121] The consumer, as one of the contracting parties, filed a lawsuit with a court (i.e. initiated litigation) on the basis of the contract.

15.69. **The trial court** held that the *Directive* itself and its horizontal effect did not suffice to render the arbitration agreement invalid. The trial court also held that the arbitral proceedings must abide by the law, even if the parties agree on how the arbitrator shall case manage the proceedings. Consequently, an arbitration clause incorporated in a consumer contract cannot *per se* impair the consumer's position. The trial court therefore terminated the proceedings based on the defendant's defence (objection) of a lack of jurisdiction (the defendant invoked the arbitration clause). However, the appellate court reversed the decision of the trial court and terminated the proceedings.

15.70. In the appeal challenging the decision of the trial court, the plaintiff argued that an arbitration clause in a consumer contract is automatically invalid pursuant to the application of Section 55(1) of the CC [CZE].[122] **The appellate court** concluded[123] that it was an unfair

---

"[...] (2) *The arbitral award shall contain the reasons for the award, unless the parties agree to dispense with reasons; this also applies to any arbitral award rendered pursuant to Section 24(2). An arbitral award rendered in a dispute arising from a consumer contract must always contain reasons and instructions regarding the right to file a petition with the court for the annulment of the award.* [...] (3) *When determining the award, the arbitrators apply the substantive law applicable to the dispute; they may, however, resolve the dispute according to the rules of equity, but only if the parties explicitly authorized them to do so. In disputes arising from consumer contracts, the arbitrators shall always abide by consumer protection laws and regulations.*" Subsection (1) of Section 25 of the ArbAct [CZE] remains unamended. No change in cases that do not concern so-called consumer contracts (a contract concluded by a consumer / a consumer-type contract).

[120] This arbitration agreement (in the form of an arbitration clause) was concluded on 12 May 2007.

[121] Section 13 of the ArbAct [CZE] is cited above in a footnote to the annotation of this decision, including information about the change effective from 1 April 2012.

[122] CC [CZE] (cit.): - Section 55 – "(1) *Contractual terms in consumer contracts may not derogate from the law to the detriment of the consumer. In particular, the consumer may not waive the rights guaranteed to him or her by the law or impair his or her contractual position in any other manner. (2) Clauses in consumer contracts specified in Section 56 are invalid. (3) When in doubt as to the meaning of consumer contracts, the interpretation that is more favourable to the consumer shall apply.*" Section 56 – "(1) *Consumer contracts may not contain terms that, contrary to the requirement of good faith, cause a significant imbalance in the parties' rights and obligations to the detriment of the consumer.* (2)

term contrary to consumer protection laws and consequently an invalid provision. The appellate court maintained that the respective arbitration clause caused an imbalance between the contracting parties to the detriment of the plaintiff as the consumer pursuant to Section 56 of the CC [CZE].[124] The clause effectively restricts the fundamental constitutional right of the plaintiff as a citizen and a consumer to assert her rights before an independent court (Article 36(1) of the Charter [CZE][125]); the plaintiff's fundamental right is restricted in a manner that the plaintiff could not control due to the fact that the contract was an adhesion contract (Article 3(2) of the *Directive*). The Municipal Court in Prague, as the appellate court, also held that the invalidity in the present case was irreparable, i.e. absolute invalidity, and rejected the possibility of voidability, with reference to the provisions of Article 6(1) of the *Directive* and the interpretation thereof in the ECJ case law. In the ensuing proceedings before the ÚS ČR [CZE], the complainant objected, *inter alia*, that the appellate court had failed to address the issue of whether the case law of the ECJ was binding on the citizens of

---

Subsection (1) shall not apply to contractual terms that define the subject of performance under the contract or the price of performance. (3) Inadmissible contractual terms are, in particular, contractual terms (a) excluding or limiting the legal liability of a supplier in the event of the death of a consumer or personal injury to the latter resulting from an act or omission of that supplier, (b) excluding or limiting the consumer's rights to make claims under liability for defects or liability for damage, (c) stipulating that an agreement is binding on the consumer, whereas the supplier's performance is subject to a condition whose realization depends on the supplier's own will alone, (d) permitting the supplier to retain the performance provided by the consumer even if the latter does not conclude a contract with the supplier or rescinds the contract, (e) authorizing the supplier to rescind the contract without any contractual or statutory reason where the same facility is not granted to the consumer, (f) enabling the supplier to terminate a contract of indeterminate duration without reasonable notice, except where there are serious grounds for doing so, (g) obliging the consumer to fulfil conditions with which he or she had no opportunity to get acquainted prior to the conclusion of the contract, (h) enabling the supplier to alter the terms of the contract unilaterally without a valid reason specified in the contract, (i) providing for the price of goods or services to be determined at the time of delivery or allowing a supplier of the goods or services to increase their price, in both cases without giving the consumer the corresponding right to rescind the contract if the final price is too high in relation to the price agreed when the contract was concluded, (j) obliging the consumer to fulfil all of his or her obligations where the supplier does not perform his or hers, (k) giving the supplier the possibility of transferring his or her rights and obligations under the contract, where such transfer jeopardizes the enforceability of the consumer's claim or the guarantees for the consumer, without the latter's agreement."

[123] The decision of the appellate court is not available and the conclusions were taken from the summary incorporated in the reasons given by the ConCourt CR [CZE].

[124] The provision is cited above in a footnote to the annotation of this decision.

[125] The provision is cited in a footnote in the opening part of the annotation to this decision.

the Czech Republic, and that the appellate court had failed to quote, or at least refer to, the relevant ECJ rulings.

[**Constitutional Complaint and Conclusions Adopted by Constitutional Court in Ruling, Including Reasons**][126]

15.71. The plaintiff filed a constitutional complaint and demanded that the appellate court's decision be set aside. The plaintiff argued, *inter alia*, that consumer disputes clearly belonged to the category of disputes that could be submitted to arbitration (they are arbitrable). These disputes meet all the conditions prescribed by the ArbAct [CZE], in particular, they are property disputes capable of being settled. The plaintiff highlighted that its clients had not been forced to accept the arbitration clause, and that the provision excluding the jurisdiction of courts was regularly omitted at the request of clients. The plaintiff's contracting practice was therefore open to proposals for changes presented by potential clients, intended to modify the *basic contract offer*. The conclusion of arbitration agreements must therefore be considered an expression of free will, because the consumer (just like other customers potentially concerned) did not request any changes in this regard.

15.72. The Constitutional Court principally dismissed the constitutional complaint, especially because any other decision would constitute undue interference with the decision-making of the [lower] courts; the Constitutional Court also highlighted its exceptional status, according to which the ConCourt [CZE] is not part of the general court structure. The Constitutional Court is called upon to protect constitutionality, not to control "common" legality, and it therefore does not examine whether the [lower] courts interpreted and applied "simple (sub-constitutional) law" correctly. Nonetheless, the ÚS ČR [CZE] did provide comments on several important issues.

15.73. Above all, the Constitutional Court CR [CZE] principally agreed with the conclusion adopted by the [lower] court in the present case (i.e. the appellate court). **The Constitutional Court, however (following its previously voiced opinions), did not classify arbitration clauses in consumer contracts as automatically invalid.** The Court only confirmed that **courts are entitled to review the validity of such arbitration clauses in particular cases,** even if the parties themselves do not raise any objection of invalidity. If the courts conclude that, in the given case, the clause is unfair; they shall hold the clause invalid.

---

[126] Further conclusions of the ConCourt CR [CZE] are summarized in the opening part of this annotation.

15.74. The author believes that the ÚS ČR [CZE] placed an emphasis on this rule, which is often neglected (and such neglect stems from an unduly undiscriminating approach). The problem is that arbitration clauses in consumer contracts are not automatically invalid; even the fact that the consumer contract (as part of the main contract) was concluded as an adhesion contract does not automatically render the contract invalid. Invalidity is a penalty for arbitration clauses that, **in the particular case**, causes a significant imbalance between the parties to the detriment of the consumer (provided that all of these conditions are met). The Constitutional Court CR [CZE] referred to its previous opinion, already voiced in several other cases, according to which an arbitration clause negating the jurisdiction of the courts does not violate the right to judicial protection if the substance thereof corresponds to the **expression of will of both contracting parties.**[127] This opinion complies with the case law protecting the autonomy of the will and the freedom of individual action. The expression of will must be entirely free, permissible and unambiguous. The courts are therefore obliged to assess each arbitration clause individually.

15.75. In connection with the rules applicable to arbitration, the Constitutional Court held that only permanent arbitral institutions are allowed to issue their own rules as standard procedural guidelines. At the same time, however, the Court expressed an opinion that probably does not feature very prominently in the respective decision. The fact is that even the parties to the proceedings conducted before a permanent arbitral institution that has issued procedural rules (*Rules*) and published those Rules in the *Business Journal* may agree to deviate from the Rules. This legal opinion has been widely recognised in the Czech Republic, but it has never been clearly confirmed. The reason is that none of the three permanent arbitral institutions in the Czech Republic incorporates provisions in their rules that are common in a number of international arbitral institutions in other countries, i.e. provisions that often enable these institutions to reject a request for arbitration if, for instance, the agreement of the parties is irreconcilable with certain procedural standards that the permanent arbitral institution considers essential.

15.76. Just like in many other cases handled by the ÚS ČR [CZE], and just like in the practice of the lower courts and in the rich case law of the SC CR [CZE], the focal point is the position of the so-called *arbitration centres*, i.e. entities *organizing* arbitration, whose status does not meet

---

[127] Resolution of the ConCourt CR [CZE], Case No. II. ÚS 2682/08 of 6 November 2008, whereby a complaint against the resolution of the SC CR [CZE], Case No. 32 Cdo 2282/2008 of 31 July 2008, was dismissed.

the conditions stipulated for *permanent arbitral institutions* under Section 13 of the ArbAct [CZE]. In the present case, the arbitration clause stipulated that the arbitrators should be chosen by the *arbitration centre* from its own list of arbitrators, without the centre being a permanent arbitral institution.[128] In its constitutional complaint, the complainant disagreed with the legal opinion that classifies such arrangement as an evasion of the law (namely the provision regulating permanent arbitral institutions); the plaintiff argued that the ArbAct [CZE] is a private-law regulation, not subject to the principle of implied prohibition (whatever is not explicitly permitted by the law is prohibited). Conversely, the complainant argued that the private-law nature of the Arbitration Act clearly requires that the application of this law must be subject to the principle of implied permission pursuant to Article 2(4) of the Constitution CR [CZE] (and Article 2(3) of the Charter [CZE][129]), i.e. whatever is not explicitly prohibited by the law is permitted. The complainant in the present case expressed an opinion that neither the ArbAct [CZE] nor any other law prohibits *ad hoc* arbitrators [appointed for the given proceedings] to organize in the [so-called] arbitration centres; the complainant even claimed this to be the arbitrators' constitutional right.[130] The complainant also disagreed with the opinion of the Grand Panel of the SC CR [CZE], Case No. 31 Cdo 1945/2010 of 12 May 2011, whereby the Supreme Court supported the opinion voiced in the

---

[128] In that connection, it is necessary to say a few words about the basically global discussion regarding the issue of whether permanent arbitral institutions should administer any *lists* of arbitrators at all. Many important permanent arbitral institutions abandoned this practice in past years, and a number of them have not been, as a rule, administering any *lists* at all. In that connection, we need to mention an extensive discussion in Austria [AUT] concerning the issue of whether the list of arbitrators ought to be renewed at all after the *validity* of the previous document expired in 2009. It is true that a new (updated) list was published again in 2010, but only as the so-called *indicative list* of experts in international arbitration. Besides, even those arbitral institutions that have maintained the practice of *lists* no longer demand that these lists be binding, at least to some extent. We must emphasize, though, that in the countries of Central and Eastern Europe, it is still a fairly common practice, with its disadvantages, but certain advantages too. Nonetheless, in the present case handled by the ConCourt CR [CZE], the key issue was not a *list* administered by an entity that would meet the statutory requirements of a *permanent arbitral institution* under Section 13 of the ArbAct [CZE] (this provision is quoted above in a footnote to this annotation).

[129] Charter [CZE] – Article 2 – [...] "(3) *Everyone may do that which is not prohibited by law; and nobody may be compelled to do that which is not imposed upon him or her by law.*"

[130] With reference to Article 20(1) of the Charter [CZE] (cit.): "*The right of association is guaranteed. Everyone has the right to associate together with others in clubs, societies, and other associations.*"

decision of the High Court in Prague, Case No. 12 Cmo 496/2008 of 28 May 2009. The latter maintains that the activities of the so-called *arbitration centres* that do not meet the stipulated requirements in order to qualify as permanent arbitral institutions, as well as their practice of issuing *Rules* and lists of arbitrators, constitute unlawful evasion of the law.[131] In the present case, the ÚS ČR [CZE] identified with the conclusion on unfairness of the given [particular] arbitration clause. In particular, the consumer may not waive the rights guaranteed to him or her by the law, or otherwise impair his or her contractual position. The Constitutional Court of the Czech Republic [CZE] upheld the conclusions of the appellate court and agreed that, considering the substance of the main contract in this particular case (the reservation contract), which can be **subsumed under the general category of consumer contracts**, the wording of the arbitration clause incorporated therein must be measured according to a more rigorous standard; the same applies to the criteria relating to the arbitrators who will decide any eventual future dispute between the contracting parties, especially the method of their appointment. Considering the nature of consumer contracts, it is necessary to place special **emphasis on the rule that both parties must have equal rights in selecting their arbitrators. Consequently, the principle of selecting one's arbitrator is not, in this particular case, fulfilled by a mere reference to the list of arbitrators.**

15.77. In this case, the parties had agreed that disputes would be resolved in arbitration with [... *a legal person other than a permanent arbitral institution under Section 13 of the ArbAct /CZE/* ...] by a single arbitrator selected by said Court. However, this "Court" is not a permanent arbitral institution within the meaning of the Arbitration Act. Section 7(1) of the ArbAct [CZE] stipulates that the arbitration agreement should, as a rule, determine the number of arbitrators and identify them by name, or stipulate the method whereby the number and the identity of the arbitrators shall be determined. The final number of arbitrators must always be odd. Subsection (2) of the respective provision stipulates that if the arbitration agreement does not set forth the requirements specified in Subsection (1), each party shall appoint one arbitrator, and these arbitrators shall elect the chairman of the arbitral tribunal. Section 13(1) of the ArbAct [CZE] stipulates that *permanent arbitral institutions* can only be established by law. Section 13(2) of the ArbAct [CZE] stipulates that permanent arbitral institutions can issue their own *statutes* and *rules*, which must

---

[131]   Here an intentional partial summary.

be published in the *Business Journal*; these statutes and rules may determine the method of appointment and the number of arbitrators, and may stipulate that the arbitrators shall be selected from a list administered by the permanent arbitral institution. The statutes and rules may also determine how the arbitrators shall case manage the proceedings and render their decisions, as well as resolve other issues connected with the activities of the permanent arbitral institution and the arbitrators, including rules regulating the costs of proceedings and remuneration of arbitrators. With respect to the substance of the particular arbitration clause and taking into account whether the parties agreed in said clause that any of their eventual future disputes (considering the fact that the legal person referred to in the clause is not a permanent arbitral institution, which can only be established under the law) would be resolved by an *ad hoc* arbitrator, we cannot dismiss the fact that the **selection of the respective arbitrator was entrusted directly to this "Court"** (i.e. the legal person in question). However, this legal person (corporation) is not a permanent arbitral institution in terms of the applicable law,[132] and it is not entitled to issue *statutes* and *rules* that would, *inter alia,* provide for rules regulating the case management of the arbitral proceedings or, as the case may be, determine the method of appointment of arbitrators, etc. If the entity carries on activities that, according to the ArbAct [CZE], are reserved for permanent arbitral institutions, **logic dictates** that this entity **clearly and intentionally violates the law.** It is a manifest attempt to impose conditions that raise reasonable and justified doubts regarding the perspective of independent and impartial dispute resolution. We cannot even postulate that the parties had perhaps agreed to have their eventual dispute resolved by an ad hoc arbitrator, because no such arbitrator was identified in the arbitration agreement, or rather the arbitration agreement contained no clear terms, in compliance with the law, that would provide for the method of selecting the respective arbitrator; the already mentioned reference to the appointment of the arbitrator by the "Court" cannot be accepted as an alternative (substitute) method of appointing an ad hoc arbitrator due to the reasons specified above, as well as with respect to the principle of equality of the parties.

15.78. The Constitutional Court of the Czech Republic [CZE] also held that the conclusion regarding the misleading, even fraudulent, nature of the clause could also be derived from the fact that the arbitration clause

---

[132] The line of business registered in the Companies Register for the given legal person was *brokering trade and services.*

referred (whether to the *statutes* or in connection with the appointment of the arbitrator) to a legal person whose name (*company name*) included the words *arbitration court*, despite the fact that it was not a permanent arbitral institution under Section 13 of the ArbAct [CZE]. In that connection, the author would like to add that an extensive Amendment to the ArbAct has been passed in the meantime, taking effect on 1 April 2012. The Amendment, *inter alia*, incorporates in the ArbAct [CZE] a new Section 13(4), which explicitly prohibits the use of such a *misleading* name by entities other than those having the status of *a permanent arbitral institution*.[133] This basically constitutes an enactment of a principle that has already been voiced by Czech courts in their previous rulings.[134]

[**Author's General Note**]

15.79. The author does not dispute and principally fully agrees with the decision of the Constitutional Court of the Czech Republic [CZE]. Whereas the legal opinions of the ConCourt [CZE] are basically stable and represent the Constitutional Court's consistent support for autonomy, as well as a balanced approach to the interpretation of the will and the protection of good faith of the parties, including the protection of the weaker party to consumer contracts, the case law of the [lower] courts still exhibits significant variances. Decisions of the lower courts often lack any individual assessment of all facts of the respective case, primarily the circumstances attending the conclusion of the contract, and they often tend towards a very undiscriminating approach. On top of that, Czech courts hardly ever examine and take into account the approach of the parties after they enter into the

---

[133] Section 13(4) of the ArbAct [CZE], the version which takes effect on 1 April 2012 (cit.): "(4) *No entity may carry out its activities using a name that evokes a misleading impression that the entity is a permanent arbitral institution under this law, unless a different law or regulation or an international agreement integrated in the legal system authorizes the entity to use the name.*"

[134] See, for instance, the resolution of the High Court in Prague, Case No. 7 Cmo 136/2010 of 22 July 2010, according to which corporations are not allowed to choose a *company name* that would include the words "arbitral" or "arbitration", unless they are a permanent arbitral institution established under a special law. This was a decision rendered by the appellate court on appeal from a resolution adopted by the court administering the Companies Register; the trial court dismissed the petition for registration of a change in the company name of the corporation, because the new name was supposed to include the words *"arbitral office"*. The decision was annotated in and the cited *ratio decidendi* is adopted from: 17 (3) SOUDNÍ ROZHLEDY (2011), Decision Ref. No. 31, pp. 100-101. As concerns the general principles governing company names for corporations, the High Court referred to, for instance, the opinion expressed in the resolution of the SC CR [CZE], Case No. 29 Cdo 201/2007 of 15 April 2008.

arbitration agreement at the moment the dispute arises and needs to be resolved. In that connection, we need to mention especially ECJ Case C-243/08 of 4 June 2009 *Pannon GSM Zrt v. Sustikné Győrfi Erzsébet (Pannon GSM)*.[135] This particular case does not concern arbitration directly; the ECJ was called upon to assess an agreement on the jurisdiction of a court different from the court that would otherwise have jurisdiction if the decisive criterion were the place of residence of the consumer (the defendant in the case). As opposed to Spanish law applied in *Mostaza Claro*[136] and *Asturcom*,[137] Hungarian law in *Pannon* required that the unfairness of the contractual term be raised by the contracting party in its defence. The Hungarian Code of Civil Procedure stipulated that the court must examine the propriety of venue *sua sponte*. But, unless the case concerns exclusive jurisdiction, the defence of improper venue cannot be raised after the defendant lodges his or her first submission on the merits. The Hungarian court therefore submitted a question to the ECJ asking whether the court is obliged, even in this particular case, to examine its jurisdiction (venue) *sua sponte*. The ECJ ruled that an unfair term in a consumer contract is invalid *per se*, i.e. the invalidity is not contingent on the defendant successfully raising the relevant defence in court. **The ECJ noted, though, that the *Directive* does not prescribe an obligation on the national court to exclude the application of the relevant unfair term if the consumer, having been properly instructed by the court, does not intend to object to it.** Consequently, the ECJ leaves it up to the consumer to decide whether he or she will be bound by the unfair term. Article 6 of the *Directive*, however, stipulates that states are obliged to ensure that consumers are not bound by unfair terms. Paradoxically, it is not certain to what extent the ECJ ruling is compatible with the *Directive* – if the consumer decides to insist on the validity of a term which, in the court's opinion, is unfair. In actual fact, the *Directive* would be breached because the consumer would still be bound by the unfair term. A contractual term in a consumer contract, although unfair *per se*, is only *voidable* (its invalidity is *conditional*). In other words, it cannot be classified as so-called absolute invalidity within the

---

[135] Judgment published in: ECJ, 2009, p. I-04713. CELEX: 62008CA0243. Language of the case: Hungarian.

[136] ECJ Judgment, Case C-168/05 of 26 October 2006 in *Elisa María Mostaza Claro v. Centro Móvil Milenium SL (Mostaza Claro)*, published in: ECJ, 2006, p. I-1421. CELEX 62005CJ0168. Language of the case: Spanish.

[137] ECJ Judgment, Case C-40/08 of 6 October 2009 in *Asturcom Telecomunicaciones SL v. Cristina Rodríguez Nogueira (Asturcom)*, published in: ECJ, 2009, p. I-09579. CELEX 62008CA0040. Language of the case: Spanish.

meaning of certain legal systems (for instance, Czech law or, with a certain difference in terminology, Austrian law, etc.) or as ineffectiveness (e.g. German law) or as nullity. **This means invalidity examined by the court *sua sponte*. However, even these situations require that the consumer perform an act aimed at raising a defence of such invalidity, after the consumer was properly instructed about the court's legal opinion. The consumer's conduct (actions or omissions) can ex post validate the invalidity caused by the unfairness.** From this perspective, even the *Pannon GSM* decision can be considered a landmark decision, although it prima facie appears to merely follow the ECJ's previous case law. Besides, the Madrid Appeals Court [ESP], for instance, arrived at the same conclusion in *Juan Pedro* v. *Metrovacesa S.A.*[138] The unfairness of the term incorporated in a consumer contract, i.e. the consequences with respect to the validity of the term, cannot be assessed merely in relation to the moment of conclusion of the contract; the subsequent conduct of and the approach adopted by the parties (especially the consumer) must be taken into consideration too. Their approach ought to significantly influence the determination of whether or not the parties' expression of will at the conclusion of the arbitration agreement was free and serious. However, in the case resolved by the ÚS ČR [CZE] under Ref. No. II. ÚS 3057/10 (the decision of 5 October 2011 annotated in this section), both the decision of the appellate court (Municipal Court in Prague) and the decision of the ÚS ČR [CZE] meet the criteria set by the ECJ in *Pannon GSM;* the consumer expressed its refusal by the very fact of being the plaintiff in the given case (on the merits).

| | |

---

[138] Decision of the Madrid Appeals Court [ESP], Case No. 28079370102010100498, 12 November 2010 (*Juan Pedro* v. *Metrovacesa S.A.*); for a detailed annotation of this Spanish decision, see the excursion into Spanish law elsewhere in this book. In the Spanish decision, the Madrid Appeals Court went even further and held, *inter alia*, that the principle of good faith protects both the consumer and the professional; the Court refused to protect the consumer if he had already had the opportunity to raise the corresponding objections during the arbitral proceedings. The court principally refused to consider the application of consumer protection laws and consider the alleged invalidity of the arbitration agreement, which did not comply with these laws, if the arbitration had in fact been initiated by the consumer himself or herself.

VI. Admissibility of Settlement on Merits as Prerequisite for Arbitrability – Separability of Arbitration Agreement from Main Contract (Czech Supreme Court Judgment 29 Odo 1222/2005 of 19 December 2007)[139]

Key words:

future disputes | optional transactions | settlement | reason for nullity| contract nullity | separability | civil status | validity of the arbitration clause | arbitration clause | settlement | dispute over the inoperativeness of withdrawal

Laws and Regulations Taken into Account in This Ruling:

➤ Czech Act No. 99/1963 Coll., Code of Civil Procedure, as amended, CCP [CZE]: Section 80,[140] Section 81,[141] and Section 99;[142]

---

[139] Published *in* Sвírка Soudních Rozhodnutí a Stanovisek (*Collection of Judicial Decisions and Opinions*), Ref. No. 103/2008 (R 105/2008).

[140] CCP [CZE] – Section 80 (unofficial translation) – *"A petition to commence proceedings may be filed with a view to obtaining a decision on, in particular, a) civil status (divorce, annulment of marriage, determination of whether or not the marriage exists; dissolution, annulment, or non-existence of a registered partnership ("partnership"), determination of paternity, adoption, legal capacity, declaring a person dead); b) the fulfilment of obligations arising from law, from legal relationships or a breach of law; c) the determination of whether or not a legal relationship or right exists, in the case of a pressing legal interest."*

[141] CCP [CZE] - Section 81 (unofficial translation) – *"(1) Even in the absence of a petition, the court may, of its own accord, initiate proceedings in matters involving the custody of minors, permission to place or detain a person in a medical institution, determining legal capacity, guardianship proceedings, declaring a person dead, inheritance proceedings, determining whether or not a marriage exists, and such other proceedings for which the law provides. (2) If a preliminary injunction was issued pursuant to Section 76a CCP [CZE], then the court of jurisdiction pursuant to Section 88 (c) [CCP/CZE/] shall initiate custody proceedings immediately upon having been referred the matter, or as the case may be, immediately after it has been found to have jurisdiction (Section 74 (4) [CCP/CZE/]), even without a formal motion. (3) Unless where the law stipulates otherwise, the presiding judge shall issue a resolution on the initiation of proceedings ex officio and deliver the same into the parties' own hands. Resolutions on the initiation of proceedings on the legal capacity of an attorney-at-law shall also be promptly delivered by the court to the Minister of Justice and the President of the Czech Bar Association. (4) A person who has been granted custody of a minor based on a preliminary injunction issued pursuant to Section 76a [CCP/CZE/] shall be served the resolution on the initiation of proceedings in the matter itself, as well as the decision rendered in the matter itself."*

[142] CCP [CZE] - Section 99 (unofficial translation) – *"(1) If the nature of the matter allows for it, then the parties may terminate the proceedings by way of a court-approved settlement. The court shall strive for a settlement between the parties; in trying to reach the*

➤ Czech Act No. 216/1994 Coll., on arbitration and the enforcement of arbitral awards, as amended, ArbAct [CZE]: Section 2 (2).[143]

Rationes Decidendi:

15.80. The following **fundamental conclusions** were drawn in Judgment 29 Odo 1222/2005 of the Czech Supreme Court of 19 December 2007:

15.81. The nature of a dispute will regularly allow for the conclusion of an (out-of-court, amicable) settlement in matters in which the parties find themselves in a typical bilateral relationship, with respect to which substantive law does not rule out that the parties organise their legal relationship in the form of optional transactions (arrangements, measures). It follows that the nature of a dispute precludes a settlement, especially in those cases in which proceedings may be initiated even without a pertinent motion (Section 81 CCP [CZE]), in which the proceedings are to decide on a participant's civil status (Section 80 (a) CCP [CZE]), or in which substantive law does not allow the participants to resolve their dispute by way of an amicable understanding.

15.82. Unless where the reason for a contract's nullity has to do with the arbitration clause that concerns disputes that may arise from the contract, the nullity of the contract has no bearing on the validity of the arbitration clause.

15.83. Where the arbitration clause (agreement) concerns all future disputes as may arise from a given legal relationship (contract), it also extends to disputes over the declaration of nullity of withdrawal from the (main) contract.

---

settlement, the chairman of the arbitral tribunal shall, in particular, discuss the matter with the parties, call their attention to the laws and opinions of the Supreme Court and decisions published in the Collection of Judicial Decisions and Opinions regarding the matter, and recommend the options for a settlement of the dispute based on the circumstances of the matter. (2) The court decides on whether to approve the settlement; it shall withhold approval if the settlement is in conflict with the law. In such a case, the court shall resume proceedings after the resolution enters into force. (3) An approved settlement has the legal effects of a final judgment. However, the court may cancel the resolution on approval of the settlement if the compromise is invalid under substantive law. An application to this effect may be filed within three years from the date on which the resolution approving the settlement entered into force."

[143] ArbAct [CZE] (unofficial translation) - Section 2 – "[...] (2) *An arbitration clause may be validly concluded if the parties are entitled to conclude a settlement regarding the subject matter of the dispute.[...]*" Section 2 ArbAct [CZE] in its entirety is cited in the annotation of SC [CZE] Decision 29 Cdo 1130/2011 of 31 May 2011.

[Comment of the Author of This Annotation]

15.84. The decision at hand concerns arbitration proceedings and is considered of fundamental importance for Czech arbitration practice when it comes to interpreting the prerequisites for arbitrability (i.e. the parties' option to enter into a settlement). It also provides essential confirmation of the separability of arbitration agreements from the main contract, though this separability really has already been established as a notorious fact in Czech law and legal practice, which in this respect does not depart in any way from international practice. With respect to arbitrability being conditional upon the possibility of a settlement between the parties to the dispute, this decision is referenced in Czech Supreme Court Judgment 29 Cdo 1130/2011 of 31 May 2011, on the arbitrability of summary proceedings on bills of exchange (which is annotated further below in this volume of the CYArb). For this reason, we decided to also include an annotation of Czech Supreme Court Judgment 29 Odo 1222/2005 of 19 December 2007 in this overview of judicature.

| | |

VII. Scope of Arbitration Clause; Petition for Determination of (Ownership) Title to Real Estate
(Resolution of Regional Court in Ostrava [CZE], Case No. 57 Co 150/2009-51 of 15 February 2010)

Key words:
purchase contract | real estate | real estate transfer contract | arbitration agreement | scope of an arbitration clause | (ownership) title | contractual relationship

Laws and Regulations Taken into Account in This Ruling:
➢   Act No. 216/1994 Coll., on Arbitration, as subsequently amended, ArbAct [CZE]: Section 1 and[144] Section 2(1);[145]

---

[144]   ArbAct [CZE] (as applicable on the day this arbitration clause was concluded, cit.): Section 1 – "(1) *This Act sets forth rules regulating the resolution of property disputes by independent and impartial arbitrators and the enforcement of arbitral awards.* (2) *This Act shall not apply to the resolution of disputes of public non-profit healthcare facilities established under special laws.*"

Ratio Decidendi:

The court reached, *inter alia*, the following conclusion[146] regarding the scope of an arbitration clause:

15.85. An arbitration clause covers not only the rights arising from legal relationships established directly by the contract, but also the issue of the legal validity of these relationships, as well as the rights associated therewith. If the arbitration agreement (arbitration clause) is included in a real estate purchase contract (real estate transfer contract), the arbitration clause also covers disputes over the determination of the (ownership) title to the real estate.

| | |

With effect from 1 April 2012, an Amendment to the ArbAct [CZE] also partially modifies (supplements) Section 1(2) of the ArbAct [CZE]; the respective provision, as amended by the Amendment to the ArbAct [CZE], reads as follows (cit.): Section 1 – "[...] (2) *This Act shall not apply to the resolution of disputes of public non-profit healthcare facilities established under special laws; this Act shall also not apply if proceedings before the financial arbitrator were opened or if a decision on the merits was rendered in such proceedings* [...]".

[145] ArbAct [CZE] (as applicable on the day this arbitration clause was concluded, cit.): Section 2 – "(1) *The parties may agree that their disputes over property, except disputes arising from the enforcement of decisions and except incidental disputes, which would otherwise fall within the jurisdiction of the courts, shall be decided by one or more arbitrators or by a permanent arbitral institution (arbitration agreement)."*

With effect from 1 April 2012, an Amendment to the ArbAct [CZE] also partially modifies (supplements) Section 2(1) of the ArbAct [CZE]; the respective provision, as amended by the Amendment to the ArbAct [CZE], reads as follows (cit.): Section 2 – "[...] (1) *The parties may agree that their disputes over property, except disputes arising from the enforcement of decisions and except incidental disputes, which would otherwise fall within the jurisdiction of the courts <u>or which can be submitted to arbitration under special laws</u>, shall be decided by one or more arbitrators or by a permanent arbitral institution (arbitration agreement)* [...]".

[146] The decision of the RC in Ostrava [CZE] annotated in this article is not available. The opinion articulated in the *ratio decidendi* was adopted from the Resolution of the SC CR [CZE], Case No. 31 Cdo 1945/2010 of 11 May 2011, which decided the cassation appeal against said decision. The SC CR [CZE] set aside the resolution of the RC in Ostrava and remanded the case for a new trial. The SC CR [CZE] did not, however, challenge the conclusion articulated in the *ratio decidendi* of this annotation; the court challenged the validity of the arbitration agreement based on a different reason. The resolution of the SC CR, Case No. 31 Cdo 1945/2010 is fully annotated elsewhere in this book.

VIII. Arbitrability of Disputes over Bills of Exchange and Promissory Notes (Czech Supreme Court Judgment 29 Cdo 1130/2011 of 31 May 2011):147

Key words:
arbitrability | conclusion of contract | written form | arbitration clause | claims from bills of exchange | promissory note (bill) | settlement | credit facility | revolving credit | imperfections of the contracting procedure | General Terms and Conditions | interpretation of the arbitration agreement | interpretation of the main contract | rules of interpretation | collateral (security instrument) | securing a claim

Laws and Regulations Taken into Account in This Ruling:

➢ Czech Act No. 40/1964 Coll., Civil Code, as amended, CC [CZE]: Section 35;[148]

➢ Czech Act No. 513/1991 Coll., Commercial Code, as amended, ComC [CZE]: Section 266;[149]

---

[147] The text of the decision in its entirety is available (in Czech only) in electronic form at: http://www.nsoud.cz/JudikaturaNS_new/judikatura_prevedena2.nsf/WebSearch/9DC585 1E454511EFC12578B700431910?openDocument (accessed on November 7, 2011).

[148] CC [CZE] (unofficial translation) - Section 35 – "(1) *The expression of will may be by acting or omitting; it may be performed explicitly or in another way that does not cast doubt on what the participant wanted to express. (2) Legal acts expressed in words shall be interpreted not only according to their verbal expression, but in particular according to the will of the person who engaged in the legal act, unless this will is at variance with the verbal expression. (3) Legal acts expressed otherwise than in words shall be interpreted according to what the particular way in which they were expressed usually stands for. The interpretation shall take into account the will of the person who engaged in the legal act, and protect the good faith of the person to whom the act was addressed.*"

[149] ComC [CZE] (unofficial translation) - Section 266 – "(1) *A manifestation of will is interpreted according to the intention of the acting party, if this intention was known or must have been known to the party to which the manifestation of will was directed. (2) In cases where a manifestation of will cannot be interpreted under Subsection (1), it is interpreted according to the meaning usually attributed to it, by a person who is in the same position as the person to whom the manifestation of will is directed. Expressions (i.e. terminology) used in business contacts (i.e. negotiations, contracts) are interpreted according to the usual meaning in such contacts. (3) When interpreting a manifestation of will under Subsections (1) and (2), due account shall be taken of all circumstances related to the manifestation of will, including the negotiations about the conclusion of the contract in question and the practice that the parties have introduced between themselves, as well as the subsequent conduct of the parties, if the nature of the case so permits. (4) A manifestation of will that contains an expression that permits different interpretations shall be interpreted, if in doubt, to the disadvantage of the party that first used the expression in the negotiations. (5) If under the provisions of this Part of the Code the decisive factor is to*

> Czech Act No. 99/1963 Coll., Code of Civil Procedure, as amended, CCP [CZE]: Section 80,[150] Section 81,[151] Section 99,[152] and Section 237 (1) (c);

> Czech Act No. 216/1994 Coll., on arbitration and the enforcement of arbitral awards, as amended, ArbAct [CZE]: Section 2,[153] and Section 3.

Rationes Decidendi:

15.86. The following **fundamental conclusions** were drawn in Judgment 29 Cdo 1130/2011 of the Czech Supreme Court of 31 May 2011 (in M.S. versus PROFI CREDIT Czech, a.s.):[154]

(1) Arbitrability of Summary Proceedings on Bills of Exchange

(1) (a) Bills receivable are fit for arbitration.[155]

15.87. (1) (b) Claims from bills of exchange have property character, in that the obligation to make payment of a certain amount of money is incorporated in them. Disputes triggered by an action for payment of a bill are therefore property disputes (Section 2 (1) ArbAct [CZE]).

---

be the seat, the place of business, the location of works or an establishment, or the residential address of a contracting party, it shall be the location (address) as stated in the contract, until a change is communicated to the other party."

[150] Cited in the annotation of the Czech Supreme Court Judgment 29 Odo 1222/2005 of 19 December 2007 contained in this volume of the CYArb.

[151] *Ibid.*

[152] *Ibid.*

[153] ArbAct [CZE] (unofficial translation) - Section 2 – *"(1) The parties may agree in an arbitration clause that property disputes between them (excluding disputes arising from the enforcement of decisions and incidental disputes) that would otherwise fall within the jurisdiction of the courts shall be decided by one or several arbitrators or by a permanent arbitral institution. (2) An arbitration clause can be validly concluded if the parties would also be entitled to conclude a settlement regarding the subject matter of the dispute. (3) The arbitration clause may concern an individual dispute that is already pending (agreement to arbitrate), or any disputes arising in the future from the legal relations between the parties (arbitration clause). (4) Unless stipulated otherwise in the arbitration clause, the arbitration clause concerns rights arising directly from the legal relations between the parties, as well as the issue of the legal validity of those legal relations and related rights. (5) Unless expressly ruled out in the arbitration clause, the arbitration clause binds the parties' legal successors."*

[154] Prior to the initiation of proceedings before the Czech Supreme Court (NS ČR [CZE]), the following decisions had been rendered in the matter:

> Judgment 55 Cm 110/2007 of the Hradec Králové Regional Court (Pardubice branch), and

> Judgment 5 Cmo 141/2008-80 of the Prague Upper Court of 20 May 2008, in the wording of Resolution 5 Cmo 141/2008-89 of 16 June 2008.

[155] The NS ČR [CZE] attributed special legal relevance to the assessment of whether summary proceedings on bills of exchange are arbitrable.

15.88. **(1) (c)** The fact that an arbitrator has no authority to render a decision in the form of a default summons does nothing to change the fact of the arbitrability of claims from bills of exchange.

(2) Admissibility of Settlement as Prerequisite for Arbitrability

15.89. **(2) (a)** The nature of a dispute will regularly allow for the **conclusion of an (out-of-court, amicable) settlement** in matters in which the parties find themselves in a typical bilateral relationship, with respect to which substantive law does not rule out that the parties organise their legal relationship in the form of optional transactions (arrangements, measures). It follows that the nature of a dispute precludes a settlement, especially in those cases in which proceedings may be initiated even without a pertinent motion (Section 81 CCP [CZE]), in which the proceedings are to decide on a participant's civil status (Section 80 (a) CCP [CZE]), or in which substantive law does not allow the participants to resolve their dispute by way of an amicable understanding.[156]

15.90. **(2) (b)** Within the context of Section 2 (2) ArbAct [CZE], only those disputes suffer from a lack of arbitrability in which the nature of the case does not allow the parties to enter into a settlement, whereas the question of whether the court is in a position to approve a (specific) settlement between the parties is of no consequence for the validity of the arbitration agreement.

(3) Interpretation of Arbitration Clause

15.91. **(3) (a)** Arbitration clauses are interpreted by applying the rules and principles for the substantive-law interpretation of legal transactions.

15.92. **(3) (b)** Following the rules of interpretation contained in Section 35 (2) CC [CZE] and Section 266 ComC [CZE] and other principles for the interpretation of legal acts,[157] there can be no reasonable doubt that the phrase "[...] authority to hear and decide any disputes that concerned such claims as may directly or indirectly arise from this agreement on a revolving credit facility or in connection with it" also extends to disputes over the payment of a promissory note that served as a collateral for the receivable from the credit agreement, in a situation in which the terms of contract contain provisions on the issue of a blank

---

[156] The Czech Supreme Court reiterated and confirmed its position rendered in Judgment 29 Odo 1222/2005 of 19 December 2007, published *in* SBÍRKA SOUDNÍCH ROZHODNUTÍ A STANOVISEK (*Collection of Judicial Decisions and Opinions*), Ref. No. 103/2008 (R 105/2008).

[157] The Czech Supreme Court refers, e.g. to the principles spelled out in decision of the NS ČR [CZE], published under Ref. No. 35/2001 *in* SBÍRKA SOUDNÍCH ROZHODNUTÍ A STANOVISEK (*Collection of Judicial Decisions and Opinions*) and Ruling I ÚS 625/03 of the Czech Constitutional Court of 14 April 2005.

note as collateral and on the terms for completing the note, as well as the arbitration clause.[158]

(4) Written Form of Arbitration Clause; General Terms and Conditions

15.93. **(4) (a)** For the requirement of the written form to be met, it suffices for the arbitration agreement to be contained in General Terms and Conditions to which the contract actually made and executed by the parties refers. Such an arbitration agreement satisfies the written-form requirement.

15.94. **(4) (b)** In reviewing whether the arbitration agreement was validly made, one has to determine whether the proposal to contract that contained the arbitration clause (and be it in the form of a reference to General Terms and Conditions) was accepted without change, or whether other imperfections occurred during the contracting process that may give rise to doubts as to the inception and valid existence of the contract. Unless there are such doubts, the arbitration agreement may be considered properly made.

15.95. **(4) (c)** An additional aspect in support of finding that the contract (including the arbitration clause) was properly made and that the contracting process did not suffer from any imperfections that would cause the main contract and/or the arbitration clause to be invalid is the fact that the parties actually rendered performances under the contract – i.e. in the case at hand, that the obliged party had access to and drew a revolving credit under the credit agreement.[159]

[Description of Facts and Legal Issues[160]]

15.96. The defendant[161] (as lender/creditor) and the claimant[162] (as borrower/debtor) had entered into a written revolving credit facility,

---

[158] In the matter at hand, this concerned Sections 6 and 18 of one and the same contractual text, i.e. the same terms of contract.

[159] The Czech Supreme Court refers, e.g. to the principles spelled out in decision of the NS ČR [CZE], published under Ref. No. 35/2001 *in* SBÍRKA SOUDNÍCH ROZHODNUTÍ A STANOVISEK (*Collection of Judicial Decisions and Opinions*) and, *mutatis mutandis*, NS ČR [CZE] Judgment 32 Odo 1259/2004 of 18 May 2005).

[160] The annotation of the actual and legal state of affairs is based on the reasons chapter of the NS ČR [CZE] decision in the matter. The author of this annotation did not have available any other information regarding this dispute, or of the arbitral award, the decision by the first-instance court, or the decision by the court of appeals. All the information in this section is therefore derived from the summary given at the beginning of the reasons chapter of NS ČR [CZE] Judgment 29 Cdo 1130/2011 of 31 May 2011.

[161] The defendant in this procedure on the motion for the annulment of the arbitral award. In the preceding arbitration, they had been the claimant (creditor).

[162] The claimant in this procedure on the motion for the annulment of the arbitral award. In the preceding arbitration, she had been the defendant (debtor).

which contained, *inter alia*, the creditor's "contractual terms pertaining to the revolving credit facility" (the "terms of contract"). In order to secure the receivables arising from the credit facility, the claimant had issued a blank promissory note, which the defendant was authorised to fill in and complete if the terms of the credit facility were not honoured. In Section 18.1 of the terms of contract, the parties agreed that the authority to hear and decide any disputes that concerned such claims as may directly or indirectly arise from the credit facility would lie with the arbitrator in an arbitration procedure conducted as single-instance proceedings (i.e. without recourse to appeals) and as correspondence proceedings, whereas the specific arbitrator would be the one to whom the defendant submitted their statement of claim. The claimant failed to duly fulfil her obligations under the credit agreement and was in default with repayment, whereupon the defendant "filled in" the blank note such that the note total was composed of the remaining outstanding portion of the credit according to the payment schedule in the amount of [CZK xxx,xxx.xx], a contractual penalty in the amount of [CZK xx,xxx.xx], and an outstanding contractual penalty in the amount of [CZK x,xxx.xx]. An *ad hoc* arbitral award was issued on 3 October 2006 in an arbitration procedure that accommodated the request for relief and required the then defendant (i.e. the debtor) to pay the note total, plus 6% interest, and to reimburse the creditor for its costs of the proceedings.

15.97. The debtor responded by filing a request for the annulment of the arbitral award, objecting, among other things, that summary proceedings on bills of exchange are not arbitrable, that the arbitration agreement had not been made in the written form, that the executed agreement had merely contained a reference to the terms of contract containing the arbitration clause, etc. The first-instance court dismissed this request for the annulment of the arbitral award on grounds of the request's lack of merit, stressing that (i) claims from bills of exchange have property character and can be the subject of a settlement and are thus arbitrable, and (ii) the arbitration clause, which had been agreed by way of a reference to the terms of contract, which contain the actual provisions of the arbitration clause, was contracted in the written form, was valid and effective, and extended also to claims from the promissory note. The (second-instance) court of appeals upheld the first-instance court's judgment.

15.98. The claimant (debtor) filed a request for appellate review of the judgment by the court of appeals, reiterating her arguments based upon which she had found the claims from bills of exchange and promissory notes to lack arbitrability, and further arguing that Section 18 of the terms of contract had granted the arbitrator no authority to *"decide in matters pertaining to bills of exchange"*, in that the arbitration clause had purportedly extended only to decisions on claims for performance under the agreement on the revolving credit facility, but not to decisions on disputes arising from collateral instruments. By referring to Section 3 ArbAct [CZE], the appellant further stressed that the *request for approval of a revolving credit facility* had not been a written contract in the proper sense of the word, but merely a proposal to contract offered by the appellant, which required acceptance by the defendant. In this respect, she pointed to the contents of the terms of contract, arguing that the notice of acceptance of contract had never been delivered to her, as anticipated by the terms of contract.[163]

[Comment of the Author of This Annotation]

15.99. The request for appellate review was rejected, i.e. the arbitral award was not set aside and the arbitrability of the summary proceedings over the bill of exchange was upheld.[164] In interpreting the arbitration clause, the Czech Supreme Court applied the same rules of interpretation as in the case of the main contract, i.e. substantive-law aspects of interpretation. While the Court did not expressly address the issue of the arbitration clause's autonomy and separability from the main contract, in no way did it call such separability into question. To quite the contrary, it is obvious that the Supreme Court considered it a *notorious fact* that required no further elaboration.

| | |

---

[163] However, as the Czech Supreme Court emphasised in its decision, proof positive of the acceptance of the "contract proposal" is inherent in the fact that the parties rendered performances to each other under the said agreement, and that the appellant asked to be granted and received credit.

[164] A constitutional complaint was later filed in the matter with the Czech Constitutional Court, where it is pending under Case No. IV. ÚS 2457/2011. As of press time for this annotation, no decision has been rendered in matters of this constitutional complaint.

3. Poland

Abbreviations used in annotations:

k.p.c. [POL]   Kodeks postępowania cywilnego [*Code of Civil Procedure*] [POL] – Ustawa z dnia 17 listopada 1964 r. [Law as from 17 November 1964], published in: Dziennik Ustaw, 1964 Nr. 43, poz. 296;

k.c. [POL]   Kodeks cywilny [*Civil Code*] [POL] – Ustawa z dnia 23 kwietnia 1964 r. - Kodeks cywilny [Law as from 23 April 1964], published in: Dziennik Ustaw, 1964 Nr. 16 poz. 93;

Pr. weksl. [POL]   Prawo wekslowe (*Bills of Exchange Act*) [POL] - Ustawa z dnia 28 kwietnia 1936 r. (Law as from 28 April 1936), published in: Dziennik Ustaw, 1936, nr 37 poz. 282.

Tomáš Řezníček

I. Limits to the Arbitration Clause: Issues of Operation of an Enterprise Limiting the Scope of an Arbitration Clause (Supreme Court (*Sąd Najwyższy*) Resolution Case No III CZP 36/11 as of 13 July 2011)[1]

Key words:
arbitration clause | scope of an arbitration clause | arbitration court | arbitration court, jurisdiction | joint debtor | jurisdiction | jurisdiction, objection | obligation

States involved:
[POL] - [Poland]. From the available annotation a relationship with another country not found.

---

[1]   Taken from the decision summary available at: http://arbitraz.laszczuk.pl/orzecznictwo/356,uchwala_sadu_najwyzszego_z_dnia_13_lipca_2011_r_iii_czp_36_11.html (accessed on November 21, 2011). On the same page is also available the text of the original decision in Polish. Cited source came from the Biuro Studiów i Analiz Sądu Najwyższego. The site is a domain of a commercial active entity. Contradicts the policy of this periodical (CYArb) to refer to such websites and their owners. Authors and editors therefore apologize to the owners and operators of sites cited. It is clear the site contains very well-prepared and updated case law of the Polish courts. Therefore the author and editors have used it as the basis for the current annotation of the Polish judicial law relating to arbitration, after review of the original sources, as well as the author and editorial processing.

Laws and Regulations Taken into Account in This Ruling:

➤ Kodeks postępowania cywilnego [*Code of Civil Procedure*] [k.p.c.] [POL] – Ustawa z dnia 17 listopada 1964 r. [Law as from 17 November 1964], published in: Dziennik Ustaw, 1964 Nr. 43, poz. 296: Art. 43 § 1, Art. 72 § 1 (1), Art. 390 § 1, Art. 1161 § 1[2];

➤ Kodeks cywilny [*Civil Code*] [k.c.] [POL] – Ustawa z dnia 23 kwietnia 1964 r. – Kodeks cywilny [Law as from 23 April 1964], published in: Dziennik Ustaw, 1964 Nr. 16 poz. 93: Art. 55,[4] Art. 366.[3]

Rationes Decidendi:

16.01. An arbitration clause concluded by joint debtor is not binding for other joint debtor.

16.02. An arbitration clause concluded by the registered partnership (*spółka jawna*) is not binding for its partner.

16.03. The buyer of an enterprise (Art. 55[4] of the Civil Code[4]) is bound by an arbitration clause concluded prior to sale of an enterprise by the seller of the enterprise with its creditor indicating all disputes regarding the obligations connected with operation of an enterprise.

| | |

---

[2] *Code of Civil Procedure* - k.p.c. [POL] Author's translation: [*Article 1161, Section 1*- The submission of a dispute for resolution by an arbitration court is subject to an agreement by and between the parties, indicating the subject of the dispute or the legal relationship from which the dispute arose or may arise (an arbitration clause).]

[3] *Civil Code* [k.c.] [POL] Author's translation: [*Article 366* - Several debtors may be liable in such manner that the creditor may claim the whole performance or a part thereof from all debtors jointly, from several of them or all of them severally, and the satisfaction of the creditor by any of the debtors frees the remaining ones (joint and several liability of debtors).]

[4] *Civil Code* [k.c.] [POL] Author's translation: [*Article 55* - The acquirer of an enterprise or an agricultural farm shall be liable jointly and severally with the transferor for the obligations of the latter connected with the running of the enterprise or the agricultural farm except for the case where, at the time of the acquisition, the acquirer did not know about those obligations in spite of due diligence on his or its part. The liability of the acquirer shall be limited to the value of the acquired enterprise or farm according to their state at the time of the acquisition, and according to the prices at the time of satisfying the creditor. Such liability cannot be precluded or limited without the consent of the creditor.]

II. Jurisdiction in Arbitral Proceedings: An Order Discontinuing the Proceedings before the Arbitration Court because of the Lack of a Valid Arbitration Clause; Arbitration Court Rules That It Lacks Jurisdiction in the Matter (Supreme Court (*Sąd Najwyższy*) Decision, Case No I CSK 231/10 as of 28 January 2011)[5]

Key words:
arbitral award | set aside an arbitration award | arbitration clause | invalidity of arbitration clause | arbitration court´s jurisdiction | discontinuation of arbitration proceedings | jurisdiction | lack of jurisdiction | order discontinuing the proceedings

States involved:
[POL] - [Poland]. From the available annotation a relationship with another country not found.

Laws Taken into Account in This Ruling:
➢ Kodeks postępowania cywilnego (*Code of Civil Procedure*) [k.p.c.] [POL] – Ustawa z dnia 17 listopada 1964 r. (Law as from 17 November 1964), published in: Dziennik Ustaw, 1964 Nr. 43, poz. 296: Art. 1180 § 1 and § 3, Art. 1190 § 1, Art. 1196 § 1, Art. 1198, Art. 1205.

Rationes Decidendi:
16.04. An arbitration court may rule on its own jurisdiction in an arbitral proceeding in which a claim has been filed (Art. 1180 §1[6] of the Code of Civil Procedure), including also in a separate order. In the regulations concerning procedure before the arbitration court, the Parliament did not provide a basis for issuance of an award dismissing a statement of

---

[5]   Taken from the decision summary available at: http://arbitraz.laszczuk.pl/ orzecznictwo/en 433/Wyrok Sadu Najwyzszego z dnia 28 stycznia 2011 I C.pdf (accessed on November 21, 2011). On the same page is also available the text of the original decision in Polish. Cited source came from the Biuro Studiów i Analiz Sądu Najwyższego.

[6]   *Code of Civil Procedure* [k.p.c.] [POL] Author's translation: [*Article 1180, Section 1 - An arbitration court may rule as to the jurisdiction thereof, including the existence, validity or effectiveness of the arbitration clause. Should the main contract containing the arbitration clause terminate or become null and void, this alone shall not imply the invalidity or expiration of said clause.*]

claim commencing a proceeding before the arbitration court, including in a situation where the arbitration court finds that it has no jurisdiction to decide the dispute. It follows from these provisions that in instances indicated in Art. 1190 §1,[7] 1196 §1[8] and 1198[9] of the Code of Civil Procedure, the arbitration court shall issue an order discontinuing the proceeding. It should thus be accepted that the arbitration court shall issue such an order also when, after beginning to receive evidence in the matter, it finds that the proceeding cannot continue because of the lack of an arbitration clause or the invalidity of such agreement. Conducting the proceeding and issuing an award then becomes impossible for a reason other than that stated in Art. 1198 §1 and the beginning of §2 of the Code of Civil Procedure.

16.05. The nature of a ruling issued by a court, including by an arbitration court, is decided by the substance of the ruling, and not the name or external form which the court gave to the ruling.

16.06. An order discontinuing the proceedings before the arbitration court because of the lack of a valid arbitration clause, or an order dismissing the statement of claim for this reason, is a ruling ending the proceeding before the arbitration court, in which the court rules on its own lack of jurisdiction in the matter. While an order by the arbitration court in which the arbitration court denies a defence of the lack of the arbitration court's jurisdiction may be challenged before the common court by either of the parties within two weeks (Art. 1180 §3[10] of the Code of Civil Procedure), the Parliament did not provide for the

---

[7] *Code of Civil Procedure* [k.p.c.] [POL] Author's translation: [*Article 1190, Section 1 - In the event the plaintiff fails to file suit pursuant to Article 1188, the arbitration court shall discontinue the proceedings.*]

[8] *Code of Civil Procedure* [k.p.c.] [POL] Author's translation: [*Article 1196, Section 1 - In the event the parties settle their dispute before an arbitration court, the arbitration court shall dismiss the proceedings. The contents of the settlement shall be included in the record of the proceedings and confirmed with the signatures of the Parties.*]

[9] *Code of Civil Procedure* [k.p.c.] [POL] Author's translation: [*Article 1198 - Save for those cases referred to in Article 1190, Section 1 and Article 1196, Section 1, an arbitration court shall rule to discontinue the proceedings if: 1) the plaintiff withdraws the case, unless the respondent objects thereto, and the arbitration court decides that there is a justified interest in the final resolution of the dispute; or 2) the arbitration court decides that any further proceedings have become unnecessary or - for other reasons - impossible.*]

[10] *Code of Civil Procedure* [k.p.c.] [POL] Author's translation: [*Article 1180, Section 3 - An arbitration court may rule on the charges referred to in Section 2 in a separate award. If the arbitration court dismisses the charge with such award, each party may ask the court for resolution within two weeks of receipt of such award. Proceedings initiated before the court do not suspend the examination of the case by an arbitration court. The provisions of Article 1207 shall apply to such court proceedings accordingly. The court ruling may not be subject to appeal.*]

opportunity to challenge before the common court an order by the arbitration court in which the arbitration court rules that it lacks jurisdiction in the matter. Upon issuance of such ruling, a proceeding before the common courts is open to the parties interested in resolution of the dispute, and they may exercise their right of access to the courts in such proceeding.

16.07. A negative determination by the arbitration court as to its own jurisdiction in a matter is a final ruling and is not subject to review by the common court. A ruling by the arbitration court finding that it lacks jurisdiction in the matter may thus not be challenged by a petition to set aside an arbitration award as provided by Art. 1205[11] ff of the Code of Civil Procedure.

| | |

III. Limits to the Arbitration Clause: Protection against the Defence that the Promissory Note Dispute Is Subject to an Arbitration Clause (Supreme Court (*Sąd Najwyższy*) Decision, Case No I CSK 112/10 as of 16 December 2010)[12]

Key words:
arbitration clause | arbitration clause may be binding | arbitration clause, limitation of | arbitration clause, succession | arbitration court | arbitration court´s jurisdiction | arbitration proceedings, defence | Bills of Exchange Act | jurisdiction, objection | legal succession | promissory note | promissory note dispute

States involved:
[POL] - [Poland]. From the available annotation a relationship with another country not found.

---

[11]   [POL] *Code of Civil Procedure* [k.p.c.] Author's translation: [Article 1205, *Section 1- An award delivered by an arbitration court in the Republic of Poland may only be annulled by a court in proceedings initiated as a result of a filed challenge of the award and under the provisions hereunder. Section 2 - If the parties agreed that the proceedings before the arbitration court should include more than one instance, then provisions in Section 1 herein refer to the final award of the arbitration court ruling with regard to the claims of the parties.*]

[12]   Taken from the decision summary available at: http://arbitration-poland.com/case-law/434,polish supreme court judgment dated 16 december 20 10 .html (accessed on November 21, 2011). On the same page is also available the text of the original decision in Polish. Cited source came from the Biuro Studiów i Analiz Sądu Najwyższego.

Laws and Regulations Taken into Account in This Ruling:

> Kodeks postępowania cywilnego (*Code of Civil Procedure*) [k.p.c.] [POL] – Ustawa z dnia 17 listopada 1964 r. (Law as from 17 November 1964), published in: Dziennik Ustaw, 1964 Nr. 43, poz. 296: Art. 1157, Art. 1161 § 1, Art. 1181 § 3, Art. 1184 § 1, Art. 1212 § 2;

> Prawo wekslowe (*Bills of Exchange Act*) [Pr. weksl.] [POL] - Ustawa z dnia 28 kwietnia 1936 r. (Law as from 28 April 1936), published in: Dziennik Ustaw, 1936, nr 37 poz. 282: Art. 17, Art. 20 § 1.

Rationes Decidendi:

16.08. Generally is considered that an arbitration clause may be binding also on legal successors with respect to the relationship under which disputes were submitted to the arbitration court for resolution, but an endorsee is protected by Art. 17[13] of the Bills of Exchange Act against defences by the promissory note debtors based on their personal relations with the prior holders of the note. This also includes protection against the defence that the promissory note dispute is subject to an arbitration clause. The promissory note debtor could assert against the endorsee the defence that the promissory note dispute is subject to an arbitration clause agreed with the prior holder of the promissory note only if the endorsee, in acquiring the promissory note, consciously acted to the injury of the debtor, i.e. knew of the existence of grounds for the debtor to assert the arbitration clause against the prior holder and also sought, to the injury of the debtor, to deprive the debtor of such defence. The promissory note debtor's assertion against the acquirer of the promissory note, without any limitations, of the defence that the promissory note dispute is subject to an arbitration clause, could come into play only in instances where the promissory note was acquired by way of an assignment agreement or endorsement after protest for non-payment or after the deadline for protest, having the effect of an assignment (Art. 20 §1 first sentence[14] of the Bills of Exchange Act).

---

[13] *Bills of Exchange Act* [Pr. weksl.] [POL] Author's translation: [Article 17 - *Persons against whom claims under the promissory note are raised may not defend themselves from the note owner by making allegations based on their personal relationship with the issuer or previous owners, unless the owner, upon purchasing the promissory note, acted to deliberately harm the debtor.*]

[14] Bills of Exchange Act [Pr. weksl.] [POL] Author's translation: [Article 20 first sentence – *Any endorsement after the payment term shall have the same result as an endorsement prior to such term.*]

16.09. Although a clause submitting a promissory note dispute to an arbitration court is theoretically permissible under Art. 1157[15] of the Code of Civil Procedure, to do so must be regarded from the perspective of the promissory note creditor as highly irrational, as it deprives the promissory note creditor of the benefits afforded it by seeking payment of the promissory note in a proceeding for an order of payment before the common court. The position cannot be accepted (...) that benefits comparable to those afforded to the party enforcing payment of a promissory note by a proceeding for order of payment may be assured in an arbitration proceeding by reference to the regulations concerning proceedings for order of payment within the parties' agreement concerning "the rules and manner of proceeding before the arbitration court" (Art. 1184 §1[16] of the Code of Civil Procedure).

16.10. In light of the irrationality of submission of a promissory note dispute to an arbitration clause, it should be accepted that the effectiveness of such a clause requires an express reservation with respect to the given promissory note claim which in each instance does not raise any doubts. These rules out extending an arbitration clause included in the agreement underlying the issuance of the promissory note, with respect to disputes connected with such agreement, to a promissory note claim against the issuer.

[Tomáš Řezníček]

Mgr. Tomáš Řezníček (*1978) works as a legal trainee in the Law Offices of Bělohlavek, Prague, Czech Republic. He graduated from the Law Faculty of Charles University in Prague in 2007, also completed foreign law studies at the Law Faculty of Jagiellonian University in Krakow. He is the co-author of various articles with prof. A. Bělohlávek published in professional journals in the Czech Republic. Field of interest: Commercial Law, Private International Law, Pharmaceutical Law.

e-mail: tomas.reznicek@ablegal.cz

| | |

---

[15] Code of Civil Procedure [k.p.c.] [POL] Author's translation: [Article 1157 - *Unless otherwise provided by a special law, the parties may agree that property disputes or non-property disputes, in respect of the subject-matter of which they could reach a settlement, shall be resolved by an arbitral tribunal; this shall not apply to proceedings in matters of maintenance.* Article 1157 - *Unless special provisions of law state otherwise, the Parties may file their property or non-property rights disputes that may be the subject of a court settlement for resolution by an arbitration court, except for suits for alimony.*]

[16] *Code of Civil Procedure* [k.p.c.] [POL] Author's translation: [Article 1184, *Section 1-Unless the statutory provisions state otherwise, the parties may agree on the rules and procedures applicable during the proceedings before an arbitration court.*]

4. Romania

Abbreviations used in annotations:
ROU   Romania

Alexander J. Bělohlávek

I. Arbitrability of Disputes from Contract on Joint Enterprise Association; Exclusion of Jurisdiction of Courts (Ploieşti Court of Appeal No. 61 of 19 January 2010)

Key words
Arbitrability | appointment of arbitrator | liquidation | jurisdictional challenge | arbitration clause | ad hoc arbitration | association | permanent arbitral institution | exclusion of jurisdiction of courts

Laws and Regulations Taken into Account in This Ruling:
➢   Code of Civil Procedure [ROU]: Sections 158, 341, 344-351, 355(1).

Rationes Decidendi:[1]
17.01.   An arbitration clause in a contract concerning property rights that determines jurisdiction over a particular dispute arising from the contract, as well as an agreement on the management of arbitral proceedings before a permanent arbitral institution, exclude the jurisdiction of courts.

17.02.   Disputes over the rights and obligations from a contract on joint enterprise (association) are also arbitrable. Arbitrators are also entitled to make decisions on the dissolution of associations and the liquidation thereof, as well as on the obligations connected with the drawing up of financial statements (balance) of associations.

17.03.   If the arbitration clause identifies a particular permanent arbitral institution, this permanent arbitral institution has jurisdiction, and the proceedings are not *ad hoc* arbitration.

17.04.   The objection of a lack of jurisdiction of a court on the grounds of an arbitration clause excluding the court's jurisdiction shall only succeed if there exists an arbitral tribunal to which the court could refer the motion as the forum competent to hear and resolve the case.

---

[1]   The decision was referred to us and the text of the judgment was provided by Professor Ligia Catuna, Timisoara, Romania.

[Description of Facts and Legal Issues]

17.05. The plaintiff requested an order declaring that the contract on joint enterprise (association),[2] which had been entered into by the parties to the dispute, was terminated; the plaintiff also demanded that the court order the defendant to draw up the balance of the association and liquidate the association. The plaintiff also demanded that the defendant be ordered to include in the balance such income originating from relationships with third parties. The case concerned a contract on joint enterprise (association) entered into between the parties. The plaintiff de facto demanded a decision on the dissolution of the association for serious disagreements between the contracting parties stemming from the fact that certain income was not recorded in their joint balance. The defendant, *inter alia*, challenged the jurisdiction of the court on the grounds of an arbitration clause incorporated in the contract on joint enterprise (association). The arbitration clause in the contract on joint enterprise (association) stipulated that if any disagreements between the parties could not be resolved by amicable settlement, the disputes were to be submitted to an arbitral tribunal and resolved pursuant to the Rules of ad-hoc commercial arbitration; the arbitration was to be conducted by the Chamber of Commerce and Industry of Romania. The trial court granted the challenge[3] and ruled that the dispute be referred to the Court of Arbitration with the Chamber of Commerce and Industry of Romania. At the same time, the trial court held that the motion concerned a claim regarding the exercise of rights from a contract on joint enterprise (association), including the liquidation thereof. The court also confirmed the existence of a valid arbitration agreement incorporated in the same contract. This arbitration clause therefore excludes the jurisdiction of courts and stipulates the jurisdiction of an arbitral tribunal. The plaintiff appealed the decision.

[Decision of Court of Appeal]

17.06. The Ploieşti Court of Appeal dismissed the appeal as groundless. The court upheld the decision of the trial court and ruled that the latter had interpreted the case correctly and in compliance with the law when the court had concluded that it lacked jurisdiction in the case, because the dispute was to be heard by an arbitral tribunal. The arbitration clause explicitly stipulates the jurisdiction of the Court of Arbitration with the Chamber of Commerce and Industry of Romania. The court also

---

[2] This contract was entered into on 20 June 2005.
[3] Resolution of the Buzău Court of 21 October 2009.

correctly referred the case directly to the arbitral tribunal. The appellate court held that the proceedings were not *ad hoc* proceedings in which the arbitral tribunal is established by the appointment of the arbitrator; in this case, the arbitration clause stipulated the jurisdiction of a permanent arbitral institution. If, and only if, the arbitration clause does not identify any permanent arbitral institution and there is no other arbitral forum that would have jurisdiction to hear the dispute, i.e. the case cannot be referred to arbitrators, the defence of a lack of jurisdiction would not succeed. In this case, however, the arbitration clause identified the Court of Arbitration with the Chamber of Commerce and Industry of Romania, which actively acts as a permanent arbitral institution. The arbitral tribunal therefore exists and operates, and the trial court correctly referred the case to this permanent arbitral institution for a hearing.

| | |

II. Post-hearing Petitions; Impossibility of Partial Annulment of Arbitral Award; Award *Ultra Petita* (Resolution of Supreme Court of Cassation (Chamber of Commerce) No. 1247/2010, Dossier No. 6136/2/2007 of 15 April 2010)

Key words
partial annulment | decision on the merits | plaintiff's motion | remedial measure | procedural rights | hearing of the case | subject of the proceedings | fair trial | ultra petita | hearing | fundamental procedural rights | annulment of arbitral award

Laws and Regulations Taken into Account in This Ruling:
➤ European Convention on Human Rights;
➤ Code of Civil Procedure [ROU]: Section 364(i), (j);
➤ Civil Code [ROU]: Section 1529.

Rationes Decidendi:[4]
17.07. An arbitration clause suspends the otherwise general jurisdiction of courts.

---

[4]   The decision was referred to us and the text of the judgment was provided by Professor Ligia Catuna, Timisoara, Romania.

17.08. Arbitration is characteristic, *inter alia*, for the expeditious hearing of a case. However, the parties must not be deprived of certain fundamental rights, which litigation would otherwise guarantee. The mechanism of observance of these fundamental rights is represented by the possibility of the annulment of an arbitral award by a court.

17.09. Statutory grounds for the annulment of the arbitral award are the subject of public policy, and the parties cannot suspend or exclude these grounds or the possibility of the annulment of the arbitral award.

17.10. Post-hearing petitions and statements of fact, incorporated only in the final briefs of the parties, cannot be considered duly heard. Such petitions are procedurally null and void (non-existent).

17.11. The partial annulment of an arbitral award (annulment of only one or more, not all, of the orders pronounced by the arbitral award) is not possible. An arbitral award may only be set aside as a whole. Grounds for the annulment of an arbitral award only applicable to one of the orders are also applicable to the other paragraphs of the order.

17.12. The motion for the annulment of an arbitral award is not a regular remedial measure. It is a revision mechanism *sui generis* used in order to guarantee fundamental procedural rights. Consequently, the grounds for the annulment of an arbitral award have effects with respect to the entire decision on the merits; as opposed to a regular remedial measure applicable in litigation, it is not possible to set aside only one or more, not all, of the orders pronounced by the arbitral award.

17.13. When the court rules on a motion for the annulment of an arbitral award based on the allegation that the arbitrators decided *ultra petita*, the court must first establish the scope of the duly made and heard petition (statement of claim) on which the arbitration was based. Only after the scope of the petition (statement of claim) is established may the court decide whether or not the arbitral award is *ultra petita*.

[Description of Facts and Legal Issues]

17.14. The plaintiff filed a motion with the Bucharest Court of Appeal on 14 November 2007 and requested the partial annulment of Arbitral Award No. 140 of 15 June 2007 rendered by the Court of International Commercial Arbitration with the C.C.I.R. The plaintiff claimed that the arbitrators had breached certain provisions concerning public policy by delivering a decision *ultra petita*. The case concerned a petition (statement of claim) for a declaration that a contract on joint enterprise (association) was terminated in consequence of serious disagreements between the contracting parties. The plaintiff further claimed that the specific paragraph of the petition (statement of claim) with respect to which the plaintiff requested the annulment of the arbitral award was only lodged after the hearing had been closed, and consequently, the petition (statement of claim) was not the subject of the proceedings. The defendant proposed that the court dismiss the motion as groundless. Later in the proceedings, the defendant also raised the reservation of the inadmissibility of a motion for annulment (of an arbitral award).

[Decision of Trial Court]

17.15. The Bucharest Court of Appeal, VI (Chamber of Commerce)[5] dismissed the defence of the inadmissibility of the motion for annulment, and granted the motion and annulled the part of the arbitral award that concerned the declaration that the contract on joint enterprise (association) was terminated. The court also ordered a hearing on the merits of the case in this regard, and directly scheduled the date of the hearing. The trial court held that the doctrine and the practice both agreed that a motion for the annulment of an arbitral award was de facto a remedial measure. Consequently, it is not possible to argue that the annulment of the challenged decision in full is the only admissible solution; it is possible to apply, without limitations, the principle of "*qui potest plus, potest minus*". As concerns the merits of the dispute, the court held that the petition (statement of claim) filed with the arbitral tribunal concerned two claims (petitions), namely (i) the declaration that the contract was terminated in consequence of a unilateral cancellation, and (ii) the petition demanding that the defendant vacate the occupied premises. The court noted that the claimant did not propose that the arbitral tribunal itself declare the termination of the contract; the claimant only proposed that the arbitral tribunal establish (find) that the contract had been terminated. Besides, it was established that the defendant had failed to mention before the arbitral tribunal that there had allegedly been significant disagreements between the partners; such statement of fact is only contained in the party's post-hearing brief. The trial court therefore concluded that the plaintiff's right to a fair trial under the European Convention on Human Rights had been breached.

17.16. The court also concluded that the grounds for the dissolution of an association under the Civil Code are not an exhaustive, but merely an indicative list.[6] The law therefore only provides examples of such cases; the doctrine and the practice agree that disagreements between

---

[5] Judgment of the Bucharest Court of Appeal, VI, No. 36 of 27 February 2008.

[6] Section 1529 of the Civil Code [ROU].

partners constitute legitimate grounds that can result in the dissolution of the association. The court rejected the defendant's argument that the dissolution of an association can only be implemented in those situations agreed upon in the contract on joint enterprise (association); the contract cannot exclude the grounds for the dissolution of the association set forth by statute. However, the actual grounds for the dissolution of the association were only mentioned in the final written brief delivered to the arbitral tribunal after the hearing had been closed. The statements of fact articulated therein indeed constitute grounds for the dissolution of the association, but they must be supported by evidence heard or read in the proceedings, and the other party must have the opportunity to present its comments on the issue.

[Decision of Court of Appeal]

17.17. The defendant filed a timely appeal. In the appeal, the defendant especially argued that the judgment summarized above had breached the restrictions applicable to the jurisdiction of a court in proceedings for the annulment of an arbitral award. The defendant maintained, *inter alia*, that the court set aside part of the arbitral award, because the petition (statement of claim) concerning that specific part had not been the subject of the hearing. The court therefore concluded that the petition (statement of claim) had not, in fact, existed. Consequently, the petition (statement of claim) cannot be the subject of a hearing on the merits scheduled by the court after the court set aside that very part of the arbitral award. In other words, the defendant argues that if a particular petition (statement of claim) was not the subject of a hearing before a tribunal, the court cannot hear the petition (statement of claim) either, because the petition (statement of claim) does not exist in law.

17.18. The Supreme Court of Cassation heard the case and concluded that courts have general jurisdiction. The legislator suspends that jurisdiction where the parties contract an arbitration clause. Arbitration is characteristic, *inter alia*, for an expeditious hearing of the case. However, the parties to the arbitral proceedings must not be deprived of the fundamental procedural rights, which litigation would otherwise guarantee, because an arbitral award is a decision on the merits with the same effects as a court judgment. The Code of Civil Procedure therefore provides for a special "remedial measure" against arbitral awards, namely a motion for the annulment of an arbitral award. The motion for the annulment of an arbitral award can only be filed on the grounds explicitly set forth in the statute.[7] Statutory grounds for the annulment of an arbitral award are the subject of public policy, and the parties cannot suspend or exclude these grounds or the possibility of the annulment of the arbitral award.

17.19. The arbitral award may be set aside if "the tribunal delivered a decision regarding issues that were not the subject of the petition (statement of claim) [...], with "issues that were not the subject of the petition (statement of claim)" meaning any and all claims that were not submitted for a hearing between the parties to the dispute, i.e. including post-hearing petitions. Post-hearing petitions cannot be considered as duly made (they are non-existent). The arbitral award can therefore be set aside if the arbitrators rendered a decision regarding issues that were not submitted for a hearing. Consequently, the Supreme Court held that if any of the orders pronounced by the arbitral award fell within the scope of any of the grounds for the annulment of an arbitral award, this sufficed for the annulment of the whole arbitral award, irrespective of whether the order suffering from the defect had any conditional or unconditional connection to the other orders. This limitation is based on the nature of the motion for the annulment of an arbitral award, which is not a regular remedial measure. Only a regular remedial measure would allow the partial annulment of the order on the merits. However, a motion for the annulment of an arbitral award is a special remedial measure, which, in case the criteria of any of the statutory grounds are met, has the result of the annulment of the entire arbitral award as a whole, because the grounds for the annulment of the arbitral award[8] are grounds consisting of the breach of the procedural guarantees benefiting the parties to the dispute, which have an impact on the entire decision (arbitral award). The Supreme Court of Cassation [ROU] therefore held that the partial annulment of the arbitral award constituted an erroneous application of the law, and as such, suffered from a defect. Contrary to a regular remedial measure challenging a decision rendered in litigation, the motion for the annulment of an arbitral award represents a special procedure that does not allow only one of the orders on the merits to be separated and annulled.

17.20. The Supreme Court of Cassation also rejected the arguments of the lower court. The lower court held that the court basically could, after the partial annulment of the arbitral award and during the hearing on the merits, adopt the results of the hearing of the case reached in the

---

preceding arbitral proceedings and thereby remedy the defects of the proceedings before arbitrators. This solution, however, is in conflict with the very nature of the motion for the annulment of an arbitral award, which is not a regular remedial measure. In this regard, the Supreme Court of Cassation accepted the reasons presented in the cassation appeal, in which the appellant claims that the lower court de facto permitted the hearing on the merits of a claim which, according to the order that pronounced the annulment of the arbitral award, has never in fact been made, because it was a post-hearing petition incorporated in the final brief. Consequently, the Supreme Court of Cassation reversed the decision of the lower court, remanded the case for a new trial, and ordered the lower court to establish, during the retrial of the motion for the annulment of the arbitral award, the limits of the arbitrators' jurisdiction based on the duly filed petition (statement of claim).

III

5. Slovak Republic

Abbreviations used in annotations:

CZE	Czech Republic
ECJ	Court of Justice of the European Union
CC [SVK]	Civil Code of the Slovak Republic – Act No\ 40/1964 Coll., as subsequently amended[1]
Directive	Council Directive 93/13/EEC of 5 April 1993 on unfair terms in consumer contracts[2]
SVK	Slovakia
ArbAct [SVK]	Act No 244/2002 Coll. [SVK], on Arbitration, as subsequently amended.

Alexander J. Bělohlávek

1. Termination of Enforcement of Arbitral Award Justified by Unfair Term in Consumer Contract (Resolution of Regional Court in Prešov [SVK], Case No. 17CoE/99/2010 of 15 February 2011)

Key words:

absolute commercial transaction | absolute nullity | consumer protection | disproportion between rights and obligations | nullity | nullity of the arbitration clause | unfair term | legal certainty | weaker contracting party | arbitration clause | consumer | consumer contract | pre-formulated standard contract/standard form contract | acknowledgment of debt | public policy | public interest | enforcement of the award | termination of enforcement

Laws and Regulations Taken into Account in This Ruling:

➢ Civil Code of the Slovak Republic – Act No. 40/1964 Coll., as subsequently amended, CC [SVK]:[3] Section 52 et seq. – primarily Section 39, Section 52, Section 53(4)(r);[4]

➢ Council Directive 93/13/EEC of 5 April 1993 on unfair terms in consumer contracts, Directive:[5] primarily Articles 3 and 6;

---

[1] The law was originally adopted during the Czechoslovak era; the version of the Civil Code applicable on 31 December 1992 was integrated in the law of the Czech Republic [CZE], as well as that of the Slovak Republic [SVK].

[2] *OJ* L 95 of 21 April 1993, pp. 29–34.

[3] See *supra* note 1.

[4] Full text of Section 53 of the CC [SVK] is quoted in a footnote below.

[5] *Supra* note 2, at 29–34.

> ➤ Act [SVK] No. 483/2001 Coll., on Banks: Section 93b(1);
> ➤ Act No 244/2002 Coll. [SVK], on Arbitration, as subsequently amended, ArbAct [SVK]:Sections 40 and 45.[6]

Rationes Decidendi:
The Regional Court in Prešov [SVK], upholding the decision of the trial court (District Court in Kežmarok [SVK]), **arrived, *inter alia,* at the following conclusions:**[7]

18.01. An arbitration clause that is not the result of a consumer's active negotiation of the terms of the contract and that does not provide the consumer with any choice as to whether to accept or decline the clause is unfair and consequently *contra bonos mores.*

18.02. If the arbitral award was delivered on the basis of an unfair arbitration clause, the court may decline to give its consent with enforcement (execution) of the award or terminate the already pending enforcement proceedings (execution).

18.03. **A so-called absolute commercial transaction,** which is obligatorily subject to the provisions of the Commercial Code, can also be classified as a consumer contract (a contract concluded by a consumer), which is **subject to special consumer protection.** Such contracts are also subject to the special consumer protection regime in terms of the *Directive.*

18.04. The consumer is no doubt the weaker contracting party, whether for his or her lack of the necessary information or for his or her weaker negotiating position.[8]

18.05. The protection of consumers against unfair contractual terms entails absolute nullity, and there is no justification for such terms. In this regard, the European Union promoted the status of consumer protection to the level of national public policy rules.[9]

---

[6] The provisions are quoted in the footnotes below.

[7] Adopted from the annotation: Edmund Horváth, *Neprijateľná rozhodcovská doložka (Unfair Arbitration Clause)*, www.najpravo.sk (24 March 2011). The electronic version is available at: http://www.najpravo.sk/judikatura/obcianske-pravo/spotrebitelske-zmluvy/neprijatelna-rozhodcovska-dolozka.html?print=1 (accessed on January 2, 2012).

[8] The Regional Court in Prešov [SVK], as the appellate court, invoked in this connection the ECJ judgment in *Mostaza Claro,* Par. (25). The Court also referred to Article 3 of the *Directive.*

[9] The court invoked the Resolution of the ECJ, of 16 November 2010, Case No. C-76/10 *Pohotovosť s.r.o.* v. *Korčkovská* [2010], OJ C 134, Par. (50), which is fully annotated elsewhere in this book. Said paragraph (50) reads as follows (cit.): "*Considering the nature and the importance of public interest, which is the basis of the protection afforded by Directive 93/13 to consumers, Article 6 of the Directive must be considered a provision*

18.06. An adhesion contract offers no choice to the consumer, here in the sense of giving preference to arbitration over litigation in case of a dispute, or vice versa.

18.07. If the obligor breached his or her obligations, the obligee has the right to enforce his or her rights. Such enforcement, however, must be exercised with the use of legitimate means of protection, which do not include procedures based on unfair terms in consumer contracts.

18.08. **Acknowledgment of debt** by the obligor only entails substantive-law effects, and does not validate unfair terms in a contract (in the present case, an agreement on the method of enforcing claims under an unfair arbitration clause).

18.09. The characteristic of a judgment as final and conclusive is the essential quality thereof, because it is associated with the important principle of legal certainty resulting from a final and conclusive decision on the merits (*res judicata*). However, in certain cases, the law itself explicitly provides that a final and conclusive judgment can be subject to review (for instance, by way of exceptional remedial measures). Such legally approved exceptions to the rule include the court's power to dismiss a petition for enforcement or to terminate already-pending enforcement proceedings pursuant to special laws (pursuant to the Arbitration Act[10]).

[Description of Facts and Legal Issues]

18.10. The present case concerned a claim arising from a consumer credit facility provided by means of a bank's credit card. The District Court in Kežmarok [SVK] (as the trial court) dismissed the executor's application for authorization to enforce the arbitral award. The reason was that the respective contract contained an unfair (unacceptable) term, an arbitration clause in a standard form contract.[11] The court invoked the basic characteristic features of consumer contracts.[12] The court highlighted that one of the characteristic features of a consumer

---

equal to national rules with the status of mandatory rules under the respective national legal system (the abovementioned judgment in Asturcom Telecommunicaciones, Par. 52)."
The author does not agree with the conclusion regarding public policy – see the commentary to the decision in the final part of this annotation.

[10]   Section 45 of the ArbAct [SVK]. This provision will be quoted in the footnotes below in connection with the annotation of this decision.

[11]   In the present case, the arbitration clause corresponded to the clause incorporated in the bank's business terms and conditions (cit.): "*Any dispute between the bank and the client arising from or in connection with the legal relations between the bank and the client, which the parties fail to resolve by their mutual agreement, will be submitted for resolution to the Permanent Arbitration Court of the Banking Association established in Bratislava ("Arbitration Court")."* This arbitration clause was concluded on 17 June 2004.

[12]   Section 52 et seq. of the CC [SVK].

contract is that the contract is drafted in advance, and the consumer has no opportunity to negotiate the terms of the agreement or any changes to the offer. This was the case here. The court also invoked the ArbAct [SVK],[13] which stipulates that the court shall terminate the enforcement proceedings (execution) upon the obligor's motion or *sua sponte* (i) for any of the reasons stipulated by special laws, or (ii) if the arbitral award suffers from defects in terms of Section 40(a) and (b) of the ArbAct [SVK],[14] or (iii) if the arbitral award orders impossible or unlawful performance or performance *contra bonos mores*. The court also invoked the indicative list of unfair contractual terms in the CC

---

[13] Section 45 of the ArbAct [SVK] (cit.): "(1) *The court competent for enforcement or execution under special laws shall terminate the enforcement or execution proceedings at the request of the defendant against whom the enforcement of the arbitral award or the enforcement of the judgment or the execution were initiated* (a) *on grounds stipulated in a special law,* (b) *if the arbitral award suffers from a defect specified in Section 40(a) and (b),* or (c) *if the arbitral award orders a party to the arbitration to provide performance that is objectively impossible, unlawful or contra bonos mores.* (2) *The court competent for enforcement or execution shall terminate the enforcement of the arbitral award or the execution sua sponte if the court discovers that the arbitration suffered from defects specified in Subsection 1(b) or (c).* (3) *The court decisions under Subsections 1 and 2 can be appealed.*"

[14] ArbAct [SVK] (cit.): Part Seven – Annulment of Arbitral Awards – Section 40 – "*Grounds for Filing a Petition* – (1) *A party to arbitration may file a petition with the competent court demanding that a domestic arbitral award be set aside only if* (a) *the arbitral award was delivered in a matter that cannot be submitted to arbitration (a non-arbitrable matter) (Section 1(3)),* (b) *the arbitral award was delivered in a matter that has already been decided by a final and conclusive court decision delivered in litigation or by a final and conclusive award of an arbitral tribunal delivered in different arbitral proceedings,* (c) *one of the parties to the arbitral proceedings challenges the validity of the arbitration agreement,* (d) *the arbitral award deals with a matter that was not covered by the arbitration agreement and the party to the arbitral proceedings raised such an objection in the arbitration,* (e) *the party to the arbitration who must have a statutory representative did not have such a representative or a party to the arbitration was represented by an unauthorized person and the person's acts were not subsequently approved,* (f) *the arbitral award was delivered by an arbitrator who was disqualified by a decision rendered under Section 9 for a lack of impartiality, or the party to the arbitration could not have the arbitrator disqualified before the arbitral award was issued at no fault of the party,* (g) *the principle of equality of the parties to arbitration was violated (Section 17),* (h) *there are reasons justifying a petition for a trial de novo under special laws,* (i) *the arbitral award was affected by a criminal offence committed by the arbitrator(s), party(ies) to arbitration or expert(s), of which the perpetrator was found guilty by a final and conclusive judgment, or* (j) *the arbitration violated generally binding laws and regulations on the protection of consumer rights.* (2) *If a party to the arbitration files a petition with the competent court, the contested arbitral award remains final and conclusive. The court called upon to adjudicate on the petition may suspend the enforceability of the arbitral award at the request of a party.*"

[SVK],[15] which also includes arbitration clauses that order the consumer to resolve his or her disputes with the professional exclusively in arbitration.[16]

---

[15]   Section 53(4) of the CC [SVK]. CC [SVK] (cit.): Section 53 – "(1) Consumer contracts must not contain terms that cause a significant imbalance in the rights and obligations of the contracting parties to the detriment of the consumer ("unfair term"). This shall not apply as concerns contractual terms that relate to the main subject matter of the performance and to the adequacy of the price, insofar as these contractual terms are in plain intelligible language or if these unfair terms were individually negotiated. (2) A term shall not be regarded as individually negotiated even if the consumer had an opportunity to get acquainted with the term before signing the contract, unless the consumer was able to influence the substance of the term. (3) Unless the supplier proves otherwise, contractual terms agreed between the supplier and the consumer shall not be regarded as individually negotiated. (4) The following terms in a consumer contract shall especially be considered as unfair, i.e. terms (a) requiring the consumer to perform with which the consumer did not have the opportunity to get acquainted before the conclusion of the contract, (b) giving the supplier the possibility to transfer his or her rights and obligations under the contract to a different supplier without the consumer's consent, where the transfer would jeopardize the enforceability or reduce the guarantees for the consumer, (c) excluding or limiting the legal liability of the supplier in the event of the death of the consumer or personal injury to the latter resulting from an act or omission of that supplier, (d) excluding or limiting the consumer's rights when invoking the supplier's liability for defects or liability for damage, (e) permitting the supplier to retain performance provided by the consumer even in case the latter does not conclude or cancels the contract with the supplier, (f) permitting the supplier to cancel the contract without any contractual or statutory reason where the same facility is not granted to the consumer, (g) enabling the supplier to terminate a contract of indeterminate duration without reasonable notice, except where there are serious grounds for doing so, (h) obliging the consumer to fulfil all his or her obligations where the supplier does not perform his or hers, (i) enabling the supplier to alter the terms of the contract unilaterally without a valid reason agreed upon in the contract, (j) providing for the price of goods or services to be determined at the time of delivery or allowing the supplier to increase the price of his or her goods or services, in both cases without giving the consumer the right to cancel the contract if the final price is too high in relation to the price agreed when the contract was concluded, (k) requiring any consumer who fails to fulfil his or her obligation to pay a disproportionately high sum as a penalty for the default on the consumer's obligation, (l) restricting the consumer's access to evidence or imposing on him or her a burden of proof that, according to the applicable law, should lie with another party to the contract, (m) inappropriately excluding or limiting the possibility of the consumer to enforce his or her rights *vis-à-vis* the supplier in the event of total or partial non-performance by the supplier, including the consumer's right to offset a debt owed to the supplier against any claim that the consumer may have against the supplier, (n) automatically extending the validity of a contract of fixed duration after the expiration of the period for which the contract was concluded, while giving the consumer an unreasonably short period to express his or her consent with the prolongation of the contract, (o) giving the supplier the right to determine whether the goods or services supplied are in conformity with the contract, or giving him or her the exclusive right to interpret any term of the contract, (p) limiting the supplier's liability if the contract was concluded by his or her agents or requiring that a contract concluded by the supplier's

agent meet a particular formality, or (r) requiring the consumer to take disputes exclusively to arbitration, subject to the arbitration clause agreed by the parties. (5) Unfair terms in consumer contracts are invalid. (6) If the subject matter of the consumer contract is the provision of finances, the remuneration must not significantly exceed the remuneration commonly required on the financial market for consumer credits in similar cases. The assessment of similarity between the cases shall primarily include the consideration of the consumer's financial situation, the manner and the extent to which his or her obligation is secured, the volume of the finances provided by the supplier and the due date. (7) Securing an obligation arising from a consumer contract by a security transfer of rights to real property is not allowed in consumer contracts. (8) If the supplier provided performance to the consumer and the consumer had not ordered the performance, the consumer is not obliged to return or retain the performance; the supplier shall not have any other claims against the consumer either. Unrequested performance also includes any repeated performance provided to the consumer under a contract concluded by means of distant communication if the consumer had not explicitly requested such performance. Unless the supplier proves the opposite, repeated performance shall always be considered unrequested. (9) In the case of performance under a consumer contract that is supposed to be provided in instalments, the supplier may exercise his or her right under Section 565 only after three months following the consumer's default on the payment of an instalment, and provided the supplier warned the consumer of the exercise of said right with at least 15 days' notice. (10) The unfairness of contractual terms shall be assessed taking into account the nature of the goods or services for which the contract was concluded and by referring, at the time of conclusion of the contract, to all the circumstances attending the conclusion of the contract and to all the other terms of the contract or of another contract on which it is dependent. (11) The terms of a consumer contract of indeterminate duration according to which the supplier of financial services under a special law reserves the right to terminate the contract unilaterally without any notice period where there is a serious objective reason shall not be considered an unfair term under Subsection (4)(g), provided there is a serious objective reason that was not caused by the supplier, that the supplier could not foresee or avert, and that prevents the supplier from performing under the contract, and on condition that the supplier agreed in the contract that the supplier would notify the consumer of the termination of the contract and the reason for the termination without undue delay and in writing. (12) Subsections (4)(g) and (i) on unfair terms shall not apply to a consumer contract the subject matter of which is (a) a transaction in transferable securities, financial instruments and other products or services where the price is linked to fluctuations in rates and indices on the regulated market or to a market rate that the supplier does not control, or (b) the purchase or sale of foreign currency, traveller's cheques or international money orders denominated in foreign currency. (13) The following terms shall not be considered as unfair under Subsection (4)(i), i.e. terms according to which (a) a supplier of financial services under special laws reserves the right to alter the rate of interest or the amount of other charges for financial services under special laws payable by the consumer or due to the latter without notice where there is a serious objective reason, provided that the supplier undertakes to inform the consumer without undue delay and in writing of the alteration and of the consumer's possibility to terminate the consumer contract and that the latter is free to dissolve the contract immediately and free of charge, (b) a supplier of financial services under special laws reserves the right to unilaterally alter the conditions of the consumer contract for an indeterminate duration, provided that the supplier is obliged to inform the consumer without undue delay and in writing of the alteration and of the

18.11. The trial court held that the arbitration clause prevented an arbitral award rendered on the basis thereof from becoming an enforceable decision, because it prevented the consumer from choosing either arbitration or litigation. The arbitration clause was, in the present case, not the result of any active negotiation of the terms of the contract in which the consumer would participate; in other words, the consumer had no choice when accepting the contractual terms. The consumer could only "take it or leave it" as a whole. The trial court therefore

---

consumer's possibility to terminate the contract and that the latter is free to dissolve the contract immediately and free of charge. (14) Subparagraph (4)(j) on unfair terms shall not apply to a consumer contract the subject matter of which is (a) a transaction in transferable securities, financial instruments and other products or services where the price is linked to fluctuations in rates and indices on the regulated market or to a market rate that the supplier does not control, (b) the purchase or sale of foreign currency, traveller's cheques or international money orders denominated in foreign currency, or (c) a price-indexation clause, where explicitly permitted under special laws and provided that the method by which prices vary is explicitly described in the clause."

[16] It is basically a literal transcript of the list of contractual terms specified in the *Annex to the Directive*. See Section 53(4)(r) of the CC [SVK]; these provisions were incorporated in the Slovak Civil Code by Act [SVK] No. 568/2007 Coll., effective 1 January 2008 (see the analysis of the new substantive-law rules regulating consumer protection in the Czech Republic [CZE] in connection with the so-called *New Civil Code*– NCC [CZE]). The trial court also invoked the conclusions of the joint session of the department for civil law and the department for commercial law of the Regional Court in Prešov [SVK] held on 27 September 2010; the judgment analysed in this annotation quotes the following passage from the opinion adopted by the joint session: "*A contractual term in a standard form contract concluded after 31 December 2007 or in general business terms and conditions incorporated in such a contract that was not individually negotiated by the consumer and that requires the consumer to resolve his or her disputes with the supplier exclusively in arbitration prevents the arbitral award issued on the basis of the term from becoming an enforceable decision, which would give the supplier the right to demand authorization for an executor to conduct the execution. The term qualifies as an unfair contractual term even if it gives the consumer the possibility to choose between arbitration and litigation, provided that the clause also allows that if the arbitration is initiated by the supplier, the consumer will be obliged to submit to arbitration or will be obliged to file a petition with the court in case the consumer wishes to prevent arbitration. There are no reasons preventing the court from adopting an analogous approach if the contract was concluded before 1 January 2008.*" The reasons justifying the opinion further read as follows (also adopted from the annotation of the trial court's decision): "*[t]he high rate of abuse and the manifest preference for efficiency over an objective decision-making process fully justify the increasingly intensive focus on arbitral awards as enforceable decisions.* [According to our jurisprudence ([...])] *"[f]rom the consumer's perspective, it is irrelevant whether the resolution of his or her disputes in arbitration is imposed on him or her by a standard contractual clause or by the supplier's conduct. The consumer ought to be protected from both. The possibility of the supplier to impose his or her will in the contractual relationship was the reason why the entire mechanism of consumer protection against standard form contracts was created.*"

terminated the proceedings,[17] because the arbitration clause was found to be unfair and consequently *contra bonos mores*.

[Decision of Appellate Court and Appellate Court's Arguments]

18.12. The Regional Court in Prešov, as the appellate court, upheld the conclusions of the trial court. The obligee's appeal was therefore dismissed. The appellate court had no doubt that the contract in the present case was a standard adhesion contract, i.e. a standard form contract that is repeatedly being concluded by the professional. The same applies to the contractual terms, as well as to the fact that the credit facility was provided (as a financial service) in connection with the creditor's business. The appellate court thereby rejected the obligee's arguments – the obligee claimed in its appeal that the contract was not a consumer contract, because the special provisions regulating so-called *"consumer contracts"* do not apply to so-called *absolute business transactions* (in the present case, a credit contract), which are subject to the provisions of the Commercial Code. These arguments were rejected by the appellate court with reference to the *Directive*. The court also analysed the consumer protection rules applicable before 1 January 2008 with respect to so-called standard contract forms (pre-formulated standard contracts);[18] these rules prohibited contractual terms *"that establish a manifest disproportion between the rights and obligations of the contracting parties to the detriment of the consumer"*. Consequently, it is not necessary to resort to the indirect effect of the Directive in order to conclude that the obligee, as the professional, was at the time of the conclusion of the contract explicitly prohibited from contracting such terms in his or her standard form contracts that would establish a significant imbalance between the parties' rights and obligations to the detriment of the consumer.[19] The appellate court concluded that an arbitration clause requiring the consumer to submit to arbitration as the only option was unfair.[20]

---

[17] With reference to Section 39 and Section 53(5) of the CC [SVK] and to Section 45(1)(c) and (2) of the ArbAct [SVK].

[18] The case primarily concerned the application of Section 23a of Act No. 634/2002 Coll., on Consumer Protection, as applicable on the day the contract was concluded (the so-called standard form contract is *a contract that is supposed to be concluded in more cases if it is usual that the consumer has no substantial control over the terms of the contract*).

[19] Section 53 et seq. of the CC [SVK]. This provision is quoted in a footnote elsewhere in this annotation of the decision of the Slovak court.

[20] The court invoked, similarly to the trial court, the conclusions of the joint session of the department for civil law and the department for commercial law of the Regional Court in Prešov [SVK] held on 27 September 2010, just like the conclusions of the session were referred to by the trial court (quoted in a footnote above).

18.13. The obligee's argument invoking the Act on Banks was not successful either. The Act on Banks stipulates that the bank is obliged to instruct the client (and be able to prove it) about the consequences of entering into the proposed arbitration agreement, and to give him or her the **possibility of a choice.**[21] The court concluded, however, that the bank had offered no such choice to the consumer.

18.14. The appellate court also rejected the plaintiff's (the professional's) arguments regarding the importance of the acknowledgment of debt by the consumer. The court correctly held that the instrument of the acknowledgment of debt is regulated under substantive law, which has effects with respect to the expiration of time periods, legal fiction regarding the existence of the debt, etc. Such acknowledgment, however, has no influence on the validity (or subsequent validation, as the case may be) of unfair terms in a consumer contract, which are consequently, in the court's opinion, null and void.

[Author's Note on Judgment]

18.15. The Slovak court's decision is not surprising. Besides, it is clear that Slovakia [SVK] belongs to those countries that have not only implemented, but also apply the *Directive* rather strictly. Nonetheless, the judgment is, in certain respects, controversial. First of all, we need to point out that **the Slovak court defines consumer protection in the European Union (under EU law) as a component of *public policy.*** The author believes, however, that consumer protection is a **component of a [qualified] *public interest*. Both concepts (*public policy* v. *public interest*) must be principally distinguished,** also from the perspective of the protection afforded to each of them. These **two different categories** are often used interchangeably even in the case law of courts; but the effects, and especially the effects, of both categories are significantly different. Besides, it appears that the Slovak court adopted a rather undiscriminating approach and rejected the arbitration clause without meticulously analysing the facts of the case,

---

[21] Section 93b(1) of Act [SVK] No. 483/2001 Coll., on Banks. The court extensively elaborated on the obligations binding on the professional under the Slovak Act on Banks as the court responded to the plaintiff's (professional's) arguments. In the end, however, the court ruled against the plaintiff (professional) by stating that the plaintiff had failed to meet the conditions prescribed under the Act on Banks. The quoted provision of the Slovak Act on Banks stipulates the obligation to submit the offer of the contract (in the present case, the offer of the arbitration agreement) in advance. In a later amendment to the law, this particular provision of the Slovak Act was amended to stipulate clearly that the bank must let its client *choose*. The court ruled that the plaintiff *had offered no choice* in the present case.

especially the circumstances attending the conclusion of the contract.[22] This does not appear to comply with the current European practice either, including ECJ case law and important opinions prevalent in most European countries. Slovakia [SVK] has apparently been undergoing certain developments (together with some other countries, especially EU Member States) that most other countries already put behind them, i.e. from the strict rejection of arbitration clauses in consumer contracts in the past to a very cautious and careful examination of the facts of the case and all circumstances attending the conclusion of the contract,[23] which can be the only decisive factor in determining whether a particular contractual term is unfair or not, and consequently determining the legal effects of such factual situation.

18.16. Nonetheless, the sources available to the author do not offer any detailed information regarding the course of the arbitral proceedings in the present case, especially whether the consumer did or did not have or use the opportunity to request the annulment of the arbitral award. The decision does mention, though, that the consumer *did not raise the objection* of the nullity of the arbitration clause during arbitration itself, without, however, indicating what opportunity the consumer had to raise such an objection and whether, and to what extent, the consumer was an active participant in the arbitral proceedings or not. The applicability of the ECJ legal opinion voiced in *Asturcom*, as well as *Océano Grupo*, which the Slovak court invokes and which are annotated in greater detail elsewhere in this book, is significantly affected thereby. The Slovak courts (both the trial court and the appellate court) do not address this issue at all, or only to an insignificant extent (based on the available annotation), and therefore do not answer the question of **what opportunity the consumer had to raise his or her objections (if any) in the course of and immediately after arbitration.** The court based its arguments on the so-called

---

[22] The author needs to point out that he only had at his disposal the source cited in the opening part of this annotation, which summarizes the respective court decision. The full text of the decision of the trial court and, especially, of the appellate court could not be obtained. It needs to be emphasized (see also the footnote above) that the Slovak court apparently did address the circumstances attending the conclusion of the contract to some extent, as evidenced by its conclusions regarding the performance (in the present case, *failure to perform*) of the professional's obligations under the Slovak Act on Banks *vis-à-vis* the client (consumer).

[23] Primarily the developments in German law [DEU], which appears to have progressed the most, compared to other European countries, towards a very sensitive and diversified approach that, on top of that, strongly emphasizes the importance of autonomy, despite the otherwise traditional protection of the weaker party in Germany, France [FRA], the United Kingdom [GBR] and other countries.

absolute nullity of an unfair term in a consumer contract. But as we have explained elsewhere in this book (see the detailed analysis of the ECJ case law), the EU interpretation practice leans toward the opinion that such arbitration clauses, and perhaps other unfair contractual terms too, are not null and void (absolute nullity), but only voidable. This issue must be addressed irrespective of which approach the Slovak substantive law (CC [SVK]) adopted with respect to unfair terms. The Slovak decision, just like many decisions adopted, for instance, by Czech courts [CZE], invokes its own (national) substantive law and the absolute nullity of unfair terms in consumer contracts. At the same time, however, it invokes the Directive and its effects. In that very connection, we must highlight the necessity of an autonomous EU interpretation, which, however, is rather inclined towards *voidability*, depending on the opportunity the consumer had in the course of and immediately after the arbitral proceedings to raise his or her objections, and the extent to which the consumer actually used that opportunity (if at all). It appears the Slovak Court unduly disregarded this issue.

| | |

Section B

Case Law of the Arbitral Tribunals

All quoted rulings and rationes have been made anonymous to the maximum possible extent. To this end, rationes and explanations have been considerably abbreviated and modified. For the sake of anonymity, some data may have been deliberately altered, where such changes have no effect on the legal pertinence of the analysis of the specific issue expressed, in particular, by legal sentences. Quotes and annotations relating to judicial practice are non-binding and cannot be construed as a reference to a law source or an obligatory interpretation of the law. Further, legal opinions voiced by arbitrators are, as a rule, of an individual nature, and arbitration courts composed of different arbitrators may come to significantly different conclusions. Moreover, the quoted rulings of [state] courts cannot be considered a binding legal source in the Czech Republic, even though their considerable importance for the standardization of the current legal practice cannot be denied.

Czech Republic

Abbreviations used in annotations:

ArbAct [CZE]	[Czech]Act No. 216/1994 Coll. of 1 November 1994;
CCP [CZE]	[Czech]Act No. 99/1963 Coll., Code of Civil Procedure;
CivCo [CZE]	[Czech] Act No. 40/1964 Coll. of 26 February 1964, the Civil Code;
CommCo [CZE]	[Czech] Act No. 513/1991 Coll. of 5 November 1991, the Commercial Code;
NS [CZE]	Supreme Court of the Czech Republic.

Alexander J. Bělohlávek

Interpretation of Arbitration Agreement; Scope of Main Contract and of Arbitration Clause; Doubts as to Jurisdiction (Resolution on Jurisdiction (Jurisdictional Order / Decision on Jurisdiction) Delivered in Arbitration before Arbitration Court at Economic Chamber of Czech Republic and Agricultural Chamber of Czech Republic in Prague, Case No. Rsp 1734/11 of 7 November 2011)

Claimant:	*Czech natural person – individual (business person)*
Respondent:	*Czech legal person (public entity – municipality/city)[1]*
Place of Arbitration:	*Czech Republic*
Arbitration Agreement:	*The arbitration agreement invoked by the Claimant was in fact an arbitration clause incorporated in the main contract executed in the second half of 2006*
Nature of Arbitration:	*Arbitration before a permanent arbitral institution (Arbitration Court at the Economic Chamber of the Czech Republic and Agricultural Chamber of the Czech Republic in Prague), domestic dispute proceedings[2]*
Applicable Law:	*Main contract[3] – Czech law Arbitration agreement – Czech law Procedural rules – Czech law*

Key words:
civil law | extensive interpretation | taking of evidence | substantive-law | Kompetenz-Kompetenz | decision on the merits | international jurisdiction | separability of the arbitration clause | costs of proceedings | nullity (of contract) | performance without any legal cause | doubts about jurisdiction | legal cause for performance | jurisdiction | jurisdictional challenge | legal fact | legal act | procedural requirement | subject matter of the main contract | separability of arbitration clause | equality of the parties | arbitral award | arbitration agreement | scope of the arbitration agreement | autonomous interpretation | court | judicial protection | main contract | structure of contract | sovereignty | domestic proceedings | constitutional right | interpretation of the arbitration agreement | interpretation of contract | termination of proceedings | annulment of arbitral award

---

[1]   For the purposes of the proceedings, the Respondent was classified as a resident. See the conclusions of the arbitral tribunal annotated below.

[2]   The ArbAct [CZE] does not distinguish between domestic and international disputes and stipulates the same rules for both types of disputes.

[3]   The case concerned a commercial relationship – running slot machines in the Czech Republic.

Laws and Regulations Taken into Account in This Ruling:

➤ CCP [CZE] – Act [of the Czech Republic] No. 99/1963 Coll., Code of Civil Procedure, as subsequently amended: Section 106[4];

➤ ArbAct [CZE] – Act [of the Czech Republic] No. 216/1994 Coll. of 1 November 1994, on Arbitration and Enforcement of Arbitral Awards, as subsequently amended: [in particular] Section 2,[5] Section 15,[6] Section 16,[7] Section 18,[8] Section 23,[9] Section 28,[10] Section 31(a), Section 31(b).[11]

---

[4]   **Section 106** – **(1)** As soon as the court discovers, upon the Defendant's objection lodged together with or before the first act of the Defendant on the merits, that the agreement of the parties requires that the case be submitted to arbitration, the court must desist from further examination of the case and terminate the proceedings; the court, however, hears the case if the parties declare that they waive the agreement. The court also hears the case if the court determines that the matter is not arbitrable under the laws of the Czech Republic, or that the arbitration agreement is null and void or non-existent, or that examining the agreement in arbitration proceedings exceeds the scope of jurisdiction vested in the arbitrators by the agreement, or that the arbitral tribunal refused to hear the case. **(2)** If the court proceedings under Subsection (1) were terminated and the same case was submitted to arbitration, the original petition for commencement of the proceedings retains its legal effects, provided the motion for the commencement of arbitration proceedings is lodged no later than 30 days after service of the court's resolution terminating the proceedings. **(3)** If the arbitration proceedings were opened before the court proceedings, the court stays the proceedings on the non-existence, nullity or expiration/termination of the agreement until the arbitrator(s) decide on their jurisdiction over the case or on the merits.

[5]   **Section 2** – **(1)** The parties may agree in an arbitration clause that property disputes between them, excluding disputes arising from the enforcement of decisions and incidental disputes, which would otherwise fall within the jurisdiction of the courts, shall be decided by one or more arbitrators or by a permanent arbitral institution (arbitration agreement). **(2)** An arbitration agreement may be validly concluded if the parties are entitled to conclude a settlement on the subject of the dispute. **(3)** An arbitration agreement may concern: (a) an individual pending dispute (agreement to arbitrate); or (b) any disputes arising in the future from a particular legal relation or from a defined group of legal relations between the parties (arbitration clause). **(4)** Unless stipulated otherwise in the arbitration agreement, the arbitration agreement covers rights arising directly from the legal relations between the parties and the issue of the legal validity of those legal relations and related rights. **(5)** Unless expressly excluded in the arbitration agreement, the arbitration agreement is binding on the parties' legal successors.

[6]   **Section 15** – **(1)** Arbitrators are entitled to review their jurisdiction. If they reach the conclusion that they lack jurisdiction pursuant to the arbitration agreement submitted to them, they shall so decide in the form of a resolution. **(2)** A jurisdictional challenge based on non-existence, invalidity, or expiration/termination of the arbitration agreement, unless the invalidity arises from the fact that it was impossible to conclude an arbitration agreement in the matter, must be raised by a party together with or before the party's first procedural act on the merits.

[7]   **Section 16** If the party asserts his or her claim in arbitral proceedings before the claim becomes statute-barred or expires and the arbitrators decide that they lack jurisdiction or the arbitral award is set aside, and if the party re-files his or her claim or

I. Scope of Arbitration Clause – Relation between Arbitration Agreement and Main Contract

Rationes Decidendi:

19.01. **(1)(a)** Unless the arbitration clause incorporated in the main contract stipulates otherwise, the scope of the arbitration clause is usually identical to the subject matter of the main contract; in such cases, the arbitration clause extends to disputes arising from the [subject matter] of the main contract).

19.02. **(1)(b)** Consequently, if the arbitration clause itself does not explicitly stipulate the scope of disputes to be covered by the clause, the subject matter and the scope of the main contract determines the scope of the arbitration clause incorporated in the main contract.

19.03. **(1)(c)** Despite its **separable and relatively independent nature (independent of the main contract)**, the arbitration clause must also be interpreted as an integral **component of the comprehensive legal relationship** established both by the main contract and by the arbitration agreement.

19.04. **(1)(d) The separability of the arbitration agreement** and its [relative] independence of the main contract cannot be interpreted as a requirement of clear separation of the arbitration clause in the text of the main contract (unless the law stipulates otherwise in special

---

a petition for a continuation in the proceedings with a court or another competent body within 30 days of service of the decision on lack of jurisdiction or annulment of the arbitral award, the original statement of claim filed in the arbitral proceedings retains its legal effects.

[8] **Section 18** The parties to the arbitral proceedings are on equal footing and must be granted full opportunity to exercise their rights.

[9] **Section 23** The arbitral proceedings are terminated by (a) an arbitral award; or (b) a resolution in all other cases; the resolution must be signed, must specify reasons for the decision, and must be served on the parties like an arbitral award; if the statement of claim filed with the permanent arbitral institution is withdrawn prior to the appointment of the tribunal or the arbitrator, a resolution terminating the proceedings shall be rendered and signed by the chairman of the permanent arbitral institution.

[10] **Section 28** – **(1)** A written arbitral award must be served on the parties and subsequently stamped with a certificate of finality. **(2)** An arbitral award that cannot be reviewed pursuant to Section 27 or because the time period has elapsed for filing an application to review the arbitral award under Section 27 without the application being filed, takes the effects of a final court judgment upon service and can be enforced by court

[11] **Section 31** – At the request of any party, the court shall set aside an arbitral award if: **(a)** it was delivered in a matter that cannot be submitted to arbitration (a non-arbitrable matter), **(b)** the arbitration agreement is null and void for other reasons, or it was nullified, or it does not cover the matter [...].

cases).[12] The arbitration clause does not even need to be incorporated in a single separate provision. **The individual parts of the arbitration clause can be incorporated in different sections of the main contract; these parts do not even have to be immediately connected in the wording of the contract, and in some cases, some of the provisions may form part both of the main contract and of the arbitration clause.** However, we must always perform an **autonomous interpretation** of both of these agreements (the main contract and the arbitration clause/agreement) as separate and relatively independent legal facts. The structure of the main contract and the method of incorporation of the arbitration clause in the main contract can be one (and probably often an important one), though not the only criterion for the interpretation of the arbitration clause.

19.05. (1)(e) If the parties included an explicit condition subsequent in the main contract with *ex tunc* effects (for the main contract, i.e. cancellation of the contract from the very beginning) and the condition was fulfilled, then any performance provided by the parties to one another constitutes performance based on a different cause (grounds) than the main contract. Disputes arising from such performance cannot be submitted to arbitration, unless the arbitration clause explicitly indicates that the clause should cover such cases and that the scope of the clause is broader than the scope of the main contract[13], because the general rule is that the scope of the main contract determines the scope of the arbitration clause. If the arbitral tribunal concludes that the arbitration clause does not extend to the dispute, the tribunal is not allowed to examine the legal cause (or lack thereof) for which the contested performance was (or was not) provided.

II. Interpretation of Arbitration Agreement

Ratio Decidendi:

19.06. In the absence of any special interpretational rules stipulated by arbitration laws, the validity and scope of the arbitration agreement must be examined pursuant to the general rules applicable to the substantive-law construction of legal acts (legal facts).

---

[12] Requirements for highlighting the text or even separating the arbitration clause from the main contract can, in special cases, be stipulated by law (for example). A typical example could be so-called consumer disputes (B2C disputes).

[13] This was not the case here. Quite the opposite, the arbitration clause did not expressly define the subject matter of the disputes covered by the clause; it was therefore necessary to conclude that the scope of the clause does not exceed the scope of the main contract.

III. Separability of Arbitration Clause and Validity of Main Contract and of Arbitration Agreement

Ratio Decidendi:

19.07.   The separability of the arbitration clause and the relative independence of the main contract and the arbitration agreement is a generally recognised principle applicable in the interpretation of the arbitration agreement and the jurisdiction of the arbitral tribunal. However, this principle does not prohibit the arbitral tribunal from drawing their conclusions regarding nullity or conclusions suggesting that the contract does not cover the respective case with respect to both of these [relatively independent] contracts, i.e. both the main contract and the arbitration agreement. The reasons justifying such conclusions can be the same.

IV. Doubts about Jurisdiction of Arbitral Tribunal and Transfer of Jurisdiction over Dispute to Arbitral Tribunal

Rationes Decidendi:

19.08.   **(4)(a)** The transfer of the jurisdiction to hear and resolve the merits of the dispute constitutes a significant deviation from the constitutional right of the parties to court; it is a deviation and an exception approved by law subject to the conditions stipulated by law. Jurisdiction must therefore be clearly determined beyond any doubt. This applies especially to cases in which the Respondent properly challenged the jurisdiction of the arbitral tribunal. No fiction or assumption has any place in such cases, except fictions or assumptions explicitly recognised by law or by an agreement of the parties (including fictions or assumptions recognised by the rules applicable to the proceedings in the respective case, if any). This is not the case here.

19.09.   **(4)(b)** In this particular case, however, the arbitral tribunal had to arrive, after taking evidence in the case, at a different conclusion, because <u>only a decision on the merits itself</u> will determine, despite the separability of the main contract and the arbitration clause, the scope of the arbitration agreement, and the parties' constitutional right (especially the Respondent's right) to have their case resolved by a court could be unduly curtailed as a result of such procedure. With doubts like these, the arbitrators are obliged to terminate the proceedings and give the parties the opportunity (preserving the substantive-law effects of the parties' claims asserted in arbitration) to have their case resolved in litigation, i.e. within the scope of general jurisdiction.

19.10. **(4)(c)** The arbitration agreement must be conceived of as a legal fact that allows, subject to the law[14] the suspension of the jurisdiction of the general judiciary to hear and resolve the merits of the case. Consequently, an arbitration agreement cannot (at least under *civil law*, namely under Czech constitutional and other laws) be considered a legal fact the construction of which could transgress the statutory limitations of the constitutional right to judicial protection. The transfer of the jurisdiction to hear and resolve the merits of the case does not cancel, but only suspends the jurisdiction of courts, and the parties may still invoke such general jurisdiction.

19.11. **(4)(d)** When making a decision on the jurisdiction of the arbitral tribunal to hear and resolve a particular dispute, an extensive interpretation of the arbitration agreement (arbitration clause) in an attempt to *"enforce (at whatever the price)"* the hearing and resolution (of a given dispute) in arbitration, can be very questionable and risky. If we apply such an extensive interpretation, we must count on the possibility of the arbitral award subsequently being set aside pursuant to Section 31(b) of the ArbAct [CZE]. Conversely, if the arbitral proceedings are terminated for the lack of jurisdiction of the arbitral tribunal, the court is bound by the resolution terminating the arbitral proceedings in the sense that the court is obliged to hear the case (Section 106(1) of the CCP [CZE]). This corresponds to the current case law of our courts.[15] Moreover, courts are by no means limited by the "defined scope" of legal relations covered by the arbitration clause (Section 2(3)(b) of the ArbAct [CZE]). Consequently, as opposed to arbitrators, courts can resolve the contested issues in a comprehensive manner within one and the same proceedings, i.e. without being limited by the scope of the relations as defined in the arbitration agreement.

19.12. **(4)(e)** The decision on the jurisdictional challenge allows and often requires that the decision-making body examines a significant portion of the facts of the case and the legal issues associated with the merits of the dispute and hears or reads the necessary **evidence**. For this purpose, it is possible to take any evidence that would be admissible with respect to proving allegations regarding the merits of the dispute.

---

[14] Here within the limits of the ArbAct [CZE].
[15] The arbitral tribunal invoked in said resolution, for instance, the judgment of the Supreme Court of the Czech Republic, Case No. 29 Cdo 1899/2008-175 of 23 February 2010 (cit.): *"If the arbitral tribunal decides pursuant to Section 15(1) of the ArbAct [CZE] that the tribunal lacks jurisdiction, the court is bound by the decision in that the court is obliged to hear the case; [...] This is also the reason why the claimants are not being denied justice, as the arbitral tribunal's decision on lack of jurisdiction does not prevent claimants to file a lawsuit or a petition for continuing the proceedings in court. [...]."*

V. Subject Matter of Resolution Terminating Proceedings for Lack of Jurisdiction of Arbitral Tribunal[16]

Rationes Decidendi:

19.13. **(5)(a)** A resolution is not a constructive decision that would allow the imposition of any (new) obligations on the parties. The same applies to compensation for the costs of proceedings (if any) in case the proceedings are terminated by a resolution for a lack of jurisdiction of the arbitral tribunal.

19.14. **(5)(b)** Only an arbitral award becomes final and enforceable and as such is subject to enforcement, similarly to a court judgment (Section 28(2) of the ArbAct [CZE][17]). A resolution terminating the proceedings does not become final and is not subject to enforcement.

19.15. **(5)(c)** Consequently, a resolution terminating the proceedings may not impose the obligation to compensate the party that succeeded with its jurisdictional challenge for the **costs of proceedings**.

VI. Equality of Parties in Arbitration

Rationes Decidendi:

19.16. **(6)(a)** The parties in arbitration are principally on equal footing.[18] The fact that one of them is a public entity (here a municipality/city) is irrelevant.

19.17. **(6)(b)** But the arbitral tribunal may and often must take account of the fact that the acts performed by one of the parties (here the public entity – municipality) must meet special criteria of form, and that the acts can be performed only by persons authorized to do so, for instance, by law (here the Municipalities Act).

[Description of Facts and Legal Issues:]

19.18. The respective case concerned the supply of construction works ordered by the Respondent (municipality/city). The claim submitted to arbitration concerned extra works. Although the Respondent did take over the subject matter of the performance itself, the Respondent claimed the extra works had not been properly approved. The Respondent also claimed the contract containing the arbitration clause had been terminated/expired.

---

[16] Section 23(b) of the ArbAct [CZE].
[17] According to the laws valid on the day the decision was rendered.
[18] Section 18 of the ArbAct [CZE].

19.19. The arbitral tribunal concluded that the Claimant did not succeed in proving that the claim concerned performance provided under the contract with the arbitration clause. The Claimant clearly provided some performance to the Respondent in the case at hand, but the Claimant failed to prove that the performance was provided under the contract containing the arbitration clause. In other words, the Claimant failed to prove that her claims were covered by the arbitration clause incorporated in the main contract. Quite the opposite, when discussing the jurisdictional challenge, the arbitral tribunal entertained serious doubts about the main contract and the possibility that the main contract itself expired and the performance was provided under a completely different contract (for instance a verbal contract), or even that the performance was provided without any legal cause. Naturally, an arbitration clause can also cover such claims (if any). But if the arbitration clause were supposed to cover such situations, it would have to be expressly agreed in the clause. The scope of the arbitration clause can therefore be broader (although it is not very common in practice) than the scope of the main contract in which the arbitration clause is incorporated. However, if this is not the case, we must assume that the arbitration clause does not cover claims under any other [main] contract than the one into which it is integrated as an integral, yet relatively separable component.

19.20. Among other things, the dispute centred on whether the condition precedent actually occurred, suspending the effects of the main contract and, in said case, the effects of the arbitration agreement. According to the agreement of the parties, the condition precedent allegedly consisted of the client's (the Respondent's) announcement that the Respondent secured financing for the respective project. Such a circumstance (this announcement) was not discovered. The arbitral tribunal did base its decision on the principle of equal footing of the parties, despite the Respondent being a public entity (municipality/city). But the tribunal admitted that this case specifically required and justified that more stringent criteria be applied to the manifestations of will of the public entity, which must meet special criteria of form. Besides, the contract itself contained a special clause with an express declaration when the main contract, as well as the arbitration clause, were approved by the municipality's bodies (officials).

19.21. No other arbitration agreement that would cover this case was either discovered or alleged by the parties. Consequently, this was a situation completely different from, for instance, disputes over claims from invalid contracts.

[Notes regarding Resolution (Jurisdictional Order):]

19.22. The arbitral tribunal concluded in this case that if jurisdiction is not proven beyond any doubt, and if doubts about the jurisdiction of the arbitral tribunal persist even after the jurisdictional challenge is discussed, the tribunal ought to lean in favour of the conclusion that the arbitrators lack jurisdiction over the dispute. Arbitrators are not allowed to construe the arbitration agreement extensively, because this could jeopardize the parties' constitutional right to submit their dispute to court. Doubts about jurisdiction must be interpreted in favour of court proceedings. The jurisdiction to hear and resolve any dispute in an authoritative manner is (at least in *civil law* countries) a **material demonstration of state sovereignty**. The authoritative hearing and resolution of disputes is a component of state sovereignty and a demonstration of state power. The right to submit one's dispute to a court is a constitutional right. Only the state (its constitutional and legislative power) can determine the scope of the state's surrender of the exclusive domain of state power and the conditions thereof. In other words, arbitrators are entitled, but are also obliged to determine, first and foremost, whether the conditions for a suspension of judicial authority to resolve the respective dispute were met, and whether this jurisdiction was transferred to the arbitral tribunal (under the *Kompetenz-Kompetenz* principle). Cases in which the arbitrators construe their jurisdiction unduly broadly, and despite the absence of their jurisdiction resolve the dispute, are protected by mechanisms such as the annulment of arbitral awards and/or the rejection or termination of proceedings enforcing the arbitral award. The arbitrators may not, however, exceed their jurisdiction intentionally. If they have doubts regarding their jurisdiction, they must surrender the jurisdiction to resolve disputes to courts. In cases where a party challenges their jurisdiction, the arbitrators are obliged to analyse their jurisdiction very thoroughly, and may only decide the merits of the dispute if they are convinced of their jurisdiction beyond any doubt. Unless they arrive at such an unambiguous conclusion supporting the jurisdiction of the arbitral tribunal, the arbitrators should terminate such arbitration. Further steps in the case then depend on the parties. If the parties (or at least one of them) wish to have their dispute authoritatively decided, they may either address a court, or they can enter into a new arbitration agreement (agreement to arbitrate), which would cover the subject matter of the dispute.

19.23. Paradoxically, in the case at hand, the decision on the merits could retrospectively affect the conclusion as to whether or not the respective arbitration clause covers the dispute. In most *civil law* countries, where jurisdiction is usually conceived of as a *procedural requirement* (not a substantive-law issue), just like under Czech law, such a solution is inadmissible. The arbitrators certainly may, to some extent, and they did in the present case, also discuss the merits of the case (especially take evidence), provided it is indispensable for the determination of jurisdiction. Such a situation usually occurs if the validity of the arbitration clause is questionable. A positive conclusion regarding the jurisdiction of the arbitral tribunal must, however, always precede the evaluation of the factual and legal circumstances of the case by the arbitrators for the purposes of examining the merits of the case. Unless the issue of jurisdiction is clear beyond any doubt, and unless it is obvious that this *procedural requirement* is fulfilled, arbitrators must terminate the proceedings. In such case, the arbitrators terminate the proceedings by a resolution (pursuant to Section 23(b) of the ArbAct [CZE]).

19.24. The arbitral tribunal thus concluded that where there are doubts regarding the scope of the arbitration agreement that cannot be eliminated, despite a thorough discussion[19] of the issue of jurisdiction, the proper procedure is to favour the jurisdiction of courts. The reason is that courts have general jurisdiction, and as the Supreme Court case law indicates, courts are obliged to accept their jurisdiction whenever the arbitrators refuse to hear the case, i.e. even if it ultimately transpires that the arbitration clause extended to the dispute. In other words, it was a case completely different from situations in which the validity of the arbitration agreement is in doubt. Where there are doubts regarding the validity of the arbitration agreement and the possibility of varying interpretations, we must prefer the conclusion favouring the validity of the contract (both the main contract and the arbitration agreement) wherever the conclusion is legally admissible. But this case primarily concerned a dispute over the scope of the arbitration agreement.

19.25. Naturally, it can be a subject of dispute to what extent the principle favouring court jurisdiction over the jurisdiction of an arbitral tribunal, in a situation where the arbitrators doubt their jurisdiction, would be applicable in **international arbitration**. In a **domestic dispute,** it is usually clear that in the absence of the arbitrators' jurisdiction, jurisdiction is vested in the courts of the respective state. But in an

---

[19]   The arbitral tribunal summoned the parties to two separate hearings merely for the purpose of discussing the jurisdictional challenge. The tribunal also took extensive evidence at the hearings, which the court considered necessary for clarifying the issue of jurisdiction and the scope of which was almost as broad as evidence necessary to prove the merits of a dispute.

international dispute, the international jurisdiction of courts of a particular state may be questionable too. Besides, international disputes may often be specific due to the fact that the parties could have intended to exclude the jurisdiction of courts, because it is an international dispute and/or because jurisdiction over the dispute could be exercised by the courts of a particular state. Nonetheless, the conclusion that the arbitral tribunal might have used different interpretational criteria in the given case if it were an international dispute is extremely speculative. In any case, it is necessary to emphasize that, in an international dispute, the arbitral tribunal, when deciding on its jurisdiction, could also take account of other criteria different from those limiting the tribunal in domestic disputes, including international customs.

19.26. In this particular case, the arbitral tribunal terminated the proceedings for a lack of jurisdiction. Under the national (Czech) law valid on the day the arbitral tribunal rendered its decision, however, the resolution of the arbitral tribunal terminating the proceedings could not contain a ruling on compensation for the costs of proceedings. Only courts, not arbitral tribunals, are authorized to rule on the obligation of one party to compensate the other party for the costs of proceedings in a resolution terminating the proceedings. As opposed to resolutions rendered by courts, resolutions terminating the proceedings rendered by arbitral tribunals pursuant to Section 23(b) of the ArbAct [CZE] do not become final and enforceable. The claim for compensation for the costs of proceedings under national (Czech) law is defined as a claim *sui generis* associated with the party's steps adopted in order to assert his or her claim (as opposed to other legal systems, for instance, in Germany and other countries, where the claim for compensation for the costs of proceedings is deemed to be a special claim for damages or a different claim of an adhesive nature immediately following the party's substantive rights discussed in the proceedings). Under Czech law, the claim for compensation for the costs of proceedings is a claim resulting from the particular proceedings in which such claim must be made. It is not impossible (though not employed in practice) for a party that challenged the arbitral tribunal's jurisdiction and proposed termination of the arbitration as a result thereof to make a simultaneous *explicit* proposal that the tribunal deliver an arbitral award ruling on the refund of the costs. The author of this commentary is convinced that this possibility follows from the *Kompetenz-Kompetenz* principle, i.e. the arbitrators' right to primarily determine their jurisdiction, as well as from the abovementioned nature of the claim for a refund of the costs of proceedings in the domestic (Czech) civil procedure as a *procedural claim sui generis*. But an *arbitral award on the costs of proceedings* cannot be rendered by the arbitrators *sua sponte*. The absence of an explicit proposal of the parties demanding that the arbitral tribunal render a separate arbitral award on the costs of proceedings, even in those cases in which the tribunal rules on the termination of the proceedings for a lack of jurisdiction, would constitute a decision *ultra petita*, which is prohibited. The arbitral tribunal may, however, include in its resolution terminating the proceedings a statement saying that the parties shall both pay their own costs of proceedings, or that the arbitration fee paid by the claimant shall not be returned; this is merely a qualification of an obligation that the parties have already performed based on their agreement or based on the applicable arbitration rules (according to the Rules of the Arbitration Court at the Economic Chamber of the Czech Republic and Agricultural Chamber of the Czech Republic governing Domestic Disputes and Principles Governing the Costs of Proceedings incorporated in the former). Special procedural rules of arbitration shall in such case apply by the very fact that the claimant initiates proceedings before this permanent arbitral institution and under these rules of arbitration. Such obligations are therefore by no means influenced by the finding of a lack of jurisdiction pronounced by the arbitral tribunal in the resolution rendered in the present case.

| | |

Zdeňka M. Nocarová

Evidence-Taking Procedure, Obligation to Negotiate Out-of-court Settlement, Court Assistance, Burden of Proof, Limits to Arbitration Tribunal's Active Pursuit of Evidence, Significance of Deeds under Substantive Law and Procedural Law (Award, RS HK ČR and AK ČR, Case No. Rsp 2408/10 of 6 September 2011: Evidence Taking Procedure)

Claimant:	*a Czech legal entity*
Defendant:	*a foreign natural person (a citizen of the Socialist Republic of Vietnam), an entrepreneur with his place of business in the Czech Republic, who holds a residency permit for the territory of the Czech Republic for business purposes.*[20]
Place of Arbitration:	*Czech Republic.*
Arbitration Agreement:	*The arbitration agreement took the form of an arbitration clause contained in the main contract, which had been made in the second half of 2006.*
Nature of Arbitration:	*Proceedings before a permanent arbitral institution (Arbitration Court attached to the Economic Chamber of the Czech Republic and the Agricultural Chamber of the Czech Republic in Prague), held as proceedings over a domestic dispute.*[21]
Applicable Law:	*Main contract*[22] *– Czech law. Arbitration agreement – Czech law. Procedural standards – Czech law.*

---

[20] The defendant was treated in the proceedings as if he had been a citizen (i.e. a domestic entity). See the arbitration tribunal's findings as annotated below.

[21] The ArbAct [CZE] does not differentiate between domestic and international disputes, and stipulates the same rules for both types of dispute.

[22] The relationship underlying the dispute was a commercial-law relationship – the operation of gambling machines on the territory of the Czech Republic.

Key words:

witness affidavit | photocopy of deed | burden of proof | intensity of this international element | deed | international element | international dispute | place of business | trial proceedings | regular court | legal representative | residency permit | court assistance | counter-claim outweighing the claim | parties' legal capacity | res iudicata | interpreter | domestic legal entity | domestic dispute | non ultra petita | acknowledgement of debt | examination of the witness | set-off

Laws and Regulations Taken into Account in This Ruling:

➤ CivCo [CZE] – [Czech] Act No. 40/1964 Coll. of 26 February 1964, the Civil Code, as amended: Section 558.[23]

➤ CommCo [CZE] – [Czech] Act No. 513/1991 Coll. of 5 November 1991, the Commercial Code, as amended: Section 323.[24]

➤ ArbAct [CZE] – [Czech] Act No. 216/1994 Coll. of 1 November 1994, on arbitration proceedings and the enforcement of arbitral awards, as amended: [here in particular] Sections 19 and 20.

Rationes Decidendi:

20.01. The defendant, in his capacity as a natural person – a citizen of the Socialist Republic of Vietnam with a proper residency permit for the territory of the Czech Republic and business operations in the Czech Republic – is for the purposes of this procedure treated as a domestic legal entity. Therefore, given that the other party to the dispute was a Czech legal entity, this is a dispute between two entrepreneurs with their respective place of business in the Czech Republic and is thus

---

[23]   CivCo [CZE]: Section 558 – Acknowledgement of Debt – *"If someone acknowledges in writing that they shall pay their debt, specific as to title and amount, then it is held that the debt existed at the time of such acknowledgement. In the case of statute-barred debt, the acknowledgement only triggers the aforementioned legal consequence if they who acknowledged their debt knew that it was already statute-barred."*

[24]   CommCo [CZE]: Section 323 – Acknowledgement of Obligations –*"(1) If someone acknowledges in writing a certain obligation of their own, then it is held that the obligation existed at the time of such acknowledgement, to the extent to which it was acknowledged. These effects also occur if the creditor's claim was already statute-barred at the time of acknowledgement. (2) The legal acts described in Section 407 (2) and (3) also qualify as the acknowledgement of a non-barred obligation. (3) The acknowledgement of obligations has also effect vis-à-vis guarantors."*

At the same time, it needs to be stressed that pursuant to Section 263 CommCo [CZE], the parties cannot contract around the cited provisions in Section 323 CommCo [CZE]. Similarly, the parties cannot deviate from those provisions that stipulate that the written form is mandatory for the given legal transaction.

considered as a **domestic dispute.**[25] Under the captioned circumstances, the defendant should be treated in the way one would treat a **domestic** entrepreneur, and there is no reason to consider the matter as an international dispute – in other words, while an international element has been identified in the matter, the **intensity of this international element** is not strong enough to pave the way for the application of foreign law or even the application of the Arbitration Court's Rules for International Disputes.

20.02. The fact that a party is considered as a domestic legal entity for the purposes of proceedings (due to their place of business being located on domestic territory) does not exclude the possibility of having the defendant accompanied by an **interpreter**, as there may exist legitimate reasons for interpreting the course of oral proceedings even in the case of a domestic legal entity.

20.03. **The legal representative of a party may at the same time act as their interpreter.**

20.04. **The undertaking of the parties to refrain from using** *any* **[procedural]** *remedy* **for resolving their dispute unless and until every effort has been made towards an amicable resolution**[26] **does not preclude the parties from initiating adversarial trial proceedings (which may also take the form of arbitration proceedings).** Rather, the above-referenced undertaking may merely (under certain circumstances) be a prerequisite for the actionability of a given claim in terms of substantive law, but cannot change the fact that the arbitration agreement has been validly made and is in force and effect. And even the (potential) substantive-law obstacle of a claim not being actionable because of such an undertaking can only be the subject of review if the party who is affected by it has invoked the lack of actionability as a defence in proceedings on the merits.

---

[25] Moreover, the agreement that gave rise to the dispute had also been agreed pursuant to Czech law.

[26] The arbitration agreement made (in the form of an arbitration clause) in the second half of 2006 read: *"The Parties shall make efforts towards resolving all their disputes in an amicable manner, and shall not take recourse to any remedies for dispute resolution unless and until they have exhausted every effort towards resolving such conflict or dispute amicably. If such negotiations prove unsuccessful, then either party (or both parties together) shall bring the dispute before the Arbitration Court attached to the Economic Chamber of the Czech Republic and the Agricultural Chamber of the Czech Republic in Prague for a decision. The arbitration proceedings shall be held in accordance with the Rules of Arbitration of the Arbitration Court attached to the Economic Chamber of the Czech Republic and the Agricultural Chamber of the Czech Republic. Decisions by the arbitration tribunal are final and binding for both parties."*

20.05. The arbitration tribunal is not required to review the **parties' legal capacity (standing)**, and it is common practice for assertions and refutations in this respect to be the exclusive domain of the parties.

20.06. If the defendant asks during the proceeding (i.e. during the oral hearing) that the claimant compensates his **counter-claim outweighing the claim** made in the claimant's statement in the same proceeding (but fails to do so in the form of a proper statement of counter-claim), then the arbitration tribunal shall consider the defendant's demand to be a procedural defence in the form of **the statutory defence of set-off** up to (but not exceeding) the amount of the claim as specified in the claimant's statement.

20.07. If a party has been instructed during a scheduled oral hearing that its earlier assertions or evidence that was presented to the arbitration tribunal and that was accepted and heard by the arbitration tribunal require further verification by additional evidentiary means, but the party fails to procure such evidence, and does not propose the procedure anticipated by Section 20 (2) ArbAct [CZE] (despite having been specifically reminded of this option), and does in fact not even attend the oral hearing without any official excuse, then such party may legitimately be considered unable and/or unwilling to bear the additional burden of proof.

20.08. A party who has been instructed of its option to propose the procedure anticipated by Section 20 (2) ArbAct (regular **court assistance in the procurement of evidence**) and has at the same time been informed that the arbitration tribunal will not by itself initiate any such court's assistance procedure, the party should understand this to be meant that the arbitration tribunal considers the matter sufficiently exhausted for a decision in the matter, which, however, may likely be negative with respect to (i.e. dismissive of) its claim, and in terms of whether the party has fulfilled its duty to procure evidence or not. Such instruction also ought to alert the party to the possibility that it should have submitted additional evidence in support of its previous assertions or bolster the evidence that was already presented. This conclusion is fair, especially if the party is represented by a professional legal advisor and therefore ought to be able to thus properly understand the tribunal's advice pursuant to the Section 20 (2) ArbAct [CZE] (court assistance in the procurement of evidence).

20.09. The arbitration tribunal does have to address whether **the matter has been exhausted in the trial proceeding to such a degree as to allow the arbitration tribunal to make a decision in the matter** (Section 19 (2) ArbAct [CZE]). Only if this question is answered in the affirmative way, the arbitration tribunal may proceed and issue a decision (award) in the matter. The arbitration tribunal has an option of asking, of its own accord, a regular court to summon and examine (i.e. take testimony from) a witness (Section 20 (2) ArbAct [CZE]). By making explicit reference to this option, the arbitration tribunal also signals that it is inclined to accommodate the parties if they were themselves to request a procedure pursuant to Section 20 (2) ArbAct [CZE]. In assessing the conflicting priorities between the parties' (i.e. in particular, the claimant's) duty to take an active approach towards their evidentiary obligations, on one hand, and the arbitration tribunal's limits as far as its active (investigative) approach towards bringing light to the facts of the case and the legal circumstances thereof is concerned, on the other hand, the arbitration tribunal must also consider which party benefits from the potential examination of any witness. If the examination of the witness may serve to substantiate the assertions of the claimant (or of both parties, as the case may be), and the claimant nonetheless – and in spite of having been suitably instructed – decides against proposing the procedure set out in Section 20 (2) ArbAct [CZE], but insists that hearing the given witness is not necessary (or that evidence in the form of an affidavit by the witness is sufficient), then the arbitration tribunal should conclude that the claimant has been unable to bear the burden of proof. If the onus is on the claimant, who has been informed of the said option, but does not ask to initiate the assistance procedure as captioned above, then the arbitration tribunal can come up with a conclusion that the claimant failed to bear the burden of proof.

20.10. If a party submits a **deed** in the form of a *plain* [photo]*copy*, in spite of having been **called upon** by the arbitration tribunal **to submit an original**, then the arbitration tribunal is entitled to consider the contents of such a deed **merely to be a part of that party's assertions,** rather than the evidence. This is warranted, in particular, if the respective other party calls the contents of the given deed into question, and if no other evidence is at hand that would substantiate the said contents beyond doubt.

20.11. The mere assertion of the defendant that they handed in certain revenues [here: the proceeds from operating gambling machines] **cannot be considered as an acknowledgement of the claim made in the proceeding**, unless the defendant also confirms the amount of the surrendered sum.

20.12. Suppose the defendant invokes the **defence of set-off**, i.e. the discharge of their obligation in substantive-law terms due to a set-off, but does not properly elevate its counter-claim to the status of a matter in dispute, then the existence and legitimacy of such counter-claim may not be separately assessed and decided once the claimant's claim has been dismissed. If the claimant's claim has been dismissed (for reasons other than due to a set-off), then the defendant's counter-claim *remains open to be raised again* (i.e. does *not* qualify itself as *res iudicata*); if the tribunal were to decide on the defendant's counter-claim under these circumstances, it would violate the *non ultra petita* principle.

20.13. **The acknowledgement of debt is a substantive-law institution** of fundamental legal importance. For an acknowledgement of an obligation to have substantive-law effects, it must meet the minimal standard pursuant to Section 558 CivCo [CZE][27] or, as it were, Section 323 CommCo [CZE][28]. **The substantive-law assessment of the given deed must be viewed separately from its procedural assessment (i.e. its assessment as documentary evidence).** To find that a given deed does not meet the substantive-law standards for an acknowledgement of debt does not necessarily rule out that the deed may still serve as evidence for certain facts of relevance for the dispute at hand – but the reverse does not necessarily held the true. The onus to show that the criteria set out in substantive law for an acknowledgement of debt have been met lies with that party that has derived such substantive-law acknowledgement of debt from a given deed.

[JUDr. Zdeňka M. Nocarová, Ph.D.]
Founding partner of the law firm NOCAROVÁ JAŠEK & PARTNERS, v.o.s ., arbitrator at the Arbitration Court attached to the Economic Chamber of the Czech Republic and Agricultural Chamber of the Czech Republic and at the Arbitration Court attached to the Czech-Moravian Commodity Exchange. Dr. Nocarová graduated from the Law Faculty in 1998 and during her studies she graduated with honors at The Marshall School, took economy classes at the University of Minnesota Duluth, in the United States and completed her undergraduate work at University of Passau, Germany. Since 1999 she also acts as a Court interpreter in both English and German languages.
e-mail: znocarova@njp.cz

| | |

---

[27] Provision cited in the introduction to this annotation.
[28] Provision cited in the introduction to this annotation.

Czech (& Central European) Yearbook of Arbitration

Květoslav Růžička

Substantive-law Standards Applicable to Examination of Validity of Contracts in Arbitration (AC, Interim Arbitral Award, Rsp 981/11 of 21 September 2011: Interim Award)

Key words:
partial award | final award | interim award | third parties | non-party | preliminary issue

Laws and Regulations Taken into Account in This Ruling:
➢   ArbAct [CZE]: Section 18,[29] Section 19,[30] Section 20,[31] Section 23,[32] Section 28.[33]

---

[29]   ArbAct [CZE] – Section 18 – „The parties to the arbitral proceedings have the same standing and must be granted equal opportunities to enforce their rights."

[30]   ArbAct [CZE] – Section 19 – „(1) The parties may agree on the procedure to govern the proceedings. The issue of the applicable procedures may be decided by the presiding arbitrator if authorized to do so by the parties or by all the arbitrators. (2) If no agreement in accordance with Paragraph 1 is reached, the arbitrators shall conduct the proceedings in the way they consider adequate. They shall conduct the proceedings keeping in mind the specific facts of the case and without unnecessary formalities and providing the same possibility to all parties to enforce their rights. (3) Unless otherwise agreed by the parties, the proceedings before the arbitrators are oral. Such proceedings are always non-public."

[31]   ArbAct [CZE] – Section 20 – „(1) The arbitrators are entitled to hear the testimony of experts, parties, and other witnesses that willingly appear before them. Other evidence may be proffered but only if provided to them. (2) Acts that cannot be performed by the arbitrators shall be performed by the court upon the request of the arbitrators; the court is obligated to grant the request unless such an act is not permitted by law. If the act requested is permitted by law, the court shall make any and all decisions necessary for the execution of the request. (3) The cost of proceedings in accordance with Paragraph 2 shall be paid by the permanent arbitral tribunal or by the arbitrators."

[32]   ArbAct [CZE] – Section 23 – „The arbitral proceedings terminated by issue of a) an arbitral award; or b) a decision in the cases when an arbitral award is not issued;[32] the decision must be signed, must include the reasoning, and must be delivered as an arbitral award; if the statement of claim filed with the permanent arbitral tribunal is revoked prior to the establishment of the tribunal or appointment of the arbitrator, the decision on termination of the proceedings is issued and signed by the chairman of the permanent arbitral tribunal."

[33]   ArbAct [CZE] – Section 28 – „(1) The arbitral award must be delivered in writing to the parties, who must be provided with a certificate of its enforceability upon delivery. (2) The arbitral award, which cannot be reviewed pursuant to Section 27 or because the time period has elapsed for filing an application to review the arbitral award under Section 27, can be enforced by the court."

I. Interim Award: Purpose, Characteristics and Requirements for Issue of Award

Rationes Decidendi:

21.01. 1 (a) The interim award usually deals with fundamental preliminary issues of substantive law related to the subject matter of the dispute and the arguments presented by the parties. This type of decision therefore enables the parties to focus, in later stages of the proceedings, on the remaining contested issues, and facilitates better and more efficient exercise of the parties' rights.

21.02. 1.(b) The arbitral tribunal may also decide in the interim award that the effects of certain agreements occurred on a particular date at the latest, if that constitutes an important preliminary issue on the merits. This does not prejudice the power of the tribunal to come to the conclusion, in later stages of the proceedings, that the effects had occurred even earlier, and if important for further hearing of the case and/or the dispute, such conclusion may be incorporated in the reasons of the final award, or if need be, in another interim award.

21.03. (1) (c) In relation to the final hearing and resolution of the parties' claims submitted to arbitration, interim awards are, to some extent, capable of fulfilling a function equivalent to the purpose of a court's *obligation to give instructions* to parties in litigation. Interim awards may not be issued before the case is examined to such extent that allows the arbitrators to deliver a binding and *final* decision on the issues dealt with in the order of the interim award (usually significant preliminary conclusions on substantive law issues). Whether the proceedings have reached that stage must always be examined in relation to the subject matter of the order of the interim award.

21.04. (1) (d) Interim awards are binding decisions on preliminary issues of substantive law, the resolution of which between the parties is necessary for the tribunal to finish hearing the case and to subsequently deliver a decision on the contested claims submitted to the particular proceedings. However, interim awards do not terminate the proceedings within the meaning of the opening sentence of Section 23 ArbAct [CZE]. It is an *intermediate stage*, the purpose of which is to (*pro futuro*) case manage the proceedings as efficiently and economically as possible, from the procedural perspective, and to lay the foundations for the future [final] award pursuant to Section 23(a) ArbAct [CZE]. As concerns the issues determined in the order of the interim award, however, this decision is also final, even though it does not terminate the [entire] proceedings. When deciding on whether it is suitable to issue this type of decision (interim award), the arbitrators are bound especially, without limitation, by Sections 18 through 20 ArbAct [CZE], and subject to the substance of these provisions, other laws and rules applicable to the particular proceedings.

II. *Inter Partes* Effects of Arbitral Awards; Third-party Interests Affecting Examination of Arguments Presented by Parties

Rationes Decidendi:

21.05. (2) (a) Arbitrators do not have the right to make any decisions on the validity of agreements between the parties, unless all of them are also parties to the respective arbitral proceedings.

21.06. (2) (b) With respect to the issues determined in its order, the interim award is final and binding and carries the effects of a final and binding court judgment upon delivery to both parties (Section 28(2) ArbAct [CZE]). However, it is not enforceable, because interim awards are not decisions on specific claims presented by the parties, or any part thereof; such claims are incorporated in the parties' petitions on the merits, and can either be resolved by a partial award, or by the final award terminating the [entire] proceedings.

21.07. (3) (a) Final and binding awards have the same effects as final and binding court judgments. However, arbitral awards are, with certain specific exceptions [inapplicable in this case], decisions with *inter partes* effects. A decision on the validity or, conversely, nullity of assignment agreements executed by and between parties, one of which is not a party to the respective arbitration, would significantly affect the non-party (the person who is not a party to the dispute (arbitral proceedings)). Such a conclusion is unacceptable. Arbitrators are not allowed to render any decision affecting the rights and obligations of third parties.

21.08. (3) (b) Nonetheless, the third person, the original party to the [main] agreement, could join the arbitral proceedings, namely as a third party to the proceedings. Such joinder is contingent upon the acts of the two original parties to the proceedings and/or the third party; however, it always requires the consent of the arbitral tribunal and the fulfilment of the applicable conditions stipulated by the procedural rules governing the proceedings.

21.09. (3) (c) If the grounds which, according to the respondent, render null and void the agreements on the basis of which the respondent was supposed to become party to the [main] agreement apply exclusively to the relationship between the original party to the [main] agreement that has not joined the arbitration and the respondent, the arbitral tribunal does not have the right to review these arguments on the merits presented by the respondent; the arbitral tribunal must avoid any conclusions in this respect. The circumstances that can be subject to review by the arbitral tribunal are exclusively such circumstances that are related to the issue of whether the respective agreement (*assignment agreements*) did or could have effects, namely whether the agreement could have given rise to changes in the person of a party to the [main] agreement (supply agreement) negotiated between the parties to this particular arbitration. Consequently, for the purposes of the particular proceedings, the arbitral tribunal must base its decision on the rebuttable presumption that the assignment agreements are valid, and as a result thereof, confine its examination only to the effects of the assignment agreements between the parties to this arbitration, in which the arbitrators must decide on the merits. The only legally relevant objections in such case could be objections such as a failure of proper notification of the change in the parties to the [main] agreement, etc.

III. Substantive-law Standards Applicable to Determination of Factual and Legal Questions

Rationes Decidendi:

21.10. **(4) When examining agreements** (the [main] agreement) **from the substantive-law perspective,** the agreements themselves are only the first approximation to the meaning of the *word* [consensus] *that the parties wish to stipulate by their acts.* A literal interpretation of the agreement may, but may not, correspond to the will of the actors. Will is the internal state of mind of the acting person, which is not directly accessible to and discernible by the interpreter of the legal act. The will must be ascertained through the medium of external circumstances associated with the signing and performance of agreements, especially circumstances connected with the signing of the agreement and the subsequent acts of the parties after signing. Objective law, although it regulates the fundamental arguments and methods of interpretation of agreements and other legal acts, does not offer a comprehensive list of arguments and principles that the court should take account of when interpreting agreements, nor does it determine in any unequivocal manner the mutual relations between the individual interpretation rules. The court must consider the mutual relations of the applicable arguments relating to the respective agreements and balance their role in the particular case with respect to the specific circumstances of the case, and refrain from applying these criteria in a routine manner. **Such** approach also complies with modern case law, which is gradually replacing the formally legalistic approach to law with an approach by which the court tries to provide such answers to the legal and factual questions posed by the parties to the dispute that are best supported by arguments. The arbitrators must adopt the same approach to the interpretation of agreements; arbitrators should strive for such an interpretation even more than the courts.

[Description of Facts and Legal Issues:]

21.11. The dispute concerned claims under a supply agreement (the provision of construction works), and the respondent, the legal successor to one of the original contractual parties, argued (*inter alia*) that he was not bound by the contractual obligations allegedly owed to the claimant. The respondent argued that the agreement executed between him and his legal successor was null and void. The arbitral tribunal therefore had to answer the question of whether the tribunal had the power to decide on the validity of the agreements that had given rise to changes in the parties to the supply agreement, whether in relation to the respondent, and the decision on whether he was bound by the contractual obligations as alleged by the claimant). The tribunal concluded that they were not endowed with such powers. The question of whether the respective agreements (*assignment agreements*) were invalid, as alleged by the respondent, could only be answered in a dispute between the assignor and the assignee (i.e. between the initial obligor and the respondent in these proceedings).[34] Other conclusions made by the arbitrators are articulated above.

[*Prof. JUDr. Květoslav Růžička CSc.*]
Professor, Dr. of law, Ph.D.; Department of Int. Law, Faculty of Law, University of West Bohemia; Dept. of Commercial Law, Faculty of Law Charles University in Prague, lecturing private international law and international civil proceedings, arbitration, international commercial law, arbitrator.
e-mail: ruzicka@prf.cuni.cz

| | |

---

[34] The arbitral tribunal identified with the opinion of the NS [CZE] articulated with respect to litigation; the arbitral tribunal concluded that that opinion was applicable to arbitration to the full extent. See Judgment of the NS [CZE], Case No. 32 Cdo 4511/2009 of 15 February 2011, annotated in, for instance: 19 (10) PRÁVNÍ ROZHLEDY 377-378 (2011); it is true that the decision deals with a case based on different factual circumstances, but according to the arbitrators, the conclusion could be applied to the present issue.

Book Reviews

Book Reviews

Natalia Ivanovna Marysheva
Private International Law

Chapter 23 – I. O. Khlestova, Международный коммерческий арбитраж [International Commercial Arbitration], in Международное Частное Право [Private International Law], Moscow: Wolters Kluver (N. I. Marysheva ed., 2011), 848-903 pp.

The publication, **Private International Law,** is a great and comprehensive textbook for the entire field, covering both conflict-of-law rules and international civil procedure. Following a *good and time-tested tradition* of how this field is taught in the CEE countries, the textbook also includes a chapter (Chapter 23) on international commercial arbitration. Teaching private international law in a comprehensive manner, i.e. by including conflict-of-law rules and international civil procedure, along with an integrated and detailed analysis of international arbitration, has a long-standing tradition in these countries, and it is regrettable that some schools appear to have abandoned it. It used to be the case that law school graduates in these countries had an excellent knowledge of arbitration – which is not all that surprising, given that arbitration continues to develop very briskly in the region.[1]

The structure of Chapter 23, on arbitration, is a masterful cross-sectional account of the matter in its entire breadth, from the concept of arbitration and its legal essence, through international sources, arbitration clauses and the

---

[1] For instance, it is estimated that up to 150,000 arbitral awards are rendered in the Czech Republic every year. Of course, the overwhelming majority of proceedings will concern domestic disputes (and thus qualify as domestic procedure), but in commercial agreements with foreign entities, arbitration clauses are also very frequently used.

enforcement of arbitral awards (which are given special attention), to – in a final section – arbitration in Russia specifically. The authors also mention specific international concepts of arbitration with a certain geographical scope that are usually ignored by the international literature outside Russia – for instance, a discussion of the Rules for International Commercial Arbitration prepared by the United Nations Economic Commission for Asia and the Far East from 1966[2]. Nor does the publication disregard the judicature – the cited decisions, as a whole, are little known. An interesting case is, for e.g. the annotation (including practical comments) of Decision 140/2003 of the International Arbitration Court at the Russian Chamber of Commerce and Industry of 16 February 2002, concerning the determinateness of the arbitration agreement in terms of a specific arbitral institution and the application of the European Convention on International Commercial Arbitration of 1961. The latter is also given substantial attention in this publication. Incidentally, it is a curious fact that this Convention, which is very useful, has fallen into neglect in practice, and is unfortunately ignored even in publications by authors of renown.

The only shortcoming in this publication (i.e. in the chapter on arbitration specifically) is the lack of discussion of the course of proceedings – which has its own important characteristics. The author of this chapter (I. O. Khlestova), under the excellent editorial guidance of N. I. Marysheva, has shown her brilliant theoretical understanding, as well as her familiarity with the practice of international arbitration. It is particularly regrettable, then, that she did not make use of her broad expertise in the matter to discuss the course of proceedings of international arbitration (there are certain minor references in further parts of Chapter 23 on procedural stages within arbitration, but they remain fragmentary). However, this shortcoming does not diminish the high standard of the publication as a whole.

[*Alexander J. Bělohlávek*]

| | |

---

[2]   With a reference to a scholarly publication on arbitration that is of fundamental character and may well be called a *classic* today, and which was published in the Soviet Union in 1976: SERGEI NIKOLAEVICH LEBEDEV, MEZHDUNARODNOJE SOTRUDNICESTVO V OBLASTI MEZHDUNARODNOVO KOMMERCESKOVO ARBITRAZHA, Moscow: Torgovo-promyshlennaia palata SSSR, Sektsiia prava, Sektiia torgovogo moreplavaniia 147-158 (1979).

Piotr Nowaczyk | Andrzej Szumański | Maria Szymańska
UNCITRAL Rules on Arbitration, Commentary

*Piotr Nowaczyk & Andrzej Szumański & Maria Szymańska Regulamin Arbitrażowy UNCITRAL, Komentarz [**UNCITRAL Rules on Arbitration, Commentary**] Warszawa: C. H. Beck (2011), 800 pp., ISBN: 978-83-255-2955-0 / eBook 978-83-255-2956-7.*

The authors are experienced and internationally renowned writers and their book is probably the first extensive commentary issued after the amendment of the UNCITRAL Rules in 2010. This detailed commentary-like publication of almost 800 pages is devoted to the analysis of all of the individual provisions of the UNCITRAL Rules, with a large volume of available case law and an analysis of the legal opinions that have been published to date. The authors also focus on the historical context dating back to 1966, and offer an overview of the entire genesis of the Rules which have evolved into probably the most important instrument harmonizing the arbitration practice outside institutionalised proceedings before permanent arbitral institutions.

It is important that the authors not only reflect, but also meticulously compare practical experience in the application of the UNCITRAL Rules in proceedings regarding claims arising from private international law and in international commercial arbitration. The fact that they attempt to provide a detailed interpretation of the individual concepts, both from the *common law* perspective and the *civil law* perspective and then arrive at an autonomous international interpretation is particularly praiseworthy. This perspective is interesting especially as concerns various status issues, such as the status of proceedings, but also the status of arbitrators, the parties and other persons involved in the proceedings. Although it is published in the standard and well-established form of the classical commentaries by C. H. Beck, the book is rather unique. As opposed to typical academic monographs (regular commentaries) most references to case law (whose cited and analysed volume is astonishing) are incorporated in the core part of the text, not the footnotes. Naturally, both methods are possible, common for academic literature and *comfortable* for users. Nonetheless, incorporating the references to case law directly in the text does have a certain advantage: it allows the reader to follow the topic without interruption or distraction. This method of academic writing, however, requires a high degree of discipline as concerns the authors' uniform approach to the text and their articulation skills. They have managed to abide by these rules and the resultant commentary meets all these criteria. The citation of case law does not impair the clarity of the text or the capacity of the reader to find the parts of

Czech (& Central European) Yearbook of Arbitration

the text to which the authors refer to the relevant case law. This achievement alone deserves a most positive commendation.

The authors did not forget to include an index, but considering the extent and the importance of the analysed issues, it might have been useful to offer a more detailed version, particularly an index of references to laws, rules and case law. On the other hand, we ought to point out that the commentary is divided into chapters according to the individual articles of the UNCITRAL Rules. It is reasonable to expect that the commentary will be used by readers who have a basic knowledge of the UNCITRAL Rules and know which issues are being discussed in this or that particular article; the needs of practitioners with respect to indices in similar books are not so demanding as in the case of monothematic academic or scientific publications focused on specific issues. It is a comprehensive and well-arranged book of very high quality. The voluminous annexes to the core part of the commentary are no less significant. To date, it has only been published in Polish, but I believe that the authors will prepare other language versions. This commentary is a unique piece of work that deserves a wider readership.

[*Alexander J. Bělohlávek*]

| | |

Alexander J. Bělohlávek | Renáta Hótová
Experts in the International Environment (of Civil and Criminal Court Proceedings, Arbitration Proceedings, and Investment Disputes)

Alexander J. Bělohlávek, Renáta Hótová; Znalci v mezinárodním prostředí (v soudním řízení civilním a trestním, v rozhodčím řízení a investičních sporech) [**Experts in International Environment (of Civil and Criminal Court Proceedings, Arbitration Proceedings, and Investment Disputes)**] *Praha: C. H. Beck, 2011, 592 pp., ISBN: 978-80-7400-395-0.*

In terms of their vocation and professional focus, the authors represent an interesting combination of legal theory and practice on the one hand and economic theory and practice on the other hand. This is not the authors' first joint work and their previous output has always highlighted interesting connections between the legal and economic spheres (that is to say, fields that quite logically intersect and overlap in many ways). The latest product from the interaction of these authors is again an exceedingly interesting piece of work, which on the one hand provides a detailed, cross-sectional account of arbitral activity in the international environment and in disputes with an international element, while on the other hand provides an account of the application of experts' methods and procedures in such disputes. This combination is truly unique in both domestic and international literature, and this fact alone renders this publication highly interesting and valuable.

Cross-sectional scope and interactivity may well serve as catchwords to describe the style of the entire publication: the issue is analysed from the vantage point of civil law (including private international law), as well as from the vantage point of public international law. Experts have never been all that involved in the sphere of public international law. The number of cases in which experts have been appointed for such proceedings is very limited – the only exception possibly being in the area of investment disputes, which the authors discuss in great detail and with in-depth knowledge. It is in this part, in particular, and especially in comparison to the other chapters, that one can clearly see how broad experience with expert work in private-law disputes also has an impact on the public-law sphere – clear evidence for a phenomenon that we have witnessed over recent years: the breaking of the previously inviolable barrier between private-law and public-law disputes, such that the two separate fields now make mutual use of the experience gained in the other. This "cross-fertilization" of legal institutions and experiences was unthinkable in the past, but is in the process of becoming a commonplace occurrence. There is no shortage of examples, for that matter. Nation states regularly and typically use private-law institutions in their disputes that public law has quite logically had little use for, such as the assignment of receivables, or set-offs, etc. In the procedural arena, we can see how disputes grounded on public international law sources increasingly draw upon institutions whose use is substantially more frequent in private-law disputes (such as arbitration). The appointment of experts is another clear example – one which the authors have analysed thoroughly.

In addition, the authors have collected, annotated, and analysed several hundred decisions rendered in various forums or by arbitration courts (with a detailed and structured index being included), and have analysed several hundred legal provisions of domestic and international origin. Part II moreover contains a very detailed excursion into the national legal framework for expertise in more than two-dozen countries across Europe and overseas. In an annex, translations of several special national laws are given (Czech Republic, Slovakia, Poland and Austria), along with comments.

For the international environment, the practice applied in arbitration proceedings is obviously of fundamental importance, and it is therefore only logical that the authors pay considerable attention to arbitration, discussing both the legal basis for expert work within arbitration and the recommended procedures for their appointment and for the assessment of expert reports and expert testimony. The publication also comprises translations and comments on the ICC's and Belgian CEPANI's special rules for expertise, as well as a translation and comments on the latest version of the IBA Rules on Taking Evidence (2010). These are likely the first translations of these rules into the languages in which the publication has appeared.

The authors, however, gave less consideration to contracts made with experts from the perspective of private international law (conflict-of-law rules). This issue would certainly have been deserving of more attention, with a view to the fact that the appointment of foreign experts even within the domestic arena has gained favour in a number of countries. That being said, the authors discuss this issue, too (if not as broadly). For instance, they look into the liability of experts in the international environment and into arbitration law within the context of the non-contractual liability of experts, especially in cases in which experts are commissioned to perform value appraisals for international investment projects. On the other hand, the authors devote a detailed analysis to the role of experts under international treaties on judicial assistance – an area that is often overlooked.

An additional interesting aspect of this work is that it has been published not only in Czech, but in the meantime also in Russian[3] and Polish.[4]

[*Prof. JUDr. Květoslav Růžička, CSc.*]

---

[3]   Kiev [Ukraine]: Taxon Publishing House (2011).
[4]   Warsaw [Poland]: Publishing House C. H. Beck (2011).

News & Reports

Czech (& Central European) Yearbook of Arbitration

Amendment to Czech Arbitration Act in Effect from 1 April 2012 – Preservation of Arbitrability in Consumer Disputes and Introduction of Stricter Conditions for Resolving Consumer Disputes in Arbitration

I. Arbitration Laws (*lex arbitri*) and Importance of Arbitration in the Czech Republic

Arbitration has a long tradition in the Czech Republic, and enjoys strong legislative support thanks to being defined under a separate law – the Arbitration Act (Act [CZE] No. 216/1994 Coll., on Arbitration and Enforcement of Arbitral Awards, as amended – 'ArbAct [CZE]'). Following a lengthy and somewhat quarrelsome debate, an extensive amendment to the Arbitration Act has been adopted and came into effect on 1 January 2012 ('ArbAct [CZE] Amendment'). The purpose of the amending the legislation was to define conditions for arbitral proceedings relating to consumer disputes (disputes arising under contracts entered into by consumers), which, for all intents and purposes, could and still can be settled through arbitration. The text of the Arbitration Act (ArbAct [CZE]) effective until 31 March 2012, however, did not contain any provision to this effect, causing numerous doubts as to the arbitrability of consumer contracts, and as to whether or not Czech law requires arbitration clauses in consumer contracts to generally be considered inappropriate and consequently invalid in the sense of the *Directive*[1] and substantive-law provisions of the Czech consumer protection legislation. Until now, interpretation according to the *lex arbitri* [CZE] has been based on the *'Kompetenz-Kompetenz'* principle.[2] The quite extensive case law of [general] Czech courts and of the Constitutional Court, annotated in detail in the final

---

[1]   Council Directive 93/13/EC of 5 April 1993, on unfair terms in consumer contracts, OJ L 95 of 21 April 1993, pp. 29–34. CELEX: 31993L0013.

[2]   See Naděžda Rozehnalová, *Zásada autonomie rozhodování rozhodců o své pravomoci-dvě stránky jednoho problemu* (*The Principle of Autonomy and the Rules for Decisions under which Arbitrators Define Their Jurisdiction – Two Aspects of One Problem*), 16 (2) ČASOPIS PRO PRÁVNÍ VĚDU A PRAXI 112–121 (2008).

section of this excursion into Czech law, contains relatively frequent references to this issue. Despite the fact that it is somewhat ambiguous and not always consistent, the case law contains numerous references that indicate that arbitration clauses in consumer contracts are essentially acceptable and that consumer disputes may generally be settled through arbitration.[3] The ambiguity concerns the approach to assessments of the inadequacy of such clauses in specific contracts and in specific disputes. Another aspect that needs to be considered is that, in light of the number of disputes settled through arbitration in the Czech Republic, the issue is sensitive from the political viewpoint. Due to the absence of the exequatur procedure in relation to domestic arbitral awards,[4] which are used as the basis for the enforcement of judgments after their delivery to the parties (after they come into legal effect) only if approved by a court, there are no exact statistics as to the number of disputes resolved in the Czech Republic. According to estimates of the Czech Ministry of Justice, however, some 150,000 disputes are heard and settled through arbitration this way every year, where most of them are resolved in *ad hoc* proceedings, and most concern consumer contracts (contracts entered into by consumers). Such a quite unique popularity of arbitration shows how delicate this issue is, and explains why the discussion preceding the ArbAct [CZE] Amendment was so extensive.

According to Section 2, Paragraph 1 of the ArbAct [CZE], **all property disputes may be settled through arbitration, provided that such disputes can be settled, with the exception of disputes related to the enforcement of a judgment relating to incidental disputes.**[5] In determining whether a private dispute may be settled in arbitration, Czech law does not take into account the status and nature of the contracting parties (parties to the dispute);[6] thus, there are no specific criteria for contracts under which one of the parties acts as a

---

[3] In the past, lower-level courts often considered arbitration clauses invalid *ex lege*, regardless of the specific circumstances of particular cases, and their decisions were overturned only after an appeal was filed with the Supreme Court of the Czech Republic [SC CR [CZE]). Conversely, the SC CR [CZE] usually did not find (at least on the general level) discrepancies between arbitration clauses and consumer protection laws (see, for example, Resolution of SC CR [CZE], Ref. No. 32 Cdo 1590/2008 of 30 March 2009). The Czech Constitutional Court ('CC CR [CZE]') has expressed numerous opinions about this issue.

[4] The concept is similar to the principles that constitute the basis of Austrian law. Austrian law, however, is restrictive as far as the arbitrability of consumer disputes is concerned, and basically prohibits the application of arbitration clauses in consumer disputes (see the separate overview of Austrian law).

[5] Disputes concerning the extent of assets in bankruptcy proceedings.

[6] An exception is disputes arising under agreements entered into by public non-profit medical establishments according to a separate law. Such disputes cannot be settled through arbitration according to Section 1, Paragraph 2 of the ArbAct [CZE]. This is the only arbitrability exception contained in Czech arbitration laws, which stems from the status (nature) of a contracting party.

consumer. Until the adoption of the amendment to the Arbitration Act [CZE], Czech law contained no explicit exception in relation to consumer disputes and their settlement in arbitration proceedings. The only interpretation regarding the validity of arbitration clauses in consumer contracts was therefore possible based on substantive-law provisions of consumer protection laws that protect consumers against inappropriate clauses in contracts. Nonetheless, the arbitrability of such disputes has not been and continues not to be restricted.

II. Amendment to Arbitration Act (Czech Arbitration Act in Effect from 1 April 2012)

II.1. Concept of Amendment to the Czech Arbitration Act

The new law preserves the existing scope of the ArbAct [CZE], and extends the application of the provisions thereof to consumer disputes. The ArbAct [CZE], however, now contains explicit provisions intended to protect consumers. A comparable conceptual approach can be found, for example, in German law, which is very similar to the principles of the current Czech legislation. At the same time, the ArbAct [CZE] Amendment takes into account the issues proposed in the Recommendation (EC).

Effective as of 1 April 2012, the new legislative definition of arbitration in the Czech Republic (ArbAct [CZE] Amendment) will introduce these **new explicit consumer protection measures** (**with regard to arbitration agreements entered into by consumers**):

➢ An arbitration agreement must be contained in a **separate document** other than the provisions that define the other rights and obligations of the contracting parties, i.e. an arbitration agreement must be in a document other than the '*main contract*' (a failure to comply with this requirement may render such a contract completely invalid).

➢ The amended law defines the **minimum obligatory content of an arbitration agreement**.

➢ The new legislation introduces **stricter requirements for arbitrators** in relation to consumer disputes.

➢ The law now expressly states that disputes under **contracts entered into by consumers may only be resolved according to valid laws,** and that all arbitral awards **must be substantiated.**[7]

---

[7] If a dispute concerns an agreement other than a consumer contract, the existing provisions apply, where the parties may agree that the dispute will be settled based on the principles of justice (*ex equo et bono*), and may demand that an arbitral award contain no substantiation.

➢ An arbitral award relating to a **consumer dispute must include explicit information** that a **motion may be filed** demanding a court to **annul the award.**[8]

➢ The amendment introduces a **publicly available list of arbitrators** who have the (sole) authorization to settle **consumer disputes** (this list is intended to provide information on whether individual arbitrators meet the qualifications for resolving disputes of this kind, and at the same time, whether they are subject to the supervision of the Czech Ministry of Justice).

➢ During proceedings pertaining to the **annulment of an arbitral award**, a court **may examine** whether an arbitrator or a permanent arbitration institution resolved a consumer dispute contrary to consumer protection laws, clearly in violation of good morals, or against public order. There has been an extensive debate about the proposed legislation regarding the options of reviewing the merits of a case, i.e. whether a judgment has been delivered in accordance with substantive law. Such a procedure would involve a special review conducted by a court, where arbitrators would essentially deliver rulings corresponding to judgments in first-instance court proceedings. **The possibility to review arbitral awards relating to the merits of consumer disputes**, however, which was strongly advocated by certain political groupings and was to be, understandably, restricted to consumer disputes, **was not accepted during the discussion on the proposed requirements for the form of arbitral awards**.

These measures expand the possibilities of protecting the consumer, and increase the extent of information on the nature and progress of arbitration proceedings. Like other forms of litigation, consumer disputes **observe the basic arbitration principles** that stem from the autonomous will of the parties. Firstly, the stronger party must, already during the stage preceding a potential dispute, fulfil mandatory conditions that consist of providing information to the prescribed extent, and secondly, the law introduces **stricter requirements for arbitrators** and their impartiality. At the same time, the consumer must realize the potential aftereffects of signing an arbitration agreement, and consequently, waiving the right to have a dispute heard and settled by a court of law. Hence, the law does not protect persons (consumers) who, despite all the information they receive, act in a careless and negligent manner.[9]

---

[8]   Section 25, Paragraph 2, second sentence of the ArbAct [CZE], as amended by ArbAct [CZE] Amendment.

[9]   The exclusion of such an approach to consumer protection is approved by the case law of the Supreme Court of the Czech Republic; see, for example:
➢Judgment of SC CR [CZE] Ref. No. 23 Cdo 1201/2009 of 29 June 2010;
➢Resolution of SC CR [CZE], Ref. No. 23 Cdo 4895/2009 of 28 April 2010.

Besides mechanisms targeting consumer protection, the ArbAct [CZE] Amendment also deals with some other problems that have emerged during the application of the *lex arbitri* in the past. Probably the most important issue that has been causing strong *turbulence* in the Czech arbitration practice for the past several years is the functioning of so-called *arbitration centres.*[10] These are entities that do not meet the conditions set out in the ArbAct [CZE] for *permanent arbitral institutions*, but nonetheless organize the settlement of disputes (they formally provide resources to arbitrators in '*ad hoc*' proceedings). Czech arbitration laws have been based on the notion that permanent arbitral institutions may only be established based on the law,[11] where a strict distinction exists between proceedings before such permanent arbitral institutions and proceedings before *ad hoc* arbitrators. This principle has not only been preserved, but also strengthened by the following explicit stipulation that aims to prevent interpretation problems (cit.): *"Permanent arbitral institutions may only be established under another law or only if another law expressly allows their establishment."*[12] At the same time, the law explicitly prohibits the use of designations in the names of legal entities based on which such entities may be mistaken for permanent arbitral institutions.[13] In addition, the ArbAct [CZE] Amendment expands the objective arbitrability of disputes. It is because, until now, only disputes in the jurisdiction of courts could be resolved through arbitration. Even though this issue has been discussed for some time, disputes in the jurisdiction of other authorities have been excluded from objective arbitrability thus far. The Arbitration Act now allows hearing such disputes, but only on condition that special laws contain provisions to this effect. Together with the ArbAct [CZE] Amendment, the legislators approved a change of the Electronic Communication Act,[14] which allows signing arbitration agreements regarding financial disputes arising under this piece of legislation (disputes with operators, in particular). Expanding the application of

---

According to the opinion expressed by the Czech Supreme Court [CZE] (cit.): "*consumer protection has its limits and can in no way be regarded as protection against the consumer's carelessness and irresponsibility*".

[10]   The controversial nature of this issue is underscored by the high number of disputes it has instigated. Some important decisions of general courts, as well as of the Constitutional Court [CZE], are annotated at the end of this section, which examines the Czech legal system ('*Case Law*').

[11]   Section 13, Paragraph 1 of the version of the ArbAct [CZE] in effect until 31 March 2012.

[12]   Section 13, Paragraph 1 of the version of the ArbAct [CZE] in effect from 1 April 2012 (ArbAct [CZE] Amendment).

[13]   Section 13, Paragraph 4 of the version of the ArbAct [CZE] in effect from 1 April 2012 (ArbAct [CZE] Amendment).

[14]   Act [CZE] No.127/2005 Coll., on Electronic Communication and on Amendment to Certain Related Acts, as amended.

the act (objective arbitrability) is therefore subject to a direct modification of other laws, which will allow negotiating arbitration clauses in disputes that are not in the general jurisdiction of courts.

Other changes introduced by the ArbAct [CZE] Amendment concern:

➢ The cancellation of the confidentiality requirement, where the procedure defines the course of action taken in the event the whereabouts of an arbitrator are unknown;

➢ The termination of arbitration proceedings; and

➢ The introduction of a new reason for deferring the effect of an arbitral award if it is apparent that that a motion to cancel an arbitral award is substantiated and will be accepted,[15] etc.

II.2.   Arbitration Agreements for Consumer Disputes

The ArbAct [CZE] Amendment is based on the notion that, in an arbitration agreement, the contracting parties waive their right to have a consumer dispute heard before a court and delegate this jurisdiction to a private entity. Consumer disputes will be subject to a separately negotiated arbitration agreement (separate document), and not to the conditions constituting the main contract (a failure to comply with this requirement may invalidate the contract). Such an approach will prevent a situation in which an arbitration clause is included, for instance, in business terms and conditions.

An arbitration agreement for consumer disputes must specify the following obligatory data (the data must be accurate and complete):

➢ Information on the arbitrator or the fact that the arbitral award will be delivered by a permanent arbitral institution;

➢ Information on the manner in which arbitration proceedings are to be initiated and conducted;

➢ Information on remuneration paid to the arbitrator, the anticipated types of expenses the consumer may incur as part of the arbitration proceedings, and the rules for claiming compensation for such expenses;

➢ Information on the place where arbitration will take place;

➢ Information on the method for delivering the arbitral award to the consumer; and

➢ Information stating that a final arbitral award is enforceable.

---

[15]   The objective of this part of the ArbAct [CZE] Amendment is to prevent obvious excesses, such as a situation in which an enforceable arbitral award is delivered without the existence of an arbitration agreement.

If contracting parties agree to the jurisdiction of a permanent arbitral institution, it is considered sufficient if the arbitration agreement contains a reference to the articles of association and rules of such permanent arbitral institution.[16]

The ArbAct [CZE] Amendment has defined in a more exact manner and, in relation to **consumer disputes, has also introduced stricter requirements for the conduct of arbitration activities by arbitrators.**[17] Like before, arbitrators must conform to the general age requirements and be fully qualified for legal acts.[18] In addition, arbitrators must have a **clean criminal record.**[19] Starting on 1 April 2012, the law will also require arbitrators handling consumer disputes to possess **university education in the field of law** at the level of either a master's or a doctoral degree obtained at a university in the Czech Republic or abroad, provided that such education is recognized by the Czech Republic [CZE] as equivalent to the applicable qualification in the Czech Republic based on an international treaty, or provided that such education is recognized under a special law, and at the same time, the content and extent of such education correspond to the general education that is obtained in a master's study program in the field of law at a university in the Czech Republic. These special conditions will be assessed by the Ministry of Justice of the Czech Republic during the registration of a person in the registry of arbitrators authorized to settle consumer disputes.[20] Such registration is a prerequisite for the conduct of arbitration activities by an arbitrator with regard to disputes arising under contracts entered into by consumers. Another condition for entry into this registry is that a person to be registered must not have been deleted from the list or arbitrators during the past five years based on a decision of the Justice Ministry.[21]

---

[16] These documents must be (like as required by the previous version of the act) published in the *Commercial Bulletin*.

[17] Section 4 of the ArbAct [CZE].

[18] As to a person other than a Czech national, the requirement concerning qualification for legal acts is subject to the law of the country whose citizenship the person has. It is sufficient if such a person is qualified for legal acts according to the law of the Czech Republic (Section 4, Paragraph 2 of the ArbAct [CZE], as amended by ArbAct [CZE] Amendment).

[19] The requirement for no criminal record is deemed not complied with by a person who has an enforceable conviction against them for a criminal offense, unless such person has received a pardon (Section 4, Paragraph 3 of the ArbAct [CZE], as amended by the ArbAct Amendment).

[20] Section 35, Paragraph 1 of the ArbAct [CZE], as amended by the ArbAct Amendment.

[21] Section 35, Paragraph 1, Letter d) of the ArbAct [CZE], as amended by the ArbAct Amendment.

II.3. Independence and Impartiality of Arbitrators

The new law that will take effect on 1 April 2012 also introduces fine-tuned provisions and stricter conditions regarding independence and impartiality in the settlement of consumer disputes. Compared to the current legislation, the amendment preserves the obligation of an arbitrator to disclose to the parties information on any circumstances liable to raise doubts about the arbitrator's impartiality.[22] As to **consumer disputes**, arbitrators must inform the parties prior to hearing a case whether they have settled a dispute involving one of the parties in the past three years (Section 8, Paragraph 3 of the ArbAct [CZE]).[23] In the event qualified information is provided to the parties (information on circumstances suggesting that an arbitrator should be excluded due to a lack of impartiality), the parties may agree on another arbitrator. If no agreement is reached, however, a motion can be filed with a court in accordance with Section 12, Paragraph 2 of the ArbAct [CZE] to dismiss the applicable arbitrator.[24]

[*Alexander J. Bělohlávek*]

| | |

---

[22] Section 8, Paragraph 2 of the ArbAct [CZE].

[23] ArbAct [CZE] (cit.): Section 8 – "[...](3) *In resolving disputes arising under consumer contracts, an arbitrator must inform the parties prior to the beginning of the proceedings whether he has issued or taken part in the issue of an arbitral award during the past three years or whether he is acting as an arbitrator in hitherto unfinished arbitration proceedings regarding a dispute in which one of the parties is or has been involved. The time period referred to in the preceding sentence starts on the date on which ended arbitration proceedings to which the information requirement applies and ends on the date on which begin the arbitration proceedings in which the arbitrator is subject to the information requirement.*"

[24] Section 12 of the ArbAct [CZE]. The ArbAct [CZE] Amendment has introduced no change regarding the replacement of a dismissed arbitrator compared to the current version of the Arbitration Act.

The Activity of the United Nations Commission on International Trade Law Working Group III: Online Dispute Resolution Model Law

I. Background

The influence of modern technologies in recent years has been enormous. Cyberspace as a mediator of global transactions has offered many different forms of communication, such as e-mails, secured direct audio / video communication or the exchange of information through social systems and other interconnected networks which have had an important influence in the rapid growth of cross-border e-commerce. The usability of these offered tools can be demonstrated by *i.a.* the rise in European retail sales, which increased by 18% from 2009 to 2010, a trend which promises to increase[25] further.

Technology easily enables individuals to exchange any data without any geographical barriers, thus this fact has also opened up an area for solving many complex conflicts in e-commerce and has created a space for Online Dispute Resolution providers. *"Traditional judicial mechanisms for legal recourse did not offer an adequate solution for cross-border electronic commerce disputes, and [that] solution (providing a quick resolution and enforcement of disputes across borders) might reside in a global online dispute resolution system for small value, high volume business-to-business and business-to-consumer disputes"*[26] geared toward making communication in any conflict easier and more efficient between businesses and consumers. Yet there is no need to restrict online dispute resolution ("ODR") to the online environment; as it can easily solve offline conflicts as well.

The ODR system can be described as altered Alternative Dispute Resolution ("ADR") integrating online communication tools in the process of solving conflicts. By its importance and position the online element creates the fourth

---

[25] Adrea Carini, *European Online Retail Forecast, 2010 to 2015.* Available at: http://forrester.com/rb/Research/european_online_retail_forecast%2C_2010_to_2015/q/id/58597/t/2 (accessed on October 29, 2011).

[26] Paragraph 25. Online Dispute Resolution for Cross-border Electronic Commerce Transactions. United Nations Commission on International Trade Law. Working Group III (Online Dispute Resolution). Twenty-second session. Vienna, 13 - 17 December 2010. A/CN.9/WG.III/WP.105. Available at: http://daccess-dds-ny.un.org/doc/UNDOC/LTD/V10/574/10/PDF/V1057410.pdf?OpenElement (accessed on April 3, 2011).

Czech (& Central European) Yearbook of Arbitration

party of ODR, probably not having the same level of importance as the parties and arbitrator(s), but serving as an ally, uplifting the convenience of the dispute solving process. It is however necessary to point out, that ODR is not a strict copy of offline ADR, because the online element creates wholly new automated negotiation or conciliation systems, which are not known to ADR and which significantly changes the offline dispute process. It also offers greater accessibility for consumers as shown by online conciliation and negotiation systems usually connected to online auctions or sellers such as eBay or Amazon.

That Online Dispute Resolution rules are developed ad hoc recently became significant and, thus there is no supervision of such rules and the systems cannot follow any rules created. The discussion as to whether such a situation is convenient or not is not the focus of this paper, yet having a set of rules is crucial despite opinions indicating ODR providers will continue to follow an ad hoc trend in the future. Foreseeing a situation where there will be only a few global systems is not realistic, because of shattered areas of usage and this could result in an enormous difference between offered services, which is not thought desirable.

The necessity of an ODR model law lead the United Nations Commission on International Trade Law ("UNCITRAL") to create Working Group III. Online Dispute Resolution in 2010 focused on development of the area and on trying to offer a suitable and flexible set of model rules.

II. The Activity of the Working Group at Its Three Sessions

On the basis of a note from the Secretariat of the United Nations and the discussions at the colloquium organized also by Penn State University and the Pace Institute of International Commercial Law a working group to *"undertake work in the field of online dispute resolution relating to cross-border electronic commerce transactions, including business-to-business (B2B) and business-to - consumer (B2C) transactions"*[27] was established to be conducted in part or in full by use of an electronic means of communication.

In the beginning the Working Group had to determine existing models of ODR systems highlighting issues of special consideration, because narrow model law does not suit every type of ODR.

It must be expressed here that the Working Group cannot cover the special process of already established and specialized working ODR systems such as the Uniform Domain Name Dispute Resolution Policy ("UDRP") of the Internet

---

[27]   *Ibid.*, para. 2.

Corporation for the Assignment of Names and Numbers ("ICANN"). UDRP[28] as a special form of dispute resolution solves disputes between domain – name registrants and trademark owners arising from cases concerning domain names which are similar or confusingly similar to the name of the trademark owner and registrant who does not have any legitimate interest or / and who is using it in bad faith which is the only scope within which UDRP can operate.[29] Yet this particular set of rules has to serve as an inspiration offering much practical experience revealing the functionality or imperfections of the ODR as a whole.[30]

The first step toward creating the rules is to describe the stages of ODR. The Working Group focused on two main stages – conciliation and arbitration, and also tried to explore automated systems.

Mainly, the stages of ODR are offered separately yet there are serious attempts to offer service from non - binding systems (conciliation) to binding systems (online arbitration), which can be shown in the ECODIR (Electronic Consumer Dispute Resolution Rules) project and which is also reflected in the draft rules.

Automated negotiation can be taken as the first stage towards settling disputes between the parties. This mechanism is determined by use of negotiating software to reach agreement between the parties without using any third party.[31] These mechanisms can be divided into two types – assisted and blind bidding negotiation. The first system helps parties through software to achieve an agreement; it tries to count the best outcome[32] proposing the parties' possible solutions. The second system allows both parties to place bids without seeing the sum offered by the other party. When those bids reach a certain level, which approaches the other, then the software automatically reveals the offers and proposes the settlement.[33]

---

[28] Dealing with domain name disputes ending with .aero, .asia, .biz, .cat, .com, .coop, .info, .jobs, .mobi, .museum, .name, .net, .org, .pro, .tel and .travel.

[29] Paragraph 4 (b). Uniform Domain Name Dispute Resolution Policy. Available at: http://www.icann.org/en/dndr/udrp/policy.htm (accessed on November 27, 2011).

[30] This is not however only ODR system, which can serve as inspiration of working system. Compliant - handling mechanisms such as eConsumer.gov, European Consumer Centres Network and International Consumers Advisory Network or dispute resolution provider such as Better Business Bureau offer another useful experience.

[31] The third party participating on the negotiations would be in the position of negotiator / conciliator.

[32] See more at: *Smartsettle, beyond win–win*. Available at: www.smartsettle.com (accessed on November 15, 2011).

[33] The example of this system is offered by Cybersettle.com, which even patented this double blind bidding system and now serves i.a. to solve disputes concerning New York City. See more at: *Cybersettle*. Available at: www.cybersettle.com/pub/home/about.aspx (accessed on November 10, 2011).

Online conciliation as a non-binding solution uses Cyberspace to communicate between the parties and conciliator(s) through e-mails, video communication, special platforms which can offer separate or shared space (a multichannel exchange of information) for the benefit of the parties and conciliator.[34] Great advantage is seen in this dynamic form which reacts to the direction of the dispute by variations in the process, thus effectively serving the parties.[35]

Online arbitration as the most promising stage of online dispute resolution offers a more effective solution than other non-binding types of ODR and is expected to become a tool for solving B2B and B2C disputes. An example of online arbitration is a project under the American Arbitration Association; however it uses Commercial Arbitration Rules and has no specific online alteration. Online arbitration as a binding instrument fully enables the use of electronic file management as "*a closed system whose access is limited to the parties and arbitrators (i.e. website) or is only used by the arbitration institution (i.e. Internet)*"[36] is utilized by the American Arbitration Association's WebFile, or NetCase which is used by the ICC International Court of Arbitration.

The need for having complaint-handling mechanisms was pointed out as being a valuable tool included in ODR systems. "*It was said that complaint-handling, negotiation and conciliation were methods of amicably resolving disputes that had proven to be very effective.*"[37]

The confidence in online arbitration should be improved by implementation of trustmarks serving to provide accreditation for online merchants and describing through use of a logo, picture or seal that they provide decent service, thus attracting consumers. "*One option was to emphasize the use of trustmarks and reliance on merchants to comply with their obligations. Another was to require certification of merchants, who would undertake to comply with ODR decisions rendered against them.*"[38] A general trustmark system is needed,

---

[34] The Working group even admits the possibility of having such exchange of information via mobile phones. However, the stage of development and trustworthiness of the ODR systems is definitely not on such a higher level.

[35] See more at: *American Arbitration Association's Webfile.* Available at: https://apps.adr.org/webfile/ (accessed on November 15, 2011).

[36] *Supra* note 2, at para. 10.

[37] Paragraph 29. Report of Working Group III (Online Dispute Resolution) on the work of its twenty-second session (Vienna, 13-17 December 2010). United Nations Commission on International Trade Law. Working Group III (Online Dispute Resolution). Twenty-second session. Vienna, 13 - 17 December 2010. A/CN.9/716. Available at: http://daccess-dds-ny.un.org/doc/UNDOC/GEN/V11/801/48/PDF/V1180148.pdf?OpenElement (accessed on November 5, 2011).

[38] Paragraph 48. Online dispute resolution for cross-border electronic commerce transactions: issues for consideration in the conception of a global ODR framework. Working Group III (Online Dispute Resolution). Twenty-fourth session. Vienna, 14-18 November 2011 A/CN.9/WG.III/WP.110. Available at: http://daccess-dds-

because we can easily find not only just a few doubtful providers in Cyberspace. The Better Business Bureau, TRUSTe, Euro-Label or Global TrustMark are private bodies promoting and strengthening global or local belief in the ODR redress system.[39]

Another part of the proposal concerns improvement in exchanging information creating an international multi-lingual communication standard for ODR. The system is called E-Commerce Claims Redress Interchange ("ECRI"). The participants will agree on the *"standardized codes for dispute cases"*[40] and the idea is that those codes will harmonize every data structure of common disputes and will also simplify and clarify the communication, which *"can be represented not only in textual and numeric form but also as symbols / images or even sounds."*[41] The system is presented in simple fact-based cases such as in ordered, but not delivered goods / services; goods / services not ordered; goods / services not as described or settlement not complied with[42] and the main aim of ECRI is to simplify B2C disputes.

III. Global ODR Rules

Current standards on ODR are offered by international non-governmental organizations, which do not provide a harmonized set of rules; hence the main intent is to provide a framework functioning most probably at some combination of a global, regional and domestic level. How to manage ODR platforms and the selection and interoperability of the platforms by customers should also be determined.

The rules are provided for different stages of a dispute settlement; it begins with negotiation and facilitated settlement on a consensual level, followed by arbitration as a binding decision. *"The Rules are intended for use in conjunction with an online dispute resolution framework that consists of the following documents: (a) Guidelines for online dispute resolution providers; (b) Online dispute resolution provider supplemental rules; (c) Guidelines and minimum*

---

ny.un.org/doc/UNDOC/LTD/V11/859/64/PDF/V1185964.pdf?OpenElement (accessed on November 11, 2011).

[39] *The Better Business Bureau.* Available at: www.bbb.org (accessed on November 15, 2011). Yet other trustmark systems are also available such as: *Euro-Label.* Available at: http://www.euro-label.com/ (accessed on November 15, 2011). *TRUSTe.* Available at: http://www.truste.com/ (accessed on November 15, 2011) or *Global TrustMark Alliance.* Available at: http://www.globaltrustmarkalliance.org/ (accessed on November 15, 2011).

[40] Paragraph 2. Creating a cross-border online dispute resolution data exchange system. United Nations Commission on International Trade Law, Working Group III (Online Dispute Resolution). Twenty-third session. New York, 23–27 May 2011. Available at: www.odr2012.org/files/system.docx (accessed on November 5, 2011).

[41] *Ibid.,* para. 3.

[42] *Ibid.,* para. 4.

requirements for neutrals; (d) Substantive legal principles for resolving disputes; (e) Cross-border enforcement mechanism"[43] as a demonstrative list.

A cross-border enforcement mechanism is crucially needed and the Convention on the Recognition and Enforcement of Foreign Arbitral Awards ("New York Convention") offers one of the best tools for enforcing arbitral awards. The question is whether the New York Convention can be applied in electronic binding decisions which were held partly or fully online. This topic needs further analysis, yet on the basis of a liberal interpretation and by using the interpretation of electronic means at the United Nations Convention on the Use of Electronic Communications in International Contracts, an electronic award should be enforceable in court either in a paper version or in the form of an online document electronically signed by the arbitrators and delivered online to the parties. This is also supported by the recommendation[44] regarding the interpretation of article II paragraph 2[45] and article VII paragraph 1[46] of the New York Convention.

In the beginning draft rules are focused on the scope of application. *"The Rules shall apply to ODR proceedings where parties to an online transaction have agreed that disputes in relation to that transaction shall be referred for settlement under the Rule".*[47] How the parties could reach the agreement and how to incorporate it, are questions yet to be decided, yet the answers will follow the general concept rooted in the alternative dispute resolution system. The list defining the terms used by draft model law will follow afterwards. The description for use of communication tools prefers electronic communication and also offers the time of receipt of an electronic communication. The time of the receipt of an electronic communication is defined as the moment when the

---

[43] Draft Preamble. Online Dispute Resolution for Cross-border Electronic Commerce Transactions: Draft Procedural Rules. Working Group III (Online Dispute Resolution). Twenty-fourth session. Vienna, 14-18 November 2011 A/CN.9/WG.III/WP.109. Available at: http://daccess-dds-ny.un.org/doc/UNDOC/LTD/V11/858/94/PDF/V1185894.pdf?Open Element (accessed on November 20, 2011).

[44] Recommendation regarding the interpretation of article II (2) and article VII (1) of the Convention on the Recognition and Enforcement of Foreign Arbitral Awards (New York, 1958). Available at: http://www.uncitral.org/uncitral/uncitral_texts/arbitration/ 2006 recommendation.html (accessed on November 20, 2011).

[45] *The term "agreement in writing" shall include an arbitral clause in a contract or an arbitration agreement, signed by the parties or contained in an exchange of letters or telegrams.*

[46] *The provisions of the present Convention shall not affect the validity of multilateral or bilateral agreements concerning the recognition and enforcement of arbitral awards entered into by the Contracting States nor deprive any interested party of any right he may have to avail himself of an arbitral award in the manner and to the extent allowed by the law or the treaties of the country where such award is sought to be relied upon.*

[47] *Supra* note 19, at Art. 1.

information can be retrieved by the addressee of the sender, thus this definition is not using such problematic and vague expression as "the time, when the message was delivered."

The process itself begins with the notice made by the claimant, which is communicated through the ODR provider to the respondent, who reacts to the notice. What the communication should contain is suggested both for notice and reaction. The language used for the ODR proceedings should be the one used in connection with the transaction in dispute or the one agreed on by the parties.

Negotiation follows as the first step of settling the dispute. The process begins with the response to the notice and it could end by acceptance of the solutions proposed by the claimant. Negotiation itself can be lead as assisted negotiation with the participation of the neutral, however there is no explicit agreement as to whether the rules will also take automated negotiation into consideration.

The appointment of the neutral is the concern of the ODR provider; the person is selected from the list of qualified neutrals. In that moment the ODR provider notifies the parties and provides all communication concerning the case to the neutral. If the parties still have not reached agreement, the facilitated binding settlement shall render a decision which will be communicated to the parties. *"The [award] shall be made in writing and signed by the neutral, and shall contain the date on which it was made. The [award] shall be final and binding on the parties. The parties shall carry out the [award] without delay."*[48] *"In all cases, the neutral shall decide in accordance with the terms of the contract, taking into consideration any relevant facts and circumstances, and shall take into account any usage of trade applicable to the transaction."*[49] The rules also include the liability of the ODR provider and neutrals, the possibility of the party to be represented. Finally it solves the question of the cost; it is the duty of each party to pay its own costs.

The position of the neutral and the process itself respects and follows the basic principles of alternative dispute resolution, yet as the ODR process is seen as flexible and innovative, neutral and ODR providers can diverge more and fully use the advantages of such a process.

IV. Conclusion

One of the most important questions, which needs to be solved is the issue of applicable law, which will be considered as essential at future meetings. *"One suggested approach was to use equitable principles, codes of conduct, uniform*

---

[48] *Ibid.,* Art. 9, paras. 2, 3.
[49] *Ibid.,* Art. 9, para. 5.

generic rules or sets of substantive provisions as the basis for deciding cases, thus avoiding complex problems that may arise in the interpretation of rules as to applicable law. The Working Group will have before it at a future meeting a paper examining the issues relating to applicable law, taking account of previous discussions on this matter."[50]

The development of the rules is still in an early phase. We find ourselves at the moment when the direction and the scope of the rules must be decided and agreed upon, after which the Working Group can take another step forward to create the set of model rules, which would be respected by the merchants, who will believe in the efficiency of the system and who will see its enormous advantages. However at the last meeting the Working Group appeared to follow the trend of creating draft rules that are less flexible and more closed. This cannot be seen as desirable and will hopefully change, because business needs less limited rules to accept ODR and consumers have higher standard of protection guaranteed by national laws.

[*Pavel Loutocký, BA (Hons)*]

Pavel Loutocký is currently a fifth year student pursuing a Master's Degree at the Masaryk University in Brno, Faculty of Law, and working as a paralegal in a law office. In 2010/2011 he studied at the University of Abertay Dundee in Scotland, UK, where he pursued a European Business Law programme. He ended his studies there with his dissertation on the Weaknesses and Strengths of On - line Arbitration Focusing on B2B Commerce and received a Bachelor's with Honours degree. He is inter alia focused on Information Technologies Law and International Arbitration Systems.

e-mail: loutocky@gmail.com

| | |

---

[50] *Supra* note 14, at para. 50.

Case Law of the Court of Justice of the European Union (ECJ) regarding the Limitation of Arbitrability and Autonomy by Arbitration Clauses and Choice-of-court Clauses in Consumer Contracts (B2C) (Comparative Overview)

Since the first decision rendered in 2000 in which the ECJ (formerly the Court of Justice of the European Communities, the "ECJ") ruled on the unfairness (validity/invalidity) of arbitration clauses in consumer contracts, several landmark decisions have been issued by said *forum*; these rulings analyse the issue of arbitrability of consumer disputes, including the autonomy of the parties in the case of contracts concluded with consumers, with respect to the possibility of submitting disputes to arbitration. These rulings naturally concern unfair terms in consumer contracts. Although the first explicit reference by the ECJ to consumer contracts dates back to 2006, the *Mostaza Claro* case, the ECJ's legal opinions are based on older case law. The arbitrability of consumer disputes and the arbitration clauses in consumer contracts must be perceived in the context of the legal opinions on unfair terms in consumer contracts, but also in unity with, for instance, the opinions on the choice-of-court clauses in consumer contracts, which exhibit many features common to arbitration clauses alike; both types of clauses are connected primarily by their similar purpose and nature.

The first ruling was **Oceáno Grupo**.[51] That case did not concern arbitration clauses, but the fairness (or lack thereof) of choice-of-court clauses. Nonetheless, the conclusions regarding choice-of-court clauses are, in the context of the issues analysed in this article, basically fully applicable to arbitration clauses. In said case, the ECJ ruled that a **national court is entitled to determine *sua sponte* (of its own motion) whether a choice-of-court clause before it is unfair when making its preliminary assessment, especially when examining its jurisdiction to hear and resolve the case.**[52]

---

[51] ECJ Judgment of 27 June 2000, Case C-240/98 through C-244/98 *Oceáno Grupo Editorial SA* et al., CELEX 61998CJ0240.

[52] It is necessary to emphasize that the ECJ otherwise honours the principle that, as a rule, it is for the parties to take the initiative in the proceedings, and that the court is only

The ECJ supported its conclusion by the fact that **the consumer's position is weak, both due to his or her weaker bargaining power and his or her lack of knowledge; the court's intervention is necessary to eliminate this imbalance.**

In another decision, **Cofidis,**[53] the ECJ primarily concentrated on the issue of whether **the defence of the unfairness of a particular term can be limited by a limitation period.** The Court concluded that such limitation was **not possible,** because it would deprive the consumer of the protection conferred by the *Directive*; the professional (the business) would simply wait and sue the consumer after the expiration of the limitation period.[54] However, the ECJ ruled in the *Cofidis* judgment that, **based on the principle of procedural autonomy, an EU Member State was allowed to, observing the principle of equivalence, maintain and create its own procedural rules.** The ECJ maintained that a limitation of the possibility to raise the defence by stipulating an applicable limitation period would, if the **principle of equivalence** were duly observed, comply with Community law (now EU law); the ECJ highlighted, though, that each case had to be examined individually and with due consideration of the factual and legal specifics of the particular case. The ECJ only expressed its opinion on a limitation period that erodes the system of protection under Council Directive 93/13/EEC of 5 April 1993 on unfair terms in consumer contracts[55] (hereinafter "*Directive*"). The Court did not clarify, though, the decisive moment at which the unfair term ceases to bind the consumer, i.e. whether a successful objection (defence) is a *conditio sine qua non* for the invalidity of the term. This issue was analysed by the ECJ in the *Pannon GSM* decision.

---

able to act upon its own motion in *exceptional cases,* where the public interest requires such intervention. See, for instance, the following rulings of the ECJ:

➤ ECJ Judgment of 14 December 1995, Case C-430/93, *Jeroen van Schijndel et Johannes Nicolaas Cornelis van Veen* v. *Stichting Pensioenfonds voor Fysiotherapeuten* [1995] ECR I-4705, marg. (21), CELEX: 61993J0430; as well as:

➤ ECJ Judgment of 7 June 2007, Cases C-222/05 through C-225/05, joined cases *J. van der Weerd et al. /C-222/05/, H. de Rooy sr. et H. de Rooy jr. /C-223/05/, Maatschap H. et J. van 't Oever et al. /C-224/05/ et B. J. van Middendorp /C-225/05/* v. *Minister van Landbouw, Natuur en Voedselkwaliteit,*[2007] ECR I-4233, par. (35), CELEX: 62005CJ0222.

[53]   ECJ Judgment of 21 November 2002, Case C-473/00 *Cofidis* SA v. *Jean-Louis Fredout* [2002] ECR I-10875, CELEX 62000CJ0473.

[54]   As concerns arbitration, however, we need to point out that stipulating a limitation period for petitions for the setting aside of arbitral awards complies with consumer protection under EU law, as the Court held, for instance, in *Asturcom.*

[55]   *OJ* L 95 of 21 April 1993, pp. 29–34. CELEX: 31993L0013.

The *Mostaza Claro*[56] case was a landmark decision; the ECJ approved the use of arbitration clauses in consumer contracts (subject to the conditions listed in the directive), if allowed under national law. As concerns the arbitrability of consumer disputes, the EU Member States are therefore free to exercise their autonomy. In the *Mostaza Claro* case, the ECJ also held that even if the laws of national origin did not provide for the possibility of the court to assess the fairness of the arbitration clause, the court could perform such assessment at least in the proceedings for the annulment of the arbitral award. As early as in the *Eco Swiss*[57] case, the ECJ ruled that if a national court was obliged to set aside, at the request of a party, an arbitral award conflicting with the national mandatory rules (laws of national origin), such obligation also applied to Article 81 TEC (Article 101 TFEU[58]).[59] In the *Mostaza Claro* case, the ECJ broadened

---

[56] ECJ Judgment, of 26 October 2006, Case C-168/05, *Elisa María Mostaza ClaroMostaza Claro* v. *Centro Móvil Milenium SL* [2006] ECR I-1421, CELEX 62005CJ0168.

[57] ECJ Judgment of 1981, Case C-126/97, *EcoSwiss China Time* v. *Benetton International N.V.* [1999] ECR I-03055, CELEX: 61997J0126.

[58] Article 101 TFEU (ex Article 81 TEC) (cit.): "1. The following shall be prohibited as incompatible with the internal market: all agreements between undertakings, decisions by associations of undertakings and concerted practices that may affect trade between Member States and that have as their object or effect the prevention, restriction or distortion of competition within the internal market, and in particular those which: (a) directly or indirectly fix purchase or selling prices or any other trading conditions; (b) limit or control production, markets, technical development, or investment; (c) share markets or sources of supply; (d) apply dissimilar conditions to equivalent transactions with other trading parties, thereby placing them at a competitive disadvantage; (e) make the conclusion of contracts subject to acceptance by the other parties of supplementary obligations which, by their nature or according to commercial usage, have no connection with the subject of such contracts. 2. Any agreements or decisions prohibited pursuant to this Article shall be automatically void. 3. The provisions of Paragraph 1 may, however, be declared inapplicable in the case of: (-) any agreement or category of agreements between undertakings, (-) any decision or category of decisions by associations of undertakings, (-) any concerted practice or category of concerted practices, which contributes to improving the production or distribution of goods or to promoting technical or economic progress, while allowing consumers a fair share of the resulting benefit, and which does not: (a) impose on the undertakings concerned restrictions that are not indispensable to the attainment of these objectives; (b) afford such undertakings the possibility of eliminating competition in respect of a substantial part of the products in question."

[59] *Eco Swiss* concerned a claim for damages made by the licensee (*EcoSwiss China*) against the licensor. The subject matter of the licensing agreement was the right to label the plaintiff's watches and clocks as *Benetton by Bulova*. The licensing agreement was prematurely terminated by the licensor (three years before the expiration of the agreed period), and the licensee (the plaintiff, *EcoSwiss China*) initiated arbitral proceedings in the Netherlands, in compliance with an arbitration agreement incorporated in the licensing agreement. The claimant/plaintiff (the licensee) was successful in the proceedings; the claimant/plaintiff also prevailed in the proceedings on the declaration of enforceability of the arbitral award (both interim and final) conducted before the competent Dutch court.

the scope of the obligation to cover Community legislation (EU laws), the nature of which is similar to public policy (provided the national court has jurisdiction to set aside an arbitral award, which is contrary to public policy). The authors believe, however, that the Court did not mean public policy, but [*only*] a specific public interest expressed through absolute mandatory rules (internationally binding rules, i.e. overriding mandatory rules from the perspective of private international law), not a component of *public policy*. This is a manifest demonstration of the fact that even the ECJ itself (unfortunately often due to terminological reasons and due to the legal and cultural diversity of the composition of the ECJ) does not carefully distinguish between public policy and a [*mere*] specific public interest, which is expressed through (overriding) mandatory rules, but is not a component of *public policy*.

The ***Pannon GSM***[60] case also does not concern arbitration directly; the ECJ was called upon to assess an agreement on the jurisdiction of a court different from the court that would otherwise have jurisdiction if the decisive criterion were the place of residence of the consumer (the defendant in the case). As opposed to Spanish law, which was applied in *Mostaza Claro* and *Asturcom*, Hungarian law required that the unfairness of the contractual term be challenged by the contracting party in its objections (defence). The Hungarian Code of Civil Procedure [HUN] stipulated that the court shall examine its jurisdiction (venue) *sua sponte*, but unless the case concerns exclusive jurisdiction, the defence of improper venue cannot be raised after the defendant lodges his or her first submission on the merits. The Hungarian court therefore referred a question to the ECJ for a preliminary ruling asking whether the court was

---

Subsequently, the Dutch Supreme Court (*Hoge Raad*) made a reference to the ECJ for a preliminary ruling based on the defendant's objection; the defendant argued that the licensing agreement was contrary to Community public policy (*ordre public*) for violating the rules of European competition law. Paradoxically, this ECJ ruling was not so important, even as concerns the issue of public policy (*ordre public*), which has been the subject matter of a number of other cases, especially in connection with competition law. The ECJ held that the obligations in terms of Article 81 TEC [Article 101 TFEU] are a component of European public policy; but the Court failed to provide any clear guidance as concerns the issue of whether and to what extent this public policy must be taken into consideration in arbitration; nonetheless, the ECJ itself principally found the resulting situation controversial, especially considering the fact that the procedural rules of the Community do not apply to arbitration at all, or only to a limited extent, at least in cases concerning regular contentious proceedings. Above all, the ECJ ruled that arbitrators themselves were not in a position to request that the ECJ give a preliminary ruling under Article 234 TEC [Article 267 TFEU]. The ECJ therefore allowed the possibility of adopting such procedure through the medium of courts within the scope of their jurisdiction, in particular, arbitral proceedings, in terms of the courts' supportive and control function *vis-à-vis* arbitrators.

[60] ECJ Judgment of 4 June 2009, Case C-243/08, *Pannon GSM Zrt v. Sustikné Győrfi Erzsébet [Pannon GSM]* [2009] ECR I-04713, CELEX: 62008CA0243.

obliged, even in this particular case, to examine its jurisdiction (venue) *sua sponte*. The ECJ ruled that an unfair term in a consumer contract was invalid *per se*, i.e. the invalidity is not contingent on the defendant successfully raising the relevant defence in court. The ECJ noted, though, that the *Directive* does not prescribe an obligation on the national court to exclude the application of the relevant unfair term if the consumer, having been properly advised by the court, does not intend to object to it. Consequently, the ECJ leaves it up to the consumer to decide whether he or she will be bound by the unfair term. Article 6 of the *Directive*, however, stipulates that the states are obliged to ensure that consumers are not bound by unfair terms. Paradoxically, it is not certain to what extent the ECJ ruling is compatible with the Directive – if the consumer decides to insist on the validity of a term which, in the court's opinion, is unfair. In actual fact, the *Directive* would be breached, because the consumer would still be bound by the unfair term. A contractual term in a consumer contract, although unfair *per se*, is only voidable (its invalidity is *conditional*). In other words, it cannot be classified as so-called absolute invalidity within the meaning of certain legal systems (for instance, Czech law, or, with a certain difference in terminology, Austrian law, etc.) or as ineffectiveness (e.g. German law) or as nullity. **This means invalidity examined by the court *sua sponte*. However, even these situations require that the consumer perform an act aimed at raising the defence of such invalidity, after the consumer was properly advised about the court's legal opinion. The consumer's conduct (actions or omissions) can *ex post* validate the invalidity caused by the unfairness.** From this perspective, even the *Pannon GSM* decision can be considered a landmark decision, although it prima facie appears to merely follow the ECJ's previous case law. In addition, the Madrid Appeals Court arrived at the same conclusion in ***Juan Pedro* v. *Metrovacesa S.A.***[61] The unfairness of the term incorporated in a consumer contract, i.e. the consequences with respect to the validity of the term, cannot be assessed merely in relation to the moment of conclusion of the contract; the subsequent conduct of and the approach adopted by the parties (especially the consumer) must be taken into consideration too. Their approach ought to significantly influence the

---

[61] Decision of the Madrid Appeals Court [ESP], Case No. 28079370102010100498, 12 November 2010 (*Juan Pedro* v. *Metrovacesa S.A.*); for a detailed annotation of this Spanish decision, see the excursion into Spanish law elsewhere in this book. In the Spanish decision, the Madrid Appeals Court went even further and held, *inter alia*, that the principle of good faith protects both the consumer and the professional; the Court refused to protect the consumer if he had already had the opportunity to raise the corresponding objections during the arbitral proceedings. The court principally refused to consider the application of consumer protection laws and consider the alleged invalidity of an arbitration agreement that did not comply with these laws if the arbitration had in fact been initiated by the consumer him- or herself.

determination of whether or not the parties' expression of will upon the conclusion of the arbitration agreement was free and serious.

In the *Asturcom*[62] case, the situation was unique, in that Ms. *Rodriguez Nogueira* was completely passive both in the course of arbitration and during the court proceedings – the case only ended up before the Spanish court because the plaintiff requested the enforcement of the arbitral award. In said case, the ECJ ruled that it was not possible to extend the protection afforded by the *Directive* to those cases in which the consumer is completely passive and fails to challenge the arbitral award; nonetheless, the Court found a way that would allow the courts to set aside the arbitral award – the same procedure as in *Mostaza Claro*.

The Court arrived at that conclusion by applying the principle of equivalence and effectiveness to national laws – if the Directive lacks any procedural rules, the Member States are free to adopt their own procedural rules (the principle of procedural autonomy). In other words, if the national court has the possibility to review the compliance of the arbitral award with public policy, the court must have the possibility to review the compliance of the arbitral award with Community law, the nature of which is similar to public policy. The ECJ fails to add, though, whether the arbitral award issued on the basis of an unfair term ought to be set aside; the Court only holds that it is up to the national court to adopt measures that are prescribed for those cases by its national law. Contrary to *Pannon*, the Court does not clarify whether or not the consumer's will (not) to be bound by an unfair term (if any) can be taken into consideration.

In the *Caja de Ahorros*[63] case, the ECJ confirmed that the standards of consumer protection prescribed by the *Directive* were only the minimum standard, which did not prevent the individual states from adopting their own national laws securing a higher level of protection for consumers.

The *GSM Pannon*[64] case was followed by the ECJ ruling in *VB Pénzügyi Lízing*,[65] in which the ECJ broadens, in the case of choice-of-court clauses, the obligations of the court that discovers a potentially unfair term in a contract. The national court called upon to hear and resolve the case is – according to the ECJ – obliged to conduct an investigation allowing the court to determine

---

[62]   ECJ Judgment of 6 October 2009, Case C-40/08 *Telecomunicaciones SL* v. *Cristina Rodríguez Nogueira* [*Asturcom*][2009]ECR I-09579, CELEX 62008CA0040.

[63]   ECJ Judgment of 3 June 2010, Case C-484/08, *Caja de Ahorros y Monte de Piedad de Madrid* v. *Asociación de Usuarios de Servicios Bancarios* [*Ausbanc*]. This decision is only briefly annotated in connection with the analysis of the Directive.

[64]   ECJ Judgment of 4 June 2009, Case C-243/08, *Pannon GSM Zrt* v. *Sustikné Győrfi Erzsébet* [*Pannon GSM*][2009] ECR I-04713 CELEX: 62008CA0243.

[65]   ECJ Judgment of 9 November 2010, Case C-137/08, *VB Pénzügyi Lízing Zrt.* v. *Ferenc Schneider*, CELEX: 62008CA0137, published in: *OJ* C 13, pp. 2-2.

whether the term falls within the scope of the Directive, and if so, whether it is unfair. The ECJ also confirms its jurisdiction to interpret an "*unfair term,*" but at the same time, the Court **restricts this power to a general interpretation only**; the assessment of (un)fairness of contractual terms in individual cases is always the task of the national court. Nonetheless, just like in the *GSM Pannon* case, the ruling in the *VB Pénzügyi Lízing* case confirms that the court is obliged to **examine** whether or not the particular term is actually unfair. In other words, the court is obliged to examine any and all circumstances of the contract, and primarily the circumstances attending the conclusion of the contract. Both these decisions, however, **warn against** a very common trait in the practice of lower courts (usually not to be found in the practice of the supreme judicial authorities), i.e. **an unduly undiscriminating interpretation**; both decisions emphasize the **necessity of (i) investigation/determination and (ii) individual assessment of the factual and legal findings.**

As concerns the **Pohotovosť**[66] case, the reference to the ECJ for a preliminary ruling was apparently unnecessary, because the answer to the question could have been inferred from the current case law; this is the reason why the ECJ resolved the case by a resolution (order) with reasons, not a judgment. The facts of the case are basically identical to the *Asturcom* case. Both cases concerned arbitration terminated by an arbitral award against the consumer, after which the plaintiff filed a petition for the enforcement of the arbitral award; the response of the competent national court was a reference for a preliminary ruling. In addition, the consumers in both cases were passive. In this judgment, the ECJ also confirmed that national courts were entitled to assess the (un)fairness of a contractual term *sua sponte*, provided they had the necessary factual and legal findings at their disposal, and provided such possibility was allowed under the national procedural rules. The ECJ also ruled that the ECJ could not assess the (un)fairness of any particular contractual term, because the Court did not have jurisdiction over that issue; the specific assessment is always the task of the relevant national court. The national court, if it comes to the conclusion that the contractual term is (un)fair, must adopt the measures prescribed in such cases by national law; the desired result is to make sure that the consumer is not bound by unfair terms. In this particular case, therefore, the ECJ does not mention at all the possibility that the consumer would voice his or her opinion regarding the unfair term and whether he or she wishes to be bound by it.

In the *Pohotovosť* case, the ECJ also expressed its opinion on the connection between Directive 87/102/EEC and the *Directive*; the satisfaction of the requirement posed by Directive 87/102/EEC to mention the APR(C) (annual

---

[66] ECJ Order of 16 November 2010, Case C-76/10, *Pohotovosť s.r.o.* v. *Iveta Korčkovská* [*Pohotovosť*] CELEX: 62010CB0076, *OJ* C 30, p. 12.

Czech (& Central European) Yearbook of Arbitration

percentage rate of charge in consumer credit agreements) may be a decisive factor in the assessment of whether the terms of a consumer credit agreement are comprehensible under the *Directive*. In addition, the national court has the possibility to directly apply the rules of national law that implement Directive 87/102/EEC; in such case, the court would not have to assess (un)fairness under the *Directive* at all.

[*Alexander J. Bělohlávek and Eliška Šrotová*]
Eliška Šrotová currently works as a legal trainee in the Law Offices of Bělohlávek, Prague, Czech Republic. Graduate from Masaryk University in Brno, Czech Republic. Study stays at Aalborg University, Aalborg, Denmark and Northwest University, Xi´an, People´s Republic of China. Former participant of Willem C. Vis International Commercial Arbitration Moot.
e-mail: eliska.srotova@ablegal.cz

| | |

The First International Scientific Conference "MEDIATION 2011 – A Cultivated Method of Conflict Resolution" in the Czech Republic

The method of resolving disputes through a mediator was the main topic of the first international conference, "MEDIATION 2011 – A Cultivated Method of Conflict Resolution," jointly hosted by the Law and Pedagogical Faculties of Palacký University in Olomouc with the support of the Czech Ministry of Justice and under the auspices of the Czech Yearbook (CYIL & CYArb®) projects. The conference took place at the Law Faculty on October 14 15, 2011 and was attended by significant specialists from the Czech Republic and other countries. The patronage for the conference was provided by the Minister of Justice JUDr. Jiří Pospíšil and rector of Palacký University in Olomouc prof. RNDr. Miroslav Mašláň, CSc.

A science conference provides one of the effective opportunities for opening an interdisciplinary discussion on mediation knowledge and skills in several fields of science, above all psychology, law, sociology, social work and pedagogy. For this reason, the organisers tried to open up space for all specialists to meet. Using a mediator to resolve disputes is successfully employed as an effective manner for preventing conflicts in developed countries. This is why specialists from abroad were invited to the conference.

A further reason for opening the discussion was to inform the public of the potential in mediation to resolve, for example, labour, family and business disputes. More discussion on mediation is necessary for the public to begin to trust this method of dealing with disputes. Mediation involves prioritising an attempt to find a suitable compromise – rather than time-consuming legal proceedings – for those involved in a quarrel. Instead of testimonies and legal negotiations, there is the attempt to introduce informal negotiations to find the best possible solution. The mediator is a qualified specialist, with a neutral opinion, with the task of coming between two quarrelling parties and creating a suitable environment for open communication and finding an agreement, which complies with the wishes of both parties. The mediator is responsible for managing processes and finding mutually acceptable agreements. Among the main aims of the international conference is the pooling of knowledge from legal and socio-psychological disciplines along with mapping the possibilities of using mediation in civil and criminal conflicts.

We must not forget the fact that the process of approving legal amendments of mediation is currently taking place. The Czech Parliament was presented with a proposal for the law on mediation, whereby this proposal is now being intensely discussed. The aim of the conference was to open an interdisciplinary discussion on the possible insufficiencies and impact of this proposal on mediation in the Czech Republic.

Although mediation as a peaceful alternative method of dispute resolution has been used since the 1990s, it is still based mostly on the experience from abroad, from states such as the United States, Canada or Australia. Currently, mediation in the Czech Republic is applicable only to disputes related to criminal proceedings and to a very limited extent and also in certain disputes relating to family law conflicts. On the other hand, the Czech Republic, as an EU member state, undertook to transpose the Directive of the European Parliament 2008/52/ES from May 21, 2008 on certain aspects of mediation in civil and business matters into domestic law. Otherwise the Czech Republic could face sanctions from the European Union. As the Czech Republic has not fulfilled this duty yet, mediation is provided only by private mediators and mediation centres, which occur within the framework of non-profit organisations. The fact that Slovakia has had a law on mediation in civil conflicts since 2004 serves as a catalyst for the incorporation of mediation into Czech Republic law as a specific instrument. Organisers of the event, among other things, stressed the aim of opening an interdisciplinary discussion on the problematic area of mediation in the Czech Republic and elsewhere and of finding a starting point for further theoretical investigation and practical application. After the introduction phase, whereby a host of Czech specialists (doc. PhDr. Irena Sobotková, CSc., prof. JUDr. Pavel Šámal, Ph.D., doc. PhDr. Martina Urbanová, Ph.D., prof. PhDr. Jaro Křivohlavý, CSc., prof. JUDr. Naděžda Rozehnalová, CSc.) and foreign specialists (prof. PaedDr. Vladimír Labath, Ph.D. (Slovak Republic), prof. Rufino Lopez, Jr. (USA)) appeared, the meeting moved on to the thematically-focused sections. The individual sections covered all basic fields in which mediation is successfully employed (mediation in family conflicts, business and other civil matters, in criminal matters and, last but not least, the very important problematic area of education in mediation and mediation in schools). More than 200 specialists from the Czech Republic and other countries participated in the conference. Detailed output from the sessions of individual sections is available on the conference website www.mediaceolomouc.eu. The meetings were conducted in Czech, Slovak, Polish and English.

In the section devoted to family mediation, contributions from a range of judges, solicitors, social workers, mediators and participants of mediation and science workers were heard. The confidentiality of the mediator became a central topic, especially with an eye on information, which could be used in criminal proceedings and mediation by the courts. Furthermore, participants discussed the interdisciplinary notion of mediation in family matters, whereby education in psychology, social work, pedagogy and law was seen as beneficial. However, the level of legal education was not specifically defined during the discussions. The section also reached the conclusion that the legal amendment should reflect the particular position of attorneys as mediators.

The large section of mediation in business and other civil matters showed that mediation in the Czech Republic has a bright future in this area. The presented contributions showed the variety in mediation for solving various types of legal disputes ranging from conflicts in the health services, insolvency disputes to disputes with foreign elements. Contributions about mediation in German and Slovak law brought a comparative outlook to the legal amendment. Such contributions were, within the framework of a very fruitful discussion, confronted with the law about mediation, which was negotiated during the conference as parliamentary press number 426 in the Chamber of Deputies of the Czech Parliament. It was shown that the prepared legal amendment of mediation leads to a number of hypothetical questions, which may, in the near future, have an influence on mediation practice, e.g. the duty of confidentiality, course of due process and financial law deadlines, performance of mediation agreements or qualification agreements for the performance of the function of mediator.

In the section devoted to mediation in criminal matters, the contributions focused on the problematic area between the assailant and the victim. The key questions about mediation between the assailant and the victim in Slovakia, especially with the developing possibility of applying mediation within the framework of the new institute of agreements on guilt and crime were presented by JUDr. Lucia Kurilovská, Ph.D., representative of the Institute of State and Law under the Slovak Academy of Sciences. Contributions summarising the practical experience of mediators in the field of criminal law and, last but not least, the contribution focused on the possibility of applying mediation in the framework for judging in cases involving youth from the point of view of the practicing judge were very beneficial for all participants.

Two topics were joined in the section called Mediation and Education, these being education and the further education of mediators and mediation in schools. Contributions and subsequent discussions were mostly centred on the question of the professionalization of mediation and the level of education of the mediators. The participants regard this problematic area as key for successfully applying mediation in practice. According to the conclusions of the section, there should be evaluating criteria for testing mediators. The section reached the conclusion that it is necessary to further educate mediators for the successful provision of mediation and those inspection mechanisms with supervision and general rules such as a code of ethics and professional standards were thought necessary.

The second conference day provided an opportunity for the participants to take part in topical workshops, which reflected the interdisciplinary overlap of the mediation. The participants were able to become acquainted with the new trends in ADR such as collaborative law and, simultaneously, to verify the psychological aspects and methods used in the process of mediation, e.g. the agreement of verbal and non-verbal expression or using the strength of emotions.

The conference showed that the problematic area of mediation is currently a very hot topic, which provokes a number of theoretical and practical questions, which shall be answered and investigated in the future. This is due to mediation being relatively new to the Czech environment. However, trends in the methods of dealing with legal conflicts are apparently aided in foreign legal affairs by mediation, leading to the conclusion that the Czech Republic should follow suit. It must be thus noted that, as mediation in the future benefits lawyers, psychologists, pedagogical specialists and other specialists, the mediation conference – a Cultivated Method of Conflict Resolution – has a deserved place in the schedule of years to come.

[*JUDr. Miluše Hrnčiříková, Ph.D.*]
lecturer at the Department of Commercial Law and International Private Law, Faculty of Law of Palacký University in Olomouc.
e-mail:miluse.hrncirikova@upol.cz

[*JUDr. Lenka Westphálová, Ph.D.*]
lecturer at the Department of Civil and Labour Law, Faculty of Law of Palacký University in Olomouc
e-mail:lenka.westphalova@upol.cz

[*Mgr. Ondřej Šmíd*]
PhD Candidate at the Faculty of Law of Palacký University in Olomouc.
e-mail:ondrej.smid@upol.cz

| | |

Report on Sopot's [POL] "European Forum for New Ideas": Summit of European Arbitration Institutions

"Arbitration is doing justice and justice is not and cannot be business."

The influence of European legislation on the future of international arbitration within the European Union, the concept of European public policy and its effect on the annulment of arbitral awards, the role for arbitral tribunals to interpret EU law in the context of proposed harmonization of contract law in the EU as well as the "European ICSID" were, among other issues, subject to the debate between leading representatives of the international arbitration community at the Summit of European Arbitration Institutions of the European Forum for New Ideas (EFNI). The conference was organized by Lewiatan Court of Arbitration under the auspices of the Polish presidency in the Council of the European Union that took place on September 28, 2011 in Poland's premier sea resort, Sopot situated as we believe not accidently near the city of Gdańsk, the place where in 1980 Lech Wałęsa started the revolutionary Solidarity movement that resulted in the restoration of democracy in the Central-European region.

As an accompanying prominent event of EFNI the Summit of European Arbitration Institutions entitled *"International Arbitration in Europe in the 21st Century: Beyond Splendid Isolation?"* was dedicated exclusively (upon invitation) to leading representatives of the international arbitration community in Europe, to discuss the position of the arbitration community on the recent European Union's legislative proposals. The summit was divided into two parts – the first part moderated by Adrian Winstanley, General Director of the London Court of International Arbitration (LCIA) was devoted to the issues concerning Commercial Arbitration, the second part moderated by Jason Fry, General Secretary of the ICC Court of International Arbitration, was devoted to the influence of EU law on Investment Arbitration.

Within the *commercial arbitration panel* the panelists first focused on the proposed legislative amendment to the Regulation Brussels I[67], specifically on whether the exclusion of arbitration from the scope shall be maintained or not, and on the controversial decision of the European Court of Justice in *West*

---

[67] Council Regulation (EC) No 44/2001 of 22 December 2000 on jurisdiction and the recognition and enforcement of judgments in civil and commercial matters, art. 1(2)(d): "the Regulation shall not apply to (. . .) arbitration."

Tankers.[68] The debate proved the need for meetings at this level as the arbitration community is still in the process of debating and is not quite united in the to be taken towards Brussels I. Whereas one part of the participants viewed such an extension of the existing scope of Regulation as not advisable and underlined that application of the New York Convention on the Recognition and Enforcement of Foreign Arbitral Awards is fully satisfactory and even proposal for legislation changes might have a critical effect on arbitration, other participants expressed opposite views arguing that the arbitration should be addressed in the Regulation to ensure a certain degree of predictability and to ensure interaction between the New York Convention and Brussels I. As the different approaches of the European Commission and the European Parliament toward amending this regulation have created "ongoing uncertainties," the arbitration exception in Brussels I shall be "retained and clarified." The debate further touched notably on the great impact of the EU on arbitration originating from the EU legislation itself as well as from the ECJ's case law and the lack of the right to refer questions to the ECJ by the arbitral tribunal. The interference of EU law therefore requires that EU institutions and the arbitration community must engage in an effective dialogue in positive and supporting ways to revisit the entitlement of arbitral tribunals to refer directly to the ECJ for the interpretation of EU law (now only national courts may do so). Also a soon to be expected formal proposal of harmonized EU contract law in the context of its optional character and issues arising from the enforceability of its principles was discussed. Finally the issue of European public order, its definition and its effect on the annulment of arbitral awards were considered in the debate.

In the second part of the Summit regarding *investment arbitration* the participants looked at the landscape of investment arbitration in the context of the Lisbon treaty. As the Lisbon treaty has extended exclusive EU competence to foreign direct investment (the term being undefined in the Lisbon treaty) it enables the EU to enter into international investment agreements or to trade international investment agreements. The Lisbon treaty brought a number of complex issues to be resolved that were discussed by the participants, such as: What type of agreements will be made by the EU in the future – exclusive between the EU and counterparty state, bilateral, multilateral, mixed treaties? What transitional arrangements as to the actual treaties shall be included to deal with an existing BIT? What kind of dispute resolution mechanism shall be included in those instruments?

---

[68] The ECJ judgment of 10 February 2009, C-185/07, *Allianz SpA and Generali Assicurazioni Generali SpA* v. *West Tankers Inc.*. The ECJ in this judgment held that, while an anti-suit injunction concerning arbitration would fall outside the scope of Brussels I, if such an injunction presumed to eliminate the jurisdiction of another member state, the regulation gave exclusive jurisdiction to the court first seized.

Despite the number of unresolved issues, a majority opinion on the future form of EU investment agreements might have been reached in favor of mixed agreements, and it is as yet unclear what model of dispute resolution mechanism the EU investment treaties shall contain as the EU is not a state and therefore does not have the capacity to become a signatory to the Washington Convention and be part of the ICSID system for the settlement of investment disputes. A variety of existing rules of different arbitration institutions suitable for application in investment cases comes into a play at least as a model for elaboration of a new set of rules for resolving investment disputes especially those of ICSID or UNCITRAL. One of the alternatives considered was establishment of a "European ICSID" although the consensus was against this possibility. Instead the view was taken that other existing institutions such as the ICC Court of Arbitration could fulfill this role if their rules were properly adapted.

An important issue of enforcement of arbitral awards was subsequently discussed with an eye on a proper mechanism in situations where the award creditors can't invoke the ICSID Convention, which provides a specific mechanism for awards to be recognized and enforced in the same way that judgments of the host state are.

The panel debate under the title "Arbitration – an emblem of civil society" was opened to all EFNI participants. The debate between arbitrators, European Union authorities and representatives of the business community was brilliantly moderated by Beata Gessel-Kalinowska vel Kalisz and by Sophie Nappert. Those who took part in the discussion were: Jacek Krawczyk, Vice President of the European Economic and Social Committee, Philippe de Buck, General Director of Business Europe, and representatives of the arbitration community John Beechey, President of the ICC International Court of Arbitration, Catherine Kessedjian, Vice Director of the European College in Paris and Audley Sheppard, Partner in Clifford Chance.

John Beechey addressed the audience with his concern on the future of arbitration in Europe which he believes to be threatened by recent European legislative policy that may lead to depriving the arbitration necessary a degree of certainty which could result in business going elsewhere as it is certainty combined with reliability and cost effectiveness that are foremost and make arbitration so attractive worldwide. Catherine Kessedjian followed John Beechey to share her worries on the lack of appraisal of all the potential consequences facing arbitration within Brussel I and her sense that after the legislative process ends with arbitration rule in Brussel I, in twenty years the contract drafter could remove arbitration clauses within the EU from the contracts. From this perspective, because no one would have sorted through all the consequences, not Brussel I but another instrument is needed. Sophie

Nappert opposed such a view, pointing out that the discussions over the Brussel I amendments have already lasted over ten years and any continuation would never lead to any solution. Philip de Buck as a representative of the business community for whom the arbitration is a solution, on the condition that it needs to be reliable for the continuation of negotiations with a partner, regretted that changes in EU law take forever. Jacek Krawczyk acknowledged the difficulties in harmonizing the law of all the EU member states and announced the invitation addressed to the Lewiatan Arbitration Court to continue with the dialog on the playground of European institutions. Beata Gessel-Kalinowska vel Kalisz concluded that arbitration institutions must be prepared to get closer to the reform process or "other people will end up deciding these questions instead of us."

Hopefully the words of Lech Wałęsa who wants to be "a last revolutionary" in Europe will be heard and dialogue at the right level between the arbitration community and EU officials on the abovementioned issues will in the future be satisfactory enough.

Participants in the Summit: "International Arbitration in Europe in the 21st century: Beyond Splendid Isolation"

Summit organiser and speakers:

Beata Gessel-Kalinowka vel Kalisz, President of the Lewiatan Court of Arbitration in Warsaw

Sophie Nappert, barrister at 3 Verulam Buildings in London

Panel on commercial arbitration:

Adrian Winstanley, director general of the LCIA (moderator)

Judith Gill, partner at Allen & Overy (introduction)

Wolfgang Hahnkamper, chairman of the Austrian Arbitration Association (on Brussels I)

Beata Gessel-Kalinowka vel Kalisz, President of the Lewiatan Court of Arbitration in Warsaw (on Brussels I)

Wendy Miles, partner at Wilmer Cutler Pickering Hale & Dorr in London (on the influence of EU law on arbitration)

Maciej Szpunar, Poland's Deputy Minister of Foreign Affairs responsible for EU law, legal and treaty affairs (on the proposed harmonisation of contract law in the EU)

Albert Henke, professor of international investment law and disputes settlement and research fellow and lecturer on civil procedure at the Universita of Milan and a senior associate at Clifford Chance in Milan (on the annulment of awards and European public policy)

Diana Droulers, President of the International Federation of Commercial Arbitration Institutions and executive director of the Arbitration Centre of the Caracas Chamber of Commerce

Jerzy Rajski, professor of civil comparative law at Warsaw University

Panel on investment arbitration:

Jason Fry, secretary general of the ICC Court of Arbitration in Paris (moderator)

Barton Legum, partner at Salans in Paris (introduction)

Alexander Bělohlávek, partner at Belohlavek Law Office in Prague

Luigi Fumagalli, professor of law of State University of Milan

Sophie Nappert, barrister at 3 Verulam Buildings in London

Dirk Pulkowski, legal counsel at the Permanent Court of Arbitration in The Hague

Other participants:

John Beechey, chair of the ICC Court of Arbitration in Paris

Jens Bredow, secretary general of the German Arbitration Institute (DIS) in Cologne

Lorraine Brennan, managing director of JAMS International in London

Philippe de Buck, director general of Business Europe in Brussels

Francois Dessemontet, professor at Lausanne University and representative of the Swiss Arbitration Association (ASA)

Marcin Dziurda, president of the state treasury solicitor's office in Warsaw

Catherine Kessedjian, professor at the University Pantheon-Assas (Paris II)

Jacek Krawczyk, vice president of the European Economic and Social Committee

Bartosz Krużewski, partner at Clifford Chance in Warsaw

Piotr Nowaczyk, partner at Salans in Warsaw

Anna Maria Pukszto, partner at Salans in Warsaw

Audley Sheppard, partner at Clifford Chance in London

Czech (& Central European) Yearbook of Arbitration

Krzysztof Stefanowicz, vice president of the Lewiatan Court of Arbitration in Warsaw

Małgorzata Surdek, partner at CMS Cameron McKenna in Warsaw

Tomasz Wardyński, partner at Wardynski & Partners in Warsaw

[*Tomáš Řezníček*]

| | |

Report on Prague's World Jurist Association's 24ᵗʰ Biennial Congress on the Law of the World – "National Legal Cultures in a Globalised World"

"A world ruled by law, not force."

In the week of October 23ʳᵈ, 2011 – October 28ᵗʰ, 2011, Prague, the Czech Republic's capital, became what one could describe as a city full of lawyers. Several hundred delegates from over fifty countries, among them members of the judiciary, representatives of the academic sphere and of course practicing lawyers gathered for the World Jurist Association's 24ᵗʰ Biennial Congress on the Law of the World. During the week the program (which was held under the motto *National legal cultures in a globalised world*) offered a wide range of panel sessions on various issues of modern international law. Given that Alternative Dispute Resolution is one of WJA's traditional themes[69] and considering that the Association has always engaged in close cooperation with other organizations, it is not surprising that commercial arbitration, investment arbitration and mediation have not only been included in the busy schedule, but definitely were the Congress highlights.

On Monday, October 24ᵗʰ, 2011, the afternoon was dedicated to the youth, as it was time of the Young Arbitrators Forum. This ICC's traditional event was organized by the ICC YAF, ICC Czech Republic, ICC Russia, ICC Poland and Department of International Law and European Law, Faculty of Law, Masaryk University, Brno, Czech Republic. Notably, this is the first time when their ICC National Committees joined forces to prepare such an event. The first panel provided a comparative perspective on the *Status and independence of arbitrators in commercial arbitration*. Dr. Iur. Filip Černý, associate of the Law Offices Bělohlávek (Czech Republic) introduced the speakers and moderated the discussion. Presentations were made by **Mgr. Ivan Cisár**, representing the Faculty of Law, Masaryk University (Czech Republic), **Dr. Rafał Morek** from the Faculty of Law, University of Warsaw, Associate, K&L Gates Jamka Sp.k. (Poland), **Mr. Matthew Hodgson**, Associate at the Prague

---

[69] For example last year, a Conference under the title International Arbitration & ADR – The Impact on the Rule of Law was held in Port Louis, Mauritius on April 5ᵗʰ, 2011 – April 7ᵗʰ, 2011.

office of Allen & Overy and **Ms. Maria Kostytska,** Senior Associate, Winston & Strawn (France). The second session which dealt with the question of *Costs in international arbitration* was chaired by **Mr. Paweł Pietkiewicz,** Partner at White & Case W. Daniłowicz, W. Jurcewicz i Wspólnicy - Kancelaria Prawna Sp. k. (Poland) who also gave his own presentation. The other speakers were **Ms. Ieva Kalnina,** Associate at Lévy Kaufmann-Kohler (Switzerland), **Dr. Iur. Tereza Kyselovská** from the Faculty of Law, Masaryk University (Czech Republic) and last but not least **Dr. Leonila Guglya,** Freshfields Bruckhaus Deringer (France).

Tuesday, October 25th, 2011 was dedicated to a whole-day ICC Conference on the topic of **Party Autonomy versus Autonomy of Arbitrators,** with all three ICC National Committees being involved in the preparations. The program was divided into four separate sessions. During the first, the discussion concentrated on *Limits of party autonomy in drafting arbitration agreement / clause* and featured the following speakers: **Mr. Ilya Nikiforov,** Managing Partner at Egorov, Puginsky, Afanasiev and Partners - Russia, **Mr. Maciej Jamka,** Managing Partner at K&L Gates Jamka sp.k. (Poland), **Mr. Jean-Christophe Honlet,** Partner at Salans (France) and **Professor Dr. Alexander J. Bělohlávek,** Partner, Law Offices Bělohlávek (Czech Republic). The second panel dealt with *Limits of party autonomy and tribunal´s power in procedural matters* with **Dr. Iur. Vít Horáček,** Partner at Glatzova & Co. (Czech Republic), **Mr. David Goldberg,** Partner at White & Case LLP (United Kingdom), **Dr. Beata Gessel-Kalinowska vel Kalisz,** President of Lewiatan Court of Arbitration and Managing Partner at GESSEL Law Firm (Poland), **Dr. Crenguta Leaua** from Bucharest University of Economics and partner at Leaua & Asociatii (Romania) as well as **Mr. Martin Valasek** from Norton Rose (Canada) all who took part in the interesting discussion.

The afternoon started with a panel titled *Limits of party autonomy in disposing of their material rights and limits of tribunal´s autonomy when deciding on the applicable substantive law.* **Dr. Iur. Bohuslav Klein,** attorney at law and arbitrator (Czech republic), **Mr. Richard Chlup,** Senior Associate, Mannheimer Swartling (Russia), **Dr. Witold Jurcewicz,** Partner at White & Case (Poland) and **Mr. Przemysław Krzywosz,** Partner, Przemysław P. Krzywosz Kancelaria Prawna (Poland) all shared their views on the subject. In the final part of the conference, the *New ICC Rules of Arbitration* were introduced in an ongoing effort to bring the current changes in the ICC arbitration practice to the arbitration community. An overview of the most important aspects of the new rules was provided by **Mr. Andrzej Kąkolecki,** Legal Consultant for ICC Poland (Poland), **Mr. Vladimir Khvalei,** Partner at Baker & McKenzie (Russia), **Mr. Piotr Nowaczyk,** Partner at Salans (Poland) and **Dr. Galina Zukova,** Counsel at the ICC International Court of Arbitration (France).

Another interesting panel mainly (but not exclusively) for members of the arbitration community was a session on *Bilateral Investment Treaties*, also held on Tuesday, October 25th, 2011. It was chaired by **Alexandre Vagenheim**, Associate at Castaldi Moure & Partners (France) who, apart from moderating the discussion, opened a very current issue, i.e. the influence of Community law on the rules applicable to investment treaties and their interaction. It was noted that this problem is not only theoretical, but has a great impact on arbitration praxis. The second speaker was **Joshua Fellenbaum**, Associate at Mannheimer Swartling (Sweden), who discussed the controversies over the interpretation of the term "investment" under article 25 of the ISCID Convention. Last, the audience heard from **Ieva Kalnina**, Associate at Lévy Kaufmann-Kohler (Switzerland) who dealt with the issue of BIT (Bilateral Investment Treaties) shopping and its impact on disputes between investors and host states.

On Wednesday, October 26th, 2011, the delegates had a chance to visit the west bohemian city of Pilsen. Apart from the social program, the working schedule continued with a panel discussing *Alternative Dispute Resolution*. **Mgr. Libor Ulovec**, Senior Associate at bnt – pravda & partner, s.r.o. (Czech Republic) described the position and role of mediation in the Czech Republic, in that unlike arbitration, mediation does not have a long tradition in the Czech Republic and is considered something rather unknown. Prof. Avv. **Antonella Antonucci**, Lecturer of Law and Economics at the University of Bari (Italy) offered a presentation on how the ADR is perceived and used in Europe and in the United States, paying special attention to disputes arising in connection with financial services.

[Mgr. Tereza Profeldová]
Tereza Profeldová (*1978) works as a legal trainee in the Law Offices of Bělohlávek, Prague, Czech Republic and is a graduate of the Faculty of Law of Charles University in Prague. Field of Interest: Private international law, arbitration and IP rights.
e-mail: tereza.profeldova@ablegal.cz

| | |

Current Events,
Past & Ongoing CYIL / CYArb®
Presentations

I. Current Events

I.1.   [GEORGIA]

[GEO] – [GEORGIA] / co-organization with [POL] – [POLAND]

BATUMI [GEO] 21-22 September 2011
Conference held by The Court of Arbitration at the Nowy Tomyśl Chamber of Commerce in Nowy Tomyśl [**POL**], The Polish Association for Arbitration and Mediation, Poznań [**POL**] jointly with The Chamber of Commerce of the Autonomous Republic of Adjara in Batumi [**GEO**], The Court of Arbitration at the Chamber of Commerce of the Autonomous Republic of Adjara in Batumi [**GEO**] and The Batumi Shota Rustaveli State University [**GEO**] from the series *"Arbitration and mediation in Central and Eastern Europe and some Asian countries"* on the topic ***The role of ADR in resolving international private-law disputes involving parties from the South Caucasus countries (Armenia, Azerbaijan Georgia).***

I.2.   [AUT] – [AUSTRIA]

SALZBURG [AUT] 14 January 2011
European Court of Arbitration: ***Workshop with Dr. Jernej Sekolec.***

VIENNA [AUT] 3-4 October 2011
Conference ***New 2012 ICC Arbitration Rules***, organised by ICC Austria.

VIENNA [AUT] 2 December 2011
ArbAut (Austrian Arbitration Association. Conference *"Arbitration in Turkey and Austria"*, an Austrian-Turkish Bilateral Conference.

I.3.   [HRV] – [CROATIA]

ZAGREB [HRV] 2-3 December 2010
18ᵗʰ Croatian Arbitration and Conciliation Days.

I.4.   [CZE] - [CZECH REPUBLIC]

PLZEŇ [CZE] 27 May 2011
International Scientific Conference organized by the Department of International Law, Law Faculty of West Bohemian University on *Actual Issues of Arbitral Proceedings. Topics: international Comercial Arbitration, Domestic Arbitration and Special Types of Arbitration (On-line, Medical and Sport Disputes).*

OLOMOUC [CZE] 14-15 October 2011
The Law Faculty of Palacký University in Olomouc *Iˢᵗ International Scientific Conference: Mediation 2011: Cultivated Dispute Resolution.*

PRAHA [CZE] 24 October 2011
International Chamber of Commerce, *Young Arbitrators Forum in Prague.* As part of the WJA 24ᵗʰ Biennal Congress on the law of the World, the European Chapter of YAF organized event dedicated to status and independence of arbitrators and costs in international arbitration.

PRAHA [CZE] 24 October 2011
Young ICCA, *Second Young ICCA Workshop in Prague,* covering the topics "Witness Statements and Document Disclosure in International Arbitration."

I.5.   [POL] – [POLAND]

WARSZAWA [POL] 7 April 2011
Conference held by the Arbitration Court attached to the Polish Chamber of Commerce on *Impartiality, Independency and Challenge of Arbitrators. Speakers and topics*: prof. Marek Wierzbowski, prof. Tadeusz Ereciński (*Challenge, Impartiality and Annulment of Award*), doc. dr. Maciej Tomaszewski (*Impartiality and Indepencency from the Perspective of Arbitrators*), Anna Krysiak (*Impartiality and Independency from the Perspective of Party´Counsel*), dr Maria Hauser-Morel (*ICC Good Practise*). Discussion chaired by prof. M. Wierzbowski, prof. Zbigniew Ćwiąkalski, Maciej Jamka,

Piotr Nowaczyk, prof. Józef Okolski, dr. Andrzej Tynel. Conclusion by Marek Furtek, President of the Court of Arbitration, and prof. Marek Wierzbowski.

WARSZAWA [POL] 12 May 2011
Conference held by the Arbitration Court attached to the Polish Chamber of Commerce on *FIDIC and Arbitration Disputes: Polish and International Perspectives. Speakers and topics*: dr Marek Furtek (introduction), Witold Jurcewiczh, Ellis Baker, Phillip Capper, Pawel Samborski, Christopher Seppala, Michal Subocz.

WARSZAWA [POL] 5 September 2011
Young Arbitrators Forum (Arbitrażowe Forum Młodych) organised by the Arbitration Court attached to the Polish Chamber of Commerce. The Forum has been opened by professor Julian Lew, the Founder and Director of the School of International Arbitration, Centre for Commercial Law Studies, Queen Mary Law school (University of London).[1]

WARSZAWA [POL] 23 -24 September 2011
IIIrd Annual Conference on Arbitration AIJA (International Association of Young Lawyers)– *Arbitration in Construction Disputes*. Organised by the Arbitration Court attached to the Polish Chamber of Commerce under the auspice of the Dean of the Faculty of Law and Administration University of Warsaw.[2]

I.6.   [RUS] - [RUSSIAN FEDERATION]

MOSCOW [RUS] 30 November 2010
Session of the Arbitration Commission of the ICC National Committee of the Russian Federation, attended by the representatives of the ICC National Committee Czech Republic, focused on the cooperation of both National Committees.

II. Past and Ongoing CYArb® and CYIL Presentations

II.1.   Past Presentations in 2010

The CYArb® [Czech (& Central European) Yearbook of Arbitration®] and the Parallel Project (Periodical) the CYIL [Czech Yearbook of International Law®] Were Presented Jointly with Their Publisher (Juris Publishing Inc.) at the Following Events in 2010:

---

[1]   Detailed informations available on www.sakig.pl.

[2]   Detailed informations available at: http://www.aija.org/modules/events/index. php?id=305 (accessed on February 13, 2012).

➢ The Washington D.C. XVIIIth International Congress of the International Academy of Comparative Law, Washington D.C. [USA].

➢ The 74th The Hague ILA Conference, The Hague [NED].

➢ The IBA [International Bar Association] Annual Conference, Vancouver [CAN], 3 – 8 October 2010.

➢ The International Conference of the Faculty of Law, Trnava University in Trnava [SVK] "Dies Iurisprudentiae Tyrnaviensis" – "Law in the European Perspective", 23 and 24 September 2010.

➢ The International Conference of the Faculty of Law, Comenius University in Bratislava [SVK] "Law as a Unifying Factor of Europe – Jurisprudence and Practice", 21 – 23 October 2010.

➢ The International Symposium regarding Selected Commercial Law Issues in a Broader Context organised by the Department of Commercial Law, Faculty of Law, P. J. Šafárik University in Košice [SVK] jointly with the Institute of State and Law, Academy of Science Czech Republic [CZE], Štrbské Pleso (Tatry) [SVK] 26 – 28 October 2010.

➢ The Masaryk University Faculty of Law IVth International Conference Days of Law, Brno [CZE], 10-11 November 2010.

➢ The JURIS Conference on Cross-Examination in International Arbitration, Vienna [AUT], 5 November 2010.

II.2. Past Presentations in 2011

The CYArb® [Czech (& Central European) Yearbook of Arbitration®] and the Parallel Project (Periodical) the CYIL [Czech Yearbook of International Law®] Were Presented Jointly with Their Publisher (JurisPublishing Inc.) at the Following Events in 2011:

➢ The 14th Annual IBA International Arbitration Day, Seoul [Republic of Korea], 3-4 March 2011.

➢ The WJA (World Jurist Association) Conference on International Arbitration and ADR – The Impact on the Rule of Law, Port Louis [Mauritius], 5-7 April 2011.

➢ The JURIS Fifth Annual Investment Treaty Arbitration Conference, Washington D.C. [USA], 5 April 2011.

➢ The JURIS Seventh Annual Leading Arbitrators' Symposium on the Conduct of International Arbitration, Vienna [Austria], 18 April 2011.

➢ The IBA/AAA/ICDR Arbitration Conference, New York City [USA], 13 June 2011.

➢ The JURIS Conference on Cross-Examination in International Arbitration, New York City [USA] at the Harvard Club, 14 June 2011.

> ➢ *The Law Faculty of Palacký University in Olomouc I^{st} International Scientific Conference: Mediation 2011: Cultivated Dispute Resolution,* Olomouc [CZE], 14-15 October 2011.
> ➢ The Masaryk University Faculty of Law *V^{th} International Conference Days of Law,* Brno [CZE], 23-24 November 2011.
> ➢ The *WJA* (World Jurist Association) *24th Biennial Congress on the Law of the World,* Prague [CZE], 23 – 28 October 2011.

II.3. Ongoing Presentations in 2012

The CYArb® and CYIL Plan to Hold Presentations (Among Other Projects) at the Following 2012 Events:

> ➢ *The Law Faculty of Palacký University in Olomouc International Conference on the Private Obligations and its Securing and the Non-contententious Proceedings,* Olomouc [CZE], 10 February 2012.
> ➢ *5th Annual Olomouc Pre-Moot,* Olomouc [CZE], 17-18 March 2012.
> ➢ The JURIS *Sixth Annual Investment Treaty Arbitration Conference,* Washington D.C. [USA], 27 March 2012.
> ➢ The JURIS *Eight Annual Leading Arbitrators´Symposium* on the Conduct of International Arbitration, Vienna [Austria], 2 April 2012.
> ➢ The Masaryk University Faculty of Law *VIth International Conference Days of Law,* Brno [CZE], 2012.

Selected Bibliography of Czech and Slovak Authors for 2011

Opening Remarks:
This overview lists only works published in 2011. The individual chapters into which this overview is divided always cover both substantive and procedural issues.
Titles in translations are indicative.

I. [CZECH REPUBLIC] – Titles Published within the Czech Republic

I.1. Monographs

Alexander J. Bělohlávek, Ochrana přímých zahraničních investic v energetice [*Protection of Foreign Direct Investments in the Energetics*], Praha: C. H. Beck, pp. 448, 2011, ISBN: 978-80-7400-000-0.[1]

Alexander J. Bělohlávek; Renáta Hótová, Znalci v mezinárodním prostředí (v soudním řízení civilním a trestním, v rozhodčím řízení a v investičních sporech) [*Witness Experts in International Proceedings (in Civil Court Litigation, in Criminal Court Proceedings, in Arbitration and in Investment Disputes)*], Praha: C. H. Beck, pp. 584, 2011, ISBN: 978-80-7400-395-0.[2]

Petr Dobiáš, Mezinárodní pojistné právo se zřetelem k řešení pojistných sporů v rozhodčím řízení (Vybrané kapitoly) [*International Insurance Law with a Special Focus on Insurance Disputes Resolution Through*

---

[1] Title published in Czech. Polish and Russian editions also availables and published by Warszawa: C. H. Beck (2011) and by Kyiv [Ukraine]: Taxon (2011). Book Review for example Alena Pauličková, *in* 150 (9) PRÁVNÍK, Praha: Institute of State and Law, Academy of Science, Czech Republic 933-935 (2011).

[2] Title published in Czech. Polish and Russian editions also availables and published by Warszawa: C. H. Beck (2011) and by Kyiv [Ukraine]: Taxon (2011).

Arbitration (Chosen Chapters)], Praha: Leges, pp. 268, 2011, ISBN:978-80-87576-04-5.[3]

I.2. Periodicals, Collections and Conference Proceedings

Bulletin advokacie [*Bulletin of the Czech Bar*], Praha: Česká advokátní komora [*Czech Bar Association*], 2011, ISSN: 1210-6348[4]

Alexander J. Bělohlávek, *Ústavní soud České republiky opustil striktní smluvní výklad koncepce rozhodčího řízení: Nález ÚS ČR z 8. března 2011, sp. zn. I ÚS 3227/07 (komentář a rozbor k nálezu ústavního soudu) [The Constitutional Court of the Czech Republic Has Left a Strict Contractual Interpretation of the Concept of Arbitration: Decision of the Constitutional Court of the Czech Republic of March 8th, 2011, Docket I US 3227/07 (Notes and Analysis of the Decision of the Constitutional Court)].* No. 12, pp. 40-44.

Jan Kocina, *Rozhodčí doložky sjednané ve prospěch "soukromých rozhodčích soudů" [Arbitration Clauses In Favour Of Private Arbitral Institution].* No. 7-8, pp. 48-49.

Obchodněprávní revue [*Commercial Law Review*], Praha: C. H. Beck, 2011, Vol. 3, ISSN: 1803-6554[5]

Luděk Lisse, *Rozhodování rozhodce (nejen) podle zásad spravedlnosti [Decision Making Process of the Arbitrator (not only) According to the Principles of Equity].* No. 7, pp. 218-221.

Miloš Tomsa, *K problematice právní úpravy rozhodčího řízení [On The Arbitration Law].* No. 9, pp. 267-270.

Obchodní právo [*Commercial Law*], Praha: Prospektrum, 2011, Vol. 20, ISSN: 1210-8278[6]

Miloš Tomsa, *Nepřiměřenost rozhodčí doložky ve spotřebitelských smlouvách [Inadequacy of the Arbitral Clause in the Consumer Contracts].* No. 6, pp. 2-8.

Karel Svoboda, *K vykonatelnosti rozhodčích nálezů doručených opatrovníku [On the Enforcement of Arbitral Awards Serviced to the Curator].* No 7-8, pp. 23-27.

---

[3]   Title published in Czech.

[4]   Papers published in Czech with abstracts in a foreign language. Abstracts in English and in German.

[5]   Papers published in Czech. Abstracts in English, sometimes in German.

[6]   Papers published in Czech. Abstracts in English.

Právní fórum [*Legal Forum*], Praha: Wolters Kluwer ČR, a.s., 2011, Vol. 8, ISSN: 1214-7966[7]

Lukáš Klee, *Řešení sporů podle smluvních podmínek FIDIC* [*Dispute Resolution According to the FIDIC Contractual Conditions*]. No. 5, pp. 212-215.

Karel Marek, *K pravomoci rozhodování sporu u ručení prodávajícího prodeje podniku při rozhodčí doložce v dodavatelské smlouvě* [*On the Jurisidiction in Disputes concerning Liability of the Contractor in the Contractor's Agreements, Sale of the Company and the Arbitral Clause in the Contractor's Agreement*]. No 7, pp. 334-339.[8]

Gabriela Babjáková, *Smlouvy uzavírané se spotřebitelem* [*Consumer Contracts*]. No 7, pp. 334-339.

Miluše Hrnčiříková, *Platnost rozhodčí smlouvy, aneb jaký vliv může mít určení povahy rozhodčí smlouvy na praxi* [*Validity of the Arbitration Agreement or What Influence Could the Determination of the Nature of the Arbitration Agreement Have for the Praxis*]. No 8, pp. 737.

Luděk Lisse, *Sjednocení či změna judikatury v rozhodčím řízení?* [*Unification or Change of the Case Law in the Arbitral Proceedings?*]. No 11/12, pp. 548-553.[9]

Právní rádce [*Legal Advisor*], Praha: Economia, 2011, Vol. 19, ISSN: 1210-4817[10]

Luboš Chalupa, *K právní povaze rozhodčího řízení před rozhodcem ad hoc* [*On legal nature of ad hoc arbitration*]. No. 4, pp. 12-13.

Luděk Lisse, *Rozhodčí řízení de lege ferenda* [*Arbitration De Lege Ferenda*]. No 1, Bohumil Poláček, *Znalci v rozhodčím řízení* [*Expert Witnesses in Arbitration*]. No. 9, pp. 25-27.

Tomáš Sokol, *K aktuálním problémům rozhodčího řízení* [*Current Problems of Arbitration*]. No 9, pp. 4-14.

René Skýpala, *Rozhodčí doložky a „jiné problémy ochrany práv slabší strany"* [*Arbitration Clauses and other Problems of the Protection of the Weaker Party*]. No 11, pp. 49-50.

Aleš Uhlíř, *Rozhodci v pracovním právu* [*Arbitrators in the Labour Law*]. No. 12, pp. 32-33.

Pavel Vrcha. *Rozhodnutí Nejvyššího soudu ČR o problematice rozhodčích doložek: Usnesení Vrchního soudu v Praze ze dne 28. května 2009, sp. zn. 12 Cmo 496/2009.* [*Decision of the Supreme Court of the Czech Republic on the Issue of Arbitral Clauses: Resolution of the High Court in Prague of 28 May 2009, docket no. 12 Cmo 496/2009*] No. 4, pp. 45-47.

---

[7]   *Ibid.*
[8]   The Author on Consumer Arbitration in pp. 336-337.
[9]   *Ibid.*
[10] Papers published in Czech, Summary in English.

Právní rozhledy [*Law Review*], Praha: C. H. Beck, 2010, Vol. 18, ISSN: 1210-4817, reg. No of the Ministry of Cultural Affaires: E 6318[11]

Luděk Lisse, *Návrh novely zákona o rozhodčím řízení – spotřebitelské spory* [*Bill Amendment of Law on Arbitration – Consumer Disputes*]. No 15, pp. 551-557.

Luděk Lisse, *K právní povaze rozhodčího řízení* [*On the Nature Of Arbitration*]. No 15, pp. 551-557.

Martin Kulhánek, Poznámky k připravované novele zákona o rozhodčím řízení [*Comments to the Prepared Novelization of the Act on Arbitration*]. No. 7, pp. 247-253.

David Slováček, *Arbitrabilita spotřebitelských sporů* [*Arbitrability of Consumer Disputes*]. No 10, pp. 364-366.

Jan Štandera, *Mediace – možná cesta z labyrintu soudního řízení?* [*Mediation-A Possible Way Out of the Court Proceedings Labyrint?*]. No. 22, pp. 803-810.

Právník [*The Lawyer*], Praha: Ústav státu a práva Akademie věd České republiky [*Institute of State and Law of the Academy of Sciences of the Czech Republic*], 2011, Vol. 150, ISSN: 0231-6625[12]

Katarína Chovancová, Švédská arbitráž od islandských ság až po súčasnosť [*Swedish Arbitration – From Icelandic Sagas until the Presence*]. No. 8, pp. 798-822.[13]

I.3. Other Publications (incl. E-Sources)

Luděk Lisse, *K otázce rozhodčího řízení bez existence rozhodčí smlouvy* [*Regarding the Arbitration without an Arbitration Agreement*], ePravo.cz, paper No. 72577, issue dtd 29 March 2011.[14]

Zdeněk Nový, *Alternativní řešení sporů prostřednictvísm internetu aneb být znamená být on-line?* [*Alternative Dispute Resolution through Internet or To Be Means To Be On-line?*], 20 (4) Jurisprudence, pp. 35-39, 2011, ISSN: 1802-3843.

---

[11] Papers published in Czech.

[12] Papers published in Czech with abstracts in a foreign language. The abstract is most often in English (exceptionally in German or French). See also www.pravnik.eu (accessed on February 13, 2012) (detailed informations on the periodical).

[13] The original title is in Slovak. Abstract in English.

[14] In the electronic version available at: http://www.epravo.cz/top/clanky/k-otazce-rozhodciho-rizeni-bez-existence-rozhodci-smlouvy-72577.html?print (accessed on May 28, 2011).

I.4. Books (Monographs) and Articles by Czech Authors and / or on the Topics regarding Arbitration and ADR in the Czech Republic Published outside the Czech Republic

Monographs

Alexander J. Bělohlávek, Międzynarodowa ochrona prawna inwestycji w energetyce [*Protection of Foreign Direct Investments in the Energetics*], Warsaw: Wydawnictwo C.H. Beck Sp. z o.o., pp. 448, 2011, ISBN: 978-83-255-3338-0.[15]

Alexander J. Bělohlávek; Renáta Hótová, Biegli w środowisku międzynarodowym (w cywilnym i karnym postępowaniu sądowym, w postępowaniu arbitrażowym oraz w sporach inwestycyjnych) [*Witness Experts in International Proceedings (in civil court litigation, in criminal court proceedings, in arbitration and in investment disputes)*], Warsaw [Poland]: Wydawnictwo C.H. Beck Sp. z o.o., pp. 626, 2011, ISBN: 978-83-255-3337-3 (print); ISBN e-book: 978-83-255-3440-0.[16]

Alexander J. Bělohlávek, Международно-правовая защита инвестиций в области энергетики [*Protection of Foreign Direct Investments in the Energetics by International Law*], Kyiv [Ukraine]: Taxon Publishing, pp. 504, 2011, ISBN: 978-966-7128-79-1.[17]

Alexander J. Bělohlávek; Renáta Hótová, ЭКСПЕРТЫ В МЕЖДУНАРОДНЫХ УСЛОВИЯХ (при гражданских и уголовных судебных процессах, арбитражных и инвестиционных разбирательствах) [*Witness Experts in International Proceedings (in civil court litigation, in criminal court proceedings, in arbitration and in investment disputes)*], Kyiv [Ukraine]: Taxon Publishing, pp. 504, 2011, ISBN: 978-966-7128-80-7.[18]

---

[15] See *supra* note 4.

[16] Title published in Polish. Czech and Russian editions also availables and published by Praha: C. H. Beck (2011) and by Kyiv [Ukraine]: Taxon (2011). See also book review *in* CYARB – CZECH (& CENTRAL EUROPEAN) YEARBOOK OF ARBITRATION, Vol. II., 2012 (book review drafted by Květoslav Růžička).

[17] Title published in Russian. Czech and Polish editions also availables and published by Prague: C. H. Beck (2011) and by Warsaw [Poland]: C. H. Beck (2011). Book Review for example Alena Pauličková, *supra* note 1.

[18] Title published in Russian. Czech and Polish editions also availables and published by Praha: C. H. Beck (2011) and by Warsaw [Poland]: C. H. Beck (2011). See also book review in CYARB – CZECH (& CENTRAL EUROPEAN) YEARBOOK OF ARBITRATION, Vol. II., 2012 (book review drafted by Květoslav Růžička).

Czech (& Central European) Yearbook of Arbitration

Other Publications

Alexander J. Bělohlávek, *Czech Republic, in* Arbitration 2010 – Global Arbitration Review – Edition *Getting the Deal Through*, London: Publishing house: Law Business Research, pp. 95-100, 2010.[19]

Andrea Carska-Sheppard, *The Interantional Arbitration Paradigm and Application of Dispute Resolution Measures – A Czech Republic Perspective*, 27 (1) Arbitration International, pp. 47-56, 2011, ISSN 0957 0411.

Martin Hrodek; Michaela Koblasová, *Czech Republic*, The Baker & MacKenzie International Arbitration Yearbook 2010-2011, Huntington (NY): Juris, pp. 187-198, ISBN: 978-1-933833-78-1.

For further publications of Czech authors also issued in the Slovak Republic – see below.

II. [SLOVAK REPUBLIC]

Monographs, Collections and Conference Proceedings

Slávka Michančová; Renáta Dolanská (eds.), *Súčasnost a perspektívy probácie a mediácie.* [*Current Situation and Perspectives of Probation and Mediation*], Prešov / Slovenská republika [Slovak Republic]: Prešovská univerzita v Prešove [University in Prešov / Slovak Republic], 2010, ISBN: 978–80–555–0162–8.

Selected works published in the particular book on arbitration and ADR:

➤ R. Brzobohatý; Lenka Poláková, *Modely mediace – výzvy a perspektivy pro řešení sporů* [*Models of Mediation – Challenges to and Perspectives of Dispute Resolution*].

➤ Tomáš Horáček, *Aktuální otázky vzdělávání mediátorů v ČR* [*Current Topics Regarding The Education of Mediators in the Czech Republic*]. pp. 291 et seq.

➤ Ernest Kováč, *Etický kódex mediátora* [*Code of Ethics for Mediators*]. pp. 127 et seq.

[19] Published in English.

III. [BULGARIA][20]

V. Ivanov, Rescision of Bilateral Contracts Due to Non Fulfilment: Court and Arbitration Practice – Arbitration Court of the Bulgarian Chamber of Commerce and Industry, Commentary and Notes,[21] Sofia: Nova zvezda, 2011.

IV. [BELARUS]

Alexander Korobeinikov, *Belarus*, The Baker & McKenzie International Arbitration Yearbook 2010-2011, Huntington (NY): Juris, pp. 165-172, 2011, ISBN: 978-1-933833-78-1.

V. [CROATIA]

Elma Beganovic, *Croatian Law on Arbitration and Uncitral Model Law on International Commercial Arbitration, in* Young ICCA Blog. 15 November 2010.[22]

VI. [HUNGARY][23]

Monographs and Collections

A választottbíróság hatvan éve: a Magyar Kereskedelmi és Iparkamara mellett szervezett Állandó Választottbíróság fennállásának 60. évfordulója alkalmából 2009. november 19-20-án megtartott konferencia előadásai: [1949-2009] [*Sixty Years of the Arbitration Court: Presentations of the Conference Held on 19th-20th November, 2009, Celebrating the 60th Anniversary of the Existence of the Arbitration Court Attached to the Hungarian Chamber of Commerce and Industry (1949-2009)*],

---

[20] Research completed with the assistance of Plamen Borissov, Sofia, Bulgaria. Based on our electronic research, research in the archives of the Arbitration Court with the Bulgarian Chamber of Commerce and Industry and the Law Faculty at the Sofia University "St. Kliment Ohridski", we have not discovered any titles dealing with arbitration published in Bulgaria in 2010. We have not, however, performed a thorough and complete research of all publications and periodicals printed in Bulgaria.

[21] Translation of the original Bulgarian title.

[22] The electronic version available at: http://www.youngicca-blog.com/ (accessed on November 27, 2010).

[23] Research completed with the assistance of Dr. Katalin Préda, Budapest, Hungary.

Czech (& Central European) Yearbook of Arbitration

Budapest, Magyar Kereskedelmi és Iparkamara [*Hungarian Chamber of Commerce and Industry*], 2010.[24]

Other Publications (Other than Monographs)

József Antal; Anna Ménes, *Hungary*, The Baker & MacKenzie International Arbitration Yearbook 2010-2011. Huntington (NY): Juris, pp. 267-280, 2011, ISBN: 978-1-933833-78-1.

Dániel Bán; László Kecskés, *Az alá nem írt választottbírósági szerződések megítélésének változásáról* [*On the Changes of Awarding the Not Signed Arbitration Contracts*]. 11 (1) Európai jog, pp. 3-21, 2011, ISSN: 1587-2769.

Tibor Cenner, *A választottbíráskodásnak nemcsak előnyei vannak* [*There Are Not Only Advantages of the Arbitration*]. 55 (3) Kistermelők lapja, pp.11, 2011, ISSN: 0238-9533.

László Kecskés, *A választottbíráskodás történeti alapjai* [*Historical Grounds of Arbitration*]. 58 (7) Magyar jog, pp. 358-396, 2011, ISSN: 0025-0147.

László Kecskés; *Dr. Horváth Éva, "Nemzetközi Választottbíráskodás" című könyvéről* [*About the Book Entitled „International Arbitration" by Dr. Horváth Éva*]. 58 (4) Magyar jog, pp. 252-254, 2011, ISSN: 0025-0147.

Józsefné Lukács, *Változik a francia választottbírósági szabályozás* [*The French Rules of Arbitration Are Changing*]. 11 (1) Európai jog, pp. 40-42, 2011, ISSN: 1587-2769.

Józsefné Lukács, *A Magyar Kereskedelmi és Iparkamara mellett szervezett Állandó Választottbíróság 2006-2010. évi tevékenységének számszerű adatai* [*Numerical Data on the Operation in the Years 2006-2010 of Arbitration Court Attached to the Hungarian Chamber of Commerce and Industry*]. 58 (9) Magyar jog, pp. 559-565, 2011, ISSN: 0025-0147.

Katalin Murányi, *Az állami bíróságoknak a választottbíróságok működéséhez kapcsolódó gyakorlata és gondolatok az esetleg szükséges jogszabály módosításokról* [*Case Law of the State Courts in Connection with the Operation of the Arbitration Courts and Thoughts on the Possibly Needed Revisions of Law*]. 58 (4) Magyar jog, pp. 193-208, 2011, ISSN: 0025-0147.

Antónia Rádi, *Korlát a választottbíráskodásnak: államosítás másként* [*Obstacle to the Arbitration: a Different Way of Nationalization*]. 33 (40) HVG, pp. 16-18, 2011, ISSN: 1217-9647.

---

[24] Published in the very end of 2010, in fact available in 2011. ISBN of the book not granted; available in some libraries only.

Róbert Szakál, *Ügynöki jutalék kifizetésének megtagadása (választottbírósági esetek)* [*Denial of the Payment of Commission Payable to the Agent (Article on the Case Law)*]. 19 (6) Gazdaság és jog, pp. 24-26, 2011,

VII. [LATVIA]²⁵

Inese Druviete, *Pagaidu tiesību aizsardzības līdzekļu loma šķīrējtiesas veselībā* [*Role of Temporary Remedies in the "Health Status" of Arbitration Court*], 36 Jurista vārds, Riga: Latvijas Vēstnesis, pp. 631 et seq, 2010.²⁶

VIII. [LITHUANIA]

Deividas Soloveičikas, *Viešųjų pirkimų ginčų arbitruotinumo problematika* [*Possible Solution of Public Procurement Cases in Arbitration*], 75 Teisė, Vilnius: Vilniaus Universiteto leidykla, 2010.²⁷

IX. [POLAND]²⁸

Monographs

Łukasz Błaszczak, Wyrok sądu polubownego w postępowaniu cywilnym [*Arbitration Award in Civil Proceedings*], Warszawa: Wolters Kluwer Polska sp. z o.o., 2010.

ADR Arbitraż i Mediacja [*ADR Arbitration And Mediation*], Warszawa: C. H. Beck, 2010, ISSN: 1898-942X²⁹

Elżbieta Bogucka; Piotr Nowaczyk, *Sąd Arbitrażowy przy Krajowej Izbie Gospodarczej na tle najważniejszych instytucji arbitrażowych w Europie* [*The Court of Arbitration at the Polish Chamber of Commerce in the Perspective of Major European Arbitration Institutions*]. No. 2, pp. 5 et seq.

---

²⁵ Selected by Veronika Leja, Riga, Latvia.

²⁶ The electronic version available at: http://www.juristavards.lv/index.php?menu =auth&id=216097 (accessed on December 1, 2010).

²⁷ The electronic version of the annotation available at: http://www.leidykla.vu.lt/ mokslo-darbai/teise/teise-2010-75-tomas/soloveicikas-d-viesuju-pirkimu-gincu-arbitruo tinumo-problematika/ (accessed on November 17, 2010). The article was pointed out to us by G. Uleviciute (ECOVIS, Vilnis, Lithuania).

²⁸ Polish bibliography concerning arbitration and ADR for 2008 and 2009 also available in Andrzej Pasek, *Bibliografia arbitrażu i mediacji za lata 2008-2009* [*Bibliography of Arbitration and Mediation for the Years 2008-2009*], (2) ADR. Arbitration and Mediation 35-61 (2010).

²⁹ Quarterly. Papers published in Polish.

Paweł Cioch, *Rozstrzyganie sporów sportowych w świetle ustawy o sporcie* [*Sport Disputes Resolution in the Context of the Polish Sport Act*]. No. 2, pp. 13.

Oskar Filipowski, *Mediacja w polskim postępowaniu grupowym* [*Mediation in Polish Collective Proceeding*]. No. 1, pp. 5 et seq.

Grzegorz Frączek, *Funkcjonowanie ośrodków mediacyjnych* [*Functioning of Mediation Centres*]. No. 2, pp. 25 et seq.

Agnieszka Górnicz-Mulcahy; Monika Lewanowicz-Machnikowska, *Mediacja w sporze zbiorowym* [*Mediation in a Class Action*]. No. 2, pp. 49-59 et seq.

Ludwina Klein, *Ochrona poufności arbitrażu inwestycyjnego* [*Investment Arbitration Confidentiality Protection*]. No. 2, pp. 37 et seq.

Małgorzata H. Kurtasz, Anna Marek, Krystian Mularczyk, *Postępowanie pojednawcze a postępowanie mediacyjne* [*Conciliatory Proceedings and Mediation Proceedings*]. No. 1, pp. 20 et seq.

Magdalena Mazur, *Moc wiążąca umów procesowych na przykładzie zapisu na sąd polubowny* [*Binding Force of Procedural Agreements on the Example of the Arbitration Clause*]. No. 1, pp. 39 et seq.

Sylwester Pieckowski, *Mediacja w sprawach gospodarczych* [*Mediation in Commercial Cases*]. No. 2, pp. 61 et seq.

Mateusz Pietraszewski, *Zdatność arbitrażowa sporu w świetle najnowszego orzecznictwa Sądu Najwyższego* [*Dispute Arbitrability in the Context of Most Recent Supreme Court Rulings*]. No. 2, pp. 87 et seq.

Anna Pułka, *Sądy polubowne szybsze i tańsze? Rozważania na marginesie postępowania arbitrażowego wszczętego przez Danish Polish Telecommunications Group przeciwko Telekomunikacji Polskiej S.A.* [*Arbitration Courts Faster and Less Expensive? Deliberations at the Side of the Arbitration Proceedings Initiated by Danish Polish Telecommunications Group against Telekomunikacja Polska S.A.*]. No. 2, pp. 99 et seq.

Agnieszka Różalska-Kucal, *Międzynarodowy arbitraż inwestycyjny - potrzeba zmian regulacji prawnych - sprawozdanie z konferencji (Warszawa, 26 X 2010)* [*International Entrepreneurial Arbitration – Need of Changes of Regulations by Law – Report of Conference (Warsaw, 26 October 2010)*]. No. 1, pp. 77 et seq.

Władysław Rychłowski, *O potrzebie nowelizacji ustawy z 23.5.1991 r. o rozwiązywaniu sporów zbiorowych* [*On the Need of Amendments to the Class Action Resolution Act of 23 May 1991*]. No. 2, pp. 113.

Karol Ryszkowski, *Orzekanie na zasadach słuszności w postępowaniu przed sądem arbitrażowym - summum ius summa iniuria?* [*Adjudication on the Basis of the Principles of Equity Before an Arbitration Court – Summum Ius Summa Iniuria?*]. No. 1, pp. 53.

Andrzej Szumański, *Nowy regulamin oraz wewnętrzne zasady postępowania przed Sądem Arbitrażowym przy Polskiej Konfederacji Pracodawców Prywatnych Lewiatan* [*New Regulations and Internal Rules of Proceeding Before the Court of Arbitration at the Polish Confederation of Private Employers Lewiatan*]. No. 2, pp. 129.

Bartosz Trocha, *Kwestia obecności arbitrażu w europejskim prawie postępowania cywilnego w świetle projektów rewizji rozporządzenia Bruksela I* [*The Issue of Presence of Arbitration in the European Civil Procedure Law in the Light of Draft Revisions to the Brussels I Regulation*]. No. 1, pp. 63.

Arbitration e-Review, 2010, Warszawa: Sąd Arbitrażowy przy Krajowej Izbie Gospodarczej [*Court of Arbitration attached to the Polish Chamber of Commerce*] in LexisNexis Polska

Yuliya Chernykh, *Poufność czy jawność w arbitrażu inwestycyjnym - perspektywa Ukrainy.* [*Confidentiality or Publicity in Investment Arbitration: Ukraine's Perspective*]. No. 3, pp. 38-42.

Arbitraż w Polsce [*Arbitration in Poland*], Warszawa 2011

Marcin Dziurda; Adam Olszewski, *Arbitraż z udziałem Państwa Polskiego* [*Arbitration with the Participation of the Polish State*]. pp. 21.

Aleksander Chłopecki, *Niektóre aspekty "branżowego" sądownictwa arbitrażowego na przykładzie Sądu Polubownego przy Komisji Nadzoru Finansowego* [*Aspects of Sector Arbitration, Judging by the Example of the Court of Arbitration at the Polish Financial Supervision Authority*]. pp. 31.

Beata Gessel-Kalinowska vel Kalisz, *Rozstrzyganie sporów korporacyjnych w postępowaniu arbitrażowym* [*Solving Corporate Disputes in Arbitration Proceedings*]. pp. 53-59.

Krzysztof Stefanowicz, *Krajobraz arbitrażowy w Polsce-widok subiektywny* [*Arbitration Landscape in Poland – a Subjective View*]. pp. 9.

Gerhard Wegen, *Arbitraż w Polsce – dlaczego?* [*Arbitration in Poland –Why?*]. pp. 63.

Artur Barczewski; Maciej Jamka, *Arbitraż w sprawach budowlanych – wybrane problemy praktyczne* [*Arbitration in Construction Matters – Selected Practical Issues*]. pp. 41.

Biuletyn Arbitrażowy [*Bulletin on Arbitration*], Warszawa: LexisNexis Polska Sp. z.o.o. 2011[30]

Sebastian Baur; Karl Pörnbacher, *The New French Arbitration Law, the UNCITRAL Arbitration Rules and IBA Rules on the Taking of Evidence in International Arbitration*. No. 4, pp. 52.

Louis B. Buchman, *Reforma francuskiego prawa arbitrażowego* [*French Arbitration Law Reform*]. No. 4, pp. 47.

Szczęsny Kaźmierczak, *O możliwości przerwania przed sądem powszechnym biegu przedawnienia roszczeń podporządkowanych kognicji sądu arbitrażowego* [*On the Possibility of the Extension of the Limitation Period for Claims Covered by an Arbitration Agreement through Commencement of State Court Proceedings*]. No. 4, pp. 82.

Zofia Kosteczka, *Amicus curiae w arbitrażu inwestycyjnym* [*Amicus Curiae in Investment Arbitration*]. No. 4, pp. 102.

Dmitry Marchukov, *Leading Ukrainian Arbitration Institution on Influence of Insolvency Proceedings on Arbitration: Has the Approach Changed?* No. 4, pp. 65.

Rafał Morek, *Przegląd orzecznictwa Sądu Najwyższego i sądów apelacyjnych* [*Selected Court Decisions Related to Arbitral Proceedings*]. No. 4, pp. 115.

Piotr Nowaczyk, *Nowy Regulamin Arbitrażowy UNCITRAL* [*New UNCITRAL Arbitration Rules*]. No. 4, pp. 40.

Anna Wolak-Danecka, *Arbitraż w Republice Czeskiej* [*Arbitration in the Czech Republic*]. No. 4, pp. 71.

e-Przegląd Arbitrażowy, 2011, Vol. 2

Łukasz Błaszczak, *Lex mercatoria, zasady prawa oraz zasady słuszności jako podstawy orzekania przez sąd arbitrażowy* [*Lex Mercatoria, Rules of Law and Rules of Equity as Grounds of Adjudication by an Arbitration Court*]. No. 1, pp. 13.

Pavlo I. Byelousov; Olena S. Perepelynska, *Uznawanie i wykonywanie orzeczeń arbitrażowych na Ukrainie: Nowy rozdział* [*Recognition and Enforcement Procedure in Ukraine: Reload*]. No. 2, pp. 24.

Piotr Bytnerowicz, *Warunki zgłaszania nowych roszczeń z kontraktów FIDIC w postępowaniu arbitrażowym* [*Conditions for Bringing New Claims to Arbitration under FIDIC Contracts*]. No. 1, pp. 27.

Piotr Drzewiecki, *Arbitraż ad hoc zakończy dyplomatyczny spór między Szwajcarią i Libią?* [*Will Ad Hoc Arbitration Terminate Diplomatic Dispute between Switzerland and Libya?*]. No. 2, pp. 53.

---

[30] Issued by Sąd Arbitrażowy przy Krajowej Izbie Gospodarczej [*Court of Arbitration attached to the Polish Chamber of Commerce*] in LexisNexis Polska.

Klaudia Frątczak; Natalia Mikołajczyk, *Nowelizacja francuskiego Kodeksu Postępowania Cywilnego: Rewolucyjne zmiany w prawie arbitrażowym* [*Reform of the French Code of Civil Procedure – Revolutionary Changes in Arbitration Law*]. No. 2, pp. 40.

Olga Horvath; Kamil Zawicki, *Poufność w arbitrażu międzynarodowym a potrzeba międzynarodowych standardów etycznych prawników* [*Confidentiality in International Arbitration and the Need for Global Ethical Standards for Lawyers*]. No. 2, pp. 9.

Marcin Kałduński, *Sprawozdanie z międzynarodowej konferencji arbitrażowej "International Commercial Arbitration. Austrian/Polish Twin Conference"* [*Report of International Arbitration Conference "International Commercial Arbitration. Austrian/Polish Twin Conference"*]. No. 1, pp. 39.

Michał Markowski, *Wpływ przestępstwa przekupstwa na postępowanie arbitrażowe w międzynarodowym arbitrażu handlowym* [*The Impact of the Crime of Bribery on the Proceedings in International Commercial Arbitration*]. No. 2, pp. 27.

Marek Neumann, *"Otwarcie i skrycie...: o poufności w arbitrażu międzynarodowym* [*Openly and Secretly...: On Confidentiality in International Arbitration*]. No. 2, pp. 58.

Łucja Nowak, *Co nowego w Sądzie Arbitrażowym ICC?* [*What's New at the ICC Court of Arbitration?*]. No. 1, pp. 32.

Jerzy Rajski, *Granice swobody sądu arbitrażowego w zakresie stosowania przepisów prawa w sprawach gospodarczych* [*The Limits of the Arbitral Tribunal's Freedom in Respect of Applying Provisions of Law in Commercial Cases*]. No. 1, pp. 6.

Jerzy Rajski, *Poufność a jawność w arbitrażu międzynarodowym* [*Confidentiality vs. Transparency in International Arbitration*]. No. 2, pp. 5.

Harald Sippel, *Odmowa przeprowadzenia rozprawy jako przesłanka uchylenia wyroku arbitrażowego* [*Austrian Supreme Court: Refusal to Conduct a Hearing Despite a Party's Motion Is Reason to Set Aside an Arbitral Award*]. No. 1, pp. 42.

Stanisław Sołtysik, *Międzynarodowe Centrum Arbitrażowe w Hong Kongu obchodzi dwudziestopięciolecie działalności* [*Hong Kong International Arbitration Centre – 25th Anniversary of Its Founding*]. No. 1, pp. 36.

Monitor Prawniczy, 2011

Adamus Przemysław. *Wynagrodzenie mediatora w postępowaniu cywilnym – wybrane zagadnienia* [*Mediator's Remuneration in Civil Proceedings – Selected Issues*]. No. 10, pp. 532 et seq.

PPC, 2010

Paweł Grzegorczyk, *W ramach której z podstaw kasacyjnych należy zarzucać naruszenie przepisów regulujących warunki uznania orzeczenia sądu państwa obcego lub wyroku sądu polubownego wydanego za granicą?* [*Which Cassation Ground Should Be the Basis for the Plea of Infringement of the Provisions Regulating the Conditions of Recognition of a Foreign Judgment or a Foreign Award?*]. No. 1, pp. 77-82.

PPH, 2010

Michał Jochemczak, *Attorney-client privilege w międzynarodowym postępowaniu arbitrażowym* [*Attorney-Client Privilege in International Arbitration Proceedings*]. No. 3, pp. 37-44.

Prawo Europejskie w Praktyce [European Law in Practice] 2010

Robert Siwik, *Zapis na sąd polubowny w umowach konsumenckich - wnioski z najnowszego orzecznictwa ETS* [*Arbitration Clause in Consumer Agreements – Conclusions Drawn from the Latest ETS Case Law*], No. 3/2010, pp. 37-43.

Prawo Spółek 2011

Marcin Tofel, *Aktualności i orzecznictwo: Zapis sporu wekslowego na sąd polubowny* [*News and Case Law: Arbitration Agreement concerning a Bill of Exchange Dispute*]. No. 7, pp. 2.

Marcin Tofel, *Aktualności i orzecznictwo: Zdatność arbitrażowa sporu o ustalenie nieważności czynnośći prawnej* [*News and Case Law: Arbitrability of a Dispute for Declaration of Invalidity of a Legal Act*]. No. 7, pp. 10.

Przegląd Prawa Handlowego 2011

Jerzy Rajski, *Granice autonomii sądu arbitrażowego w odniesieniu do stosowania przepisów prawa w sprawach ze stosunków gospodarczych* [*The Limits of Arbitral Tribunal's Autonomy in Respect of Application of Provisions of Law in Commercial Cases*]. No. 1, pp. 6.

Jerzy Rajski, *Zagadnienia transparentności w międzynarodowym traktatowym arbitrażu inwestycyjnym* [*Problems of Transparency in International Treaty-Based Investor-State Arbitration*]. No. 3, pp. 4.

Andrzej Szumański, *Magna Carta międzynarodowego arbitrażu handlowego w świetle art. 17 Regulaminu Arbitrażowego UNCITRAL z 2010 r.* [*Magna Carta of International Arbitration in the Light of Art. 17 of UNCITRAL Arbitration Rules as Revised in 2010*]. No. 7, pp. 4.

Glosa, 2010

Paweł Błaszczyk, *Glosa do uchwały SN z dnia 7 maja 2009 r., III CZP 13/09. Zdatność arbitrażowa sporów ze stosunku spółki handlowej [Capacity to Arbitrate over Corporate Disputes – Commentary on the Supreme Court Resolution of 7 May 2009, III CZP 13/09]*. No. 1, pp. 22-29.

Other Publications

Rafał Adamus, *Upadłość z szansą na układ a arbitraż [Insolvency Open to Arrangements and Arbitration]*, (6) Jurysta, pp. 20, 2011.

Michalak Arkadiusz, Marcin Mioduszewski, Janusz Raglewski, Justyna Rasiewicz, Małgorzata Sieradzka, Jarosław Sroczyński, Marek Szydło, Michał Wyrwiński, Marian Zdyb, Ustawa o zwalczaniu nieuczciwej konkurencji. Komentarz *[Act on Counteracting Unfair Competition. A Commentary]*, Warszawa: Wolters Kluwer, 2011, ISBN: 978-83-2640-393-4.

Marcin Aslanowicz; Joanna Jasiewiczy, The Baker & MacKenzie International Arbitration Yearbook 2010-2011. Huntington (NY): Juris, pp. 325-334, 2011, ISBN: 978-19-3383-378-1.

Dorota Dzienisiuk, *Mediacja a specyfika spraw z zakresu prawa pracy [Mediation and Specific Character of Labour Law Cases]*, (1) Praca i Zabezpieczenie Społeczne, pp. 19, 2011.

Jacek Gołaczyński, *Wybrane zagadnienia na tle ustawy z 4.2.2011 r. – Prawo prywatne międzynarodowe [Selected Issues of Act of 4 February 2011 on International Private Law]*, (11) Monitor Prawniczy, pp. 573, 2011.

Dariusy P. Kała, *Zażalenie na postanowienie w przedmiocie uznania wyroku sądu polubownego wydanego za granicą. Glosa do postanowienia z dnia 24 czerwca 2009 r. (I CSK 538/08) [Interlocutory Appeal Against a Ruling on Recognition of a Foreign Arbitration Award. Commentary to the Ruling of 24 June 2009 (I CSK 538/08)]*, (2) Przegląd Sądowy, pp. 118, 2011.

Marek Neumann, *Klauzula porządku publicznego a treść wyroku sądu polubownego - glosa do wyroku Sądu Najwyższego z 9.09.2010 r. (I CSK 535/09) [Public Policy and the Content of an Arbitral Award – Commentary on the Supreme Court's Ruling of 9 September 2010 (I CSK 535/09)]*, (2) Glosa, pp. 61, 2011.

Grzegorz Skowroński, *O pojęciu arbitrażowości sporu – zarys prawnoporównawczy [A Comparative Brief on Objective Arbitrability]*, (2) Przegląd Ustawodawstwa Gospodarczego, pp. 32, 2011.

Karol Weitz, *Zdatność arbitrażowa sporów o ustalenie nieistnienia stosunku prawnego z powodu nieważności czynności prawnej [Arbitrability of*

Disputes for Declaration of Non-Existence of a Legal Relationship due to Invalidity of an Act in Law], (5-6) Palestra, pp. 128, 2011.

Andrzej W. Wiśniewski, Międzynarodowy arbitraż handlowy w Polsce. Status prawny arbitrażu i arbitrów [*International Commercial Arbitration in Poland. Legal Statute of Arbitration and Arbitrator*], Warszawa: Wolters Kluwer, 2011, ISBN: 978-83-2641-209-7.

Paweł Wrześniewski, Charakter prawny zapisu na sąd polubowny [*Legal Nature of an Arbitration Agreement*], Oficyna Wydawnicza, 2011, ISBN: 978-83-930375-5-1.

Andrzej Zieliński; Flaga-Gieruszyńska Kinga, Kodeks postępowania cywilnego. Komentarz, [*Civil Procedure Code. Commentary*], Warszawa: C.H. Beck, 2011, ISBN: 978-83-2552-274-2.

Andrzej Zielony, *Istota prawna wyroku sądu polubownego* [*Legal Substance of Arbitration Court Judgements*], (1) Polski Proces Cywilny, pp. 46-78, 2011.

Adam Zienkiewicz, *Mediacja jako sposób konsensualnego rozwiązywania sporów. Perspektywa niemiecka, polska i ukraińska. Międzynarodowa konferencja naukowa (Ratyzbona, 25–26 VI 2010)* [*Mediation as Form of Consensual Dispute Resolutions. German, Polish and Ukrainian Perspective. International Research Conference. (Ratisbon, 25-26 June 2010)*], (6) Państwo i Prawo, pp. 124, 2011.

X. [ROMANIA][31]

Monographs[32]

Alina Mioara Cobuz-Bagnaru, *Arbitrajul ad-hoc conform regulilor Comisiei Natiunilor Unite pentru Dreptul Comercial International* [*Ad hoc arbitration according to the United Nations Commission on International Trade Law rules*], Bucuresti: Universul Juridic, 2010.

Revista Română de Arbitraj [*Romanian Review of Arbitration*], București [Bucharest], Curtea de Arbitraj Comercial Internațional de pe lângă Camera de Comerț și Industrie a României [*International Court of Commercial Arbitration attached to the Chamber of Commerce and Industry of Romania*], 2011, Vol. 5, Reg. No. 9059/5.11.2008

---

[31] For further articles on arbitration in Romania see also *Revista Română de Arbitraj* issued by the International Commercial Arbitration attached to The Chamber Of Commerce And Industry Of Romania (see http://arbitration.ccir.ro/engleza/index.htm).

[32] All titles published in Romanian. The research for CYIL performed by Dr. Ligia Catuna, Timisoara, Romania.

Issue No. 17; Issue No. 1 within the volume:

Şerban Beligrâdeanu, *Temeiul legal şi condiţiile de admisibilitate a unei clauze de neconcurenţâ dupâ încetarea contractelor – comerciale – de administrare încentarea de către societăţile comerciale cu persoane fizice [Legal Basis and Conditions for Admissibility of Non-compete Clauses after Termination of Management Agreements between Companies and Individuals]*. pp. 1-7.

Doug Jones, *International Dispute Resolution in the Global Financial Crisis.* pp. 8-28.

Derek Roebuck, *The Life and Death of the compromissum.* pp. 29-39.

Alina Oprea, *Excepţia de arbitraj în Regulamentul 44/2001: câteva observaţii privind decizia CJCE în cauza West Tankers [Arbitration Exception under Regulation No. 44/2001: Notes on the ECJ Decision in the West Tankers Case]*. pp. 40-46.

José María Alonso Puig, *Recent Decisions in Spanish Law.* pp. 47-50.

Issue No. 18; Issue No. 2 within the volume:

Paolo Michele Patocchi, *Modificarea Regulilor de arbitraj UNCITRAL. [Revised UNCITRAL Arbitration Rules]*. pp. 32-40.

Irina Adriana Poncracz, *Teoria "Grupului de companii" între mit ş realitate ["Group of Companies" Doctrine – between Myth and Reality]*. pp. 1-10.

Mauro Rubino-Sammartano, *De ce un arbitraj diferit poate oferi rezultate mai bune [Why Different Arbitration May Have Better Results]*. pp. 11-14.

Levana Zigmund; Cristina Metea; Matei Purice, *EDF Services Limited v. Romania – o analiză [EDF Services Limited v. Romania – Analysis]*. pp. 15-31.

Curierul Judiciar [*Legal Courier*], Bucharest, Vol. 2010, ISSN: 1582-7526[33]

Cristian Gheorghe, *Limitele arbitrajului în materie societară [The Limits of Arbitration in Company Matters]*. No. 8.

XI. [RUSSIAN FEDERATION]

Vladimir Khvalei; Ekaterina Solomatina, *Russian Federation, in* The Baker & MacKenzie International Arbitration Yearbook 2010-2011, Huntington (NY): Juris, pp. 325-358, 2011, ISBN: 978-1-933833-78-1.

---

[33] All titles published in Romanian. The research for CYIL performed by Dr. Ligia Catuna, Timisoara, Romania.

XII. [SLOVENIA]

Spomenka Hribar, *Vsakdo se bo na referendumu moral odločiti sam: oktroirani arbitražni sporazum* [*Everyone Will Have to Make Up Their Own Mind at the Referendum: The Imposed Arbitration Agreement*], 52 (122) Delo, pp. 16-17, 2010 (29 May 2010), ISSN: 1580-3007.[34]

XIII. [UKRAINE]

Svitlana Romanova; Nataliya Demir; Taras Aleshko, *Ukraine, in* The Baker & MacKenzie International Arbitration Yearbook 2010-2011. Huntington (NY): Juris, pp. 441-460, 2011, ISBN: 978-19-3383-378-1.

---

[34] The published material is informative and serves popularization purposes. This published information was pointed out to us by Mojca Muha (Senica), Ljubljana, Slovenia based on the research in the NUK database.

Important Web Sites

http://www.czechyearbook.org

Czech Yearbook of International Law® and Czech (& Central European) Yearbook of Arbitration.®

The web site is currently available in nineteen languages: English, Bulgarian, Czech, Chinese, French, Italian, Japanese, Korean, Hungarian, German, Polish, Romanian, Russian, Portuguese, Slovak, Slovenian, Spanish, Ukrainian, Vietnamese. This web site allows access to the annotations of all core articles and to information about the authors of these articles as well as to the entire remaining contents (except core articles) of both yearbooks (CYIL and CYArb®).

I. [CZE] – [CZECH REPUBLIC]

- http://www.cnb.cz
  Česká národná banka
  (Czech National Bank as the Central bank of the Czech Republic).[1]

- http://www.compet.cz
  Office for the protection of competition.[2]

- http://www.concourt.cz
  The Constitutional Court of the Czech Republic.[3]

- http://www.csesp.cz
  Czech Society for European and Comparative Law.[4]

- http://www.csmp-csil.org
  The Czech Society of International Law.[5]

- http://www.czech.cz
  Portal "Hello Czech Republic." Basic information about the Czech Republic and news interesting for foreigners. Rather a promotional portal.[6]

- http://www.czso.cz
  Czech Statistical Office.[7]

- http://dtjvcnsp.org
  Česko-německý spolek právníků. [Czech-German Lawyers Association]. Deutsch-Tschechische Juristenvereinigung e.V.[8]

- http://www.ekf.vsb.cz/en/
  Faculty of Economics, VŠB Technical University of Ostrava.[9]

---

[1] Website available in English and Czech.
[2] Website available in English and Czech. Basic laws and regulations on the protection of competition in the Czech Republic are also available at the website, both in Czech and in English (unofficial translation).
[3] Website available in English and Czech. Part of the (significant) case law also available in English.
[4] *Supra* note 1.
[5] Website available in Czech. In English only a brief summary of the webpages.
[6] Website available in English, Czech, French, German, Russian and Spanish.
[7] *Supra* note 1.
[8] Website available in German.
[9] Website available in English and Czech. Some information (regarding post-graduate studies) also available in German. Department of Law available at:

- http://ftp.pse.cz/Info.bas/Cz/Predpisy/brs_statut2.pdf
  Statute of Burzovní rozhodčí soud při Burze cenných papírů Praha, a.s.
  [Exchange Court of Arbitration at the Prague Stock Exchange].[10]

- http://www.hrad.cz[11]
  Website of the Office of the President of the Czech Republic.

- http://www.icc-cr.cz
  ICC National Committee Czech Republic.

- http://www.iir.cz
  Institute of International Relations Prague.[12]

- http://www.ilaw.cas.cz
  Ústav státu a práva Akademie věd ČR, v.v.i. [Institute of State and Law
  of the Academy of Sciences of the Czech Republic].[13]

- http://www.jednotaceskychpravniku.cz
  Jednota českých právníků [Czech Lawyers Union].

- http://www.icc-cr.cz
  ICC National Committee Czech Republic.

- http://justice.cz
  Czech justice portal including both courts and the Ministry of Justice,
  prosecution departments, Judicial Academy, Institute of Criminology
  and Social Prevention, as well as the Probation and Mediation Service
  and the Prison Service.[14]

---

http://en.ekf.vsb.cz/information-about/departments/structure/departments/dept-119 (in English, accessed on February 13, 2012).

[10] The Statute is available in Czech. One of the three permanent arbitration courts established in the Czech Republic by law (statute), in compliance with Section 13 of Act No. 216/1994 Coll., on Arbitration and Enforcement of Arbitral Awards, as subsequently amended.

[11] Website available in English and Czech. This website also allows access to the personal webpage of the President of the Czech Republic.

[12] Website available in English and Czech. This Institute was founded by the Ministry of Foreign Affairs of the Czech Republic.

[13] *Supra* note 1.

[14] Website available in Czech. The individual websites of the institutions covered by this portal also contain pages or summary information in English.

- http://www.law.muni.cz
  Faculty of Law, Masaryk University, Brno[15]

- http://www.mzv.cz
  Ministry of Foreign Affairs of the Czech Republic.[16]

- http://www.nsoud.cz.
  The Supreme Court of the Czech Republic.[17]

- http://www.nssoud.cz
  The Supreme Administrative Court of the Czech Republic[18]

- http://www.ochrance.cz
  Public Defender of Rights (Ombudsman).[19]

- http://www.ok.cz/iksp/en/aboutus.html
  Institute of Criminology and Social Prevention.[20]

- http://portal.gov.cz
  Portal of the Public Administration.[21] This website allows access to the websites of most supreme public administration authorities (including ministries).

- http://www.prf.cuni.cz
  Faculty of Law, Charles University in Prague.[22]

- http://www.psp.cz
  Parliament of the Czech Republic. Chamber of Deputies.[23]

- http://www.rozhodcisoud.cz
  The Arbitration Court attached to the Czech-Moravian Commodity Exchange Kladno.[24]

---

[15] *Supra* note 1.

[16] Website available in Czech. Important information from this portal also available in English.

[17] Website available in Czech. Some basic information also in English and French.

[18] *Supra* note 1.

[19] *Ibid.*

[20] *Ibid.*

[21] *Ibid.*

[22] Website available in Czech. Basic information available in English.

[23] *Supra* note 1.

[24] Website available in English and Czech. Website of one of the three permanent arbitration courts established in the Czech Republic by law (statute), in compliance with

- http://www.senat.cz
  Parliament of the Czech Republic. Senate.[25]

- http://www.society.cz/wordpress/#awp
  Common Law Society.[26]

- http://www.soud.cz
  Arbitration Court attached to the Economic Chamber of the Czech Republic and Agricultural Chamber of the Czech Republic.[27]

- http://www.umpod.cz
  Office for International Legal Protection of Children[28]

- http://www.upol.cz/fakulty/pf/
  Faculty of Law. Palacký University, Olomouc.

- http://www.vse.cz
  The University of Economics, Prague.[29]

- http://www.zcu.cz/fpr/
  Faculty of Law, Western Bohemia University in Pilsen.[30]

II. [SVK] – [SLOVAK REPUBLIC]

- http://www.concourt.sk
  Constitutional Court of the Slovak Republic.[31]

Section 13 of Act No. 216/1994 Coll., on Arbitration and Enforcement of Arbitral Awards, as subsequently amended. This arbitration court was established by Act No. 229/1992 Coll., on Commodity Exchanges, as subsequently amended.

[25] *Supra* note 1.

[26] Website available in Czech.

[27] Website available in English, Czech, German and Russian. Website of one of the three permanent arbitration courts established in the Czech Republic by law (statute), in compliance with Section 13 of Act No. 216/1994 Coll., on Arbitration and Enforcement of Arbitral Awards, as subsequently amended. This arbitration court was established by Section 19 of Act No. 301/1992 Coll., on the Economic Chamber of the Czech Republic and the Agricultural Chamber of the Czech Republic, as subsequently amended.

[28] The Office is the Central authority responsible for protection of children in civil matters having cross-border implications. Website available in English and Czech.

[29] *Supra* note 1.

[30] See *supra* note 26.

[31] Website available in English and Slovak.

- http://www.flaw.uniba.sk
  Faculty of Law, Comenius University in Bratislava (SVK).[32]

- http://iuridica.truni.sk
  Faculty of Law. Trnava University in Trnava (SVK).[33]

- http://www.justice.gov.sk
  Ministry of Justice of the Slovak Republic.[34]

- http://www.nbs.sk
  Národná banka Slovenska (National Bank of Slovakia as the Central bank of Slovak Republic).[35]

- http://www.nrsr.sk
  National Council of the Slovak Republic (*Slovak Parliament*).[36]

- http://www.prf.umb.sk
  Faculty of Law. Matej Bel University, Banská Bystrica (SVK).

- http://www.prezident.sk
  President of the Slovak Republic and Office of the President (SVK).[37]

- http://www.test.sopk.sk
  The Court of Arbitration of the Slovak Chamber of Commerce and Industry in Bratislava.[38]

- http://www.uninova.sk/pf_bvsp/src_angl/index.php
  Faculty of Law, Pan European University (SVK).[39]

- http://www.upjs.sk/pravnicka-fakulta
  Faculty of Law, Pavol Jozef Šafárik University in Košice (SVK).[40]

---

[32] *Ibid.*
[33] *Ibid.*
[34] Website available in English and Slovak. This website also allows access to the following portals: Courts, Slovak Agent before the European Court for Human Rights, Slovak Agent before the Court of Justice of the European Union, The Judicial Academy.
[35] *Supra* note 31.
[36] Website available in English, French, German and Slovak.
[37] *Supra* note 31.
[38] Website available in Slovak. Some basic information available in English.
[39] Website available in English, German and Slovak.
[40] *Supra* note 31.

- http://www.usap.sav.sk
  Institute of State and Law, Slovak Academy of Science.[41]

III. [AUT] – [AUSTRIA]

- http://www.arbitration-austria.at
  Österreichische Vereinigung für Schiedsgerichtsbarkeit. Austrian Arbitration Association.[42]

- http://www.internationales-schiedsgericht.at/
  Wiener Internationalen Schiedsgerichts (VIAC). Vienna International Arbitral Centre (VIAC).[43]

IV. [BLR] – [BELARUS]

- http://www.cci.by/ArbitrCourt/AboutCourt_en.aspx
  International Arbitration Court attached to the Belarusian Chamber of Commerce and Industry.[44]

V. [BGR] – [BULGARIA]

- http://www.bcci.bg/arbitration/index.html
  Arbitration Court at the Bulgarian Chamber of Commerce and Industry.

- http://www.lex.bg
  Information server on Bulgarian law.

VI. [EST] – [ESTONIA]

- http://www.koda.ee
  Arbitration Court attached to the Estonian Chamber of Commerce and Industry.[45]

---

[41] Website available in Slovak.
[42] Website available in English and German.
[43] Website available in English, Czech, German and Russian.
[44] Website available in English and Russian.
[45] Website available in English, Estonian and Russian.

VII.   [HRV] – [CROATIA]

- http://www2.hgk.hr/en/about_cce.asp?izbor=pac
  The Permanent Arbitration Court at the Croatian Chamber of Commerce.[46]

VIII.   [HUN] – [HUNGARY]

- http://www.mkik.hu/index.php?id=1406
  Court of Arbitration attached to the Hungarian Chamber of Commerce and Industry.[47]

- http://www.mkik.hu/index.php?id=1409&print=1
  Act LXXI [Hungary] of 1994 On arbitration. Nonofficial English translation published on the portal of the Hungarian Chamber of Commerce. [**Law on arbitration**].

IX.   [LVA] - [LATVIA]

- http://www.chamber.lv
  The Arbitration Court of the Latvian Chamber of Commerce and Industry LCCI.[48]

X.   [LTU] – [LITHUANIA]

- http://www3.lrs.lt/pls/inter3/dokpaieska.showdoc_l?p_id=56461
  Law on Commercial Arbitration of The Republic of Lithuania No I-1274 as of 2 April 1996.[49] Official translation by Lietuvos Respulikos Seimas (on the portal of the Parliament of the Republic of Lithuania).

- http://www.arbitrazas.lt
  Vilniaus komercinio arbitražo teismas. Vilnius Court of Commercial Arbitration.[50]

---

[46]   Website available in Croatian. Basic information available in English. See the English presentation of the arbitration court at the website.
[47]   Website available in Hungarian. Basic information available in English.
[48]   Website available in English, Latvian and Russian.
[49]   Published in: Parliamentary record, 1998-04-01, No. 4 (*Teisés aktą priémé - Lietuvos Respublikos Seimas*).
[50]   Website available in English, Lithuanian and Polish.

XI.   [MKD] – [MACEDONIA]

- http://www.mchamber.org.mk/%28S%28bqz5fz45uu52szfwzrwaa055
  %29%29/default.aspx?lId=2&mId=50&smId=0[51]
  The Permanent Court of Arbitration attached to the Economic
  Chamber of Macedonia [*Стопанската комора на Македонија*].

XII.   [MDA] – [MOLDOVA]

- http://www.arbitraj.chamber.md/index.php?id=93
  Curtea de Arbitraj Comercial International pe linga Camera de
  Comert si Industrie a Republicii Moldova.   The International
  Commercial Arbitration Court of the Chamber of Commerce and
  Industry of the Republic of Moldova.[52]

XIII.   [POL] – [POLAND][53]

- http://www.sakig.pl/
  Sąd Arbitrażowy przy Krajowej Izbie Gospodarczej w Warszawie.[54]
  Court of Arbitration at the Polish Chamber of Commerce in Warsaw.

- http://www.iccpolska.pl/
  Polski Komitet Narodowy Międzynarodowej Izby Handlowej. Polish
  ICC National Committee.

- http://oirp.bydgoszcz.pl/index.php?page=statut-2
  Sądu Polubowny przy Okręgowej Izbie Radców Prawnych w
  Bydgoszczy. Court of Arbitration attached to the Regional Chamber of
  Legal Advisors in Bydgoscz.[55]

- http://www.gca.org.pl/x.php/1,392/Arbitraz.html
  Sąd Arbitrażowy przy Izbie Bawełny w Gdyni. Arbitration Court
  attached to the Gdynia Cotton Association.[56]

---

[51]   Website available in English and Macedonian.
[52]   Website available in English, Moldovan and Russian.
[53]   Operation and accessibility of all websites were last checked on 17 November 2010.
[54]   Website available in English, German, French, Polish and Russian.
[55]   Website available in Polish.
[56]   Website available in English and Polish.

- http://oirp.gda.pl/portal-dla-przedsiebiorcow/sad-polubowny
  Stały Sąd Arbitrażowy przy Okręgowej Izbie Radców Prawnych w
  Gdańsku. Permanent Court of Arbitration attached to the Regional
  Chamber of Legal Advisers in Gdańsk.[57]

- http://www.igg.pl/1/node/39
  Sąd Arbitrażowy przy Izbie Gospodarczej Gazownictwa. Court of
  Arbitration attached to The Chamber of the Natural Gas Industry.[58]

- http://www.ihk.pl/index.html?id=1635
  Sąd Arbitrażowy przy Polsko-Niemieckiej Izbie Przemysłowo-
  Handlowej. Court of Arbitration attached to the Polish – German
  Chamber of Commerce and Industry.[59]

- http://www.iph.krakow.pl/?a=page&id=31
  Sąd Polubowny przy Izbie Przemysłowo-Handlowej w Krakowie.
  Court of Arbitration attached to the Chamber of Industry and Trade
  in Krakow.[60]

- http://www.iph.torun.pl/index.php?aid=113837484143da38b99fb66
  Sąd Polubowny przy Izbie Przemysłowo-Handlowej w Toruniu. Court of
  Arbitration attached to the Chamber of Industry and Trade in Torun.[61]

- http://isap.sejm.gov.pl
  Legal information (laws and regulations) system on the portal of the
  Sejm [Parliament] of the Republic of Poland.[62]

- http://www.kigm.pl/index.php?option=com_content&task=view&id
  =60&Itemid=65&lang=p
  Międzynarodowy Sąd Arbitrażowy przy Krajowej Izbie Gospodarki
  Morskiej. International Court of Arbitration attached to the Polish
  Chamber of Maritime Commerce in Gdynia.[63]

---

[57] *Ibid.*

[58] Website available in Polish. Some basic information, especially about the Chamber,
also available in English and German.

[59] Website available in German and Polish.

[60] *Supra* note 55.

[61] Website available in Polish. The portal also offers English version which, however, was
not available during our last visit (17 November 2010) (we cannot rule out technical
problems but we could not verify that before handing over this manuscript to CYArb for
printing).

[62] Website available in Polish. See also: http://sejm.gov.pl (accessed on February 13,
2012).

- http://www.knf.gov.pl/regulacje/Sad_Polubowny/index.html
  Sąd Polubowny przy Komisji Nadzoru Finansowego. Court of Arbitration attached to the Polish Financial Supervision Authority.[64]

- http://www.liph.com.pl/index.php?body=7
  Polubowny Sąd Łódzkiej Izby Przemysłowo-Handlowej. Court of Arbitration attached to the Chamber of Industry and Trade in Łódz.[65]

- http://www.nig.org.pl/sa/pl1.html
  Sąd Arbitrażowy przy Nowotomyskiej Izbie Gospodarczej w Nowym Tomyślu. Court of Arbitration attached to the Chamber of Economy in Nowym Tomyśl.[66]

- http://www.nsa.gov.pl/
  Supreme Administrative Court.[67]

- http://oirp.olsztyn.pl/content/blogsection/23/73/
  Stały Sąd Arbitrażowy przy Okręgowej Izbie Radców Prawnych w Olsztynie. Permanent Court of Arbitration attached to the Regional Chamber of Legal Advisors in Olsztyn.[68]

- http://www.piit.org.pl/piit2/index.jsp?layout=1&news_cat_id=62&place=Menu01
  Sąd Polubowny ds. Domen Internetowych przy Polskiej Izbie Informatyki i Telekomunikacji w Warszawie. Arbitration Court for Internet Domains attached to The Polish Chamber of Information Technology and Telecommunications.[69]

- http://www.polubowny.org/index.html
  Centrum Mediacyjne oraz Stały Sąd Polubowny przy Fundacji Adwokatury Polskiej i Ośrodku Badawczym Adwokatury im. adw. W. Bayera. Mediation Center and Permanent Court of Arbitration attached to the Donation of Polish Bar and Center for Bar Research of W. Bayer.[70]

---

[63] Website available in Polish. Some basic information available in English.
[64] *Supra* note 56.
[65] *Supra* note 55.
[66] *Ibid.*
[67] *Ibid.*
[68] *Ibid.*
[69] *Supra* note 56.
[70] *Supra* note 55.

- http://www.pssp.org.pl/index.htm
  Polskie Stowarzyszenie Sądownictwa Polubownego – Polish Arbitration Association.

- http://www.riph.com.pl/index.php/Company/sub32
  Sąd Arbitrażowy przy Regionalnej Izbie Przemysłowo-Handlowej w Gliwicach. The Permanent Court of Arbitration at the Regional Chamber of Commerce & Industry in Gliwice.[71]

- http://www.sadarbitrazowy.org.pl/
  Sąd Arbitrażowy przy Polskiej Konfederacji Pracodawców Prywatnych Lewiatan. Court of Arbitration at the Polish Confederation of Private Employers Lewiatan.[72]

- http://www.oirpwarszawa.pl/kategoria/pokaz/idk/612/ida/520/strona/
  Stały Sąd Polubowny przy Okręgowej Izbie Radców Prawnych w Warszawie. Permanent Court of Arbitration Attached to the Regional Chamber of Legal Advisers in Warszawa.[73]

- http://www.rig.katowice.pl/default.aspx?docId=30
  Sąd Arbitrażowy przy Regionalnej Izbie Gospodarczej w Katowicach. Court of Arbitration attached to the Chamber of Economy in Katowice.[74]

- http://www.sa.dig.wroc.pl/sa/index.php?option=com_content&task=view&id=69&Itemid=28
  Sąd Arbitrażowy przy Dolnośląskiej Izbie Gospodarczej we Wrocławiu. Court of Arbitration attached to the Lower Silesia Chamber of Economy in Wrocław.[75]

- http://www.sejm.gov.pl
  Sejm Rzeczypospolitej Polskiej. Sejm [*Parliament*] of the Republic of Poland.[76,77]

---

[71] Website available in Polish. Some basic information also available in English and German.

[72] *Supra* note 56.

[73] *Supra* note 55.

[74] *Ibid.*

[75] Website available in Polish. Applicable Rules of proceedings available in English and German.

[76] *Supra* note 56.

[77] See also http://isap.sejm.gov.pl – legal information system available through the portal of Sejm.

- http://www.senat.gov.pl
  Senat Rzeczypospolitej polskiej. The Senate of the Republic of Poland.[78]

- http://www.sn.pl/
  Supreme Court of the Republic of Poland.[79]

- http://www.ssp.piph.pl/
  Stały Sąd Polubowny przy Pomorskiej Izbie Przemysłowo-Handlowej w Gdańsku. Permanent Court of Arbitration attached to the See [*Maritime*] Chamber of Industry and Trade in Gdańsk.[80]

- http://www.trybunal.gov.pl
  Constitutional Court.[81]

- http://www.wib.com.pl/index.php?idkat=11
  Sąd Arbitrażowy przy Wielkopolskiej Izbie Budownictwa. Court of Arbitration attached to The Wielkopolska Chamber of Construction.[82]

- http://www.wiph.pl/content/view/69/53/
  Sąd Arbitrażowy Izb i Organizacji Gospodarczych Wielkopolski. Arbitration Court attached to the All Polish Chamber of Industry and Trade.[83]

- http://www.zbp.pl/site.php?s=MGM0YzkzYWY1MTc3Nw
  Sąd Polubowny przy Związku Banków Polskich. Court of Arbitration attached to the Polish Bank Association (ZBP).[84]

- http://www.ziph.pl/strona,19,polubowny-sad-gospodarczy
  Polubowny Sąd Gospodarczy przy Zachodniej Izbie Przemysłowo-Handlowej w Gorzowie Wielkopolskim. Court of Arbitration attached to The Western Chamber of Industry and Commerce in Gorzow Wielkopolski.[85]

---

[78] Website available in English, French, German, Polish and Russian.
[79] *Supra* note 56.
[80] *Supra* note 55.
[81] *Supra* note 56.
[82] Website available in Polish. Basic information, especially about the Chamber, available in English.
[83] *Supra* note 55.
[84] *Supra* note 56.
[85] Website available in Polish. Basic information and information about the Chamber also available in English, French, German and Russian.

XIV.   [RUM] – [ROMANIA]

- http://arbitration.ccir.ro
  The Court of International Commercial Arbitration attached to The Chamber of Commerce and Industry of Romania.[86]

XV.   [RUS] – [RUSSIAN FEDERATION]

- http://www.iccwbo.ru
  ICC National Committee Russian Federation.

- http://www.spbcci.ru/engarbitaltribunal
  The Arbitration tribunal at Saint-Petersburg Chamber of Commerce and Industry.[87]

XVI.   [SVN] – [SLOVENIA]

- http://www.sloarbitration.org
  The Permanent Court of Arbitration, although attached to the Chamber of Commerce and Industry of Slovenia [CCIS].[88]
- http://www.sloarbitration.org/english/introduction/organization.html
  Nonofficial English translations of Slovenian law on or related to arbitration published on the portal of the Permanent Court of Arbitration, although attached to the Chamber of Commerce and Industry of Slovenia. (i) Code of Civil Procedure of Slovenia.[89] (ii) Private International Law And Procedure Act.[90] [**Law on arbitration**].

---

[86]   Website available in English and Romanian.
[87]   Website available in English and Russian.
[88]   Website available in English and Slovenian.
[89]   Published in the: Official Gazette of the Republic of Slovenia, No. 26/99.
[90]   Published in the: Official Gazette of the Republic of Slovenia, No. 56/99.

Index

504

| 505

CALL FOR PAPERS FOR VOLUMES 2013

Did you find the articles in the second volume of CYArb interesting?
Would you like to react to a current article
or contribute to future volumes?

We are seeking authors for both
the Czech Yearbook on International Law® (CYIL) and the
Czech (& Central European) Yearbook of Arbitration.®

The general topics for 2013 are the following:

CYIL 2013
*Regulatory Measures
and Foreign Trade*

CYArb 2013
*Borders of Procedural
and Substantive Law
in Arbitral Proceedings
(Civil versus Common Law
Perspectives)*

More general and contact information available at:
www.czechyearbook.com